THE
ETIQUETTE
ADVANTAGE
IN BUSINESS

THE
ETIQUETTE
ADVANTAGE
IN BUSINESS

PERSONAL SKILLS FOR
PROFESSIONAL SUCCESS

PEGGY POST
AND
PETER POST

HarperResource
An Imprint of HarperCollinsPublishers

FIRST EDITION

Designed by BTD NYC
Illustrations © LAURA HARTMAN MAESTRO

Library of Congress Cataloging-in-Publication Data
Post, Peggy
        The etiquette advantage in business : personal skills for professional success / Peggy Post
and Peter Post. — 1st ed.
                p. cm.
        Includes bibliographical references and index.
        ISBN 0–06–273672–8
        1. Job hunting. 2. Business etiquette. 3. Success in business. I. Post, Peter. II. Title.
        HF5382.7.P68 1999
        650.14—dc21   99-346344

---

03 BTD/RRD 10 9 8 7 6 5

Contents

ACKNOWLEDGMENTS

With our special thanks, we want to recognize Fred DuBose for his invaluable insight and diligence. It's hard to imagine bringing this book to fruition without him.

We also thank the following for their research and great ideas: Courtney Denby, Inge Dobelis, Martha Leslie Hailey, Tad Harvey, Beth Landis, Alexis Lipsitz, Dierdre Van Dyk, and Bryce Walker.

Our appreciation goes to those who shared their expertise in their respective professional or business fields: Regis Canning, Lois Ebin, John Fowler, Greg Gregory, Dr. Judy Harkins, Mimi Irwin, Nancy Maniscalco, Knox Massey, James B. Miller Jr., Bob Moore, Susan Onaitis, Morgan Rich, and Evan P. Spingarn.

Thanks to these for their critical eye: Linda Ambrose, Keith Anderson, Kate DuBose, Stacy Kravetz, Kenneth Santor, and Burke Stinson.

Not least, we want to thank the following for their helpful suggestions: Katherine Cowles, Elizabeth Howell, Alfred Kennedy, Janet Kenny, Nelson Kenny, Alan Klavans, Anne McCarver, Larry McCarver, Allen Post, Anna Post, Tricia Post, Carl Raymond, Monica Sapirstein, Cindy Post Senning, and Sally Dee Wade.

INTRODUCTION

If people can arrive at work in jeans without causing a stir, does that mean our grandparents' rules of etiquette are obsolete? Or is it that people have ceased to care? Actually, the answer is "No." Changes in the business world mean that etiquette is more in demand than ever. And there is more than enough evidence that exhibiting social skills in business is its own reward.

In truth, "business etiquette" is little more than common sense coupled with consideration for others. Here's what making it part of your portfolio can enable you to do:

- Negotiate the tricky ground of a job search
- Gain confidence in yourself
- Dress appropriately for the situation, no matter what your professional field
- Use your people skills to interact effectively with your coworkers and business associates from outside
- Handle with ease the conflicts inherent to the workplace
- Get along better with your boss
- If you're a boss, gain the respect of those you supervise
- Communicate effectively with people in both speech and writing
- Acquit yourself well when dining out and when hosting or attending a business party
- Respect the cultural differences you encounter when traveling overseas
- Increase your chance of success if you're striking out on your own

What we call the "etiquette advantage" in business doesn't stop there. Many of today's office workers have missed out on learning the basics of manners in an era of dual-income and single-parent families, and their concern about manners is well-founded: Etiquette can make the difference between getting ahead in the workplace or being left behind. To that end, this book seeks to instill self-confidence by first delineating the basics of good manners. Throughout, the underlying lesson is that the right behavior elicits the right response from those being dealt with in a business transaction of any sort. We also strive to give workers the security to judge for themselves just what constitutes "right behavior" in a given situation—the kind of self-confidence that contributes to the strong presence that propels people to the top.

Emily Post was concerned with business etiquette from the start. As she wrote in 1922, "To make a pleasant and friendly impression is not only good manners, but equally good business." No doubt she would have eagerly confronted the challenges of today: the job insecurity that megamergers, reengineering, and downsizing have left in their wake; the question of sexual harassment; and the technological advances that have us working and communicating in ways we hardly could have imagined.

Our own professional backgrounds (combined, more than 55 years of experience in finance, service industries, and public relations) gives us a true appreciation of Emily Post's belief that everyday manners and workplace manners are inseparable. Just as people everywhere want to make personal encounters pleasant, so they strive to adhere to standards of behavior that make professional relationships productive—especially in a business world where the "team" concept has become increasingly important.

WHAT YOU'LL FIND

The Etiquette Advantage in Business serves people across the board—from those who work from a home office to those who regularly do business overseas. While devoting considerable space to the needs of employees in the junior to mid-level range, the book also advises top management on how to maintain good relations with their employees. Section by section, here's what is in store:

- **THE PATH TO EMPLOYMENT.** Four chapters show you how to use etiquette to your advantage as you apply for a job, prepare or update your resume and cover letter, and withstand the anxieties of job interviews.
- **LIFE AT THE OFFICE.** The topics in these seven chapters include getting along with your coworkers and supervisors; your attitude toward your workspace, be it a cubicle or an office; relations between the sexes; and your personal privacy.
- **BUSINESS DRESS.** What clothes are "correct"? The rules governing dress are constantly changing, and in no area of business are the changes more obvious. Two chapters—one for men, one for women—show you how to judge what's appropriate to wear in any situation.
- **EXECUTIVE ETIQUETTE.** Addressed primarily to those at the managerial level, these three chapters focus on the manager's responsibilities and obligations to the workers he or she supervises, with special attention given to assistants.

- **THE WORLD OUTSIDE.** Establishing good relations with customers, clients, contractors, and vendors is the subject of the first chapter, with business gifts covered in the second. Rounding out the section are chapters on business travel and behavior at conventions and trade shows.
- **THE SPOKEN WORD.** Three chapters focus respectively on the importance of introductions, the art of conversing well, and the appropriate use of the telephone in its many forms.
- **THE WRITTEN WORD.** These four chapters offer valuable lessons in expressing yourself skillfully in the traditional way (on paper) and the modern way (electronically).
- **THE BUSINESS MEETING.** The first of two chapters shows how effectively planning and leading a meeting is a courtesy to everyone concerned. The second concentrates on meeting manners for participants.
- **BUSINESS ENTERTAINMENTS.** The practical advice offered in these four chapters helps the businessperson feel confident and at ease when entertaining or being entertained—whether at a formal or informal business meal, at home, at the theater, or even at a baseball game.
- **DOING BUSINESS ABROAD.** Three chapters addressed to international travelers stress the importance of cultural understanding, the first step in achieving successful business negotiations overseas.
- **THE HOME OFFICE.** The practicalities of self-employment and the interaction between home-based workers and their customers, family, and friends are the topics of these three chapters.

The goals of *The Etiquette Advantage in Business* are many: to bring a level of comfort to the businessperson who never had the chance to learn the basics of etiquette; to provide a refresher course for those who did; to equate good manners with good business sense; and to instill the self-confidence that sets you on the road to success. We hope our book will make a difference for employees and executives everywhere, a helpmate that grounds people in the timeless fundamentals as they work their way through a fast-changing world.

PEGGY POST
PETER POST

October 1999

PART I

THE PATH TO EMPLOYMENT

*I*t's a tough world out there—and tougher for some job hunters than others. Whether you're clutching a new business diploma or have twenty years of experience under your belt, you face a corporate world that has decimated its middle management ranks. On the other hand, if you're a computer whiz or a medical technician you may be able to write your own ticket with employers. Yet in another decade, these positions can be reversed as the employment landscape bucks and sways.

Today's job hunters enter a volatile environment, and for the unprepared, job hunting can be full of disappointment. But take heart: Knowing and applying the etiquette of the job search can often distinguish you from the anonymous herd of applicants and increase your chance of getting what you really want. This section starts with a chapter about taking stock of yourself, then proceeds through the job-hunting process, stressing that first impressions are crucial—in everything from telephone queries and application letters to your proper demeanor in interviews. Today's job market may be unpredictable, but self-confidence and polished manners exert a powerful effect on the people who hold your future in their hands.

CHAPTER 1
THE REAL YOU

A saying sprang to life in the mid-Twentieth century: "You are what you eat." It could as well have been "You are where you work." It's hardly a surprise that your sense of self is tied to how you earn a living. The arrival of electronic commuting notwithstanding, the great majority of people spend more time at work than they do at home—and that means striking a balance between holding on to your identity while becoming part of a larger whole.

Whether he or she is a first-time job hunter or a worker who is looking for a change (or has no choice but to make one), the smart job seeker is going to approach this important task with eyes wide open both to personal needs and to the business world as it exists today. This means going about finding your dream job with enthusiasm and drive but, at the same time, accepting that a measure of compromise is sometimes necessary.

THE RIGHT FIT

When you look for a job, you're looking for a fit: a fit for your talents, your skills, your interests. But there's something more. No doubt you're hoping your job will be *meaningful*—that you'll be one of those few who can honestly say, "I love my job so much I can't believe I get paid for it." Another concern may be remaining true to yourself. "Selling out" became a buzzword thirty-odd years ago because people who joined "the establishment" were seen by some as putting money and ambition before integrity and principle.

If you're lucky enough to gain such intangible rewards, congratulations. But it is your attitude and behavior toward your coworkers, your bosses, and your business associates from outside that will make the difference—an essential part of how contented and successful you'll become.

Naturally, doing your job well is vital. But answering to other people (even the CEO answers to the board of directors) and interacting every day with a diverse group of coworkers necessitates keeping your social skills in excellent working order—"etiquette" being a crucial advantage on the way to both personal and financial fulfillment. First, though, let's put things in perspective.

NEW ATTITUDES

The workplace has undergone tremendous changes in the last two decades. For one thing, it is moving away from hierarchy and individualism toward a structure of teamwork and collaboration. There's also a trend toward shorter work-weeks, longer vacations, and more focus on life outside of work. Increasingly, people place less emphasis on the monetary rewards of working for someone else and more on thinking of and for themselves.

It's no surprise, then, that there is a boom in entrepreneurship, especially among the young, from whose lips the word "entrepreneur" falls as regularly as "peace and love" did from their baby-boomer parents'. The last decade has seen a sharp rise in the number of small-business start-ups, fueled by the success stories of people who have yet to see thirty making fortunes by selling everything from software to soda pop. But even the person who successfully strikes out on her own has to play by the rules: While she has the freedom to make her own decisions, she still has to answer to the world outside, and do it with civility and grace. Worthy in its own right, the simple act of being considerate to others is integral to getting ahead.

A Willingness to Bend

Short of starting your own business, the first thing to decide before taking a job is how much you're willing to bend—not only once you're employed but while you're in the process of becoming so.

Today the business world is far less uniform, with standards differing according to each company's unique culture. A prime example: A growing slice of the labor force works in information technology, where the degree of individuality in dress and behavior is miles away from what is often expected in more traditional businesses. But no matter how free-spirited the individual and the field he or she seeks to enter, certain standards of behavior apply: that you take your relationships with people seriously; that you treat them respectfully; that you are even-tempered and fair; and that you abide by the company's rules so long as they remain ethical and aboveboard.

MAKING AN IMPRESSION

Despite what some people think, a concerted effort to make a good impression doesn't have to mean putting on airs, playing games, betraying yourself, or compromising your integrity. Phoniness and pretentiousness are one thing;

observing rules of behavior that have evolved over time to serve the common good is quite another. Good manners are based not on elitism but on simple common sense: The more considerate business people are to one another, the better their relationships with coworkers, employees, customers, and suppliers. Manners grease the wheels of social interaction. And who could object to that? It's not a stretch to say that what we now call "etiquette" might have played a role in how we evolved, with those who saw to the needs of others favored over those who did not.

Conforming to certain customs and principles hardly means forsaking who you are. You may not like some of the things expected of you—whether changing from what you normally wear or being expected to start work at nine o'clock sharp—but pragmatism dictates that you must. Only the most rigid of individualists won't make some accommodation to the demands of the workplace—and in most companies, refusing to do so means, as they say, cutting off your nose to spite your face. With that fundamental precept in mind, begin your search for employment armed with the knowledge that being willing to

---

THE DANGERS OF STEREOTYPING

The workforce of today is more diverse than ever, and in whole new ways. First, women joined men in the white-collar ranks, and before long the landscape of American business blossomed into a multifaceted ethnic mix. Yet a decade or so ago, age was an issue only when someone was too wet behind the ears to step up to a manager's job or was perceived as over the hill. Now, thanks to the technological revolution, a generation with a whole new set of skills has entered the workplace, yet another subgroup.

Never has it been more important for one generation, be it older or younger, not to make knee-jerk assumptions about the other. Each has its own things to offer, both in skills and attitude. The voice of experience and the view to the future don't have to be mutually exclusive but can merge to create a rich company culture that benefits everyone.

The job hunter who is quick to stereotype gets off on the wrong foot. Human beings are infinitely complex and don't always reveal themselves by how they wear their hair or clothes. Although the assumptions people have about one another may be right on the money, they may often be nowhere close—and assuming that a workplace "isn't your type" because of what you see on the surface is a snap judgment that could keep you from a rewarding job. Not accepting this truth is shallow and could cut you off from people who could help you grow. A person who knows to delve beneath the surface is the one who is more likely to succeed.

adapt makes the difference between getting a job or doing without one—and between keeping a job or being fired.

TAKING STOCK

Whether you're searching for your first job or making a change, take time to honestly assess your attitudes and strengths. Then decide what it is you want to say about yourself and why someone should hire you. Start with a list of your personal assets, past accomplishments on the job or in volunteering, and any leadership positions you have held. Use the following questions as a springboard to exploring the real you:

- What are your most unique experiences and skills? Were you the star debater in high school? You scored highest in math? Do your interests lean toward the everyday or the intellectual?
- What kind of activities would your ideal job involve? Do you prefer the creative thought that is required in knowledge industries or more straightforward, task-based work?
- What were the best and worst aspects of any job you held before? Working in a structured environment where others made the decisions, which is just the way you liked it? Or were you chafing at the bit to make decisions yourself?
- Are you the practical type or the artistic type? Is being part of the mainstream your goal or do you fear being seen as average?
- What are your professional goals? To make money first and then assume the rest will take care of itself? Or is it the other way around?
- How do you define success? Does it mean making loads of money or doing what is most fulfilling? If you put money on the back burner, are you certain you won't regret it in the long run, no matter how happy you are in your job?

Asking yourself these questions and mulling over the answers will not only give you a context within which to view a potential job but also make it easier to convey to others your enthusiasm, confidence, and motivation. You'll soon be telling everyone you know—and probably those you've just met—that you're looking for a job, so be prepared to articulate your goals, speak about your strengths, and convince others that you would be an asset to their organization. In short, become a person who knows what you want, why you want it, and how to get it, all the while conducting yourself in such a way that will not only make you feel good about yourself but also smooth the way to realizing your full potential.

CHAPTER 2

THE JOB SEARCH

So what does etiquette have to do with a job search? Much indeed. Your stops along the path to employment include meeting new people, communicating your abilities, and proving you not only have what it takes but also would be nice to have around. Etiquette gives you confidence, letting you focus on the tasks at hand instead of worrying about how to comport yourself.

This chapter takes you on a quick tour through job-hunting territory, with pointers for traveling it with self-assurance and civility. Forming the framework are the ins-and-outs of networking, setting up informational interviews, answering want ads on the Internet and in the papers, making cold calls, and consulting an employment agency. Advice is slanted toward how you should act in the process and applies to job hunters of any kind: the new college graduate seeking her first job; the worker looking for a change; the unlucky soul who suddenly finds himself out of a job. (For more on the last two cases, see Leaving Your Job, page 123.) Even though on the surface job hunters have little in common in attitude and style—compare the buzz-cut computer genius sporting a Hawaiian-print shirt to the budding stockbroker in the expensive Italian suit—their concerns and course of action are more or less the same.

NOTE: Bookstores offer a wealth of job-search guides that leave no stone unturned. The classics of the genre are often updated and take you through the finer points of job hunting in a way that, because of space limitations, this book cannot. Browse the shelves until you find a guide that appeals to you and then strike out on your search with the all-important tenets of good behavior firmly in place—the finer points that give you the competitive edge.

THE SAVVY NETWORKER

Networking—the buzzword for making contact with people and exchanging information, ideally to the mutual benefit of everyone—isn't something you sign up for. Rather, it is an effort and a state of mind. Networking occurs anytime you meet someone in your field of interest, when you write a letter to a potential helper whose name you've found in your college alumni list, when someone picks up the phone to tell you of a job opening, and any other time someone advances your job search in any way, shape, or form.

How you behave when networking is as important as the effort itself. The smart networker respects the opinions (and time) of others, helps other people as much as he is helped, and establishes rapport long before asking a favor or even offering a business card. A bad networker is a name-dropper who brags about his connections and comes across as being more concerned about what can be done for him than what he can do for someone else. Is it so hard to guess which of the two has a greater chance of success?

CAST YOUR NET

Start creating your network by making a list of people you know well, any you admire professionally, and any you'd like to meet. Cast a wide net, using all of your connections—professional, academic, familial, and social, right down to the local librarian. Then narrow the list to the following:

- People whom you know would be glad to help you
- People who might be interested in your search and be willing to make an introduction
- People who may not help you directly but may hear of a job opening

Remember that you don't have to limit yourself to friends and acquaintances. Try to contact (first by e-mail or letter and then by telephone) someone who has been successful in the field you hope to join. Almost any connection—attendance at the same high school or college, a mutual friend, or a shared professional or cultural interest—can be used as a springboard for introductions.

Many people will feel some obligation to help someone from their former school, and obtaining your college's alumni list is one way of finding them. Scan the list for people whose jobs are within the field or profession that interests you. If notations in the list don't include occupations, look up alumni in the city where you live. A friendly call to ask someone if he or she knows of a school chum who works in your field of choice may well lead to the right person. Another good source is the database of a social or service organization to which you belonged in college.

A second way to widen your circle of contacts is to join professional organizations, volunteer groups, or social clubs, which can provide personal satisfaction and even a bit of fun. Going a step farther and becoming a leader in such groups has three benefits: Your visibility is increased, making people want to know you; you enhance your leadership skills; and you show your skills to people who otherwise would not know your capabilities.

STAYING IN TOUCH

The first rule of networking is to do it all the time, not just while job hunting. Keeping in touch, as well as helping out people on your list whenever possible, ensures that when you actually do need help finding a job you can easily call in your chits. When that moment comes, tell everyone you know you're job-seeking and then leave it at that. As eager as you'll be to whip out your resume, it's up to someone else to ask for it. Also be careful not to come off as a shameless self-promoter, grabbing every chance to spout off your accomplishments. A low-key mention of your job search is all that's needed; anyone who's interested will probably ask questions or offer to help.

Following are some ways to stay in touch with people in your network, even when you're not actively looking for work. (Note that passing along the lame joke that was forwarded to you on e-mail by your ex-college roommate from New Jersey isn't one of them.)

- Meet for a bite to eat
- Invite to a party
- Invite to a baseball game or play when you have an extra ticket
- Mail an article that would be helpful or interesting
- Send holiday, birthday, congratulatory, and get-well cards when appropriate
- Share information about job openings

When anyone, either inside or outside your network, says he'll be happy to help, graciously accept. If the helper says he wants to tell a friend about you, follow through immediately by sending him or her a resume, along with a brief letter detailing your career goals. If the helper gives you the name of someone to call, tell that person you're calling at the suggestion of [helper's name]. If you're lucky, you might have found the first link in a chain that leads to an informational interview (see page 10) or even a job interview.

Note the type of job you want in a handwritten or e-mail note to your helper or referral, pointing out whatever qualifications and experiences make you think you can handle it.

Write or e-mail a thank-you note to everyone who has offered help in any way. If, for example, you chat with someone at a cocktail party who says he thinks he'll mention you to his boss, your note will serve as a reminder. Just remember to never assume the favor has already been performed.

Notes like this one can set the stage for things to come:

Dear James:

I enjoyed meeting you at Sharon Stewart's party last weekend—especially since I never dreamed of crossing paths with a Braves fan in Pittsburgh. Of course,

THE INFORMATIONAL INTERVIEW

The purpose of the so-called informational interview is to learn about a person's career, company, or industry, with the ultimate aim of advancing your job search. (This kind of meeting is not—repeat, *not*—an opportunity to flash a resume or ask for a job.) Through your networking contacts or your own research, identify several successful people within your field of choice or an influential person within a company that you'd like to learn more about. Then begin the process of requesting a brief meeting:

- Send a brief letter of introduction (or, in fields that don't stand on tradition, do it via e-mail) stating your background, your career goals, and your reason for wanting to meet.
- End the letter with a promise to call.
- Follow through later in the week, phoning to ask about scheduling a meeting.

GETTING IN
The easiest way to get an appointment is to already know someone or to be referred by a mutual friend. If you're making a cold call (ringing up a person who doesn't know you or doesn't expect your call), you'll have to work much harder, since getting a response may mean writing more than one letter and making several phone calls to an assistant. With each call, strike a balance of politeness, deference, charm, and self-confidence, but be careful not to become a pest: Use your intuition to gauge whether the person you're calling is rolling her eyes at yet another entreaty. While persistence with charm can pay off, with the wrong person it can backfire.

PREPARING
Once a meeting is scheduled, make the most of it by preparing thoroughly, scouring the Internet and publications. Learn as much as you can about both the company and the field, and be ready

I also really appreciate your offer to mention me to your boss. Your company sounds like the kind of place I'd be interested in knowing more about. Thanks!

Sincerely,

Chris Cavanaugh

If you're using stationery or a correspondence card and it isn't printed with your address and phone number, write them under your signature. Even if you exchanged cards with the recipient, he may have lost or misplaced yours.

Keep a list of the people who have helped you (or even expressed interest in your job search) so that as soon as you're hired you can deliver the good

1) to state what you hope the meeting will accomplish, and 2) to talk about your career goals. Put your questions in writing, keeping in mind that your aim is to learn as much as possible while making a good impression.

Call the morning of the meeting to confirm the start time and then arrive five minutes early. Dress professionally, giving as much attention to looking spiffy and well-groomed as you would for an actual job interview. Bring a resume in a folder or briefcase, but don't offer it unless it is asked for. Also bring paper and a pen to take notes. (Forget your tape recorder, which would not only set the wrong tone but probably make the person you're speaking with less inclined to open up.) Wear a watch, since you'll want to be the one to end the meeting when the allotted time is up.

MEETING
During the course of the meeting, play up the pupil-teacher relationship—particularly if you're a recent graduate. Without seeming to pry, ask the person what she learned along the way before succeeding in her career. Take note of any career moves she says were beneficial, plus any that were not. If you can convince the person that you want her advice because you admire her accomplishments, you may well gain a mentor and an ally—a contact who knows just the people who can open doors for you.

THANKING
Follow up an information interview with a thank-you note. (Send it on the same day of the meeting or, at the latest, the morning after.) Thanking the person for her time—and for sharing insights into her career or company—not only makes her feel good about helping you but also reinforces the positive impression you hope you made.

news to all. A note of thanks also lets you say, "Please call on me if I can ever help you in any way"—an obligation for the nice-guy networker.

THE RIGHT TOOLS

Finding a job is first and foremost an exercise in communication, both oral and written. Today, most companies expect job applications to be faxed or e-mailed, but that doesn't mean that an honest-to-God letter is a thing of the past. Correspondence on high-quality paper, when done right, can make an especially good impression—especially when the inclusion of your e-mail address shows that you could have taken the easier way out.

- **VOICE MAIL/FAX/E-MAIL.** Make it easy for people to reach you over the telephone by having an answering machine or a voice mail service at home. Leave a professional-sounding message by clearly announcing your first and last names and phone number. Speak as you normally do; you don't want to over-enunciate and sound as if you're trying too hard. Don't get creative: You have no way of knowing what a prospective employer will think of background music or jokey spiels explaining why you're not at home. (See also Recording a Greeting, page 301.)

    Having a fax machine or e-mail at home isn't essential (the cost may be prohibitive), but you should know how to gain quick access to either. Regular mail will usually do when sending a resume and cover letter, but if an employer asks you to fax or e-mail material ASAP, get moving to the nearest all-service copy shop.

- **PERSONAL BUSINESS STATIONERY.** When you're sending by regular mail, never use company letterhead to conduct personal business—especially when looking for a job. For all job search letters, buy the best quality personal business stationery you can afford; the favorable impression made by a heavy bond 100% cotton paper is worth the cost. Business stationery can be either 8½ by 11 inches or 7½ by 10 inches and makes the best impression when printed (black ink is the fail-safe choice) with your name, address, telephone number, and e-mail address and fax numbers. (See also The Stationery Drawer, page 314.)

- **CORRESPONDENCE CARDS.** A handwritten note makes an indelible impression in the electronic era, especially in more traditional fields. While cover letters and other formal correspondence should be word-processed on your business stationery letter sheets, thank-you notes and personal notes to business associates can be written on a correspondence card. (See also The Stationery Drawer, page 314.)

- **PERSONAL "BUSINESS" CARDS.** Job or not, a job seeker should have a printed card of some kind—the most efficient way to give someone you meet enough information to reach you in the future. Make sure the card is of high-quality stock printed with a readable font. Include your full name, home address, home phone number, and if applicable, a home e-mail address and fax number. Once you've had cards printed, put a few in each coat, suit, handbag, or briefcase, so that you'll have one handy when needed.

If you are employed but simultaneously looking for another job, consider having a personal card printed with only your name, home and e-mail addresses, and telephone and fax numbers. Having both this card and your company card at the ready lets you choose between handing out one or the other as called for. (See also Your Trusty Business Card, page 226.)

TAKING ACTION

Networking is the underpinning of your job search, but not an end unto itself. Sooner or later, it's time to take action. When that moment arrives, you're charged with the work of learning what's out there, whether this involves calling a company directly, settling into a chair to check out the want ads or surf the Net, or enlisting the services of an employment agency.

Before you make your attempt, find out as much as you can about the company or firm. What do they do? How big are they? Where are they located—a single site or several cities? Have they made any news lately that you might mention in your letter or call? If a company you're interested in is publicly held, try to find the most recent annual report. A trip to the business department of your library is a good investment of your time. You might also be able to talk to a current employee or even a supplier who has a steady working relationship with the company. Do your homework: Knowledge will give credibility to your application letter and prepare you for interviewing.

LETTERS AND PHONE CALLS

Your first contact with a potential employer may result from successful networking, in which case you'll probably have a referral. Alternatively, you may be starting out cold. If the latter, you'll be writing an unsolicited letter or phoning a potential employer who has never heard of you. A well-composed letter on paper may give you a leg up, if only because it allows you to show off your writing skills in a time when good business writing is at a premium. (Job application letters are given full treatment in Resumes and Application Letters, page 28.) When it comes to picking up the telephone, the chance of a cold call paying off may be only a little better than being struck by lightning—but, as they say, "You never know. . . ."

COLD CALLS

Because any office open for business expects to take incoming calls during business hours, don't be shy to call and inquire about potential job openings, whether you've been given the name of a contact or not. If you haven't, your initial call's purpose is to get the name, title, address, and extension number of the person who does the hiring in the department you're looking to join— research, perhaps, or marketing. This information will usually come from an assistant who, if unable to help, will transfer you to Human Resources or Personnel. (Note: Calling either Human Resources or Personnel first off is not the best idea; in many companies, one of their jobs may be to screen out job applicants, not assist them.)

After preparing for your call (see Taking Action page 13), take the plunge. Don't worry too much about having to make repeated efforts to reach someone: polite, positive persistence is an admirable quality in the business world. At the same time, listen for signs of exasperation from the assistant when he realizes it's you yet again. If you sense any, make your next contact a letter.

Once you've been put through to the person in charge of hiring, don't jump into a discourse: Someone who tags you as longwinded is unlikely to be eager to meet you. Simply introduce yourself, give the name of whoever referred you (if applicable) and a brief description of relevant professional experience and your current job (if any), and say that you're interested in learning about potential openings in his or her department. If the person seems receptive, ask if you can go ahead and send a cover letter and resume (check to

---

TELEPHONE TIPS FOR JOB SEEKERS

Whether you're trying to get through to someone to schedule a job interview or an informational interview or to ask about job openings, keep in mind the following tips. (See also On the Telephone, page 288.)

- BEST TIMES OF DAY TO CALL. Typically, the best time to reach someone is between 11:15 A.M. and noon, when morning meetings have adjourned and the lunch hour hasn't started. Another time when people are more likely to be free is after 4:00 P.M.
- VOICE MAIL AS A TOOL. Placing your call very early or very late in the day, when the call screener (typically a 9-to-5 employee) isn't likely to answer, often gives you the opportunity to leave a voice mail message on the person's direct line. Play on the person's ego by mentioning positive things you've heard or read about him that make you want to meet him.
- THE RIGHT ATTITUDE. Be friendly and upbeat every time you call. Never act annoyed that someone from whom you need a favor hasn't returned your call, much less acknowledged your existence. Always be considerate of other people's time by being direct, courteous, and to the point.
- THE CALL SCREENER. Don't try to become friends with a call screener, but do sound friendly and positive. A secretary or assistant who finds you to be aggressive or curt will undoubtedly find reasons to not put your call through. State that you know the person you're trying to reach must be very busy and then ask the most convenient time of day for her to be reached. If your mission is accomplished, a second thank you to an especially cooperative and cordial call screener is deserved.

see whether he prefers e-mail or paper). Don't bring up meeting unless you perceive some genuine interest. Before hanging up, thank the person by saying something like, "I know how busy you must be, and I really appreciate your taking the time to talk with me."

CHECKING OUT WANT ADS

If networking is casting a wide net and seeing what comes in, answering want ads and looking for job postings on the Internet cut straight to the chase, if only as a part of the larger job-seeking picture. Be aware, however, that companies usually post ads only as a last resort, preferring to either hire from within the organization, through referrals, or through employment agencies; at the same time, untold millions of workers owe their jobs to scouring the want ads.

Don't think "newspaper" first off: The ads in trade publications and industry journals in your field of professional interest will often relate better to what you do than those found in the paper. To find job postings on the Internet, use your browser and a search engine, type in "sales careers," for example, and then follow the links that will lead you to related Web sites.

There are two basic types of want ads and job postings:

- **OPEN ADS.** These list the name of the company advertising a job, along with an address or phone number.
- **BLIND ADS.** These show no company name; instead, you respond to an anonymous post office box address. Companies run blind ads for a variety of reasons: to avoid being bombarded by applicants showing up in person; to keep plans to replace a current employee confidential; or to covertly determine job satisfaction among their own employees (which means, of course, that responding to a blind ad is too risky if you're currently employed).

Keep in mind that a want ad, whether open or blind, is most trustworthy when it gives specific details about the job and employer; the smaller the type and the more vague the job description, the more leery you should be.

Some companies give post office box addresses to respond to, others fax numbers and e-mail addresses. A company that lists only an e-mail address expects you to be fully wired, while one that gives only a post office box would probably be impressed by a perfectly executed letter on good-quality stationery.

Be sure to read a job advertisement carefully and try to figure out what kind of employee the company wants, and then use your cover letter to sell yourself accordingly. Such careful attention to detail will make your letter—not-

WHILE YOU'RE LOOKING

Even when you're unemployed, you can gain experience that could increase your chances of getting the job you want. Here are two ways:

- **VOLUNTEERING.** Sometimes it pays to work for free. Volunteering is an excellent way to broaden both your base of contacts and your experience. If, for example, you're a college student or recent graduate whose interest is public relations, you might volunteer to do PR for a nonprofit group. Many nonprofits can't afford to pay for services such as PR and welcome an energetic student with a desire to succeed. During your stay, shining in your work and developing at least one solid relationship within the organization means you'll have a strong reference when you eventually need one.
- **FREELANCING.** Consider setting up shop at home if you're skilled at computer graphics or programming, writing, design, financial planning, or public relations. Use your network to let people know you are taking on clients or projects on a freelance basis. To increase your chances of getting work, make it known that you're willing to charge less than the going market rate. The positive references you will accumulate are likely to pay off later on.

ing, when possible, experience and accomplishments that meet their needs— stand out among the potentially hundreds of responses. Actually, so will expressing a letter to a post office box, which is money well spent.

If the ad lists a phone number and nothing more, call and ask for the name and title of the person to whom your resume and cover letter should be sent. And make sure everything about the name is correct: Getting the spelling of an unusual name right just may give your letter the edge in a time when many people aren't prone to such tender loving care.

SIGNING UP WITH EMPLOYMENT AGENCIES

Just what do employment agencies do? First, you should understand that most private agencies represent not you but rather companies that are looking for employees. Clearinghouses of a kind, private employment agencies act as both recruiter and screener of prospects, most of whom have responded to ads placed by the agency, others who contact it cold.

In most cases, you do not pay a private employment agency to help find you a job; the tab is paid by the companies enlisting the agency's help. It goes without saying that this is something you should find out up front. Also be aware that free services are provided by government-run state employment agencies, of which there are some 2,000 nationwide. These maintain lists of job openings, most often for entry-level workers but also for professionals.

Private employment agencies typically work with entry-level job seekers, too. But take note: Companies looking for employees generally list job opportunities and find prospects in the open market, so you'll be missing out if you rely too heavily on openings provided by an agency. Consider agencies as only a part of, not the be-all, of a job search.

ANOTHER BIT OF ADVICE: Never sign up with a private employment agency without doing a little detective work. Ask for recommendations for agencies from any friends who have experience with them, or even from a friendly interviewer who isn't able to offer you a job. On your own, find out something about the agency's history: how long they've been in business and the professions they specialize in. Also make a call to the Better Business Bureau, who will tell you if any complaints have been filed against the firm.

MEETING THE RECRUITER

Try to meet in person with an employment agency recruiter before she presents you as a candidate to an employer. This meeting is as important as a job interview, so dress the part, arrive on time, bring a resume and list of references, and be prepared to speak succinctly about your goals, accomplishments, and skills. Also do everything you can to show respect for the recruiter's expertise and time. Courteous behavior will reap benefits; like a potential employer, a recruiter is looking for strong social skills as part of the package.

One explicit difference between an *employment agency* interview and a *job* interview is how forthcoming you are about unfavorable information in your personal or job history. While you would never actually lie during a job interview, you wouldn't necessarily bring up being fired, for example, unless you were asked the question. Not so with a recruiter. Present yourself in a positive light, but avoid unwelcome surprises by telling the person anything about your employment or personal history that could be construed as negative. Because recruiters are answering to the employer, they don't want to be caught unawares after giving a glowing recommendation. Similarly, if your radar tells you a former supervisor might give you a less than flattering recommendation, prepare the recruiter for the possibility.

Remember that the recruiter's job is finding the perfect employee for the employer, not the perfect job for you. With this in mind, be as specific as possible when describing your needs so that you aren't seen as fitting a job that doesn't appeal to you. Also face the fact that the recruiter is not a job counselor. Expect an agency to represent you positively to companies, to keep your job search confidential, and to tell you why a particular employer isn't offering a job—but not to provide career advice.

HEADHUNTERS

Executive search firms, better known as headhunters, are hired by companies to seek out people who fit the specifications for certain executive positions or creative jobs requiring exceptional skills. While headhunters sometimes place ads, their usual modus operandi is the aggressive mining of executive ranks in an effort to lure individuals away to their client. Unlike employment agencies, they don't invite job hunters into their stable of candidates. You could approach such a firm with a resume and letter, but seeing it come to something is a long shot for even the most qualified job hunter.

JOB COUNSELORS AND CONSULTANTS

Other kinds of agencies or firms go by the name of career counselor, job counselor, job consultant, professional placement specialist, or management consultant. To varying degrees, their purpose is to assist in determining career goals, to give direction in finding the most suitable occupation, and to package a person's skills and accomplishments into a salable resume and cover letter. What all have in common is payment in advance by the job seeker (or, in some cases, by a company financing outplacement assistance for an employee who has been laid off), regardless of the outcome of the search.

If you go this route, try to find a firm with experience and contacts in your particular field. At the very least your consultant should stay current with industry trends and have access to trade publications and journals. You become the employer, so to speak, when hiring consultants, so ask plenty of questions regarding their experience, results with other clients, and education.

NOTE: If an agency of this kind won't furnish references, citing client confidentiality, take it as a sign you should look elsewhere.

The Yellow Pages are full of professionals who specialize in speech coaching, table manners, and personal appearance. If you feel you need help in any of these areas, consider signing up. While not job consultants, they aid you by polishing off any rough edges—a boon in these competitive times.

ORGANIZE, ORGANIZE, ORGANIZE!

If you are without a job, make your search for one your full-time work. Likewise, if you're currently employed and looking, get busy during your off-hours and weekends. Be methodical in the process and take it one day at a time. To maintain a sense of control (and to seem in control to others), set daily or weekly goals for the number of calls and letters you'll put forth.

Effective time management is crucial to the job search. Begin each day or week by writing a list of specific tasks to accomplish: "Call Douglas Denby about scheduling an interview. Follow up with Anne Banks regarding letter and resume." Even if on a certain day—or worse, within a week—no one returns your calls or responds to your letters, you will probably still feel a sense of daily accomplishment because you've made five calls, reached two people, learned of a new opportunity, or scheduled a networking lunch.

TEMPORARY EMPLOYMENT AGENCIES

A temporary employment agency provides companies with qualified workers on short notice and job seekers with temporary employment. Becoming a temp has its benefits when you're in the midst of a job search: It can provide additional job experience; it can pay the bills until you find a permanent job; and it might even lead to permanent employment.

Approach an interview at a temp agency just as you would any job interview; the more impressed they are, the better the assignments you'll be offered. An agency will need copies of your resume, so have it ready before calling. Then be specific about what kind of job you're looking for and in what field. If, for example, your goal is to work as a paralegal at a law firm, you could shoot for *any* job (secretary, for example, or receptionist) at *any* law firm. Working as a temp is a way to get your foot in the door and meet the people who can hire you permanently, assuming they're going to recognize your skills and talents. Once inside, you'll be privy to job openings in other departments and able to apply for positions as they become available.

ABOUT SALARY: When working through a temp agency you'll be paid an hourly wage consistent with the industry standard for your geographic location and level of experience. (It is the agency that determines your salary, not the company.) Salaries aren't set in stone, and it's acceptable to negotiate an hourly rate with the temp agency that meets your needs and expectations.

CHAPTER 3

RESUMES AND
APPLICATION LETTERS

As you prepare to fax, e-mail, or post your resume to points near and far, face up to a blunt reality: In today's time-conscious world, people are looking for reasons to dispose of it. The person who receives your resume is under no obligation to actually read it or respond—and is all the less likely to if it's not well-presented or contains a misspelled word. To lessen the chance of your resume being directed toward the wastebasket or deleted with the click of a mouse, make it easy to read and error-free. Remember that the care with which it's done announces your professional abilities loud and clear.

For all the attention that goes into creating a resume (ideally, tailored to the desired job), the end product should be short and sweet—one page or, if you have extensive work experience, two. A "quick take" shows consideration of the time of the reader, a fundamental of business etiquette. This is true whether you're applying cold for *any* job opening within a particular company, a *specific* job opening you found in an ad, or you are sending your resume and cover letter to someone to whom you've been referred.

The cover letter of your resume is actually a letter of application, ideally a well-crafted piece of salesmanship that separates you from the pack. While the resume effectively telegraphs the bare bones of who you are and what you are seeking, the letter allows you to expand on how your background makes you a good fit for a certain company or job.

THE BASICS

Paring down your resume and letter means taking the trouble to organize and present information so that it's readily accessible; likewise, making sure that it's free of any grammatical and spelling errors shows you as not only meticulous but respectful—the compositional equivalent of not slouching in your chair. Your dictionary, a brush-up on grammar, and perhaps one of the myriad resume- and cover letter-writing guides on the market (each with a somewhat different theory of what's best) will be your tools. No matter which style or format you choose, be mindful of these four basics:

- Make certain your resume and cover letter are completely accurate and a true reflection of your experiences.
- Illustrate your skills and abilities by relating your specific accomplishments instead of merely listing the jobs you held.
- If you're mailing your resume and cover letter, use 8½" x 11" sheets of good-quality (high cotton-fiber) paper in white, off-white, or a muted neutral color.
- Use a readable typeface. Steer clear of trendy or unusual fonts, and keep the size at 12 points—no larger, and never below 10 points.

CHRONOLOGICAL OR FUNCTIONAL?

The two classic resume styles are the reverse chronological resume, which lists the jobs you've had from the present one to the first, and the functional resume, which describes your skills, abilities, and accomplishments as they relate to the job you seek. Employers are most accustomed to the chronological style, but if you have little work experience or some gaps in employment, a functional resume shows your skills and talents in the best light. Both styles have these elements in common:

- **THE HEADING.** This gives the potential employer what he needs to reach you—your full name, address, phone and fax numbers, and e-mail address, if any. Most people use a slightly larger or bold font to highlight their name in the heading. Three things to note:
  - If any of this vital information changes, update it immediately so that no one has difficulty finding you.
  - Let the style of the company determine whether you should add still more: your cell phone number or even a personal Web page. A company that relies heavily on electronic communication may expect such information, whereas those that stick close to tradition may see it as overkill.
  - If you are currently employed, don't use your business address or phone number; it's hardly appropriate to conduct your job search on another employer's watch. Also, don't hesitate to say that you want to keep your job search confidential; confidentiality may not always be assumed.
- **A STATEMENT OF YOUR OBJECTIVE.** This lets the reader quickly assess the kind of job you're looking for and the experience or skills that make you qualified for it. (If you're applying for a specific job, tailor the

objective accordingly.) Be as brief as possible when describing why you're a prime candidate, limiting yourself to one or two concise sentences: "Seek entry-level position in sales that provides the opportunity to use my communication skills and my ability to reach and exceed quotas." Unless you want a lateral career move, write an objective that elevates you one or two rungs on the ladder: "Goal is to work as an inside-sales support manager, putting to fuller use the managerial skills and technical knowledge I gained as assistant manager at TurboTech Systems."

- **EXPERIENCE AND EDUCATION.** Whichever of these is more substantial in your curriculum vitae is listed first.

    Recent college graduates with no work experience or only one or two previous jobs should start with their education, including such details as GPA (but only if it's above 3.0 on a 4.0 scale), academic honors, major, and any college leadership positions.

    - Education takes a backseat in the resumes of people who have gained real on-the-job experience. Occupations and accomplishments are listed in reverse chronological order (present job first), followed by education. The education notes should be limited to name of school, degree(s) obtained there, and date of matriculation.

    When listing your past jobs, include the name and location of each company, your job titles, and dates of employment. On a separate worksheet, list your responsibilities, accomplishments, skills, and unique talents; then select for your resume those that best fit the job, along with two or three of your most outstanding accomplishments. (Don't include any routine responsibilities, which will be assumed. If, for example, you were an administrative assistant, there's no need to mention photocopying, taking messages, and fetching coffee.) Just take care not to misrepresent yourself or your experience.

- **OPTIONAL ADD-ONS.** Including one line of special interests, skills, or hobbies may inspire small talk during the interview you hope takes place. Be sure the interests you list are a positive reflection of your abilities and personality and have some relevance to the job. This is also the place to list language proficiencies or knowledge of work-related computer programs.

    Adding more detailed education history, such as grades, leadership roles, or relevant course work, is up to the individual. Including your college GPA is hardly necessary after you have acquired several years of work experience, but is optional even if you have just graduated. Realize, however, that if you are a recent graduate and leave out your GPA, the reader will assume it was less than a 3.0 on a 4.0 scale.

Theresa Montalvo
211 Elmwood
Houston, TX 75110
(713) 555–1212

OBJECTIVE
Entry level position in accounting, where exceptional math skills, mastery of applicable software, attention to detail, a willingness to work hard, and a positive attitude are required.

EDUCATION
Currently enrolled in night classes at University of Houston, working toward degree in accounting that will enable me to reach my goal of becoming a CPA.
Graduated in 1994 from Hillsboro Junior College, in top 15 percent of class.

EXPERIENCE
1995 to present   Assistant bookkeeper, Moonbeam Computers, Katy, TX
- Created linked spreadsheets to track travel and entertainment using Excel
- Maintained an Access database to record additions to fixed assets
- Downloaded mainframe queries to Excel for account analysis
- Designed an information systems improvement that made cost reports available 20 percent sooner

SUMMARY
Creative problem solver who works well with people. Fluent in Spanish. In junior college, awarded Moore Math Medal two years in a row.

This aspiring accountant shows she's serious by including her eventual goal in her resume—to become a CPA. While her experience is thin, she specifies her duties in bulleted entries, with the last showing her as the kind of person who does more than is required. The inclusion of her math award backs up her claim to superior math skills.

OPPOSITE: *This manager in the heating, ventilation, and air conditioning (HVAC) business is looking for a higher position in another company. Because he is experienced, his educational background is placed at the end. His track record shows him to be a self-reliant person who continues to advance.*

Michael Collins
4620 Carroll Street
Laramie, WY 82002
(307) 555-1212

OBJECTIVE

Join a leading company in the HVAC industry in a key sales-management position, with responsibility for sales and service administration for both domestic and international markets.

SUMMARY

Over 8 years of customer service and inside sales experience in the HVAC industry, with emphasis on hydronic systems and mechanical components. Advance training in the application of chillers, boilers, pumps, and related equipment.

EXPERIENCE

1995–present   Manager of Customer Service, Cool Breeze, Inc., Laramie, WY

Key responsibilities include processing of all orders, dealing with representatives on technical issues, coordinating deliveries with production, and reviewing all purchase orders and other legal documents. Initiated regular weekly meetings with purchasing and production departments to reduce lead time on orders. Recognized as employee of the year, 1998.

1991–94   Manager of Warranty, Cool Breeze, Inc.

Reviewed all incoming claims under the standard warranty policy. Approved payments or arranged for appropriate action. Reported to senior management on a weekly basis a summary of all claims and reported any critical areas of concern or developing trends to the Engineering and Corporate Safety Coordinator. Reduced the cost of warranty claims by 35% compared to budget for 3 years running.

1986–91   Field Service Technician (repairing HVAC equipment), Cool Breeze, Inc.

Managed field service and start-up crew working in the Southwest. Responsible for work-order scheduling and crew training. Devised a job-planning program that reduced average service time by 30%. Received company award as top service team 4 out of 5 years.

KEY SKILLS

Experience in telephone sales

Good working knowledge of order entry

Proficient in use of Internet and Excel, Word, and PowerPoint

EDUCATION

Bachelor of Business Administration, University of Wyoming (1993)

Associate Degree in HVAC systems design and operations, Holbein Institute (1990)

Certificate in advanced air-conditioning repair, Vo-Tech of Laramie (1986)

Summer intern, Hot Stuff Pump Company (1990). Worked with Chief Engineer on the development of a new heat exchanger. Prepared drawings using AutoCAD 13. Earned 60% of funds needed for college expenses.

NO JOB EXPERIENCE?

Don't despair while gazing wanly at the "Experience" line on your resume, thinking you have nothing to put down. Everyone has to have a first job, and no one expects a recent graduate to have years of professional experience. If you're just striking out on your search, let your education, academic honors, leadership roles, volunteer work, and summer jobs be the sum total of your resume. Don't be embarrassed to include any summer jobs or internships you held in high school or during college; it may so happen that, like you, your potential employer was a camp counselor and feels it's great leadership training for the corporate world. And don't forget volunteer work. Just because you weren't paid for a job doesn't mean it isn't valid experience. Helping, say, to run a homeless shelter at your church or synagogue shows experience in management, budgeting, and organization.

CONCERNING REFERENCES

While it's a good idea to have four or five references who can speak to your capabilities and accomplishments, remember not to incorporate them into your resume or cover letter. Instead, list them on a separate page, double-checking the addresses and phone numbers. Take the list to an interview in case you are asked for it; if you're caught without it, have it delivered by the next business day.

ASKING FOR A REFERENCE

Choose your references carefully: Go with people who know your professional skills and capabilities but aren't threatened by your success. Though it's tempting to include relatives and friends, they are never suitable as references unless you've actually worked for them. If you are a recent graduate, you might include professors who can confirm your academic accomplishments and contributions in the classroom.

Once you've made up a list, call potential references and ask if they are willing to be named. If they are, show concern for their time constraints by asking if they'd rather have their home or office phone number listed. If you receive anything less than an enthusiastic response, reevaluate your decision to include the person and consider finding someone else.

After the initial call, offer to get together for a cup of coffee or lunch (your treat, of course) so that you can personally hand over your resume. If the invitation is accepted (and don't be surprised if it isn't in these harried times), be as aware of your clothing and personal image as you would for an interview (see page 35). Think of meeting with a reference as an exercise in networking; he or she may be able to give you a referral as well.

If a face-to-face meeting isn't feasible, mail your resume to a reference. In a separate note, include examples of your work so that the person will be prepared to speak about your capabilities in specifics: "She doubled her sales quota every month" will have more impact than "She's a real go-getter."

THANKING REFERENCES

Thank each reference twice: when he or she accepts the role of reference and when you accept a job. A typed letter is appropriate, but a handwritten note on

---

WHAT TO LEAVE OUT

As important as knowing what to put in your resume is what to leave out. Just as you want your writing to be concise, the style and content of your resume should follow the classic dictum "less is more."

- **THE WORD "RESUME."** Putting this at the top of the page is not only unnecessary but takes up precious space. The same applies to the line "References available upon request," which is generally understood.
- **REFERENCES.** Don't add these to the resume (or cover letter) itself. List them on a separate page and keep it until references are requested.
- **A PHOTO.** Even if you're drop-dead gorgeous, you want to be hired for your mind, experience, and accomplishments—not looks. Remember, too, that pictures are usually scrutinized and commented on by all who see them.
- **AGE, ETC.** Don't list strictly personal information that is not related to the job, such as age, height, weight, marital status, or health.
- **YOUR GPA?** At some point, usually five years after your graduation, leave off your college accomplishments and your GPA, even if it was a 4.0. Use your own discretion: A 40-year-old would seem foolish noting that he served as president of his social fraternity, but a 21-year-old with limited job experience should include such an accomplishment because it demonstrates leadership skills.
- **SALARY NEEDS.** Avoid including salary needs unless the advertisement you're responding to specifically asks for them. In that case, include them in the cover letter. Your resume is never the place to broach the subject of salary.

your best stationery is more personal. By all means, keep your references abreast of your job search, especially when you've had success.

Once hired, it's acceptable to ask your new employer which references he or she contacted, so you can write a second note of thanks. Even if references weren't called, thank them for offering their assistance; your diligence will pay off in the future if you need to call on them again. Mention in your correspondence (and in person, when possible) your eagerness to return the favor in some way whenever you can.

THE APPLICATION LETTER

Consider the goal of the cover letter—technically an employment application letter—to successfully apply for an interview. It is not, in fact, going to get the

---

AN EXEMPLARY COVER LETTER

The following letter is an example of a professional and attention-getting application. It is written on the recommendation of a supervisor. It is also an unsolicited letter and must consider the fact that no position may be available. Note that the writer focuses on her account work rather than her lengthy experience as a traffic director because account service is the area in which she desires employment. She cites specific, though not confidential, numbers to demonstrate the success of the project she has managed. The writer's one personal remark—returning to her hometown—is relevant to the job because it establishes her roots in and knowledge of the recipient's territory.

Winston R. Smith
Vice-President, Account Services
Big Bang Advertising Agency
4321 Creative Boulevard
Chicago, IL 00000

Dear Mr. Smith:

Meredith Gregory, my supervisor at Flotsam, Jetsam & Associates, has recommended that I contact you about an account service position with Big Bang. During six years as Flotsam's traffic director, I have had behind-the-scenes involvement in virtually every aspect of the business. But direct client contact is what I do best.

Two years ago, in addition to my normal duties, I became the account manager for Fido Dog Food, then a small division of the Ms. Gregory's Big Cheese Food Products account. The work has been long, hard, and always satisfying, and now I plan to move into account service

job for you. A good application letter, supported by a concise resume, should make the reader *want* to meet the writer in person. (See also Effective Business Letters, page 314.)

Whether you are writing unsolicited, responding to an advertisement, or writing with a personal referral, be sure you have the full name and courtesy and business titles of the recipient correct. If "M.J. Jones, Human Relations Director" is Mary Jane and your salutation is "Dear Mr. Jones," your carefully written letter may hit the recycling bin. If you do not know the correct person to address (as often happens when you respond to a blind ad), call the company and ask. If you cannot find a person's name, then it's appropriate to address the company or a specific department or position.

---

full-time. It is the area where I can make the most productive use of my organizational skills, my persistence in bringing every project to successful completion, my commitment to measurable results for the client and the agency, and the "grace under fire" that is the chief asset of every traffic manager worth her salt.

I am very proud of what I've accomplished on the Fido account, especially my direction of the repositioning campaign that has raised the brand from near-generic status to a major regional name. In two years, Fido has expanded distribution, enlarged its product line, and seen a remarkable 73 percent growth in sales. Flotsam has benefited as well, with a fourfold increase in billings, from $500,000 to $2 million.

Why do I want to leave such a booming account? I am known at Flotsam as "the traffic director who does account work," and a full-scale transfer to the account side would be difficult to achieve here. I can bring Big Bang a broad-based knowledge of product and service accounts—as you know, Flotsam has a diverse client list. I am also a great admirer of Big Bang's strategic planning and implementation as well as the creative work that you consistently provide. And on a personal note, I would like to return to Chicago, the city of my birth.

Mrs. Gregory tells me that she is looking forward to appearing with you on the research panel at the marketing convention next week. As I know how exhausting these events can be, I will call you in two weeks to see if we can arrange a meeting. (My daytime number, should you want to reach me, is 312–555–1212.) I realize that you may have no immediate openings, but I would like to discuss future opportunities with Big Bang.

Thank you very much for your consideration.

Sincerely,

[SIGNATURE]
Dorothy B. Gale

TO TELL THE TRUTH

A cardinal rule for the job applicant: Don't even think of lying or exaggerating anything in a resume or cover letter. Assume that the truth will come out and have severe, even lifelong, consequences. But given that, how do you write about something in your background that is less than favorable—or at least sounds like it?

Just how negative that "something" is determines what to write. For example, when an applicant has family obligations that make relocation impossible, it's best to make this point up front. If, however, you were fired or laid off from your last job, it's probably better not to explain. Chances are good that anything written about this kind of experience will sound defensive and even hostile. But be prepared to confront the question in an interview.

Women who left the workforce to raise a family, even for several years, have nothing to be ashamed of. When bringing up such gaps in employment in your application letter, put them in the most positive light by noting any continuing education, volunteer work, or life experiences that would be viewed as beneficial by a potential employer.

THE COMPANY'S NEEDS

As you compose your application letter, keep firmly in mind what you're selling—your abilities, your skills, your experience, and your education *as they relate to the employment needs of the company*. There will be many things about you that a potential employer does not want to know. Your family, hobbies, politics, religion, and personal traits are of interest only if they bear directly on the job. You have to convince the reader that you may well be the best person for the position; do that by stating what you can do for the company, not what the company can do for you. (An employer, for example, doesn't want to hear that an applicant regards a job as "an opportunity to improve my financial management skills.")

A GOOD START

First of all, use personal stationery and your personal address. Writing on the letterhead of a current employer is deceptive—and will make a potential employer question your common sense. Make every letter an original. You may be sending out dozens of resumes, but each cover letter should be individualized. The computer makes it easy to develop a basic format for application letters, but a format is not mere duplication.

Make your opening sentence and paragraph dynamic. "I am applying for the position of customer services representative . . . " is informative, but it is also clichéd and lacking in energy. Your application may be one of dozens, or hundreds. What can you say in your first sentence that will compel the recipient to read on? When journalists speak of a "grabber lead," they are referring to an opening sentence so intriguing that it grabs the reader's full attention. An example: "I realized I wanted to be a salesman in the summer of 1981, when my lemonade stand put everyone else's in the shade." A second example: "It was my philosophy professor who told me I should think of becoming a lawyer some day." Aim for a grabber lead, and avoid openings that are predictable, dry, and hackneyed.

If you are writing as the result of a personal referral or recommendation, say so in the first sentence. Use the full name of the person who is making the referral: "Our mutual friend, Bob . . . " will not impress the employer who knows several Bobs as well as Roberts. Include any titles or information that will immediately identify your referral: "Our friend Dr. Robert 'Bob' Johnston, who is still the best physician ever to care for us Western College football players, recommended that I contact you about the sports reporting position with your newspaper." This opening not only identifies the referral by name and title, but it also establishes a connection between the writer and the reader, provides a key piece of information about the writer, and clearly states the purpose of the letter.

KEEP IT SHORT

Never write more than one page. If there is lengthy information you need to include (such as a history of publications or a catalog of technical capabilities), list the data on a separate sheet and make reference to the listing in your cover letter. At the same time, don't simply repeat the facts in your resume; instead, use your cover letter to point out and expand on information that is directly applicable to the job you're seeking. You'll also want to briefly explain specific experiences or capabilities, such as overseas service or fluency in a foreign language, so long as they are relevant.

NO APOLOGIES NECESSARY

Remember that you're seeking a job, not begging for clemency. Even for first-time job applicants, cover letters should reflect self-confidence and competence. You don't have to humble yourself or plead—and never apologize. On the other hand, demonstrating self-confidence should not become arrogance. Letters that tell an employer "You'll never find a more productive worker than me" or "There's no task I can't accomplish" are cocky, boorish, and at bottom, false. "My experience as a radio producer has taught me how to deal with last-minute problems and still meet every deadline" shows confidence and professionalism without being boastful.

Bringing Up Salary

In general, address the issue of salary in an initial letter only when the employer asks for your salary requirements or when the amount of your compensation is your first consideration. If you have to make $50,000 a year, you might as well say so in the beginning and let the chips fall.

Many potential employers use salary figures as a means to cull applications, and it's frankly pointless to pursue a job that can't meet your financial needs. If an employer asks for salary requirements, you may give the actual amount of your present salary or a range. It is perfectly acceptable, however, to say that your current salary is "consistent with standards in the market" or that your needs are negotiable.

Closing the Letter

Notice that the sample application letter on pages 28–29 closes with a commitment to act. It also includes a telephone number where the writer can be reached during business hours. If you're available only at certain hours, give that information as well. If you can't take calls during business hours, say so and provide a number for an answering service or machine or an e-mail address. (If you use a machine or voice mail, be sure that your answering message is clearly audible and professional and that you include your name.) Do not, however, expect an employer to track you down. Make your follow-up calls on schedule.

End with gracious, but not effusive, thanks. Concluding sentences such as "Thank you for your time and consideration" and "Thank you for considering my application for the position" are always correct.

Never send photocopies, and always sign each letter. (If you're of the old school and want to send an actual letter, you should never hand-write it, although you may address an envelope by hand.)

Finally, don't automatically blame your letter if you fail to get an interview. There are many reasons why you may not get to the next step in the process:

USING A RESUME SERVICE

Your expertise in drawing blueprints or translating languages may be a wonder to behold, but your resume will be judged first by how it looks and reads. It's not a stretch to say that its appearance is vitally important: If the person reading your resume feels, even after a glance, that it's too hard to find what he needs, he may stop right there. Computer technology to the rescue: The ability of computers to make information more accessible with boldface types and bulleting can create a supremely user-friendly resume.

If your design skills on the computer end with word processing, consider hiring a resume service. But be aware that there are two schools of thought on the wisdom of pursuing this route. Proponents say that besides adding technical finesse, a service can take your list of previous jobs and wordsmith it into a maximum-impact marketing tool. Skeptics say it will end up looking like it came off the assembly line. If you are considering hiring a service, ask to see several samples—not just one—of their work. Then politely suggest that your participation in the creative process would be a condition of signing up.

TWO ADDITIONAL SOURCES OF HELP: 1) Web sites on the Internet that walk you through the process of writing your resume; and 2) special software programs that will format your resume for you.

The position may have been filled; the employer may have received applications from more qualified people; there may have been no job in the first place. (For corporate visibility, some companies continuously run classified ads even when they have no openings.)

PROOFREADING YOUR WORK

Any mistake in your letter can cost you the job. There is no excuse for misspelling, poor grammar, or bad punctuation. Unless you're very secure with your writing skills, have someone else proofread your resume and all cover letters. A new, objective pair of eyes can find mistakes and give suggestions for rewording or deleting information. Another trick is for you to read the letter from right to left, one line at a time; this forces you to look at each word separately. Move a piece of paper down the page to track each line.

Always wait at least one day between creating a document and proofreading it so that your eyes become new and objective. This waiting period between creating and proofing allows you to be less biased about your own work.

*Resumes
and
Application
Letters*

CHAPTER 4

THE INTERVIEW

You've gotten to the interview stage, so count your resume and cover letter as your first successes on the path to employment. Congratulations are in order, but now it's time to put your best foot forward and show who you really are. What you've put down on paper is going to be backed up and expanded by how you present yourself in person, and that's where social skills—another name for etiquette—enter the picture. Your expertise, experience, and ability to field questions are vital, of course, but your attitude, your appearance, and how you handle yourself can either clinch or ruin your chances.

IMPROVING YOUR ODDS

Don't let anyone tell you an interview isn't stressful. How on earth could it not be, considering you're being judged on your looks, your life history, your intelligence, and your ability to think on your feet—all in unfamiliar surroundings? Some interview questions you can anticipate, others you can't. The best way to stay calm is to recognize what you *can* control and prepare for that. Improve your odds with some research and self-examination:

- **READ UP ON THE COMPANY.** Resources such as Dun & Bradstreet, leading business magazines, and the company's annual report (and possibly its Web site) will fill you in on the company's profile and its general attitude. Collecting information not only helps you anticipate the qualities your interviewer is looking for but gives you ideas for questions to ask the interviewer (see page 44). Ideally, you'll be able to talk about the company's chief products, prime markets, and even plans for future growth. If you're applying for a specific job, ask Personnel for the job description beforehand, so you'll be able to answer questions in that context, highlighting any skills that directly apply.

- **KNOW THYSELF.** With your newfound knowledge of the company and your own resume in mind, take stock of your qualities. Because you'll be asked about your strengths, aptitudes, and experience, it's essential to have a concrete idea of them before articulating them to your interviewer. (See also Taking Stock, page 6.)

Spend some time reviewing your resume (refreshing your memory of dates of employment and exact job titles) and, if necessary, revising it to highlight the most relevant areas of your experience. Know your resume by heart. During the interview, having it firmly in your head enables you to point out or discuss certain parts of it without consulting a hard copy.

- **PRACTICE.** Ask yourself the questions you're likely to be asked (see page 40), and practice answering them aloud: What are your strengths and weaknesses? What are you looking for? What qualifies you for this job? What is the hardest challenge you've faced, and how did you overcome it?

THE RIGHT CLOTHES

Like it or not, the clothes you wear to your interview invite snap judgments that are hard to overcome, no matter how well you acquit yourself as a conversationalist and thinker. Gold chains or pinkie rings alone may screen out a male before a word is spoken, and a female wearing pink patterned hose is also jeopardizing her chances. Yes, dressing is personal and a way of expressing yourself, but clothing yourself for a job interview often requires a measure of compromise, especially in traditional fields. Even if the field is of the type known for breaking the mold (the traditional dress code included), you'll need to sharpen up—a jacket and tie need not be from Brooks Brothers to look smart and in good taste. Dark or neutral colors, natural fabrics, appropriate footwear in tip-top shape, and the judicious (if any) use of scent combine to make a positive impression virtually anywhere.

DRESS TO FIT IN

When putting together your interview outfit, consider the kind of office you're visiting: Your clothes should be a conservative version of what you would wear to work there if your job level were one notch above. (If it's possible to scout the office out beforehand without looking conspicuous, drop by on any workday but Friday, the typical dress-down day, to get an idea of the general standard of dress.) In short, you want to look as if you'll fit in.

Remember to plan for *all* of your wardrobe; any coat, umbrella, handbag, or briefcase should be as presentable as the rest of your outfit. Try to carry as little as possible, so you don't find yourself loaded down as you walk into your appointment. Do bring a small leather notebook or planner: You shouldn't take notes during the interview, but it's smart to have a presentable notebook on hand in case you need to take down phone numbers and such at the end. Also carry with you at least one copy of your resume—clean, unsmudged, and ready to make a powerful impression on whoever receives it.

The advice that follows is slanted toward businesses on the conservative side, and will usually put you on safe ground. At the same time, dressing *too* traditionally could hurt your chances in fields such as information technology, music, and fashion. Again, tailor your wardrobe to the expectations of the company.

INTERVIEW CLOTHES FOR MEN

Following are the best interview clothing choices at most companies. (See also Business Clothes for Men, page 149.)

- **SUITS.** Unless you're interviewing in a field where a suit would look out of place, wear one. At most places, an open-collar shirt and jacket may be fine for daywear down the line, but not when you need to make a good first impression. Natural fabrics in solid dark blue or gray suggest authority and quality, while all but the most subtle of patterns are risky. Also make sure your suit hasn't gone out of style; three-piece suits were the business fashion in the Eighties but wouldn't look so spiffy today. In any case, it must be perfectly clean and pressed; spots and wrinkles leave a poor impression.
- **SHIRTS.** As a rule, the simpler the better in conservative environments—no bright colors, no patterns, no French cuffs, no monograms. White or pale blue are preferred choices for color, and you can't go wrong with a 100 percent cotton fabric—preferably laundered with medium starch.
- **TIES.** In general, now is not the time to use your tie as an expression of your individuality. To play it safe, choose the traditional silk tie in relatively muted colors and patterns (foulard, stripes, paisley, or solid). It may also be wise to avoid ties with images and designer logos.
- **SOCKS.** These are easy: Choose a color that coordinates with your suit (usually black, dark gray, dark brown, or dark blue), and make sure they're long enough not to expose bare skin when you're sitting or crossing your legs.
- **SHOES.** Wing-tips or slip-on dress shoes in black or brown leather are the classics. Avoid any "dress" shoes with thick rubber soles. As important as the style is the condition: Shoes should be newly polished, and heels shouldn't be visibly worn down.
- **JEWELRY AND COLOGNE.** With either of these optional accessories, less is more. Limiting jewelry to a wedding band is the safest choice. In some creative fields, a small earring is more acceptable than a pinkie ring, neck chains, or bracelets, which are a bad idea most anywhere. As for cologne, splashing on too much can be the kiss of death. Confine any scent to a subtle aftershave, used sparingly.

- **BRIEFCASE.** A slim leather attaché or portfolio is the best choice. Make sure the contents are orderly in case you have to open it.

INTERVIEW CLOTHES FOR WOMEN

Women have more to think about, and often have to spend more than men. On the other hand, they have a wider range of clothing choices than men, especially in colors, patterns, and fabrics. (See also Business Clothes for Women, page 165.)

- **SKIRT SUIT.** This is the risk-free choice for an interview. While natural fabrics were once the only way to go, today knits and natural-synthetic blends are perfectly acceptable; not only will they stay unwrinkled, but modern science has made synthetics such as Rayon lose their not-so-tasteful sheen.
- **BLOUSES.** Choose a long-sleeve blouse that shows a little cuff beyond the jacket sleeve. Short sleeve blouses may be fine for work in summer, but not for your interview. A sleeveless blouse? Never—at least in conservative fields. Many of the old color and fabric taboos no longer apply to blouses, but for an interview, a cotton or silk blouse in a neutral color and with a simple collar is still the safest choice.
- **SCARVES.** A classic 34-inch-square silk scarf that complements your suit in color and pattern brings an elegant touch to your outfit. Just make sure the colors aren't too loud or the patterns too large.
- **SHOES.** Pumps with a 1½-inch heel (and in perfect condition) are standard. Choose a color that complements your suit and handbag—black, brown, burgundy, or navy. Avoid open-toe shoes.
- **STOCKINGS.** Fashions change, but in the late Nineties, sheer skin tones were in and patterns and opaques were out. Choose a shade that approximates your skin color or is a bit darker.
- **BRIEFCASE.** A status briefcase is preferable to a purse for an interview, conveying more authority. A small purse kept inside the case will hold your lipstick and other grooming essentials.
- **JEWELRY AND PERFUME.** The advice for male interviewees to rein in the showiness of their ties applies twice over to women and their jewelry. Earrings or bracelets that dangle, sway, jangle, or gong should be left at home, as should any rings other than a wedding band, an engagement ring, and perhaps one more of simple design. Multiple piercings up the ear (not to mention any in the nose or eyebrow) will be greeted with alarm at the more traditional workplaces, and necklaces should be confined to small-scale silver or gold chains or classic pearls. Minimalism is the rule for perfume as well: Choose a light, not romantic, scent—and wear it very sparingly.

- **MAKEUP.** Subtle makeup that doesn't call attention to itself is without doubt the best choice in any but the most nonconventional workplaces. Save the brown lipstick and heavy eyeliner for weekends.

GROOMING AND HYGIENE

While you want to be *seen* to your best advantage during an interview, you never want to be *smelled,* except for perhaps the slightest hint of perfume or cologne. Shower or bathe, wash your hair (or, if you're a woman, pay a visit to the hairdresser), and use deodorant. And don't forget your breath: Try not to eat before the interview—nothing should come between it and your last tooth-brushing (especially alcohol, which will "loosen you up" right out of a job). Avoid eating garlic or onions even the night before; in some people, the odor of both can emanate from the pores for up to 18 hours or more. The same applies to liquor, beer, and cigarettes: If you've overindulged the night before, your interviewer's nose may tell him so—and he'll mark you as undisciplined or worse. Don't rely on breath mints to mask such a serious lapse in judgment.

Men's hair. Scouting the workplace culture for clues on the issue of hair is a good idea. Is the traditional business look the rule, or is personal expression given free rein? Whatever the style (and whether you decide to follow suit), your hair should be neat and clean.

Women's hair. The idea that a businesswoman's hair shouldn't be longer than shoulder length has gone by the board in most professions. Nevertheless, special care should be taken to make long hair look well styled and cared-for. For an interview, wearing hair pinned up or tied back using simple clips, combs, or other hair accessories may be the least risky choice. Whatever the length of your hair, the idea is to have it so clean and well combed that you're not tempted to "fuss" with it during your interview.

THE BIG MOMENT

Now that you're scrubbed and dressed to the nines, double check that everything is in order. Allow yourself plenty of time to get to the interview meeting in case you have trouble finding the room; you'll also want to freshen up in the rest room beforehand. Don't make your entrance too early, though, or your wait in the reception area may make the interviewer feel rushed or intruded on. Five to ten minutes early is ideal timing.

While waiting, be cordial but professional (in other words, not overly familiar) with everyone you meet. You never know how much influence the

READY? SET? BEFORE YOU GO . . .

Here's a checklist of things you should remember before you set out for your interview. Tick them off one by one and you're all set. (See also Interview Faux Pas, page 41.)

- Your shoes are clean.
- Your clothes are pressed and stain-free.
- Your nails are clean.
- Your hair is neat.
- You've removed all extra jewelry.
- You have clean copies of your resume.
- You have the address and phone number of the meeting place.
- You know how to get there and how long it will take.
- You know the names of everyone you are meeting, and how to pronounce them.
- You have your notebook and pen.
- There is nothing extraneous or bulky in your bag.
- You are prepared for rain or sleet or snow, and your coat is in good condition.
- For women, you have a powder compact, lipstick, and an extra pair of panty hose.

receptionist or assistant might have, especially if the interviewer can't make up her mind about you and asks for an opinion. When you come face to face with the interviewer, extend your hand in greeting: "Hello, Ms. [Mr.] Philpot. Thanks for calling me in." Be composed, and don't forget to smile. Although you shouldn't try to get too chummy, do your best to act friendly and relaxed. (See also The All-Important Handshake, page 269.)

Once you're seated (stand until you're offered a chair), the interview will no doubt begin with small talk. (If you find yourself at a loss for words and the interviewer isn't coming to the rescue, look around for an opening gambit; the office's pictures, books, or plants may provide common ground for conversation.) Then come the pertinent questions.

The first piece of advice: Don't panic. The interviewer is likely to be at least a little nervous, too, since she's representing the company. But even if a supremely self-confident interviewer goes beyond a slightly imperious manner to aggressiveness, you're not entirely at her mercy. She'll be orchestrating the conversation, but remind yourself that you have some responsibility for it as

The Interview

well: By asking questions and subtly directing them to your strengths, you have at least some measure of control.

Don't be surprised if you're interviewed by two people at once, or by two or more people separately. If you're faced with a panel of interviewers, make eye contact with all of them at different points, and don't concentrate your attention on one at the expense of others. Instead of letting a multiperson interview cow you, consider it an opportunity to find out even more about the company. The more answers to your questions, the better.

ANSWERING QUESTIONS

Answer questions in a clear and confident manner, but be careful not to come off as a know-it-all. Start your statements with "I think . . . " or "I imagine . . . " or "As far as I can tell . . . " instead of "There's no doubt that . . . " or "Everyone knows that . . . " or "It's clear that . . . "

Also, take a moment to phrase the answer in your head when even an obvious question is posed—for example, "Why are you qualified for the job?" If you've practiced as you should have, your well-rehearsed response will look more spontaneous. Here are three questions that are usually asked, either directly or in a roundabout way:

- **WHAT ARE YOUR STRENGTHS?** This question can be answered in two ways: 1) with a list of your virtues, or 2) with concrete examples of your good points at work. The latter is far more effective in making a lasting impression; the interviewer is more likely take note of your anecdote about how you took charge of the office when your supervisor was ill than something on the order of "I'm good at assuming responsibility when I see a job that needs doing."

- **WHY DO YOU WANT A NEW JOB, AND WHY WITH US?** Put a positive spin on this one. For example, if you're currently employed, avoid saying you feel your talents aren't sufficiently appreciated, you dislike your boss, or anything else negative; instead, say you've gained enough experience in your current job to make you ready to tackle new challenges, and you believe this new position could give you the chance. Back this up with your knowledge of how the company operates (something you've learned in your earlier research). Woe to the interviewee who is asked "What do you know about us?" and finds himself at a loss for words.

- **WHAT WAS THE HARDEST THING YOU EVER FACED IN A JOB?** This question *demands* previous preparation. The idea is not to recount the story of a disastrous situation but to talk about a problem that

INTERVIEW FAUX PAS

As important as the dos that apply to an interview are the don'ts, both in dress and behavior. You may be partial to chewing gum and wearing loud-colored clothes, but doing either is a major faux pas in all but the most unconventional companies. Here are some things to avoid.

FOR WOMEN	FOR MEN	FOR ANYONE
• cocktail dresses, or anything suggesting nighttime revelry • flowing or flowery dresses • microminis and tight pants • open-toed shoes • corduroy, denim, Lycra • beyond one on each earlobe, any visible piercings • jewelry that calls attention to itself • a highly unconventional hairstyle or color • anything scuffed or in less than peak condition	• short-sleeved shirts with a tie • any jewelry other than two (at the most) rings • too much cologne • too creative facial hair • beltless slacks • piercings in general, depending on the field	• arriving late • bringing shopping bags or boxes • loud colors in your outfit • plopping into a chair before the interviewer offers you one • using first names unless asked to • chattering on and on • chewing gum • smoking • jiggling your knee • playing with your hair • fidgeting in general

you were instrumental in solving. This shows that you are ready and able to cope with difficulties that may come your way.

FIELDING INAPPROPRIATE QUESTIONS

The Equal Employment Opportunity Act outlaws questions about age, national origins, marital status, sexuality, and religion. Most interviewers know the law and won't ask. Still, be prepared for the possibility. First, decide whether you'll confront or deflect the issue. If confronting, realize that acting offended or invoking the law will jeopardize your chances, even though you're within your rights.

If a question offends you, you could thank the interviewer for her time and indicate that, based on the question, this is not the kind of company you're interested in. A less rash course is to give her the opportunity to reexamine the appropriateness of the question. But do it by questioning the *question*—not the questioner: "I'm surprised by that question. I thought it was off limits."

Or try humor. "How old are you" answered by "Old enough to have seasoned like a good wine" won't sound confrontational. However you respond, ask yourself whether you want to work for a company that not only asks questions that are personally invasive but also flout the law in the process.

- **HOW OLD ARE YOU, AND WHERE WERE YOU BORN?** Age discrimination is prohibited by law, so this question is unlikely; anyway, the interviewer will be able to judge your approximate age from the dates on your resume. If you're over forty and the interviewer alludes to your age in any way, turn it to your advantage: "I really feel I'm at the top of my form now that I'm in my forties and have so much experience under my belt." If you're a member of an ethnic minority and are asked "Where were you born?," just give the name of the city and state if you were born in the U.S. If you were born elsewhere but are a citizen, say "I was born in Paraguay but am proud to say I became a U.S. citizen in 1991." If you're not a citizen, say you're in the process of becoming one, if this is the case. Understand that by law the potential employer has to check documentation of your citizenship or valid alien status.

- **MARRIED WITH CHILDREN?** At the heart of the questions "Are you married?" and "Are you thinking of having children?" is another: "Are family obligations going to affect your job?" Answering the first one is easy: Just say something on the order of "Yes, I'm married, but my husband and I have known from the start how important it is to keep our family and work lives separate." The second one, almost always directed to women, is thornier. Instead of questioning the relevance of a question about having children, answer honestly but with qualification: "No—not at present, at least." Or "Yes, some day down the line. But it really depends on how my career goes."

- **WHAT'S YOUR SEXUAL ORIENTATION?** If you are openly homosexual, being asked this question is your answer to whether you want to work there—and the answer is almost always "No." Accordingly, politely pose a question of your own: "I'm gay, but what does that have to do with my fitness for this job?" Don't get into a conversation about how you're "gay, but don't follow the homosexual lifestyle." The very fact that the question was asked shows that the company, if it's not actually antigay, considers sexuality an issue; in some states they are also ignoring the law. If you're closeted but refuse to lie, look surprised and lightly brush the question off with "Gee, is that question really appropriate?" Then let the chips fall where they may.

- **WHAT'S YOUR RELIGION?** Answering this question directly risks stereotyping you to those who think in terms of Christian versus Jewish or

Muslim, Catholic versus Protestant, believer versus atheist. If you choose to answer, be general: "My own spirituality is important to me, but I make a practice not to discuss it, especially at work."

OFF-THE-WALL QUESTIONS

Some interviewers try to test your ability to operate under pressure. A classic method is to ask a question for which you're completely unprepared: "How many pages are in your local newspaper? Which three valuables would you carry out of your house in a fire? If you were a leafy green . . . " The aim of the

---

THE HOLE IN THE RESUME

If you have a gap in employment of more than a year, you may be asked why. The reasons for dropping out of the workforce range from matters of choice (taking time off to raise kids or earn an advanced degree) to the unavoidable (being injured, downsized, or fired).

If you chose to stop working, dwell less on justifying why you thought it a good idea than how your time off improved you—juggling a houseful of kids honed your organizational skills, for example. Taking off time for an MBA or other degree speaks for itself, showing that you're serious about making the most of your career. Likewise, absences from work because of serious injury or downsizing are self-explanatory. It's only when you've been fired for misbehavior or poor performance (not job elimination) that you have your work cut out for you when you're asked "You weren't employed in '95 and '96? Why?" If you were fired, you don't have to say so unless asked directly. Saying something like "I was eager to get out and see what other opportunities were out there, and want to keep looking until I find the right place" could either placate the interviewer or arouse suspicions; let your intuition tell you whether to try it. If he asks "Did you leave of your own accord?" be done with the evasion tactics. Answer that you and your boss were having differences and couldn't resolve them (which is true)—so you were let go. The worst thing you can do is say anything negative about your former employer or claim that you were wronged. Approach it from the positive side, saying you've grown from the experience and have corrected any shortcomings and are eager to put your newfound knowledge to work.

Whatever the reason for a gap in your employment, it is important to present yourself as someone who has not been living in a cave for several years but who remains interested and involved in your career. You should also use the functional-style resume (page 22), which won't emphasize the obvious hole in employment the way a chronological resume would.

interviewer is twofold: first, to see how you handle pressure, and second, to see how logically you work toward an answer.

In short, prepare to be unprepared. Listen carefully to the interviewer, acknowledge the question ("Well, I haven't thought of that . . . "), and then take a minute to think before you speak. Let the interviewer hear your thought process: "Hmm. . . . there are usually four sections in our daily paper. The front section is between 20 and 24 pages, and the others are about half as large, so I'd say there's an average of about 55 pages a day." In the end, the answer itself is unimportant (and most likely wrong): Your ability to keep your cool and display a logical train of thought in making a guess is the real goal.

ASKING QUESTIONS

At the end of the interview, you'll more than likely be asked whether you have any questions of your own—not merely as a courtesy but as a continuation of the interviewer's investigation. Make your questions specific to the company or the job; they should also reflect your respect for the interviewer and your seriousness about your job search. Rely on the interviewer to have insights about the company and its employees, but don't ask for the kind of information that could easily be gleaned from the company's annual report; otherwise, you'll

---

YOU'RE OVERQUALIFIED?

If you are interested in a job but overqualified, your interviewer will doubtless want to know why you're willing to take a step down and, in most cases, accept a lower salary. You can explain that you're simply happier with a less demanding position, want to spend more time with your family, or do more volunteer work, whatever the case may be. But realize that employers are wary of hiring overqualified candidates, seeing them as less likely to be satisfied and therefore more likely to leave. For this reason, convey a message of real dedication to the job, along with a valid reason for wanting it.

You may also want to change the format of your resume from the traditional chronological form, which stresses the upward direction your career has taken in the past and highlights the fact that the new position would be a step down. Instead, organize your employment history by areas of experience, which shows your qualifications without pointing out the downward move. (See also Chronological or Functional?, page 22.)

reveal that you haven't done your homework. Here's a sampling of pertinent things you might ask about:

- **YOUR RESUME.** No, the question isn't what the interviewer thought of your resume, but whether she has read it. A surprising number will not have, covering the lapse with something like "Actually, I haven't had a chance to go over it that thoroughly." This lets you know that you have to verbally recap your qualifications, highlighting the assets that best fit the job.
- **JOB RESPONSIBILITIES.** You may have read a job description for the position you're applying for, but a boilerplate outline often fails to reflect reality—primarily, which of the duties are most important. The interviewer's elaboration on the written description helps you to tailor your discussion of your skills to the job's most significant aspects.
- **COMPANY STRENGTHS.** Ask the interviewer her opinion of the company's strong points. This allows you the chance to demonstrate your knowledge of the business, which you gained in your preparation stage.
- **THE JOB'S BIGGEST CHALLENGES.** This is another way of finding out what problems are normally faced in the job and showing how you might go about solving them. Draw on any experience you have, but don't propose a solution to any problems unless you're sure you're on firm ground.
- **WHAT'S EXPECTED OF YOU.** Learning time frames for project deadlines, production quotas, and any other concrete standards of performance gives you the chance to say you're sure you can meet them. It might also open the door to recounting something similar you've done in a previous job.

DISCUSSING SALARY AND BENEFITS

Let the interviewer bring up salary. If he does, it won't necessarily mean you have the job, but it's a good sign. The rationale for waiting: If you broach the subject, the interviewer may not have had time to decide that you're a prime possibility for the job, and he therefore may quote the lower end of the range.

It's fine to respond to the interviewer's salary question with a question: "Could you give me an idea of the range?" Once you have an idea of your market value and the company's resources, offer a range of about $5,000 to $10,000 within which you're willing to negotiate. Wait until you've discussed other benefits and compensation before you make your decision on what you would accept. And remember that you don't have to answer on the spot: It's perfectly fine to ask for more time to consider the amount.

WAITING TO HEAR

Waiting to hear whether you've been accepted for the job is one of the most stressful parts of the job search. But face up to the fact that you must do just that: Wait, and be patient. Sending in still more samples of your work or yet another reference can make you look pushy. No matter how important the job is to you, remember that you're only one of the hiring manager's many concerns. Nevertheless, it's best to have some contact with the company (including your always-essential thank-you note) within three weeks of your interview, lest you appear to have drifted off to some greener pasture. Limit yourself to the following while waiting to hear:

- **A POST-INTERVIEW THANK-YOU NOTE.** This is a must for applicants. A thank-you note shows good manners and reinforces your interest in the job. Write it as soon as you can; aim to have it on the interviewer's desk within two or three days of your meeting. Remember that the interviewer may be seeing a number of people, so include the date of your meeting and the position you are seeking.

  Your thank-you need not be lengthy: Three or four brief paragraphs should do the trick. Although many personal business thank-you notes (for gifts, social occasions, and the like) are handwritten, post-interview thank-yous follow standard business letter format and are typed or printed. There's no reason to restate your qualifications, although you may want to address any specific requirement that came up in the interview. (If, for example, you learned that the position involves some contact with trade press, you would want to mention that you were editor of your college newspaper and are familiar with the fundamentals of press releases and interviews.)

  Use your thank-you letter to recall strong points from the interview, to answer any questions that may have arisen, and to provide information you have promised: "I was very impressed during my tour of your facilities, and my conversation with Dr. Mitchell was particularly helpful. I am enclosing a copy of my paper on 'Car Phone Safety Issues' that we discussed." End on an upbeat note by thanking the interviewer and expressing your hope for a positive outcome: "Thank you for your time and interest. I look forward to the possibility of joining your staff." Or "Thank you again for meeting with me last Friday. I look forward to hearing your decision about the position."

- **ONE PHONE CALL.** If you haven't heard from anyone within the time frame the interviewer specified, make a brief call saying that you're just

BUCK UP!

Discouraged, disillusioned, down-in-the-dumps, and blue? If you've just gotten yet another rejection letter, remember there's plenty of company out there, given that it's the rare job hunter who doesn't go through the same thing to one degree or the other. Instead of slumping, buck up. Even if you get *two* negative responses in one afternoon, answer positively when people ask about how your job search is going. Be upbeat about the people you're meeting and what you're learning. A positive attitude will make you feel better and leave the person who inquired with an affirmative feeling about you and your ability to handle the challenge. If you give others the impression that you can stand up to the difficulties and disappointments of job hunting, they will probably think more highly of your ability to accomplish other things.

checking in to see if there's anything else you should send. If you know when the company intends to make a decision and you haven't been notified, call a day or two after that date has passed to ask whether a decision has been reached, and to reiterate your interest in the job.

RESPONDING TO AN OFFER

If you are absolutely, positively, 100 percent certain you want the job, accept it on the spot. Otherwise, you needn't succumb to pressure to give an answer right away. If you prefer to ask whether you could do a little more exploration, say something to the effect of "Thank you for the offer. This is very exciting! But would you mind if we met again before I give you the answer?"

Now is the time to find out more about the company, your immediate supervisor, and the team of people who will be your workmates. This is when you have the most leverage, so be sure to hammer out the details of your benefits package and salary.

It's also the time to ask about the potential for upward mobility and growth. If you're currently employed elsewhere, seek agreement from your potential employer to start at least two workweeks after your acceptance so that you can give your present employer adequate notice.

The
Interview

47

RESPONDING TO A REJECTION

So it didn't work out this time? Sending a brief note acknowledging that you've been rejected is better than just slinking off and acting as if you'd never had personal contact with a company. Thanking the company for considering you will show you are a person of substance and good manners. And who knows? There's always the chance that you missed being hired by a hair and could be considered for a job in the future.

PART II

LIFE AT THE OFFICE

Navigating the day-in-day-out of the workplace can be an adventure fraught not only with questions but with hazards. Should you hold the door for a female executive, or will she take it as an insult? Is the worker in the next cubicle a peer or a boss? Is there a surefire way to duck office gossip? And what do you do when someone steals your lunch or your ideas?

As the modern office becomes both more technical and more egalitarian, the rules of conduct have changed. This section looks at the minor and major dilemmas—from coping with life in a cubicle to dealing with problem peers—and how to manage them with confidence and grace. Etiquette is the secret that enables you to get through difficult situations at work with both your professional reputation and your sanity intact.

As simple as "being nice" sounds, using office etiquette to your advantage requires more than good instincts. In the seven chapters that follow, you'll find advice on managing conflicts with your coworkers, understanding your boss (and deferring to him or her without losing your your dignity), and handling matters as varied as making small talk, sharing equipment, and asking for a raise or promotion. Also here are tips on dealing with the thorniest issues of male-female relations, how to make sure your private life remains private, and how to keep those petty annoyances so common to office life from being blown out of proportion.

CHAPTER 5

YOU AND YOUR COWORKERS

Whether you're starting a new job or have been settled into one for years, you probably find yourself occasionally asking a question: "So just who are these people, anyway?" Here you are for forty-odd hours a week, sharing your time and space with a group of individuals whom you had no part in choosing. The fact that you work in the same field should give you at least one interest in common, but not necessarily—not in an age when more and more people regard their jobs as a means to a wholly unrelated end. The office secretary may be taking dictation only until her screenplay is sold. The accountant in the next cubicle may be crunching numbers but thinking about his plan to win the Boston Marathon. How do you get to know these people? What are the secrets to getting along with them?

Those questions aside, an ill wind blows in some quarters of the workaday world, spawning a fashionably cynical attitude about the people we work with: "My job is terrific. It's the people I can't stand." But as fashions go, this is an unwise and possibly dangerous one, rather like platform shoes. Even the evolution in work styles—temporary employment and electronic commuting—does not free employees from making the best of things with their fellow workers and working toward a harmonious atmosphere. Whatever the worker's title or level of responsibility, nowhere is the Golden Rule more in need of polishing than here.

THE SAME SOUP

You and your coworkers are in the same soup, and whether you sink or swim has a great deal to do with your ability to treat your workmates—even the difficult ones—with courtesy and respect. From a strictly self-serving perspective, it pays to have allies rather than enemies and to assume that everyone you work with can give you a boost up the corporate ladder. (That fumbling mail boy might turn out to be the boss' grandson and heir apparent. The caustic secretary could have a direct pipeline to the CEO.) Even if you don't regard yourself as a "people person," you can win friends and gain influence by observing the common courtesies and being tolerant when others do not. Work to appreciate the contributions your coworkers make instead of focusing on their failures, and recognize that you are all part of a larger company culture with its own rules, standards, and eccentricities.

This chapter sets the stage with a brief discussion of company culture and then delves into the situations that arise when people are thrown together in the workplace. Respecting personal space and rank, the role of small talk, the polite handling of disagreements, the squelching of gossip and inappropriate comments—these are among the topics. Others range from dealing with temp workers to after-hours socializing with your fellow workers and behaving yourself at the office party. Some of the situations faced by you and your coworkers are given their own chapters—sharing facilities and equipment (Around the Floor, page 93); coming to terms with your workspace (In Your Workspace, page 82); your relations with coworkers of the opposite sex (Women and Men Together, page 126); and keeping your private life private (Your Personal Privacy, page 135).

GRASPING COMPANY CULTURE

Kate learned firsthand about company culture when she was interviewing with three prospective employers in her town. Going from one to another was like moving from "the mountains to the prairies to the oceans white with foam." When Kate had a meeting at Heavy Duty Corporation, an industrial company, she found an environment as tightly buttoned as the collars of the Oxford cloth shirts that all Heavy Duty managers wore. Across town at Good Vibes Inc., a major music label, the atmosphere bubbled like a soft drink, and Kate could never quite figure out who was in charge. The working environment at Friends in Deed, a national charity, was friendly but more professional and was staffed with personnel passionate in their mission.

Kate's three potential employers, with their three distinct operating styles, represent what has come to be known as "corporate culture." A culture is broadly defined as a group that shares beliefs, interests, values, goals, and living styles. Applied to businesses, culture expresses the common characteristics that set one workplace apart from another. It affects everything from how major decisions are made and communicated to how the lowliest cubicle is decorated. When Kate, like all new employees, accepts a position, she will not only have to learn a new job but also how to adapt.

In business, culture is hierarchical—the rules of the game come from the top down. Even those companies that tout their participatory management and flattened pyramidal structures are not exactly democracies. Good intentions notwithstanding, business cultures develop over time, become ingrained, and are slow to change. In fact, CEOs who attempt to radically alter a well-established corporate culture will find themselves frustrated and sometimes tossed out of the executive suite on their golden parachutes.

In the days when workers had one or two employers during an entire working lifetime, accepting the prevailing company culture was relatively easy. But today, workers are likely to have many employers and even several career changes during their employment years; every change requires adaptation, often to wildly varying business styles and manners.

Success in a new job can depend on how quickly you master the company culture. Along with taking your cues from your bosses, interacting with coworkers gives you all the practice you need. Your coworkers are all individuals—people from diverse backgrounds and with diverse ambitions and objectives. Some you will like; others you won't. But you can learn something from every one of them about how to get along inside the company and, in turn, the business world in general—a lesson that will work to your advantage.

FACE-TO-FACE

Your interactions with your coworkers begin with considerations as basic as respecting their personal space, understanding rank, and giving thought to the way you handle everything from small talk to humor to disagreements.

PERSONAL SPACE

When you engage in conversation—chitchat or strictly business—one of the quickest ways to alienate others is to violate their physical space. Instead of crowding the people you talk to, step back (about 18 inches is a reasonable distance). If someone is very soft-spoken, you may have to lean in to catch his or her words, but back away when you speak. Make solid eye contact. An open and interested expression, which begins with the eyes, is far more engaging in any face-to-face meeting than an in-your-face stance or posture.

Be conscious of height differences: Stand sufficiently far away so that the person doesn't get uncomfortable having to look up or down at you. Be especially considerate of people with physical handicaps—a person in a wheelchair or with a hearing impairment—and don't expect coworkers on crutches, in casts, or with "football knees" to stand around chatting for any length of time. If you deal with international coworkers, be sure that you know and observe their conversational customs and taboos.

RESPECTING RANK

In business, rank is power, so be conscious of the position of the person with whom you're talking. On the one hand, you don't want to be overly familiar with peers and superiors. Maintain a respectful conversational distance: no back-slapping, nudging, hugging, elbowing, or other touching that implies

---

SMALL-TALK TIPS

S mall talk is one big deal—an important part of building business relationships. It is when you and your coworkers let down your guard while sitting at a cafeteria lunch table, waiting for a meeting to begin, or hanging out in the copier room that your personality and real interests come to the fore. Almost any topic is up for grabs so long as it's not malicious, derogatory, inflammatory, or indiscreet.

By being open to opportunities for small talk, you'll discover who is the resident expert on grand opera or NASCAR racing, who is the movie buff, the gourmet cook, the night-school scholar. If you're attentive, you can learn in a matter of minutes who is the office gossip, the snob, and the backstabber. Through small talk, your coworkers also become better acquainted with you, finding out if you're social, and easy to talk to—something that's to your advantage in the workplace. (See also The Smart Conversationalist, page 275.)

- When initiating small talk—say, as you wait for the elevator, or before the start of a meeting—be attuned to the other person's receptiveness. If he or she seems distracted or unresponsive, take the hint and back off.
- Even when the person is willing to chat, don't overstay your welcome. Remember that small talk should not get in the way of business.
- Whatever the subject—sports, movies, the latest political scandal—don't try to dominate the conversation. Ask for the other person's opinions and show genuine interest in his or her ideas.
- If other people come along, make an effort to include them in the conversation. You may need to switch topics to something that everyone can discuss. Whatever the subject, don't leave the impression that the newcomers interrupted a more important conversation.
- Think before you speak and avoid subjects that are too personal. It's okay, for example, to share war stories about raising teenage children. But if your coworker's son recently flunked out of

nonexistent intimacy. Just because you're chatting with your supervisor about the Super Bowl, don't assume that the casual nature of the conversation allows you to dispense with the common courtesies: Don't prop your feet on the desk, drop down on the couch without an invitation, or fidget with the bric-a-brac on the coffee table.

On the other hand, when talking with workers in subordinate positions, you don't want to abuse your rank. Use of courtesy titles is often dictated by company culture, but it is always polite to address people who are considerably older as "Mr." or "Mrs." or "Ms." whatever their jobs may be (and unless they insist you do otherwise). A twenty-five-year-old junior executive

college, stay far away from any talk about the irresponsibility of today's young people. If a sensitive subject does come up, be guided by the attitude of your conversation partner.

- It's fine to disagree with someone, but phrase your comments politely. "You're wrong!" is hostile and combative, while "Actually, I just don't agree with you about that but I'd like to hear more of your opinion," is tactful.
- Don't overuse "I." Once you've told a story about yourself, ask a question that allows the other person to take his turn as the subject.
- Be careful not to repeat yourself. Telling the same story again and again or going back over details is overkill, to put it mildly. Many things are of interest when told for the first time, but the twice-told tale quickly becomes boring. A good conversationalist remembers what he or she has said, and takes care to avoid repetition.
- Keep abreast of the world outside. Reading a daily newspaper and a weekly news magazine to learn what's happening beyond the office supplies you with subject matter for small talk and shows that you aren't a mere drone.
- Be aware of the impact of small talk on those working around you. Keep the sound volume under control, and read the body language of anyone nearby you to judge whether to keep talking or to take the conversation elsewhere. Whispering may suggest gossiping or secretiveness, leaving a bad impression on others.
- To end small talk, leave after you, not the other person, has made a statement. It's rude to create the impression, however unintentional, that your chat partner said something that drove you away. Conclude with a remark such as "Well, I think it's time I got back to work" or "This was really interesting. We'll have to talk again."
- If a coworker who just wants to chat interrupts you while you're working, suggest another time. "You've caught me at a bad moment. Can we touch base after I've finished these letters?" If you do the interrupting, be sensitive to the other person's reaction. If she says she can't stop, take "no" for an answer and don't take offense or feel rejected.

may get a power rush by addressing his sixty-year-old secretary by her first name, but in a very conservative organization the rush could be short-lived if his boss doesn't approve.

REQUESTING AND OFFERING HELP

No one likes the office shirkers who never seem to get their own projects finished on time and habitually impose on peers for assistance. Everyone avoids the employee who can never learn the filing system and is constantly seeking on-the-job training. As a result of these bad eggs, good workers sometimes hesitate to ask for help because they fear being lumped in with the shirkers, the indolent, and the incompetent. But in most workplaces, coworkers will willingly volunteer to lend a hand to someone who has helped them.

The best way to get help is to give it. For instance, if you see an officemate working through lunch to collate a large client packet and you pitch in to help, your generosity will likely be returned in kind. Be mindful that a voluntary act is not overtime; your reward is a coworker's gratitude, not extra pay. Don't store your own good deeds away in your mental favor bank, awaiting repayment, or remind everyone what a good person you are.

When you receive a helping hand, a thank you is always necessary, no matter how small the favor. If a coworker gave up his lunch hour to help you, a funny card, a little gift, or an invitation to lunch may be in order. When possible, you might also compliment helpful coworkers to their superiors.

HELP FOR THE NEWCOMER

Be particularly conscious of newcomers. New employees may have crackerjack skills, but they will have a lot to learn about how your business works—names to remember, places to locate, policies to master, reporting relationships to understand. Be helpful and forgiving within reason. Try to recollect how you felt when you were first employed and what information you needed. Volunteer answers, even if the questions haven't been asked yet: "Ms. Hernandez wants those weekly reports in a folder, but Mr. Wilson prefers a memo." Or "If you have a doctor's or dentist's appointment, tell Mrs. Shipman, and she'll clear your schedule." Just remember that help doesn't include office gossip; leave it to the newcomer to make his or her own judgments about coworkers and bosses. (See also The Welcomer, page 97.)

GIVING AND ACCEPTING COMPLIMENTS

You and everyone you work with need occasional pats on the back. Corporate executives hire consultants and take courses to learn how to give compliments, but the real key is being an empathetic person, capable of feeling with and for others. This is no touchy-feely exercise. Paying compliments when and where compliments are due is a kind of day-to-day justice. Saying "well done" or "good job" to coworkers raises their spirits a notch or two; it also communicates that you are a thoughtful and observant person, capable of giving and sharing credit where it is deserved. Just don't overdo it; handing out compliments too freely and too frequently devalues both your words and your sincerity.

"Aw, Shucks!"

Receiving compliments graciously is hard for many people. Taught from childhood not to be show-offs, they have the impulse to negate good comments by going into great detail about why the compliment is undeserved. But this is the

---

Star Players
THE CREDIT SHARER

The Credit Sharer has a finely turned sense of justice and wants to see credit given where it is due. Coworker or boss, she gets her greatest kick when the group is lauded for its merits and achievements. Her team approach can irritate coworkers with private agendas, and she can cut the office brown-noser down to size with a simple, well-aimed remark: "Rob did a great job on that report, but I know he'll second me when I say it wouldn't have been half so good without José's research and Angelica's excellent writing."

The Credit Sharer is an observant type; she listens carefully and pays attention to who is doing what and how well. She won't reward slackers with her praise, but she is willing to sing hymns for the unsung workers, particularly those who are not in prominent positions or are psychologically unsuited to blow their own horns. She is also quick to respond when a coworker is unfairly blamed for a problem that was not his doing or was caused by more than one person's failure. She can be tough as nails when she spots an inequity, so the Credit Sharer often makes enemies faster than other star players. In some companies, she suffers when her superiors mistake her sense of fairness for lack of personal ambition and drive. But if the Credit Sharer becomes a boss, she can be a dream because she instinctively understands the first principle of management—that good managers succeed *because* of the people they supervise, not in spite of them.

kind of modesty that rings hollow. In fact, a momentary burst of genuine immodesty ("I did handle that well, didn't I?") is usually preferable to the calculated obsequiousness of rejecting a reasonable compliment.

Two simple words can solve all compliment dilemmas: "Thank you." Unless you are receiving an Academy Award or a Congressional Medal of Honor, those two words, delivered with a smile, are always up to the job.

WHAT TO SAY WHEN . . .

Hearing news of one kind or another about your coworkers' personal lives is inevitable. In some cases you will want to congratulate, in others, commiserate. If the person is a close friend, you'll probably have no trouble in coming up with something to say; for those you know less well, little more than a simple acknowledgment will usually do. (See also Your Personal Privacy, page 135.) Before venturing any comments, consider the following whenever . . .

- **SOMEONE BECOMES ENGAGED OR MARRIES.** "Congratulations, best wishes, all happiness." Genuinely wish your coworker well. Don't be too inquisitive about his or her choice of spouse (that's what in-laws are for), and don't be too free with marriage advice or horror stories.
- **SOMEONE IS PREGNANT.** Be happy for your coworker, but don't pry. Avoid giving advice that may conflict with current medical opinion; future parents need confidence in their physician, and it is unfair to undermine that relationship even from the best of intentions. Also refrain from sharing terrible labor and childbirth stories.
- **SOMEONE MISCARRIES.** A miscarriage is a death that requires grieving. Be sympathetic by recognizing the depth of the loss. Never offer up phrases such as "It was for the best" or "It was just God's will." And never, under any circumstances, imply that the miscarriage may have resulted from something your coworker did or did not do.
- **SOMEONE DIVORCES.** Divorce is another kind of death. Don't ask for the reasons or get into conversations about what a loser your coworker's ex seems to be. It's better to listen than to talk, although you might offer practical advice (how to find child care or file income tax as a head of household) when needed. (See also Your Divorce, page 138.)
- **SOMEONE IS ILL.** If a coworker or a coworker's relative is seriously or terminally ill, your actions will speaker louder than words. Show sympathy by helping the person on the job. Don't complain about absences from the office. Be alert should anyone else try to undermine your coworker's position

during an illness or loot his office or files. (It happens.) Keep the person informed about business happenings.

- **SOMEONE DIES.** When a coworker loses a loved one, write and speak your condolences. If you are close, attending pre-funeral and funeral services will be comforting. But just working with someone is not a reason to take a funeral day off. Never make comments such as "It was really a blessing" or "Be thankful his suffering is over." Offer practical assistance where you can, and be understanding. The death of a loved one will change your coworker, so don't expect him or her to bounce back in the space of a few weeks to become the person you used to know.

- **SOMEONE IS FIRED OR DOWNSIZED.** Be sympathetic, but don't prolong the agony by talking it into the ground. Accept your coworker's official explanation for a firing, and don't engage in speculation. If you can give practical assistance, do—a recommendation, help with a resume update, information on other job openings. But don't let sympathy lure you into encouraging or participating in destructive behaviors such as binge drinking or firing off threatening letters. Finally, don't be surprised if a former coworker drifts out of your life; he or she needs to move on, and because you are still part of the old workplace and old hurts, you may be left behind.

ANIMOSITIES AND SQUABBLES

It is going to happen. Sooner or later, you'll find yourself at loggerheads with a coworker, or you'll be dragged into somebody else's quarrel. Either situation is a real test of your mettle as a mature adult.

The first rule is *not* to avoid disagreeing when you feel strongly about an issue. If you have honestly and critically reached a position that is contrary to your coworker's, you have an ethical obligation to state your case as strongly as you can. But it is also wise to pick your battles with care. If it doesn't really matter to you whether the office soda machine stocks Coke or Pepsi, leave that disagreement to others.

Ideally, a disagreement between coworkers is handled in private, but there are times when conflict is integral to the work process—during a brainstorming session, for example, or a policy meeting—so be considerate of bystanders. State your case clearly and engage in debate if necessary, but don't be mulish. Pay attention to the reaction of others: As soon as you pick up signals of resentment or annoyance, bring the conversation to a close for the time being; otherwise, it could degenerate into personal attacks. "Actually, I think it would be

*You
and
Your
Coworkers*

better if we talked about this later" is one way of defusing the situation. Or you could try, "Let's take this up when we can get [the supervisor] to help us figure out the direction the company wants to go."

Don't get drawn into other people's disagreements, but do not feign ignorance if you can really help find a resolution. If, for example, you have factual information that can settle an argument, speak up. Remember that telling what you know or offering reasonable compromises is not the same as taking sides. Expect to be attacked, but maintain your objective role even if the parties to the disagreement unite against you.

DON'T MAKE IT PERSONAL

Never allow a disagreement to become personal. Apart from being rude, name-calling and personalizing weaken your case in any argument. The instant you call Joe an "idiot" for preferring to file alphabetically rather than by invoice number or make a snide reference to Marcia's lack of higher education during a lunchtime political discussion, guess what happens? Joe or Marcia

---

Star Players
THE MEDIATOR

The Mediator knows better than to involve himself in employee-employer conflicts. His forte is negotiating the troubled waters when coworkers collide. While everyone else in the office is taking sides ("Mary never stays a minute past five! She leaves all her extra work to us!" says Joan; "But Mary's a single mom. She has to pick up her child!" says Jill; "She's unbelievably selfish!" "NO! You're unbelievably callous!"), the Mediator is willing to step in and referee. If the office is plagued with politics, he is the Supreme Court—an island of sanity and safety for those other workers who wish not to become involved.

The Mediator is a star because he is not afraid of confrontation; rather, he plays fair and has a knack for unearthing the real facts underlying office squabbles. People quickly learn to trust his objectivity and, more often than not, tell him the truth. A real Mediator isn't a Goody Two-Shoes but a diplomatic conciliator with a talent for cutting through other people's anger, frustrations, and jealousies to get at the heart of a problem.

How do you explain his goodwill? It's a good bet that the Mediator genuinely enjoys the people he works with and the job he holds. By the same token, he believes that harmony creates the best environment for both.

just won the war, even if you won the battle. If someone calls you a name or challenges your competence, chalk it up to frustration in the heat of conflict and try your best not to hold grudges.

Three more bits of advice:

- **STICK TO THE SUBJECT.** Don't allow a disagreement to wander into non-germane issues. Especially avoid referring back to old conflicts. Remember that even if you were proved right in the last argument, you may be wrong in this one. Beware when others try to sidetrack an issue; diversion, deflection, and tossing red herrings onto the trail are classic tactics of those with the weak side of an argument. If you fall for the trick, learn from your mistake and listen more closely next time.
- **BE OPEN TO COMPROMISE.** Although you may not get everything you want, resolution is usually better than continual hard feelings. Be sure to document the outcome of the disagreement; if it is business-related, you should also confirm the final resolution with a memo to your "opponent." Documentation and confirmation are important if it becomes necessary to take the matter to a higher level of authority.
- **DON'T GLOAT.** Avoid the temptation to gloat or say "I told you so." If everyone recognizes that you were right, you will only undermine yourself by engaging in petty smirking and arrogance. (You want your colleagues to say "Josh really knows his stuff," not "Josh knows his stuff, but he's still a jerk.")

HANDLING GOSSIP AND RUMORS

The probability that people will refrain from gossiping is about the same as finding them arriving at work naked, and all on the same day, at that. The grapevine, the scuttlebutt, the dish, the buzz—call it what you will, gossip is inevitable among people who often spend more time with one another than with their nearest and dearest. What's going to happen at the next board meeting, who's going to be promoted or let go, and the direction of management's game plan are natural subjects for speculation, particularly in times of uncertainty. Whether to gain reassurance or make it easier to prepare for the worst, employees are going to gossip about the workplace.

THE HARMFUL KIND

Gossip becomes malignant when it does someone harm, no matter how slight or unintended. Talking about a coworker's sex life may raise questions about his or her sense of propriety or choice of mates, but it is unlikely to affect the person's status at the office. (See also Your Personal Privacy, page 135.) But tongue-wagging about who's kissing up to the boss, taking credit for someone else's work, or going to the movies on their telecommuting days demeans the person in the eyes of coworkers and can result in serious, job-threatening consequences. This kind of gossip is at bottom a self-serving act on the tale-teller's part—an attempt to make himself or herself look better in the light of someone else's questionable behavior or to retaliate for real or perceived slights.

PROTECTING YOURSELF

What can you do to avoid becoming the subject of office gossip? Keep personal information to yourself. Answering even seemingly innocuous questions about your age, income, personal relationships, sexuality, and politics can set you up for gossip and innuendo. You don't have to answer, but be warned. Dedicated rumormongers can turn your most polite "no comment" into grist for their gossip mill. (Can't you just hear this: "That new guy wouldn't say what his salary is, which makes me think he's coming in at a higher grade than the rest of us. And the boss tells us we have to tighten our belts. Harrumph!")

If you become the subject of gossip or a rumor, you'll want to uncover the source when the story is false. Begin your detective work by talking to the person who clued you in; explain to him or her that the story is untrue and you want to stop it. If you promise confidentiality, there's a good chance you will learn the name of the initial source of the falsehood.

CONFRONT AND RESIST

You should confront the gossip, but stage your confrontation in private. Adopt an attitude of concern rather than anger: "Sally, I hear you told a couple of people that I'm looking for a new job and I've been meeting with a headhunter. The truth is that I had lunch last week with my old college roommate, and he happens to work for an employment firm. But I am *not* looking for a job, and that story could really cause me a lot of trouble here." Even if the gossip denies spreading the tale, she'll be stung because she has been caught, and she'll think twice before gossiping about you again.

Remember that it takes two to tango; a person who is eager to hear the latest gossip is an active participant and hardly blameless, even if he or she doesn't spread the story. Gossiping can be hazardous to your professional reputation. You never know who's chummy with whom, and you could wind up covered in mud if you dish dirt about the wrong person. If asked to gossip with colleagues, be tactful but firm: "I honestly don't want to hear the details of anybody's pri-

Star Players

THE ANTI-GOSSIP

I f much of gossip is harmless, bad gossip (false, cruel, negative, divisive talk) can infect the workplace as quickly as an *e. Coli* outbreak. There is no vaccination, but the Anti-Gossip can often be the antidote. The Anti-Gossip is no sweet "I just don't want to hear that" type. Instead, she is an aggressive truth-seeker, an empiricist who demands proof of every rumor. Like Missouri, her motto is "Show Me." The Anti-Gossip may not be a likable person—particularly to dedicated whisperers and story-passers. But she knows that most gossip is nine-tenths assumption, presumption, and exaggeration.

Her objective is to get to the bottom of things, and she's perfectly willing to ask for answers rather than deal in suppositions. You might even find her cornering the boss in his office with her questions about the next company layoff or his divorce. She is often tactless and occasionally tasteless, but the Anti-Gossip knows what her gossipy workmates never learned—that rumor-mongering is a far more egregious social error than a little impertinence. She is relentless, and once she has tracked down a false rumor, she will stop it in its tracks. Her coworkers may not love her, but her dogged pursuit of the truth will earn the Anti-Gossip a gold star every time she spares a colleague the pain and grief of heedless, needless blather.

vate life." You should politely refuse to listen—"Oh, that sounds interesting, but I'd just rather not know"—and quickly excuse yourself.

SQUELCHING OFFENSIVE COMMENTS

There are times when you can't walk away from inappropriate office talk, particularly when you or someone else is being defamed, insulted, or patronized. What do you do when a coworker makes blatantly sexist or racist remarks, calls you (or someone you know who is trustworthy) a "liar" or a "cheat," or treats coworkers and subordinates with snobbish and arrogant disrespect? A couple of centuries ago, you might have challenged the offending person to a duel. Today, you must rely on your wits.

You have an obligation to yourself and your company to confront or report verbal offenders, just as you would a thief or arsonist. If you only sit back and listen, you become a collaborator—passive, but nonetheless guilty. Also, your company can be held liable for the hateful remarks of employees, and while you are in its employ, you owe loyalty to the greater good.

ONE-ON-ONE

If you can talk with the person in private, do so. Frame your statements as criticism of the remarks, not the person, and be specific: "You probably didn't realize, but that comment you made about Leslie's short skirts really was sexist, and I could see that she was offended and hurt." People who repeatedly offend or degrade others are rarely subtle and usually don't take hints. But they may respond if you indicate that your concern is for their own welfare and reputations.

When a close colleague offends, seek an opportune time to speak to him or her in confidence. If your colleague is not a fool, he or she will get your point and understand that you're speaking up out of friendship.

IN THE OPEN

Some remarks require immediate and public response. Be direct, but remember to confront the *remark* rather than the speaker. However great the temptation, control your anger and avoid patronizing the person. For example, if a coworker's subject is racial politics run rampant, try something on the order of "People are treated fairly here, Ralph, and I know that your boss got his job because of his ability, not because of his race." If you can (it isn't easy), give the person a graceful way to retreat from his or her offensive remarks: "I think we talk too much about people's races, don't you, Ralph? Hasn't your boss recommended two promotions for you this year?"

Whatever you do, don't become involved in a shouting match. You simply cannot out-shout a dedicated bigot or snob. If the offending remarks are habitual, it's time to take the matter to a superior. If you fear retaliation, make your complaint in confidence. On rare occasions, a situation is so bad that an anonymous disclosure to management may be necessary.

LANGUAGE MOST FOUL

Attitudes toward profanity and verbal obscenity are grounded in company culture. But even if your company is lax in the language department, you don't have to indulge yourself or put up with offensive terms. Be reasonable: If "damn" and "hell" offend your ears, you might consider another career path. There are, however, certain Anglo-Saxon and irreligious words and phrases that are intolerable, especially when directed at individuals.

When obscenity and profanity are permitted in the workplace, their use tends to be widespread, and you can't correct everyone. Signal your distaste by never using these words yourself and by excusing yourself politely from office gatherings whenever the language becomes too raw. Some people will label you a prude, but you may be pleasantly surprised by others who welcome your attitude and even imitate your behavior.

DEALING WITH PETTY ANNOYANCES

Some things people do are not worth a full-fledged workplace showdown, but they can nonetheless drive you up the wall. The secretary with the voice that can shatter glass, the marketing guy who smacks gum with all the finesse of a cow chewing its cud, the intern whose perfume is like a biological weapon of war. Although you have to grin and bear most of your coworker's follies and foibles, you can try, with courtesy, to correct problems that literally affect your work. Before tackling the failings of others, however, it's a good idea to take a look in the mirror: Is it possible that you annoy your coworkers every bit as much as they annoy you?

Problem Peers

THE VICTIM

A portrait in paranoia, the professional Victim reveals himself in many ways: by the chip that remains firmly in place on his shoulder; by continually complaining about his lack of advancement; by trashing coworkers who have already attained the job level to which he aspires; and by claiming he's never given credit for his talents. In departmental meetings, the Victim darkly hints at Machiavellian plots on the part of management and looming disasters for workers at all levels. Over lunch, he's the doomsayer who is always reading "the writing on the wall." Female Victims are often quick to take the most innocent displays of friendliness from male coworkers as less than honorably intended. Working with the Victim, male or female, is like being sentenced for eternity to be an audience member of the worst of the afternoon TV talk shows. Worse, the Victim can taint an entire office with his suspicions, accusations, and conspiracy theories.

Don't be afraid to take issue with the Victim's more vicious or paranoid statements, but deliver your comments wrapped in kid gloves: "Edgar, I really can't imagine Mr. Cassidy's lying when he says he hasn't heard about any more cuts. He's a straight-shooter, you know, and just because he's a boss doesn't mean he's a liar." A healthy dose of provable facts is the grenade that shatters the professional Victim's delusions.

Smokers are the literal outcasts of most businesses these days—banished to the out-of-doors in rain, sleet, snow, and hail for periodic puffing. Yet tension still persists among smokers and nonsmokers, with consideration on the part of both more necessary than ever before.

If you're a smoker, understand that some people have "smoker's breath" that is more powerful than others—and yours may be on the high side. If you aren't sure, put a little extra distance between yourself and anyone you're talking with. Breath mints may help, but a good tooth brushing and a dose of mouthwash is better. There's also the problem of smoke-permeated clothing. If you smoke, try not to do it in tightly enclosed spaces, or take a stroll in the fresh air before you re-enter a smoke-free space.

Cigar and pipe smokers should exercise all the same cautions as their cigarette-smoking colleagues. The remnants of cigar smoking are particularly unpleasant, even to cigarette smokers, and can linger for a very long time. The best course is to save the stogies for your own home or a cigar club. (See also A Battle Royal, page 145.)

If you are a non-smoker, show a little tolerance. If you want someone to put out a cigarette, ask *politely*. Most smokers have no desire to offend or to cause discomfort or health problems for others, and unless you encounter the

---

THOSE EMBARRASSING MOMENTS

Spinach stuck in the front teeth, an open fly, an unbuttoned blouse, a dangling false eyelash—these are the staples of situation comedy and very real embarrassing moments. When they happen to you, all you can do is laugh and blame bad luck. When you realize they are happening to others, step in and help. Discreetly, tell the victim (privately if possible), and if need be, help to repair the damage. If you are a woman and are too shy to tell a male colleague that his zipper is undone, quietly get another male to do it. When a coworker alerts you that there's a blob of mustard on your tie or a poppy seed in your teeth, don't take offense or get huffy. Be grateful; a friend has just saved you from another embarrassing moment.

Some problems should just be left alone. Someone's dandruff, a hairpiece that looks like a shag rug, or raccoon-eyes makeup do not affect the workplace in any serious way and are really nobody else's business. It's up to the person with the problem to realize that it may be jeopardizing his changes for advancement. Only if you're close to the person should you gently suggest that something he is doing might be hurting his career.

occasional nicotine Neanderthal, there's no reason to act like a storm trooper. Another caveat: Before you criticize a colleague's smoker's breath, remember the garlic salami sandwich you had for lunch.

OTHER ODORS

A coworker's body odor, bad breath, or smelly feet are extremely sensitive issues. They can be the result of poor hygiene, but there is also the possibility that personal odors can be caused by medical conditions, medications, or dietary deficiencies. (A popular high-protein diet some years back brought remarkable weight loss and terrible breath.)

Be very cautious before you raise a stink about personal odors. Ask yourself if the problem is long-term or recent. Has the person been ill, or is he taking medicine? If the problem becomes unbearable, you can talk with someone who is close to the malodorous coworker and may be willing to speak to him or her. Or discuss the problem with a sympathetic supervisor or Human Resources manager. (This is an instance when a group of concerned employees is more impressive to a boss than an individual complainer.)

Perfumes, aftershaves, colognes, and other cosmetics are meant to be pleasant but can quickly become oppressive in a crowded office. Many companies are adopting policies regulating the use of scents on health grounds. But you can help by not overdoing your own toilette. Don't spritz in the office. Test a new scent before wearing it to work because body chemistry affects the power of fragrances and can intensify them. Save the musky, heavy scents for nights on the town. (See also Perfume, page 177; Your Cologne, page 164.)

CHEWING GUM

There's nothing inherently wrong with chewing gum; the problem with doing it at work is the constant risk of annoying people who think your gum-chewing is socially graceless or simply a disgusting habit. Chewing gum when you're alone is fine, of course, so long as your smacking or bubble-popping can't be heard in the next cubicle. But chewing gum in business meetings or with clients and associates is a little like eating with your mouth open: It feels better to you than it looks to everyone else.

Be a bit circumspect about other workers' gum habits. With so many people giving up smoking, the gum may be a literal lifesaver. There are times, however, when it is advisable say something to a gum-chewer; for example, if you are about to enter a client meeting with a colleague who is chomping away, you might politely suggest that she dump the gum. Chances are, the chewer is unconscious of having it and will appreciate your warning.

TEMPS AND PART-TIMERS

One of the most dramatic changes in the contemporary workplace is the growing use of nontraditional employees. Once, and not that long ago, the typical office was filled with nine-to-fivers who worked for one company for years and received the traditional compensations of salary or hourly wage plus a package of benefits that ranged from vacation and sick days to health, life, and insurance and pension plans. Today, however, the person working next to you is just as likely to be a temporary worker or a part-time employee. The use of temps and part-timers appears to be a trend rather than a fad, and permanent and full-time employees have to adapt their thinking about and behavior toward these new-fashioned coworkers.

WORKING WITH TEMPS

It's a fact that many traditional employees resent the arrival of a temp from the reasonable fear that their own jobs may be the next to be converted. But it is important to separate the individual from your company's hiring policy. If you want to protest the use of temps, take it to senior management or the corporate board. Do not take it out on the temporary employee.

Welcome temporary employees graciously, and be ready to offer your assistance as they settle into the job. Assume that the temp worker is both skilled and ready to learn, and treat him or her with the professional courtesies you would extend to a permanent employee. Be aware that temp workers may well expect a chilly reception, and it is largely the responsibility of the staff to bring them into the team, show them the ropes, and introduce them in a positive way to the company culture.

If it is your workplace custom to take a new employee to lunch in the first week, also take the temp worker who is on an extended assignment. Include the temp worker in normal office socializing. Get to know them and you may be pleasantly surprised to discover that temps are not so different from you. In fact, temps are often very interesting people who take temporary assignments in order to support themselves as they pursue other interests. Your new temp may be an actor or an artist, a future film director, or a writer finishing a novel.

Just as coworkers should avoid blaming temps for company hiring policies, you want to be careful not to draw temps into office debates about company policies. Don't subject them to your complaints and insecurities or try to elicit their sympathy and support. The temp is employed by a different boss—possibly a large national or multinational employment service—and has no direct pipeline to your topmost management. In truth, the temp's employment may be a good deal less secure than yours, so don't get mad when the temp refuses to engage in gossip or bull sessions.

If You're a Temp

Temporary employees should do their best to adapt to the customs and culture of a new office as quickly as possible. If you are a temp, your agency should provide you with basic information about your new assignment. Sometimes, though, your assignment may come too quickly for a thorough orientation and your agency may be unfamiliar with the personality of the workplace they are sending you to. Until you get the lay of the land, dress conservatively and behave with maximum decorum. You'll quickly learn whether the office style is casual or formal.

Try not to judge your new coworkers too harshly if they are cold or stiff with you. You may have dropped unwittingly into a major downsizing or a shift in company employment. Unfortunately, temps are easy targets for the resentments of long-time employees who sense that the rug is being pulled from under them. A thick skin can help, but you don't want to be so aloof that coworkers avoid you or, worse, undermine your job. Keep your antennae up, and respond when someone makes a friendly overture. It can't hurt to accept offers of assistance, even when you don't really need the help; doing so shows collegiality and respect for the knowledge and experience of long-timers.

In questions of socializing with coworkers, be guided by the policies of your agency and explain your situation to the people you're working with. Never discuss salary or benefits, because comparisons will inevitably be drawn. Because you have two bosses—the service employing you and the company contracting with your agency—keeping confidentiality is doubly important.

Working Part-Time

Part-timers are employed by the company but work nontraditional schedules—coming in for a few hours a day, for a few days a week, or telecommuting from home at least part of the time. Some part-timers share a single job.

One of the part-timer's biggest challenges is to prove to coworkers that you are just as serious about your work as any full-time employee. Usually it's easier to gain acceptance if you are hired as a part-time employee than if you switch from full-time to part-time work. Coworkers who are accustomed to seeing you from nine to five may become irritated that you are no longer readily available. Some may regard your change to part-time as slacking off or an example of company favoritism. Even if your reason for going part-time is to care for an elderly parent or a sick child, a few coworkers will be green-eyed with envy at what they perceive as your "escape" from the daily grind.

ON YOUR TOES

Good work habits are the best offense for the part-time worker. Be where you are supposed to be, when you are supposed to be there. Although your life no longer revolves around your job, be focused like a laser when you are at work. Your supervisor will doubtless announce the part-time arrangement to the entire office, but be sure that everyone has a copy of your schedule, including the company receptionist who will have to field your business calls when you are not there. (You should also make it a habit to check your messages and voice mail regularly in your off-hours.)

You may want to give your home e-mail address to colleagues, so you can receive memos and announcements. Be flexible; if there is an important departmental meeting scheduled on your off-day, make plans to attend, and check in occasionally with your supervisor so that you don't miss out on news and information that affects your job. Do not drop out entirely from the social side of the office, although you will probably have to reduce on-the-job breaks in order to get your work done.

Whatever you do, don't complain about being overloaded with work; your full-time coworkers will be hard-pressed to sympathize with your plight when they visualize you lounging in the sun or cruising the mall during your off-hours. If you are overburdened, talk with your supervisor as soon as possible and be specific about your problems. (In businesses where part-time work is a new phenomenon, employers often have a hard time determining appropriate workloads and may expect more productivity than is possible.)

When you discuss your off-hour activities with coworkers, be very careful that you don't appear to gloat; keep in mind that a perfectly normal remark about having lunch at your son's school or volunteering mornings at the food bank may strike coworkers, who feel chained to their desks, as insensitive. And avoid scheduling any non-work-related activities such as doctor appointments or haircuts during your work hours.

COURTESIES FOR THE DISABLED

The largest minority group in the United States—some 17 percent of the population—comprises people with disabilities. But they're not statistics; they are more than 45 million individuals who are human beings first and have special needs second. So put aside any anxiety you might feel when you work with someone who's disabled ("Am I saying the wrong thing?"), and be yourself. Act just as you would with anyone else, and if the disability is brought up, it should be the disabled person who does it, not you.

SENSITIVITY IN LANGUAGE

You don't have to be excessively sensitive about your language: The words "deaf" and "blind" have not been banished from the vocabulary, but "handicapped" may be on its way out. It's perfectly fine to ask a blind person "See what I mean?" and to invite someone in a wheelchair to "go for a walk." Trying to eliminate common words and phrases like these from your conversation is

---

Problem Peers
THE BACKSTABBER

The most adept Backstabbers are often the last people you'd expect. Charming and personable, they win over coworkers and genuinely seem to enjoy the company of their peers. But charm is a common quality among the ambitious, and the ambitious are not always above turning on a colleague if they think it's to their benefit. What distinguishes the Backstabber from ordinary people of charm and ambition is his or her lack of human feeling: They might not literally run over their grandmother, but they wouldn't hesitate to steal the old girl's life savings. Skilled Backstabbers are hard to detect and even harder to combat because they cover their tracks so well and rarely leave fingerprints at the scene of the crime. Until superiors catch on to the Backstabber's methods (it usually happens, though often too late to avoid problems), the only way to cope is to smile when you are together and to watch your back at all times.

A first cousin of the Backstabber is the Tattletale, who is not necessarily malicious but merely unthinking. This person divulges confidences because telling a good story is more important to them than respecting other people. Trace a rumor and there's an excellent chance the source is a Tattletale. Take care, however, not to confuse him or her with a coworker who reports genuinely serious problems.

awkward and implies that the person with disabilities should be treated differently from everyone else.

Never leave people with disabilities out of a conversation because you feel uncomfortable or you assume they will. Include them as you would anyone else, and let it be their decision whether to participate.

To Offer Help?

It is always courteous to ask if a coworker with a disability would like assistance, but don't automatically provide help that may be unwanted. Follow the person's cues, and don't be offended if your offer of aid is refused: It is everyone's choice to be as independent as he or she can be. For example, don't push someone's wheelchair unless you are asked. But do offer to push if the two of you are approaching a steep ramp or an obstacle.

Don't pet guide dogs or try out equipment the person with a disability may be using. But do feel comfortable asking a blind person if he or she would like to take your arm when navigating an unfamiliar area. Remember that people with disabilities are people first and generally understanding of your need for guidance. Whenever you are in doubt, ask the person with a disability what he or she wants.

With the Deaf or Hard-of-Hearing

Face the person, maintaining eye contact throughout your conversations, since many people with hearing loss can get a lot of information by both listening and reading lips. If the person is hard-of-hearing, it's helpful to speak up and speak clearly, but never shout or exaggerate your lip movements. If speech alone is not working, it is perfectly acceptable to gesture or write notes.

If you have dealings with a deaf person who has an interpreter, always direct your attention to the deaf person rather than the interpreter. (This can feel uncomfortable because the courteous worker doesn't want to exclude anyone from the conversation. Don't worry; trained interpreters, including those for non-English speakers, understand their role and won't expect to participate.) Speak at your normal rate, being sure the interpreter can hear you clearly.

With Wheelchair Users

When you meet, offer a handshake if you would normally, unless it is clear that the person does not have the use of his or her arms. Under the Americans with Disabilities Act (ADA), most businesses are legally required to accommodate the physical needs of people who use wheelchairs. Even so, don't hesitate to offer your help if you spot someone in a tight situation.

WITH THE BLIND OR THOSE WITH LOW VISION

When you greet a blind coworker in the early days of his or her employment, identify yourself by name; your voice will be recognized before long. Whenever necessary, offer to read written information, such as the latest office memo or the cafeteria menu. It's appropriate to offer your assistance with selecting food from a buffet or getting coffee when everyone is gathered around the conference table. But be an observant friend, and follow your blind or sight-impaired coworker's lead as to how far to go.

WITH THE SPEECH IMPAIRED

Listen patiently and carefully to someone with a speech impediment. Your understanding of his or her speech (or of any device used by the person) will improve as you continue to listen. Remain attentive to the conversation even if there are delays. Don't complete the person's sentences unless he or she looks to you for help. If you don't understand, ask a question to help the person clarify the part you missed.

EXCHANGING GIFTS WITH COWORKERS

Holiday gift-giving is such a long-standing tradition in some workplaces that it can't be ignored. If you decide on your own to give gifts to colleagues you're close to, something to brighten up his or her workspace is usually the best choice. Tailor gifts to the individual: You probably know what types of ornaments or gadgets would make someone's office more pleasant. But remember that diplomacy requires that the gifts appear to be of similar value. If you're giving a polyvinyl troll to someone in your department, keep it quiet that you've given the person in the next cubicle a nice fountain pen. (See also Gift Choices, page 238; Accepting and Declining Gifts, page 241; "Thanks!" page 242; Gifts for Bosses, page 125.)

SECRET SANTAS

To ease the financial strain of providing every coworker with a gift, some companies have a holiday grab bag or Secret Santa systems that ensure everyone gives and everyone receives, with expenditures limited. Just be sure to abide by the limits; if your gift is more expensive than it should be, whoever receives it

Here we go again," you murmur as he appears at the door, with what may as well be a tin cup in hand. Next comes the inevitable plea: "It's Nancy Dixon's birthday this Friday, and we're getting her a cake from Layers Unlimited. Want to chip in?" It's not that you have anything against Nancy—nor birthdays, for that matter—but sometimes you think to yourself that enough is enough.

Office collections by workmates for birthdays, weddings, the birth of a baby, or school charities are perfectly acceptable but can nickel-and-dime people to the point of distraction, if not penury. If the frequency of collections seems to be getting out of hand, you might want to adopt a personal policy to give only for certain events, like showers. (Don't refuse across the board or your workmates may make negative assumptions about your generosity.) Chances are, other employees feel office collections are an undue burden, too. If a bit of discreet investigating confirms that they indeed do, go as a group to talk to a supervisor about setting up or enforcing some collection guidelines. One idea: A general office "kitty" to which everyone contributes.

may feel embarrassed. It is fine to give humorous (but not off-color) gifts to coworkers at holiday time, and homemade gifts are a thoughtful and frugal way to spread good cheer.

PLANNING AND ATTENDING OFFICE PARTIES

The days of office parties where coworkers drank too much, talked too much, and ended up with the metaphorical lampshade on their heads are virtually over and gone. Today's office parties have matured, by and large, into calmer occasions that serve as much to build morale and showcase the company as to share camaraderie. Office parties, especially the informal variety, also provide employees with the chance to become better acquainted and even to forge the bonds of real friendships—an important side effect in a time when the workplace has become the principal venue for social contacts.

INVITATIONS

Whoever in the department is in charge of the party (or if it is a company-wide affair, the company event planner) will send a memo on paper or by e-mail to each staff member. An example: "The production department will celebrate a good year and a Merry Christmas on Friday, December 23rd, in Meeting Room C. All work stops at 3:30 P.M. sharp for cocktails and a buffet. Will you join us?" When the party is to be held in a restaurant, hotel, or club, more formal invitations may be sent—handwritten for small groups, printed for large ones. Details of party arrangements—generally, the food and drinks—are often delegated to staff members. Look for hidden talents among your workmates: Someone who has a reputation for knowing music, for instance, can be put in charge of getting the band, booking the DJ, or selecting the recordings.

OFFICE PARTY PITFALLS

People who drink too much at office parties risk serious harm to their professional careers. Sloppiness and lack of self-control become obvious to superiors, who will think twice—or worse, never—about giving a big drinker future responsibilities. Belligerent and unruly behavior or sexual aggressiveness can lead directly to dismissal. Even relatively benign behavior under the influence—laughing too loudly, talking too much, acting giddy, becoming quietly morose—will be remembered and can soil reputations. A good host keeps a careful eye on employees during an office party; fellow employees can help, too, by watching out for the coworker who is overindulging and steering him toward the coffee or even taking him home before the situation becomes obvious.

Drug use or possession at the office or a business-related social function is grounds for both instant dismissal and legal action. Alcohol has one virtue—it is legal. Marijuana, cocaine, and so on through the controlled-substances list are not. An employee who thinks that a party is just the place to light up a reefer will learn differently when he finds himself looking for a new job.

An eternal danger for office partygoers is becoming too intimate with colleagues or superiors. In the spirit of seasonal abandon and fueled by one too many drinks, men and women often place themselves in compromising positions, of which actual sex is just one possibility. Excessive flirting, inappropriate soul-bearing, too-eager touching—amorous adventures in all forms lose their romance in the clear light of the office workday. The safest way to avoid embarrassment and regret is to be well aware of the dire consequences that can result. Stay in control, starting with strict limits on your drinking.

If you and your coworkers decide to party on after the office party has ended, keep the previous warnings about alcohol, drugs, and intimacy firmly in mind. Also give thought to people's transportation needs; if a coworker faces a long or dangerous commute after a party or no designated driver will be available, you should arrange in advance for sleepovers or make hotel reservations. No party is good enough to put anyone's life in jeopardy.

Spouses and dates may or may not be invited. If spouses and dates are included, the party invitation should be clearly addressed to "Mr. and Mrs. Brown" or "Miss Green and guest."

OFFICE PARTY DRESS

At a party held after work in the workplace, both men and women can simply show up in the clothes they have worn all day. Or they may change to fancier dress in anticipation of the event. Although overdressing and underdressing are generally out of place, people like to dress up their officewear with jewelry, a spiffy new tie or silk scarf, or other accessories.

At an office party held outside the office, both men and women may properly change from work clothes into dress clothes. Because this is a business affair, overly dressy or revealing clothing is in poor taste. It's advisable to err on the side of conservatism: Wearing high-tops or a tee-shirt with your tuxedo may get a laugh from coworkers but could earn something else from the boss. If you are unsure about the proper dress, check with a colleague who has attended these off-site social events in the past.

OTHER OFFICE OCCASIONS

Employers and employees often throw parties when someone leaves or retires, when a coworker is going to be married or have a baby, and to honor individual achievements. Office sports teams celebrate with postgame get-togethers. Many businesses have regular birthday parties for workers.

Special-occasion parties may be given by the boss or by the staff and should include the entire department and possiby any special friends of the guest of honor in other areas of the company. While spouses aren't necessarily included, especially if the party is given within regular office hours, the spouse of the guest of honor should be invited.

These informal parties may be given in the office, a conference room, or the cafeteria. Alternatively, a lunch or dinner can be held at a nearby restaurant. A staff committee or the boss' executive assistant is usually designated to handle details including time, place, menu, entertainment, and gifts. Bills should be given directly to the boss if he or she is giving the party; if the staff is hosting, the bill is split among them. (If you are a party organizer, it's a good idea to collect party funds before you wind up with out-of-pocket expenses.)

There are several important rules to remember when planning a special occasion party. First, before you do anything else, clear the event with your superior. Be certain that the scheduled date and time do not conflict with important business. Second, reserve the party space well in advance. Don't expect the conference room to be available just because you want it to be. Third, don't impose your party planning on people who are trying to work. Be considerate of your coworkers' time and responsibility to the job.

Don't tie up the copy machine or the printer with your party favors or drape public spaces with crepe paper and tinsel. Finally, don't overdo your party privileges; a weekly or even a monthly party is just too much. So is throwing a workplace bridal shower for a coworker's sister's granddaughter. The best office parties are always those that are planned and executed in a businesslike manner.

RESTAURANTS, BARS, AND AT-HOME PARTIES

Because your coworkers might be personal friends as well, it's normal to social-ize with them at lunch, after work, or at home. Shoptalk will often be the focus of such gatherings, with things said that would be risky to discuss at the office. At other times, work will merely be threaded through the conversation; and occasionally—blessedly—work will be left behind.

Letting your hair down in a social setting should be done with care. In a relaxed atmosphere—especially if alcohol is present—tongues are loosened and defenses are dropped. The temptation to say more than you intend is beguiling. But don't make the mistake of believing that off-the-premises conversation is off-the-record. If you pass a rumor, take potshots at an absent coworker or boss, or reveal a workplace confidence, you can be sure that what you said will get back to the office, sometimes faster than you.

DINING OUT WITH COWORKERS

When you lunch or have dinner out with coworkers (see Business Meals, page 391), the big question is generally who will pay and how much. If you choose a Chinese restaurant where every dish is shared, there's no problem: The bill is split, and everyone pays the same amount. But what if you have a soup and salad and everyone else has meat, veggies, and dessert? The more people with larger appetites than yours, the greater—and more disproportionate—your share becomes if the bill is simply split evenly. Some diehards maintain that it's bad form to quibble about a restaurant bill, but if you are paying for ten or fif-teen dollars' worth of food you didn't eat or for several rounds of cocktails you didn't drink, you have a right to ask for relief.

The absolute best way to handle fair payments is for the group to reach an agreement *before* placing any orders. If Lucy eats like a bird and everyone else is up for the Surf 'n' Turf, then tell your server to bill Lucy separately, and split everyone else's bill even-steven. If orders will vary significantly, ask for separate bills for everyone. (A restaurant that will not provide separate checks might be scratched off your group's list.) If you are blessed with a willing mathematical genius at the table, let that person handle the bill division, and don't quarrel when he or she rounds off numbers. Tips should be evenly divided, because everyone received the same service, but bar bills should be divided among the drinkers only.

It is inappropriate to ask a server for separate checks at the end of the meal or to invite a newcomer to dine without being clear that the meal is Dutch treat. Be conscious of what you order compared to your companions; if you owe more, take the initiative by speaking up and paying the piper. If someone offers to put the whole bill on her credit card in order to save time, be sure to pay back immediately. People tend to forget small debts, but it is rude and thoughtless to expect a generous coworker to come around with hat in hand when her credit-card bill arrives. And if it's the Thursday before payday and you really can't afford a meal out, politely ask your coworkers for a rain check rather than borrowing from someone who is probably as short on funds as you.

AT THE BAR

The British and Australians call it "shouting"—taking turns paying for each round of drinks. But be warned that too much shouting results in hoarseness: If you're with six people and each feels obligated to buy a round of drinks, everyone will end up inebriated. Besides, a great many people just don't drink much anymore, and it's discourteous to expect abstemious folks to pay for other people's evening of fun.

In groups of three or more, the smart course is to agree in advance to split the total bill at the end and control the impulse to buy a round. When a coworker agrees to be the designated driver for your group, be eternally grateful and pay for his or her iced teas, colas, and bar snacks.

AFTER-WORK PARTIES AT HOME

Perhaps the most delightful office gatherings of all are those that take place in someone's home. Often these get-togethers are celebratory—when the mem-

CAREFUL WITH THE JOKES

A mature sense of humor enables people to tease and laugh with others in a kind and gentle way, and to laugh at themselves without any trace of self-consciousness. The ability to make others smile is a gift; the ability to elicit laughter is also a business tool. But you should always use humor with care.

Whenever you feel like injecting a joke into a conversation, make sure it is at no one's expense; ethnic, racial, religious, or gender-based humor is not worth the risk of hurting someone else's feelings or soiling your reputation. Also, be careful about naming names, insulting your own and other companies, or attacking causes. Telling that hilarious joke about Alcoholics Anonymous will mark the jokester as an insensitive boob when a coworker is in treatment or has lost a loved one to alcoholism.

Until you get to know people very well, it's probably best to leave the jokes at home. Remember, too, that humor and jokes are not the same thing. The workplace is not a comedy club; if you can't get a punch line straight, don't step on stage. Some of our greatest humorists, from Mark Twain to Garrison Keillor, have rarely told jokes, instead dealing in sly observations on the whole human condition. They understand that good humor, unlike bad jokes, is natural, healthy, and best when shared with others.

bers of an office team want to toast the end of a major project, the winning of a new account, or the promotion of a fellow worker. In times of uncertainty and change in the workplace, the purpose of at-home parties may be simply to spend a few carefree hours together, away from the daily grind. Here are some ideas for successful and low-stress at-home events:

- **THE "WINE-AND-CHEESE" PARTY.** Despite its name, this party doesn't demand that only wine and cheese be served. The beauties of a wine-and-cheese-type party are its informality, ease of preparation and clean-up, and relatively low costs (especially if coworkers are sharing the expenses). So long as you have an adequate and tidy space, comfortable seating for every-one, and a well-stocked grocery store or deli nearby, you can throw a wine-and-cheese party on very short notice.

    Depending on your budget, chose a selection of reds that run from heav-ier types (Burgundy and Bordeaux) to lighter Côtes de Rhône or Beaujolais. Likewise, whites could range from sweet (Sancerres and sweet Sauternes) to dry (Sauvignon Blanc and white Burgundy). Uncork a bottle or two of red a few minutes before the party starts so that the wine will have had time to breathe. Leave open bottles on the serving table and invite guests to help themselves, although you should occasionally make the rounds of the party to refill the glasses of those who are unable to tear themselves away from a talk. Be sure to provide beverages for nonalcohol drinkers—bottled waters and soft drinks, fruit juices, and coffee make a good selection. Sparkling grape juices add spirit to the party, without the buzz.

While cheese should certainly be on the menu, any finger foods are appropriate. You can set out rolls of pepper salami and blocks of hard cheese with a basket of sturdy, good-size crackers alongside, so your guests can make their own finger sandwiches. The possibilities for snacks are endless—thin-sliced pumpernickel or oat bread, soft and hard cheeses, small pots of mayonnaise and a choice of mustards, prepared dips with raw veggies for dipping.

If the party is running longer than you expected and people are having a good time, be prepared to help with transportation. You may wind up with a guest on your couch, especially someone who has sampled a bit too much of the wine. Be sure that no one attempts to drive while tipsy.

- **THE INFORMAL COCKTAIL PARTY.** This is an ideal way to entertain workmates within a restricted time period. Friday is the best day: It's a traditional time to unwind, and some guests will probably continue on to dinner at a restaurant. The cocktail party can be as informal as you like, to the point of having guests mix their own drinks. Depending on your climate and the season, outdoor parties are an excellent way to accommodate more guests than your living room can handle. Seating should be adequate, but most people expect to stand at a cocktail party.

If you are supplying the liquor, you're hardly obliged to have every type under the sun. Let your workmates know you will provide the basics, and if they want their exotic personal favorite they'll have to bring it themselves. The basic home bar includes scotch, bourbon, gin, and vodka (and, to cover your bases, beer and wine), along with tonic, seltzer or club soda, sweet and dry vermouth, lemons, and limes—a hefty initial investment, but you can probably count on some of it being saved for later use. For those who don't want alcohol, have bottles of mineral water (both sparkling and still), fruit juices, and soft drinks. Provide some edibles such as small bowls of Italian olives and salted nuts or platters of chips and dips.

If you decide to serve hors d'oeuvres, the simplest solution is to buy them already prepared, or provide cold cuts, sliced cheese, and dense breads for finger sandwiches. Other choices include elegant spreads made from smoked mozzarella and sun-dried tomatoes or goat cheese and chives. To accommodate vegetarians, try tofu spreads flavored with vegetables—surprisingly tasty and reasonably priced.

To make sure your party doesn't wind on beyond the allotted time, specify that it will last from six to eight when you extend your invitation. Because many people leave work before five on Friday afternoons, an earlier start may be possible, but be considerate of how far people must drive and the state of rush-hour traffic.

- **THE POT-LUCK PARTY.** This is the most informal party of all—a true BYO. The charm of a pot-luck is that it enables coworkers of all levels—and even your bosses, if you are inclined to invite them—to mix and mingle in an atmosphere as comfortable as an old-fashioned church supper or picnic. Sometimes, having a pot-luck is the only way someone with a full-time job can manage to entertain. With others pitching in, a party becomes possible.

Any officemate whose house or apartment is large enough to accommodate the group can provide the space and act as the organizer, while the guests will supply most of the food. The participants can bring prepared dishes from a market or deli, or casseroles, vegetable dishes, or desserts they've whipped up themselves—especially if they want to show off a specialty they're known for.

If you're the organizer, take care to see that the menu is coordinated: You don't want four people bringing Italian sausage dishes and no one showing up with a vegetable or salad. Those who don't cook may prefer to bring bags of chips and a carton of dip. Or they can volunteer to supply the beverages—soft drinks, juices, beer, or wine, depending on the group's tastes. (Since the emphasis is on good food and good company, pot-lucks are the perfect opportunity to avoid serving alcohol at all.) By the day of the party, you should have decided who will be responsible for what: If something is missing from the menu—a sweet, perhaps—prepare it or buy it yourself.

When organizing a pot-luck, be conscious of coworkers' personal needs. Will the location accommodate a colleague who uses a wheelchair, for example? Should spouses, dates, and children be included? Single moms or dads may have difficulty getting a baby-sitter and organizing young children while preparing food for the party. (Let them off the hook by asking them to bring the paper napkins.) If business is not the purpose of the event, a pot-luck is a comfortable setting to meet the significant others in coworkers' private lives.

CHAPTER 6

IN YOUR WORKSPACE

An irony for the new millennium: As the hierarchical pyramid of the workplace flattens out, who resides at the junior level is made all the more evident by the physical space where they work—the cubicle, the symbolic soul of the cost-cutting business ethic of the late 20th century. On top of that, a surprise: Not everyone who works in a cubicle is a junior level employee. In a few companies, workers from the vice president on down occupy cubicles in the name of teamwork and equality. Such forward thinking notwithstanding, in most organizations the "hard wall" versus "soft wall" debate (i.e., office-with-door versus cubicle) has been a major issue over the last several years. Along with this abiding concern, this chapter discusses practical matters. What messages does your office decor send? How proprietary should you feel? What does your attitude toward your cubicle say about you? What rules of behavior apply when a workmate or visitor enters your space?

YOUR OFFICE

"My office." The words trip off the tongue as easily as "my house" or "my family." Tinged with white-collar pride, the O word takes on still more luster with additional words attached: A window office ratchets the occupant up another notch on the status scale, while the corner office speaks of power. Today, having a hard-wall office of any kind is a precious feather in one's cap. An upshot of this phenomenon: Modesty on the part of the haves is all the more important when interacting with the have-nots.

A DOSE OF HUMILITY

The fact is, the window office/cubicle divide doesn't always equate with senior/junior. In some companies, cubicle dwellers at a certain job level graduate to window offices whenever one becomes available; whoever is next in line wins the prize. If this explains your good fortune, humility, not gloating, is the demeanor to strive for. When a workmate who sits in a cubicle comes into your office, don't play the self-satisfied fat cat who puts his feet up on the desk and surveys his domain. That you have an actual desk (not a modular work surface) may not bother your visitor in the least, but getting up and leaning or perching yourself on the edge of the desk or taking a chair next to him or her is nonetheless a good idea; it de-emphasizes the inequities, if only subliminally.

No matter who the visitor or what the situation, anytime you come around from behind your desk and sit near someone, you set up a friendly climate for a more relaxed discussion (see also page 92). The behind-the-desk position is formal and signifies that this is your turf. Bosses, too, will do well by occasionally removing themselves from behind the desk and democratizing the scene.

CLOSING YOUR DOOR

Keep in mind that a closed door is a stark reminder to cubicle dwellers that you have a door and they don't; for this reason, close yours only when there's a legitimate reason to do so. As a rule, privacy is warranted when you need quiet to concentrate, when you're meeting with a visitor, or when you're discussing a confidential matter with an employer or coworker.

Furthermore, don't abuse the privilege. A closed door doesn't give you the license to make personal calls all day long or to complete personal tasks. As much as it feels like your home away from home, your office is still the property of your employer—and you're there to do the business you were hired to do.

ANOTHER REMINDER: No slamming! If you're bothered by a conversation going on outside your door, either wait it out or take the opportunity to run an errand elsewhere on the floor. If it drags on, get up and shut the door as softly as possible; the talkers will no doubt catch on. If your idea of sending a message to a knot of jabberers is to slam the door, you'll come off looking childish and short-tempered.

YOUR CUBICLE

Just as the term "firing" goes by any number of names, so does the cubicle and its variations, from the euphemistic "open-plan officing," "soft-wall office," and "work station" to the slang "geek ghetto," "cube," and "pod." Labels aside, these workspaces of the millennium are the subject of much contention. Listen to the views from both sides of the fence, with the pro-cubicle camp's defense coming first:

- Cubicles are less costly for businesses, some of which justify the arrangement by plowing the savings into more pressing needs.
- The cubicle is the great equalizer. A few companies are committed to the concept of cubicles for staff at every level, with the idea that erasing all visible signs of hierarchy makes for better feelings and more productivity.
- Close quarters spur team energy. Some companies build cubicles on the premise that putting people in close proximity feeds the "faster" third of the "faster, cheaper, better" business mantra.
- Cubicles point the way to the next century. Some futurists hold that even cubicles are being made superfluous by technological advances that facilitate greater mobility and allow people to stay in touch from remote locations. "Task-based" environments, where space is designed to follow function, not rank, are already in place in group medical practices, and some law firms are beginning to see how to increase performance and productivity by using such "alternative officing."

Cubicle critics beg to disagree, contending the following:

- Cubicles amount to little more than an invasion of privacy, resulting in the lowering of both productivity and creativity.
- Cubicles lead to an intimacy that many workers find uncomfortable.
- The dissatisfaction of the cubicle worker with his space creates bad feelings towards management and erodes whatever loyalty remains.
- Cubicles serve as a constant reminder of a worker's marginality to the company as a whole.

The truth naturally lies somewhere in between. Regular walls support the heads-down kind of work done by engineers and people in knowledge industries and are best suited to their type of work. People performing tasks based on teamwork, such as getting out a daily newspaper, run the risk of being out of the loop unless they work in an open arrangement.

In any case, cubicle workers usually have no choice but to make the best of it. Short of looking for a job elsewhere and making a window office a stipulation of employment, they can ease the frustrations and inconveniences common to "life in the cube" by taking the bull by the horns.

A MATTER OF ATTITUDE

The ease with which you handle having to work from a cubicle says much about your resiliency. It also slots you somewhere along the personality scale that runs from crybaby to stoic—and don't think your attitude won't be noticed: When the time comes for raises and promotions, the person who accepts his fate with good graces has the edge over the perennial whiner. Regardless of how you really feel, rolling with the punches doesn't mean you're a weakling; it demonstrates a firm grasp of the realities of life in business.

Resentment toward management is usually misplaced, since decisions on office design are probably beyond their control. Don't hesitate to make your wish for a window office known to your supervisor, but at the same time say that you understand that the possibility is contingent on other factors. Stay upbeat, as if you know she'll do what she can when the opportunity arises. Looking bitter and defeated may leave a sour taste and work to your disadvantage.

Territorial Imperatives and Privacy

Because the worker in a cubicle is so visible (and all the more so in the half-wall design), there is a subconscious assumption on the part of passersby that he is automatically available. But this notion couldn't be farther off the mark. Some companies have gone so far as to distribute red baseball caps for workers to don whenever they don't want to be disturbed.

However compact or noisy your cubicle domain, you still have the right to expect visitors to respect your time and space. The cubicle is your office territory and should be treated as such. Just as visitors refrain from barging into an office or opening a closed door, they shouldn't sashay into your cubicle without knocking lightly or saying "May I come in?"

The same applies to your next-door neighbors. The phenomenon that has come to be known as "prairie-dogging"—standing up or hanging over cubicle walls to communicate—can get annoying and invasive. Here, plain common sense is called for: Employees intensely involved with coworkers in team projects may find prairie-dogging the best and most efficient way to communicate quickly, while employees working on individual projects usually prefer that others respect their need for privacy.

If prairie-dogging seems out of line and bothers you, choose your words to a coworker with care: "Bruce, I know it's easiest for you to talk over the wall, but would you do me a favor and come around? The fewer reminders that we're without walls, the better, don't you think?" Sitting face-to-face and talking is a way of showing you're giving your full attention.

Noise is the enemy of the cubicle dweller, a constant threat to concentration in a space that can't be soundproofed with the closing of a door. Hear, hear:

- Even hard walls and doors are no match for some people's voices, which have a timbre much like the throbbing bass in a sound system. If you have such a voice, get in the habit of speaking more softly in open-plan offices.
- Many people tend to unconsciously talk louder when they're on the phone. As silly as it sounds, a Post-it marked "Sotto Voce" or some such message will remind you to lower your voice.
- Never shout a request or response to someone in a nearby cubicle. If it's too much trouble to walk over, pick up the phone instead.
- Radios blaring in cubicles are another form of intrusion. If you must listen to music, use headphones. Then again, if your neighbors find the music from your favorite classical station soothing, play it but keep it low.
- No clicking! Don't click the clip of a pen while talking on the phone. Nor should you clip your nails while phoning or reading.
- When you ask the people in the next cubicle to quiet down, do it as politely as possible. Remember that minor resentments are magnified by someone who is dissatisfied at being consigned to a cubicle and can quickly lead to frayed tempers.

CHATS, PHONE CALLS, AND EAVESDROPPING

An unfortunate byproduct of cubiclization is the ability of those around you to hear everything you say—and vice versa. It takes a very strong-willed individual to tune out the voices around him, which often is possible only with the help of earplugs or earphones. But remember, it cuts both ways:

- Group conversations are particularly problematic. When entertaining visitors, go to a common area so as not to disturb the neighbors. Also try to dissuade people from loitering or socializing around your cubicle. (A polite "Larry, I'm working on something right now that demands my full concentration" should do the trick.) And be discreet—a cubicle is not the place to talk about sensitive matters; discuss anything confidential in a private place.
- Phone calls are a touchy matter, too. Whenever you don't want to be overheard, find an empty office or a pay phone in the lobby, or make the call after hours. If that's impossible and a next-door neighbor seems to be listening to even your most mundane calls (evidenced by under-the-breath chuckles or mutterings of surprise), try drowning out your voice with an air filter or a

white noise device. If that doesn't work, take the matter up: "Don, we're in close quarters, but would you mind giving me privacy when I'm on the phone?" Don may not stop eavesdropping, but at least you've made your point.

- If you walk up to someone in a cubicle and find he's on the phone, don't hover there waiting for him to hang up. Leave and try again later.

MORE UNWELCOME SOUNDS

Radios and loud voices are often the least of it. One of the stickier wickets in the culture of cubicles is the officemate who makes inappropriate or offensive sounds. Burping, the slurping of soup or coffee, loud yawning, and worse are amplified in close quarters.

Be thoughtful of neighbors by maintaining some decorum at your desk. The rest room, of course, is the place to relieve yourself of any physical discomforts. Even if you only have the sniffles, leave and blow your nose often enough that you're not going to be sniffing and snorting like clockwork.

CREATIVE ADJUSTMENTS

Many cubicle residents have found smart ways to achieve some level of privacy and mute some of the noises around them. Removable entryways can be arranged into a kind of semi-maze entrance, for example. Plants or corkboards placed strategically can help to muffle outside noise and create a sense of privacy at the same time. But before moving panels or putting up makeshift sound buffers, be sure to get permission from your employer or office manager. It can be humiliating to have to disassemble your alterations after everyone has complimented you on your ingenuity.

PIN-UPS

Cubicle walls often become billboards and a way to share a cartoon, joke, or article that's particularly apropos. But be careful with your choices: While something a little risqué may be permissible in your office, never put up materials that cross the line to gross or obscene. Anything with racist or sexist undertones is equally beyond the pale.

A FURTHER NOTE OF CAUTION: Never pin anticorporate articles from magazines or newspapers to your cubicle wall, whether they are written about your own company or the corporate world in general. Those in view of anyone passing constitute a direct affront to management. While no one should be expected not to speak freely, such displays mark you as someone who's distrustful of your superiors, sees himself as a victim of larger forces, and is probably bitter to boot. Even if this is true, advertising it jeopardizes your chances of survival if a round of layoffs occurs.

WORKSPACE DECOR

The decoration of your workspace depends on a number of things, with the type of work and the amount of customer interaction conducted there being some of the most important. If you deal face-to-face with clients and customers on a daily basis, the decor is generally customer driven. In a service industry such as banking, for example, the environment is often homogenous, with personal effects kept to a minimum. In offices where creative work is done, such as a graphic design studio, decor is often more personalized. That's because many employers feel a sterile environment is anathema to creative work.

YOUR THINGS? OR THEIRS?

Because you probably spend more time in your workspace than at home, it stands to reason that you develop a feeling of propriety about everything around you. But just how freely can you use office supplies and equipment—as well as that precious commodity, time—for your own personal needs? Preferably never, but that is all but impossible.

- PERSONAL PHONE CALLS. A long-term employee might consider his extension number as part of his identity, but remember who is paying the bills. Personal long distance calls should either be charged to your calling card or made from home. The exception is when your company presents you with a monthly log of your long distance phone calls and you check off and pay for the personal ones. Remember, too, that you are there to work.

- OFFICE SUPPLIES. Small items have a way of becoming interchangeable between the office and home, and finding a few in both places is little to worry about. Taken only occasionally and a few at a time, pens, paper clips, and staples are generally not going to cause anyone alarm—but whole boxfuls will. Don't fool yourself into thinking that you're owed office supplies because you're such a hard worker. No matter how entitled you feel, secreting a stapler or a ream of bond paper in your briefcase is nothing less than thievery.

- DOCTOR'S APPOINTMENTS. It's usually impossible to always keep doctor's and dentist's appointments to your off time, but scheduling them for the beginning or end of the day will prevent mid-day interruptions and save transit time in the bargain. You can ask your supervisor if you can work late or through lunch to make up your lost time.

These factors come into play in the decoration of individual spaces, including cubicles. (Even though cubicle dwellers and their guests usually adjourn to a meeting room, frequent visitors will have occasion to be in the workspace.) Experts believe that employees who feel an element of control over their physical space are happier workers; after all, work is the place where most of us spend the majority of our time. Accordingly, most employers have no problem letting employees display personal photos, colorful posters, and knickknacks, and even adjust the lighting if possible. Some employers even take it to another level, filling the common areas with such leisure-time toys as jukeboxes and Ping-Pong tables to foment a comfortable atmosphere and encourage creativity.

In other offices, that sort of freewheeling, personalized ambiance isn't appropriate. Much depends not only on the type of work being done there but on the preferences of the people at the top. And these can be extreme: One corporate philosophy dictates that soft-wall offices remain just as the designer intended them, reasoning that an attempt to heighten a waist-high wall with a bulletin board or a row of potted plants defeats the purpose of the open-office plan. (Floor managers would be wise to remember that not allowing cubicle dwellers to creatively adjust their space can magnify the feeling that they have no privacy, much less individuality.)

MORE WORKSPACE MANNERS

There are some things that apply to workspace etiquette in general, without regard to walls and doors. Within this grab bag of concerns are whether you should stand when someone enters, how to play the good host to visitors, and the more mundane (though no less potentially annoying) matters of using a speakerphone and lunching at your desk.

WHEN TO STAND?

Male or female, a well-mannered person rises when either a superior or someone elderly enters the workspace. You also rise for clients and customers, of course. It's even nice to stand to greet any workmate who hasn't dropped by your office or cubicle for a while. Rising is not an empty gesture done for the sake of "etiquette," but a way of showing respect.

At most other times, however, you can remain firmly in your chair. Assistants and other people who come and go would no doubt find it strange if you popped up every time they walked in.

Eating at Your Desk

Eating at your desk is often unavoidable, particularly in busy offices or those without cafeterias. Besides eating quietly (especially in a cubicle), think "smell." Odoriferous foods such as fried fish and freshly microwaved members of the cabbage family (including broccoli and Brussels sprouts) are no respecters of walls. Whether emanating from the desk in a hard-wall office or a cubicle, the odor of some foods is an equal opportunity offender once it gets into the air conditioning system. (See also Cooking and Microwaving, page 99.)

Using a Speakerphone

For some people, the effort of picking up the phone receiver is too great; they rely instead on talking or listening to messages by speakerphone. This forces everyone around to suffer the noise, especially those who work in an open-plan office or have thin walls. A speakerphone should be used only in closed offices and ideally when more than one person is on the receiving end.

If possible, make conference calls using speakerphones from a conference room. Even closed doors can't always muffle voices, since people talk more loudly to be heard. (See also Using a Speakerphone, page 289.)

Office Appointments

Meetings around your desk can be highly productive if you observe a few courtesies. First, is your space really conducive to discussion? A doorless cubicle in a busy office may be your domain (like it or not), but the hustle and bustle that you hardly notice can be nerve-shattering to a client. Evaluate your private space. Is it comfortable physically and psychologically? If not, reserve a meeting room for appointments.

When the receptionist calls and says your visitor has arrived, go out to greet him—or, if you have an assistant, send her to escort him in.

Early arrivals. If a visitor arrives more than ten minutes early and you are not ready, try to keep her from feeling awkward. If there is a receptionist, ask him to make the visitor comfortable, telling her you'll be out as soon as possible. If you work in a small office without a receptionist, come out of your office, greet the visitor, accept her apologies for arriving early, offer her an available chair, and give her a magazine to read while she waits.

Late arrivals. If a visitor arrives so late you won't be able to squeeze him into your schedule, accept his apology and arrange another meeting. Or should he arrive after you are already indisposed, ask the receptionist or an assistant to tell him you waited as long as you could and that you would like to schedule another date and time to meet.

Keeping someone waiting. Never keep a visitor waiting more than five or six minutes past the appointed time. If you have no choice but to do so, walk out and apologize in person. (People today are smart enough to know a power play when they see one, and remaining out of sight contributes to the assumption that you're making one.) An offer of a cup of coffee and a magazine is also a nice gesture. If something has come up that is going to delay your meeting for

---

THE BLACK HOLE

I f business is moving toward the paperless office, it isn't there quite yet: Clutter remains the enemy of the efficient worker. True, there are those who have random piles of paper stacked almost to the ceiling, yet in the flash of an eye burrow in to find exactly the memo they need. Then there are the workers who drown in a sea of paper, covering every surface with a short stack here, a single page there. To them, things magically disappear, often never to be seen again—sucked into the dreaded black hole.

It's one thing to lose the scrap of paper with the phone number of your dry cleaner, but another if a business associate from outside the office calls for a discussion and you're frantically rifling though papers on your desk for your notes. Overcome the problem by doing the following:

- KEEP A PAD BY THE PHONE FOR JOTTING. Most lost jottings have been written on an envelope flap, the margin of whatever sheet is handy, or on the back of a printed sheet and thrown away. Even if you have to nail it down, keep a notepad for just this purpose next to the phone on your desk.
- CLEAR THE DECKS DAILY. Straightening up the office at the end of the day serves two purposes: You're likely to find something you thought was missing, and you'll find it satisfying the next morning to walk into an uncluttered space. The latter provides a bonus: a psychological effect that's more positive than most people realize.
- USE FOLDERS. Besides the business papers, letters, and data sheets you put in your filing cabinet, there's the flotsam and jetsam that collects over a couple of weeks: circulated journals and magazines, schedules from the production department, postcards mailed from traveling friends. Keep a box of manila folders in a drawer and assign a different label to each. Then keep them in one place—a desktop standing file purely for miscellany.
- ASK YOURSELF WHETHER YOU REALLY NEED IT. If you can't come up with a specific reason for keeping a piece of paper, throw it away. Also, if the memo was sent via e-mail, remember that you may keep a permanent record in your computer.

more than 15 minutes, apologize for taking up your visitor's time and ask if he prefers to reschedule on another day.

YOUR MEETING

In addition to extending your greeting, there are two things you should always do when a business associate from outside enters your workspace: 1) Offer to hang up his coat, if he has one, and 2) ask him to be seated. Remember that sitting behind a desk is less personable than taking a chair next to him (see page 83). If you want the meeting to remain private, close your door; if you're in a cubicle, go to a common area or meeting room, which you should have reserved in advance.

Be sure to have all the necessary materials at hand, so that visitors won't have to navigate through piles of files. If coworkers are participating in the meeting, arrange for them to be present in your office when the guest arrives and then make introductions.

If the phone rings, it is generally bad form to answer it when a visitor is present. If you have a do-not-disturb button on your phone, use it. If you have an assistant and he considers a call important enough to interrupt your meeting, use your intuition to decide whether this particular visitor will mind or not. (See also Phone Call Faux Pas, page 295.) If you expect the meeting to be a long one, you might offer the visitor a beverage. Keeping a coffee maker, tea bags, and a couple of china cups and saucers in your office simplifies things by saving you from having to rely on orders from outside, which are difficult to time.

If a visitor overstays his or her welcome, you can politely end the meeting by stating that you have another appointment or duty.

SEEING VISITORS OUT

Walk the visitor back to the reception area. Do this even if it's a straight shot and he won't have to make his way through a maze of corridors. Exchange a few pleasantries when saying good-bye, but if he shows signs of chatting at length you can simply say you have to go back to work.

CHAPTER 7

AROUND THE FLOOR

C rossing paths with your workmates all day and sharing floor space, office equipment, and facilities demands more than patience. As a cog in a larger wheel, you'll want to maintain your presence and identity without getting on people's nerves. Find the middle ground: A glad-hander or backslapper can be wearying to be around, while aloofness could make you look as if you think you're above it all. The trick is to be quietly pleasant and mindful of any personal qualities that have the potential to annoy—a booming voice, a radio that plays all day, a propensity to read other people's faxes or hog the copier, or a grating laugh that could drive people up the wall, assuming they have one.

In the common areas of your office—the corridors, the copier and fax rooms, the kitchen or cafeteria, the rest rooms—your relationship with your coworkers shifts from that of team members with a common goal to one of competing for space and equipment, if only subconsciously. How you handle yourself and treat others in the process will keep the workday less troublesome, resulting in a lighter mood that eases the daily grind.

IN THE CORRIDORS

Creating a workplace where courtesy reigns doesn't mean feeling obligated to say hello every time you pass someone in the hall; being preoccupied with what you're doing is only natural when you're busy and shouldn't be taken as an affront. Naturally, you'll want to greet coworkers the first time you see them with "Good morning" or "How's it going?," but after that a quick smile or nod will do. It can be tiresome to work in the kind office where everybody walks around being relentlessly cheery and threatening to hug you at the drop of a hat. More important is what *not* to do when passing people in the hall—staring straight down at the floor with a sour look on your face. Even though it's unlikely to be taken personally, ignoring people does little for the kind of atmosphere that makes the day go better.

HALLWAY SCHMOOZING

Say you're walking down the hall and see someone you've been meaning to talk to schmoozing with a friend. Your most polite choice is not to interrupt at all, but whether you do depends on how friendly you are with the people. In any case, instead of just jumping in, wait for an opening in the conversation. If the conversation seems to be an intent one, make sure your interruption is for something substantial—where the data sheets for a mutual project can be found, not what the corner soup place has as today's special.

When chatting in the halls, stand to the side so as not to block traffic—an obvious courtesy, but one that a surprising number of people ignore. If that includes you, remember that making busy coworkers detour around you a couple of times is little to worry about, but after three or four it can start to get annoying. Less obvious is what people might be thinking when your conversation goes on for more than 10 minutes or so; besides disturbing people in nearby offices, you could be seen as a slacker if you make a regular habit of gabbing away in the corridors.

If you bump into your boss in the hallway and have been meaning to talk with her about something, weigh whether the setting is conducive to the conversation. Depending on your office environment, it may be better to just mention your need to speak to her and ask if you can set up a time.

COMMUNAL EQUIPMENT

Communal office equipment, which has a way of needing maintenance more regularly than it should, is a lightning rod for the "it's not my job" attitude among workers. Keeping it in good working order is assumed to be the responsibility of someone else, and probably is. (Besides, in many offices you probably don't have access to toner cartridges and such.) Even if it's technically not your responsibility, you should take care of things if you know how. If the signal lights show that a fax machine, printer, or copier needs toner or has a paper jam, either do the job yourself or call the person in charge of machine maintenance right away. This applies twice over in a small business, where, in the spirit of team players, everyone—including the boss—should pitch in.

A CERTAIN PROBLEM

What if the person who's supposed to be responsible for seeing to the equipment isn't doing his job? Raise the issue politely—and to the person, not his boss: "Rob, I hate to complain, but the 'replace cartridge' sign has been lit on the marketing department fax for two days now, and it has really become a problem. Can you tell me when you'll be able to install it?" If he answers he can't get to it till tomorrow, ask if there's anyone else who can do the job. If there isn't—or if he says he'll do it in a couple of hours and doesn't—tell him that you'll have to ask the floor manager for a solution.

If even this doesn't spur him into action, deliver on your promise. Tell the floor manager that repeated requests to replace the cartridge have come to naught and leave it at that. Rob's action speaks for itself, and the chance to vent your frustration isn't reason enough for berating him to his boss. When it comes to office machines, the last thing you need is an enemy.

COPIERS

Copying machines run at different speeds, with some processing 30 pages in half the time an older machine does. Those that are slow are just waiting to create frustrations, if not conflicts. But even the use of state-of-the-art copiers requires remembering the needs of others.

The most obvious courtesy is for someone who has a large copy job—say, 20 pages or more—to let anyone who has only two or three interrupt the job (or if you've gotten to the machine at the same time, to go first). It's another matter if you've set the machine for finishing (sorting, stapling, enlarging, or the like) and you need 4 copies of a 20-page manuscript. In this case, give anyone who comes to use the machine an estimate of how long it will take. A new-

---

RESPECTING PRIVACY

Don't snoop! As you sift through a fax in-box or remove someone else's just-transmitted document from the machine, look only at the cover sheets. Similarly, if you open the lid of a copier and find someone has left an original sheet, don't get curious if it looks like something private. While the page would usually go in a communal receptacle for forgotten sheets, this is one time when you should deliver it in person. Save the person any worry by volunteering, "I didn't read this when I opened the copier lid, but I could tell it was private. Thought I'd drop it by."

Pay special attention if faxing or copying something personal, especially if having someone else see it will cause you any embarrassment. Medical or legal papers, once left behind and seen, could start the gossip mill grinding.

comer who sees that someone has just set the machine for a major job should automatically be the one to defer.

Jobs of any real magnitude are best done either early in the morning or just after quitting hours, when the machines are freer. An alternative is to do the job on a copier that's off the beaten path. After any large job, check the paper drawer and top it off as necessary.

Also check company policy for personal copying jobs. If you work for a small business with a "no personal copies" policy, always abide by it or ask special permission from your boss. If you are doing it secretly and a coworker reports it, be angry with yourself, not the tattler.

FAX MACHINES

When faxing, abide by the office rules. Some companies allow fax machines to be used only for business, not personal, communications; others care not a whit, although you'll show consideration by sending personal faxes after hours. If your company falls somewhere in between, it's a good idea to ask permission from a supervisor when you need to use the office fax for personal correspondence.

Unlike a copying job, a fax transmission cannot be interrupted, meaning that sending extra-long faxes will tie up the machine for what seems like forever. Follow the same "who goes first" rule that applies to using copiers. Likewise, if you have a fax of 20 pages or more, try to send it early in the morning, just after closing time, or when most people have gone to lunch. Better still, check your options for an e-mail attachment before blindly dumping a job in the fax machine. A bike messenger is another choice for a large job being sent locally.

Most offices keep in and out boxes near the fax machine to bring some order to an exercise that most people rarely stick around for. One box is for pages already faxed but not picked up; the other box, for incoming faxes that have yet to be collected. Feeling obligated put a fax in a workmate's mailbox or to let her know her fax has arrived is a recipe for inefficiency for anyone who's busy; people should take responsibility for checking for any faxes they expect or occasionally sifting through the in-box. Still, if it's no trouble to drop off a business fax to someone (or mention they have one) as you pass by his or her office or cubicle, by all means do.

A practical note: Faxes that use thermal (heat sensitive) paper produce copies that fade after a few months. When you receive a fax to be filed, photocopy it and file the photocopy with the fax copy.

Star Players

THE WELCOMER

This person is a godsend to new employees, temps, contract workers, and suppliers. He knows how it feels to be a stranger in a strange land and goes out of his way to welcome newcomers and make sure they get the lay of that land. When the personnel department's obligatory tour of the office or plant is done, it is the Welcomer who is happy to review details of the operation and clear up the newcomer's questions and confusions. The Welcomer understands that ignorance of small details—where to find the paper clips or how the kitchen clean-up schedule is rotated or who handles supply requisitions—can turn a new coworker's early days on the job that much more difficult. The true Welcomer invites questions and is never averse to explaining things more than once, and no one is beneath his concern. While others may regard temp workers and suppliers as so much furniture, the Welcomer is grateful for their presence; he learns names quickly and is eager to introduce new workers to the veterans of the office.

People who are more accustomed to cold greetings in new places may mistakenly question the Welcomer's motives. But the real Welcomer is a person of compassion and good manners. He may not become a friend for life, but he can take the chill off of any new job.

FAX ETIQUETTE

Despite the rise of e-mail, faxing remains the preferred form of rapid transmission for many types of documents and materials. Bear in mind that a faxed message is less personal and usually less convenient than a telephone call. Nevertheless, faxes can be very helpful when you need to contact someone who can't be reached by telephone or pager. For example, you may not want to call an executive who is in transit or attending an important out-of-town business meeting, but you can easily send a fax to his or her hotel.

Proper fax etiquette is relatively simple, with five main points:

- **USE A COVER SHEET.** Don't be tempted not to use one or a fax could get lost in the shuffle. The cover sheet includes the name of the recipient, his or her fax number, the total number of pages being transmitted, and the date. If you're sending to a company, indicate the recipient's title, department, and phone or extension number. Include the sender's name as well as fax and telephone numbers. Cover sheets may also include special notations, such as "Urgent" and "For Immediate Delivery," plus exact instructions for what to do if there is a problem with the transmission.

Around the Floor

- **DON'T COUNT ON PRIVACY.** You can mark a fax CONFIDEN-TIAL or PERSONAL, but remember that your fax may pass through many hands before reaching the intended recipient.
- **NUMBER THE PAGES IN YOUR DOCUMENT.** This allows the recipient to ascertain that all pages have arrived. If the fax is incomplete, you can resend the missing page or pages rather than the whole document.
- **BE CONSIDERATE OF THE RECIPIENT.** Sometimes you have to send extremely long documents. Rather than tie up the recipient's office fax machine, send your fax before or after office hours if possible. If you must send a lengthy fax during business hours, call the recipient first. There may be a number for an alternate fax machine that is not in heavy use, or the recipient may want to alert others that a long document is expected.
- **TEST THE IMAGE.** If you're sending an image that may not repro-duce clearly (a photograph, for example, or a poor photocopy), test the image by using your fax's copy function. Also test anything printed on colored paper or with colored inks. Some felt-pen highlighting will not reproduce, so high-lighted information should be underlined in black ink.

PRINTERS

Avoid printing out lengthy jobs on a printer that you know to be heavily used. If your job is for 8½" x 11" paper, direct it to a laser printer that handles only that size, leaving the other printers free for 11" x 17" printouts.

If a job hasn't been picked up by a coworker, don't just throw it aside. Place it face up where it can be clearly seen or put it in a space designated for finished jobs—a metal rack or an in-box large enough to accommodate big sheets. As with faxes, it would be a nice gesture to drop off a job if it's obvious whose it is, although going out of your way isn't always practical.

When the printers are down, don't take out your frustration on the techni-cal support staff, who are doubtlessly doing all they can. Remember that these haggard souls are more frustrated than you are, and when technology decides to show us who's boss it usually gets its way. Alert them at the first sign of trou-ble (or call the Help desk, if you have one), and then turn your attention to something else productive until the problem is solved.

FURNITURE

Treat any tables in the reception room, conference rooms, or the kitchen as you treat your furniture at home. That means putting a soda can or a sweating glass on a napkin or coaster to avoid leaving a ring on a table made of wood. The same goes for your office furniture, which may be expensive and will more than likely be inherited someday by someone else. Don't wipe greasy fingers on a fabric-covered chair, and don't let the crumbs of your morning muffin fall on the floor and be ground into the carpet, where they can leave unsightly oil stains.

IN THE KITCHEN

The kitchen has the potential for being the messiest room on the floor, so it's only fair that everyone does his or her part to keep it clean. If you spill something—on the counter, in the fridge, on the floor—*wipe it up.* Don't leave your dirty dishes in the sink. If necessary, wipe down appliances after you use them.

Besides cleanliness, there's courtesy. If your fridge doesn't have an ice maker, refill the ice cube trays when you empty them. (Also be sure to pick up any ice cubes that fall to the floor, so they don't melt and make a puddle that could make someone slip.) If there's a communal coffeemaker, refill it and start a new pot if you take the last cup. Report any problems with the vending machine; if management hasn't made it clear who to tell when the vending machine is on the fritz, find out from whoever is responsible for maintenance, report it, and post the information for the future benefit of others.

STORING FOOD

When it comes to the refrigerator, one rule is paramount: Don't leave milk or leftovers inside until they start to smell. In a time of cost-cutting measures, the cleaner who cleans out the refrigerator every Friday may be cut back to once a month, but in any case it's your responsibility to dispose of food you never got around to eating. If you regularly bring your lunch to work, invest in some airtight plastic containers. Neglected food wrapped in aluminum foil will spoil faster and start to smell that much sooner.

COOKING AND MICROWAVING

Just as you're responsible for washing your own dishes, you're responsible for cleaning up any appliances you use. If anything you've placed in the microwave boils over or splatters, wipe down the inside of the oven with a wet paper towel. Likewise, if sauce has bubbled over in a conventional unit and burned to a crisp on the surface, wipe it off. Remember in particular that the toaster oven and the grilled cheese sandwich are a match made in hell: The charcoaled cheese drippings become room odorizers every time the toaster oven is turned on—the goop that keeps on giving.

Around the Floor

Problem Peers

THE FOOD THIEF

You could wring somebody's neck, couldn't you? Nothing is more frustrating than finding the smoked turkey sandwich your mouth was just set for has mysteriously disappeared from the fridge. "How could they?" you think. As maddening as having your sandwich or leftover lasagna purloined is the pilfering of milk—a splash here, a splash there by people who think of it as "borrowing just a little" for their coffee or tea. What they become are partners in crime when the carton that was supposed to last you a week is almost empty after two days. Personalizing a food package by clearly labeling it with your name may disabuse the potential thief of the notion it's communal, but don't count on it. The annoying little white-collar crime of food theft is all too easy for some people to commit.

It is almost impossible to catch a food thief unless your kitchen has surveillance cameras. (The evidence, after all, has probably already been digested.) Your only way of getting back is to announce the deed to the world. Compose a note for the refrigerator door and leave it posted there for a few days. While you'll be tempted to write something witty ("Who's the turkey who took my turkey"), don't let the seriousness of the matter be lost in the tone; this is one time when it does not pay to be nice. Try something on the order of "To whoever stole my sandwich on Monday, March 22: Taking other people's things just might to be grounds for firing. Was a tuna salad sandwich worth the risk? Signed, An irate coworker."

While the smell of popcorn popping or leftover macaroni and cheese being heated up may do little more than make people hungry, foods with unpleasantly distinctive smells are another matter. Frying fish on the stove top (which people have actually been known to do at work) is a major error, but seemingly benign foods can cause just as big a stink. The main culprits are members of the cabbage family, including the pretty little Brussels sprouts that were so good last night. The sprout's cousins (broccoli, head cabbage, cauliflower, collards, and kale) release varying degrees of odor when being reheated, but remember: Wherever they end up being carried—the desk in your office, the communal lunch table—the smell is sure to follow.

WASHING DISHES

Don't leave dirty coffee mugs in the sink or food scraps in the garbage disposal. It's each person's responsibility to wash his own dishes as soon as he has finished his meal. The food residue on dishes that sit in the sink for days starts to smell, as any poor housekeeper can tell you. A group could get together to assign biweekly kitchen cleanup shifts, but giving in to people's dereliction of their own duties sets a bad example. To avoid the awkwardness of confronting mess-makers in person, post a reminder sign above the sink.

COMMUNAL LUNCHES

Having lunch together in the cafeteria is a great time to get to know your coworkers. More important, it's a great time for them to get to know *you*—and if you use your lunch hour as an opportunity to start a juicy rumor, brag on and on about your kids, or inhale your food in one fell swoop, they're not going to be impressed. Both the quality of your small talk and decent table manners help contribute to your reputation as someone who's a pleasure to be around.

Having a regular group to lunch with is only natural, but occasionally mix your lunch partners so that you don't become too isolated from your workmates as a whole. Either invite workers from another department or try going at different hours so that you'll encounter a wider range of people.

If you bring your lunch and always eat at your desk, becoming too much of a creature of habit can start to make you look unsociable. If a coworker who eats in the cafeteria (especially if he or she is your boss) sometimes drops by and asks if you want to go get a bite, think seriously about leaving your sandwich in the fridge and having it tomorrow.

TABLE CONVERSATION

Avoid sensitive work topics, since people at other tables may overhear. Things that are too personal are also not a good idea—the hot date you had last night, the trouble you're having with a child. For the benefit of your lunch partners, don't talk about your or anyone else's skin conditions, stomach problems, or operations—not exactly appetizing subjects at the best of times. Lunch is a time for relaxing and taking a break—not the place for conversation that would be better conducted in a bar after work, if at all.

Kitchens that have a dining table or two often have "regulars" who lunch together there. If two officemates make a ritual of jointly tackling the daily crossword puzzle over their take-out lunches, you can greet them in the kitchen, but don't distract them with conversation while you're waiting for your food to finish microwaving.

Some cliques make a habit of venting their unhappiness at the kitchen lunch table, seemingly oblivious of people walking in and out. If you're there waiting for your food to heat or the kettle to boil, try to ignore what they're saying. But when the talk turns to criticism of a superior or workmate, a polite reminder is not out of line: "Theresa, I don't mean to butt in, but shouldn't you save what you're saying about Veronica for another time? You never know when she's going to walk in." Also take what you're hearing with a grain of salt, since there are always two sides to a story.

IN THE REST ROOMS

Depending on the frequency of maintenance, the office rest rooms can be more disorderly than the kitchen. With cutbacks common and cleaning staff curtailed, users often find the floor littered with paper towels, the soap dispensers clogged, the toilet-paper rolls missing, and the place a general shambles. Do your part by always using the trash can, wiping up water that splashed out of the sink, and replacing toilet paper rolls as necessary.

Your Toilette

A woman putting on her makeup, a man shaving, or anyone tooth-brushing in a workplace rest room should remember that they are not at home. The important thing is to go about things discreetly and not take over the space. Better still, find a rest room that's out of the way and rarely used if you can.

- A woman should do her daily makeup routine at work only if the rest room has enough sinks and surrounding counter space to allow her room.
- A man who wants to get rid of his five o'clock shadow before a late afternoon meeting will find an electric razor much less messy than shaving cream. Any hairs that fall into the basin should be wiped out.
- Anyone who suspects he has bad breath or wants to practice good dental hygiene should keep a toothbrush and toothpaste at work and give teeth a good brushing every day after lunch. But don't let foam run down your chin or make hawking noises while spitting; it can be disgusting to any witnesses. Flossing your teeth is better done when no one is around.
- Creatures of habit can grow annoying through overexposure. A man who goes into the men's room every afternoon, fills the sink with water, bends down, and washes his face for so long you'd think he'd just come in from a cattle drive can quickly grow tiresome. The same goes for a woman who takes a tweezer to her eyebrows in midafternoon like clockwork. Some things are best left to private moments.

Problem Peers
THE HALL MONITOR

The Hall Monitor exacts order and discipline at all times—not only from coworkers but from the custodians, mailroom staff, receptionists, and even vendors and guests. Loud laughter from a neighboring office, a knot of schmoozers blocking the hall, and dirty plates in the kitchen sink may not be desirable, but a modern-day office is hardly the Reading Room of the Library of Congress. The Hall Monitor, however, respects nothing but the rule of law. She is likely to be a stickler for company policy, constantly pointing out that "Human Resources doesn't allow that" or admonishing lax colleagues to "read the employee manual!" The Hall Monitor has a particular horror of things that aren't done in a proper manner; she can spot a dusty ficus plant from a hundred yards, and an overflowing wastebasket or paper-clipped rather than stapled memo will cause her an attack of apoplexy. E-mail is her new medium, and she loves firing off dire warnings or prim critiques that usually begin "Some inconsiderate persons have been . . . "

Most Hall Monitors are benign folks, and they can be handled with a nod and a wink. But if the Hall Monitor reports to a fault-finding boss, the combination can be caustic—so stick to the rules, dust your plants, and wash your dishes.

THE TOILET

Briefly, don't have conversations from a stall. Don't leave the lid up. If you are obsessive about germs and arrange sheets of toilet paper on the seat, dispose of them when you leave instead of letting them litter the floor. Always flush.

Then there's the inescapable but rarely acknowledged problem of a more delicate nature: odor. Even if you're unfamiliar with the military term "courtesy flushes," you should have no trouble figuring out what it means. Frequent flushes help keep olfactory problems to a minimum, as will using any air freshener that is kept there for the purpose.

CHAPTER 8

YOU AND YOUR SUPERVISORS

Despite endless jokes and situation comedies to the contrary, bosses are people. As Shakespeare might have said, prick them and they bleed the same as everyone else. Whatever name he or she goes by (boss, supervisor, employer, manager, middle manager, executive), there's not a boss in the world who doesn't have a boss. The CEO must report to the board of directors, the board of directors to the shareholders. Even the highest-flying entrepreneur must answer to his lenders and his market. What separates you from your boss is power and responsibility. He or she has the power to direct and demand your performance; your boss is then responsible for your performance to everyone above him or her on the chain of command.

THREE STEPS TO COMPATIBILITY

Over a lifetime of work, most of us will have good bosses, mediocre bosses, and a few truly atrocious bosses. In every case, three straightforward steps will set the stage for getting the relationship off on the right foot.

- **STEP 1.** Understanding that bosses are people is the first step in getting along with them—and getting ahead in business. People who supervise are driven by the same complicated mix of ambitions, fears, hopes, and quirks as the rest of us. Being human, they will make mistakes.
- **STEP 2.** Accept the reality that your supervisor is in charge. She is, in the hierarchy of business, the superior, and that position requires deference. "Deference" is an interesting word; it can mean respect and esteem for a person in a higher position, or it can mean an insincere or ingratiating attitude. A smart employee defers in the first, positive sense by showing respect for the boss' opinions and decisions without grumbling or groveling. Assume that the person in charge became so because she has expertise in both the work and in the management of employees; by being respectful, you can learn a thing or two about being a boss yourself, whether you've risen to the supervisory level or not.
- **STEP 3.** This step should be obvious, but it is omitted with surprising regularity from career guides and management texts: If you want to get along

with your boss, *do your job.* Before you begin to take on extra tasks that will flatter and please a boss, as is often advised, *do your job*—and to do your job means to *do it on time.* Nothing is more important to your relationship with the person who supervises you than these two simple rules.

HAIL TO THE CHIEF

When you take a new job or a new position within your company, you want to master your own duties. But you must also uncover your new supervisor's modus operandi. Different bosses have widely differing ways of operating: Your old boss required written project reports delivered punctually at the end of each week; your new boss prefers verbal updates and only occasionally asks for written reports. Your old boss got a kick out of the rubber crocodile collection on your desk; your new boss frowns on cluttered cubicles. When you step into a new job, be open to your new boss' ideas. Remember that there's no absolute right way to run an office, and stay flexible.

You can quickly pick up on the most obvious characteristics of your new boss' style by observing your coworkers and their interactions with him. Don't be hesitant to ask questions, because your job description will tell you only what is expected of you, not how to do it. If the boss isn't available, it's fine to talk with your fellow workers about office procedures. Just be sure that your questions don't carry implied criticisms. Avoid the "At my last job, the boss would never tolerate . . . " approach.

THE NEWCOMER

The situation can be more difficult when a new boss takes over. Being courteous is a breeze when she is a welcome addition, but employees not infrequently resent a new supervisor, especially when they perceive that their previous boss was mistreated or when a deserving colleague has been passed over for the position. Resentment always seems aimed at the new arrival, yet there's a very good chance that she had nothing to do with past problems. What do you do when the office is in such turmoil? Be fair and be open. Allow your new boss to start with a clean slate.

If you can, try to discourage negative comments and gossip among your peers. Don't become embroiled in your coworkers' petty rebellions—it's the boss' job to straighten out the problems with the staff in her own way. Welcome the new boss. Provide assistance when you can, but give her a little breathing room to settle in. And most important, do your job. In fact, the most helpful

Exemplary Bosses

THE PEACEKEEPER

A project doesn't measure up to expectations, and recriminations fly. "We didn't do as good a job as we could have on the Rodwell report because *you* didn't give us what we needed!" yells an account manager in one department. "I beg your pardon, but it's not our job to spoon-feed you," replies her counterpart from down the hall, leveling a withering stare. "The information is right there in the annual report for you to look up for *yourself!*"

Understanding that job descriptions have a way of bending with the wind after a while, the Peacekeeper prevents such contretemps by repeatedly making clear who is responsible for what. How? By dropping into offices, keeping her ear close to the ground, and sensing any explosions that might be in the offing, whether they are between individuals or departments. She then takes steps to defuse them, outlining responsibilities for a specific project in writing. If a larger problem with a neighboring department is perceived, the Peacekeeper moves to work with the department head to find a solution.

While you surely admire the Peacekeeper's skills, don't assume that they should extend to purely personal conflicts among you and your coworkers. A boss of this kind is still only your manager, not your psychiatrist or counselor.

thing you can do for a boss when there's trouble in the office is to lay low and perform. You may not be the center of attention during the fray, but your steadfast dedication to the work will be remembered and appreciated.

ONE-ON-ONE WITH THE BOSS

Frankly, how you get along with supervisors is more your responsibility than theirs. Their job is to get the work done in the most productive and profitable manner. Your ambitions and goals are your concern. The question facing all workers is how to get the most out of their relationships with bosses.

One answer is to respect the superior-subordinate roles without becoming obsequious. Apart from a few Neanderthals, most bosses do not want to employ yes-men types; the business world is far too complex and competitive for a boss to be surrounded by office sycophants. Showing respect means respecting the boss' intelligence and experience. You may not be the boss' peer, but neither are you a servile flunky. How to act:

- **SPEAK UP AND OFFER IDEAS.** Bosses generally welcome fresh thinking from the people they supervise.
- **BE PREPARED.** Bosses appreciate the difference between those who shoot from the hip and those who do their homework before speaking.
- **DON'T WASTE YOUR BOSS' TIME.** Be concise and clear. Have your materials and support documents ready, and have copies of pertinent papers made ahead of time. You'll not only save your boss' time but also show yourself as organized.
- **LOOK FOR PROBLEMS YOU CAN SOLVE.** Bosses favorably regard employees who show initiative.
- **ASK FOR HELP WHEN YOU NEED IT.** Most bosses enjoy teaching and guiding their employees. Asking your superior for help is not a sign of weakness; it is an appropriate recognition of the boss' broader knowledge and experience.
- **BE A TEAM PLAYER.** It may be a cliché, but bosses prefer directing a cohesive group rather than a hodgepodge of self-centered individualists. Prima donnas may be high achievers, but many bosses believe that a group of steady workers is ultimately more productive than the loftiest star.
- **SHOW ACCEPTANCE.** Accept your boss' final decisions graciously even when they are contrary to your thinking.

A MEASURE OF SUPPORT

It's logical to make the boss look good. You do that partly by doing your own job well. You can also help the boss by being sensitive to his or her needs and work style. You don't have to be good buddies with the boss—just observant. If, for example, you see that your boss is snowed under with reports to read before a big meeting, you might offer to help by summarizing one or two.

Compliment the boss every now and then, and sing his praises to others when the opportunity presents itself. Support your boss' decisions in public. Even when company politics become brutal—a reorganization or management-level housecleaning—it's generally wise to stay loyal to the person above you. Whatever the outcome (and even if your supervisor gets the ax), your loyalty will be noted by others. No one forgets a Benedict Arnold, and the next boss is highly unlikely to trust an employee who betrayed a former boss.

Some career guides advise covering up for a boss' mistakes or flaws. But there's covering, and there's lying. If the CEO calls you and angrily demands why your boss missed an important meeting, you can politely claim ignorance even if you suspect he was at the gym. At the same time, you should warn your boss that the CEO is on the warpath. But don't make up a cover story—

the boss was with a client, for example—because it traps you both in the falsehood. Besides, if you show a willingness to lie for your boss, he may come to expect it.

DO NOT UNDERMINE

Never try to undermine your supervisor's position. There are a few legitimate situations when you must go above or around your boss (see pages 111 and 118), but it is extremely dangerous when ambition drives an employee to connive. Keep in mind that a company has a large investment in a supervisor or department head. In a conflict between boss and worker, the boss will almost always win, and the loser will only gain a reputation for ruthlessness and deceit.

THE ART OF COMPLAINING

There are times when you have to go to your supervisor and complain, whether it's as minor as grumbling about a messy rest room or as major as being sexually harassed. You may have a private gripe or your dissatisfaction may be shared by

---

Problem Peers
THE SYCOPHANT

Usually referred to in vulgar terms, the Sycophant flatters and flutters around anyone who has the power to advance her career. She's easily identified by her propensity to gravitate to top-level employees at office functions, grab a seat next to the boss at meetings, worm her way into a place at the head table at the company dinner, and agree enthusiastically with anything her supervisor says whenever her supervisor is within earshot.

The Sycophant is a dedicated reader of business advice books, especially the *How to Succeed Through Kissing Up* variety. She's the classic fair-weather friend, cozying up to coworkers on the rise and leaving everyone else in the dust. While her yes-man attitudes can be irritating, the Sycophant is rarely sufficiently smart or sophisticated to be a real threat. In fact, she may be her coworkers' favorite office entertainment (not that she realizes it) as she practices her painfully obvious manipulations and maneuvers. Male or female, the Sycophant is much like the "bad girl" character in an ongoing soap opera, constantly scheming to get her way but oblivious to the fact that millions of people know her every move before she makes it.

others. In any case, the boss is almost always the person to talk with. To complain effectively is something of an art, and by asking yourself the following questions, you can avoid some common pitfalls.

- **IS YOUR COMPLAINT WORTHWHILE?** Before you rush into the boss' office, calmly examine the problem in the light of common sense. Is the problem persistent and serious enough to warrant intervention by a supervisor? Does it affect the quality of your work or overall productivity? Is it worth the boss' time, or will you be perceived as crying wolf? Too many business complaints arise from personality conflicts and minor irritations; when the facts come to light, it's sometimes the complainer who suffers.

- **HAVE YOU DOCUMENTED THE PROBLEM?** What is your evidence that a problem even exists? It is extremely important that you be able to support your complaint, both to show your seriousness and to validate your claims. It is not a question of your honesty—it's that no boss worthy of the title would accept every complaint at face value. Your boss may have to take the issue to higher levels; union rules may be involved; legal action may be required. Serious accusations such as office theft or sexual harassment require proof—and suspicions and gossip aren't proof. Keep a journal or diary of events; assemble paper evidence; find others who can back up your claim. (Be discreet when you discuss the issue with others; you're looking for confirmation and support, not a reputation as the office busybody.)

- **ARE YOU THE RIGHT PERSON TO MAKE THE COMPLAINT?** A worker who has been reprimanded for tardiness in the past would be on shaky ground complaining about a coworker who habitually takes long lunch hours; it would smack of sour grapes. Be honest with yourself, and if you lack the credibility to make the complaint, see if there's someone else who can do it. Again, this is not a reflection on your honesty; credibility is usually a matter of who is best positioned to make a solid case.

- **WHAT RESULTS DO YOU WANT?** The Office Whiner prize goes to the person who is full of problems, not solutions. Whatever your dissatisfaction or complaint, be sure you have suggestions for correcting the matter. You may not want to include them in the initial complaint (problem-solving is a manager's job), but you should be ready to respond if and when the boss asks for your ideas. Be reasonable. If your complaint is that Jane fails to meet a deadline once in awhile, "I think she should be shown the door!" is not a recommendation likely to impress.

- **WHAT'S THE BEST APPROACH?** Bosses are commonly classified as "readers" (those who want to see it in writing) and "listeners" (those who prefer to get information through conversation and oral reporting).

A well-prepared, confidential memo is probably the best way to take a complaint to a reader type, whereas a private meeting to discuss the problem will work better with the listener. Regardless of how you initially present the problem, if it's serious you'll almost certainly have to meet face-to-face at some point—so be prepared to do so.

- **WHAT'S THE RIGHT TIME?** If the issue isn't urgent, give the boss a chance to have her morning cup of coffee before you hit her with a problem. Don't wait until the whole office is tied up in a crash project to express your dissatisfaction. By respecting your boss' other obligations, you greatly improve your chances of being listened to.

- **HOW LONG SHOULD YOU WAIT FOR A RESPONSE?** Never expect immediate action on a complaint. You may not see results for a long time, as when your complaint involves changing a company policy. There are occasions when nothing is done. A good boss will eventually tell you what came of your complaint, but understand that there may well be consequences that he or she cannot discuss. For example, if your complaint resulted in the discipline of another employee, the action is confidential. If your boss hears you out and then says, "I'll handle it," you should trust his or her word. Just because you haven't been informed of the results doesn't necessarily mean nothing has been accomplished or changed.

If a problem persists after you've registered your dissatisfaction, carefully weigh the pros and cons of further complaints. What seems like reasonable follow-up to you may quickly become pestering to a boss. There are times when it is better to back off, face reality, and let the issue drop.

COMPLAINING ABOUT CONDITIONS

Complaints about workplace conditions can involve anything from poor janitorial service to excessive overtime. If you have a union, many working conditions are covered by your agreement, and you will report problems to your steward or union representative. Otherwise, go to the boss, his assistant, or the office manager. Minor problems with the physical environment (maybe you need a new chair, or the photocopier consistently malfunctions) can usually be covered in a brief memo or e-mail. More serious or physically threatening problems (loss of a security card, locked fire doors, the presence of unauthorized persons) should be reported as quickly as possible by the fastest means available. Don't hesitate to call the boss directly if the situation is potentially dangerous.

Overtime and Workloads

Problems such as excess overtime or short-staffing are a bit trickier. Don't jump to the conclusion that the boss is at fault. She may already be working to get relief. If the boss is unaware of the problem, it's wise to inform her in a polite, conciliatory manner. Send a credible representative and provide adequate documentation of the problem. (No angry mobs at the castle gate!) You may get the results you want if you frame the complaint in terms of productivity: For example, show your boss how the lack of staff is causing missed deadlines and increased work errors.

The Group Complaint

If conditions don't improve, it may be time to gather your troops and meet as a group. The advantage of a group (made up of department representatives or the whole department) is that numbers can impress even the most insensitive supervisor; most bosses want to avoid serious and widespread morale problems. If group complaining doesn't work, you may have to go over the boss' head, but if you take this step, be sure to let the boss know what you are doing.

Exemplary Bosses
THE STRAIGHT SHOOTER

It didn't take the mergers and downsizing of the Nineties to engender a mistrust of management. The idea that managers will make decisions that are in the best interest of their employees has never enjoyed much currency, and the belief that management regards workers as little more than pawns in a game of corporate chess has hardened into cynicism. A good manager makes the effort to breach that wall of cynicism by answering honestly the concerns of workers and refusing to lie. When asked about looming layoffs, he frankly tells you that he can't guarantee that there won't be any more. Your morale may not improve, but the fact that he has dropped the pretense that cuts aren't forthcoming helps you start adjusting to the possibility.

Going hand in hand with truthfulness is timeliness. In short, when a company makes the news because of rumors of an impending merger or poor quarterly earnings, you shouldn't have to learn of it from the paper or the TV. Instead, a good manager either sends memos out to the staff or sees to it that the public-relations department includes timely details of the matter in the office newsletter or bulletin.

Copy him or her on all letters and memos to higher-ups. Document the problem, and keep the tone of all communications professional. When the problem is resolved, your boss is still the boss.

COMPLAINING ABOUT COWORKERS

Scott is late to work nearly every day and expects you to cover for him. Rachel is driving everyone crazy with her bad moods. Ben's divorce is really affecting the quality of his work. And somebody is stealing food from the office fridge.

Problems with coworkers are the everyday stuff of business life. Many of these difficulties can often be worked out among the staff, but sometimes you'll want the boss to step in, especially if the problem is serious or has legal implications. Sexual harassment, racist remarks, religious proselytizing, theft, lying, fighting, threatening behavior—these are examples of serious problems that can affect the entire company, and your direct supervisor needs to know about them immediately. You may not have the time to document such regrettable incidents, but if you become aware of a serious problem, go straight to your supervisor. Be precise; don't elaborate beyond what you actually know; don't feel obliged to cover for coworkers or explain their behavior. Then leave it to the supervisor to manage the situation.

IS IT WORTH IT?

As for run-of-the-mill, irritating, obnoxious, difficult coworkers, you'll have to decide whether complaining about them is worth the effort. Ask yourself if others have a problem with the person or the behavior. Does the behavior affect the way the person or other workers do their jobs? Is the problem persistent or short-term? Is there an underlying condition such as alcoholism or drug use that may be the cause? Finally, can you talk to the person and work things out, or is the boss' intervention necessary?

In other words, if you complain about a coworker, be sure that your complaint is valid and not a mere personal issue. When you complain about a colleague, arrange a private meeting with your boss instead of writing a memo. (Never complain via e-mail unless you are prepared for your words to become public property.) In your meeting, be calm and focus on the troubling behavior, not the person: "Roger leaves a half-hour early at least three days a week, and we're having a problem getting his time sheets" is far better than "Roger is totally irresponsible and deceitful." Be as objective as you can, and don't be tempted to express moral judgments.

Like it or not, sometimes you must simply grin and bear it, tolerating difficult people whose value to the business outweighs their quirks. The egomaniacal salesman who is always the top producer, the temperamental art director who wins the prestigious awards, the sharp-tongued secretary who is a genius with complex computer programs—they may irritate your boss even more than they bother you. But bosses have the responsibility to balance the general good against the individual.

YOUR PERFORMANCE REVIEWS

Bosses are supposed to evaluate their workers' performance periodically, often in connection with salary reviews. In larger companies with full-fledged Human Resources departments, reviews are conducted religiously, and PAs (performance appraisals) become part of each employee's file. Yet many bosses, especially in smaller businesses, believe they don't have the time for face-to-face reviews and therefore avoid them. Because there are more small companies than ever today, there's a good chance your boss may delay or overlook reviews.

Consider, for example, the case of the business school graduate who was hired for a six-month probation period. A year later, he had received two unsolicited salary increases, yet no one had actually said that he was on the permanent staff. In fear and trembling, he finally raised the issue with his boss. The boss was amazed by the young man's concern. "But nobody fired you after six months," the boss declared in all innocence. "What else did you want?"

Most employees do want and need reviews in order to measure their own performance vis-à-vis company expectations. Performance reviews also give the employee the opportunity to address work-related problems and to clear up any mistakes or misconceptions. You have every right to challenge inaccuracies (as when a coworker blamed you for mistakes she committed) and to have your response included in your file.

A Gentle Reminder

When your supervisor is the review-resistant type, you may have to force the issue. If your six-month or annual review date has come and gone, make an appointment to see the supervisor and discuss your performance. If your boss cancels the appointment, be persistent and make another. When you finally get the meeting, you may have to guide the boss with your questions. "What would you say are my strong points? Any areas where I can improve? When do you think I can take on more responsibility?" Et cetera. Just remember that the

WHEN YOU TELECOMMUTE

In an age when electronic communication can sometimes make offices seem almost superflu-ous, many companies are allowing workers to work part-time from home, usually one or two days a week but virtually full-time in some cases. If you have joined the community of telecom-muters, you're part of the wave of the future.

By being attentive to the details of the telecommuting arrangement from the start, you and your employer or supervisor can see to it that the arrangement is positive. Anticipate problems. Imagine situations that may cause conflict and misunderstanding. If, for example, it's important that your boss be able to reach you at any time during the work day, he or she may be willing to provide you with mobile phone service. If you're expected to attend in-office meetings, your employer might agree to at least a day's notice. Clarify all deadlines and project delivery schedules.

It is important for you to take your telecommuting responsibilities seriously. If you've promised, for instance, to call or e-mail your boss at a predetermined time every day or each week, do it punctually. Don't hesitate to alert your employer if you're becoming overloaded with assignments. Supervising a telecommuting employee may be a new experience for your boss, and he or she is adapting to the situation, too. Be sensitive to your boss' concerns, and remember that although you're working at home, you have to be as self-disciplined as you are at work. (See also Family and Friends, page 550.)

---

meeting is a performance review, not a soul-bearing or gripe session. Stay focused on your job and your responsibilities.

DEALING WITH CRITICISM

It's an inevitability—you will be criticized by your boss. It helps to keep in mind that "criticism" doesn't necessarily mean negative comments. In the best of all possible worlds, criticism is closely reasoned judgment based on careful evaluation of all available evidence. "You idiot! Can't you do anything right?" is abuse, not criticism.

In today's culture of self-esteem, many younger workers don't know how to deal with criticism simply because they haven't been subjected to it. Assum-ing that your boss is not neurotically abusive, however, it is part of his or her responsibility to be critical of employees. This implies making and communi-cating positive as well as negative judgments. Nevertheless, thin-skinned employees usually miss the positive remarks altogether and read miles of mean-ing into mere inches of negative comment. This might be termed the "Woe is me" attitude, which leads directly to worst-case-scenario thinking: "The boss said I should reorganize the conclusion of my report. He hates my writing. He thinks I'm disorganized. He thinks I'm dumb!"

In order to learn and profit from criticism, it may be necessary to grow a little armor over that thin skin. Learn to listen to what the boss is really saying without inferring hidden meanings. Learn not to react until you have digested the criticism. Control the instinct to become defensive; defensiveness in the face of legitimate criticism is about as productive as the infantile instinct to suck your thumb. Count to ten or recite the Preamble to the Constitution before launching a counter-offensive. It also helps to hone your sense of humor; don't take the boss' favorite joke about "the bumbling junior executive" as suggesting something negative about *you*.

When receiving criticism, the rule is to listen and think, not hear and react. It's not easy to learn to value criticism, but doing so is a triumph of intellect over raw emotion. In fact, receiving criticism well—understanding that criticism is an opportunity to learn and improve—is a classic characteristic of good and excellent bosses, and it no doubt helped them to rise.

RESPONDING TO CRITICISM

Along with accepting criticism, it is perfectly reasonable to respond to it, especially if you think it unfair. But frame your response in friendly, collegial terms if you can. In a staff meeting, for example, your supervisor, Mrs. Johnson, incorrectly associates you with a project she is criticizing as inadequately prepared. Don't jump to your feet, yelling that it wasn't your project or your fault. Instead, say something such as "I agree that the Alpha project could have used some fine-tuning. You'll remember, Mrs. Johnson, that I was working on the Omega account at the time. I did hear that the Alpha team was working on a really short deadline, and maybe that accounts for some of the difficulty." Mrs. Johnson will get the message that you are not accountable for the problem. But by returning the point of your remarks to the Alpha project, and not ending on Mrs. Johnson's error, you lessen the embarrassment for the boss. (You may even score points with the Alpha team by deflecting blame to a deadline problem.)

Whether to correct your boss in public or private depends on his or her threshold for criticism. The Mrs. Johnson example illustrates how public response can be handled without ruffling anyone's feathers. But if the boss is sensitive or if you need to discuss the criticism in some depth, arrange a private meeting, preferably when the boss is at ease. Try not to be confrontational. Even if the criticism was totally unjustified, phrase your response in terms of

Difficult Bosses

THE TANTRUM THROWER

The Tantrum Thrower yells, screams, and threatens. He's a grown-up child who never got past temper tantrums. If he's merely a difficult boss, he probably feels genuinely sorry after each incident. But if he's a true abuser, he's happiest when demeaning a subordinate, exercising the power of his position most brutally. His eruptions lack both rhyme and reason; he usually catches his victims off-guard, and his employees often have no idea what he's ranting on about. He has little sense of decorum and is as likely to pitch his fits in public as in private.

No business should tolerate a boss who is physically brutal, and any form of physical assault should be reported immediately to the highest level. Serving as the object of the Tantrum Thrower's public ravings may be humiliating, but it also means you have witnesses. Document every incident in detail. If you decide to meet with the boss in question, go in a group; a difficult boss may get your message, while you need witnesses for any confrontation with an abuser. If you have no options, keep firmly in mind that the Tantrum Thrower is out of control, and you can no more blame yourself for his behavior than for a change in the weather.

what you can do to remedy the situation: "When you were criticizing the Alpha project yesterday, I know you forgot that I didn't work on it. But you've said often enough that these short deadlines hurt everybody. It could be my group next time, and I want to get your ideas for avoiding the problem." You have corrected the boss, but you've also given her an "out" and moved the discussion forward to a more productive area.

You can learn from valid criticism, even criticism directed at others. But sooner or later, there's a good chance you'll have a boss who is just plain mean and abusive. In this case, your options are limited; you can take it, or you can get out. If you stay in the job, you'll have to work hard not to become a victim of the boss' evil ways. Be your own critic, and don't take his or her complaints to heart: The criticisms of a truly abusive boss are neither valid nor well-intentioned.

DEALING WITH DIFFICULT BOSSES

There are tough, demanding bosses who drive you to perform above and beyond anything you thought yourself capable of. A tough boss, however, is not the same as a difficult boss—bosses who range from the merely hard-to-get-along-with to just plain abusive.

Bosses in the "difficult category" drive you, sure—they drive you crazy with their quirks or demands. They may be control freaks, credit hoggers, or pass-the-buck types. But difficult bosses are not, as a rule, out to get you, and they are generally unaware of how their behavior affects their employees. Entrepreneurial types, for example, are notoriously difficult to work for because they simply cannot comprehend that employees are not wholly obsessed by their own brilliant visions. Even good bosses can become difficult when they are under severe pressures, such as impossible productivity demands or potential layoffs. The problem with most difficult bosses is that they are not skilled or competent managers of people. They missed the lectures on leadership and team play. (See also Difficult Bosses, pages 116, 117, 119; Exemplary Bosses, pages 106, 111, 122.)

Difficult Bosses
THE BLAMER

The Blamer doesn't erupt, and you may not suspect her actions until you get a peek at your employment file or pick up on office gossip. She never accepts personal responsibility and blames others for her failures and flaws. She's particularly hard on low-level employees, assuming they're defenseless, though she'll blame anyone to get herself out of trouble. If she holds you accountable in a public forum, you might be able to defend yourself. But if she is truly an abuser, she'll praise you to your face while twisting the knife in your back. Difficult or abusive, the Blamer's forte is poisoning the well by spreading false impressions of a worker's competence.

The Blamer can be particularly hard to deal with when she genuinely believes her own interpretations and falsehoods. This makes heart-to-heart talks with her problematic because she simply can't see your point of view. It can also be hard to document the Blamer's actions because she most likely assigns blame to you when you're not there. Performance reviews can provide solid clues to her fabrications, especially if you can refute a bad evaluation with paper evidence and the testimony of others. Luckily, most Blamers will sooner or later trip themselves, if you can wait that long. They will eventually blame someone who could not possibly be at fault or become so tangled in their lies that they hang themselves, or their superiors will simply grow weary of their constant refusal to take responsibility.

Discussing the Problem

It can help to talk with a difficult boss in a nonconfrontational meeting. You may want to include several office representatives in the meeting to demonstrate that the problem is widespread—as when both salaried and hourly workers are suffering from excessive workloads or overtime. Be specific about your complaints and show the boss how the problem is affecting overall productivity and morale. Try not to blame; instead, offer to help. Be aware that defensiveness may be the first reaction, and change may come more slowly than you'd like. But if your boss shows a willingness to make adjustments in his or her behavior, be ready to meet him or her with cooperation. (A few compliments on your part won't hurt either.)

Going Over His Head

If you have to go over or around a difficult boss, be sure to keep the boss informed of your actions. Let him know that you are meeting with his superiors. If your business has an experienced Human Resources staff, they may be able to help you decide on the strategy that is most likely to achieve the results you want within the unique structure and culture of your business. Keep in mind that your objective is positive change for everyone, including your difficult boss—not a bloody palace revolution.

Abusive Bosses

Abusive bosses are neither tough nor merely difficult; they are mean and hateful and sneaky and unpredictable. They pick their victims for no apparent or logical reason. They afflict their workers with physical and emotional tortures (from ulcers and migraines to failures of self-confidence) that are more akin to the Spanish Inquisition than the workplace. Call them brutal, toxic, beastly, atrocious—abusive bosses are deliberately harmful to the people around them.

Abusive bosses often make excellent hatchet men because they are willing to do the jobs most bosses loathe, including mass terminations. What makes them abusive also makes them valuable to some companies and accounts for their upward mobility. They can fire a thousand people in a half-hour meeting and not let it bother them.

Before you personally tackle an abusive boss, it's always wise to gauge his or her role in the company. How are your boss' superiors likely to respond to your challenge? Is your boss a bad seed who will be rooted out, or is he or she regarded as the company's necessary evil?

The best defense when you can't leave your job is to identify your boss as an abuser and to understand in your heart and mind that you are not the cause of the problem (remember that abusive bosses hurt people, tough bosses don't, and difficult bosses don't mean to). It won't be easy, because the worst bosses are like domestic abusers; they use their power to demoralize their victims and batter self-esteem into self-doubt. Employees may be able to combat abusers through group action. (If you have a union, try taking your issues there.) Documentation and unity are powerful weapons, but face up to the fact that even they may not solve the problem.

For employees with abusive bosses, there may be no totally happy solution other than escape, but it is not always possible or desirable to transfer or find a new job. Normal complaint and reconciliation mechanisms don't often work with abusive bosses; heart-to-heart talks are rarely helpful and may even be counterproductive if the boss labels you as "the enemy."

Difficult Bosses
THE BIGOT

The Bigot hates people in groups. He's full of jokes and snide remarks about people of different ethnicity, nationality, or religious heritage. He can be a sexist, racist, or ageist. If his bigotry were limited to comments, he might be tolerable because he's so pitiable. But his prejudices permeate the workplace and affect his every decision: This group never gets the plum assignments; that group can forget promotions and merit raises. Worse, he often draws people of goodwill into his bigotry, using his superior position to coerce his workers into silent acceptance of his unfair and demeaning behavior, thereby demoralizing everyone.

Fortunately, the Bigot is his own worst enemy. Why? Because the law of the land—as well as most corporate policies—is firmly against him. By documenting his words and deeds, workers can put him on the hot seat with senior managers and, if necessary, in court. If the Bigot is socially and culturally ignorant, but otherwise a decent-enough chap, he may be salvageable through company-directed diversity and sensitivity training. If, on the other hand, he's prejudiced to the core, he should be dismissed. In either case, the company, which is liable for his words and deeds, should be notified of his actions immediately.

YOUR CAREER PATH

Your supervisor will have a major impact on your career. He or she has the power to satisfy your immediate objectives and influence your long-range goals. But when you deal with the boss on issues that affect your career, remember that his or her primary concern is not your future or your personal situation, but things that are happening here and now.

ASKING FOR A RAISE OR PROMOTION

When you feel ready move upward, begin by determining exactly *why* you deserve more money or a loftier position. In a time of corporate belt-tightening and downsizing, more money and new titles are not automatic, even for high achievers. The good old days when employees with families got raises whenever their families increased in size are done and gone.

Merit is your best leverage. Before you talk to your boss about a raise or promotion, conduct a personal performance appraisal. Look at your accomplishments and your failures. Naturally, you'll focus on your strong points when you talk with the boss, but he or she may raise problem areas and weaknesses—so be prepared. What have you done to correct deficiencies? Maybe you took a computer training course to upgrade your skills or attended an anger-management seminar. Maybe you're taking college business courses at night, you've read all the business books your boss recommended, or you've expanded your contacts in the business community. Let your boss know that you are a determined self-improver.

If you can, calculate your contributions to the company. Perhaps you can document how a particular program you initiated affected departmental productivity. Show off your sales figures. Recall the new business you have brought in. Remember that if you don't sing your own praises, no one else will carry the tune for you. There are times to be self-effacing, but a meeting where you are asking to advance isn't one of them.

AT THE MEETING

If ever a meeting needs to be conducted professionally, it is the salary or promotion discussion. Never, ever bring up personal issues. The boss doesn't care about your second mortgage, your kid's orthodontia, or your grandmother's nursing-home bills. When you are seeking a promotion, be ready to tell the boss what you can bring to the job. Show that you are prepared for the responsibility by knowing what the new position entails and how you plan to manage it. What can you achieve in the new job that you can't do now? How will the company benefit by your appointment to the position?

If you're asking for more money, decide what you'll do to earn it. Don't sell your soul, but think about responsibilities you can reasonably assume to justify a larger pay packet. Depending on company attitudes, you can ask for a specific dollar amount or name a salary range, but be sure that your bottom figure is one you can live with. You might consider asking for other forms of compensation, performance bonuses or stock options, for example.

You may want to provide information about the general market standards for a person with your responsibilities. Your boss may not know, for instance, that the average salary for OS managers in your region is $4,000 above your current pay level. It may be risky, but if you have received nibbles from headhunters or recruiters at other companies, you can tell your boss about their offers—particularly if you have a decent relationship with your boss and a good track record. Be careful not to bring up other offers as a threatening or coercive tactic; threats can blow up in your face. Present them as a means of helping the boss to evaluate your position relative to comparable companies. If you're genuine in your representation, the boss will not be riled—and if he or she senses that you may be in demand elsewhere, so much the better.

Your Wishes Weren't Granted?

Don't be too upset if your increase is below your expectations or your request is turned down. Even when the general economy is booming, your company may simply not be in a position to give large raises. There may not be a promotion open. (Just because Joe the accounts supervisor is resigning doesn't mean that his position will be filled. Downsizing in large corporations has eliminated many middle- and even upper-management positions, making promotions a lot harder to get than in the days when every third person was vice president of something.) If your boss explains that there is a wage freeze in effect or that the position you qualify for is being eliminated, realize that negotiations are ended and graciously accept defeat. Keep your eyes and ears open, and when circumstances change, you can always try again.

REFUSING OFFERS

What do you do when the boss makes you an offer you have to refuse? For example, the boss wants you to develop and conduct a new training program that includes night sessions three times a week. You're a single mom; you can use the extra money. But night sessions will create a child-care nightmare, and you barely see your children as it is. Or your boss wants you to take over a new account: It's a plum, but the job involves constant travel or a relocation, and you don't think your family can handle the added stress. What do you do?

You think about it very hard. Weigh all the pros and cons. Talk with the people who mean the most to you. If you really cannot take on the added hours or excessive travel, turn down the offer. But be forewarned. You will, of course, be gracious and grateful when you reject the offer, but there's every chance your boss will not understand your decision. Even good bosses may think that you're throwing away a career opportunity and letting them down at the same time. No matter how reasonable your reasons and how sympathetic the boss, your refusal of an offer may well stall your career ambitions for a time. You may face a period of repair work, rebuilding your image with the boss.

THE POSITIVE SIDE

But there is a positive side to refusing an offer. Choosing between job and family, for instance, is a kind of forced confrontation with your priorities. It's not always easy to decide what matters in one's life, but most people can learn and grow from the experience. As more and more employees look for a satisfying balance between their personal and professional lives, bosses are hearing "no" more often—and perhaps getting used to the sound.

JUST SAY NO

There are other kinds of offers that you must refuse in no uncertain terms. If you are asked, or possibly expected, to participate in activity that is unethical, immoral, or illegal, just say no. You don't have to consider the offer. You don't have to be polite. Just say no, and say it loud and clear. Then report the offer to someone in a position to take immediate action. By asking you to do something that violates your moral or ethical standards, your boss has broken the most basic human contract. He or she no longer deserves your loyalty or respect. You'll also want to take an unflinching look at your entire company. Is the boss' behavior an aberration, or is it reflective of the general corporate culture? How the company handles the situation will tell you whether you want to continue your employment or go elsewhere.

LEAVING YOUR JOB

Nowadays, Americans change jobs so frequently that a whole industry has been created around outplacement. Even getting fired has lost some of its sting in an age characterized by corporate reengineering and downsizing. Whether you leave a job at your own initiative or someone else's, you should handle your departure with care.

OF YOUR OWN ACCORD?

If you're leaving your job by choice, don't signal your intention too early or to the wrong people. If you are looking for a new position, be discreet. Don't, for instance, leave your updated resume in the office photocopier or get your secretary to type your application letters. Ask headhunters to phone you at home. Don't schedule a luncheon interview with a potential new employer at your current boss' favorite bistro. People love to gossip about who is planning to head for the door, and your boss will soon get wind of your plans. He or she probably won't fire you before you can resign, but you'll lose your advantage in any final negotiations. (And heaven forbid you should change your mind at the last minute and decide to stay put.)

If you've been fired or asked to resign, not only should you not leave mad, you shouldn't leave the *impression* that you're mad. Ranting and raving only confirms unfavorable opinions. If you're part of a mass cutback, your boss is probably as upset as you (and his head may be the next one on the block). From fear of litigation, companies are inclined to reveal as little as possible about the causes of firings, but if your boss is a good soul he or she may be able to provide you with reasons and advice that can help you correct problems. Remember, too, that you'll want recommendations and references. It goes without saying that getting fired hurts. But try to be fair, accept your own role in the job loss, and don't go for the boss' throat.

This chapter opened with the statement that bosses are people. So are you—a person with gifts and talents and interests and dreams. Getting fired is not the end of the world; it's not even that unusual in this day and age. Give yourself some time to grieve for the loss, and to indulge in some healthy venting if you like. But be on your guard against the impulse to see yourself as a victim. Martyrdom is a job qualification only for sainthood; when you begin your new job search, you will be in the real world, dealing with real world bosses again. It is vital to approach your next opportunity with confidence and enthusiasm. You won't include a firing on your resume, of course, but be honest and as open as necessary in interviews. Don't show resentment or cast blame on your old boss. You have a lot to offer your next boss, so focus on your strengths and what you can bring to the table.

THE EXIT STATEMENT

Whether you are resigning or were fired, you should work with your boss on an appropriate exit statement. It is important for you to participate in the writing, even if the statement is for in-office circulation only as opposed to wider distribution, including news releases. By working with your supervisor on the exit statement, you'll make certain that you and your former employer are telling the same story. Naturally, it's a good idea for the statement to include something about your achievements. If you've been fired, it is unnecessary to explain why. A generic statement is adequate: "Jerry will be leaving Acme this Friday to pursue new career opportunities." An exit statement for a person moving to a new job can be more specific: "All of us at Acme will miss Rebecca, but we know she will be a great success in her new position as Human Resources Director of Manderley Enterprises."

If you're resigning, be courteous and appreciative in your meeting with (or let-ter to) the boss. The point is to leave with all your bridges unburned. You may want to sound off about every rotten moment you've endured and every idiot you've had to work with (the "Take This Job and Shove It" syndrome). Don't do it. You never know when you might need your boss' help down the line, and old employers have a way of becoming new customers if you haven't alienated them. You might even want to return to the company in the future. So make sure you leave on a grace note, no matter how you truly feel.

GIFTS FOR BOSSES: YES OR NO?

It is usually inappropriate to present a gift to your employer, especially if it looks too personal or expensive. (Your boss knows how much you make, and spending too much may appear sycophantic at best; at worst it may seem evidence of poor business sense and impractical finan-cial habits.) On the other hand, taking part in a group effort with other employees who pool their money for a holiday, birthday, or anniversary gift is a nice gesture to a supervisor. A group gift also lacks the hint of favor-currying that a personal gift may have. Two other exceptions: First, when someone has worked closely with the same boss for several years, a small inexpen-sive gift is appropriate. Second, when the boss has an extended illness or is hospitalized, flowers or a card are always thoughtful.

You and
Your
Supervisors

CHAPTER 9

WOMEN AND MEN TOGETHER

The idea of a "weaker sex" has been rightly consigned to the dustbin in a business world where women have proved themselves as capable as men. Driving home the point, more women than ever are leaders: Not only have they reached the top in corporations, but they also own almost 50 percent of small businesses. But with their rise in the workplace has come a new set of concerns. How do women react to men who have yet to adjust to the change? And is chivalry dead, a casualty of equality? More important, how do both sexes deal with sexual attraction, which has nothing to do with one's work but only with being human? (See also Gender-Free Chivalry, page 134.)

ROMANCE IN THE WORKPLACE

It is naive to think that romance, whether your own or someone else's, won't be a factor in the workplace, no matter the field. When people are thrown together in the same building for most of the day and often into the night, flirting and relationships will be inevitable. Statistics tell the story: Roughly half of married couples first met at work.

While it is true that romances are an eternal part of office life, relations between the sexes have become a potential minefield. Going hand in hand with the growing number of women in the workplace is a heightened awareness of discrimination and harassment, making office affairs touchier and more dangerous than ever. Questions of conflicts of interest, distraction from work, and the unpleasant ramifications of a fling's sour ending are very much on the minds of workers and Human Resources departments alike.

Given this tricky state of affairs, how do you—as a woman or a man—proceed when you find yourself attracted to an officemate, or vice versa? Is even flirting off-limits? No. Does the manner in which you flirt matter? Yes. Does the fact that your love interest and you are at different job levels matter? Yes. It goes without saying that not all relationships are fraught with danger or even

The Etiquette Advantage in Business

126

trouble, but entering into a romantic involvement requires no small measure of thought and care. (See also Your Love Life, page 136.)

THE FLIRTER

Someone new to your workforce is physically attractive, dresses well, seems pleasant, and is single—and so are you. If you find yourself drawn to him or her and want to explore the possibility of taking things a step further, wait to flirt until you know the person well enough to predict the response. In most cases, it is perfectly acceptable after you've become acquainted to extend an invitation for drinks or dinner. But if the invitation is declined, stop and leave it there— unless, of course, the person seems flattered and genuinely disappointed not to be able to accept. Otherwise, repeated bids not only show you as a pest but could end up putting you at significant risk. Remember that you're in an office, not a singles bar, and persistence is neither charming nor seductive. What's more, you can never be sure when your attentions might be perceived by someone as sexual harassment.

THE FLIRTEE

If flirting by a coworker is welcome and your company doesn't outlaw office dating, it's fine to flirt right back and—who knows?—maybe find the love of your life. You're *not* interested? Then try to be as honest as possible without causing offense. A white lie is an easy way out, but think twice before you deliver one. If, say, you pretend to keep your business and personal lives separate, you might paint yourself into a corner: If you take up with another workmate later, the flirter will be faced with the hurtful realization that you lied.

How does the object of someone's affection distinguish an innocent invitation to see a movie or have a drink after work from one with a motive other than friendship? One clue is when it comes out of the blue from someone you barely know. Beyond that, go with your gut: Most people can sense when an invitation is proffered because of romantic interest.

A SECRET TO KEEP?

If your company trusts you to date coworkers, return the favor by proving your work remains paramount during the day; you have no more license to canoodle at the vending machine than you did before. It's in poor taste to subject coworkers to displays of affection, not to mention unprofessional.

If your office bans romances between workers at different levels, consider the options: You could continue the affair in secret, at the risk someone will discover the truth and spread the news; you could ask to be transferred to another department without giving the real reason; you could end the relationship; or you could find a new job.

Many people prefer to keep even permissible office romances under wraps at the beginning of the relationship, loath to provide food for gossip before they themselves know whether things will work out. But once the relationship promises to last, one or both of you should speak confidentially to a supervisor to discuss your options.

Then there are the couples who prefer to hide their relationship when they feel people wouldn't approve of it. The truth is that even though it's against the law to discriminate, many offices are less than welcoming to nontraditional relationships—to be specific, interracial or homosexual couples. If you feel uncomfortable revealing your relationship to coworkers, remember that you have no obligation to do so. A simple "I'm sorry, but I try to keep my personal life private" is a good enough answer to someone who pries, although some couples

---

Problem Peers
THE LOTHARIO

The man who thinks he's God's gift to women may be just that. But in the real world, he's usually not even close. It's only when this harmless delusion is translated into action that it becomes a problem. A male signaling interest in a female workmate with suggestive looks, off-color remarks or jokes (which can count as sexual harassment), or repeated (and declined) requests to go out will get his just desserts: a reputation as a lecher. Needless to say, this automatically puts him out of the running for winning the affection—much less, the respect—of *any* woman in the office.

If there's no mistaking that an officemate is coming on to you, try a polite rebuff: "Really, Dan, there's no chance of our going out"—followed by either "I have a boyfriend" (if true) or "I'm just not interested in changing our friendship into something else." If he's persistent, be frank: "Dan, we're friends. Period. Will you *please* stop asking me out?" If this doesn't shame him into backing off, threaten to inform a supervisor or Human Resources, who will more than likely realize it is their interest to confront the offender.

DATING POLICIES

Reflecting an acute awareness and even paranoia of lawsuits, most companies now have written anti-discrimination policies that include outlawing sexual harassment. (See What Is Sexual Harassment?, page 130; Harassment Seminars, page 195.) But policies on *dating* in the workplace are a different kettle of fish. According to a 1998 survey by the Society for Human Resource Management, most offices have no written dating policies. Yet there are often unwritten understandings, usually born of anticipation of situations where harassment might become an issue.

Whatever the shape of a company dating policy, a couple should enter into a relationship with eyes wide open to it. For one thing, the policy may require disclosure, especially when workers of unequal rank are concerned. Some offices require one partner to transfer to another department if the relationship continues, or both partners to sign a contract of consent. If you find any regulations of this kind in your employee handbook (or are unclear about how they apply to your situation) speak to a representative of Human Resources or to your supervisor.

Remember, dating policies are designed partly to protect all parties against discomfort and legal liability. But they should also serve to clarify the company's culture: The standards of behavior between men and women in a young, liberal company are likely to be quite different from those in a starchy, conservative firm. If you feel any dating policies are inconsistent with the company culture, it may be worth taking up with your supervisor. (See also Office Policy, page 136.)

find it easier to deny everything. Prejudice against nontraditional couples is an unfortunate attitude, but exist it does, and it may limit how open you can be in a conservative workplace.

ROMANCES BETWEEN MANAGER AND EMPLOYEE

No matter how professional a front you maintain during the work day, a relationship between two people of unequal power in the office will raise suspicions of unfair treatment or questionable motives. Inherent here are issues of power, preferential treatment, and manipulation, which don't necessarily play a part in a romance between equals.

If the relationship is serious, one of you (almost certainly the partner of lower rank) should consider requesting a transfer. If this seems rash, look at the alternatives: If the relationship were to continue for any length of time, the more junior partner could never be promoted without the risk of people crying unfair advantage. On the other hand, if the relationship ends badly there could be issues of harassment or misuse of power that would be traumatizing to both parties.

Some companies require that the managerial partner disclose the relationship to Human Resources. This is intended to protect both partners should the relationship go awry; disclosing the affair means that accusations of sexual harassment or unfair treatment, if they arise, can be examined by HR with an understanding of the ex-couple's background.

ROMANCES WITH ASSOCIATES FROM OUTSIDE

If you work closely with someone from another company, you face a difficult situation if a romantic relationship results. Because you're responsible for doing business together, the inordinate amount of time you spend with the person may be little more than cause for gossip among your coworkers. But if the relationship becomes serious, consider removing yourself as the company contact; otherwise, there could be charges of preferential treatment. Also bear in mind that if the relationship *doesn't* last, it may cause tension or even the loss of an account.

WHAT IS SEXUAL HARASSMENT?

Because sexual harassment is often in the eye of the beholder, the government goes to lengths to define it. According to Title VII of the Civil Rights Act of 1964, sexual harassment occurs in three forms:

- **QUID PRO QUO.** This translates as "this for that" harassment, in which a supervisor 1) offers a job, promotion, or raise in return for a date or sexual favors, or 2) a supervisor threatens negative consequences if his or her advances are not succumbed to.
- **HOSTILE ENVIRONMENT CLAIMS.** More of a catch-all, this section of the law refers to cases of flirting, touching, unwanted e-mail, nudie pinups, inappropriate comments, lewd gestures, foul language, and comments on one's dress or appearance.
- **ACTIONABLE HARASSMENT.** Having more serious criteria is actionable (illegal) harassment, which demands a more serious response. Anyone subjected to it should bring the matter to the attention of a supervisor or Human Resources. Harassment is actionable in these cases:
  - If it is conveyed, explicitly or implicitly, that obtaining or keeping a job is contingent on your submission to the behavior.
  - If any employment decisions are based on your response to the behavior.
  - If the behavior creates a hostile or abusive work atmosphere that alters the conditions of your job.
- **MORE ON "HOSTILE ENVIRONMENT."** It is particularly important for workers to remember that what they consider funny may be insulting to someone else. For instance, telling dirty jokes or describing the previous night's sexual activity around the water fountain or at the lunch table may seem perfectly innocent and natural to the person doing the talking—but

---

SEXIST LANGUAGE

Thankfully, the days when "girl Friday" could be considered a job title are long gone. A secretary is no longer "my girl" and female colleagues are neither "sweetie," "honey," nor the atrocious "little lady." Today's girl Friday is just as likely to be a man, and women are no longer restricted to roles that gave rise to condescending tags. If such terms are used today, they're more likely to be on the level of the gender-free "kid" and "kiddo."

In another bow to change, words ending or beginning with -*man* have been banished. It matters not that the suffix meant *person* in Old English and Anglo-Saxon and that the earliest form of *wo-* (not -*man*) in *woman* denoted gender. Knowledge of the history of English will not erase the fact that words such as *chairman, spokesman,* and *foreman* are understood today to refer to a male and a male alone. For this reason, it is common practice to replace -*man* with either -*woman* or -*person* when necessary. If the result seems especially awkward and contrived, as in *waitperson,* use the alternatives: waiter or waitress.

appalling and offensive to others. A smart office worker carefully considers the wide range of sensibilities inevitable in any group of individuals.

RESPONDING TO HARASSMENT

Given the open-ended nature of the law as stated, it is important to understand more about the nature of harassment before deciding to make a claim. The National Organization for Women offers guidelines to help clarify the definition. Harassment is said to occur if *all four* of the following things happen:

- Remarks are made about your gender or sexuality.
- Offensive behavior is intentional and/or repeated.
- The behavior is unwanted and not returned.
- Your work is being interfered with, or your office environment becomes uncomfortable.

If all four criteria are met, you need to decide what action to take next. You may not be comfortable talking directly with the person doing the harassing. In this case, talk with your supervisor or with a person from your company's human resources department. Or you may choose to discuss the situation directly with the person doing the harassing. It's possible there has been a simple miscommunication, which can be cleared up with a frank and open discussion. Tell the person to cease, and state in no uncertain terms that you don't condone his or her advances or comments. Depending on the response, you may choose to give a warning or two, but make it clear that if the behavior continues you will report him.

Keep a record of the encounters you've had with the person. It may seem paranoid to jot down the nature of every talk the two of you have, but if the harassment continues you need to have accurate and detailed examples: what was said and done, and who may have been a witness. It's also wise to keep copies of your performance reviews at home for safekeeping; if your harasser tries to discredit your work, your documentation of good performance will speak for itself. More advice:

- Check your employee handbook and follow the instructions for combating sexual harassment outlined there. You can also speak to a supervisor or a member of the Human Resources staff. Representatives of the company should find it in their best interest to support you, especially when you show them that you are serious in your complaint.
- If the company doesn't take your complaint seriously, consider contacting an outside agency as a step toward ending the harassment. Among the

organizations offering help are the Equal Employment Opportunity Commission (EEOC), the National Organization of Women (NOW), Women's Legal Defense Fund (all three are based in Washington, DC), and the National Association of Working Women, based in Cleveland, Ohio.

CHARGING HARASSMENT

If it comes to charging harassment, consider what you're up against. How will your actions affect the way your coworkers (both the accused and those content not to cause a stir) treat you? Do you want to defend your job, or do you consider it more important to challenge (and, you hope, change) the status quo? Is it worth your time, effort, and money to fight a company that appears to have no real interest in promoting a harassment-free workplace? It is important to understand that if the case gets as far as a courtroom, the burden of proof is on you. You must show you were 1) treated less well than similarly situated workmates; 2) the discrimination was intentional; and 3) there was no legitimate business reason for denying you the promotion.

NEGATIVE REACTIONS

For a woman to take on a sexual harassment charge is no small feat, and while women everywhere will doubtless applaud your efforts, other men and women will find them grounds for grudges. Many women choose to change jobs rather than gain a reputation as litigious and difficult. Furthermore, other companies may be loath to hire a woman with a history of rocking the boat, however right she may have been in doing so.

A person can usually expect this kind of unfavorable reaction when she or he decides to bring a suit against a coworker or superior. If not actually dismissed from the company, she or he may be made uncomfortable enough so that leaving is seen as an attractive option. Be prepared for this, and weigh your options carefully before you decide how to proceed (one possibility, if you're ostracized, is a claim for "constructive termination"). Resources such as NOW and the EEOC should be able to help you make your decision.

IF YOU'RE FALSELY ACCUSED

Some accusations of sexual harassment are patently false. A typical scenario, with a male as the accused: You are a male middle manager and a female employee accuses you of sex discrimination because you failed to promote her. If you are innocent of the charge, go immediately to your boss and to the Human Resources department to tell your side of the story. Remember that the burden will be on the claimant, who will have a tough case to prove (see Charging Harassment, page 133). As a rule, a company that believes that a manager accused of discrimination or harassment has done nothing wrong will back the person to the point of covering his or her legal costs should both the manager and company be sued.

GENDER-FREE CHIVALRY

At the opposite end of the pole from harassment stands chivalry—not anachronistic but merely gender-free, especially in a professional setting. It wasn't so long ago that rising when a woman entered the office, carrying her packages, walking to the other side of the car to open her door, and other small acts were simply expected of men. Where did they go? They fell by the way because they suggested a need for protection, something that women have been proving unnecessary for more than a generation.

Thankfully, chivalry itself has not gone out of style. Instead of men taking care of women, today's ideal is people taking care of people. Holding the door for someone, helping to put on a coat, standing to greet a newcomer—a polite person extends such gestures to everyone, regardless of sex. Nevertheless, many men still insist on playing the perfect gentleman, and a woman who is treated to the old courtesies should never consider such behavior an affront. Kindness is kindness, whatever the motive behind it. Among the chivalries that today are gender-free:

- HOLDING A DOOR. Whoever arrives at the door first holds it for others.
- GETTING OFF AN ELEVATOR. The person closest to the door exits first.
- HELPING PUT ON A COAT. Anyone having difficulty putting on a coat or sweater should be helped, regardless of gender.
- PAYING FOR A MEAL. The old "a gentleman pays for a lady" etiquette is obsolete. Today a *host* of either sex is expected to pay the bill.
- STANDING. Standing to greet someone is always polite—and is especially important when the person is of higher rank, a client, or elderly.
- WALKING ON THE OUTSIDE. The custom of a man taking the outer position on a sidewalk dates from the days when carriages splashed mud and ladies needed shielding. Needless to say, the practice is, if not already obsolete, waning.
- HELPING TO SEAT. Pulling out someone else's chair at a restaurant table and helping to push it in is called for only when the person is elderly, incapacitated, or could simply use some help, as with a heavy chair.
- HELPING TO CARRY SOMETHING. A workmate who is overloaded with books or packages will appreciate an offer of help from *anyone* nearby.

CHAPTER 10

YOUR PERSONAL PRIVACY

When it comes to talking about personal matters, employees can be their own worst enemies. Without intending to, they often divulge private information about themselves that winds up becoming water-cooler wisdom. How and how much you talk about personal issues—dating, marriage, children, divorce, sexual preference, death, personal finances—is up to you.

Of course, today when you talk about privacy in the workplace you're talking about two different things. First is how close to your chest you keep information about your family and your private life—the subject of this chapter. The other is the right of your company to monitor your activities, and whether that counts as an invasion of privacy. For the answer (generally "no"), see A Right to Privacy, page 358.

YOUR FAMILY

Who you are is intimately related to your family. Some people will be genuinely interested in your background—that your grandmother was a Suffragette, that your father fought in Vietnam, that your uncle once worked for Elvis—but beware of imposing any family problems on your workmates. People you work with will be concerned that someone close to you is suffering a serious illness, for instance, and you may want to tell colleagues as a way of explaining periodic absences from the office. But they neither expect nor want daily updates on Grandpa's arthritis or Aunt Tillie's gynecology. Be especially careful about discussing medical matters that may come back to haunt you. If, for example, news of your family history of a serious disease reaches your employer, you can't be fired, but you may become known as a "health risk"—affecting future employment or promotion opportunities.

THE FAMILY TREE

Employees who use family background to aggrandize themselves may impress a few people but will annoy many more. When it is natural to disclose a piece of family information, do so. (If your father is a member of the state legislature, for example, it is appropriate to give his name to a colleague who is seeking information about a state highway project.) Yet, workers who are constantly announcing to all and sundry that "Daddy's ancestors came over on the Mayflower" or "my brother Bubba is a brain surgeon" are in immediate danger of becoming the office joke. Besides, relying on family pedigree or history to impress is a sure sign of personal insecurity.

YOUR LOVE LIFE

They say that all the world loves a lover; everybody wants to know who sent the beautiful bouquet of roses on your birthday or who was the charming woman on your arm at the company picnic. But discussing the details of your love life, especially with coworkers you don't know well, can be obnoxious. Moreover, employees who are too free with intimate details can be putting themselves in danger of sexual harassment charges.

Don't expect your workmates or supervisors to be your romance counselors or to keep your deep, dark secrets confidential. In the throes of romantic difficulties, you may feel compelled to unburden to coworkers, but remember that you will have to work with these people long after the breakup is healed or you've tossed the bum out. Will your thoughtless confessions become an infinite source of embarrassment? Also, if you do find a sympathetic ear, don't bend it to the breaking point. Just because colleagues are kind and understanding during coffee breaks at work doesn't mean that they want to continue the conversation on their private time.

OFFICE POLICY

Your employer, on the other hand, may be vitally interested in your love life if you are dating another employee; a client, supplier, or someone connected with the business; or a competitor. Your boss' concerns can range from office morale and potential nepotism to perceived or actual conflicts of interest. It may seem none of your employer's business whom you date, but consider the possible problems. Imagine that someone in your company's purchasing department becomes romantically involved with the salesperson for a parts supplier. Even if the relationship has no effect on your company's future purchasing decisions, the *appearance* of favoritism will be created.

Now that the general balance between working men and women is relatively equal, romance in the workplace is becoming a commonplace occurrence, but companies are only learning how to deal with it. Many bosses frankly hate interfering in their employees' personal lives and tend to work on a case-by-case basis (an inconsistent approach that frustrates workers). Smart companies, on the other hand, have clearly defined policies on dating and office relationships. In either case, you should talk with your Human Resources manager or supervisor before you risk discipline, transfer, or dismissal. Don't let news of your relationship filter through the office grapevine before you have a chance to make your own case. (See also Women and Men Together, page 126.)

YOUR MARRIAGE AND CHILDREN

Marital and parental status are usually the first two pieces of personal information that circulate about a new employee. A wedding ring, family photos on your desk, the "Baby on Board" sticker on your car—all are invitations to questions. It's up to you to tell how much or how little you want about your spouse or your children.

Family relationships can forge bonds with other workers. They can also explain and ameliorate some behaviors. (For example, knowing that you have children whom you must pick up from day care or after school will help colleagues understand why you cannot schedule late afternoon meetings.) But if you bring family problems to work, be prepared to become the subject of office talk, attract unwanted advice, and risk more serious consequences.

LEAVE IT AT HOME

In a typical situation, Caroline was so upset with her teenage son's bad attitude and poor grades that she confided her frustration and anger to several coworkers. They commiserated and shared similar experiences. But imagine Caroline's surprise when she was summoned to her supervisor's office a few weeks later. Her boss came straight to the point: Was Caroline's problem with her son affecting her performance at work? He'd noticed a couple of small things—her last project report had seemed a little less comprehensive than usual, her expense invoice was a day late. Caroline defended herself, and the supervisor seemed satisfied. But the experience was humiliating and also a little frightening because Caroline was a single parent and sole breadwinner. At bottom, however, Caroline had no one to blame but herself. By discussing her home life at work, she had essentially forfeited her privacy.

Not every problem is so dramatic, but in most cases, the best plan is to leave home matters at home. Certainly avoid imposing your family on others.

Don't expect your colleagues to buy your daughter's Girl Scout cookies by the dozens or sponsor your son's soccer team. A few photos are fine, but don't turn your office or cubicle into a family portrait gallery; it's distracting to visitors to see your children's smiling faces and artworks on every inch of wall space. Don't bring your children to work unless it's allowed; even then, be sure that your youngsters are quiet and respectful of the privacy of others.

YOUR DIVORCE

The failure of a marriage is traumatic in the best of circumstances. Psychologists have long told us that divorce is a type of death, but for divorcing workers, the question is how much denial, anger, and grieving should be shared with coworkers and supervisors. The answer: As little as possible, especially in the early stages of separation and any legal wrangling that ensues. Turn to friends, family, and professionals outside the office for support and guidance rather than letting yourself become the subject of office gossip and the target of bosses (who may watch you like hawks if they expect performance problems related to the divorce).

You should, however, talk with your supervisor if the divorce process is likely to affect you on the job—requiring time off for meetings with lawyers, court appearances, the sale of house and property, the care of children. If you experience any emotional or behavioral difficulties (occasionally being short with coworkers, forgetting appointments, becoming distracted in meetings), discuss it with your supervisor. A good boss will be understanding and may be able to help by shifting some of your workload for a while. There is no need to go into details about the cause of the divorce—and never berate or demean your ex- or soon-to-be-ex-spouse to colleagues or bosses. Simply state the facts and any problems you have or anticipate having. By the mere act of approaching your supervisor and honestly apprising him or her of the situation, you will be demonstrating a degree of control over your life that will reassure your superiors of your stability.

IN THE SAME COMPANY

When a divorce happens between two employees of the same company, the stress can affect everyone. The worst circumstance is when a divorcing couple expect their coworkers to take sides, thus turning a private matter into a companywide tangle. Hard as it may be, divorcing couples have an obligation to keep their personal lives private, except for appropriate notification of supervisors. It may be necessary to consider a change of job or transfer for one or both parties if their acrimony is likely to infect an entire office.

When and how do you tell coworkers? If you can, save the news until the last possible moment—the time of the final decree or the separation of households. If word leaks out, confirm what is obvious and keep the gory details to yourself. When you tell, it is best to go to supervisors and close associates first. On the theory that the sooner the news is out, the sooner it dies, you might mention your divorce to the office's biggest gossip and let him do your dirty work. It's not necessary to stop every Tom, Dick, and Harry in the hall and regale them with your story. Nor is it wise to send out divorce announcements or, as one divorcing couple did, to write personal notes to every coworker. Remember that a divorce, however painful, is a private sorrow, and not everyone will be sympathetic or even care.

YOUR SEXUAL ORIENTATION

Revealing sexual orientation or preference to an employer is tricky. Although some states and localities have enacted laws that protect gay and lesbian workers against employment discrimination, the majority of jurisdictions do not recognize them as a protected class. The issue is a political and social minefield, and court decisions as yet offer little consistent guidance.

Legal status and fairness aside, homosexual employees must take a hard look at their individual workplaces and corporate cultures when deciding whether to disclose. It is not easy to leave a life partner at home when the company hosts its annual family day or to be denied insurance coverage for a person who is your true dependent. It's terrible to be denied employment because you received a less than honorable discharge when you were "outed" in the military. Fortunately, enlightened employers realize that sexual orientation, whether heterosexual or homosexual, is irrelevant to job performance, and in an age when productivity is king, the ranks of enlightened employers are growing.

OTHER PERSONAL ISSUES

Your religious beliefs and practices, your politics, your racial and ethnic culture, even your finances—all these issues seem like logical subjects for office chat. But are they? The law may protect your privacy in hiring and allow some areas of workplace accommodation to your personal beliefs. But an employee who inflicts his or her personal issues on coworkers—proselytizing for a faith, for example, or constantly whining about lack of money—is both indiscreet and discourteous.

CHAPTER 11

OFFICE BUILDING ETIQUETTE

The smart businessperson knows that manners aren't just something you switch on for the benefit of your officemates and your business associates from outside. In terms of your at-work behavior, good manners extend to the people in the rest of the office building as well. Your nerves may be frayed by the rush-hour traffic or your mind preoccupied with the tasks looming ahead, but try to give some thought to those whose paths you cross as the day begins. Many people in your building are likely to be strangers who work for other companies; others are service personnel whom you know by face if not by name. True, some of these individuals may know which company you work for, but treating everyone who surrounds you with courtesy has less to do with polishing the company image than it does with simply being nice.

IN AND OUT

First, to that most mundane of acts: opening a door. Who holds it for whom? Today, whoever gets there first—the most obvious sign that chivalry isn't really dead, but only gender-free. (See also Gender-Free Chivalry, page 134.) That doesn't mean that a man should *not* hold the door for a woman, of course. Any woman who takes offense when he does would do well to examine her perspective: Men of a certain age find that old habits die hard, and they deserve the benefit of the doubt. Most cling to tradition because they were taught there are some things that a gentleman does as a matter of course, not because they see a woman who accepts such courtesies as submitting to the "stronger" sex.

ANOTHER BIT OF DOOR ETIQUETTE: Stand away from entryways and elevator doors whenever you're biding time in the lobby. If you're waiting for someone, stand against a wall so as not to impede traffic. This matters all the more when a group is gathering in piecemeal fashion to go to lunch. Even three or four people standing in front of the elevator or outside doors will become a frustrating roadblock, especially at the busiest times of day.

REVOLVING DOORS

A generation ago, revolving doors posed a dilemma for thoughtful men: Didn't it make sense to cast the ladies-first rule aside, step in, and take on the strenuous task? Or, if a gentleman did so, would everyone mistake him for a rube?

The fact that such puzzles have disappeared doesn't mean you shouldn't be careful with revolving doors. At busy times of day, people rushing through them tend to think of the meeting that's starting, the lunch date they're late for—anything but the person in the tiny compartment behind. Yet inattention could lead to injury if your unknown partner in transit happens to be disabled or elderly. Be aware of your surroundings, and remember to think of other people when your movements can so directly affect theirs. Another consideration is never to squeeze into a revolving door compartment that is already occupied.

ELEVATOR ETIQUETTE

The old-style elevator operator, nattily attired in a jacket with gold braid, has gone the way of the Edsel in most office buildings. But however casually he or she is clothed, any operator is due a "please" and "thank you" whenever you request a floor or debark—and that's not all to remember as you ride.

GETTING ON

The rules for entering an elevator are much the same as those for going through a door—gender is not as much of an issue as it once was, and the elderly or incapacitated go first. After pushing your floor button, move as far to the back as possible, leaving room for others. If you're unable to reach the button to push it, don't be embarrassed to ask someone else to do it for you.

If the elevator is already jammed with people before you get on, don't squeeze your way inside, even if you work in a building where the elevators seem to take forever to arrive. Getting to your floor a couple of minutes earlier than you might have isn't worth irritating the other passengers.

Likewise, patience is a virtue when you find the door closing as you approach. Although it's a nice gesture for a passenger to hold the door for you or push the "door open" button, it's equally thoughtful of you to allow the passengers already aboard go ahead and get to their floors.

Also mind your manners. Don't stare at other people, smack your gum (which you should hesitate to chew in public anyway), or sing along with your Walkman. If there's a mirror or reflective wall in the elevator, women and men alike would do well to leave their primping for later.

CHATS IN TRANSIT

If you're on the elevator and you see someone you know, say "Hello." Say "How are you?" Say "How 'bout those Broncos?" But be careful about going further unless you're the only two people aboard. A quiet chat is fine, but talking and laughing loudly may annoy fellow passengers, trapped as they are for the length of the ride. (Whispering isn't the answer; in the presence of others it is rude, even among strangers.)

As important as the volume is the subject: Discussing a client's business or anything else confidential while riding a crowded elevator is on the same level as not having the sense to come in from the rain. If you need to talk about personal matters or exchange trade secrets with someone you see on the ride up or down, wait until you can have your discussion in private.

GETTING OFF

When the elevator door opens, common sense prevails: Those nearest the front exit first. One exception to this rule is when there is some obvious power differential that suggests you do otherwise—the receptionist stands back to allow the CEO to exit first, for example. If an elderly person is aboard, the other passengers might see to it that he or she can exit as easily as possible.

RIDING ESCALATORS

Escalator manners are more obvious: Keep to one side so that other people are able to continue up or down. If you're the one in a hurry to get off, don't be surprised to find that most people are standing square in the middle of the steps. Unless the escalator is so clogged that it's useless to make the attempt, politely say "Excuse me, please" to every person you want to move past. Squeezing by with a sour look does little but add one more minor annoyance to the workday.

BUILDING PERSONNEL

Naturally, the people who maintain your building—doormen, front-desk personnel, cleaners, security guards—deserve the same cordiality as anyone else you see on a daily basis: A morning hello (or at least a smile and a nod) and a thank you when they've helped you in any way. You may never have actually been introduced to them, but that's no reason to treat them as if they were part of the lobby furniture. Here are some things to consider.

- For security reasons, many buildings require workers to sign out if they leave after a certain hour. No matter how impatient you are to get home, don't sigh loudly and repeatedly look at your watch when you have to stand in line.
- If passes are needed for bringing visitors to your office on weekends or after hours (or for carting a large box out of the office), don't take it out on the desk keeper if you forgot to obtain one. Many desk keepers will overlook the lapse if you're a longtime employee; others may be by-the-book drill sergeants determined to teach you who's in charge. If you are dealing with one of the latter sort and his interdictions become so rigid as to be nonsensical—he won't allow your six-year-old in on a Saturday morning without a pass—try complaining to the building manager. But issue a gentle warning first: "Howard, I think that's really unreasonable. I want you to know I'm considering talking to the building manager about the situation." He might just curb his behavior; if he doesn't, you've taken the high road by not going behind his back.
- If you're in the habit of working late, be courteous to the regular cleaning person by saying hello or asking his or her name and introducing yourself. You're not obliged to get involved in a conversation, but being respectful makes the cleaner feel less anxiety about intruding on your space and interrupting your work.

TIPPING

Some building staff may attend to you more personally: the parking attendant who always has a pleasant word, the security guard who walks you to the bus stop late at night, the woman from the mailroom who makes a late round to pick up your outgoing packages. If so, consider giving a small gift or a tip at holiday time.

Nice tins of holiday goodies are an obvious choice, but if you have known the person for a long time you may be able to give something more useful—an attractive vase or picture frame, for example. As for tips, some businesspeople like to give $10 to $20, especially to the kinds of workers who are tipped elsewhere but not in an office building, such as doormen and parking attendants. Put the check in a card on which you've written something such as "This is for all of your help during the past year." Then sign it with "Thanks."

BUILDING MANAGEMENT

Although the doormen, security guards, and other building personnel are out in the open, building management is usually ensconced out of sight. But that doesn't mean you can't get in touch with them when you need to, whether for concerns about the air-conditioning system, noise, or another problem.

COMPLAINING ABOUT NOISE

There's little you can do about noise from outside that's unrelated to your building, but construction noises from *inside* the building are another matter. If your building is undergoing renovations and you're disturbed by the sound of drills and hammers, let this be known to your supervisor, who will take the complaint to the building manager. Storming into the building manager's office and confronting his assistant is not the route to go.

Cost considerations will most likely keep the work from being confined to after-hours and weekends, but it's possible that the problem could be somewhat eased—construction schedules rejiggered so that work on the floor above would take place mostly in the early morning or late afternoon hours.

SICK BUILDINGS

If you and your coworkers are convinced that your building suffers from sick building syndrome, don't start criticizing and demanding changes until you have some proof. Approach your supervisor and tell her of your concerns. If enough workers feel the same, the company should have tests run to detect whether gases or particles are causing sickness or allergic reactions.

If the temperature on your floor is too hot or cold, remember that opening your window may contribute to throwing off the whole system. If you have other complaints about the way the building is maintained, find out from a supervisor how to deal with the problem. There may be an official means of conveying comments to the staff in charge of building maintenance.

SIDEWALK SMOKING

Now that smoking has been banned in most offices, front sidewalks have become salons of sorts for smokers, who puff and schmooze on intermittent breaks. If you're a sidewalk smoker, be mindful of those who aren't. If, for example, your building entrance is recessed from the street and has an overhang, stand out on the curb so that a curtain of smoke won't collect in the space. In fact, you should stand away from doorways, no matter what the layout of your building. If there's no out-of-the-way spot to indulge, consider taking a walk around the block or into the parking lot.

A NOTE OF CAUTION: Don't think people don't notice when you're outside having a cigarette several times a day. Someone who's seen standing outside virtually every time anyone walks in or out of the building is going to gain a reputation not only as a slave to the weed but a slacker. This is one time when a smoker's behavior can reflect on his company: "If this guy's allowed to spend most of the day on the sidewalk," people might be thinking, "what does that say about the way things are run inside?"

SMOKING CLIQUES

Sidewalk smokers tend to form cliques—not necessarily with workmates who smoke but with smokers from other offices. As with any other business socializing, you shouldn't feel awkward about exchanging pleasantries or striking up a casual conversation—but be careful not to discuss with your smoking buddies any company business that's best kept private.

A BATTLE ROYAL

Note to the cigarette smoker: Some people hate with a passion the cloud of smoke you generate. Note to the cigarette hater: Smokers think you are the thin wedge that will lead to a totalitarian state. The battle lines are drawn, and if the combatants can't call a truce they can at least make an effort to accommodate one another.

If you're a sidewalk smoker, your most diplomatic move is to take a walk around the block (and get some exercise in the bargain). But don't be surprised when you see pedestrians hurrying past you to escape the smoke you're leaving in your wake. Try to take puffs in a moderate enough fashion to keep the air clearer than if you were puffing away like a chimney.

If you're a nonsmoker, first give credit to sidewalk smokers for smoking where they're supposed to, not inside. If you really hate the smoke, discreetly take a deep breath of fresh air before breaching the curtain of smoke you'll have to pass through on your way into the building, and then hold it unobtrusively till you get inside. (Be careful not to make a show of it, or you'll look like the world's worst prig). When walking behind a smoker on the sidewalk, by all means speed up to get past him, but refrain from casting a dirty look, which will accomplish nothing more than making the *both* of you annoyed.

Now to the cigar. If you're a cigar smoker you've probably been let in on the secret that many people, far from being impressed, find your habit distasteful—and that's putting it mildly. A particular object of scorn is the stogie-smoker who stands in front of the building puffing for all he's worth, generating a noxious cloud that can be smelled half a block away. Again, a walk around the block is a solution, but even then remind yourself that cigar smoking is something that is best left to your own home, a cigar bar, or the poker table.

BUTT DISPOSAL

Don't think cigarette butts aren't litter. They are. If no receptacles for cigarette butts are placed outside your building, find a public trash can, thoroughly extinguish the cigarette, and throw it away. Tossing the butt into the street or grinding it into the sidewalk could be said to cause insult to injury (read, litter to pollution) and will be especially resented by the building management.

PART III

BUSINESS DRESS

The English aphorist Oscar Wilde once said, "It is only shallow people who do not judge by appearances," and Shakespeare warned in Hamlet that "apparel oft proclaims the man." True then, true now. Fair or not, how you dress and accessorize speaks volumes about you. In the business world, your attire sends instant messages to others about your status, profession and professionalism, self-image, self-confidence—even your work habits and workplace. For years, entire sociological categories were identified by clothing terms—the now outdated "blue collar," "white collar," and "pink collar."

Fashions in business clothing have evolved and broadened since the days of the three-piece corporate uniform and "the man in the gray flannel suit"—and the woman's copycat version. Today the move is to "situational dress," which means adapting your appearance not only to the day-to-day flow of life at the office but to the expectations of those with whom you do business.

The following two chapters—one for men, the other for women—help you make wise wardrobe choices that suit your job, company, and specific business occasions. At the same time, they stress how you can express your individuality while staying fashionable and comfortable in any business situation.

CHAPTER 12

BUSINESS CLOTHES FOR MEN

I f your father isn't choking over what men wear to the office today (he has probably donned khakis, too), your grandfather might be clutching his throat and turning purple. Open collars, khaki, denim, sweaters, and rubber-soled shoes are the most in-your-face clue to the major changes in the business world over the last two decades—the rise of information technology industries whose lifeblood is the young; the loosening of the chain of command; the attitude that a job isn't necessarily forever; and the fact that whenever it's an employee's market companies bend to the workers' will. If the jacket and tie aren't dead yet (and don't fool yourself that they are) their survival is by no means assured. At the rate dress codes are changing, it may not be too long before the term "casual Fridays" is retired to that crammed buzzword attic where the Jazz Age expression "twenty-three skidoo" resides.

Does tremendous change mean "anything goes"? Of course not. Figuring out which clothes are appropriate for business isn't exactly brain surgery: It boils down to 1) dressing to fit in at your company, and 2) dressing to meet the expectations of those with whom you do business. In a word, it's situational. But that doesn't mean you should get complacent. Some things about clothing never change: First, people judge you by your clothes, a vital ingredient in making a good first impression and a signifier forever after. Second, dressing as your peers do but with more style often gives you an advantage no matter where you work. The first truism speaks to the situational bent of today's dress, the second to projecting an image that will help you get ahead.

ATTITUDE AND ADAPTATION

Today the big picture of business dress is more complex—or simpler, depending on how you look at it—than traditional versus nontraditional. In short, the dresser is chameleonlike. What you wear to work depends on what you're doing that day: if nothing special, your usual open-collar shirt; if meeting with clients who are sure to be wearing ties, you wear one too. If the CEO is visiting the floor or a new boss is arriving, you get out your *best* suit and tie. The same goes for special situations: If you're selling a financial concept to the board of directors, your appearance needs to reflect the same attention to detail that your presentation does. At the other end of the pole, if you're going downtown to meet with male clients who wear jeans and earrings, you know that wearing a suit could build a wall between you.

A CAVEAT: Dressing for "what I'm doing today" can be risky. You never know when an invitation to see a valued customer, client, or contractor may come out of the blue. Avoid getting caught by either 1) keeping a change of clothes in your office or 2) dressing daily in a way that's appropriate, regardless of the situation—the wiser of the two choices.

ORGANIZATIONAL STYLE

Every organization has a style, and you adopt that style to belong. If it is "traditional business dress" (a suit and tie), then there's plenty of room for gradations within its definitions, a latitude you can use to your advantage.

To compare the extremes within the range, think first of a banker who's a dyed-in-the-wool (gray flannel, of course) conservative dresser. His shirt, its collar crisply starched, is pure white; his dark suit comes with pants that are pleated and cuffed; and his tie is a dark navy with diagonal rep stripes of maroon. The look is high-contrast and fairly full. Now think of an advertising copywriter: His shirt is a warm beige; his slim tie rust-colored; and his thinner-lapel cream-colored suit has flat-front pants, without cuffs. The look is low-contrast and more streamlined. Each of these businessmen dresses within a certain code and range while remaining firmly "traditional."

Understanding the code and how to shine within it not only lets you express your individuality but sends a subliminal message that you're forward-looking and confident. Ideally, you work within the bounds of what is appropriate to express who you are and where you see yourself headed, adapting your clothes as necessary.

WHAT OF THE SUIT?

The suit may spend more time hanging in the closet than it used to, but it remains an essential, if only for weddings and funerals. And one is not enough: the weight of the fabric should fit the season—for spring and summer, cotton, gabardine, or crepe; for fall and winter, worsted wool. When you're choosing, subtle color in a fabric of appropriate weight is the aim (navy is the most favored color, with black or dark gray close behind). While you want to choose a suit with care, think less of making a fashion statement than of finding something that fits well and feels comfortable.

STYLE AND CUT

At the end of the Nineties, men's fashion has become less about the choice of shirt and tie than the cut, or shape, of the jacket and pants. Suit cuts fall into three categories: American, Italian, and British.

- **AMERICAN CUT.** This is the classic medium-contour, center-vented or unvented jacket with a natural shoulder. The pants have a moderate, or straight, line.
- **ITALIAN CUT.** The jacket has more shape, with a shoulder that is fuller and more rounded with a slightly fuller chest. It is unvented in back, and the pants are slightly wider.
- **BRITISH CUT.** This cut is slightly squarer and stronger in the shoulder and more shaped at the waist. The jacket is frequently side-vented or, more classically, unvented. The pants are slimmer than those of the Italian and American styles.

All three cuts come in two- or three-button jacket styles. (Note: When wearing a three-button suit, you can either button the top two buttons or just the top button; for a more relaxed look, use only the middle button.) Another variation is the vent at the back of the jacket. At the end of the Nineties, unvented jackets were considered more up-to-the-minute in less traditional fields, while the vented jacket is the conservative choice.

SUIT FABRICS

Rule number one for a suit fabric: No matter the color, the surface should be matte—not shiny or iridescent. The choice in fabrics boils down to wool, cotton, and either of these blended with the new microfibers, synthetic fibers that have made polyester's tacky reputation obsolete.

- **WOOL.** With its many textures, wool is the suit fabric of choice because of its ability to stretch but still keep its shape; its matte finish; its ability to breathe (keeping you warmer in winter and cooler in summer); and its long shelf life. What are called *woolen* fabrics are made from loosely twisted, fuzzier yarn and go by the name of tweed, flannel, and melton; *worsted* wool yarn is twisted more tightly, is finer, and is the basis of gabardine and crepe.

Business Clothes for Men

Wool blends (wool combined with synthetic fibers such as polyester) are popular because they wrinkle less. The higher the percentage of wool in the fabric, the richer its look. But looks aren't everything: Nylon blended with wool has a particularly nice "hand," or feel.

- COTTON. In summer, cotton and linen are popular suit fabrics because they're so comfortable. But unless you aspire to the fashionable nonchalance associated with wrinkles, remember that linen will look as if you slept in it after only a few hours. A hint: Not only will wool wrinkle less, but a lightweight wool is actually cooler than cotton for summer.
- MICROFIBERS. Synthetic fibers, made from petroleum-based chemicals, have undergone a change for the better in the last decade or so. From the time nylon was introduced in 1938, the point of synthetics has been to resist wrinkles (remember the term "wash and wear," which meant no ironing?) and to last virtually forever. Today the industry has retooled them to lose their undesirable sheen and whatever connotations it carried.

COLOR AND PATTERNS

Black, in a matte fabric, has become a new business standard, joining navy blue and gray. Before, black worn in day was associated with two extremes: at one end, the clergy; at the other, the shady character.

Dark colors have always been associated with authority, but tradition has also embraced suits in lighter shades of brown (tan and beige) and gray. Pastel-colored suits in blue, mint green, or rosy beige just won't do in a traditional work environment.

Solids are always a safe choice, but it would be a boring world if they were all men wore. Bankers and stockbrokers still favor pinstripes, with a very thin, light gray stripe preferred; wider chalk stripes are more than a little risky. Plaids range from the almost indiscernible to the clearly patterned but, like stripes, should be subtle in both design or color.

OTHER GARMENTS

The following notes on clothes and accessories will help you make choices when you shop, no matter what your field. Choosing suitable fabrics and materials has to do with seasonality and practicality, but what is "in style" is more than ever in the eye of the beholder. Nevertheless, until all standards vanish, erring on the side of subtlety is the best course, a philosophy reflected in the notes that follow.

SPORT JACKETS

Although the sport jacket is descended from the English hunting jacket, today it is simply a jacket without matching trousers—no athletic activity required. It switches roles with ease, dressing up a pair of corduroy pants or a flannel shirt or making the traditional jacket and tie look more casual. The most versatile style is the single-breasted jacket with a classic shape, with the three-button version as the more modern. Small checks, muted patterns, and tweeds are the usual patterns, while solids come in almost every color imaginable.

> **FABRICS OF CHOICE**
> *Wool, hopsack weaves, microfiber, or sueded solids; for warmer climes, silk blends*
> **THINGS TO AVOID**
> *Loud colors, bold patterns, trimming*

BLAZERS

If the sport coat is the most casual item of business wear and the three-piece suit the dressiest, the navy blue blazer occupies the middle ground. It comes in the American, Italian, and British silhouettes (vented or unvented), with navy blue and black the colors of choice. In Europe, blazers are worn with slacks that have low color contrast, but in America a blazer paired with gray flannel slacks (preferably darker charcoal gray) creates a casual look that's unsurpassed.

> **FABRICS OF CHOICE**
> *Lightweight gabardine or crepe; flannel*
> **THINGS TO AVOID**
> *Brass buttons on a blazer (the "bandleader look") are on their way out; buttons with a designer's monogram*

VESTS

The taste for vests comes and goes, and in the late Nineties vests were making a comeback, especially as a way to dress up a suit. When worn with a three-piece suit, the vest traditionally matches (not contrasts or coordinates with) the other pieces, preferably in dark navy or gray. Vests are meant to dress up an outfit, so think twice before using them as attention-getting accessories.

SLACKS

The *way* you wear suit pants and slacks of any kind matters. Pants worn on the hips, like jeans, make your stomach look bigger, while pants hiked to the waist are more slimming. (Hiking up your pants doesn't mean the "pants up to the armpits" look, but merely having your waistband high enough to rest the waistband over

> **FABRICS OF CHOICE**
> *Wool, microfiber, and wool/microfiber blends*
> **THINGS TO AVOID**
> *Box pleats, inverted pleats*

VARIATIONS ON THE CASUAL

If one were to group men's dress styles today, the people who work outside of the most traditional fields and are no longer counted among the tie-wearers could be thought of as falling into four categories. Those categories could be called, from the least casual to the most, the Blazers, the Khakis, the Black Turtlenecks, and the Jeans. The smart company knows that an eclectic mix of styles contributes to the richness of the whole.

THE BLAZERS

Often employed in the advertising, architecture, or publishing fields, these are the spiffiest of the casual dressers. If they have a uniform, it is the navy blue blazer with gray flannel slacks—a classic look that hints of all things yachty. Other pants of choice are corduroys or khakis, frequently with classic pleated styling. Shirt choices lean toward the comfortable: nonfitted, unstarched twill or Oxford button-down in solid, plaid, or check. The Lacoste-style knit shirt is another staple.

> **FROWNED ON**
> *Bold colors and patterns, baggy silhouettes*

THE KHAKIS

Unlike the Blazers, the Khakis don't consider a jacket central to their look. The sporty image they project depends on the quality and fit of the slacks (often the more modern flat-front, non-pleat style) and the shirt that contrasts with it—a white or muted tone sport shirt of Oxford cloth or poplin. A lightweight knit,

> **FROWNED ON**
> *Tank tops, T-shirts, sandals, shorts*

your hipbones.) Another way to keep pants from making you look fat: Instead of double pleats, choose flat fronts, which are also more modern.

Cuffs are a personal preference, but you should choose cuffs whenever you're not sure what's appropriate; cuffs are more classic, no cuffs more modern. (Note: When you're wearing high demi-boot style shoes, slim line pants look best and don't need cuffs.)

DRESS SHIRTS

Shirt collars at their most basic: Spread collars are the dressiest and shouldn't be worn without a tie. The point collar is the most versatile, looking fine when worn open or with a tie, and is the more modern choice. The button-down collar on a dress shirt is seen as somewhat fuddy-duddy today by the fashion con-

V-neck sweater T-shirt underneath is also part of the look. Outerwear is usually a leather jacket or a nylon parka. The Khakis' hair is often a little longer and more relaxed than the Blazers', and ties are worn less frequently.

THE BLACK TURTLENECKS

Often working in retail, fashion, or the arts, these men draw their inspiration from the showrooms of Milan—a casual but sophisticated look with echoes of bohemia. The wardrobe is monochromatic, with slimmer pants and a cleaner silhouette. The black dress slack with sport coat is a staple, and an open-collar dark or white shirt is worn under a sport coat or dressy casual outer shirt. Occasionally, a solid matching tie may be added. The trend in jackets for these kinds of dressers is toward a slim cut, a narrow lapel, and a center vent.

> **FROWNED ON**
> *Anything shiny or too tight; sandals*

THE JEANS

Earning their bread in fields such as music and information technology, these men are partial to jeans or retro synthetic-fiber slacks, Hawaiian print or fitted nylon shirts, long hair, creative facial hair, earrings and other piercings, and tattoos. T-shirts with graphic designs or expressions are also a part of the look. While they choose to dress outside of the mainstream, the Jeans also know that they may have to meet with someone who's part of what used to be called "the establishment" at any minute and change their look accordingly.

> **FROWNED ON**
> *T-shirts with offensive expressions; extreme piercings and tattoos*

scious. (A note of interest: America is the only country where button-downs are worn as dress shirts.) The hidden button-down, which has a snap or button that is out of sight, is a popular new design that combines the contemporary flair of the longer point with the neatness of the button-down.

As a whole, dress shirts have become more subdued today, with the jacket more important to the overall look. Not so long ago the standard dress shirt colors were white, blue, yellow, and pink. Today's preferred choices are white, shades of blue, shades of gray, tan, and muted khaki-greens. White remains the dressiest.

The traditional amount of cuff to show under the jacket sleeve is a quarter-inch, but

> **FABRICS OF CHOICE**
> *Pure cotton, quality cotton/microfiber blends*
> **THINGS TO AVOID**
> *Wearing a spread collar without a tie; wearing a short-sleeve shirt with a tie; bright colors, heavy textures, retro dog-ear collars*

today the trend is toward more suit sleeve and less cuff. French cuffs seem silly to many men today, but for a real dress-up occasion, they add an elegant touch. Just make sure the cufflinks are unobtrusive.

OVERCOATS AND RAINCOATS

The traditional and safest length for an overcoat is just below the knee, the midcalf style having waned in the early Nineties. Shorter knee-length coats such as peacoats, parkas, and duffel coats are perfectly fine to wear with casual clothes or even a suit, especially in colder climates where practicality has to prevail over style. With any overcoat, be sure the shoulders aren't overpadded since, on top of suit shoulders, they can make you look like a linebacker. The same applies to double-breasted models, which are smart but risk looking too tight when worn over a suit.

> **FABRICS OF CHOICE**
> *Wool (soft velours), camel hair, alpaca; if you can afford it, cashmere; for raincoats, microfiber and coated cotton*
>
> **THINGS TO AVOID**
> *Extreme lengths, shiny fabrics, trimming on collars and shoulders, fur or velvet collars; for raincoats, clear plastic and poncho styles*

One of the most popular coats for cold weather is the trench coat, which is actually a raincoat. If you're a serious dresser and don't want to look as if you have only one coat, wear your trench coat only when it rains. The wool liner is intended for cold *rainy* days, not for converting the garment into a winter overcoat. (Traditionally, the beige trench coat has been the standard of taste, while black carried more working-class connotations.)

SHOES

From the dressiest on down, the traditional business shoe is the Oxford (plain toe or cap toe), the wing tip, and the plain or tasseled loafer. Save your penny loafers for casual days.

Your shoes shouldn't so much contrast with your outfit as harmonize with it: black with gray, brown with tan. Black is the dressier color of the two, and is dressier still in suede. (Note: True black suede dress shoes have leather, not crepe, soles.) With gray or navy blue clothes, wear black or dark brown shoes; with tan clothes or khakis, wear a lighter brown shoe.

SOCKS

Beyond these three basics, few rules apply to socks: 1) Use dark socks for business wear, 2) match them to your pants, and 3) make sure they're high enough not to show your bare shins when you sit down. Natural fibers such as cotton and wool are preferable to synthetics because they are better insulators, keeping feet warmer and deterring foot odor.

ACCESSORIES

As basic as a tie, as small as a pen, as infrequently used as an umbrella—the smaller items of the businessman's wardrobe can dress up a look, dress it down, make it look expensive, make it look cheap. And, like garments, these accessories should change character according to the situation.

THE TIE

The tie has hardly disappeared, but more and more men are questioning what a tradition supposedly inherited from the court of Louis XIV has to do with the world of today. That, time will judge, but for the great majority of men who dress for business the tie remains the most important of all accessories.

In fashion circles, there are two schools of thought about ties: The first says that your tie allows you to express your individuality. The second says that defining your personality with your tie may make you feel good, but nobody else really cares; plus, some people find idiosyncratic ties unprofessional. (Though your coworkers get a kick out of your tie with the mermaid motif, some of your customers may not be amused). The solution to this problem is to keep a "safe" tie in your office—and safe in the tie realm means silk, either in a solid color or with an understated pattern. Fashion tip: Coordinate the width of your tie with your lapels—wider with wide, slimmer with slim.

> **FABRIC OF CHOICE**
> *Silk*
>
> **THINGS TO AVOID**
> *Big knots such as the Windsor; tying your tie too short or too long (the tip should reach just to the top of your belt buckle); if wearing a tie lighter than your shirt, keep the contrast to a minimum to avoid the shady-character connotation*

If you're fond of bow ties, be careful wearing one to a meeting with conservative clients you don't know well; on anyone but a professor emeritus, this seemingly benign choice can be seen as dated or affected. On the other hand, many men—including more than a few public figures—have made the bow tie their signature look with great success.

HATS

Hats carry more connotations than other accessories, so choose them with care: a fedora that suits you can look smart, while one that doesn't can make you look a little disreputable. Avoid hats that are too large or unusual. As for baseball caps, those with team insignias should be worn to baseball games and out-door barbecues, not to the office.

BRIEFCASES

The care you put into your presentation shouldn't be compromised by the briefcase from which you pull it, so go for a quality model, preferably in soft leather. For a simple sheaf of papers, an option is a leather envelope carried under the arm. Laptop computer cases are also more in evidence today and have room for more than the machine.

BELTS AND SUSPENDERS

The fact that belts should be coordinated with your shoe color means you need more than one—a black, a brown (both dark and light), and possibly a cordovan. The standard width is 1¼ inches, and anything wider should be saved for clothing other than your suit.

THE UBIQUITOUS BASEBALL CAP

The baseball cap—no longer necessarily stamped with the team insignia—has become an integral part of the wardrobe of millions of American men, from the manual laborer to the captain of industry. And why not? Since business hats have largely gone the way of the dodo bird, *something* needs to be kept on the head to keep it warm. (Your mother was right: A surprisingly high percentage of your body heat *is* lost through the head.) As a bonus, the billed cap serves the functional purpose of shading the eyes from the sun. The cap is also relatively connotation-free, unlike the Borsalino (associated with slippery types), the Stetson (appropriate for ranchers, but potentially silly on cowboy wannabes), and the English sports cap (calling to mind tweeds and hunting dogs).

The most important consideration for the cap-wearing businessman is to know when to take his cap off. Wearing a baseball cap to work is perfectly fine, but keeping it on once you've stepped in the door is not. The cap is so much a part of some men that they forget they have it on, and more than one worker has come to an early morning meeting and had to be reminded to remove it. Also, if a conservative client comes in and you take him to lunch, leave the baseball cap at the office. It's a good idea to keep a more traditional piece of headwear in a drawer at the office in case you need it unexpectedly.

The alternative (not companion) to a belt is suspenders, which have about as much to do with holding up your pants as ties do with keeping the middle of your chest warm: They are not about function, but style. Suspenders are coordinated to the tie, and the quietness or wildness of the pattern is determined by the company culture in which the wearer operates.

JEWELRY

Two words sum up the well-dressed businessman's use of jewelry: minimalism and subtlety. A wedding band and a good watch aren't quite the limit, but they're close. Anything else on the hands or wrists should be limited to a very simple ring (no stones, and never on the pinkie finger) and cufflinks (the quietest of designs in silver or gold).

Chains around the neck are never suitable in a conventional work environment, and are often out of place, even in casual settings. Bracelets of any kind are not a good idea at most conservative companies, although thin and expensive ID bracelets usually won't cross the line. When wearing more than one metal item, match metal to metal—silver to silver, gold to gold.

WATCHES

A watch is often the only piece of jewelry a man wears. Some people think of a top-of-the-line brand as a status symbol, and the thrill of having a true timepiece, with its many intricate working parts, has been likened to having your first electric train. Others think that a sleek quartz watch at a hundredth of the price is by far the more sensible choice. Whatever you decide, do not pay for things you don't need: an alarm, a date indicator, and other gadgets, examples of which are gauges that measure depth and speed on diver's watches.

The style and band color of the watch should be coordinated to your outfit. Thin faces and leather brown or black bands go best with a suit, while watches with metallic bands are more at home with casual wear. Watches with leather or suede bands also go well with the khaki/plaid shirt outfit, although with brown as the preferred band color over black.

*Business
Clothes
for Men*

TATTOOS AND PIERCINGS

Fads come and go, but tattoos are forever. If you're certain you'll love your tattoo for all eternity, you may be right. But it is equally true that people change as they grow older, and doing something permanent to your body can come back to haunt you.

A tattoo on a part of your body that no one will see is not an issue, but one on a hand or cheek is different. Will the exotic salamander tattooed on your arm or upper neck affect your chances of getting a job or being promoted? No one knows for sure, but as soon as the tattoo becomes part of the image you project it cannot help but affect what people think of you. Also bear in mind that tattoo removal is not only extremely expensive but somewhat imperfect; in most cases, it leaves unsightly traces that will never go away.

By comparison, most body piercings are benign. Unlike tattoos, piercing ornaments can be removed at will, which means that people who like them can have their cake and eat it, too. In many workplaces today, such ornamentation is not only accepted but expected—a sign that you're "in the club." Most American businesses, however, still think piercings are strictly for earlobes. Over time, body piercings have moved from the earlobe to the edge of the upper ear, to the nose, eyebrow, tongue, and beyond. The smart man in business takes cues from his peers and bosses before wearing any piercings to work.

EYEGLASSES AND CONTACTS

Don't let your glasses date you. Frame styles move with the times, having shifted from the aviator styles of the Seventies to rounder frames in the Eighties to more rectangular ones in the Nineties. Observe what well-dressed people are wearing to gauge where the trend is headed.

When buying glasses, remember that a round face looks better with square frames, and a square face better with round. If your eyes are close together, choose a frame with a clear bridge but a noticeable temple piece. Men who have wide-set eyes need a more obvious dark, thick bridge over the nose and thin temple pieces; wire is a good choice. In traditional business environments, classically shaped frames in tortoiseshell, metal, or dark plastic are the usual favorites.

Whether to go with contact lenses depends on how good you look in glasses. An advantage with contacts is that tinted lenses can deepen eye color, though you don't want the artificiality to be obvious.

SUNGLASSES

Don't wear sunglasses with people you're meeting for business unless you're walking outside in bright sun. Obviously, you should make eye contact, and sunglasses make that impossible while making you look inscrutable (or worse, suspicious) at the same time. Wearing sunglasses indoors is an affectation that's going to make most people think you're trying to shout "Hollywood!"—unless, that is, you're really lunching with a movie mogul.

UMBRELLAS, WALLETS, PENS

These three items still make a statement, even though their purpose is entirely functional. The black umbrella is the classic for business, with golf umbrellas and bright colors saved for off time. Wallets, with dark leather the most traditional, should be thin enough not to cause an obvious bulge in your back pocket. A better solution is to have a very thin wallet for a few cards and a money clip for bills, which you keep in a side pocket. (Remember that there's no real need to carry every credit card you own at all times.)

Pens should be of high quality, not the $1 plastic ball-point. Another reminder: Always carry a pen in your jacket pocket, not your shirt pocket.

STAYING WELL-GROOMED

Most men learn not to be a mess when they start to date as teenagers: The better groomed they are, the better their chances of having a girl on their arm. As adults, the better groomed men are, the more points they score in business.

Staying well-groomed doesn't mean getting a weekly manicure and styling your hair to within an inch of its life. It simply means staying clean, odor-free, and untousled. It's a practical thing: A man with greasy hair and dandruff is going to be less appealing to be around, his sloppy personal habits erecting a wall of sorts between him and his coworkers and—perhaps even more important—his business associates from outside. The idea is to attract, not repel. Here's an everyday grooming checklist, with some items to keep on hand.

- **HAIR.** Wash your hair often enough to keep it from looking greasy. Avoid both the super-blow-dried look and the gelled to the skull look. If you tend to have dandruff, use a dandruff shampoo and keep a small brush in the office for whisking it off your shoulders.
- **FINGERNAILS.** Keep a nail clipper with a cleaning tool in your desk drawer. Dirt can mysteriously appear under your fingernails when you least

*Business
Clothes
for Men*

161

expect it. Nails should be trimmed straight across with about $\frac{1}{16}$ of white showing; push back the cuticles occasionally, too.

- **FIVE O'CLOCK SHADOW.** This can be a problem if you have very dark hair. An electric shaver will smarten you up if you have a late afternoon meeting, so keep one in your desk drawer if necessary.
- **NOSE AND EAR HAIR.** One morning a week, check to see if your nose hairs need clipping (special blunt-end scissors are made for the purpose) or your earlobes tweezed. Your barber can take care of the ear hair; otherwise, do it yourself at home, not in the office rest room.
- **BODY ODOR.** A daily bath is the best defense against body odor, and a deodorant or antiperspirant is the second best. Deodorants only mask odor (and can actually make body odor worse when used as a bath substitute), while antiperspirants block sweat. Combination deodorant/antiperspirants are available, but don't apply them too thickly or the scent could become obvious later in the day.
- **BREATH.** To keep your breath fresh, bring your toothbrush to work and brush after lunch. Brushing the back of the tongue helps control odor, and a breath mint or two during the day should keep you from offending.
- **NAIL BITING ET CETERA.** Nail biters should keep their nails short so that they don't look ragged. Nail biting also brings up the subject of other nervous habits: scratching your head or face around someone else, which with some people will take your image down at least one notch.
- **WELL-HEELED SHINY SHOES.** Shoes with the heels worn down should be worn at home. As for shoe-shines, your shoes needn't be mirrorlike, but they shouldn't be noticeably scuffed or dirty either.
- **IRONED CLOTHES.** The wrinkled look may have been fashionable in casual wear a few years ago, but at the office it makes you look like you're not tending to business. A touch-up with an iron before work will take a coat-hanger crease out of slacks and make any less-than-smooth shirts more presentable.
- **CLEAN CLOTHES.** Don't be tempted to wear that shirt, tie, or pair of pants with the grease spot, thinking that no one will notice. If it turns out you have to meet a client, you'll regret the decision. Wearing clean clothes is as essential as combing your hair.

YOUR HAIR

Human hair enjoyed unprecedented power as a symbol of rebellion in the Sixties. So where does it stand today? If the idea in the Sixties was to prove that how long you wear your hair ultimately doesn't matter in the great scheme of things, the battle was won. The baby boomers who flouted convention are now the measure of what's "conventional," and they say that so long as a man's hair is neat, clean, and not too extreme, it can fall over his ears to his shoulders, be pulled back into a ponytail, or be shaved into a buzz cut without eliciting a negative reaction in most workplaces.

There is room today in most corporate cultures to accommodate most styles. But not all. Hair over the ears? Yes. Rastafarian braids? No. A ponytail? Sometimes, but often risky. The important thing is to pay enough attention to your hair and scalp that you remain well-combed and dandruff-free.

BEARDS AND MUSTACHES

Facial hair has had a checkered history in the workplace. While the clean-shaven look was still the choice in most workplaces of the late-Nineties, a well-trimmed beard will be of little concern. Long or straggly beards are best left to professors, musicians, and artists. The fad among the young is to have a mere patch of hair here and there—a Van Dyke or a goatee (by comparison, the plain old mustache looks rather passé). Extreme mustache styles—Fu Manchus and handlebars—are out of place in most work environments.

WHAT SAY YOUR CLOTHES?

Clothes and grooming choices not only send messages about your personality and mind-set but provide other clues as well. Say the top of your shoe has a drop of dried soup that stays there for two days. Could the message be that you don't pay attention to more important details either? Say your hairstyle was extremely cool in 1989 but hasn't changed since. If you're oblivious to this, might you be slow to catch on to things in general? Say you make a political statement by continuing to wear a tie every day of the week when everyone else has gone casual. Are you stuck in a rut instead of looking forward? Or say your shirt is unironed and your trousers show a grease spot. If you're slovenly about your clothes, are you slovenly in your work? Or if you're a really hard worker, are you so disorganized you have to let everything else go?

At times it's not the clothing items themselves that give someone a positive or negative impression so much as how you wear and tend to them. And remember: Because the receiver of your message when you're 20 is different from the receiver when you are 40, the message evolves.

THE PENDULUM OF STYLE

In fashion, the mechanism of the style swing is that of attraction and repulsion, of push and pull. First, the younger generation takes it upon themselves to dress in a way that distinguishes them from their elders; next, the elders adopt the look to make themselves look younger. Challenged, the young adopt yet another look that the old will eventually co-opt. Back and forth, back and forth.

But it's not quite so simple. Working alongside generational push and pull is the law of supply and demand, which today allows the elders to hold sway. The perfect illustration of this phenomenon is the "pant pleats make you look fat" paradigm. Youthful and skinny, baby boomers made pleated pants the fashion of choice in the Seventies because they looked so good in them. Flash to 30 years later: The boomers are the bulge in the population in more ways than one, and their demand for flat-front pants that de-emphasize the paunch has swung the pendulum back.

Other examples of style swings? The baseball cap, lug-sole dress shoes, khaki pants, and the three-button suit. Understanding a little something about the pendulum of style puts fashion trends in context and helps you judge whether to jump on the bandwagon or greet them with a yawn.

YOUR COLOGNE

If some scents for men are meant to conjure up a woody glade or a citrus grove, they should merely hint at those bucolic places, not plop you down in the middle. No element of the businessman's wardrobe requires more subtlety than cologne. Filling a meeting room with the smell of citrus, balsam, or musk is the job of an air freshener, not you. Wearing too much cologne is even worse at an interview, where the "moderation in all things" approach is key. The toilet waters that refresh the skin after a shower are probably the best choice for the workday, with full-fledged cologne saved for night.

BUSINESS CLOTHES FOR WOMEN

Remember the days when the preferred business look for women was the man-tailored dark skirt suit with the floppy bow tie? Such lock-step uniformity went the way of disco, and women everywhere shout hallelujah. Today the idea is situational dress, with a woman's choice of what to wear to work determined by her profession and the attitudes of her company. Fields such as finance, law, banking, insurance, and health call for traditional business clothing in almost every case, whereas industries that provide design or content—advertising, for example, or publishing, entertainment, fashion, and information technology—allow for more personal expression.

Whatever the environment, businesswomen have more room for choice than do men when it comes to dress. For men, a pair of pants, a shirt, decent shoes, and a jacket and tie are generally the most that have to be considered in any but the most nonconformist workplaces. Women, on the other hand, are able to choose from a broader range of colors and styles and to work endless variations on the overall look with jewelry and accessories.

This advantage aside, a woman's approach to office attire is the same as that for men: The unique culture of her workplace—and the expectations of the people with whom she does business—defines the borders of what is acceptable. While some companies have written codes of dress with very specific guidelines, many others do not. So how do you stay on safe ground? Simple. You discern the "rules" by observing over the course of a few weeks how your workmates and senior management dress. Meanwhile, keep your dress on the conservative side until you've had time to size up the standards. (See also Attitude and Adaptation, page 149.)

SIX KEY POINTS

Whether your workplace is stodgy and conservative or determinedly avant garde, there are some timeless axioms that always apply to dress:

- **KEEP IT UNDERSTATED.** Understatement—or allowing your clothes to speak without shouting—has always been the hallmark of the well-dressed. Yet this, too, is relative. What is considered too flashy by a conservative law firm is no doubt a far cry from what's too "out there" at a recording studio. Still, the philosophies of these very different environments have at least one thing in common: In both, bosses and coworkers alike may view veering wildly from the resident norm as an act of flippancy or even contempt—behavior that's unwelcome anywhere.

- **REPRESENT YOUR COMPANY.** Whenever you deal with people from outside, your clothes reflect on your company. No matter what the dress at the office, be prepared to look your best. What happens if you've worn your favorite casual outfit to work and your boss tells you a prospective customer is dropping by for a meeting? You might keep a change of clothes in your office for just such an emergency. A better solution is to dress every day to be prepared for any situation that comes your way.

- **KEEP IT NEAT AND CLEAN.** The blouse with the ripped seam and the trousers with the grease spot should stay in the closet until they can be mended and cleaned. The same goes for footwear, even on casual days: Dirty canvas shoes should be saved for gardening or puttering around the house, not for wearing to work. Obviously, clean clothes are just as essential in fields where standards of dress are the most relaxed (information technology and music, for two). Soiled jeans and an unironed T-shirt speak more of slovenliness and poor personal habits than of rebellion and cool.

- **DON'T REVEAL TOO MUCH.** Clothes that are too revealing are unsuitable in any workplace. Whether intentional or not, low-cut blouses, too-tight pants, and see-through fabrics send a sexual message. The smart business dresser knows that the key is to look authoritative, highly competent, and as if she knows what she is doing and can be relied upon to do it. Dress for the promotion you hope to get, not to look alluring.

- **DRESS FOR THE TIME OF DAY.** Arriving at work in clothes more suitable for evening is a bad idea. If you choose something dressier than usual because you have an important lunch, forget the black cocktail dress with the beadwork. Knowing which kinds of clothes are appropriate for daywear is one of the first lessons any woman in business should learn. A velvet, charmeuse silk, or lace shell under a suit jacket is perfectly fine, but a head-to-toe outfit in one of these fabrics should be worn only in evening.

- **DON'T BE A FASHION VICTIM.** Because your work clothes are the kind of investment that should last for several years, don't let what's hot be your guide. Besides, following a trend can be a giant mistake if it doesn't fit who you are. Bear in mind that many of the designer clothes pictured after the major fashion shows are intended to push design to the limit, and are rarely meant as daywear (or even evening wear, for that matter) for the average working woman. Instead of rushing to jump on the bandwagon, simply let what looks good on you be the deciding factor as you shop for clothes.

THE TRADITIONAL CODE

The traditional dress code has taken a beating ever since the Sixties, and things are changing at an ever-faster clip. Hats and gloves? Gone. The classic dark suit with the spread-collar blouse? On the endangered species list. The white-collared dress? Still a nice look, but too stuffy for most offices.

Be that as it may, the principles underlying the traditional dress code are still in place in most professional fields—to wit, that good taste is never showy, whether in color, fabric, style, accessories, hairstyle, or makeup. Yes, customs are rapidly changing, but the smart woman in business will ground herself in the traditional rules and then branch out from there.

Here's a basic wardrobe for almost any working woman to start with:

- A three-piece suit: jacket, trousers, and an interchangeable skirt
- A white or cream-colored blouse
- A sweater set
- A "status" silk scarf—standard size, 34" square
- A microfiber all-weather coat
- A good-quality handbag
- A pair of 1½"-heel black leather pumps
- A pair of good-quality loafer-style shoes
- Tights and/or stockings
- An umbrella (arriving for a meeting soaked isn't impressive)

To these you can add garments and accessories that will individualize your look without taking it outside of your workplace norm.

COLOR CONSIDERATIONS

When it comes to color, what is considered appropriate varies by region as much as professional field. As always, the smart dresser starts by taking her cues by observing the conventions in her area and her workplace. But she also knows something about the general perception of various colors.

Business
Clothes
for Women

- Navy blue, burgundy, black, charcoal gray, and taupe are the traditional colors of the businesswoman's wardrobe, with the darker hues worn through the winter. Neutral colors, or tonals, are preferable to pure colors—sea green over kelly green, for example, or peach over orange.
- As for other colors, red is strong and assertive—the reason it's known as a power color. Bright orange, magenta, and other loud and flashy colors cross the line into tackiness in conservative businesses if not worn with care.
- White was once saved for spring and summer and used only for blouses—not jackets, skirts, or slacks. But in the late 1990s so-called winter white (various shades of off-white) became trendy—an illustration of the new thinking that color has less to do with seasonality than fabric. Today white is considered appropriate in gabardine and crepe garments in winter.

COORDINATE AND ACCENT

Coordinating color in an outfit is equally important. For the more traditional look, start with basic business colors for the major garments and then accent them with brighter colors in small amounts—an eye-catching ensemble that ensures you won't fade into the background. A classic example is the paisley scarf used with a gray or camel suit. A brighter-colored blouse with complementary earrings, necklaces, and bracelets serves the same purpose and balances the overall look.

PATTERNS AND PRINTS

It's not easy to achieve a pleasing mix of patterns in different garments, so either use a single pattern or avoid patterns altogether. Remember that patterns can send messages: Flowered prints can look prissy, while stripes convey sportiness. When you're not sure, move toward small-scale plaids, checks, and dots over large-scale versions. Stay away from big, bold patterns, especially if you're petite—they can easily overwhelm you.

In general, prints are very much a matter of personal taste and are viewed much as people look at paintings—either loved or hated. In the workplace, they are best limited to dresses, blouses, and scarves. Prints are appropriate for jackets and pants only when very subtle. As for printed two-piece ensembles, a top and a skirt work better than a top and a pant.

WHAT'S YOUR BEST COLOR?

The simplest way to determine which colors are most flattering to you is to think in terms of warm versus cool, and the colors in their range of tones.

- **WARM COLORING.** A person with warm coloring (olive or gold skin tones) will look better in warm colors such as red, yellow, orange, and rust.
- **COOL COLORING.** Someone with cool coloring (light skin tones) will be flattered by cool colors—blue, lavender, and green.

Different tones of the same color will have a different effect on your skin. Blue, for example, runs all the way from navy blue, which is often nearly indistinguishable from black, to robin's egg blue, one of the gentlest pastels. Even if garments of a certain color don't suit you, you can still use the color to accent—in a blouse instead of a suit, for example, or in a pattern or accessory.

Finding your most flattering colors is as easy as holding a piece of clothing up to your face—or better still, wrapping it around your face in the privacy of the fitting room and studying how you look. You might also want to enlist a friend and solicit her advice. A flattering color will make your eye color more intense, your skin tone more vibrant, and give you an energetic look; an unflattering color will make your eyes look dull, your skin sallow, and your face tired. (If you have a tan, remember that when it fades you'll get a somewhat different reading.)

FABRICS

The enduring preference for natural fabrics is rooted in the fact that cotton, wool, silk, and linen breathe while keeping the wearer cool or warm. In contrast, the old polyesters had trouble breathing, turning sweaty and smelly in the process. The new microfibers are synthetics reborn, providing breathability, comfort, and ease of care. (Note: Always check the garment label for instructions on cleaning; surprisingly, cotton/spandex blends often require dry cleaning.)

While woven fabrics once cornered the market, knits became fashionable in the Eighties. Among the garments acceptable in the office today are the knit sweater constructed like a jacket, the knit dress with a knit jacket, and the tailored knit suit, all of them usually in cotton, wool, or silk blends.

The acceptance of synthetics and knits is particularly good news for working women: These fabrics that were once thought of as suitable only for casual wear can now go into the workplace depending on how they're styled. It's even better news for businesswomen who travel: A garment that blends a natural fiber with a synthetic is more flexible, easier to care for, and less seasonal, making it perfect for wearing on a trip that goes from chilly Boston to steamy Houston. New fabrics with a bit of stretch to them, such as spandex, can give a clean, fitted appearance without the need for expert tailoring.

The Wrinkle Test

Look for fabrics that wear well, are easy to care for, and drape well; avoid any that are stiff or too flimsy or sheer. To test for wrinkles, squeeze the fabric with your hand; hold it for a few seconds and then release. How long does it take to recover? Do the wrinkles fall out? If they don't, you may want to skip this piece of clothing. Wool knits, crepes and gabardines, microfibers, and cotton jersey generally wrinkle less and are easier to care for than linen (notorious for wrinkling but still coveted), silk, and garments with embroidery or beading, which are generally meant for evening.

Leather, Metallics, and Sheers

Leather in the workplace is largely worn by workers in fields where one wouldn't be caught dead without it, including media, recording, and fashion industries. But remember that a well-tailored leather skirt by Chanel is a far cry from a biker's leather jacket. In conservative workplaces, variations on leather are seen: a leather vest or leather trim may be fine, but showing up in a leather garment is appropriate only if your peers are known to do so. In many businesses, leather's renegade connotation puts it in the same class with body piercing and tattoos.

Metallics or other fabrics that glitter or shine aren't acceptable in most workplaces. Likwise, sheer fabrics are risky for the office because they inherently look suggestive, even when worn with undergarments. (The same goes for silk jersey, which can be too clingy and also tends to snag.) Stretched-lace T-shirts, worn under a jacket, are an exception; if the women senior partners at your office are wearing them, you can follow suit.

What About Fur?

If you want a fur coat, the first thing to determine is whether it is considered appropriate in your workplace. Look to the company leaders for your cue, and remember that making a mistake could be disastrous. What happens, for example, if on the first day of winter a new associate at a law firm dons her brand-new fox coat, only to learn after arriving at work that her firm represents an animal-rights organization? A faux pas of the first order.

SMART SHOPPING

Buying a business wardrobe is an investment. It is also expensive. But fashions can change before you know it, and the little frock you love so much today could be out of style in a year or two. One way around the problem is to solicit the aid of a "personal shopper" at a department or clothing store. These consultants will help you build a wardrobe by working with you to identify styles that look good, are appropriate for your workplace, and will stand the test of time. They can also help identify the color palette that suits you best. The service usually is paid for by an additional commission on the value of your purchases. Be aware, however, that some personal shoppers charge the customer a set fee. So that there's no discomfort at the checkout, make sure you know what the charge will be before engaging a personal shopper. (Note: Some personal shoppers will also help you choose business and personal gifts.)

If a personal shopper isn't available or you decide not to use one, try consulting regular salespeople, many of whom are well qualified to help you put together a wardrobe. First, visit several different stores and look at the clothing styles offered by each. Identify the styles you think match your personality and the demands of your job. Once you've made your choice, approach the store's personnel about your needs. The more specific you are in describing your needs and your office environment, the more they'll be able to help you.

NOTES ON ACCESSORIES

The wide range of accessories that you're able to select from gives you more leeway to achieve a look of authority and style. Choose them to reflect both your own style and that of your organization. Remember that accessories, conventional or not, project an image, and you want that image to be positive.

HANDBAGS

A quality handbag is a valuable accessory that need not break the bank. Focus first on neatness and functionality, making sure the bag is large enough to hold all the items you carry with you other than makeup—a day planner, for example. A good handbag is something most women can afford while making them feel good about themselves. An expensive brand may be hard on a working woman's budget, however, if a choice need be made, the investment doesn't compare to that of a top-of-the-line suit or watch.

> **THINGS TO AVOID**
> *Poorly made or badly designed handbags, which will downgrade your outfit; jeweled or sparkling bags are off-limits at all but the most nonconformist offices.*

BRIEFCASES

A good-quality, soft leather model is the most professional choice for a briefcase. Canvas and suede cases are acceptable in casual settings, with black nylon an alternative. To convey a uniform and sleek appearance, coordinate your briefcase and handbag, either by using the same materials or same colors.

One fashion change in the aftermath of the electronic revolution is that businesspeople no longer carry paper unless they must—meaning the briefcase's days may be numbered. Supplanting it is the protective laptop computer case, the purchase of which demands the same attention to good design and quality as you would devote to a briefcase. Built to make room for more than a laptop, these cases will accommodate pens, paper, a spare computer battery, a mouse, and a small handbag, which can be removed and used as necessary.

BELTS

When a woman's outfit requires a belt, the classic style is ½- to ¾-inch-wide leather, but whatever width is most becoming should be the deciding factor. Buckles can be metal or leather in any simple, quiet shape; if metal, match it to other metal—earrings, necklaces, watch bands, buttons. The belt's color should be harmonious with shoe and garment colors. When you wear a printed dress, make sure the belt picks up one of the visible colors in the print; check in the mirror from a few feet away to see whether it does. Wear belts loose enough to ride with the waistband of your skirt, not above it.

SCARVES

A scarf can heighten focus on the face or provide visual relief in a monochromatic outfit, with silk and silk blends—which hang better than cotton—the preferred fabric for day. Scarves can also dress up a casual outfit or soften a tailored look. Coordinate a multicolored scarf to your ensemble by making sure it picks up a color in the outfit.

A large silk scarf—the classic is 34 inches square—looks smart under a jacket and over a jewel-neck sweater; drape it around the shoulders of your blouse or top and knot it in front. A scarf also looks good tied as an ascot under a blouse, with or without a jacket. Some stores sell a ring to hold the ends of a scarf together, which can make for a neater look.

- The many ways to tie a scarf around one's neck go in and out of fashion. In the Seventies, the large, drooping bow was the pioneering business-woman's choice, while in the late Nineties simpler styles are favored. Choose the shape of a scarf according to how you plan to tie it. (Note: You'll find that salespeople are a great resource for teaching you a variety of scarf looks. They also often have available small instruction booklets.)

JEWELRY

If you have a passion for jewelry, curb it during the workday—at traditional offices, at least. Keep in mind that jewelry should accent, not take center stage, meaning you should let nothing dangle, jangle, sparkle, or be gaudy. (See also Tattoos and Piercings, page 160.)

- **EARRINGS.** Simple button earrings in silver, gold, and pearl are classic because they harmonize well with jacket outfits. Diamond, pearl, or gold studs or small drops are also always correct. Hoops that are hollow are lighter and more comfortable to wear, while heavy earrings will stretch your earlobes over time. Another consideration: large clip-ons can make talking on the telephone difficult.

  Make earrings compatible in size and shape with a necklace.

  If you wear glasses, small earrings that won't compete with your frames are the best choice.

> **THINGS TO AVOID**
> *At conservative offices, putting studs or hoops in more than two piercings per ear*

- **NECKLACES.** Two necklace styles are traditional for business wear—small-scale silver or gold chains or classic (i.e., small) pearls in white or off-white. Let the neckline of the garment decide the shape: V-shaped neckline, V-shape necklaces; rounded neckline, rounded necklace. To coordinate a colored necklace with your outfit, make sure its color is repeated somewhere—in a print, the belt, or the skirt or blouse color.

> **THINGS TO AVOID**
> *Large faux pearls, a look too bold for work; also avoid heavy pendant necklaces, which can hit the table when you bend down at meetings*

- **RINGS.** With simplicity as the guiding principle, the maximum number of rings for traditional business wear is one per hand (wedding and engagement count as one ring).

> **THINGS TO AVOID**
> *Large sparkling stones, which are never appropriate at most offices unless they are set in an engagement ring*

- **BROOCHES AND PINS.** Choose either a brooch, pin, or a necklace; in a traditional workplace, understatement is key, and it's best not to wear any of these adornments together. Brooches and pins should also be coordinated to jacket shape, buttons, and neckline. Geometric edges go well with square or vee necks; curved edges go with jewel or round necks.

- **WATCHES.** Two kinds of bands are preferred in conservative offices: leather in black or brown or metal in matte stainless steel, silver, gold, or a mix of both. (Match the metal of your watch to that of your other jewelry.) Most jeweled watches can look gaudy, but small diamond chips are fine. Sport watches have become more acceptable so long as they're not the heavy deep-sea diver type. A watch worn with a bracelet is fine, but a watch with multiple bracelets is not.

EYEGLASSES

Now considered a fashion accessory, glasses allow businesswomen a way of differentiating themselves in the workplace. The trend was once toward big frames but now has moved to small. Conservative frames (tortoiseshell and wire in particular) are the best choice, even with sunglasses, since on the very day you decide to wear your leopard-print sunglasses with rhinestones you could be called out to a business lunch—all the more reason to keep an all-purpose pair of glasses in your desk drawer.

To keep your glasses from competing with your jewelry, choose post earrings over hoops; hoops will echo the shape and make for too much adornment. (A simple necklace may also be worn with glasses, but if you have doubts about how it looks, let your glasses be your jewelry.) Follow the same metal to metal rule that applies to watches: gold frames with gold necklaces and bracelets, silver frames with silver.

FOOTWEAR

Earning the working woman's eternal gratitude, shoemakers have designed styles that allow her to be both fashionable and comfortable. Shoes no longer have to look orthopedic to keep back and arch problems at bay. Beyond this development, the traditional taboos against open-toed shoes, backless shoes, slingbacks, and other informal styles still exist in conservative workplaces but have gone by the board in most others. Figuring out what's undesirable in most offices is simple: clogs, hiking boots, boat shoes, or chunky, thick-soled shoes. Knowing what's appropriate anywhere is equally easy: the pump.

PUMPS

The classic business pump has a 1- to 1½-inch-high heel (and the wider, the more comfortable), but any becoming height can be appropriate depending on the workplace. Extreme spikes (3 inches or higher) and flat heels look the least professional. Shoe color is less of an issue than it once was, but the traditional business colors remain black, navy, chocolate brown, and taupe. (Note: Very inconspicuous trim details can be appropriate but might limit the number of outfits that go with the shoes.) Whatever the color, under no circumstances should you wear shoes that are dirty, scuffed, or have worn-down heels.

> **THINGS TO AVOID**
> *In conservative workplaces (with the exception of casual days), white or other bright colors, ankle straps, sandals, wedges, fancy cutout shapes, and materials such as canvas and plastic; extreme patterns, including leopard or zebra, bright gold, or metallic are appropriate only in the most unconventional offices*

Save heels over 1½ inches to wear with skirts; they look too dressy for the office when worn with slacks. Other choices for pants are an Oxford-style shoe and a sleek leather loafer that covers the instep.

BOOTS

Boots are acceptable in some workplaces but aren't part of the classic business image. There are changes afoot, however. New boot styles designed with commuters in mind are cross-functional: The upper portion is less casual, while the Vibrum soles grip the pavement securely. These new styles make it possible to wear boots to the office without having to change to heels.

> **THINGS TO AVOID**
> *Ankle boots with a skirt*

When wearing boots, be sure there's no gap between the bottom of your skirt and the boot tops. And keep boots clean—especially in northern climates,

*Business
Clothes
for Women*

where salt and mud can be a real problem. Many women keep a pair of shoes at the office or carry them in a tote bag to change into at the office.

ATHLETIC SHOES

Athletic shoes at work are a definite *never* except at the most nonconformist companies and on some casual days. To wear them to or from the office, however, is fine, especially in cities where heels become a problem when negotiating sidewalks and public transportation. Even then, the shoes should be clean and good-looking.

STAYING WELL-GROOMED

Grooming is every bit as important as what you wear, from tip to toe. Hair, in fact, has proved its potential to make a statement as well as or more strongly than clothes do. The amount of makeup applied sends an unavoidable message, too—and in most workplaces, understatement in both is key.

HAIR

A woman will attract attention with her hair when she has a flattering cut or healthy, shiny hair that simply begs to be admired. (A tip: Switching shampoos and conditioners once every week or so will keep hair from looking weighted down and limp.) While extreme styles are out of place in most workplaces, it has become more acceptable to have a kind of signature look for the hair—the wet look, for one.

What about length? There's no longer a true rule, but on the job, hair should be kept out of the eyes: Tuck it behind your ears, pull it back in a ponytail, or pull it out of your eyes with a barrette. Hair bands will work, but be careful: These look good on some people but make many women look like schoolgirls, which can read as inexperience.

As for hair ornaments, simple is best—a neat clip or a barrette. Unusual ornaments are risky unless you're a senior vice-president who has earned the right to be a little au courant. The clamps that create an instant up-swept twist are also popular and make for a nice professional look.

> **THINGS TO AVOID**
> *Strangely colored (excepting auburn and the like) or oddly streaked hair, along with extreme cuts—lopped off on one side, for example—unless this is the norm in your workplace; too-showy hair clips, pins, and bows*

MAKEUP

As a rule, use a light touch—makeup should enhance, not dominate. Extreme eye makeup, very unusual lip color, a lot of lip liner that is in obvious contrast to the lipstick—these are poor choices in most workplaces.

As with dress styles, makeup styles change, and you'll need to update yours accordingly. As of the late Nineties, a neutral palate has been the favored look. At the same time, don't trust everyone wielding a makeup brush to show you your best looks—often they want to teach you the latest trends when what you want is something else. Keep foundations light. Concealer is especially important today because businesswomen are more conscious than ever of circles under the eyes, which are exaggerated by the harsh light in most offices; just be sure to choose a high-quality concealer.

> **THINGS TO AVOID**
> *In more traditional workplaces, avoid extreme makeup fads and anything that looks artificial; when using eye shadow, avoid glitter, frost, and unnatural colors such as pink, green, or blue; as for lip liners, one that's visible outside the lipstick looks unprofessional in most offices.*

If you don't have time for a full makeup routine each morning, at least apply a little lipstick, which adds color and a lift. Go with a subdued lip color—one that is just a few shades darker than your natural lip color. A neutral gloss applied over moisturizer is also a good idea. Look for one that falls somewhere between gloss and matte, since glossy lipsticks fade quickly and leave messy imprints of your lips on coffee cups at meetings.

NAILS

The best length for nails in most business environments is just over the tip of the finger. The appropriateness of talons, extreme colors (black, blue, purple, neon), and fake nails decorated with designs or pictures is in direct proportion to the conservatism of your workplace, running the gamut from simple/conservative to gaudy/unconventional. Clear nails with off-white tips are the best choice if you're uncertain. In conservative offices, it's not so much the painting of nails that matters but the colors that are chosen: a clear red, an understated pink, or clear polish are all fine. Still, remember that red on a simply manicured hand is one thing while bright red on talons is another.

PERFUME

Like it or not, the perfume you wear to the office in these times of extreme sensitivity may be offending someone's nose. At the same time, there has been an appreciable jump in the number of people who claim they are "allergic" to most smells in general, especially manufactured ones. But you don't have to be cowed into going to work scent-free, especially if you consider a scent to which you've grown accustomed as a part of your image. Just make sure the scent is light and clean, not one of the more exotic or muskier "romantic" blends more appropriate for evening. And use it sparingly: If your scent still lingers in the room when you leave someone's office, you're wearing too much.

CASUAL DAYS

Might "casual Fridays" not be long for this world? That question doesn't ask whether people will start dressing up on Fridays, but whether they'll be going casual every day of the week—something that has already happened in at least half of American workplaces. What once seemed a complex issue is today merely part of the situational-dressing philosophy: Adhere to the dress standards of your company, adapting them as necessary for the people with whom you do business. "Casual," after all, runs the gamut from jeans to khakis and blazers to the garments of the Italian designer of the moment.

Regardless of your company culture, casual items are not the ones you wear to mow the lawn (for the time being, at least) but rather those you might wear to dinner with your neighbors on the weekend. For lack of a better standard, the following items would be judged either acceptable or unacceptable in a conservative business such as finance or law.

ACCEPTABLE

- A casual blazer and a T-shirt, with a neat belt and a neat pair of loafers, and perhaps socks
- Open-toe pumps
- Tailored pants or Bermuda-length shorts
- Jumper-shape dress (long or short) in corduroy or other casual fabric
- Twin sweater set with khaki trousers and canvas shoes
- Tunic sweater with wash linen pants

UNACCEPTABLE

- T-shirts with slogans, sayings, or cartoon characters
- Tatty jeans
- Spandex miniskirts and strapless, stretchy bandeau tops
- Shorts or skirts shorter than 3 inches above the knee
- Exercise clothing, sweatpants, or sweat suits
- Tank tops

FASHION EMERGENCY KIT

The smart business dresser keeps a stash of emergency items in her office, ready to dress up an outfit or execute a quick fix. (Tip: Flight kits from airlines or sample gift kits from cosmetic companies are good for holding small items.) Here's a checklist:

- wash-and-dry towelettes
- magic marker for touching up shoe scuffs
- lint roller
- tape to hold up skirt hems
- safety pins
- small sewing kit
- extra knit top (black or off-white)
- neutral-colored jacket
- extra pair of hose
- brushes for hair, clothes, shoes
- spot remover
- nail polish—clear for panty-hose runs, your current color to repair chips
- lipstick and compact
- eyeglasses with a conservative frame
- static guard
- toothbrush and toothpaste

AFTER DARK

Evening business functions allow women more opportunity to step out from the pack. First, determine whether the event you're attending is a short-dress cocktail affair or a formal occasion and then proceed accordingly. Just as companies may have a hard and fast rule on slacks for day, they may have an equally strict rule for slacks at night. Find out from someone who has a long history with the company about the best course to take.

When choosing what to wear, take special care with how you'll be perceived, erring on the side of safety. Remember that at evening functions you'll be sized up by managing partners and their spouse or dates—in fact, it's often said you're truly dressing for the significant other.

A NOTE FOR TRAVELERS: Pack a jacket that will cross comfortably from day to evening in case you're invited to a soirée. A dressy top or jacket that will work with a daytime black pant or skirt is a particularly good idea. You may also need to take a dressy handbag with you for the evening.

Business Clothes for Women

WHITHER THE OLD TABOOS?

At what time of year, exactly, are you not supposed to wear white shoes? Did your mother say after Easter, or was it Memorial Day? A few taboos and customs hold fast, while most others have either relaxed or fallen by the wayside on the road to sartorial correctness.

SEASONAL COLOR

The answer to the white shoes question? Apply common sense. If the shoes are strictly summer-wear—white straw sandals, for example—you might want to follow the Memorial Day to Labor Day mandate. This seasonal injunction against white applies only to fabrics and materials—and loosely, at that. White suede pumps in November? Sure, if they go with your outfit. The white gabardine skirt is fine for winter, too. (See also Color Considerations, page 167.)

- Lighter colors are more acceptable at all times of year and are not limited to spring and summer, especially in seasonless fabrics. Forest green, for example, was considered a fall and winter color but is now perfectly fine for a linen springtime garment.

FABRICS

Objections to certain fabrics for business clothing have largely disappeared, with style a more important issue than "natural versus synthetic" or "woven versus knit."

- As recently as the early 1980s, knitwear was perceived as too casual for the traditional business look. But after top designers put knit suits on the map, the attitude changed. Knit also gained favor because it doesn't wrinkle, making it ideal for business travel.
- Linen is still mostly worn in spring and summer, but as a linen blouse paired with a winter jacket it is perfectly acceptable in winter.
- Velvet is still a fall and winter fabric, for both shoes and clothes. At one time velvet was never to be worn to the office but is now acceptable in the correct seasons; the barrier was broken after velvet began to be used as trimming on coats and collars.

SUEDE AND PATENT LEATHER

First, suede: It is no longer worn just in fall and winter, yet it remains seasonal for handbags. Second, patent leather: For shoes and handbags it is no longer a spring-and-summer-only choice. Patent leather in black and dark browns and other earth colors (but not bright ones) have traditionally been the colors of choice, with white patent leather reserved for little girls. But guess what? White patent leather roared into style in 1999, as if to prove that whatever has been designated taboo will eventually have its day.

PART IV

EXECUTIVE ETIQUETTE

A business equation for the times: Smart management equals tending to workers' needs, equals keeping them happy, equals lower turnover and increased productivity. Sum total: Higher profit margins and a workplace that runs like the proverbial well-oiled machine.

Enlightened companies are moving in new directions, focusing more on the individual and viewing human capital as a resource to be, if not coddled, treated with respect and understanding. In light of this evolution, the following pages consider the responsibilities and obligations of managers to their subordinates, both in day-to-day behavior and the shaping of company policy. In many cases, these principles—more important than ever as the workforce diversifies not only in sex and nationality but in attitude and expectations—apply as much to the CEO and the junior-level team leader as to the middle manager. They include setting high ethical standards and teaching by example, being accountable for one's actions, forgoing manipulation, and choosing plain English over corporate-speak. A separate chapter addresses the manager's relationship to support staff.

It was magnate Sam Walton who called executives "the servants of those we supervise"—a catchphrase implying neither fawning nor saintliness, but an acknowledgment of the importance of accommodating workers to the successful conduct of business.

CHAPTER 14

THE MANAGER'S RESPONSIBILITIES

It could be said that the boss in the ivory tower, if not a thing of the past, belongs to a dwindling breed. Over the last two decades the trend in management has been away from the command-and-control model, wherein a captain directs the workings of a complex machine from on high, to a less hierarchical structure and the diffusion of responsibility.

If bosses aren't what they used to be, neither are their employees. A strong economy and plentiful jobs have given rise to new attitudes among American workers, especially those who are in demand in such hot-button fields as information technology. The relationship between boss and employee is increasingly seen as a two-way street: Just as a company is going to reengineer, merge, or do whatever else is necessary to compete globally, so workers of any age are saying that their needs must be seen to as well. Many join corporations with a contingent, if unspoken, commitment—"So long as I'm treated well and can do better here than anywhere else, I'll stay."

NEW ATTITUDES

Even the loyal go-getter who is determined to scramble up the corporate ladder may no longer think a paycheck is enough. The nine-to-five job is progressively viewed as something to be kept in proportion—an integral part, but not the ultimate goal, of an existence that incorporates family, leisure-time activities, and personal pursuits. Understanding this reality, smart managers strike an unspoken bargain: If employees pull their weight and give their all during work hours, their needs will be met in return, whether they involve taking maternity or paternity leave or telecommuting from home.

In concert with this new attitude, enlightened top-level executives, middle managers, and supervisors of any stripe tackle everything they undertake in a straightforward yet sensitive way: the hiring of new employees, the setting of standards for job performance, the difficult task of firing. This approach, grounded in honesty and clear communication, is all the more necessary in a time when savvy employees are quick to spot hypocrisy. Managers worth their salt also bear the responsibility of motivating employees, inspiring them, and by their own actions setting a standard of behavior that will trickle down to the most junior levels. (See also The Manager's Obligations, page 200; Exemplary Bosses, pages 106, 111, 122; and Difficult Bosses, pages 116, 117, 119.)

SETTING STANDARDS

At least two kinds of standards are expected in every workplace: 1) ethical standards, which go the very heart of behavior in the workplace—day-to-day dealings and decision-making that are informed by values, character, and respect; and 2) job performance standards, essential to increasing a company's productivity and profitability.

SETTING AN EXAMPLE

As leaders, managers set an example by their own business dealings and behavior. Good examples aren't necessarily conveyed to employees through announcements in the interoffice newsletter ("We are proud to say we've taken the high road in the Weidmann dispute . . .") but by always making the principled choice, whether disciplining an employee caught pilfering office supplies or forgoing a questionable tax deduction. Smart managers understand that their own and the company's integrity are going to become apparent to employees over time. A consistent viewpoint on ethical conduct is the unwritten counterpart to the policy manual, communicating "This is how we do things."

A message of this kind is all the more important in a time when a corporate slip of any kind can end in a lawsuit. Doing what's right should be done as a matter of course, but what's "right" must be perfectly clear to employees so that they won't plead ignorance. Vagueness could increase the likelihood of unhappy workers taking legal action if they've done something that warrants firing.

DEALING WITH OFFENSES

When standards are violated, it's your duty as a manager to guide the offender back to the right path. However serious the offense—dressing inappropriately, smelling of liquor at 10 o'clock in the morning, making sexually suggestive remarks to a coworker, or leaking a confidential bit of information—have a heart-to-heart talk with the person to discuss how to rectify the problem. Hear the person out, be understanding, and stay calm—but deliver your message

"THE BEST PEOPLE"

I t is often said that "the best people want to work with the best people." What a company stands for is important in an employee's eyes, and an organization that maintains a high ethical standard—and is a good corporate citizen in the bargain—says something about the caliber of everyone who works there. In turn, the more pride employees have in their companies, the more productive and contented they become. Creating such an environment requires that management set standards of behavior, let them be known (see The Policies and Procedures Manual, page 196), and teach by example.

The best managers aspire to ethics that are based on values, not just on compliance with such legalities as the Occupational Health and Safety Act (OSHA) and the Employment Opportunity Act. Yet today's stream of news stories about misconduct at the highest levels of business might lead observers to conclude that a lackadaisical attitude toward ethics is not the exception but rather the rule. How to explain, then, the dramatic rise in the number of ethics officers in companies? (Ethics officers are watchdogs whose job is to make sense of ethically questionable situations in the workplace and then enlighten people about the consequences of their actions.) Cynics view this trend as a case of the fox guarding the henhouse: A 1991 change in sentencing guidelines allows companies convicted of committing any white-collar crime to receive reduced fines if they've put comprehensive ethics programs in place. The presence of corporate ethics officers aside, the best people see compliance with a code of ethics as value-based, not forced.

---

loud and clear: "What you've done is against company policy, and you must not do it again." At times, it also has to be pointed out that a repetition will be grounds for termination.

Many companies make it possible for workers to consult employee assistance programs, which aid them in overcoming such problems as substance abuse. Some of these programs are under the auspices of state agencies, others of the company itself. If you believe a subordinate's poor job performance is caused by a drug, alcohol, or gambling habit, such programs are one route to a solution. (It goes without saying that the matter should be kept confidential among you, your subordinate, and whoever is approving the expenditure.) At many companies, the benefits program subsidizes all or part of the ensuing treatment.

JOB-PERFORMANCE STANDARDS

Standards of another kind are those that measure job performance. In some cases, these are cut and dried: A sales company, for example, may set a mini-

The Manager's Responsibilities

mum quota for its salespeople, which clearly sets out what is expected from each. Many other people are in lines of work that don't lend themselves so easily to gauging performance—the administrative assistant who has multiple duties, the editor in a publishing house who slogs away at a manuscript day after day, the graphic designer at a small record company who acts as a jack-of-all-trades until he's called on to deliver an album cover.

In these grayer areas, a good manager devises a means by which he and his employees can measure whatever productivity is required to satisfy the needs of the company's bottom line. It is the manager's responsibility to make sure his employees have a concrete notion of what is expected of them, whether it is written down or simply conveyed and reinforced through his day-to-day interaction with an individual or a team. (See Make a List, page 207.) Even the most amorphous kind of work can be measured by quantity (the amount of work produced) and timeliness (how quickly it is done). Setting goals based on these will give a reasonable picture of performance.

To Evaluate Performance

A good company sets explicit goals for itself (to improve productivity in a certain area, for instance, or to lower outside costs to subcontractors) and then spells out the employee's role in meeting them. The gauge of success? The performance review, the source of much hand-wringing and debate. There are generally two types of job reviews:

- **The Once-A-Year Appraisal.** In most large organizations, appraisals are done once a year and are based on numerical rankings from 1 to 4—the coveted (and rarely awarded) 1 meaning "superior performer"; the feared 4 meaning "not meeting objectives" or, in the language of the floor, "outta here." These appraisals have been found by many forward-thinking companies to be wanting, and very much separated from their purpose.
- **The Continuous Appraisal.** Ideally, the review process seeks to make sure an employee does her job (and well, at that) and develops in a particular way. So it stands to reason that the best appraisals are those given informally and frequently—short review sessions at opportune times and constructive criticism or praise at others (a gentle calling-onto-the-carpet when a worker has handled a customer's request less than politely, a pat on the back when she has excelled at writing a report). Continuous appraisals tie in with the need of companies to focus more on the individual.

Performance appraisals need not be an either/or proposition. While some companies do away with the numerical ranking altogether, others use it as the culmination of the continuous review, with the rationale that last year's 3 needs to be told she's moving to a 4 so that she can turn things around before it's too late—the number acting as, in the words of one executive, "a two-by-four that's going to get someone's attention."

EVALUATION SESSIONS

Before you set up an evaluation session, give the employee plenty of advance notice that you want to talk about his work, so he can prepare any notes or thoughts he may have. Self-appraisals in writing are particularly revealing and useful in helping identify any gaps in performance.

- **MINIMIZE YOUR AUTHORITY.** You'll want to talk *with* the person you're reviewing, not *to* him, and to minimize the trappings of authority. Sessions will feel more informal if you sit at a table with the employee or beside him in a chair; your desk is a symbolic divide. Ask a question first so that the employee opens the discussion: "So how are things going?" will get the ball rolling. Listen carefully to any complaints and don't let your body language and expressions make him think you're merely waiting patiently to begin your critique.
- **DON'T OVERLOOK ANY WEAKNESSES.** If you know the employee is coming up short in some regard, you're doing him no favors by not saying so. In effect, your review is part of his training (training being the obligation of any company to its employees), and unless you point out a flaw, his career could be affected down the road. Tell him you want him to succeed and that you think he certainly will, but a particular shortcoming needs to be worked on for the benefit of both the company and himself.
- **BE POSITIVE AND TACTFUL.** Whenever possible, couch any criticism in positive terms so as not to undermine the employee's confidence.

THE 360° EVALUATION

Supplanting the traditional performance appraisal in many companies is the 360° evaluation, by which employees and bosses alike are anonymously judged by their peers, their supervisors, and their subordinates; only in the case of the boss' evaluation does the employee know who is saying what. This two-way feedback gives employees the sense that their voices are being heard while lessening the feeling that they are at the mercy of one person. Another plus: Because 360° assessments are usually monitored by someone outside the company, such as a consultant or a trainer, they are more objective.

Say, for example, the person is a researcher who gets so immersed in his work that he overdoes it, making it impossible to keep to the schedule. Tell him, "You're the best researcher we have, and that's part of the problem. As much as we'd like to delve as deeply as we can into a subject, we have to make do with what we can and still make our deadlines. I know it will be hard for you, but I also know you can do it." If, however, the problem is one that might require professional help—a drinking or drug problem, for example—urge him to take advantage of any employee assistance or counseling programs (see page 185), the fees for which are usually paid by the company.

- **PRAISE HIS STRONG POINTS.** At some point during the session, touch on the employee's general strengths and say how much you appreciate them. Wrap up the session by reassuring him that you value his work and then end by complimenting him on a strong point: "Your punctuality and willingness to work late are really appreciated, you know."

WRITTEN APPRAISALS

Unfortunately, the standard performance appraisal form is often written in such a way that it is irrelevant to actual performance, a document rife with noble aims and unreachable goals. Asking a manager to judge how well a lower-level employee "drives corporate change" or "contributes to shareholder value" is questionable at best. When you, as a manager, are faced with such a form, you can detour around the brick wall of jargon by creating a separate worksheet written in plain English. List criteria based only on what the person actually does day to day and then rate his performance accordingly. This gives you a clearer picture of his overall abilities, which will in turn determine his rating. An associate editor, for example, might be rated on points as fine as sentence structure, knowledge of grammar, and bringing coherence to a muddled manuscript.

Once you've rated an employee in these terms, graft the information onto the official form, tailoring it as necessary to fit into a particular category. Challenged with having to come up with how someone has looked after the interest of shareholders, you could pen something on the order of "Chris' exceptional writing skills ensure that our products are going to compete in the marketplace and increase profits." Human Resources will be satisfied, and Chris' performance will have been fairly appraised.

WHEN YOU HIRE

Hiring is handled differently in different workplaces, but it often falls to a company hiring officer or the head of a department. Whatever the system, having more than one person interview the applicant is the best route to take. As for the interview itself, the finer points of the process could fill a small book, and in fact do: If you haven't been trained in the art, buy a reputable guide to learn the basic dos and don'ts. A key thing you'll learn: Avoid becoming too enthusiastic. You want to be personable, of course, and a poker face isn't necessary, but you don't want to set the interviewee up for disappointment.

Another must: Read the resume. It's only respectful to do so, and not reviewing the resume beforehand might not only put the person at an unfair advantage but could hurt his feelings as well.

A good way to learn more about a prospect for a mid- to senior-level position is to take him to lunch after or during the interview. This will give you a more rounded picture of how well he handles himself socially. Sometimes, lunching with the interviewee will tip the balance between him and an otherwise equally qualified candidate.

TELLING CURRENT EMPLOYEES

If it's common knowledge around the office that you are looking to fill a new job from outside and no staff jobs are in jeopardy, employees who see a string of well-dressed strangers being escorted in day after day will pay it little mind. If, however, everyone suspects that someone's going to have to go to make room for a newcomer, do your interviewing over breakfast or lunch at a "neutral location" to avoid lurching the gossip mill into action. Keeping the process under wraps is important for another reason: If the interviewee is currently employed and word gets back to his boss, it could have a negative effect on his career if he ends up staying where he is.

MAKING AN OFFER

Inviting someone to come work with you is a pleasant task, infinitely easier than telling someone he didn't make the grade. Do it first by phone and then by letter. The phone call shortens what might be an agonizing wait for the prospect. Putting the job offer in writing makes it seem all the more real and concrete, and an event this important deserves to be documented on paper.

A job-offer letter will not only confirm the decision but invite the applicant to a meeting to negotiate salary and other practicalities. The letter should also acknowledge that the applicant may not accept the offer; for this reason, it should be sent soon enough to allow the applicant a reasonable waiting period before he makes up his mind. (See Job-Offer Letters, page 337.)

Rejecting the Prospect

When telling an interviewee that he or she is not being hired, make sure you do it yourself, whether by letter, by phone, or, in the case of someone who came within an inch of getting the job and was confident that he would, by asking him to your office. If he is underqualified or overqualified, the task will be fairly easy: Be specific about why he's not yet ready at this stage of his career or why his experience would be underused in the job. However, if his personal qualities didn't measure up, don't go into detail. In a time of constant litigation, a minimalist approach is the wisest choice.

WHEN YOU FIRE

There's no question that firing is the task a manager hates most—or, at least, should be. A stream of books on difficult bosses, news reports of rich CEOs wielding the ax with glee, and horror stories of slave-driving top executives who make life impossible for their employees before dismissing them at the drop of a hat paint a sorry picture of the abuse of power. The fact that such people can succeed is an outrage. Thankfully, the fact is that most managers are the kind of people who are going to feel human compassion for anyone who is fired and trepidation about performing the task.

Each Case Unique

Some cases are worse than others. Just as people are fired for many reasons, their reaction to being fired is variable. Consider these firees:

- The loyal worker who has three kids in college and has devoted his life to the company is not only having his job taken away but is also losing his sense of self, his peace of mind, his standing at home.
- The young, single employee who knows there are plenty of jobs in his field, feels he has the world on a string, and welcomes the chance to leave a company he's not so happy with anyway.
- The junior-level employee who has lived for three or four years with the constant threat of being laid off but realizes that getting out from under the black cloud could be the best thing that ever happened.

Another part of the equation is that each of these people may have been let go because his job was eliminated because of cuts or reengineering, because his performance didn't measure up, or because he committed a fireable offense.

Accordingly, the manager's task is going to range from slightly awkward to uncomfortable to extremely difficult.

THE LAID-OFF LOYAL WORKER

In these days of reengineering, many employees are let go merely because their jobs have been eliminated. Firing under these circumstances is the task a compassionate manager dreads most, one that doesn't come easier with practice. First, make it clear to the person that it is the job that's being eliminated, not him (something he'll already understand, but which needs to be reiterated). Then praise his performance and tell him how much you regret the hard realities of business today and that you'll be happy to write a letter of recommendation as he searches for a new job.

Lessen the angst by proceeding as follows:

- Deliver the news quickly and straightforwardly. Grit your teeth and try your best not to get sentimental, which you'll be tempted to do.
- Don't rush him out. You owe it to the person to devote sufficient time to help him recover from the shock. Don't protect yourself from the unpleasantness by cutting the session short—think of his feelings, not yours.
- Do it late in the day, so that any unpleasant reactions can be managed after hours. Friday is the best day, since the person will have the weekend to let the reality of the situation soak in.
- Do it in private. Firing over lunch is a particularly bad idea: While you may think you are softening the blow, you are putting the employee in the awkward position of having to deal with bad news in public.
- Do not delegate firing to a subordinate. Having the courage to do it yourself is the mark of a good boss.

Many large companies today arrange for outplacement centers, where employees can be set up in their own workstations (equipped with a computer with Internet access and a phone) for up to eight weeks. Job counselors are also made available for this period. An official package is given to employees that explains severance arrangements and instructs them on the use of the outplacement center.

FIRING FOR POOR PERFORMANCE

If the elimination of a job is not the reason for firing, poor performance usually is. A series of warnings are naturally in order in this case, with performance appraisals and individual consultations making it clear to the employee exactly how he has to improve. If performance continues to fall short, it is your responsibility to issue a concrete warning that the employee's job is in jeopardy unless a certain standard is met within a certain time frame.

If firing becomes necessary, get straight to the point when the person sits down in your office. A good boss will have long before gone over any shortcomings, and they need not be repeated. If the employee still questions the dismissal, briefly recap the reasons as constructively as possible and don't get into personal issues. Focus instead on severance arrangements and any other particulars involved in the termination.

DELIVERING BAD NEWS

Bad news could be the death of a key executive, the announcement of a layoff or sale of the company, a plant closing, a poor earnings report to shareholders, or even the beginning of a project that will require a lengthy period of overtime. As you, as a manager or supervisor, decide how to address bad news, keep two facts in mind:

First, the chance that your announcement will be a complete surprise is small. All executives are to some degree isolated, and they often fail to comprehend the pervasiveness of rumor and gossip within their own companies. Employees are quick to sense trouble, and if they can't get straight answers within the workplace, they may turn to others, including the press. So don't hide or delay bad news or minimize its seriousness. Straight talk is called for, as soon as is feasible. Don't delegate the responsibility for in-house delivery of bad news to low-level supervisors or PR people, and never use memos. Whether you hold a companywide meeting or smaller departmental meetings, be prepared to answer questions and to explain when you cannot answer.

Second, it is foolish to demand "business as usual" after a bad news announcement. For example, if you announce that your company is planning to close several offices but you cannot yet say who will be affected, don't expect your employees to go happily back to their routine duties. Morale will be affected, so it is important to be sensitive to the feelings of all. Don't be like the corporate cost-cutter who announced the moving of a factory to an offshore location and in the next breath informed his factory staff that they would be expected to train the foreign workers who would soon be taking their jobs. Also, don't try to put a "positive spin" on patently bad news. Employees, stockholders, and suppliers always deserve to be treated as mature adults.

A BRIEF NOTE ABOUT TIMING: There is really no best time to deliver bad news, but it amounts to adding insult to injury to schedule a bad news meeting outside regular business hours, or at the tail end of the workday.

NOTE: When firing someone under these circumstances, it is vital to keep a written record of all the steps you take and the problems you have raised with the employee. Log the dates and times of meetings and then write a summary of each so that there will be no question of what has transpired.

Firing for an Offense

A third category of firing comes when someone has committed an act that qualifies as a fireable offense, such as sexual harassment. While you should stay cool while explaining to the person exactly why such behavior is grounds for dismissal, the person who has asked for sexual favors, for example, or committed sexual harassment of even a semi-egregious kind should receive a clear message from you: In so many words, "So long, farewell, good luck, and get out." It is necessary to let it be known to the company at large that there are certain things that will not be tolerated.

SETTING COMPANY POLICY

Just how a company fulfills the responsibility of letting its employees know what is expected of them in terms of conduct and appearance differs from workplace to workplace. Some provide employees with manuals that leave no stone unturned, setting standards for office cleanliness and laying out the dress code garment by garment. Other companies put certain policies in writing and convey others by example, although the wisdom of doing the former is becoming more and more apparent: In these litigious times, executives who once set standards primarily through their actions are now driven to make policies official in writing, spelling out everything to the letter.

Office Dating

Many companies lay out policies on office dating in detail; others write down some things and leave the rest as unspoken understandings; others make policy only on harassment and discrimination; but none can ignore this critical issue. The most important question is whether a supervisor can date a subordinate, which is off-limits virtually everywhere. In any case, the smart manager approaches such problems situation by situation, sitting down to talk with the person concerned. While being candid, he speaks in a way so that it becomes *our* problem, not *your* problem, and sorts things out in that context: "Ralph, we know that your relationship with Cathy is your business and hers, and ten years ago nobody would have thought anything about it. But today we have no choice but to transfer one of you to another department." (See also Women and Men Together, page 126.)

DRESS

Even the most conservative company must face the fact that a whole generation that wears what it wants is coming into the workforce. In these more cautious days, when meeting in singles bars is largely a thing of the past, many workers dress to attract others, which often means veering from the traditional business dress code. But so long as certain standards are maintained, the smart company gives their employees leeway in their dress.

Some companies have no written dress code, while others fill 16 pages with what's permissible and what's not on casual days. The important thing is to let employees know how far they can go. Managers can either directly deliver the message of what's considered inappropriate or can make it nonpersonal by putting it in the office newsletter. Make it clear that dress relates to customer expectations and is more than just an arbitrary in-house standard. (See also Business Clothes for Men, page 149; Business Clothes for Women, page 165.)

TELECOMMUTING

Catching the please-the-employee wave of the late-Nineties, telecommuting from home is increasingly an option in most workplaces. Still, managers are divided on the wisdom of this arrangement. Some find that home-based employees are just as (or even more) productive than those on-site. Others believe it is essential for workers to have day-to-day interaction with their workmates. In any event, the arrangement should not be approached casually, but with clear rules of what work is to be produced within a certain time frame. (See also When You Telecommute, page 114.)

FLEXTIME

Another way to accommodate the worker's needs is flextime, which means that workers can start and end their workday early, or start late and end late. In jobs where teamwork is important, flextime can cause problems. Someone who arrives at 8:30 A.M. eager to get going and then finds that the Quark file he needs is checked out of the server onto the hard drive of a coworker who doesn't come in until 10 is understandably resentful. Another shortcoming with flextime: Workers whose day ostensibly begins at 10 have a way of straggling in at 10:30, or even later, by which time the earliest arrivals have put in a quarter of a

HARASSMENT SEMINARS

The heightened awareness of sexual harassment and discrimination has made office romances touchier and more dangerous than ever, given the propensity for lawsuits. The result is a boom in yearly sensitivity seminars that train workers in the tenets of respectful behavior. These may be put on by hired seminar leaders or by personnel from Human Resources or another department. Serious top-level managers see to it that prevention programs are mandatory for all employees and are presented frequently enough so that the information stays up-to-date and relevant. (The company's labor lawyer is a prime candidate for giving occasional briefings to people at higher levels.)

Such prevention programs can be invaluable in opening lines of communication and arriving at an understanding of what constitutes sexual harassment. In role-playing and question-and-answer exercises, employees not only are forced to examine their own responses to a questionable situation but also gain valuable insight into how their coworkers are apt to respond. This may be the only forum in which Bryan realizes that Anne sees any physical contact as threatening, or for Anne to come to understand that Bryan's back pats are an innocent act of gratitude for her good work. From here, the group can discuss which actions are appropriate and which are not and then, it is hoped, go forward with their new understanding.

Another benefit of prevention workshops: They provide a common language for bringing up sexual harassment questions. If an incident occurs between colleagues that makes one of them uncomfortable, it may be much easier to refer to exercises previously undergone than to broach the subject cold. "Well, if this isn't eerily reminiscent of the role-playing Mimi and John did last month" should be enough to imply to the perpetrator a connection between the situation in question and sexual harassment. The connection made, any reasonably perceptive person will understand that he or she should cease and desist.

day. A smart company will consult with their labor lawyer on this issue; otherwise, the "fairness" aspect looms large.

RELOCATION AND TRANSPORTATION COSTS

Of the half million job-related moves each year, about 20 percent are company-sponsored, and employers have developed some fairly standard benefits. It is an expensive proposition, considering that the typical relocation package includes the cost of house-hunting, financial help for obtaining a mortgage, temporary living expenses (usually limited to 30 days, but extended if necessary), and moving costs from one location to another.

The Manager's Responsibilities

Many companies also cover the costs of shopping for a new home, including travel expenses for house-hunting trips. Some large companies buy the home themselves; others arrange for a third-party relocation firm to make the purchase. Other organizations even offer help to the spouse—career counseling, help in preparing resumes, or job-lead contacts. Despite the cost, it is often in the company's interest to make the move as easy as possible: Sparing the employee headaches means he stays concentrated on the job.

As for transportation to and from work, some companies build these costs into base salaries, ensuring that even the lowest-paid employees' budgets won't be too strained by the cost of public transportation, gas, or child care.

Gift Giving

Few companies have policies restricting gifts between managers; employees' policies more often apply to gifts from outside. Many companies have policies

---

THE POLICIES AND PROCEDURES MANUAL

The more thorough the policies and procedures manual, the less the chance of misunderstandings—not only of what is expected of employees in the way of behavior (sexual discrimination or harassment, for example) but also what obligations employees bear, such as maintaining confidentiality. Unfortunately, many employees are going to stash the manual in a drawer and more or less forget about it. For this reason, reminders by way of memo are sometimes necessary when it comes to such matters as dress and punctuality.

A complete policies and procedures manual begins with a nutshell history of the company, a statement of purpose, and an outline of the company's organization, then follows with personnel policies, benefits, business expenses, principles of conduct, and miscellaneous policies.

- HISTORY. When the company was founded and by whom, the track of its growth, and its current place in the market.
- STATEMENT OF PURPOSE. Also called a mission statement, this states the company's aims in ethics and quality. A concise, to-the-point statement is preferable: "Our mission is to be recognized by clients, investors, and competitors as the leading developer of industrial real estate by building relationships and projects with service that is focused on excellence." Be careful here: A jargon-riddled statement that rambles on in the search for nobility is likely to invite cynicism from employees.
- COMPANY ORGANIZATION. This briefly explains the relationship of one department to the other, and who is responsible for what.

stating that an employee receiving a gift worth more than $25 must declare it to management. (See also Business Gifts, page 236.)

Outlawing all token gifts from outside is rare, given that during the holidays returning a gift risks insulting the sender. Some companies require that any foodstuffs sent or brought in by customers be divided up and shared; this is because the usual recipients are employees who deal face to face with clients or customers, and in many cases the people who have actually done most of the work are inadvertently overlooked.

CHARITABLE DONATIONS

Many companies believe being a good corporate citizen is highly important, with the idea that a successful company should give some money back. Top executives also give on a personal basis, seeing a charitable attitude as a plus for the company's image and an aid to running a thriving business. Many compa-

---

- **PERSONNEL POLICIES.** Among the things outlined here are the company's various job levels; hiring and firing (or "termination") procedures; the terms on which base salary and overtime compensation are paid; and policy regarding transfers. An addendum may outline the particulars of the observance of such laws as the Americans With Disabilities Act and Equal Opportunity Employment Act.
- **BENEFITS.** This section begins with the minimum service requirements for eligibility and then sets down the rules for vacation time, sick leave, extended medical leaves of absence, and parental flextime programs. Also outlined are company insurance plans and such options as profit sharing, long-term disability insurance, tuition reimbursements for continuing education, and 401(k) or similar saving plans.
- **BUSINESS EXPENSES.** This section cites job levels that are eligible for reimbursement for business travel and entertainment; spending ceilings for food, lodging, and other expenses; the reporting and approval of expenses; and moving expenses for employees who are being relocated.
- **PRINCIPLES OF CONDUCT.** Herein are set down the standards of behavior, from nonharassment policies to the definition of conflicts of interest to the misuse of company property. Addenda here may include the definition of sexual harassment and the names, addresses, and numbers of Human Resources personnel to consult if the situation arises.
- **MISCELLANEOUS OFFICE POLICIES.** This catchall category includes such issues as media relations, office security, office supplies and equipment, smoking, food and beverages, and professional appearance, including dress.

nies also have a matching-gifts policy, matching or doubling contributions to nonprofit charities, up to a thousand dollars.

Under most circumstances, solicitations for charity should not be made directly to employees, who could resent it. A better tack is to distribute brochures on the charity, then let employees decide whether to participate. The most a company can do if it wants its employees to give to a particular charity, such as United Way, is to let it be known that they have done it themselves. This sets an example, while monitoring whether an employee has given is intrusive.

DRINKING

Among businesspeople, there is a growing consensus that having drinks at lunch is a bad idea. For one thing, it loosens the tongue ever so slightly; for another, it sets a bad example and affects an employee's work for the rest of the afternoon. Many organizations have written policies against lunchtime drinking, some quite specific. An example: At some companies, an employee whose intuition tells him he must order a drink if his clients do may do so with impunity—but should not return to work for the remainder of the day.

DRUG TESTING

Whether an employee should undergo a drug test before being hired is seen as a matter of principle from both sides: Some of the most skilled and creative employees will consider it an invasion of privacy—not because they fear failing the test but because they object on principle—and an indication that the company is philosophically at odds with their thinking. On the other hand, some of the most forward-thinking companies see drug tests as necessary screening processes that ultimately benefit all of their employees. This is one issue where never the twain shall meet, and it serves as an indicator to the potential employee and the company alike whether they are a good match.

The employer should be aware of state laws on drug testing, since some states restrict random testing to safety-sensitive positions; others restrict it by case law. The employer who decides to test employees for drugs should invite them to ask questions about who will be conducting the test and who will have access to the results. A justification for drug testing is that it protects not only the company's safety and financial interests but the employees'.

The courts have given wide latitude to public and private employers to search employees' offices and files when there is a valid concern. But 50 states have 50 different sets of codes regulating privacy. County and municipal laws and ordinances add another layer at the local level, and special governmental units such as school districts and transportation authorities can regulate their employees. And all these laws and regulations are subject to interpretation by the courts.

It is incumbent on companies to not only be aware of state laws but to let employees know when e-mail is being monitored and surveillance of any kind is being conducted. Employers considering surveillance should first answer "yes" to any of the following questions:

- Is theft by employees a problem? American businesses lose tens of billions of dollars each year to theft, and experts say that most of this purloining is done by employees.
- Is there a drug or alcohol problem in the workplace? Drinking or taking drugs at work immediately affects performance and productivity, and often leads to accidents or other situations that can endanger the abuser, coworkers, customers, and innocent bystanders.
- Is the workplace plagued by low productivity, misbehavior, or violence? If workers aren't performing up to snuff, consistently arriving late, being rude to customers, failing to follow safety rules, the employer needs to know, and monitoring on-the-job activity is a reasonable course of action.
- Are workers excessively using company property for their private purposes? Employees who go overboard playing computer games, surfing the Internet or e-mailing friends, and clogging office telephones and fax machines with personal messages can become a problem for any company.
- Are employees acting in a way that can jeopardize the company? Under the concept of "negligent hiring," employers are liable for the acts of their workers—for example when a teacher with a history of child abuse molests a student or a drug-using delivery truck driver causes an auto accident.
- Is workplace crime an issue? Workers' compensation fraud, for example, affects everyone—from the employer who pays for the system to workers who legitimately deserve compensation for on-the-job injuries. Employers have wide latitude in the actions they take to protect against fraud and other illegal behavior, including industrial espionage.

The Manager's Responsibilities

CHAPTER 15

THE MANAGER'S OBLIGATIONS

There is more to being a high-performing manager than simply carrying out the duties listed in a Human Resources-sanctioned job description—those familiar managerial functions of hiring and firing, evaluating performance, tracking results, making bottom-line targets, and so on down the line. To be an effective manager requires a host of less quantifiable skills. Today's smart manager not only knows when to lead and when to get out of the way but she also respects her employees as people. She uses praise when she means it — and usually gets better results in the bargain. She can also be an enforcer when necessary, but she knows that managing by fear and threats is hopelessly out of style and that egomaniacal know-it-alls with no time for the basic civilities do not climb very far up today's corporate ladder.

One key measure of a manager's success is how adeptly she earns and *keeps* respect in the workplace—from clients as well as from everyone top to bottom in her department and company. Why is respect so important? Because showing (and earning) respect brings results. It's good for the business. The best companies look for managers who score high in people-related skills—managers who can't wait to train employees and inspire them to do their best.

Much of the secret of successful management is simply keeping your eye on the company's targets while applying common courtesy, respecting other people, communicating clearly, and keeping calm under pressure. But when the pressure starts to build—whether from your boss, your staff, or your inner voice—all that is easier said than done. This chapter looks at several kinds of behavior that can affect a manager's performance, for good or ill, and draws on the practical experience of other managers to suggest ways you can successfully steer around the inevitable danger zones.

AVOIDING MANIPULATION

It is hardly surprising that using fear and threats is counterproductive, and something the wise manager avoids. Striking fear into the hearts of workers has been blamed by some observers for "turning the American business world into a jungle," where the fearful compete with one another for their own survival. Trying to manipulate employees by constantly brandishing the threat of firing or demoting them may sometimes work in the short run, but it very rarely brings long-term success to the organization.

People respond to constructive, positive criticism much better than to threats of demotion or firing. The effective manager knows this and employs it. Why? Because ultimately the manager is responsible for the output of the employees assigned to him. Threats can have their place in severe cases, but they had best be used very carefully and with no doubt about actually carrying them out if the unacceptable behavior continues.

A POSITIVE CLIMATE

Although the relationship between employee morale and productivity is always shifting and difficult to pinpoint exactly, there is little doubt that the psychological environment of the workplace directly affects the productivity of employees. Creating a negatively charged atmosphere will lead sooner or later to reduced performance—and that is counterproductive.

"Creating a positive climate in my office is so important to me," says the head of a cutting-edge Internet company, "that when I hire people I tell them that one of the non-negotiable requirements for working at my company is being able to get along with their coworkers. If they can't, that is grounds for dismissal. Work is already pressure-packed enough. No one should have to tolerate the additional pressure of a negative atmosphere created by people who can't get along."

The way a manager manages directly affects the atmosphere of the workplace. Manage in a positive manner and the atmosphere is positive. Manage with fear and threats and the atmosphere becomes pressure-charged and negative. Efficiency, quality, and productivity all go down the drain.

MANIPULATION'S MANY FACES

Not all manipulative managers use fear and threats. Some use more subtle kinds of pressure. One of the most common ones is "Everybody is saying that . . . [you don't seem to be a team player . . . you don't seem to respond well to criticism . . . you seem less interested in manufacturing than marketing . . .]" Another common ploy is preceded by the apparently gentle question "Don't you think that . . . ?" which implies that if you really *don't* happen to think what follows the question is true, you are in the minority. Subtle and crass manipulation both originate from the same source: a person who wants his own way more than anything else.

BEING ACCOUNTABLE

Every good manager should have the courage to be accountable for his or her own actions. Owning up to your staff that you made a mistake—say, admitting that you misread the deadline for a project, causing you and several of them to work late into the night—is the mark of the strong, not the weak. Making the occasional mistake is only human: Taking blame for an error—and immediately setting about correcting it—shows you as an effective problem solver, not a dodger. Blaming another person, another department, or "circumstances beyond your control" marks you as a whiner and buck-passer—and raises a serious question about your integrity. Respect is too valuable an asset for you to risk it just to save some embarrassment or pretend that you're infallible.

Of course, owning up to your mistakes doesn't mean you shouldn't take credit for your successes—bringing a project in under budget, for instance, or delivering on a promise to step up monthly production. Don't be so modest that you undersell your achievements. Just remember to recognize other people's contributions and acknowledge them quickly, openly, and generously.

The smart manager is also willing to admit he's not all-knowing, whether about the business at hand or otherwise. When he doesn't have the answer to a question that has been posed in a meeting—the approximate quarterly sales figures of a competitor, perhaps—a straightforward "I don't know" is perfectly acceptable. At the same time, he acknowledges that he's accountable for finding the answer: "I'll find out and let you know by five o'clock today." Pretending to know more than you actually do makes you look not only phony but insecure, characteristics that stand no leader in good stead. If you claim always to have the answer, you lose credibility among your employees and that ultimately weakens your ability to lead.

"TRY THE TRUTH"

A top executive in a Texas public relations firm has a favorite saying for clients who are at a loss about what to reveal: "When all else fails, try the truth." In business, as in life, telling the truth—no matter what the short-term consequences—is far more beneficial than getting caught in a deception. People are generally forgiving, almost to a fault. But deceive them and they will remember it for a long, long time. "Try the truth" applies to everyone in the workplace: the boss, the manager, the new employee, the client, the contractor.

INSPIRING AND MOTIVATING

The smart manager doesn't leave it to the Human Resources department to inspire employees to do their best, to remain loyal to the company, and to maintain high standards. Making yourself available to answer questions and concerns, along with giving frequent feedback about job performance, is really the best kind of motivation, and it keeps the employee headed always in the right direction. The old-style taskmaster who treats employees as little more than cogs in a wheel is asking for low morale and low productivity.

Enlightened companies also realize it's incumbent on them to expose up-and-coming managers to a number of different ways of doing things. Some companies still tend to look at their business as a set of boxes arranged according to fixed rules, where one size fits all, what works for most must work for

The Manager's Obligations

everybody, and what worked yesterday will work today. Conversely, providing several models instead of one encourages eager and creative employees to mold their own style. A confident executive in a healthy company hires diverse people—and their very diversity demonstrates that there is more than one good way to bring a job to the desired conclusion.

In short, every successful company must strike a balance between establishing set ways of doing things and letting managers or employees build their own systems or processes for accomplishing tasks.

MENTORING PROGRAMS

The staffing structure of some companies makes it difficult for top managers to have frequent contact with employees—especially with employees at the junior levels. Appointing mentors is one solution. In a typical mentoring setup, a top manager asks mid- to senior-level employees who aren't overextended to serve as mentors. Each mentor is then assigned four to six employees. The mentor's responsibility is to keep in touch on a regular basis with his "mentees." He can do this in any way that fits his style, so long as it is done regularly: by holding bimonthly meetings with each individual, by dropping in whenever the opportunity arises, or by some other more or less formal means. Mentors provide an ear, help to solve problems, and can act as mediators between employee and boss if necessary. They may also contribute to the completion of the employee's

---

THE MISSION STATEMENT

Good mission statements tell everyone associated with the company—its employees, customers, clients, and stockholders—what the company stands for, why it makes certain decisions and not others, and why it takes some paths and avoids others. As such, they can separate a vigorous company from a sluggish one and help managers keep employees focused on the basic goals of the company. A mission statement should be easy to read, easy to understand, and not easily forgettable. It should broadly motivate and guide employees—keep them working in the direction the company wants to go.

The effective mission statement forgoes jargon and stands as a statement of purpose, not as a battle cry to be emblazoned on drinking cups and wall posters. When it figuratively becomes part of the wallpaper, employees will give it all the attention it deserves—namely, none.

annual performance appraisal, adding a perspective that may be not only more objective but also more accurate.

THE RIGHT NUMBER

Companies that have tried mentoring programs have found that each mentor can manage about six employees effectively; add a seventh and all of a sudden the mentor can't quite give each employee the time he deserves. As a result, the mentor feels the need for a second in command who can give the promised individual attention to some of the employees. That, of course, begins to defeat the purpose of the system, and it's a perfect example of how those infamous corporate flow charts—with boxes and duplicated names and overlapping functions and solid and dotted lines—get started.

Mentoring can in fact be an alternative to adding layers of assistant managers. Before initiating a mentoring program, however, the executive in charge either should be very sure that prospective mentors have the time available to do the job or must relieve the prospective mentor of some responsibility so that the time for mentoring opens up. Both the executive and the mentor should also be perfectly clear about the scope of the duties and responsibilities of the mentor before the mentoring begins.

TRAIN, TRAIN, TRAIN

Two common mistakes made by managers: 1) assuming that employees know exactly what their jobs are and 2) failing to provide adequate training. A new worker must be given a job description that includes every duty that is expected of him. No one, neither the boss nor the employee, should suppose that certain tasks come with the territory and certain ones do not. Even an employee who has been doing the same job at another company is going to need direction, since expectations vary from workplace to workplace.

Likewise, when someone is promoted to another level, smart managers have a detailed written job description waiting for the promoted employee. The manager should not assume that the employee is already versed in every responsibility and duty of the new job. The employee may have been so focused on excelling at his own job that he paid little note to that of his boss. (See also The Peacekeeper, page 106; Make a List, page 207.)

The Manager's Obligations

THE ULTIMATE TIME-SAVER

Investing time up front in training an employee will pay off in fewer hassles later, ultimately *saving* time. A manager should meet, if only briefly, with the employee every day for the first month, if possible, or at least three times a week, providing him with a list of activities that are important for him to engage in to get a solid start. Make sure he understands why each activity is important, how you want it handled, and what level of proficiency you expect of him—now and six months from now. In follow-up meetings, review his progress to date. These meetings afford an opportunity for intensive one-on-one training and allow you to reinforce desired approaches and skills. While the employee is learning exactly what you want, you're discovering his strong points and weaknesses. Keep your advice practical, specific, to the point.

Just be sure that you never renege on a promise to give feedback. If you do, you show the employee that follow-through is not important to you. That sets a bad example, and it could come back to haunt you.

RECOGNIZE AND COMPLIMENT

If a job is truly well done, give it all the praise it deserves. Mentioning one or two specific things that especially impressed you makes your praise all the more convincing. It shows that you understand the difficulties the job posed. And do not delay. Leaving your compliment for a few days keeps the worker in suspense, and you may risk forgetting to deliver it.

If a job is done well enough but parts of it would benefit from a little constructive criticism, save the latter for later. Allow the recipient to bask in the praise until next time the subject comes up; then say something such as "As great as that proposal was, I think it could've used a few more examples of outside competition. Do you think you could find a few and add them?"

THE POWER OF COMPLIMENTS

The power of a compliment is greater than you might realize. It makes people feel good—and people who feel good generally are better, more productive employees. That means, of course, that giving compliments is good business as well as the nice thing to do. For the owner of a small business on a tight budget, praise often is the only reward she can afford. In that case it becomes just that much more important to recognize and compliment a job well done, an effort above and beyond, or a great idea.

MAKE A LIST

It is not overstating a point to say that job training begins and ends with a careful, complete listing of job duties and responsibilities. It helps you, the manager, to clarify exactly what the job should entail and what you should expect of someone in that position. If the job includes menial and "gofer" tasks such as photocopying and fetching coffee, don't leave those out because you fear they might be a turn-off to a good candidate. If they are a turn-off, it's better for someone to find out up front rather than later, when he would be justified in feeling you deceived him. Always lay out the whole job, warts and all. Doing so makes your job easier because the people under you have a clear understanding of their responsibilities.

Make your compliments count. Just as important as giving them is *not* giving one for every little thing any employee does which will cheapen the value of your praise. For the giver and receiver, compliments are best when they are not only sincere but also well deserved.

WHAT'S YOUR STYLE?

Sometimes, the medium amplifies the message. Many managers like to deliver their highest praise face to face. Others prefer to put it in writing. It's a matter of personal style—and usually employees know which style their manager uses when she is most pleased. For managers of the terse kind, it can be a brief phone call or e-mail, or even just a handshake and a "Nice job" when passing in the hall. Others go further. One executive, when extremely pleased, composes a handwritten message, seals it in an envelope, and then delivers it person. She gives the compliment verbally and then hands over the written note as well. Employees will hold on to those notes as part of their official record.

BE AVAILABLE

Remember that your first priority as a manager is to get results, and the way to get results is through managing people, not paper. Instead of hiding behind a closed door and your desk, surrounded by a defensive barricade of paperwork, keep your door open—and especially your eyes and ears. You learn much about employee attitudes and morale by simply being alert.

The Manager's Obligations

COMMUNICATING DOWNWARD

In the executive suite, being available also means communicating downward, as well as sideways and upward. Most managers are most comfortable talking with their organizational peers about shared interests and common concerns. And few want to miss a chance of schmoozing with their bosses. That leaves people below them last in line. Be that as it may, every manager should make an effort—at least once a day—to hear what's on the minds of employees further down the corporate food chain.

Communicating downward is not only good for office morale, it's very good for the business. Those front-line employees who rarely see the inside of an executive office—salespeople, customer-service reps, telemarketing personnel—are usually the first to know what's going right and what's going wrong. A smart company makes them feel they have access to the planners and decision-makers—a chance to tell the unvarnished truth as they see and hear it every day, unfiltered by middle managers who might try to tone down bad news before it reaches the top.

There is no better way of finding out who's feeling overlooked or overwhelmed than watching the passing parade and tuning in to the office chatter—and you can ask unhappy workers in for a chat on the spot. That way, their discontents have less chance of spreading to the rest of the staff.

The telephone can be just as effective a barrier to people management as paperwork. So can e-mail. (Try talking to a manager's back hunched in front of a computer screen!) The best managers learn to take control of their telephone and e-mail time, rather than having it control them. This means time for face-to-face meetings and spontaneous conversations—the source of almost all the good ideas that arise in a corporation.

One energy company manager tries to allot no more than one hour every day to the telephone and e-mail. She gives her e-mail a half hour in the morning and makes her telephone calls in a half-hour slot in the afternoon. People she deals with inside and outside the company know she's a paragon of organization, and if they don't hear from her today, they'll hear from her tomorrow. Some days her calls and e-mail take a little longer, but some days she's done in minutes. It evens out, she says—and the discipline makes her a better manager.

BE COURTEOUS

More often than not the small courtesies get lost in the shuffle of today's do-it-now, faster-better-cheaper business world. But saying "hello," "please," and "thank you" is not just an empty gesture. Adding the word "please," for example, before "Come to a meeting in my office at 10:00" or "Fax this to Bob Johnston" is a pleasant reminder that the basic civilities of human interaction are something you and your employees share, despite the insular nature of the world you inhabit at work. You also set a good example, showing that manners are part and parcel of a successful person's repertoire.

Manners project a kind of easy confidence. They say, "No matter how crazy our jobs get, let's not forget the social amenities that hold our lives together. Let's not let a bad day destroy our mutual respect. If we keep our heads, things always work out." One manager on the news desk of a national newspaper makes a habit, no matter how harried or exhausted he feels, of greeting everyone he passes in the corridor with a smile and his or her name. If he knows an employee's relative has been in the hospital, he asks, "How's your mother doing?" He has a reputation as one of the most demanding managers on the paper—but he is also one of the most respected and admired.

THANKS, AND THANKS AGAIN

"Thank you" are two indispensable little words that you can use indiscriminately without seeming unctuously overpolite. When the mailroom clerk puts a magazine into your in-box, when a maintenance man holds the door for you, when someone runs an errand for you, say "thank you."

If a customer or client has done a favor for you—say, faxed you a copy of a business journal article the two of you were discussing—a telephoned thank you is in order, and within 24 hours. If a larger favor was performed—a supplier has compiled his last two years of sales reports for your benefit, for example—write a brief thank-you note.

SHOWING DEFERENCE

A good manager understands the protocol of the business world outside, follows its rules, and knows when to defer to people of higher rank. These social skills can provide a quick boost to one's career, as the following story shows.

The president of a toy company invited a recently hired manager to "meet the competition" at the industry's big international trade show. The manager and his boss stuck closely together all through the day until, at a particularly popular booth, another top toy executive came up to the boss and asked, "Sarah, could we talk a little high-level business?" Hesitating, the manager's boss said only, "Well . . . " and cast a brief look at the manager. Sizing up the situation at once, the manager excused himself and moved on. Later his boss complimented him on his savvy. "You certainly made that easy for me," she said. "I won't forget it. Seems we have a promising joint venture brewing, something I think you'd be just perfect for."

COMMUNICATE CLEARLY

A manager is responsible for two kinds of communication with his staff. The best managers are masters of both, though each poses somewhat different challenges.

- **CLARITY.** First, the manager must make sure that his instructions to his staff are absolutely clear and utterly accurate, so much so that only one interpretation is possible. That's a lofty goal, but there are some simple rules that make it easier to attain. Think through what you are going to write or say. Don't let any inconsistencies creep in, such as saying "ten days" in one paragraph and "two weeks" later on, when referring to the same time frame.

  As for style, the best approach is to say it as simply and directly as you can. Don't say, "At this point in time"; say, "Now." Don't say, "It has come to my attention"; say, "I know." (See also Wretched Excesses, page 313.) When you have a choice of using a longer word or a shorter word, use the shorter

THE EUPHEMISM SCOURGE

The fact is that many employees are ready to distrust any "official" statements that come out of the company front office. Why? One reason is because companies tend to speak in a convoluted, self-protective way, employing euphemisms by the dozen. Corporations use euphemisms for basically two reasons: to sugarcoat bad news and to spare feelings. Used in moderation, euphemisms can amount to simple good manners. Most people would probably rather hear "We are eliminating your position" than "You're fired," even though both mean you're out of work. But is it really necessary or helpful for companies to talk about "right sizing" and "reengineering" when what they mean is mass firings?

Many management experts attribute worker cynicism to the fact that most employees see right through the euphemisms and conclude the company thinks it can pull the wool over their eyes. If a manager faces such a climate of distrust, perhaps the best he can do is tell his staff the unadorned facts as he understands them and ask them to ignore the irritation they feel about euphemistic company pronouncements.

BUDDY OR BOSS?

Most managers have found, some through bitter experience, that it is best not to form close friendships with subordinates. Here are the perspectives of three executives who have faced the situation and reflected on it.

- **"PROFESSIONAL ONLY."** The thoughts of the president of a design firm: "As my firm has grown, I've found relationships with my employees have become more professional and less personal. When it was three of us, we knew everything about each other, and we worked closely together in one big open space with no secrets. Now, with nine people and doors and offices, the relationship between me and the employees is much more 'professional only.' I do care about each of them, but I also care about the business. And no matter how hard I would try, the business would be part of any outside-the-office friendship we might have. So I don't seek or encourage close office friendships. In some ways that's a little sad. But it keeps things simple."

- **AWKWARD VS. REWARDING.** From the president of a bank: "Any manager has to be extremely careful about becoming too friendly with an employee. For starters, if you're trying to socialize with your subordinates, they could feel obligated to socialize even if they don't want to—and you've put them in an awkward position. Any socializing should be for the purpose of learning from employees things that will help you do your own job better. That's not the same as socializing with people for the fun of it. Just as you don't want to be your child's friend instead of his parent, you want to be a boss first and a friend second."

- **FUN, BUT WITH LIMITS.** From the president and CEO of a real estate development company: "I'm a people person, so personal contact with my employees is very important. It's how I learn about what's really happening in the company, because the information isn't filtered through other levels. In-house lunches, special outings, and an occasional office party are fine—and I saw nothing wrong with taking a bunch of my accounting people recently for drinks at my house and then out to dinner, since they were getting ready for a very tough time with long hours. But even though I get to know my people in a personal way, I usually don't socialize outside the office, with the exception of a few senior managers."

one. Write simple straightforward sentences—the shorter the better. (See also The Good Writer, page 305.)

- **INFORMATION.** The second kind of communication a manager deals with is informing his staff about company decisions, policy, and directions. Some employees want a great deal of such information (or at least say they do); others want very little. What most employees do *not* want is to feel that information is being withheld from them because they can't handle it or couldn't understand its implications.

This is where the manager can use some finesse. Rather than handing out reams of paper about company policy, he can simply say, "If anybody is interested in talking about this further, I'd be more than glad to tell you what I know—which is far from everything. Please drop by if you want to talk about this company announcement."

CHAPTER 16

YOUR SUPPORT STAFF

In an age of fast-track electronic office services—e-mail, voice mail, faxes, and high-speed modems, among others—the customary roles of the secretary and receptionist are almost unrecognizable when compared to those of their counterparts of a generation ago. For the most part, traditional secretarial duties—handling paper correspondence, taking messages and dictation, mailing manuscripts, and typing—have for the most part been absorbed into the realm of electronica. In many companies, it is only the highest-ranking executive who requires the full-time services of a secretary or assistant, with a sole office assistant often assigned to multiple bosses.

This is not to say that the positions of secretary or assistant are no longer relevant: It is the work itself that has evolved. As always, an executive's assistant may still be expected to handle the boss' correspondence and phone calls, schedule meetings, and make travel arrangements. But with the help of electronic services, the assistant's time is freed for more challenging demands.

Today's assistant is likely to be something of a generalist, involved in much more than just secretarial work. Increasingly, he or she is put on a career track by the company, with the understanding that the eventual goal is to graduate to a higher position or even a managerial one. Such changes make it all the more understandable why the term "secretary" has fallen from favor, symbolizing as it does the era of the low-level, low-paid "gal Friday." Today the preferred titles include "administrative assistant" and "executive assistant."

YOUR RESPONSIBILITIES

Part of most executives' daily routine is to spend time with an assistant going over projects, dictating letters, discussing appointments to be made. It's easy to forget the basic courtesies that make your interaction more pleasant. Shouting "David, come in here!" or running through the litany of things to do without a smile seems demanding if not overbearing. "David, when you're finished with that letter, would you please come in so that we can discuss the next project?" shows recognition that he is busy, and turns an order into a request.

Likewise, using "you" rather than "I" when making requests implies that David has a participatory place in the process. "I want you to work on the Welt project this afternoon" is better phrased as "David, the Welt project needs some attention—would you fit it into your schedule this afternoon?"

A SPECIAL RELATIONSHIP

Because you, as a manager, spend more time with your assistant than with other employees, you have the opportunity to give him or her a day-by-day performance evaluation of sorts—the ideal situation for any employee, but impossible in all but the smallest offices. The same goes for the receptionist, whom you come into contact with every morning and occasionally during the day. A compliment for a job well done and a little constructive criticism when a lapse is noticed are both to their advantage and yours.

Some secretaries are of the old school and take pride in having mastered secretarial duties to a tee. Your relationship with an assistant of this sort is relatively cut and dried, with there being no question of each other's duties and obligations. Other assistants are often those who aspire to a higher level, and it is here that the definitions become less clear.

BE A MENTOR

If there is an agreement that an assistant will graduate to a higher job level after proving her abilities, the smart manager acts as her mentor—that is, encourages her interest in the profession and helps her cultivate her talents.

A typical scenario: You are a senior editor in a publishing house and your editorial assistant is in line for an associate editorship. Help her along by giving her small research or writing jobs whenever you can and then give her a friendly critique. Take a positive approach, first pointing out the strong points—enthusiastic praise for a particularly nice turn of phrase will soften the sting of any coming criticism. Then direct attention to the weaker parts, explaining how they can be improved. You owe it to the budding writer to be frank, but be careful not to quash her dreams. Show even more interest in her aspirations by giving her one of your favorite books on the writer's craft, which she can keep at her desk as a reference. The book will likely raise talking points about grammar and word usage among the two of you, gradually strengthening her skills while freeing more of your time.

YOUR ASSISTANT'S DUTIES

The conduct of your secretary or assistant is a reflection of you and the way you do business. Similarly, there are certain things you should expect of him, and other things you should not. It is your obligation to be as clear as possible in communicating your expectations to an assistant, right down to the tone he should use when answering the phone—warm and cheery or no-nonsense and straight to the point.

- **AS A COMMUNICATOR.** You'll want your assistant to present a well-mannered, cordial voice to the outside world. But remember that it's your duty to tell him just what to communicate—including where you are. Keeping your assistant informed about your whereabouts will keep both outside callers and office personnel from being frustrated when they can't reach you. You may think you're doing your assistant a favor by not burdening him with your schedule. Not so. By providing him with it, you're actually causing less trouble for other people and keeping him from becoming the one who's blamed when he doesn't have the needed information.

    Discretion is essential: The two of you share sensitive and personal information by necessity, and it's essential that your assistant keeps it under his hat. At the same time, you want him to pass on any office undercurrents that you would benefit from knowing about—which brings up the subject of gossip.

    If your assistant spends an inordinate amount of time talking in a whisper to other employees, you have a right to be suspicious, and a gentle reminder that confidentiality is essential is in order. If you discover your assistant was the source of a leak, let the punishment fit the crime. Starting the rumor that the CEO wasn't all that pleased with the work of a consultant deserves a stern reminder; leaking the news that layoffs are imminent calls for telling the assistant that such a serious lapse, if not being grounds for dismissal, will be reflected in his next performance appraisal.

- **IN APPEARANCE.** If your secretary or assistant isn't doubling as a receptionist, the casualness of his or her attire generally is determined by company or office policy. Many executives have their own personal dress code, one they may encourage an assistant to adopt. To state the obvious, the assistant's clothing should always be presentable no matter how casual the dress code: neat, clean, and professional.

    As a manager, you can treat a lapse in sartorial judgment on the part of your assistant—say, 6-inch-long Day-Glo earrings—with humor while making your point. With a chuckle, say something such as "Tell me, Jackie. Whatever made you wear those earrings to work? We're not exactly MTV." The earrings will come off, your mission accomplished without any hurt feelings.

- **AS A CALL SCREENER.** For busy executives, one of the most important duties an assistant performs is answering and screening calls. An ace assistant knows which calls to put through and which calls to defer till later. (Remember that it's your job to give him or her the authority to let callers know when they can expect to be called back.) He or she will also remind you to return phone calls or respond to voice-mail messages.

  If you detect in your assistant's voice a note of officiousness (or anything but politeness) as he screens your calls, give him clear directions as to how he should sound. It's up to you to decide how cheery the tone, so let him know what you expect and then offer some suggestions for wording.

  From the beginning, the assistant should learn exactly who does what in the office lineup so that he can transfer cold calls to the appropriate department, thereby sparing you the trouble. You should also provide him with any information he might need on a daily basis: that if anyone calls to ask about the market test results review, tell them it will be distributed tomorrow, or that you won't be able to meet at 3:00 tomorrow because you already have an appointment scheduled.

- **AS A GOFER.** Gofer *[go + for]:* Slang for an employee whose duties include running errands; not to be confused with a small burrowing animal. Definitions of the word notwithstanding, an assistant should always be informed from the time he or she is hired whether the job entails fetching cof-

---

WHITHER SECRETARY'S DAY?

Secretary's Day provides employers with an opportunity to show their assistants how much they appreciate them by doing something special: presenting them with a card, flowers, a small gift, or an invitation to lunch. The idea for the observance came in 1952 from the Professional Secretaries International trade association—not, as widely assumed, from greeting card companies and florists. Despite this, the holiday remains a poor stepchild in the days-of-remembrance family. The name alone makes many businesspeople dismiss it, and the more politically correct "Administrative Assistant's Day" and "Support Staff's Day" sound little more than contrived. In the minds of other executives and employees, the day is an idea that was too long in coming, regardless of its origins and name.

Controversy aside, the observance has the virtue of being nonreligious and straightforward. Instead of giving one-on-one gifts, supervisors who work with a secretarial pool may want to band together with others to provide each assistant with a flower arrangement or small gift. A colleague, customer, or vendor may also choose to recognize a client's assistant if he or she has gone beyond the call of duty or has been particularly helpful.

fee, picking up your starched shirts from the laundry, going to the box office to buy tickets for a play you plan to attend, shopping for your son's birthday present, or performing any other services that have little to do with actual work. Such mundane chores as photocopying and faxing are to be expected, but in the opinion of many managers, having an assistant run personal errands is not only inappropriate but goes beyond the pale.

A GIFT FOR YOUR ASSISTANT

If you're a manager in a large office, the company may provide annual holiday gifts for employees, but you may also want to reward your secretary or assistant yourself. The gift choice depends on his or her length of service: If it is less than five years, a gift costing $25 is sufficient; with longer-term assistants, you may want to be a little more generous.

The number-one rule for employer-to-assistant gifts, be they for holidays or birthdays, is to make sure they're not too personal—but that doesn't mean picking the most impersonal item you can find. Always consider your assistant's interests when choosing. Below are a few choices—some good, some bad. (See also Whither Secretary's Day?, page 216.)

TIME ON JOB	GIFT SUGGESTIONS	TOO PERSONAL
UNDER 5 YEARS	*Books, CDs, personal organizers, fruit baskets*	*Perfume, earrings*
5 TO 10 YEARS	*Theater tickets, gift certificates (movies; furniture, home, garden, or appliance stores)*	*Lingerie*
MORE THAN 10 YEARS	*Spa getaway, leather briefcase*	*Expensive jewelry*

THE RECEPTIONIST'S DUTIES

No company of any kind can underestimate the importance of hiring the right office receptionist. The person who holds this position is literally the front door of the business—the face with which the company greets the public day in and day out. It therefore stands to reason that there are certain qualities and behavior an executive expects from this employee in particular.

- **AS THE GREETER.** The receptionist's demeanor should reflect the image any healthy, customer-driven business wishes to project—a manner that is friendly, helpful, and capable. The best receptionists project a confident professionality. The virtue of patience, too, is also part and parcel of the job.

THE GREAT COFFEE DEBATE

S hould an employer expect a member of the support staff to make and serve coffee daily? The great debate continues. A recent survey revealed that only 7 percent of administrative assistants now consider making and serving coffee to the boss a part of the job description. This "duty" is now considered a courtesy, similar to offering to get coffee for a coworker. The bottom line? Serving coffee to the boss is not expected and generally not considered part of an assistant's job description. Nevertheless, it is always polite, if anyone—and that includes the boss—is going for coffee, tea, or snacks, to offer to bring something back for other people in the vicinity.

If rude, boorish people come to call, it is imperative that the receptionist remains calm, tries not to take it personally, and keeps smiling.

A good receptionist is also expected to behave cordially while greeting and accepting packages from messengers. At the same time, she should not end up chatting with delivery persons at length. Some messengers who frequently drop in develop a friendship with the receptionist, which can lead to minor problems: Not only can talk and laughter from the foyer disturb workers, but the messenger may be delayed from his next round.

NOTE: Some companies are a little too forgiving of receptionists who have been around for so long they are said to be "an institution." A brusque manner is overlooked because, as everyone knows, "She might get a little irritated sometimes, but she really has a heart of gold." People from outside, however, have no way of knowing this, and tolerating the receptionist's imperfections may end with negative impressions among clients and customers who come to call. In extreme cases, a transfer to another job, where interaction will be only with employees, is the best solution.

- **IN APPEARANCE.** The American office has undergone a sea change in business wear in the last 10 years. More emphasis has been placed on casual comfort, the type of functional and classic sportswear that is deeply rooted in the American lifestyle. While many companies enforce specific dress codes, an equal number have adopted a fairly lax company policy on office wear, allowing employees to don such previously taboo clothing as rubber-soled shoes and to forgo ties and jackets. In either case, as the company greeter and the person who deals with the outside world on an ongoing basis, the receptionist should maintain an appearance that conveys the company image.
- **AS A CALL ANNOUNCER.** Make sure the receptionist understands the importance of getting things right. Whether greeting someone in person or on the telephone, the efficient receptionist carefully writes down or

types in the name of the person (making sure the spelling is correct), the company he represents, and the time of his call. Immediately writing down the caller's name helps the receptionist properly announce the caller and provides a record of the call or visit in case the recipient is out.

- **AS A CALL SCREENER.** The receptionist of a large company with a large staff cannot be expected to know which callers to screen and which to let through; that is the assistant's job. In smaller offices, however, where the receptionist often doubles as the assistant, screening the boss' calls may be a more common procedure. (See also Screening Calls, page 293.)

PART V

THE WORLD
OUTSIDE

O utside the cocoon of your office is the world in which you do business, whether you are crossing town to meet with a customer or hopping a plane to Kansas City to hammer out a deal. This section takes a look at how to interact when you're dealing with people who are not from your home turf. It starts with those you serve with the aim of generating profit—your customers and clients—and shows how to make "customer service" more than an empty promise. Your relationship with suppliers is also touched on.

The sometimes sticky question of gift-giving is given its own chapter: just what is appropriate, and what is not? A separate chapter on business travel shows you that it doesn't have to be a necessary evil; in fact, with smart preparation, close attention to logistical details, and genuine consideration for your hosts and business associates, every business trip can be smooth sailing, whether you're traveling by car, plane, or train. This final chapter offers advice on how to take care of business and keep your priorities straight while still enjoying yourself at these often hectic but convivial convocations.

CHAPTER 17

PLEASING THE CUSTOMER

Just as Olympians fervently compete for their trophies, so today's companies vie for a singular prize—the best customers. The most successful go to great lengths to keep their customers happy and coming back for more, and that effort to please extends to clients, contractors, and vendors. Without satisfied customers and suppliers, no profit-seeking organization is going to survive for long. With everybody happy, the sky's the limit.

The first rule is to treat everyone with your full respect. In essence, make each person you deal with feel that he or she is important in your eyes. The need to behave this way with customers goes without saying, but some companies make the mistake of treating contractors and vendors as if they were lower down the pecking order. Given that contractors and vendors can make or break multimillion-dollar programs, giving them anything less than that due a customer or client is a serious blunder for the smart businessperson.

Customer satisfaction is the subject of this chapter. Although much of the advice is directed to managers, practically all of it applies to anyone in the workplace who crosses paths with people from the world outside, be they customers or couriers. But all is not sweetness and light. There are times when a businessperson must lay down the law, especially where missed deadlines and late payments are concerned.

THE ART OF LISTENING

How well you listen to your customers and clients is one of the most important talents a person in business has. What it takes is illustrated by this scenario:

A young woman named Leigh, then recently hired by a large bank based in Denver, had been looking forward to taking a vacation day on Friday. But she changed her plan on learning that she and a small group of other employees were invited to a Q & A session with a financier of some note. She was also nervous. "I'm really thrilled to be invited," she confided to a friend, "and you can bet I'll listen as hard as I can. But I just hope I *hear*."

THE HAZARDS OF BADMOUTHING

Although it shouldn't, it happens in every office. A couple of employees start talking about the difficult situation that just developed with a contractor or, worse still, a customer. Venting is the order of the hour: "Can you believe that jerk had the nerve to deliver that sorry excuse for a report and then blamed us for the problem? And he calls himself a professional!" Then there's the annoying behavior variation: "She talked my ear off again today. I swear, that woman never shuts up. She's driving me nuts!"

Disparaging the offender may relieve the employees of some of their own frustration, but it has the potential to do real harm. For one, it can prejudice coworkers who overhear the ranting, possibly affecting the way they behave with the object of scorn the next time they talk or meet. Worse yet, the ranters' comments may make their way back to the customer. What happens if a phone call that was meant to be on hold actually isn't, and the customer overhears the following? "Hey, Tom, it's that cantankerous old fool you were just talking about on the phone for you." End of relationship.

In her own way, Leigh perfectly described the three essential pieces of what psychologists call active (as opposed to passive) listening. They apply to telephone conversations as well as face-to-face meetings.

- BE THERE. Even if attending a session where valuable information will be exchanged is scheduled at an inconvenient time, don't enlist a surrogate. Make that important telephone call yourself. Don't count on someone else to tell you about what was discussed. Be present mentally and emotionally as well; if your attention wanders, you're not really there.
- LISTEN *CAREFULLY*. Listen to every word, every tone, every pause. Take notes if the situation permits it. (Taking notes isn't usually a problem during telephone conversations—keep pencil and paper handy.) If you're not sure about the propriety of notes (at lunch, for instance), the simplest thing to do is ask: "Mind if I jot down a couple of your points?"
- HEAR. If you're doing the first two, this part will be the easiest. It is really an elevated form of hearing—fully mulling over and absorbing what the speaker is saying, why he is saying it, and what it means for your future association. With this step you become an active participant in an exchange of information, even though you may not have uttered a word for half an hour.

The Etiquette Advantage in Business

As for the young banker, she was there, she listened, and she heard—very successfully, it turned out. Her questions so impressed the financier that a year later when she applied for a higher position at another bank, the financier wrote her a glowing letter of recommendation that eased her climb up the ladder. (See also The Good Listener, page 286.)

THE ART OF QUESTIONING

Asking the right questions can set you on the road to success, whether you're dealing with an irate customer or evaluating a new client, contractor, vendor, or other prospective business partner. Some people make the mistake of thinking that if you ask questions, you cede control of a discussion to the person answering. Producing answers, they reason, is more impressive than questioning. But that's plainly wrong. If you use questions creatively, they become a way of guiding the discussion in the direction you want.

Besides, in business as much as in social situations, most people really love to talk about themselves—their likes and dislikes. (Anybody with a reputation as a good conversationalist is less likely to be a raconteur than a person who asks thoughtful questions and listens well.) If you encourage someone to talk, you almost always learn things about her or him that you wouldn't learn if you chose to dominate the conversation.

GENTLE GUIDANCE

The simple technique of seeming interested in what a person has to say can dissolve barriers of suspicion and build feelings of friendship and trust, allowing people to open up. It is a skill long used by successful diplomats, winning politicians, and the best salespeople. If you move the conversation along with gentle, intelligent questions, you'll more than likely gain valuable information, given freely, without seeming nosy or intrusive—information that makes all the difference in the outcome of a business transaction of any kind. Here are some conversational gambits that will help you get into areas that might be sensitive, making people more likely to be forthcoming:

"I hope you don't mind my asking, but . . . "

"I was talking to an old friend the other day and he said the marketing plan looked a little weak, and I don't know if I agree. What do you think?"

"I read an interesting report the other day about Behemoth Booksellers that claimed a merger was in the offing . . . Have you heard anything like that?"

"If you don't think it's a good idea to tell me, please know I completely understand, but I was wondering . . . "

Pleasing the Customer

"My boss was delighted to hear that I was having lunch with you today. She's really sorry she couldn't join us, and she asked me to ask you if your company still plans to bid on the Epsom & Saltz project."

Note the frequent mention of third parties—"an old friend," "my boss," "an industry report." This helps remove your questions from the realm of personal curiosity to a more general, shared level of interest.

HANDLING DEMANDING PEOPLE

Whole books and training manuals have been churned out that tell how you should deal with demanding people. These texts usually go into great detail about various personality types (the "feeler," the "thinker," the "doer," and so on), and how you should tailor your response to each type and resolve an uncomfortable situation most effectively.

Understandably, your anxiety level may rise when you're told that it's essential to figure out how to recognize various types of difficult people. Other-

---

YOUR TRUSTY BUSINESS CARD

Handing out business cards serves many of the same purposes as the Victorian custom of leaving calling cards (with the butler, yet) to announce you had dropped by for a visit and were looking forward to an opportunity to sit and chat. That fine old convention accomplished several objectives:

- Told the recipient you thought he or she was worth your time and attention.
- Respectfully placed the decision of whether to see you in the recipient's hands, rather than forcing yourself into his or her day at an inconvenient time.
- Gave the correct spelling of your name, and sometimes a title or affiliation.
- Allowed room for a brief note, such as "in town at the Navarro Hotel until Saturday noon" or "will call back at 3 P.M. tomorrow."

The business card of today incorporates all the uses of the old-fashioned calling card and does still more:

- Invites a new business acquaintance to get in touch with you.
- Defines your position and responsibilities (e.g., Vice President, Sales).
- Provides as many as four ways or more to reach you: mailing address, telephone, fax, e-mail address, and sometimes your assistant's telephone number and alternate phone numbers for you.

wise (it is darkly hinted), you may not be doing your job and hurting your employer's relationship with customers.

LISTENING IS KEY

You don't have to guess about the best way to act with difficult people, nor do you have to take a psychology course to teach you about personality types. All you have to do is listen very carefully to what a customer with a complaint or a client with an attitude is saying and *how* they are saying it. Then keep your emotions in check. Once you do, difficult people will tell you how to respond.

Here's how it works. When someone gripes about a product or service or criticizes your company for a real or imagined lapse, listen to the words the person uses. Then use the same (or similar) words, in your response. If you hear "I thought I could *trust* your company, but now I have my *doubts*," a good response would be "Your *trust* is tremendously important to us, and I'd like to hear more about your *doubts*." Or if a demanding client takes you to task for a lack of communication, tackle the subject head-on: "Communication is the

---

The smart businessperson shouldn't be without at least a few cards in a jacket pocket—and the cleaner and newer-looking they are, the better. You never know when you might need a card (at a dinner in a restaurant, say, or sitting next to someone in a baseball stadium's bleachers), and they should be in perfect condition when you present them. Stationery and department stores sell business-card holders that prevent smudging and creasing.

How to hand out business cards, and to whom?

- If you're reasonably sure you'll be dealing with someone in the future, ask for a business card and give yours in return. Probably the one exception is a top executive who clearly outranks you; if such a senior person wants your card, or wants you to have hers, she will tell you so.
- When given a card, don't just snatch it and jam it into your pocket. Take a moment to look at it, perhaps complimenting its design. Then slip it into your wallet or datebook.
- Offer cards one to a person—not a fistful as if you were trying to flood the market with the wonder of you and your title.
- Offering your card privately to someone at a social event is perfectly fine—but suggest holding off on detailed business talk until another day. Don't pop out a card in the middle of dinner that has nothing to do with business; if you want to present one, wait until you've left the table.

Like the old calling cards, business cards almost always benefit from a personal touch. If you have a special day of the week when you're not reachable, a note on the back of your card ("Tough to get hold of on Wednesday mornings") shows you as thoughtful.

CONTENT VERSUS TONE

Listening to complaints from irate customers often triggers an immediate defense mechanism, leading you to reject what the person is saying because of the *way* it's being said—not because of what it means. Don't let a person's tone of voice prevent you from getting to the gist of the matter. The problem may be real, and it may need real attention regardless of how it's presented. Even if you can't win back the irate customer, by hearing him out and actually understanding his complaint you may prevent someone else from calling with the same problem—something that's good for business in the long run.

lifeblood of our business. Let's talk this through right now." This is as sure a way as any of convincing an irate person that you are on his wavelength and on his side—and that's the best way out of a difficult business situation, for you, the dissatisfied customer or client, and your company. With a little experience, letting the other person's words guide your response will become second nature.

If you pick up the phone and get a tirade about a defective product, the caller obviously wants action immediately. If you can promise to send him a replacement, that's what he wants to hear—not some general discussion about warranties or your company's excellent quality-control procedures. (That might come later, but not first.) If you can't promise an immediate solution, stress the urgency you feel about the customer's problem by using words and phrases on the order of "I'll look into it immediately . . . " or "I'll ask my supervisor the minute I hang up . . . " or "I'll ask our technical staff what could have happened."

Ask for a time you can call back to tell him what you've found out. It's particularly effective—and good manners to boot—to promise an irate customer that if for some unforeseen reason you can't call him back at the specified time, he should call you collect or at an 800 number. Though this courteous act may seem as if it's letting you in for trouble you could avoid, it is the kind of graciousness you would expect from a friend in the business—and that's exactly what an irate customer feels he doesn't have.

DEALING WITH ANGRY CALLERS

A lot of people at the office get them occasionally: calls from a customer who has a bone of some sort to pick. Luckily, most customers with a problem are not out of control or insulting. They realize that mistakes and oversights occur and that you are not the one to blame. If you sound genuinely interested in helping them, they will usually keep their cool.

But then there are the firecrackers with short fuses, the ones who literally explode in your ear. Add to them the frosty types who icily dissect your company's reputation and calmly cut up you and the way you do your job. In situations like these, try to keep from taking any remarks personally, even though you may in fact be under personal attack. If you reach a point where you've had enough ranting, personal abuse, or profanity, you are fully justified in saying goodbye and hanging up. Report the incident, in as much detail as you can, to your boss, quoting the abusive caller verbatim if possible.

Fortunately, it's rare that callers behave so badly. Most, infuriated as they may be, will calm down before you're driven to desperation. Here are some tips on getting past a customer's (or anyone's) anger as fast as possible:

- Let the angry caller rant for a minute or two. That usually relieves the rage he has built up.
- Don't interrupt even if he pauses or says something that sounds like the beginning of an apology, such as "I don't like to get this mad, but . . . " A comment by you at this point may set off another round of explosions.
- As the caller is venting, try to detach yourself from the emotional context of what he is saying and, almost like a scientist, objectively consider and remember the words he uses.
- When you sense the caller's anger has run its course, make a brief comment that demonstrates you've listened closely and understand how important the problem is to him.
- If that goes well, introduce yourself if necessary and say that you want to help solve the problem. This may pleasantly surprise the caller, part of whose fury may have come in anticipation of a hostile reaction to his plight. Spell out your name and give your title.
- If the caller explodes again, it's probably a good idea to ask for his number and say you'll call back in a couple of hours or at a specified time the next day. Use this breather to collect your thoughts and talk to your coworkers or supervisor about how you should proceed with this tough case.
- When you've decided how to resolve the situation, always emphasize to the caller the actions you *will* take (even if they don't fully meet his demands), not the actions you *can't* take. Never promise to do something you can't deliver on.
- If the problem turns out to be the customer's fault, such as not following a basic instruction, never adopt a superior tone. Doing so implies that if he'd been smarter he could have saved you both a lot of turmoil. Instead, patiently walk the customer through the required steps.

Pleasing the Customer

DON'T TAKE IT PERSONALLY

At a busy passport office in a major Southern city, the U.S. government has decided that one employee is enough. There are times when the waiting line snakes out of the cavernous main hall and spills into the long main corridor of the vast old post office building. "Disgruntled" is a mild description of most of the waiting people. Meanwhile, behind the passport window, Polly, the one employee, is also responsible for answering telephone inquiries—and the line never stops ringing. Yet when she answers the phone she is unfailingly courteous and helpful. Incredibly, she maintains the same calm pleasantness when passport applicants, some of whom are ready to explode, finally reach her window.

How does she do it? "I keep telling myself not to take it personally," Polly explains. "Being the only one here is not my fault. It's not under my control. I think these people have a right to be mad, but all I can do is be as quick, careful, and helpful as I can." Once in a while, after standing in line for an hour or more, a passport applicant gets to her window so hot under the collar he can't stop venting. When that happens, Polly says, "I ask them to go talk to my supervisor down the hall and tell him that I need help. That often makes people feel better, though it really doesn't get me any more help. I'm lucky because my supervisor *does* have a nice manner."

This harried but even-tempered postal worker's experience illustrates the two most important rules of dealing with unhappy customers or clients—in fact, almost any peeved person:

- Don't ever take a customer's anger or criticism personally. If you do, you will probably lash back in kind—and that makes everything worse.
- Always remember that you are not alone—you have coworkers and supervisors you can turn to for support when you need it.

Sometimes, despite your best efforts and extraordinary self-control, nothing you say satisfies an angry caller, and your company loses a customer. It happens to everybody. Don't let it eat away at you, because it's not your fault.

MAKING PROMISES

With the aggressive, the angry, and the puzzled customer, it is absolutely essential to tell the truth (without revealing company secrets) and to follow through on any offer or promise you make. Not to do so is almost as bad as losing your temper and yelling or slamming down the phone. If you say you'll call back, do it. If you say you'll ask someone else about a problem, ask that person. If you explain why you can't do what the customer wants done, be sure your facts are accurate.

Keeping your word is not just common courtesy, it's common decency—and 9 out of 10 people respond to it favorably. It's also very good business.

WHEN YOU'RE WRONG

In his bestselling book *The 7 Habits of Highly Effective People,* Stephen R. Covey recommends both admitting your mistakes and apologizing for them. "The proactive approach to a mistake is to acknowledge it instantly, correct and learn from it," Covey writes. "It is one thing to make a mistake, and quite another thing not to admit it. People will forgive mistakes, because mistakes are usually of the mind, mistakes of judgment. But people will not easily forgive the mistakes of the heart, the ill intention, the bad motives, the prideful justifying cover-up of the first mistake."

Handle with Care

When it comes to admitting mistakes and apologizing in your business life, however, some top managers would take issue with Covey. They cite incidents where an apology by an employee was interpreted as owning up to liability for a defect or a problem and the apology led to a lawsuit against the company.

The danger in being afraid to apologize is that customers will view you and your company as hard-hearted and unsympathetic and take their business elsewhere. One compromise tactic is to choose your words very carefully, to show your empathy without actually admitting a mistake or apologizing. For instance, if a customer calls and tells you she just bought your new-model toaster oven and it doesn't toast, you could say "I very much appreciate your concern about the toaster oven. I want to do all I can to see if we can get it toasting just the way you think it should." This is preferable to "We apologize for this company's part in putting this defective toaster oven in your hands."

The cautious, self-protective tack is clearly the safest and best from a legal standpoint: It assumes no liability but offers help anyway. It acknowledges that you understand why the person is perturbed and that you are committed to actively seek a solution. That may be as good or better than an apology. If you choose a more openly apologetic response, remember you're taking a risk that could come back to haunt your company.

DEALING WITH MISSED DEADLINES

Missed deadlines and ignored delivery dates can bring companies to their knees. If the holdup is internal, you can apply several kinds of pressure to the tardy individual or group, from gentle nagging and prodding (don't be afraid to ruffle feathers; the stakes are too high) to a company's ultimate weapon: the threat of firing. If you are a manager, you may be able to reallocate people and other resources to get the job done. But remember, when a major company program is in jeopardy, courtesy often has to take a backseat to coercion.

With an outside contractor or vendor, you have less control—and all the more reason to be extremely alert to deadline slippage. As you do with an internal project, set a schedule up front with deadlines that must be met. Have everyone concerned buy into and sign off on the schedule. A paper trail is essential so that nobody down the line can claim they "weren't consulted" or "weren't informed" about a deadline. (It's a good idea to try to get stiff penalty clauses into a contract, though they may be difficult to enforce and they may be small consolation if the project fails to meet its final deadline.)

A good manager is on top of things enough to know when a contractor's work is falling behind, and at the first danger sign he should meet with the project team and ask what it needs to get back on schedule. At this point, you betray no lack of confidence that the project will go smoothly after a few minor adjustments. In fact, let it be perfectly clear that there is simply no alternative—because, you remind the group, "everybody here knows the dire consequences of not bringing this project in on time."

Soft Speech, Big Stick

As long as the contractor demonstrates the ability to meet the schedule (or get back on it quickly if there is a slipup), you can be Mr. Nice Guy. But remember Teddy Roosevelt's remark about speaking softly and carrying a big stick. Your big stick is the schedule and any upcoming payments linked to it. No matter how pleased you are with the creativity of the team and the quality of its work, always keep the schedule at the forefront of discussions. Not-so-subtle remarks like this are not out of line: "I'm very pleased with progress so far, Mr. Henry. I see we have a delivery of prototypes due nine days from today, on the 15th, and a review session on the 22nd. I'm assuming you have no problem with those dates. We're very tight on this one, as you know."

If, despite all your watchfulness, a critical deadline is missed, don't make the often fatal mistake of trying to keep it a secret between you and your contractor. You should tell your direct superior, and if he or she agrees, you should bring in the lawyers. Keeping quiet about a lagging project could cost your company millions, and cost you your job.

COLLECTING MONEY YOU'RE OWED

Collecting overdue payments that people owe you for services performed or products delivered is never a pleasant task. As uncomfortable and frustrated as you may feel putting pressure on a slow payer, you should know that suing and going to court are not always—if ever—a better solution than trying to work it out yourself. "If a payment dispute goes to court," a plain-speaking old lawyer once said, "both parties have already lost." What he meant was that any dollar amount the court eventually decreed had to be paid (or not paid) was seldom worth the combination of court costs, lawyers' fees, emotional stress and strain on the litigants, and countless hours of exasperating arguments and counter-arguments. Here are several steps to consider before going to court.

- If you have received no payment after your second monthly billing (and no request for a payment extension), either call the person who pays the bills or write a personal letter to her attention. Ask if there is some problem with making the payment.
- If the overdue payer mentions a temporary cash shortage, offer to discuss an extended payment schedule, with installments spread out over months or even years.
- If, to your complete surprise, the problem payer claims that you did not perform the work as expected and agreed, hold your temper. Suggest that you sit down and discuss the matter. Make sure you say that you will be bringing along another person to sit in on the discussion.
- If the late payer is a large company, you may be told that your check request is "hung up somewhere" in the accounting department. That may be true, but impress on the company employee that you need the money and ask him to please do everything he can to expedite your payment. If you don't get your check within ten days, call the company's treasurer directly.
- If you continually get excuses and evasive answers about when your check is coming, consider hiring a lawyer to write a stern letter.

Hiring a collection agency to do your dunning can save you the stress of doing it yourself. Collection agencies, however, take a big cut of any payment they receive in your behalf. You might be better off accepting partial payment directly and either postponing full payment or settling for the partial payment. Sometimes it's better and cheaper in the long run just to put a deadbeat behind you and move on.

Actually, the best policy is to never be in the position of having a potential deadbeat customer, especially if you own a small business. Start a new relationship by politely requesting payment up front for the first services or products ordered. Then, as the relationship grows, move towards partial payments for work in progress and payment on delivery of the job.

When establishing the relationship, be up front about your expectations concerning bill payment. Then stick to your guns. If your policy is bills are due at 30 days, call on day 31 if payment isn't received. Usually a gentle reminder can get the situation corrected.

For the chronically late payer, politeness may have to take a backseat to toughness. Don't stoop to shouting or ranting, but tell the deadbeat in no uncertain terms that you'll have to cease work on a work-in-progress until past due invoices are paid. Continuing to do work without payment—or else a firm schedule for payment—simply puts you into a deeper hole. The late payer is making his problems your problem and stealing from you in the process.

YOUR OWN BILLS

A hazard for the person who owns a small business: When you hold payment to vendors even though you have collected from your customer, you can easily begin to believe that the money you are holding is really yours. The next thing

SIX STEPS FOR KEEPING CONTRACTORS HAPPY

Treating your contractors well pays major dividends, especially when you need their extra effort on a project. Here are six simple steps you can take to assure extra service from any contractors with whom you do business.

1. Treat the contractor courteously at all times.
2. Be reasonable with deadlines. Don't ask for the impossible. (When you do ask for the impossible, make sure the contractor knows how grateful you are for the extra effort he is giving you.)
3. Don't ask for a rush job when you don't need it.
4. Let the contractor know when the job isn't time sensitive.
5. Pay promptly.
6. If you ask for a favor, be ready to return the favor in the future.

you know, you've spent it. You then have to use a payment from someone else to pay the vendor who is now overdue. The cycle continues until you end up in bankruptcy. It happens all the time.

When it comes to bills, pay them. On time. It's really that simple, and in the long run it is absolutely the best policy. Contractors and vendors will bend over backwards for you because you treat them well.

STAYING IN TOUCH

You work hard to develop good business relationships with people outside your company—those sometimes demanding but always indispensable customers, clients, contractors, and vendors who can make or break your job. Don't let that carefully nurtured stock of mutual respect and goodwill wither away from neglect. Stay in touch after you've closed a big deal or sold a major program. Follow up to see how the initiatives you helped set in motion are standing the test of time. Offer your services to troubleshoot problems. Treat old customers and clients like old friends. Keep the lines of communication open to former contractors and vendors. In business, staying in touch with your past is a blue-chip investment in your future.

CHAPTER 18

BUSINESS GIFTS

For many companies, the practice of sending business gifts waned in the 1990s, a victim of time pressures and the attendant decline in socially oriented business activities—a turn of events that threatened to make even "doing lunch" more rare. For others, in particular vendors and global businesses, the long-standing custom of gift-giving held its own or became even more important. (See also Gift Giving, page 478.)

Today's business gifts are more likely to be foodstuffs or tickets to a play, concert, or sporting event than something more tangible. Companies are increasingly sensitive to avoiding the appearance of "softening up" clients, and tangible gifts are more suspect than ephemeral ones—giving rise to an attitude that might be expressed as "It's okay if you can *eat* it, *drink* it, or *do* it."

Gift policies vary widely from company to company, but generally fall into two categories: First, gifts given by the corporation as a whole, usually to create goodwill or as a charitable donation; second, gifts given by individuals in the company for the same purpose. Gifts exchanged among employees and supervisors are covered in Exchanging Gifts (page 73); A Gift for Your Assistant (page 217); and Gifts for Bosses (page 125).

GIFTS TO OUTSIDERS

Gifts from the company or its individual senior employees range from standard holiday gifts sent to customers and clients to those thanking business associates for a favor or entertainment. Other gifts might be sent to congratulate a client on a promotion or award or as an expression of sympathy for an illness or death.

FROM THE COMPANY

Clients and customers are the usual recipients of gifts sent by the company as a whole—annual holiday presents or tokens of appreciation as varied as coffee mugs, appointment calendars, paperweights, pen and pencil sets, T-shirts, and

Besides good taste, two things determine the appropriateness of a business gift: its cost and how personal it is. Cost is mostly an issue when giving to customers and clients, with the smell of bribery or favor-currying growing in direct proportion to expensiveness. Too-personal gifts are also out of place in business, including any exchanged at work. Consider carefully your relationship to the person to whom you're giving and what he or she will think appropriate. If you're unsure, it's safer to err on the less personal side.

- Gifts that "show," such as jewelry and clothing, are less appropriate than consumable or perishable items, such as food or flowers. (There are two schools of thought about jewelry: A gift of cufflinks to a man or a pin to a woman may seem fine to some people, while others say even jewelry of this kind crosses the line.)
- Tickets to an event are appropriate, but airplane tickets are not.
- Gifts of perfume, roses, or lingerie have obvious romantic overtones and should never be given in a business environment.

umbrellas. If gifts of this kind are going to bear the company logo, they should be of a certain standard—well-made and in tasteful colors, with the logo understated enough not to look like an advertisement.

- Giveaways, including those given to prospective customers at trade shows, are promotional items. They range from key chains and golf balls to tennis hats and playing cards. These, too, should reflect the company image and be tasteful enough that the recipient will want to keep them.
- In a different league are corporate donations to charities. Financial gifts are a way for successful businesses to give as well as receive—to be a good corporate citizen. Corporate giving also engenders pride in the company and sets an example for employees.

FROM INDIVIDUALS TO CUSTOMERS AND CLIENTS

Individuals in the company who give gifts to outsiders are usually at the executive to mid-manager level. If this includes you, it goes without saying that you abide by company policy and follow company traditions. Make sure your gifts don't seem too stingy or expensive compared with those given by your colleagues, and that the gift doesn't exceed the financial limit set by either your own company or the recipient's. Many businesses don't allow employees to

Business
Gifts

accept anything costing more than $25, and sending a gift to a client who's unable to keep it is awkward for both giver and receiver. (See also Accepting and Declining Gifts, page 241.)

GIFTS FROM OUTSIDE

Rather than setting a ceiling for the cost of gifts received, some companies have policies stating that those costing more than $25 must be disclosed to management. This is a way of keeping tabs on what's coming in from outside and seeing to it that everything stays aboveboard.

Most companies allow employees to receive token gifts from customers and clients because sending them back could insult the giver, especially during the holidays. Some businesses require that any foodstuffs received from outside be divided up and shared; this is because the usual recipients are employees who have the advantage of dealing face-to-face with customers, whereas the people who've done most of the work oftentimes go unrewarded.

GIFT CHOICES

Whether you're giving to a coworker or a business associate from outside, your choice of gift depends on the occasion, your relationship to the recipient, and your position in the company. Besides cost, consider 1) whether the gift is personal or professional, and 2) whether it's temporary or long-lasting.

PERSONAL OR PROFESSIONAL?

The personal versus professional determination depends on how well you know the recipient. At most times, you'll be able to give a personal gift to anyone with whom you're in a close working relationship. Knowing something about the person's hobbies or family may be all the insight you need to make the best choice. An avid biker would no doubt enjoy a bicycle pump and maps of the local bicycle paths; a gardener could be given packets of heirloom vegetable seeds or a set of good-quality garden tools. If you want to send a personal gift but feel you don't know enough about the recipient's likes and dislikes, ask his or her assistant or spouse (if you've met) for suggestions.

A professional gift, on the other hand, is the better choice for someone you don't know very well or with whom you don't work directly. Select a gift that can be used in the workplace—perhaps a reference book, a nice calendar, a pen and pencil set, or a picture frame.

TEMPORARY GIFTS

Flowers, foodstuffs, candy, and beverages fall into the temporary, or perishable, gift category. These are appropriate for most occasions—but especially when a more enduring gift could become a lasting reminder of an illness, a hospitalization, or the death of a family member.

- **FLOWERS.** A great all-purpose gift, flowers can be sent to anyone at any time, thanks to credit cards, teleflorists, and the Internet. You can also pair cut flowers with another gift (say, a vase or a mug) or attach theater tickets or a gift certificate to the arrangement. But don't choose flowers without thinking: A classic spring arrangement is appropriate no matter what, but a delivery of long-stemmed roses will imply romantic sentiments. Similarly, when sending flowers internationally, take care to learn about local customs so that you don't choose flowers with the wrong connotation.

  At any time, consider the occasion and circumstances before choosing what flowers to send:
  - For a host or hostess gift, send cut flowers before your visit or on the following day; you don't want your hosts having to hunt down a vase while they're tending to greeting their guests.
  - For an officemate, choose either an arrangement or a potted plant.
  - For someone who is hospitalized, cut flowers are traditional. If you send a plant, send one that's easy to care for; the last thing the patient or worried family members need is a failing plant that needs reviving.
  - For a funeral, check the obituary to find out whether flowers are desired and to which funeral home they are to be sent.

- **FOOD.** This is one gift that can be shared with others and, with a little research, can be personalized. Find out from the recipient's assistant or spouse if there are any particular favorites; at the same time, make sure the person has no food allergies. If time isn't a consideration, scan catalogs and the backs of magazines for mail-order firms, which offer everything from prime steaks to out-of-season fruits, specialty cakes, and smoked salmon or trout. Or you can keep things economical and impart a special touch by preparing the food yourself—your prized recipe for cheese sticks or brownies, perhaps, or a basket of exotic fruits—and packaging it attractively.

- **WINE AND LIQUOR.** Before sending a gift of wine or liquor, find out whether the recipient drinks—and, if so, what. (Mutual friends will probably supply the answer, but if you are at all unsure, opt for something else.) When sending champagne, go for high quality. Unless you can afford the real article from France's Champagne region or the best versions California has to offer, it's better to give a bottle or two of still wine.

Unlike flowers or chocolates, a gift that endures will last for years as a reminder of an event, a special milestone, or long service to the company. Naturally, the

---

MARKING MILESTONES

Your business associates from both outside and inside the office may live in different worlds, but all share life's major milestones. Acknowledging birthdays, weddings, and other events shows you respect someone's life outside of work. You're not expected give a gift for every significant day in every client's or colleague's life, of course, but some occasions call for at least a card. While chipping in for a group gift is perfectly fine, you might want to also send a separate card to people to whom you are especially close.

- A BIRTHDAY. Though you may have ignored a colleague's or client's birthday in previous years, it's a good idea to recognize a significant one—say, 40 or 50. But note that within the office there exists a double standard for birthdays: It's appropriate for a boss to give an employee a gift, but when it's the other way around, a birthday gift might be interpreted as kissing up. Use your judgment to decide whether a simple card is the better gesture.
- A WEDDING. If you've received an invitation from a coworker or client, send a gift, even if you don't attend. (There are exceptions, though, including an invitation from someone you barely know.) Then again, it may be that you know of an associate's wedding but aren't invited. If so, don't be offended; some prefer to keep their work and personal lives separate. If you still want to send a gift, either do so or organize a group gift from the office or your department.
- THE BIRTH OF A BABY. Unless you're close to the parent(s), a group gift is the best idea. Standard gifts include baby clothing, stuffed animals, toys, picture frames, and receiving blankets—but try for some originality. A gift with a truly timeless quality is a hardback edition of a classic children's book; inscribe it with a message that will be understood by the child when she reaches reading (or read-to) age.
- AN ILLNESS. A get-well card is usually a sufficient gesture when someone is ill unless you have a close relationship with the person. If sending flowers or a potted plant, check with the hospital to make sure they are allowed.
- A DEATH. The standard gifts of condolence when a business associate is dealing with the death of a close relative are 1) flowers with a card, 2) a donation to the deceased's favorite charity or a related medical organization, or 3) food, which gives the family one less thing to think about as they grieve. Consult the obituary to see whether it includes instructions on where to send flowers or donations. Remember that when someone is mourning the death of a family member, the most important thing is to offer condolence and support. This can be done effectively through a note or a simple verbal acknowledgment; express your sympathy and your willingness to help as soon as you hear of the person's loss.

nature of the occasion will help you make your choice. When honoring a retiree, for example, you're not only recognizing her service to the company but acknowledging the start of a new life phase, one with more freedom to enjoy the simple pleasures. Choose a gift the retiree can take long-term advantage of—a high-quality putter (or if it's a group gift, a set of golf clubs), a set of expensively bound books, or membership in a travel club.

THE ART OF PRESENTATION

Even a gift that's thoughtfully chosen, timely, and wonderful in itself can have its effect dulled by sloppy presentation. Wrap it carefully; if you're unable to do a professional-looking job, have it wrapped at the store or ask a proficient friend for help. Two other things to remember:

- Modesty may be an attractive quality in other situations, but never belittle a gift you are giving; be as positive as possible, emphasizing that you thought especially of the recipient when choosing it. Gifts mean more when you're proud to give them.
- Whether a gift is sent or given in person, attach a card—especially if the gift is one of many the person is receiving. Cards serve not only as an expression of your sentiments but also as a useful reminder when thank-you notes are written. A correspondence card is ideal, but a business card can also be used. With the latter, draw a line through your printed name and write a short, personal note. A mere phrase will do: "Best wishes, Beth Landau."

ACCEPTING AND DECLINING GIFTS

When receiving a gift at the office, you may open it as soon as possible; usually, the giver will want to see your reaction and be thanked on the spot. At a shower or retirement party, the opening of presents is often a party in itself. If the occasion for giving is formal, however—a wedding or an official ceremony—gifts are generally put aside, to be opened later.

Act delighted when receiving a gift, regardless of what you actually think of it. Effusing comes naturally if you're thrilled with the gift, but not so easily when you're not. Even if the present is the last thing you wanted, thank the giver for his or her thoughtfulness, letting the actor in you mask any disappointment. Be pleasant but noncommittal: "It's so nice of you to think of me this way!" or "What an imaginative choice!" Do the same in your thank-you note, the sending of which is mandatory.

When thanking someone verbally for a gift, emphasize their thoughtfulness, not your gain. Besides the usual "I love it," praise the giver with "You were so thoughtful" or "You always think of the perfect gift."

Like the verbal thank-you, a note of thanks should be sincere and enthusiastic, and preferably sent within a day or two of receipt. (Try not to let a thank-you note languish on the shelf of good intentions: A late one is not only more difficult to write, but can sound less enthusiastic.) Handwrite the note, making it short, personal, and familiar enough to sound as though you're saying it aloud. And, mention the gift.

A personal handwritten thank-you note should be written in response to flowers and donations sent for a death in the family, and also as thank-you for receipt of a personal condolence note.

To acknowledge a gift given by an entire department, it's fine to offer a general thanks to the group, either by posting a note on the bulletin board or sending out an e-mail message. Make certain, though, that whatever the medium, your message recognizes everyone who contributed.

DECLINING GIFTS

Having to pretend a little pales in comparison to the discomfort of declining a gift, which may be necessary for either of these reasons: 1) Its cost is over the limit allowed by your company, or 2) it is too personal or sexually suggestive.

In the too-costly case, there is really no need for embarrassment: In effect, it is the company, not you, who is declining. A note clearly stating this is all that's needed, regardless of the giver's motivation. The note that follows is an example of one that will spare hurt feelings on the part of someone who had good intentions yet, at the same time, dissuade anyone who was trying to curry favor from doing so again.

Dear Mr. Sharpley:

I found the carved bowl you sent delightful, but I'm afraid the rules here won't let me keep it ($30 or more at Kettle & Black and it's automatically "return to sender"). I'm sure you understand that I really have no choice. Still, I greatly appreciate your thoughtfulness and look forward to maintaining our productive business relationship.

Sincerely,

Diana Dickson

A gift with obvious romantic overtones is more difficult. You don't have to return a dozen long-stem red roses, but you could let the sender know (verbally or via a note) that while you know he meant well, sending such gifts are inappropriate in light of your professional relationship.

More serious is something sexually provocative, like lingerie. If you're given such a gift in person by a member of the opposite sex, return it on the spot, making it clear that the gift is improper: "Honestly, I don't know what you were thinking. I can't accept this, and I think it's obvious why." Then put it in writing and send it. Make a copy of your note and keep it as a record in case any repercussions arise down the line; you may need evidence of your reaction in an era when legal ramifications are an ever-present possibility.

CHAPTER 19

THE THOUGHTFUL TRAVELER

Men and women caught in the throes of making travel plans, packing, and preparing for whatever business is in store probably have etiquette as the last thing on their minds. After all, isn't behaving well a given? The answer should be a resounding yes, but business travelers will do well by themselves and other people when they take a few extra things into account. One is self-reliance, which places fewer burdens on their hosts. Another is choosing well what to take along, a habit that helps make the trip glitch-free.

Just as important is remembering to respect the rights of fellow travelers, a dictum that today includes coping with the growing frustrations of airplane travel and keeping your cell-phone calls in check. The less bumpily things run on a business jaunt (and, to be sure, the less annoyance you cause in the process), the easier it is to focus on the trip's objectives. (See also Doing Business Abroad, page 459.)

BE SELF-RELIANT

Unless a corporate travel office is handling your travel arrangements, build self-reliance into all your plans. Your hosts shouldn't have to tend to things you could handle for yourself.

- Once the date and time of the visit are set, tell the host you'll make your own hotel reservations. Or if your company has a travel department or an affiliation with a travel agency, leave it to them. If your host insists on making them herself, let her do so; the hotel chosen will no doubt be in a place convenient to you both, which is what you want.
- Don't overlook the fact that many large hotel chains offer special rooms for business travelers. Amenities range from data ports for laptops to two-line phones to highlighters and Post-it pads. Another hotel innovation is the on-site business center, equipped with copiers, fax machines, and computers—all for the benefit of businesspeople. Ask the reservationist about special services of this kind and any other perks. You might find the hotel caters to solo busi-

ness travelers by setting aside group tables in the restaurants; a few even organize wine tastings.

- Businesswomen will be wise to ask about other amenities. Today some 40 percent of business trips are taken by women, and large hotel chains have introduced a number of conveniences and services that cater to them—concierge floors with private elevators, bathrooms with well-lit mirrors, skirt hangers, and ice packs to soothe tired eyes. Even baby-sitting services and creative programs to keep children occupied are offered for women who take their kids along, a choice becoming more common among those who travel frequently.

- If you're going to meet a client at your hotel, arrange in advance for the use of a meeting room. A note of caution: Having a business meeting in your hotel room is usually considered too personal these days, especially when it is with a member of the opposite sex.

- If the journey is a long one, plan to arrive in town the day before the meeting, so you'll be refreshed and at your best. If you have an appointment scheduled for the day you arrive, book a flight that leaves plenty of room for unexpected delays. The same holds true if you're driving: Get an early start.

- Make your own arrangements for traveling from the airport to the hotel. If you must go straight from the airport to your meeting, think twice about taking a taxi; the line at the taxi rank may be long on a busy day. A safer alternative, if cost permits, is to arrange for a car service; the driver knows your destination in advance and will be waiting when you arrive.

- If you're scheduled to give a presentation, take any visual aids with you, send them ahead or arrange for them to be available to you. Don't assume that the office you're visiting has, say, an overhead projector for your slides.

- When all of your arrangements are final, prepare an itinerary for your hosts, your office, and your family. Include the following:
  - Your flight schedule, with flight numbers and times of departure and arrival
  - The name, address, and telephone number of your hotel
  - The times and locations of your meeting, with telephone numbers where you can be reached
  - The name and telephone of the contact person in the office you're visiting

TROUBLE-FREE CLOTHING

Pick out the clothes in your wardrobe that are best suited to business travel. They should be lightweight (unless the climate dictates otherwise), wrinkle-resistant, and stylish but not flashy.

- Choose washable shirts or blouses.
- Wear comfortable shoes, but take along a better pair for business meetings and evenings. Leave the sneakers at home.
- Pack at least two sets of underwear and socks or panty hose; don't rely on having the time to rinse out small items at night.
- Make sure you have everything you need in your cosmetic or shaving kit; unlike leisure travelers, business travelers often can't afford the time to buy items they forgot.
- If exercise is part of your daily routine, pack your swimsuit or workout gear; a hotel that offers exercise and sport facilities will provide towels at the gym or pool.
- Pack a collapsible umbrella.

What to wear on a plane? Both men and women may be tempted to don jeans and sneakers for the flight, especially since they know they'll be squeezed into a tight seat and could run into delays. But unless your wardrobe is packed in carry-on luggage, choose khakis and loafers or woolen pants and a blouse. If a checked bag is lost, you won't have to arrive at a meeting looking as if you've just come from mowing the lawn or shopping for groceries.

DIFFERENT CLIMATES, DIFFERENT STYLES?

Choosing a travel wardrobe becomes trickier when you travel to a part of the country where the climate is different from yours. You might assume, for instance, that if you're going to the Deep South you'll find businessmen in shirt sleeves in summer. But you probably won't, since business dress codes are fairly standard throughout the country, with long-sleeved shirts the rule—especially now that air conditioning is ubiquitous. Guard against sartorial missteps by asking the advice of workmates or friends who are familiar with the region's customs.

Dressing for evenings calls for more attention. Men might learn, for example, that a blazer is expected with the usual khakis-and-sport shirt uniform worn for casual events. Likewise, in some places women dress more formally in evening than during the day, with a beaded top instead of a twin set; accordingly, a woman should pack a dressier garment than she might be wearing. As a practicality, those who travel several times a year can invest in one of the stylish daytime-to-evening outfits that are designed with the traveling businesswoman in mind.

On Fridays, don't dress down—unless, that is, you are visiting one of your own company's offices and have no doubts about the dress code. If you are

z

PRESCRIPTION MEDICINES

Nothing can create quite so much havoc as leaving essential medications at home—except losing them. Your insurance when traveling is to divide a particular medicine into two portions, which you put in different places. (A woman can put half in her handbag and the other half in her cosmetic kit; a man, half in his shaving kit and the rest in his briefcase.) If a piece of luggage is lost or stolen, the chances that your medicine goes with it decrease. On a lengthy trip, you may also want to take along a prescription from your doctor. Similarly, if you find it impossible to function without your eyeglasses, take an extra pair; if you don't have one, carry a lens prescription with you for trip-long peace of mind.

making a presentation or attending a meeting at another company, wear your usual business clothes; then wait until you are invited to remove your jacket before taking the liberty to doff it.

EN ROUTE

Trains, planes, and automobiles: Each of these modes of transportation presents its own set of concerns for the business traveler.

UP, UP, AND AWAY

Airline travel is complicated by 1) the penchant airlines have for changing their rules, and 2) the fact that airports have stricter rules regarding security. But take note: If there's one place on earth where an ordinary citizen must always follow directions, it's an airport. News reports in the early 1990s told of a businessman (an assertive type, yet otherwise unremarkable) who lunged through the security gates without being checked. Afraid the man might be armed, authorities evacuated two terminals, and thousands of passengers were delayed for hours. Whether the cause was impatience or sheer stupidity is open to question, but the chaos that resulted speaks for itself.

Luggage and ID. So there won't be any surprises, check with the airline about size limits for carry-on luggage and the number of pieces allowed before you pack your bags. It's also common procedure for you to be asked for photo identification when you check in, and by law you will be barred from boarding if you can't produce a driver's license or some other form of photo ID. If this happens, you can exhibit your first courteous act of the trip by not arguing

The Thoughtful Traveler

with airline employees or making a scene. As prevention, get in the habit of jotting down a checklist before you leave for the airport—wardrobe items, toiletries, business papers, and personal documents, with your photo ID at the top of the list.

In the air. Once you're aloft, the real test of your civility begins. Every frequent flier can conjure up a long list of annoying, rude, and even dangerous acts he or she has witnessed. As amazing as it seems, the behavior of some passengers qualifies as a threat to safety, with alcohol often to blame. Notorious case studies abound: The man who wrestled with an attendant for a liquor bottle, shouting obscenities; the enraged woman who knocked an airline attendant to the floor because there were no more sandwiches; and incidents even more appalling. As for minor incivilities, you might as well grin and bear them. If you don't respond to boorish behavior with similar reactions, your journey will at least *feel* a lot smoother. Any truly unacceptable behavior should always be reported to the flight attendant.

Some airplane dos and don'ts:

- **DO** tell the flight attendant if you need to deplane quickly. He may be able to move you to a seat closer to the front.
- **DO** carry on at least a brief conversation with the stranger next to you only if you are sure he or she invites it. Conversely, politely cut off unwelcome chitchat by excusing yourself to read a magazine or to do your work.
- **DO** ask anyone seated next to you whether he or she will be bothered by the clicking of your laptop computer.
- **DO** treat airline attendants politely. Be patient when you make a request, say "please" and "thank you," and thank them when you deplane.
- **DON'T** try to board before your seat number is called. Never try to push ahead of fellow passengers while walking down the boarding ramp, and be careful not to block the aisle for more than a few seconds when putting luggage in an overhead compartment.
- **DON'T** crush other people's belongings in an overhead compartment to make room for your own. If there's no room for your luggage, ask the flight attendant for help. If he has no solution, accept that you must check the bag; personnel are usually standing by to make sure it gets into the cargo hold.
- **DON'T** embarrass the helpless parents of a crying child. If a noisy infant or restless youngster disturbs you, leave your seat and scout the plane to see if a vacant seat is available. If, as a rule, you find crying babies intolerable, add ear plugs to the items in your carry-on bag.
- **DON'T** overdo the alcohol. Watch your drinking or avoid it altogether, especially if you're going to attend a meeting after arriving. No matter how

liberal your corporate culture, you don't want to be met by a colleague—or even more important, a client—with liquor on your breath.

ON A TRAIN

Businesspeople who travel between the major cities of the Northeast have the luxury of choosing rail over air. Naturally, the tenets of courteous airplane travel apply equally to travel on a train, whether for a business trip or the daily commute. One is key: the use of electronic devices. Unlike airline passengers, railroad travelers are able to use their personal cellular phones to conduct business, ring up friends, or to check the football scores if they so wish. The most thoughtless have a way of turning their seats and nearby vacant ones into an office of sorts, spreading out papers and tapping away on a laptop when not shouting into a phone. So it is that an extended trip on a train has even more potential than an airline flight to make life miserable for travelers. (See also Cellular Phones and Pagers, page 297.)

ON THE ROAD

It's stating the obvious to say that someone driving to another town for a meeting should allow plenty of time to reach the destination. If you realize you're

---

PUBLIC NUISANCE NUMBER ONE?

Today, respecting the rights of fellow travelers almost threatens to boil down to one overriding rule: Keep to a minimum your calls from a cellular phone, especially when you're on a train or any other enclosed area trapping those around you as unwilling listeners. Declaring a moratorium on cell phone use while traveling is unrealistic, for some, but remember that in an airport lounge or equally crowded place, idle phone chats with friends contribute to the din. Do your part to keep the peace by making your call in an out-of-the-way place.

If you must use your wireless phone on a train, speak softly and briefly and save any calls that aren't urgent for later. (If the world didn't fall apart when calls had to be placed from ordinary telephones, it surely won't do so now.) When it comes to airphones, which are fitted into every few seat backs on a plane, remember that they aren't a toy. Calls made from one of these devices are not only expensive but disturbing to anyone within reach of your voice; talking over the engine noise of a plane means you are going to be perceived as shouting. Use airphones only when really necessary and try to keep your voice to a reasonably low level.

going to be late, call ahead and give your estimated time of arrival. Notification enables your clients or colleagues to continue with their own routine until you arrive; not only will they appreciate your thoughtfulness but your anxiety will also be relieved.

Another reason to build extra time into your schedule is concern for your own safety: You won't have to floor the gas pedal to make your appointment. The most common cause of accidents is speeding, which is responsible for 20 percent of automobile fatalities. Drive at the speed limit, turn on your blinker before changing lanes, and don't tailgate cars in front of you. Keep in mind that speeders and tailgaters run the risk of eliciting so-called road rage on the part of other drivers, an eventuality to be avoided at all costs.

In a Taxi or Limousine

Don't automatically be suspicious of a taxi driver who pegs you as an out-of-towner. At the same time, remember that drivers who are quick to take a more circuitous (read, more lucrative) route to your destination surely number more than a few. Before you leave, call your host or hotel and ask the most direct route from the airport or train station and the usual approximate fare.

Paying. Make sure you have small bills in your wallet in case the driver is not able to make change; although it is the driver's responsibility to be able to

---

POINTERS FOR CAR PASSENGERS

A car passenger traveling with fellow businesspersons should watch his p's and q's. Jabbering on about something can distract the driver, who may be reluctant to tell you so. You'll have to use your experience or intuition to gauge the appropriate level of conversation. Other hints:

- Don't lose yourself in your laptop unless there's urgency to make a deadline that the driver shares. Withdrawing completely is as discourteous as talking someone's ear off.
- Before turning on the radio, ask your companion's permission and what kind of station he or she prefers. Naturally, the same goes for the driver.
- Use your cell phone only when really necessary or when a business call is being made on behalf of you both. If you are the driver, remember that safety comes first.
- By all means don't smoke, especially in someone else's car. If you must have a cigarette, wait for a rest stop.

change at least a $20 bill, there are no guarantees. The problem can be avoided altogether by using a car or limousine service, which allows you to pay with a credit card. Also, the cost is determined up front, which means no surprises.

All-day service. Travelers with hectic schedules should consider a third alternative: hiring a limousine and driver for a full day or even the whole trip. The driver will be at your service for as long as necessary, patiently waiting at the curb whenever you have to be picked up. This kind of arrangement doesn't come cheaply, but the peace of mind you gain is worth the extra cost.

N O T E : Even though you'll be sitting in the backseat of a taxi or limousine, be amicable and do not condescend to the driver. You're not expected to develop a friendship, but occasional small talk not only shows you as thoughtful but can improve the service in the bargain.

AT YOUR DESTINATION

No matter how weary you feel, be gracious as you check into your hotel. If you have to make any special requests, a polite demeanor will get you further than a brusque one. If, say, you failed to reserve a meeting room in advance and one isn't available, you may need to ask whether you can use a table in the dining room or cocktail lounge during off hours.

Remember these tips as you check in and get settled:

- For safety's sake, don't confirm your room number aloud when you are given your key, electronic or otherwise. On the off chance a disreputable character in the lobby has spotted you as a likely target, the whereabouts of you and your belongings will remain a secret.
- If you find something about your room you don't like, call the front desk and ask for a change, giving the reason: The room is too noisy, too near the elevator, or you prefer a better view. Most hotels will try to accommodate your requests, depending on availability.
- Call your host to let him or her know you've arrived. Confirm the time of your meeting: "I'll be there at 8 o'clock sharp tomorrow morning. Look forward to seeing you then!"

DEALING WITH HOTEL STAFF

Large hotels have full-service staffs to assist their customers. Although the staff may be extremely deferential and willing to handle most requests, don't treat them as servants of a kind. Instead, make a point of being courteous and not skimping on your tipping. Not only is this the right thing to do, but word

The Thoughtful Traveler

spreads about rude or difficult guests, who can expect no more than the minimum of attention. (See also How Much to Tip, page 254.)

- **THE DOORMAN.** This may be the first hotel employee you encounter as you step out of your car. Besides greeting you, doormen can help you with directions and will hail or call taxicabs.
- **THE PARKING ATTENDANT.** If you are driving a car, an attendant may take it to the garage. Find out if valet parking is required; if it isn't, you can save tip money by taking it in or out yourself for the rest of your stay. At the same time, keep in mind that the attendants rely on tips as part of their salary.
- **THE CONCIERGE.** Large hotels have a concierge's desk to provide information and services that are given informally at other hotels—directions, ordering theater tickets, suggesting restaurants (and making the reservations), even ordering flowers to send your mother on her birthday.
- **FRONT-DESK PERSONNEL.** In hotels without a concierge, the personnel at the front desk are a source of help—for directions and information about the city and restaurants. They often wear name tags and will greet you more warmly if you call them by name.
- **THE BELLMAN.** The bellman takes your luggage from the car to the front desk and then from there to your room. Unless you have only a light bag or the hotel is especially busy, don't deprive him of his tip by lugging your bags yourself. If during your stay you have to ask a favor—having a package picked up, perhaps—a bellman will be sent to run your errand.
- **HOUSEKEEPING.** In addition to keeping rooms clean, this office handles complaints or requests about your room—not enough towels, for example, or requests for an ironing board or other equipment. If you need service of any kind for your room, call the housekeeping number on your room telephone, not the front desk.
- **ROOM SERVICE.** Tempting though it may be, room service should be kept to a minimum. It is expensive at any hotel, and at some the costs are sky high—not to mention a shock to the person at your company who reimburses expense accounts. If there is no room service menu in your room, don't hesitate to ask about prices before you order.

In some hotels you'll find a basket of snacks and a fridge full of beverages, already there for the taking. The guest selects an item and checks it off an attached bill; the mini-bar and food costs are added to your room charge at checkout. The markup for this convenience is considerable, and if you aren't careful, it will add a surprising amount to your bill.

DINING OUT

On a business trip, dining out is an inevitable part of the package, whether the occasion is a business meal or a social one. If you find yourself dining solo in your hotel, don't feel awkward. (Remind yourself that in Europe and much of the rest of the world, dining alone is nothing to be embarrassed about.) A book will keep you occupied while you're waiting for your food. If, however, you prefer to have company, check with the front desk to see if group tables are set aside for business travelers. (For full treatment of dining out, see Business Meals, page 391.)

WHEN YOU'RE THE HOST

When you're the visitor but are playing the host, ask your hotel's concierge or front-desk personnel for restaurant recommendations. You'll want a place reputable enough to do your company credit but where you won't have to watch what your guest orders. Even if your expense account has no limits, avoid very expensive restaurants; your client may take it as a sign of fiscal irresponsibility. When calling for a reservation, it's fine to ask the average cost of a meal or how prices range for main courses, appetizers, and wine. Having made reservations, you'll also find it easier to resist a guest's suggestion of a pricey restaurant.

If your dining partners are customers or clients, it's understood that you will pay the tab. Use a credit card, having made sure beforehand that the restaurant accepts the one you plan to hand over. (Although it's the rare restaurant that doesn't take credit cards, never take a chance; the embarrassment of being caught without enough cash is one of the business traveler's worst nightmares.) If you and your guests have overcoats, check them and pay the tip when you leave. To keep a guest from insisting on paying for the retrieval of his coat, go quietly ahead to the coatroom and tip the hostess.

WHEN YOU'RE THE GUEST

It is likely that you'll be invited to dinner by the business associate you've traveled to meet, which means that he or she expects to pay. Accept graciously, even if your expense account is the bigger one.

Even if you're taken to a five-star restaurant, be modest in what you order. Never go straight to the highest end of the menu, which might put your host in an uncomfortable position later down the road. A case history of the perils of careless ordering centers around an art director at a global advertising agency

The Thoughtful Traveler

who was asked by the president to invite some of her staff members and a visiting colleague to dinner. Eager to impress the guest of honor, she chose a well-known restaurant and, after everyone was settled, asked him to choose the wine. He selected a $200 bottle of Chateau Lafitte, its price unknown to the hostess until the check arrived. Although her guest worked for the same company (connoisseur extraordinaire though he was), it was she who ended up in the doghouse when her expense report was submitted.

In addition to being wined and dined, business travelers are entertained in other ways. For tips on attending private clubs, the theater, and sporting events, see Other Entertainments, page 419.

HOW MUCH TO TIP?

Whether to tip—and how much, of course—is always a matter of concern when you're traveling on business. Remember three key things: First, tip discreetly. Second, the longer the task takes, the larger the tip. Third, don't tip too much; anyone who flashes tip money or lavishes inappropriate tips on waiters, doormen, or anyone else will show himself as foolish in the extreme. Some rules of thumb for tipping:

- **SKYCAP AT AIRPORT.** The standard tip for the skycap who checks your bags at curbside is $1 per bag. A skycap who carts your bags to the check-in counter inside or elsewhere deserves double that.
- **TAXI AND LIMOUSINE DRIVERS.** The standards for tipping cab and limousine drivers vary from place to place, with some local drivers expecting no tip at all. Unless you're in a cab with someone who can tell you what's customary, assume a tip of 10 to 15 percent will be enough. Be sure you have enough change and small bills on hand at all times so that you and your companions can get out without delay.
- **DOORMAN.** It's not necessary to tip a hotel or restaurant doorman on arrival unless he takes your bags out of the car and readies them for the bellman. Follow the $1 per bag rule. If he hails a cab for you, tip him $1 for every person in your party. If the doorman has been particularly helpful during your stay, you may decide an extra $5 is in order.
- **BELLMAN.** When the bellman arrives at your room with your luggage, give him $1 or $2 for every bag he has carried.
- **PARKING VALET/ATTENDANT.** At your hotel or elsewhere, the attendant who parks and retrieves your car gets $1 or $2.
- **HOUSEKEEPER.** If you happen to see the person who cleans your room, you may hand her an envelope with your tip and thank you. Most

hotels suggest leaving an envelope containing your tip at the front desk at check-out time. The standard is $2 for each night.

- **CONCIERGE.** In large hotels, this is the staff member to ask for help with theater tickets or dinner reservations; a $5 (or $10 for hard-to-get tickets) tip will do for these services or any other special help. Whenever the concierge gives you directions around the hotel or the city, no tip is expected.
- **WAITER.** The waiter receives 15 to 20 percent of the tab (excluding tax), regardless of your opinion of service provided. This applies across the board, from the corner coffee shop to a posh restaurant. If the service was unacceptable, you may reduce your tip, but not too drastically. Sometimes, poor service is the result of a problem that the wait staff can't control. If you quietly express your displeasure, sometimes the headwaiter or manager will make amends, perhaps by saying your coffee and dessert are on the house.
- **HEADWAITER, CAPTAIN.** These employees usually receive 25 percent of tip to your waiter, but only if they have been actively involved in serving you. Either tip them separately or increase the amount of your tip to reward the extra service.

THE SAFETY-MINDED BUSINESSWOMAN

If you're a woman on a business trip, don't be lulled into thinking that your briefcase, laptop, and no-nonsense attire protect you against unwanted attention. Keep more or less to yourself, at least where strangers are concerned, and keep what conversation you do have impersonal. Don't be frightened (and above all, don't look frightened), but remember that women are more vulnerable to danger. Doing the following will increase your sense of security.

AT YOUR HOTEL

Electronic keys have reduced the incidence of hotel room break-ins dramatically since their introduction, but you can take extra measures. Some hotels have club or concierge floors with keyed elevator access. At hotels lacking such facilities, it's a good idea to ask for a room near the elevator, so you won't have to travel down a long corridor. Have your key or door card in hand before you arrive at your room to avoid fumbling through your handbag at the door. If you stay in a motel, make sure it's one with only interior entrances to the rooms.

Once you're settled, don't allow anyone into your room unless he or she is expected and you're absolutely positive you know who it is. The chambermaid who comes in the evening to turn down your bed will have a key, but other

TRAVELING WITH YOUR BOSS?

If you find yourself setting off on a business trip with the boss, keep two words in mind: respect and deference. No bowing and scraping is in order (nor should your boss expect it), but holding doors, seeing to it that she has the more comfortable seat, and letting her initiate a conversation shows an unspoken understanding of your respective ranks. Unless your executive traveling companion insists on doing them herself, you should take charge of various tasks—hailing cabs, checking in at the hotel, making restaurant reservations, and tipping service people. Stay on your toes in all regards: traveling with the boss gives you the opportunity not only to let her get to know you better but also for you to shine.

hotel personnel should be announced by the front desk before showing up at your room. Never open your door before checking through the peephole to confirm that it is either a service you ordered or someone you know.

Use discretion when getting into an elevator with a sole male occupant. If you become uneasy once inside, push the button for the next floor and get out. Many hotels will see to it that you are escorted to your room at off hours.

OUT AND ABOUT

If you've driven to your destination and find yourself driving at night, park in a visible, lighted place. Look around before getting out of the car. Get your car keys ready when returning to the car, and then glance under the car and in the backseat before getting in.

If someone appears to be following you as you're walking to your car, walk past it to find help. Likewise, if you're walking on the street and sense you're being followed, do an about-face, cross the street, or duck into a store.

CHAPTER 20

AT CONVENTIONS AND TRADE SHOWS

W hat's called in common parlance a "convention" embraces the trade show, but these are gatherings of two different kinds. The aim of a typical convention might be to bring together the far-flung managers of a multi-branched company or to direct attention to certain issues in a professional field as a whole. The trade show has a sole purpose: for vendors to display and promote their wares to prospective customers. Semantics aside, both occasions usually dwarf most any other kind of business convocation, held as they are in hotels or cavernous conference centers and lasting for as long as two to five days.

The following pages begin with a few precepts of general conduct at conventions and trade shows. The focus then shifts to the practicalities of the latter, with pointers largely directed to exhibitors in charge of display booths.

HOW MUCH FUN?

Because attending a convention or trade show usually means traveling to another city or a resort, a social aspect is always present. A holiday spirit takes hold after hours, with merriment the rule in hospitality suites—rooms rented by participating companies to provide their delegates with a space where they can relax and entertain. Golfing and group excursions to city restaurants and tourist sites are other standard activities.

While the chance to have fun is an integral part of the convention experience, smart convention-goers won't let their hair down too enthusiastically. The last thing you want to be is a stick-in-the-mud, but bear in mind that a delegate's conduct reflects on his or her company—after hours as well as during the formal proceedings. Remember, too, that poor opinions of someone who drinks too much or dresses in a way that attracts the wrong kind of attention have the habit of finding their way back to the home office.

TRAVELING WITH YOUR SPOUSE

If your spouse or partner is coming along to an out-of-town convention, make sure he or she understands that this isn't just another vacation, especially if the company is footing the bill. Although wives, husbands, and significant others are free to entertain themselves by shopping or sightseeing during the day, the company may be hosting evening receptions or other events that everyone is expected to attend. To fit in, the well-meaning spouses make an effort to learn something about whatever topics are the focus of the convention, allowing them to join in conversations in a reasonably knowledgeable way. Making the effort demonstrates an appreciation of the convention's actual purpose.

After-hours activities not sponsored by the company—a foray into the entertainment district, for example, or a group visit to a dance club—are another matter, and neither the delegate nor spouse should feel an obligation to take part. Dancing away the wee hours at the hottest new nightclub in town may be an experience to remember, but it may also have consequences the next morning, when there are meetings and conferences to attend.

DOWN TO BUSINESS

It goes without saying that the meetings are the real business of a convention, which means you should practice more than your golf swing in advance. In a word, go prepared. (See also When You Attend, page 380.)

- Review the agenda beforehand. You might discover a subject you feel passionate about to be the focus of one of the seminars, and you are eager to get involved. List the points you want to make (if only in the question-and-answer period) and arm yourself with any facts and figures that can back up any contentions you put forward.
- If you have questions you want answered or issues you think worth bringing up, write them down. Then practice asking them until each is the very model of conciseness. Rambling on at the mike won't win you points with anyone present and may garble your question to boot.
- Learn as much as you can about the principal speakers, not just by reading their biographies in the program but also by asking workmates if they can flesh out the speakers' backgrounds in any way; doing this will allow for a more meaningful conversation if you happen to be introduced to one.
- If you're going to make a presentation, remember to give credit to any other people who helped you prepare it, stating their names in full.

Once the convention is in progress, observe two important rules: The first and most obvious is to show up for the meetings you're scheduled to attend. Even if the topic isn't all that pertinent to your daily work back home, you have the obligation to participate after money has been spent to get you there. The second rule is to be punctual. Coming in late is disruptive, and you are representing your company—the name of which, remember, is emblazoned across your name tag.

At meetings, keep your mind on the subject and not on the coming night's activities. The more you concentrate on the proceedings, the more relaxed and carefree you'll feel afterwards. Also make a point of taking your own notes, since relying on the minutes to be distributed later can be a big mistake. Many of the points and insights you find important may be overlooked by the minutes taker, and even the company genius may find it impossible to mentally summon up every single one.

Networking

A convention hands you a networking opportunity on a platinum platter. During breaks, make it a point to meet people from other companies or from out-of-town branches of your own. It may be tempting to spend all your time with your chums from the home office, but remember that the very fact that you and the strangers around you work for the same company—or in the same field—means that you have something in common. You never know when a perfunctory first meeting may someday blossom into a valuable business relationship. (See also "How Do You Do?" page 267.)

TRADE SHOWS

No business event has quite the buzz of these extravaganzas, with their endless maze of display booths and throngs of people trekking to and fro. Exhibitors compete against one another to lure the curious and interest them in a desirable product, be it a new kitchen gadget pitched to a hardware retailer or an upcoming nonfiction release for booksellers.

Crowds, banners, color, music, noise: An atmosphere this overwhelming can grow wearying before long, making it all the more important for exhibitors who tend booths to keep their cool and treat even casual browsers as their best customers. As an exhibitor, remember that you are seen not as an individual but as the embodiment of your company.

NAME TAG ETIQUETTE

However negligible the contribution of a name tag to the overall impression you make, these unassuming little plastic badges are subject to certain rules. One potential courtesy falls not to you but to the company person in charge of ordering name tags: He or she will do everyone a favor by picking the necklace-style models, which are fitted with a string that loops around the neck. No longer will your nice gray jacket have to be punctured by a pin.

Two basics for name tag wearers:

- Wear a pin-on name tag on the right side of your chest, about four inches below the shoulder. This positioning will ensure it is in clear view when you are shaking hands during introductions.
- Don't wear your name tag outside the convention hall. Ideally, the tags should be small enough to be easily slipped into a pocket or handbag while you go to and from meetings.

Name tags are almost always preprinted these days, but there may be an occasion where you have to take on the task yourself. If so, proceed as follows.

- Don't write "Mr.," "Mrs.," or "Ms." in front of your name on the card. Technically, a professional title such as "Dr." may be added, but this is determined by how much the wearer wants to advertise his or her credentials.
- At business (not social) events, it's appropriate to add your title under your name: "Bryce Walker, Production Manager." Unless the convention is confined to fellow employees, add your company name as well.
- A spouse's name tag should include the company members name, which is placed in parentheses on the second line: "Gretchen Bell," followed by "(Terry Bell)." If a female spouse has retained her name, the tag would read "Gretchen Iglehart" with "(Mrs. Terry Bell)" below.

WITH PROSPECTIVE CUSTOMERS

At a trade show, it's the nature of the beast for people to make snap judgments when they pause at a booth, meaning it is doubly important for you to demonstrate good business etiquette even as you demonstrate your product. Always stand when talking to a prospective customer, shake hands, express interest in the person, and give him or her your undivided attention. Also remember that for any man or woman tending a booth, business clothes are essential. Even if the show is held in a conference center in a famously casual resort town—and the attendees' attire is in keeping—dress as if you were meeting an important client back at the office.

Whenever you have the chance to demonstrate a product to a dealer, retailer, or wholesaler, take pains to draw the prospect in. If you're taking her through the operation of a new miracle blender, for example, hand it over for her to examine. Ask questions to make sure she understands how it works and what its advantages are; doing this gives you the chance to talk about her needs and objectives. Don't hover, and don't come on with a hard sell. A personal, more sociable discussion will not only achieve better results but it can show that you are an interesting person and a pleasant potential business associate.

The trickiest part of your job is balancing several customers at once without offending any one of them. Have business cards at the ready, using them to momentarily placate any visitors awaiting their turn. Much in the manner of putting someone on hold on the telephone, utter a quick "Please excuse me" to the person you're talking with, turn to the bystander and hand her a card, and say, "Would you mind waiting a bit? I'll be right with you." If you see that a boothmate is free, direct the person to him or her. Or, if possible, quickly set up an appointment to meet later in the day.

Even if you're making small talk with a potential customer, it's not a good idea to invite another one to join in unless your intuition tells you otherwise: The best tack is to give undivided attention to one person at time. The same rule applies for product demonstrations. If someone is standing by observing, that's fine, but you should direct your demonstration to the person you're with at the moment. At the same time, make it clear to the other person that you'll turn to him as soon as you have finished.

WITH OTHER EXHIBITORS

If you attend trade shows regularly, you'll more than likely be acquainted with many of the boothtenders from other companies. While you'll no doubt want to catch up with them, and maybe make plans for the evening, remember that you're not at a high school reunion. The less time you spend schmoozing with old friends, the fewer potential customers back at your booth will be waiting their turn with one of your overextended boothmates.

For the sake of your fellow boothmates, be punctual when it is your turn to take over the post. Getting sidetracked at a huge show is easy, and keeping people waiting can cause a ripple effect for some time afterwards.

THE WELL-EQUIPPED BOOTH

In addition to the tables where your products and promotional brochures are displayed, a well-equipped booth is stocked with other materials and items. Optional extras are entertainment, prizes, and giveaways.

- **PROSPECT CARDS.** These preprinted cards ensure that a prospective customer who stops by the booth without a business card gets into your records. Inexpensive to print, the cards look more professional than asking the person to write his or her name on a piece of scrap paper or the back of your own business card. Too, if you add to the card an "Anything to note?" line beneath the lines for name, title, company, address, and phone number, you may glean more information than an ordinary business card would yield—another contact, perhaps, or the best time of day to reach the person.

- **PEN AND NOTEPADS.** Have plenty of pads and pens available in case anyone wants to jot something down. Notepads with the company logo are a good idea, not only as a convenience for the attendees but as a lasting reminder of your organization.

- **ICE WATER AND CUPS.** Keep a filled pitcher of ice water on the display table alongside plastic cups and a small sign that says "Help Yourself"—a nice gesture and a customer magnet in the bargain. Thirsty attendees will stop at the booth and probably strike up a conversation while accepting your hospitality, something they may not have done otherwise. The addition of coffee, cookies, or candies makes the booth all the more welcoming.

- **MEETING TABLES.** If you have enough space, put out two or three small folding tables (each with two or three folding chairs) so that potential customers can sit comfortably while you talk with them about your product.

- **ENTERTAINMENT.** Be careful here. Having a ponytailed folk singer strum a guitar and warble a couple of numbers may attract attention to your booth, but remember that your objective is to generate strong leads, not to entertain. Offer prospect cards to people who have gathered to listen if they haven't handed over business cards of their own.

- **PRIZES.** Staging a raffle or contest for which the "entry fee" is a business card has proved highly effective at trade shows. Prizes range from an elaborate flower arrangement to a trip to Bermuda. Golf prizes—a putter or a sleeve of balls, for example—are especially good draws. Note that contests often require the addition of a separate boothtender, whose job is to see to the contestants and the equipment. One idea for a contest is a daily putting competition, which requires little more than adequate space, a synthetic putting green, a putter, and a couple of sleeves of golf balls. The contestant with the highest percentage of successful putts at the end of the day is the winner. This is a good example of an attraction that keeps people coming back to your booth throughout the show.

- **GIVEAWAYS.** A simpler way to attract attention is to give a small souvenir or favor to anyone who leaves his business card or fills out a prospect card. Single carnations or roses are nice, and inexpensive but tasteful key chains with the company logo may be worth the investment.

FOLLOWING UP

A handwritten note to each prospective customer you talked with will have more impact than a typewritten one, which looks suspiciously like a form letter. Tell the recipient how nice it was to meet him and that you hope the interest he expressed in your product will someday result in an order. A reference to a nonbusiness topic you discussed—a new grandchild, for example—personalizes the letter further and lets it stand out from the norm.

PART VI

THE SPOKEN
WORD

---

*J*ust as walking is walking, talking is talking. True? Well, not really. Almost everyone can talk, but the number of people who are truly well spoken seems to be dwindling. In business, verbal communication is always an exercise loaded with opportunities and pitfalls. A lack of clarity, slurred words, poor grammar, and a wandering mind may be tolerated by your friends, but will do you no favors in the workplace.

It is no exaggeration to state that communicating is central to success in business, and an inability to do it well can break a job candidate, stunt career advancement, and cause serious credibility problems for both the speaker and the company. From the moment you offer a hello, what you say and the way you say it will determine how you're perceived both individually and as a representative of your employer. The following section begins with the all-important first impression made in introductions, proceeds to the many components of speaking correctly and getting your message across (both verbally and nonverbally), and ends with the proper use of that most efficient business tool, the telephone, now portable, omnipresent, and ripe with the potential for misuse.

CHAPTER 21

"HOW DO YOU DO?"

Although the ways of going about an introduction are less rigid than they once were—a reflection of the casualness that's entered all segments of American life—the act itself remains as important as ever. Failing to introduce a newcomer or a stranger, whether a business associate at a meeting, a visitor to the office, or a guest at a party, is a serious social error. That said, learning the basics for introducing yourself and others helps you feel more secure in business situations and, as a bonus, appear more polished.

WHO'S INTRODUCED TO WHOM?

Today it is rank, not gender, that plays a role in deciding who's presented to whom. The more "important" person "receives" the other person, and his name is mentioned first: "Mr. Biggins, this is Susan Loftin, our art assistant." Importance has nothing to do with snobbery and can be defined in many ways: by job level, age, experience, and degree of public recognition. (An exception to the person-of-importance rule is made when introducing peers of equal status, in which case either can be presented to the other.)

Senior executives, members of the clergy, and high-ranking dignitaries are obviously persons of importance. But in business settings, so are clients, whose goodwill is essential to the health of a company. Also keep in mind that today's business climate is more easygoing; for this reason, don't be quick to judge someone to be out of bounds if his technique doesn't follow standard protocol. With an introduction, the most important thing is to *do* it!

If you're uncertain about who to deem "important," fall back on the following guidelines, which should put you on safe ground.

- Introduce a younger person to an older person.
- Introduce a coworker to a client or to a worker from another company.
- Introduce a layperson to an official.
- Introduce anyone at a party to a guest of honor.

Remember to mention the "important," or senior-ranking, person's name first. For instance, when age is a factor, the choice would be "Mr. Sixty, I'd like you to meet Mr. Forty."

THE FOUR ESSENTIALS

Whether introducing yourself or being introduced by others, smile and stay relaxed. A warm smile, eye contact, a firm handshake, and a sincere greeting are essential to a successful first meeting. Always do the following:

- **STAND UP.** Today this rule applies to men and women alike. If you are seated, failing to rise could suggest that you think the other person unimportant. Even if there's no room to stand—you're wedged behind a table at a restaurant, for instance—briefly lift yourself out of your chair while extending your hand; otherwise, you may seem uninterested or aloof.
- **SMILE AND MAKE EYE CONTACT.** Your smile conveys warmth, openness, and interest in the person you're meeting. Making eye contact shows that you're focused on her and her alone.
- **STATE YOUR GREETING.** The direct "How do you do?" or "Hello" have long been regarded as standard. Save "It's so nice [great] to meet you" for those you've heard something positive about. And add such phrases as "I've heard so much about you" only if they are true. A good idea: Repeating the person's name—"How do you do, Ms. Dowd?"—is not only flattering but serves as a memory aid.
- **SHAKE HANDS.** A proper handshake lasts about three seconds; the clasped hands are pumped once or twice and then unclasped, even if the introduction drags on. Leaning in slightly expresses more enthusiasm, but your smile and tone of voice should have already conveyed this by themselves.

WHEN YOU'RE THE INTRODUCER

When it falls to you to make an introduction, remember two things: 1) Offer snippets of information about the people you're introducing (their professions, perhaps, or where they're from), and 2) state their names in full. "Ms. Dawson, this is Scott Bernstein our marketing assistant. Scott, meet Carol Dawson, from Wilde and Wooley." Information about the person (in this case, the client) puts him or her into a context and provides an opening for conversation: "Wilde and Wooley? They've been going great guns lately, I hear." Or "Do you know Karen Nelson? I used to work with her before she joined your firm."

Your choice of words when making an introduction is flexible. "I'd like you to meet ... " or "May I introduce ... " or any other reasonably gracious phrase you feel comfortable with is fine. When you are introducing people of unequal rank or age, use professional titles if they are called for. For example, a young salesman meeting a physician would be introduced to *Dr.* Michael Yamaguchi. Official titles such as governor, congressman, or one of the various military ranks are retained even if the position is no longer held.

Once the people you've introduced have begun chatting, you can excuse yourself at the first opportunity. Just wait for an opening in the conversation before bidding them adieu.

THE ALL-IMPORTANT HANDSHAKE

Most people are sizing you up as they shake your hand. What's more, a handshake is in order not only when you're being introduced but also when you welcome people into your office, when you run into someone you know outside of work, when you say good-bye, and when another person offers his or her hand. As straightforward as this everyday gesture may seem, take into account the following:

- **THE GENDER QUESTION.** Until recently it was considered polite for a man to wait for a woman to extend her hand, but this is no longer customary—especially in business. Furthermore, women should shake hands with other women, even if hesitant to do so. Today a handshake is usually expected, regardless of one's gender.
- **THE PROPER GRIP.** Your grip speaks volumes: A limp one suggests hesitance or mousiness, and a bone-cruncher can seem overly enthusiastic or domineering—not to mention painful. A medium-firm grip conveys confidence and authority. Also make sure your shake is palm-to-palm (not fingers-to-fingers), and keep your hand perpendicular to the ground. An upturned palm may subconsciously signal submissiveness; a downward palm, dominance.
- **THE TWO-HAND SHAKE.** This involves clasping the outside of the greeter's hand with your free hand. While this kind of handshake signals warmth, it can seem presumptuous or insincere when used in a first meeting. Take care: Some people consider the two-hand shake too intimate for business, while others see it as a "power" move, intended to subtly intimidate the recipient.
- **GLOVED HANDSHAKES.** When winter gloves are worn outdoors, common sense prevails: You needn't take them off to shake someone's hand. A woman attending an event that calls for formal attire leaves her gloves on when shaking hands, but she takes them off when it comes time to eat.
- **AN OFFER REFUSED.** If you extend your hand to an able-bodied person and he or she doesn't respond in kind, simply withdraw your hand and continue your greeting. Unless there's a extenuating circumstance, your behavior is correct and the other person's is not.

INTRODUCING SOMEONE TO A GROUP

If you find yourself introducing someone to a group—a circle of friends at a cocktail party, for example—wait for a conversational opening to present itself and then grab your chance: "Hi, everybody. I'd like to introduce you to Sandy Vail, who's in from Tennessee." If, however, the person you are introducing is one of your clients and the group is made up of colleagues, the client is the "important" one to whom the others are presented: "Linda Ambrose, I'd like you to meet our sales staff."

WHEN YOU ARE INTRODUCED

When you are being introduced, don't be surprised if you have to come to the rescue of the introducer. If he forgets your name, save the situation by extending your hand and doing it yourself. Then again, if you've already met the person to whom you're being introduced and *she* doesn't remember you, remind her of where you met. "We chatted for a little while at the Kansas brainstorming meeting last March." There's no reason to feel awkward: Just smile, put out your hand, and state your name.

If an introducer gets your name wrong, mispronounces it, or relays inaccurate information about your job or background, politely make the correction without embarrassing him. "Actually, it's June, not Joan." Getting your name straight matters most when 1) you expect to see the person you're being introduced to again, or 2) if the person will be introducing you to others. If you're permanently parting ways, it's better to let the error slide.

INTRODUCING YOURSELF

If you are attending a business meeting or social gathering and no one introduces you, jump right in. The fact that you were invited is justification enough to extend your hand and greet anyone there. (At parties, the host is responsible for introducing people but may have so much on his hands that he's unable to get to everyone.) Just step up and say, "I don't believe we've met. I'm Mary Buchwald from Hill and Dell." Be sure to state both your names and, if necessary, ask others to state both of theirs.

Refrain from putting a courtesy title or honorific before your name when introducing yourself: "Hello, I'm Mary Buchwald"—not *Mrs.* Mary Buchwald. Doctors and Ph.D.'s show themselves in a better light if they drop the "Dr." and use only their names. Leaving a title unstated suggests self-confidence and humility, and one's credentials are revealed in due course.

CONCERNING NAMES

Although many people have no problem moving to first names with new acquaintances, the practice may be unacceptable in the minds of some whom you encounter in a business setting. Etiquette says you shouldn't use a person's first name until he asks you to do so; at the same time, rigid adherence to this custom can make you look obsequious or pretentious.

Whether you should call a just-introduced person by his first name depends on a number of things, including regional social customs, age, and rank. In some parts of the United States, it is customary to use first names right off the bat. And in the South, "sir" and "ma'am" are often heard. Before traveling to a business function in an unfamiliar part of the country, it's a good idea to bone up on the local social customs—especially if your destination is a small town, where people will probably adhere more to tradition than do those in the larger cities. A colleague who grew up in the area should be able to give you an idea of the liberties you can or cannot take.

Also take your cue from the person you're greeting. If he immediately calls you Jack, there may be an unspoken understanding that you're on a first-name basis. When in doubt—if the person is elderly, for example, a top-level executive, or even a public figure—test the waters before taking the plunge. One use of "Mr. Quinby" will usually give you the answer. Unless he says "Please call me Roy," either keep using "Mr." or the appropriate honorific; alternatively, simply refrain from using his name for the rest of the chat.

REMEMBERING NAMES

For many people, names go in one ear and out the other during introductions. Their minds suddenly go blank and nervousness sets in the moment they have to shake hands. If they concentrate on anything, it's themselves—the impression they're making and whether they're saying the right thing—rather than mentally registering the other person's name.

Overcome this problem by putting the focus on the other person. When someone offers his hand, make a point of listening to his name, repeating it in your greeting, and then imprinting it in your mind by visualizing how it would look written down—or even emblazoned across a billboard.

Associating a person's name with something about his appearance—a method advised by some experts—is trickier than it sounds. If you're lucky, the person's name will easily lend itself to associations: for Mr. Green, a golf course or green piece of clothing; for Miss O'Hare, a rabbit or a head of bushy hair;

"How Do You Do?"

271

for Mr. Baker, a loaf of baking bread or a chef's toque; for Mrs. Threadgill, a spool of thread. But what of the Johnsons and Lewises and Schneiders? Of the Joneses and Rothbergs and Gonzaleses? Unless you can forge a mental link with friends of the same name, you're better off remembering the key word—*concentrate*—than playing the association game.

FORGOTTEN NAMES

If you suffer a memory lapse when greeting someone you've met before, don't be ashamed to admit it. Be honest and calm: "I remember meeting you, but I simply can't recall your name." Instead of concentrating on your own embarrassment, try to put the other person at ease.

Try to avoid bluntly saying, "What did you say your name is?" Better excuses are "I've just drawn a blank" or "My memory gets worse by the day," which puts the blame on you. If you recall anything at all about the person, bring it up: "I clearly remember the conversation we had about Fiji, but your name seems to have slipped my mind. What is it again?" Or you could look incredulous and utter something such as "I can't *believe* I've forgotten your name. I'm so sorry!"

DIFFICULT NAMES

If the name of someone to whom you're being introduced is misunderstood or highly unusual, ask for it again: "I'm sorry, I didn't quite catch your name." Making sure that you have a name correct shows respect and consideration. If the name is especially complicated and you expect to see the person again, ask him or her to write it down or give you a business card.

If someone mispronounces *your* name and does it more than once, gently correct her (in private, if possible) with a word association: "It's SHILL-er, as in thrill." You could also make a joke of it: "I've heard people pronounce my name 30 different ways, but it's actually . . . " A smile on your face as you say it shows that you don't take the mistake personally.

WHEN INTRODUCTIONS ARE UNNECESSARY

If you're walking with a group and meet someone you know coming in the opposite direction, etiquette says you're not required to pause and make intro-

HUGS AND KISSES

In the entertainment and fashion fields, greeting with hugs and kisses is positively de rigueur. But in more traditional business settings, greetings should be less demonstrative, with kissing and hugging generally avoided.

In some cases, business associates who have not seen each other in a long time may feel a hug or a kiss on the cheek is in order, but they should be discreet or avoid such greetings entirely. Another consideration: No matter what profession you're in, avoid close contact with another person when you are ill. It's more welcoming to tell someone you have a cold and keep your distance than to risk infecting him or her.

Hugs and kisses in greetings usually take these five forms:

- **THE KISS.** Kisses on the cheek are better left to social situations. In business, men and women executives should refrain from kissing in public, since even a peck on the cheek might sometimes be misconstrued. The occasional peck on the cheek is the exception when the parties know each other well, especially when they greet each other at a quasi-social event like a convention.
- **THE AIR-KISS.** What began as a way of avoiding lipstick traces and smudged makeup is now a fad. The lips are puckered and the cheek is put alongside the other person's cheek; a full-fledged air-kiss repeats the gesture on the other cheek. The habit of air-kissing often looks artificial in a business setting: To the person watching, it looks insincere; to the recipient, it may seem all the more artificial.
- **THE BEAR HUG.** Save this two-arm hug for old friends or for business associates with whom you're especially close and haven't seen for a long time.
- **THE SEMI-HUG.** Engaging in a momentary clutch (each person placing his or her arms briefly around the other person's shoulders) is sometimes appropriate among businesspeople of the same sex, but only if they have a close personal friendship as well.
- **THE SHOULDER CLUTCH.** This involves grabbing each other's right upper arm or shoulder with the free hand while shaking hands. It is best used by business associates who haven't seen each other for a long time but maintain a warm relationship.

ductions. If you stop to briefly chat, the group should continue on until you finish and catch up. Likewise, if you're dining with a group and someone you know walks by your table, you're not obliged to introduce him to your assembled friends. If you want to exchange a few words with the person, step away from the table. If, on the other hand, your intuition tells you that introductions all round are expected, then by all means make them.

"How Do You Do?"

GREETINGS IN GENERAL

When greeting people you already know, what you say or do depends on the situation. A high-five, for example, is a perfectly acceptable way to greet a peer passing down the hall, but it's inappropriate for clients and customers. A simple "Hello" or a variation thereof ("Howdy!") is fine on most occasions.

In a more formal atmosphere—perhaps a board meeting where you're meeting people for the first time, or a banquet where you pass through a receiving line—"How do you do?" is the standard greeting. This is also the preferred response from anyone being introduced to a dignitary or elderly person. (See also Adjusting Your Cultural Lens, page 479.)

CHAPTER 22

THE SMART CONVERSATIONALIST

In even the most unconventional fields of business, is being a good conversationalist really so important? In a word, yes. How you speak, the quality of your voice, and your choice of words are fundamental to how you're perceived. People who have poor grammar, are indifferent listeners, or talk mostly about themselves are seen in a less-than-positive light. Whether you're making a sales presentation or chatting with your supervisor, the ability to reach and influence a listener is one of the most valuable assets you have.

Poor speaking, on the other hand, can have serious consequences: Eighty percent of executives questioned in a recent study by a Midwestern university cited a lack of communication skills—not technical expertise and overall performance—as the reason employees were held back in their careers. Compounding the problem is the boss who won't hesitate to tell you when your job performance falls short yet is reluctant to criticize your way with words. That said, it's usually up to you to determine whether your speaking skills need work. Find out by broaching the subject with a coworker you're close to; he, too, may be uncomfortable about offering criticism, but when you assure him he'll be doing you a favor, he may very well consent.

THE IMPRESSION YOU MAKE

Every time you speak the listener is subconsciously registering the quality of your voice, your enunciation, your grammar, and your choice of words. Most often, it is only when one of these elements deviates from the norm that it's noticed, for better or worse.

Voice

Your voice reveals more than meets the ear: It can hint at your self-confidence or lack thereof, your background and level of education, the region where you grew up, and the mood you're in at the moment. Several components, from pitch to accent, contribute to overall voice quality. If you perceive a serious problem with any of these, you might consider seeking professional help from a speech therapist or purchasing an audio voice-training program.

- **PITCH.** This is the term used to describe the highness or lowness of sound, including the human voice. At one extreme is the high, nasal quality of the "chipmunk" voice; at the other, the mellow baritone.
- **VOLUME.** It goes without saying that a midrange between loudness and softness is most desirable. A too-loud voice almost always annoys or unnerves other people, while a too-soft delivery can make you seem mousy, vulnerable, or shy.
- **TONE.** Don't speak in a monotone, which not only flattens your message but the listener's interest as well. Remember, too, that putting stress on certain words can change the tone of a remark: "Do you really believe that?" is a direct question, whereas "Do you *really* believe that?" may express doubt or disagreement.
- **RATE.** The rate at which you speak is important, too. Fast talkers are harder to understand than slow talkers, and they frequently have to repeat themselves. Slow talkers merely make the listener impatient. Something else to consider: Pausing too often between words can make you seem uncertain, scatterbrained, or distracted.
- **ENUNCIATION.** This is the distinctness with which you pronounce a word. Don't swallow syllables, slur words together, or drop final letters. Dropping letters—with the "g" in *-ing* the prime example—should be reserved for informal talks among friends; when speaking over the phone or engaged in a business conversation, enunciate the entire word. But be careful not to exaggerate: Enunciating too perfectly will make you sound affected.
- **ACCENT.** So long as your grammar and word usage are correct, you should never be embarrassed by a regional, ethnic, or foreign accent. Your accent is a drawback only when it's strong enough to hamper communication. Still, a businessperson whose accent is so thick it exceeds regional standards will benefit from softening the edges, especially when traveling.

PRONUNCIATION

Changes in pronunciation are part of the natural development of language. Moreover, what is considered standard (preferred) pronunciation may vary by region or socioeconomic or ethnic group. The dictionary handles such variations by listing more than one pronunciation for words whenever necessary; the word listed first is standard in American English, viewed as "correct" by the leading members of a community—"community" meaning the American population at large. Alternate, or secondary, pronunciations appear because a substantial portion of the public commonly uses them. You may want to avoid these, however, unless they correspond to the pronunciations used by everyone in your region, across the socioeconomic spectrum.

Just how important is pronunciation to the well-spoken person? That depends. When among peers, few people mind if someone pronounces "nuclear" as noo-ka-lur, "athlete" as ath-ah-lete, or even "pronunciation" itself as pro-*noun*-ciation. On the other hand, people of some education are likely to notice the errors, though not necessarily see them as a shortcoming.

There are times when pronunciation may be crucial. In a job interview, for instance, saying an often-mispronounced word correctly may give you the edge over an equally qualified candidate. Why? Because knowing the finer points of speech suggests an attention to detail, and she who cares about the smaller things is perceived as someone able to handle the larger ones.

GRAMMAR AND WORD USAGE

Some grammatical rules have relaxed in recent years, more so in conversation than in writing. But don't be fooled into thinking that correct grammar no longer matters: It does, and a lot. Although putting a preposition at the end of a sentence is no longer frowned on (with "That's the store I went to" now preferred over the awkward "That's the store to which I went"), the basic rules hold fast. (See also Grammar Alert features, pages 307, 308, 311, 320.)

A few grammatical errors are increasingly apparent in everyday speech, with these four among the most widely heard:

- **MISUSE OF PAST PARTICIPLES.** The past tenses and past participles of certain verbs are often confused, as in the conjugation of the verb "go": "I should have *gone*" is replaced by the erroneous "I should have *went*." Other examples: the endings "-ank" and "-unk" are frequently switched, resulting in the incorrect "The boat *sunk*" (should be "sank"); "I shouldn't have *drank* so much last night" (should be "drunk"); and "My blouse *shrunk* in the wash" (should be "shrank").

- **LACK OF SUBJECT-VERB AGREEMENT.** Remember that a singular noun or pronoun takes a singular verb. The ungrammatical "One of the best things about this party *are* the hors d'oeuvres" should be phrased " . . . *is* the hors d'oeuvres" ("one," not "things," is the subject). Likewise, "An array [the singular subject] of exciting items *are* up for bids" should be " . . . *is* up for bids."

- **CONFUSING AN ADVERB WITH AN ADJECTIVE.** The suffix "-ly" is frequently tacked onto a word where it doesn't belong.

No grammar lesson is required, but suffice it to say that if you are ill or must express regrets, saying "I feel *bad*" is correct and "I feel *badly*" is not. (In this case, "feel" is a linking verb and takes the adjective "bad"; the adverb "badly" is used when you feel something with your fingers.) A similar error:

"CORRECTLY" PRONOUNCED, OR NOT?

When it comes to pronunciation, words can be said to fall into three categories. First are those whose pronunciations are frequently mangled, voiced in a way considered incorrect in any region or group. (An example: "mischievous," often mispronounced *mis-CHEE-vee-us.*) Second are words with more than one "correct" pronunciation, such as "either" and "mature." Third are words that are borrowed from other languages (often French), some of which retain their original pronunciations and some that have changed over time.

In the following lists, preferred pronunciations are shown in informal phonetics, with capitalized syllables indicating stress. Boldface letters help you spot the difference between one pronunciation and the other.

WATCH OUT FOR THESE . . .

Here's a sampling of pronunciations that fall into the "just plain wrong" category, regardless of the speaker's background—regional and otherwise. Substandard pronunciations follow the correct ones.

- **athlete.** ATH-leet, not ATH-**uh**-leet
- **February.** FEB-**ru**-ary, not Feb-**yew**-ary
- **escape. Ess**-CAPE, not **ex**-CAPE
- **genuine.** JEN-yoo-**un**, not JEN-yoo-**wine**
- **heinous.** HEY-**nus**, not HEY-**nee-us**
- **interesting.** IN-**tur**-est-ing, not IN-**nur**-est-ing
- **jewelry.** JOO-**uhl**-ree, not JOO-**luh**-ree
- **library.** LY-**brer**-ee, not LY-**behr**-ee
- **mischievous. MIS**-chi-**vus**, not **mis**-CHEE-**vee-us**
- **nuclear. NYOO**-klee-ur, not **NOO**-kyuh-lur
- **pronunciation.** pro-**NUN**-see-AY-shun, not pro-**NOUN**-see-AY-shun
- **realtor.** REE-**ul**-tur, not REE-**luh**-tur
- **similar.** SIM-**i**-lur, not SIM-**yoo**-lur
- **vehicle.** VEE-**ihk**-uhl, not VEE-**HIK**-uhl

In the statement "We wanted all the designs to look *differently,*" the final word should be "different."

- **CONFUSING I, ME, AND MYSELF.** Fearful of misusing the word "me," many people wrongly substitute "I" or "myself," thinking them

---

TAKE YOUR PICK . . .

No real right or wrong applies to the pronunciations of some words. In some of the cases shown here, what is standard depends on the region; in other cases, both choices are perfectly acceptable, no matter where you live.

- **aunt.** While **ANT** is generally preferred in American speech, **AHNT** is used in certain parts of the East Coast.
- **banal.** **BAY-nul** was once preferred and remains correct; however, **buh-NAL** is more current today and is preferred over a third choice, **buh-NAHL.**
- **either/neither.** Although the pronunciation of the first syllables of these words as **EE** and **NEE** is standard in American speech (and listed first in most dictionaries), the trend in recent years has been to the British **EYE** and **NYE.**
- **harass.** The pronunciations **huh-RASS** and **HAR-us** are equally correct.
- **mature.** Both mah-**TYOOR** and mah-**TOOR** are fine.
- **vase.** **VAYS** or **VAYZ** is standard American, while **VAHZ** is standard British.

"PARDON MY FRENCH . . . "

Most Americans know the French word "chic" is pronounced the same way in English as it is in French (*sheek,* not *chick*), but fewer are aware that the second half of "chaise longue" (translation: long chair) is pronounced *long,* not *lounge,* even though the latter is listed in the dictionary as a folk etymology. Should you care? Yes—enough, at least, to check the dictionary for the pronunciation of a foreign word before adding it to your vocabulary. But watch your step: Showing off your newfound knowledge may make you look pretentious. Instead, hold the correct pronunciation in reserve—a kind of ace in the hole. While most people you're talking with probably neither notice nor care about such things, what if someone who's important to your career actually does? If, say, at a business lunch you order a certain potato-and-leek soup, it just might be to your advantage to ask for the vee-shee-*swahz.*

- **chaise longue.** shayz-**LAWNG**, preferred over shayz-**LOWNJ** or chayz-**LOWNJ**
- **chic.** **SHEEK**, not **CHIK**
- **clique.** **KLEEK**, preferred over **KLIK**
- **corps.** **KOHR**, not **KORPSE**
- **coup de grâce.** koo-duh-**GRAHS**, not koo-duh-**GRAH**
- **forte.** As a strong point, **FORT**; as a musical term, the Italian **FOR-tay**
- **vichyssoise.** vee-shee-**SWAHZ**, preferred over vee-shee-**SWAH**

safe alternatives. The phrase "between you and I" is the most ubiquitous error of this kind, with statements such as "Daddy passed the lemonade to Sally and I [or myself]" a close second. Both of these examples require "me," which in either case is the object of the preposition; conversely, "I" is a subject. Remember that "myself" is a reflexive pronoun: It directs action back to the subject of the sentence, as in "I congratulated myself." It is also used to emphasize: "I baked the bread myself."

Brushing up on grammar doesn't have to be a chore. A number of easy-to-understand and entertainingly written wordbooks are sold today, and they bear little resemblance to the dry textbooks you probably remember. Buying one is a particularly smart investment for anyone in business.

VOCABULARY

A broad vocabulary (the store of words you draw on) is a plus for any businessperson, and expanding it is not that hard. Whenever you come across a word that's new to you or you don't quite understand, look it up in the dictionary; then try it out in conversation. After you've used the word three or four times, it should begin to come naturally. You can also consult the vocabulary-building aids found in some wordbooks and magazines.

If you have any of the following habits, your vocabulary needs work:

- You overuse words such as "cute," "interesting," "nice," "great," and "awful" and fillers such as "you know."
- You regularly mistake one word for another while talking (see Commonly Confused Words, page 281).
- Your choice of words sounds pretentious or pompous.

When it comes to the last point, remember that having a good vocabulary doesn't mean using big words in place of small ones; it's the precise meaning of a word, not its length, that matters. In most conversation, saying "endeavor" for "try," "conclude" for "end," and "prognosticate" for "predict" sounds unnatural and forced. Strive instead for a vocabulary that's wide-ranging yet direct, one that will improve communication and leave the listener with a positive impression in the process.

Interjections to banish: "y'know," "uh," "er," and other fillers. Even the broadest vocabulary is sabotaged by continually dropping these meaningless utterances between words. The habit is a subconscious one, so consider taping your voice to see whether you're prone to using them; for a truer reading, leave the tape recorder on long enough so that you forget it's there.

JARGON, ET CETERA

The agile speaker searches for the precise word that best conveys his message. But for better or worse, our speech is chock-full of jargon. In one sense, the word "jargon" means specialized language used by the members of such fields

---

COMMONLY CONFUSED WORDS

Certain words are frequently confused, some more glaringly than others—"infamous" for "famous," for example. Others that, until recently, had entirely different meanings—"disinterested" and "uninterested," for example—are now almost interchangeable because of increased usage. Confusing "who" and "whom" "further" and "farther" are also no longer the eyebrow-raisers they used to be. Still, watch out for these mix-ups:

- DISINTERESTED/UNINTERESTED. Someone who is disinterested is neutral, impartial, or has no self-interest in something; someone who is uninterested lacks interest or is bored. "I was a *disinterested* party when it came to the will, but that doesn't mean I was *uninterested* in seeing who got what."
- FAMOUS/INFAMOUS. Famous means well-known or celebrated. Infamous does *not* mean not famous; it describes someone (or something) notorious. "She was *famous* for her years on the silent screen, but the discovery that she was a gangster's moll made her *infamous*."
- FARTHER/FURTHER. Farther refers to physical distance; further indicates a greater extent or degree and can apply to abstract ideas. "As I walked *farther* down the path, I wondered whether I should pursue the issue *further*."
- FEWER/LESS. Fewer means a smaller number of individual things; less means a smaller degree or quantity. "When there's *less* water in the lake, *fewer* boaters will show up."
- FLAUNT/FLOUT. To flaunt something is to show it off; flout means to treat with indifference or scorn. "She *flaunted* her new hairstyle, which *flouted* convention with its streakings of hot pink and lime."
- LIE/LAY. To lie is to recline; to lay is to place something, as on a table; lay also serves as the past tense of lie. "After I *lay* my towel on the sand, I'll *lie* down on the beach for only a few minutes. I got sunburned as I *lay* there yesterday."
- WHO/WHOM. The distinction between these words matters much less today, but it doesn't hurt to know the difference. Think of "who" as a subject (it *does* something, as in "*Who* brought the cheesecake?") and "whom" as an object (something is *done* to it, as in "the person to *whom* the gift was given").
- REGARDLESS/IRREGARDLESS. There is only one choice here: "Irregardless" is not a real word, no matter how many times you've heard it spoken. It is substandard because it contains two negatives: "ir-" and "-less."

as science, trade, law, and the arts—"insider" words and terms that say to a member of the group something that could take a sentence to communicate to anyone else. When its only intention is conciseness, jargon serves a legitimate purpose. In every other sense, "jargon" has a negative connotation. Today, its meaning has blurred around the edges, absorbing vogue words (also called buzzwords), euphemisms, common slang, and even some clichés. The word is also used to label words believed by the speaker to sound more important than their everyday counterparts—to name but a few, "dialoguing" for "talking," "utilize" for "use," "implement" for "do," and "attain" for "get."

The world of business has done more than its share to inject jargon into American speech. "Corporate speak" is responsible for enshrining words such as "leveraging," "reengineering," "empowerment," and "developmental" in the jargon pantheon and, at the same time, turning the nouns "impact" (as a replacement for "affect"), "transition" (for "change"), and "reference" (for "refer") into verbs. An example of this brand of verbosity: "If it's transitioned at the developmental stage, it will impact the leveraging of the attainment stage" is jargon's convoluted way of saying "If it's changed, it will get better results." (See also Communicate Clearly, page 210.)

A **C A V E A T :** Stating things directly is preferable to couching them in jargon, but not in every case: For example, if everyone in your company uses a certain term—"media opportunity" for "press conference"—it's better to grit your teeth and adopt its use; a stubborn refusal to join the crowd will make you look more than a little priggish.

Vogue Words

Vogue words and terms are those that become popular catchalls and do multiple duty for synonyms with finer shades of meaning. Common examples of this lazy approach to speech include "bottom line," a substitute for "outcome," "essence," "crux," and "gist"; "address," for "discuss," "consider," "ponder," and "weigh"; and "empower," for "enable," "grant," "authorize," and "permit." (As a matter of fact, "jargon" is a catchall, having come to describe multiple undesirable word usages.)

Not all vogue words are catchalls. Some are better described as buzzwords: words that appear suddenly, gain currency, and sometimes burn out as quickly as they caught fire. Recent buzzwords and terms in business speech include "outside the box" (used to describe a forward-thinking course of action) and "branding," with which individuals undertake to market their set of talents much as one would a laundry detergent. Examples of buzzwords of longer standing are "paradigm," for an especially clear example, and "parameter," once an obscure mathematical term but now used to mean a conceptual boundary—the upshot of the word's confusion with "perimeter."

Other buzzwords come from the slang of the young, and include the retro "cool" and "groovy"; "diss" (from the verb form of "disrespect"); and "sweet" (for any desirable object). While you may think using such expressions shows you as cutting-edge, overdoing them—not to mention hanging on to them after they've gone out of fashion—can make you look silly and immature, especially when you're talking business. A worker over 30 would be wise to stick with old standbys such as "Great!" instead of the groan-inducing "Awesome!"

SLANG

There is nothing inherently wrong with slang, which lends vigor to speech so long as it doesn't descend to the vulgar. In fact, American speech is peppered with more slang words than most people realize—"bus," for example, was originally slang for "autobus," and the compact "movies" replaced "moving pictures."

More obvious slang words, terms, and phrases—"dough" for "money," "uptight" for "tense," "rip-off" for "cheat," "honcho" for "boss," "shades" for "dark glasses," "in the ballpark" for "approximate," and innumerable others— are far more at home in speech than in writing. Nevertheless, use them sparingly during a serious business discussion. Whenever you talk business, how much slang is appropriate depends on both the demeanor and vocabulary of your conversation partner.

EUPHEMISM

Euphemism is the substitution of softer words or terms for certain words people are reluctant to use for one reason or another. The purpose of euphemism is to avoid giving offense and make conversation more civil. Some euphemisms are used out of delicacy: for example, the substitution of "perspire" for "sweat" and "expectoration" for "spit"; "restroom," "washroom," and "bathroom" for "toilet"; "golden years" and "senior citizen" for "old age" and "old person"; "expire" and "pass away" for "die"; and "mortician" for "undertaker." In business, euphemism has sought to blunt the ugly reality of "firing" with such terms as "laying off," "letting go," "downsizing," and "outplacing."

Euphemism is also the hallmark of political correctness, with "crazy" softened to "insane" and "mentally ill," and "fat" to "portly," "heavyset," and "full-figured." While many of these new terms have their place, other terms have gone to such extremes that they've become the stuff of parody, spawning such joking references as "vertically challenged" for "short" and "spatially perplexed" for "intoxicated" (itself a euphemism for "drunk"). Unless plain speaking offends, it's invariably the preferred approach. (See also Communicate Clearly, page 210.)

THE ART OF CONVERSING

In the multifaceted corporate world of the 1990s, the line of chatter in a recording studio may seem almost a different language from that of a law office. But one thing hasn't changed: Being a good conversationalist is less a matter of eloquence than of adequately hearing others out and getting one's message across—something vital to conducting business.

This idea is hardly new. In the 1937 edition of *Etiquette,* Emily Post wrote, "Ideal conversation must be an exchange of thought, and not, as many . . . believe, an eloquent exhibition of wit or oratory." She held that the secret to an effective dialogue with another person was not cleverness, but learning to "stop, look, and listen." "Stop," wrote Mrs. Post, means "not to rush recklessly forward"—that is, not to start talking merely for the sake of filling dead air. "Look" means to look the person to whom you are speaking in the eye. And "listen," means exactly that; it is, she said, "the best advice possible . . . since the person whom most people love . . . is a sympathetic listener."

Besides observing these timeless fundamentals, the businessperson who strives to become a good conversationalist remembers to do some things and avoid doing others. The pointers that follow apply equally to workers in a software company where unconventionality reigns and to those in a workplace where staidness is more the style.

TALKING BUSINESS

Whenever you are discussing a contract, forging a deal, or doing business of any kind, think of your conversation in terms of three stages: the warm-up, the core, and the wrap-up.

- **THE WARM-UP.** Once you and your business companion have said your hellos and taken your seats, engage in a little small talk—chat that ranges from the day's top news story to your golf handicap to, yes, even the weather. A minimum of five to ten minutes is usually devoted to this opening stage. Throughout, camaraderie is punctuated by smiles and laughter, but only when genuinely called for. (See also Small-Talk Tips, page 54.)

- **THE CORE.** Now the talk turns to business. Make clear your personal investment in this longer portion of the conversation by sitting erect and making eye contact. As the conversation gets rolling, remember that you are engaged in a dialogue, not a monologue. Even if you must explain a complicated new technology, draw the other person in by asking questions to see whether he or she understands. Also be careful to use the word "you" as often as "I"; this conveys a subliminal message to your partner that you consider him not tangential, but integral, to the business being discussed.

    Although you should put smiles aside during this stage for the most part, don't abandon altogether the occasional snippet of small talk; leavening the conversation with the occasional funny aside or pertinent anecdote keeps things more relaxed and helps you get your message across. Hammering your point too aggressively or relentlessly will have the opposite effect.

- **THE WRAP-UP.** A brief recapitulation of any decisions that were made during the conversation ensures there are no misunderstandings. But when you resume your small talk, stick with it. Letting go of the business topic and ending the conversation on a purely social note is an implicit acknowledgment of the friendly nature of the business relationship.

ABOUT BODY LANGUAGE

What you're actually saying is also conveyed by what is called body language, a field of study that appeared in the late 1950s and was dubbed kinesics by its earliest researchers. While some body language sends a definite signal—the person who stands straight appears self-assured, for example—many other signals are ambiguous. Some examples:

- Arms folded across the chest are often said to denote defensiveness or disagreement. Consider, however, that the person talking may as easily be assuming this pose out of habit, without subconscious motivation.
- Some body language experts hold that scratching the back of one's neck suggests uncertainty—but sometimes an itch is just an itch.
- When an employee talking with his boss holds the supervisor's eyes a little too long, it might either be interpreted as a sign of respect or as a subtle challenge to authority.

The smart student of body language looks for patterns in the larger picture, not for a single gesture. Also, the wisdom of letting one's movements be

THE GOOD LISTENER

In business, it's not only discourteous but bad business practice to be an indifferent listener. Supervisors claim they can easily tell whether a subordinate has been listening by the quality of the questions asked at the end of a discussion, along with the accuracy of his or her summation. Score high as a listener by remembering to do the following. (See also The Art of Listening, page 223.)

- CONCENTRATE. Pay close attention to what the other person is saying, no matter how tempted you are to let your mind wander. Also try your best to be patient with someone who's speaking too slowly or faltering in getting his message across.
- RECONFIRM. To show you understand, occasionally paraphrase what the speaker is saying. After you've picked up the rhythm of the other person's speech, you should be able to do this without seeming to interrupt.
- WAIT. In conversation, patience is a virtue and interrupting is a sin. Remember that there's a fine line between the occasional interruption made to confirm or question a particular point and one that's made because the speaker is bursting to throw in his two cents' worth.
- QUESTION. If you don't understand something, ask for an explanation. A likely time: when talk turns to computers or other technical subjects.
- RESPOND. Use positive body language to show you're paying attention. Lean slightly toward the speaker, and react to what he says with the occasional nod, smile, or cocked eyebrow.
- KEEP STILL. If you're at your desk, don't shuffle papers or make a halfhearted effort to continue whatever you're working on. When standing, refrain from any distracting gestures, such as rattling the change in your pocket.

dictated by what is read in books is questionable; you don't want to become so acutely aware of your gestures that they no longer look natural.

BODY LANGUAGE BASICS

At times the words and tone of the speaker may be enough to gauge the meaning of what is being said, but a person's posture, facial expressions, and gestures do indeed send messages—some of which are open to interpretation (see preceding examples), others that come through loud and clear.

- STANCE. Someone who stands with back straight, shoulders back, and chin up is the very picture of self-confidence and ambition. Also note that standing with your hands clasped behind you is a more graceful and authoritative pose than sticking your hands in your pockets. Do not stand with your ankles locked, nor should you hold onto one of your arms at the elbow; both of these poses signal shyness and insecurity.

- **SITTING.** Slouching in a chair conveys laziness, tiredness, even disrespect. Some body-language experts see crossing one's legs while seated as a defensive gesture, yet many people (men and women alike) simply find this position more comfortable. A less ambiguous signal is jiggling the knee, which communicates insecurity or fear, especially during an interview.

- **FACIAL EXPRESSIONS.** A smile denotes warmth, openness, and friendliness. But don't overdo it. False smiles make you look phony, whereas never-ending smiles invite suspicion. On the other side of the coin, a frown or a furrowed brow suggests anger or worry, even if your words are positive.

  Then there is the poker face. The lengths to which some businessmen have gone to achieve this blank, noncommittal expression—believed by many to be an advantage when negotiating a deal—gave rise to a mini-trend in the 1990s: Some males began seeing plastic surgeons to receive facial injections of a bacterial substance called Botox (short for botulism toxins), which became highly sought after by many upper-income urban women for cosmetic reasons. The substance works by paralyzing certain facial muscles and eliminates wrinkles for a period of three to five months. Enthusiasts of the procedure—an extreme measure, but one that speaks to the temper of the times—have claimed that it keeps tension frowning to a minimum and makes them look more relaxed, with the dent it puts in their wallets apparently of no concern.

- **EYE CONTACT.** Looking into the other person's eyes shows your interest in the conversation. Do not, however, go to the other extreme: Staring can look threatening, not to mention strange. The desirable middle ground is reached by shifting your focus to other parts of the face from time to time.

- **GESTURING AND FIDGETING.** Go easy on the gestures: Using your hands to emphasize a point is fine, but overdoing it makes you look too excitable. Gestures and fidgets to be avoided include playing with your hair, tie, or jewelry; biting your lip; drumming your fingers; unconsciously snapping the clip on a ball-point pen; and jiggling the change or keys in your pocket.

- **NODDING.** Nodding doesn't necessarily mean you agree, but that you understand. But be careful: Too much positive head-nodding can make you seem like a kiss-up, especially when it's directed to your boss.

CHAPTER 23

ON THE TELEPHONE

Thirty years ago, who could have dreamed that placing a call to a private business, a government department, or an office of any kind would be as frustrating as it is today? Being put on hold or hearing a recorded voice telling us to "Press 1 for . . . " slams an electronic door between us and our simple wish to connect with a human being. We press and press again, our blood pressure rising until we finally reach the desired person—as often as not, on an answering machine. But take heed: When we're unsuccessful in completing a call, frustration must be brushed aside. Smart businesspeople treat even a recording device with courtesy. An upbeat tone of voice gives the recipient of your call confidence not only in you but in your company as well; an irritated tone does quite the opposite.

PLACING BUSINESS CALLS

If your call will deal with facts and figures, prepare by writing down any questions to ask or topics to cover. Then gather data sheets or other reference materials you might need. Even if some of the things you want to bring up are minor, jot them down; it's easy to forget something once the conversation starts rolling. Have a pad and pen handy, so you can take notes, and a desk calendar in case you need to set dates.

No matter who answers your call—the person you're trying to reach, a receptionist, an assistant, or a machine—identify yourself at once. Unless you're calling someone with whom you regularly do business, identify your company, too: "This is Katherine Bowlin of Sellmore Marketing." Give your name even if you talk with the person fairly often, since he may not be as familiar with your voice as you think. Another tip: Using your first and last names each time you call will reinforce your name recognition.

Quickly explain why you've called and ask if it's a convenient time to talk. (Note: Failing to ask this question is one of the most common telephone errors.) The person may not want to be interrupted or is about to leave the office. If he says talking now is fine, state the purpose and estimated length of the call: "Mr. Peterson, I have a question about the marketing proposal. It should take about five minutes." Try to be honest: If you suspect five minutes is a conservative estimate, say so.

If he says he's busy, ask when you might call back. Try to avoid having him return the call, which may put you in the awkward spot of not having your thoughts collected or notes at hand when the call comes out of the blue.

WRONG NUMBERS

If you've dialed a wrong number, admit it and apologize. Don't just hang up; little is more irritating than being on the receiving end of a wrong number and hearing nothing but an exasperated sigh and a click.

If getting a wrong number upsets you, don't direct your displeasure at the person who answers, who is not at fault. Simply deliver the line that has done service in the cause of good manners for generations: "I'm sorry. I must have dialed the wrong number." Then give the person the number you were trying to reach to make sure you don't make the same mistake twice.

YOU'RE PUT ON HOLD?

If you reach a receptionist who transfers incoming calls or an assistant who takes calls for his boss, chances are, you'll be put on hold. Most receptionists and assistants will try to make the best of the situation by keeping you updated as you wait (see The Art of the Hold, page 292). If pressed for time, simply leave a message with your name, your company name, the reason for the call, and either when you can be reached or when you'll call back.

If you are calling long distance, say so. While a long-distance charge may seem negligible to a large company, it's good business sense not to ever waste money. Identifying a call as long distance is especially important for those who work from a home office and bear the cost.

When you are on hold and more than three minutes pass, it's perfectly proper to hang up and call back later. Even though you've been treated badly, try not to betray your annoyance. Politely say that you were unable to hold and then leave it at that: No explanation is required.

USING A SPEAKERPHONE

A cardinal rule for using a speakerphone: Immediately tell the person who you are calling that you are using one. If he or she expresses any hesitation, explain why you feel it necessary—because you'd like other people in the room to be included in the conversation, for instance, or that it makes it easier for you to take notes. Most callers won't mind as long as they're asked beforehand and they understand the reason for using the device.

If others are present, identify them first off: "There are three people from Marketing who'll be joining in—Leslie Marshall, Andy Armistead, and Kathy Kincannon." The participants should then introduce themselves so that the listener can begin to link voices to names—sometimes a difficult task, since voices emanating from these devices often sound as if they were coming from a well. Confusion will be kept to a minimum if a participant identifies himself when he speaks to the listener: "Tom, Leslie here." You can also make it clear who's talking by saying "I agree with what Kathy just said" or "I see Andy has a question for you."

ANOTHER IMPORTANT TIP: Close your office door. Even though voices are amplified by a speakerphone, people generally tend to talk louder than usual when using one. The result? Workmates within earshot are disturbed by the noise.

ANSWERING BUSINESS CALLS

Don't underestimate the importance of the way you answer a call. You never know when it may be the first from a potential client or customer; your attitude and demeanor, in turn, form her initial impression of your company, and you want it to be positive, not poor. Two other considerations:

- An incoming call answered by an actual person instead of a machine will not only make a good impression but earn the caller's eternal gratitude by not putting her in electronic limbo.
- Forget your personal problems. Your voice should sound pleasant and calm whenever you answer the phone, no matter how overworked or rattled you feel. You're speaking for the company, not yourself.

Whenever possible, answer promptly—that is, by the third ring. Answering with your full name is an absolute necessity whenever a call is coming from outside. Then what to say? Although "Helen Bonner speaking" is not impolite, "This is Helen Bonner" may sound somewhat less abrupt to some ears. Then say something on the order of "Can I help you?"

If you work in a company with several departments, state your department after your name: "This is Angela Dixon, Rights and Permissions." Identifying yourself and your department saves time for both you and the caller, eliminating the need for the question "Is this Mr. Worsham's office?" or "Have I reached the accounting department?"

You're terribly busy? If you don't have an assistant to take incoming calls and a client or customer calls at an inconvenient time, give him precedence over any work you're doing if at all possible. If this is impossible, explain your predicament and tell him you'll phone back whenever it suits him. Agree on the time, and then keep your word. If you *do* have an assistant, ask her to take messages or route calls to your voice mail when you're busy; or if your phone system allows, press the "do not disturb" button.

IF YOU SHARE AN EXTENSION

When answering a phone shared by others, state the department name before giving your own: "Quality Control, Bill Fryer speaking." If the call is for someone else, say "Just a moment, please" before handing over the receiver. If the person isn't in, tell the caller when he's expected back, if you know, and offer to take a message. Don't volunteer gratuitous information about why someone's not available. If the person is in a meeting or on vacation, say so. Otherwise, don't feel you have to explain his whereabouts. "He's not back from lunch" and similar comments risk raising questions about his work habits.

If you go in search of the person being called, tell the caller how long it will take: "If you can wait two minutes, I'll try to find him." If you haven't located the person within the allotted time, return to the phone with your update. "I'm sorry, but I couldn't find him. If you give me your name and number, I'll leave them on his desk." An alternative is to ask if the caller wants to be routed to the person's voice mail to leave the message himself.

RETURNING CALLS

The number of businesspeople who are prone to hide behind voice mail is growing by leaps and bounds. Don't be one of them. If someone leaves a message asking you to call back, do so as soon as possible or at least on the same day the call was received. Twenty-four hours is as long as a call can go unreturned without violating the precepts of good manners. This golden rule is also good business practice—yet it has been broken more than almost any other. (See also page 302.)

If it's an especially busy day and you suspect the call will take more time than you can spare, call the person back, explain the situation, and ask if you can set a time to talk later. Or, if you have an assistant, ask him or her to call

When you take a telephone message, both the caller and the person you are leaving it for will appreciate it if you do the following.

- **GET THE NAME AND NUMBER RIGHT.** Ask the caller's complete name. Also ask for the spelling, since many names can be spelled more than one way—for example, Jean or Jeanne, Allen or Alan, Deborah or Debra, Anderson or Andersen. Then read the phone number back to the caller.
- **ASK THE NAME OF THE CALLER'S COMPANY.** This may help the person for whom you're taking the message identify the caller more easily. It also provides an idea of what the call may be about.
- **NOTE THE DATE AND HOUR.** Jot down the time the call came in, so the person knows how long the message has been sitting there.
- **ADD YOUR INITIALS OR NAME.** Do this in case the person the message is for wants to know more about the call.

back and explain the delay and then to arrange a callback time that will be convenient for both parties.

TRANSFERRING CALLS

If whomever you're talking with needs to be transferred to someone else in the company, first give the caller the correct extension in case he is disconnected. Then tell the person to whom the call's being transferred who is on the line, and why he is phoning; this spares callers having to repeat themselves.

Assistants whose jobs entail fielding general inquiries have a more challenging task. Their first job is to understand the duties of the company's different divisions and know who in each can best handle a particular call. They can then give callers the name, title, division, and extension number of the person to whom they're being transferred, ensuring that if a disconnection occurs the caller can dial the right person directly.

THE ART OF THE HOLD

By merely voicing the word "hold," receptionists, assistants, or secretaries who field incoming calls can become instant pariahs, if only in the mind of the frustrated caller. For their own and the caller's benefit, they should be sympathetic to the holder's dilemma and try to assuage the frustration. Doing the following will help keep annoyance to a minimum.

- Never tell someone to hold; ask him instead. More important, wait for the answer. The question "Could I please put you on hold?" is doubly irritating to the callers when immediately followed by silence or recorded music.
- Give the reason for the hold. "She's on another line," for example. Or "She's somewhere nearby, so I'll have to page her" or "I'll have to check to see who can handle that."
- When someone is holding, deliver a progress update every 20 to 30 seconds: "I thought she was almost done with her call, but she's still on the line." At the second or third check, ask whether the person wants to keep waiting or would rather leave a message.
- When you finally transfer the call, give the caller the name and extension in case he becomes disconnected.

SCREENING CALLS

Assistants also bear the burden of screening calls for their bosses and others. Touchiness abounds. For one thing, a caller who's asked his name, put on hold, and then told the desired person is unavailable may feel he has been deemed unimportant. For another, a caller who's asked "What does this call concern?" might resent having an assistant determine whether his call is worth putting through. (By the way, if you're the caller who is asked that question, it's your obligation to answer even if the matter is a complicated one; the briefest précis—"It has to do with the new banana importing law"—should be satisfactory.)

It is up to those whose calls are being screened to furnish their assistants with the language to be used. It's then the assistant's job to deliver that language in a courteous tone. When inquiring why the call is being made, a direct "May I ask what this call is in reference to?" may be favored by some executives, while others prefer the more gracious "I'm terribly sorry, but she's so busy at the moment she can't accept calls. Will she know why you're calling?" It's the assistant's duty to make whatever he says sound friendly and polite, especially when he's unable to put the caller through. (See also Dealing with Angry Callers, page 228; Your Assistant's Duties, page 215; The Receptionist's Duties, page 217.)

CALLER ID

Caller ID devices, which attach to the phone and display the number and sometimes the name of the person placing the call, can be both beneficial and bewildering. A positive: They allow you to prepare for a call before returning it. A negative: Answering your phone and using the caller's name at the outset may throw him off guard; you may come off as being sneaky—plus, the caller may not be the person identified on the screen.

Another potential negative: When you answer a business call and greet the caller by name before he has had time to identify himself, it may look as if you're trying to flaunt how technologically advanced you are. Only when you are friendly with the caller should you answer "Hi, Jim."

BUSINESS CALLS IN PROGRESS

Keep in mind that the impression you make rests entirely on your voice and choice of words, not your appearance; this makes it all the more important to sound professional and personable. Even when rushed, make an effort to speak slowly and distinctly. One much-advised technique for sounding upbeat calls for smiling as you speak, the theory being that a smile makes the voice brighter and more pleasant. Even the way you hold the receiver matters: Tucking it under your chin or holding it below your mouth makes you harder to understand.

Follow cues from the person you're speaking with to establish the call's tone. If someone is all-business and no-nonsense, you should be, too. Others may be informal and chatty; in the latter case, indulging someone who strays off the business subject may lead to the discovery of common interests or backgrounds. People who've never met face-to-face sometimes "click" and establish a kind of telephonic bond. The goodwill that results makes it all the easier for you to keep the business relationship running smoothly.

CALL WAITING AND OTHER INTERRUPTIONS

Being interrupted by a second call is less common than it once was, now that most office phone systems have switched from busy signal- and call waiting-options to voice mail, which records a message while you're on the phone. If your office phone still has call waiting and it clicks on, apologize to the first caller and say you'll return *immediately;* put her on hold and *quickly* explain to the other caller that you'll have to call back.

When you switch to the incoming caller, try your best to keep a conversation from starting: Your responsibility is to the first caller, who should never be left on hold for more than 30 seconds; even this brief period can seem like an eternity when a conversation that's going full steam is interrupted. If the incoming call is extremely urgent or from overseas, however, explain to your first caller why you must hang up and set the time you'll call back.

When you must put someone on hold for other reasons—retrieving data sheets from another office, for example—apologize and tell her how long you'll be off line. Then return when promised, even if you haven't found what you're looking for. If necessary, tell her you'll need a few more minutes and will call back as soon as your search is successful.

PHONE-CALL FAUX PAS

Following are telephone errors made by even the best-behaved businesspeople. Most apply to phone calls in general, not just those from the office.

- Don't do other things at your desk while talking on the phone. Typing and shuffling papers suggests your attention is elsewhere.
- Eating while on the phone is not only distracting but subjects the other person to unnerving smacks and crunches. Because sounds are magnified over the telephone, even a cough drop in the mouth can make its presence known.
- Don't leave a radio playing or office equipment running in the background. These sounds, too, are magnified over the phone.
- Never chew gum while talking on the phone. While gum chewing may not be offensive to some people, you have no way of knowing whether your phonemate considers it unprofessional and crass.
- Don't sneeze, blow your nose, or cough directly into the receiver. Either excuse yourself for a moment or turn your head away.
- If you have to put the receiver down during the conversation, set it gently on the desk to avoid startling your phonemate with a sudden bang.
- Don't address a business associate by his or her first name in sentence after sentence: It sounds insincere and patronizing.
- If you're holding a meeting in your office and the phone rings, don't answer unless you're expecting an important call. Then apologize to those present for the interruption. If possible, make arrangements before the meeting to have calls channeled to voice mail or to an assistant's or coworker's phone; or if you have a "do not disturb" button on your phone, use it.
- For practical reasons, some executives have assistants stay on the line for the entire call. Even if the conversation is about business and business only, letting your phonemate know that someone else is listening in is without doubt the best thing to do.

When a coworker arrives at your office door and sees you are on the phone, he should have the courtesy to leave. If he hovers and becomes a distraction, stop the conversation at an opportune moment and say, "Will you excuse me for a moment? There's someone at the door." Then quickly determine why the other person is there or mouth, "I'll see you later."

MECHANICAL GLITCHES

Most phone line disconnections occur when someone is being put on hold or being transferred. Lessen the risk of cutting someone off by mastering the buttons on your office phone. As a bonus, handling the phone with finesse makes you look more professional.

When a disconnection occurs, it is the caller's responsibility to call back. If you initiated the call, immediately redial the person and apologize, even if you're not at fault: "I'm sorry; we somehow got disconnected. I think we left off with the annual report." Redial even if the conversation was nearing an end; not calling back is like walking off in the middle of a face-to-face talk. Furthermore, the person may have more to say.

If you're the one who was called, stay off the line. If the person who made the call doesn't ring back within five or six minutes, you may call him, saying, "I'm not sure we were through talking when the line went dead."

If a bad connection or static on the line makes it difficult to hear, don't be embarrassed to ask the other person to hang up so that you can try again. A second call often solves the problem, even when placed right away.

USING VIDEOPHONES AND TDD DEVICES

Workplaces staffed largely with young, technology-minded employees are more likely to be equipped with videophones, which use a built-in camera to project your image to the caller. The devices can also be used as regular phones by simply switching off the camera. No special rules apply: A call on a videophone involves no more preparation than getting ready to answer the front door—looking presentable enough for a face-to-face encounter.

Other special tools are telephone communication devices for people who are deaf or hard of hearing—text telephones, also called telecommunication devices for the deaf (TDDs). These look like small typewriters and permit two people to communicate by typing back and forth in a conversational manner over a phone line.

If your office isn't equipped with a TDD, you can still communicate with the deaf or hard of hearing by using a relay service. In this case, the hearing caller speaks to a mediator, who relays words to the recipient by teletyping them into a console; the words then appear in the display window of the recipient's device.

If conversing with a deaf or hard-of-hearing person over a TDD, keep the following two things in mind:

- Address him or her directly, as if the mediator weren't present. Do not say, "Tell him that . . . " or "Ask him to . . . "
- As with any other call, adhere to the precepts of telephone etiquette.

For most people the chances of receiving a relayed TDD call at the office are slim, but you should be prepared for the possibility. The mediator will begin the call by saying that she is phoning from a relay service and then will ask you whether you're familiar with the TDD system. Avoid the error made by many—mistaking the mediator for a telephone solicitor and hanging up.

CLOSING A CALL

When you end a business call, don't leave matters hanging. Wind things down with a conclusive statement: "I'll get the final figures to you by noon Friday" or "I think we agree we need more research. Shall we talk again, maybe tomorrow?" Then sign off on a positive note with a polite acknowledgment: "Thank you for calling" or "It's been nice talking with you."

A few minutes spent discussing things that have nothing to do with the business at hand are perfectly in order after callers have established a friendly relationship. But don't overdo it: Without any visual clues from your phonemate, it's hard to tell when you're wearing out your welcome.

CELLULAR PHONES AND PAGERS

Now that the novelty of using a phone anytime, anywhere, has worn off, cellular, or wireless, phones offer the benefits of increased productivity and convenience, and come in handy in emergencies. At the same time, some 70 percent of Americans surveyed identify loud talking in public places as a major irritant. Seen as especially rude is using a cell phone during restaurant meals, meetings, concerts, plays, movies, and worship services.

For cell phone users, the solution is simple: Speak quietly and don't let your phone ring where it can disturb people. Either turn off the ringer or carry

POINTS OF POLITENESS

As you mind the more obvious p's and q's of telephone manners, adopting the three practices below will help you make an even better impression.

- **HOLD BACK ON FIRST NAMES.** If you haven't met someone and have some reason to suspect he doesn't share your informal nature, don't call him by his first name straight off. Unless he has started the talk with "Call me Ron. What can I do for you?" address him as Mr. Jones. An assumption from the outset that the two of you are on a first-name basis can be a mistake; to many people, especially those who are older, it is overly familiar and impolite.
- **GO EASY ON "YOU."** During the course of the call, be careful not to overuse the word "you"—especially when your phonemate hasn't met a deadline or taken care of a problem. "You forgot" or "You neglected to" can sound accusatory on the phone, even when said in a pleasant tone. Putting your comments in the form of a question is preferable: "Could you get that to me by Friday?" or "Did you complete the report on that project?"
- **LISTEN CAREFULLY.** The impersonal nature of a phone call makes it easy for you to tune out, even when a business call requires your utmost attention. Listening closely is not only courteous but ensures you won't miss any details—some of which, if overlooked, can come back to haunt you. Also let the caller *know* you're listening. Because you can't show that you're paying attention with a nod, a smile, or other visual response, use verbal responses instead: "Yes, I understand," "Of course," and "I see."

a model with one of the following features: 1) A vibrating function that alerts you to an incoming call; 2) a caller ID feature, which lets you to see who is calling and either answer the call or let it go to voice mail; 3) an alphanumeric function, which shows lines of text even when the ringer is off. As a general rule, keep your ringer to its lowest setting.

Also, when you're making calls on your phone, don't overdo it. The person who chats away on call after call earns the ire of virtually everyone nearby. A considerate businessperson remembers that all but the most urgent calls should be made from a more private location as a matter of course. (See also Public Nuisance Number One?, page 249.)

IN CLOSE QUARTERS

When you're using a cell phone on a train, plane, or bus, remember that everyone around you is privy to your conversation. It is hardly the hearer's responsibility to refrain from eavesdropping, since you're the one who created the situation; it is you who are obliged not to say anything that will offend listeners, be it foul words or talk of an intimate nature.

ANOTHER CAVEAT: When discussing business, don't risk violating the privacy of an associate or client by mentioning him or her by name; while the chances that someone within earshot knows the person are infinitesimal, you never know for sure. It is also wise to avoid discussing sensitive or confidential business for all to hear, especially at meetings or on trains.

ON THE STREET

Cell phones come into their own on the sidewalk or in a cab, when there is often good reason to use one: when you've left the office and are delayed for an appointment, when you've forgotten to relay an urgent piece of information to someone, or when you suddenly remember you need another set of figures before a meeting. Just remember not to shout into your phone while walking down the street: It's you, not your phonemate, who is contending with traffic noise. What's more, talking loudly may leave the impression to passersby that you're eager to call attention to yourself. Another consideration: Remember safety, especially when crossing intersections or maneuvering on crowded sidewalks.

IN RESTAURANTS

If cell phones have a place in business, using them in a restaurant is another matter. That old rule of "a time and a place for everything" applies especially here, where people come to relax and dine as a respite from the workday grind. Some restaurants, in fact, require that cell phones be checked at the door or be used outside the dining areas. There are exceptions to the rule, of course—for one, a mother who needs to check with the baby-sitter. But unless you are with close friends, excuse yourself and make the call in an anteroom or rest room. At business and social meals alike, making or receiving a phone call at the table is both inconsiderate and intrusive.

So what if the person at the next table is gabbing away on a phone while you're trying to talk business? If his voice is rising above the ambient noise, a dirty look probably will be little more than water off a duck's back. Motioning to him and politely asking if he would mind lowering his voice a little is perfectly within your rights; the friendlier your tone, the better your chance for success. If he ignores you, you could get up and complain to the maitre d', but consider first whether the scene that could ensue is really worth it.

In the Car

Phoning from moving vehicles brings up not only the question of etiquette but of safety. Carrying on a phone conversation diverts the driver's attention from the road, and driving with only one hand is dangerous. In fact, a Canadian study in 1998 showed that people who are talking on car phones are four times more likely to be involved in an accident. The use of a portable speakerphone, a built-in phone, or a hands-free device (a head band with a mouthpiece that plugs into a cell phone) will lessen the risk, but the smartest choice is to pull over to the side of the road before making a call.

Keep in mind that the connection from a cell phone being used in a car can be poor, making your phonemate less than pleased to have his time wasted if you have to repeat or delay your discussion as you travel to an area with better reception. If you must speak on the phone while driving, tell the person you're talking with that you may be driving out of the cellular coverage area or encountering interference—and that, if so, you'll call back as soon as you can.

ANOTHER NECESSARY COURTESY: Let your phonemate know if there are other people in the car who will be privy to the conversation.

Pagers

The annoyance potential for pagers, or beepers, is as high as that for cell phones. Those who use them should remember that however urgent the page, the pager should be turned off at once, especially at a public gathering.

Happily, the days of the audible pager are numbered. Just as the boom box was replaced by cassette players and earphones, noise-making pagers are being supplanted by ones that signal a page with a light, a low-volume tone, or a silent vibration; newer models can also give voice mail and numeric and alphanumeric messages.

ANSWERING MACHINES AND VOICE MAIL

As workdays grew more hectic in the 1970s, assistants and secretaries whose job was to answer the phone balked at taking anything more than a name and a number. The hapless caller who begged "But there's more I have to say!" was simply out of luck. The upshot? Voice-mail systems, in which office phones are connected to a computerized message-storing system—an innovation so successful that surveys reveal that by the late 1990s, people calling a business office were met with a voice-mail recording three out of every four times.

Whether you use an answering machine in a home office or are connected to a voice mail service at your company, remember that there are certain practicalities and civilities to keep in mind.

RECORDING A GREETING

On your home phone, your answering machine greeting can be as creative as you like, complete with sitar music and jangling bells if you so desire. But on your office phone, a no-nonsense, straightforward greeting is the better choice by far. Short and sweet is the goal—your full name, your company name, and a request that the caller leave a message: "This is Miguel Hernandez at Johnson-Cowles. Please leave a message and I'll call you back."

You may also want to change your greeting daily so that callers have an idea of your schedule: "On Tuesday, July 12, I'll be in a meeting in the early afternoon but should be in my office for the rest of the day. If you leave a message, I'll call you back as soon as possible." You might also refer callers to an assistant or someone else in your department: "Or you may call Cassandra Reagor on extension 7131."

When you're going away on a business trip or vacation, change your greeting before you depart. After identifying yourself, say "I'll be out of the office until Monday, August 17. Please call back then." You could also give the name of someone else in your department to talk with if the issue needs to be discussed before you return. Asking that the caller leave a message will more than likely result in a full voice-mail mailbox.

LEAVING A MESSAGE

A cardinal rule when leaving a message is to state your name and number *first.* Many people ramble on until they realize they're about to be cut off and then give their number so quickly that it's often indecipherable. Also, keep it short: Most people have little tolerance for long messages, which may be passed over or deleted if the speaker doesn't get straight to the point. Worse still, long messages can overwhelm a system.

Think of your message as you would a letter. Start with your name, phone number (in this case, your "address"), and the date and time of your call. State what you're calling about and then close by repeating your number as a "return address"—a sign-off that allows the listener to jot it down without having to replay the message.

RETURNING CALLS

Return calls left on your answering machine or voice mail within 24 hours. If you reach a machine, lessen the potential for "telephone tag" by stating where you can be reached and when—then make it a point to be available at that time. If something comes up and you can't keep your promise, leave a second message explaining the circumstances and then say when you plan to call again. And *do* it: Not calling back is the equivalent of standing someone up.

PART VII

THE WRITTEN WORD

Today, businesspeople who benefited from the strict educational standards of previous generations are likely to cite "bad writing" as one of the things that has changed for the worse. The reliance on lightning-fast, electronic communication—e-mail—has given rise to a breezy style that has little to do with the formal composition of traditional business letters and reports.

While e-mail is driven by speed, traditional business writing demands absolute clarity, accuracy, and coherence. There is obviously a place for both in the fast-paced business world of today, but it pays to bear in mind that thoughtful and well-written business communications are the most persuasive and impressive to the reader.

Should you doubt the importance of writing to job success, studies have shown that college graduates with good writing skills will earn at least three times more than their less skillful classmates. And human resources specialists will tell you how many job searches terminate with a badly written application letter.

The following chapters review business writing in its many forms, starting with composition, detailing classic business letter form, and ending with the advantages and pitfalls of writing and transmitting e-mail.

CHAPTER 24

THE GOOD WRITER

Many executives will tell you that good business writing is a dead art. Not so. But there is no question that this is a craft under siege. Bad writing is everywhere—writing so poorly constructed that it is nonsensical; so ungrammatical that it is illiterate; so obfuscating that it is unintelligible. Yet in our so-called Information Age, no skill is more important than the ability to organize and convey information with clarity and coherence. Despite the abundance of new technologies for purveying information, the simple truth is that writing is a human activity: Good writing requires active intelligence, imagination, and commitment to do the work.

Frankly, effective writing isn't easy, but it's probably not as hard as you think. In fact, the key to good writing is thinking: You have to know what you want to say before you can say it. Good writing requires time and patience, and nothing in the writer's tool kit can compensate for poor research, inept planning, or fuzzy thinking.

"EVERYBODY'S A CRITIC . . . "

Virtually everyone in business has to write—letters to clients, memos to coworkers, reports, requests, recommendations, manuals, newsletters, even notes for the office suggestion box. Some types of business writing are highly formalized, such as the financial section of a company's annual report to shareholders. Others are extremely informal: interoffice e-mail, for example. But the bulk of material today's businessperson is expected to write falls into the category of "general writing"—more organized and attentive to correct grammar and construction than spoken conversation, but not nearly so rigid and rule-bound as legal or scientific writing.

All writing, however, should be good enough to meet these basic tests:

- Is it clear? (Have you said what you intended to say?)
- Is it unified? (Have you stuck to your point?)
- Is it coherent? (Will it make sense to the reader?)

The Good Writer

When writers take up pencil and paper or sit down to a keyboard, they often forget that their objective is not to please themselves. The purpose of writing is to communicate with someone else, and the old saying "Everybody's a critic" applies. Anyone who reads your communication—whether the chairman of the board or everyone on the mailing list for the employee newsletter—will judge not only you but your company by the quality of your writing. When you get your message across in a manner that doesn't try the patience or waste the time of your reader, you are 90 percent of the way home. If you can truly interest your reader with your engaging and (when appropriate) entertaining style, you have hit one out of the ballpark.

Before getting down to the subject of specific types of business writing (see Effective Business Letters, page 314), it is useful to look briefly at some of the fundamentals—grammar, organization, and consistency.

THE IMPORTANCE OF GRAMMAR

It is interesting how often, when discussing writing, we use the language of building. We "construct" sentences. We "structure" paragraphs. Words are the basic building blocks of writing, and grammar is the blueprint.

There are actually two principal fields of grammar: word formations (how "happy" becomes "happier" and "sane" can turn "insane"), and syntax, which concerns the structure of sentences. These distinctions may interest linguists and grammarians, but for the business writer, it's enough to remember that language has structure—a sentence must have a subject and a predicate, for example, and a personal pronoun must agree with its antecedent noun in number and gender. (See also Grammar Alerts, pages 307, 308, 311 and 320.)

Does this sound vaguely familiar? Chances are that at least one English teacher tried to drum the rules of grammar into you at some point. But think for a minute about the importance of those rules. You can read the latest edition of the *Wall Street Journal,* a chapter of a Tom Clancy novel, a recipe for pineapple-upside-down cake, specifications for installing a new computer program, and a chatty letter from your grandmother—and so long as each piece of writing is grammatical, you can understand them all. That's communication! Yet if your grammar is poor, you won't be able to say what you mean; you may even convey messages that you don't intend. Your audience—the reader—may form an erroneous opinion of your competence or your seriousness. It is not exaggerating to say that the writer of an ungrammatical letter (a job application, for example) may live to regret it.

If you are unsure about your grasp of standard grammar or want to hone your skills, seek out a good reference guide at your bookstore or library. Look for texts with plenty of examples (most of us learn best by example) and make it a habit to check the rules when you are actually writing. You'll also need a dictionary, with one that offers more than definitions as the wisest choice. A comprehensive dictionary can answer grammatical questions, such as how to form the past tense and past participles of irregular verbs, and supply accurate synonyms (words that have the same, or nearly the same, meaning) and antonyms (opposites).

Your company may even offer financial assistance for a writing course at a local college. (Be sure to register for a composition course, not creative writ-

---

Grammar Alert
HE, SHE, OR THEY?

Noun-pronoun conflict is a minefield for the careful writer. Personal pronouns and the nouns they refer to must agree in number (singular or plural) and gender (masculine/he; feminine/she; or neuter/it). Singular pronouns always refer to singular nouns, plural pronouns to plural nouns. But the advent of gender-neutral language has complicated other decisions. Jack still writes his report, and Jane still tracks her expense account. But what happens when every employee does something?

EVERY EMPLOYEE RECEIVES *his* PAY ENVELOPE ON FRIDAYS.
   This is the old style—now regarded as sexist stereotyping—in which the masculine
   pronouns were used to signify human beings in general as well as men in particular.

EVERY EMPLOYEE RECEIVES *his or her* PAY ENVELOPE ON FRIDAYS.
   This usage is preferable to the ungainly "his/her" and the awkward "his and/or her,"
   but it can become irritating when used repeatedly in a single piece of writing.

EVERY EMPLOYEE RECEIVES *their* PAY ENVELOPE ON FRIDAYS.
   This style has become popular because it is easy. But it is also ungrammatical to
   use a plural pronoun, "they," to refer to a single noun, "employee."
   The best solution may mean rethinking the sentence:

ALL *employees* RECEIVE *their* PAYCHECKS ON FRIDAYS.
   In this case, switching to a plural noun preserves correct grammatical construction
   without the risk of offending.

ing.) Read good writing, both nonfiction and fiction, and pay attention to the language and structure. Here's a hint: Read aloud. Voicing the works of others literally forces you to slow down, skip nothing, and hear the way the words are put together. Better still, have a coworker read your writing out loud or read it aloud yourself; you'll quickly see where it needs improving.

ORGANIZE AND OUTLINE

A great many people can write a grammatical sentence, but they are unable to put together a coherent paragraph. Their ideas tumble around like clothes in a dryer, and the reader can't sort the shirts from the socks. Even the most indulgent reader will not put up for long with confused, chaotic writing.

Organizing is always in order before you ever write a word, and outlining is an excellent way to gather your thoughts. Begin by jotting down the main points you want to make; then look over your notes and decide how best to organize them. Here are two ways:

- **THE STEP-BY-STEP OUTLINE.** This works best when you want to explain a process. Make an outline, and if a step is out of order, you will spot it in your outline and make the correction.

Grammar Alert

I BEG TO AGREE

Every clause in every sentence has a subject and a predicate, and these two essentials must agree in number. A singular subject (one person, place, thing, idea, or quality) is always matched to a singular verb: "Jim *works* long hours." A plural subject always take a plural verb: "The guys *work* long hours."

- Problems of subject-verb agreement often crop up because of words that come between the subject and the verb. "A group of union members is protesting the tax increase" can easily and erroneously be written as "A group of irate members are protesting . . . " But the subject of the sentence is "group": All those citizens may be very angry individuals, but their group is singular.
- Pronoun subjects can also cause the writer fits. Some indefinite pronouns ("anyone," "everybody," "something," "each," "either," "neither," "one," "every") always take singular verbs. Others ("both," "few," "others," "many," "several") always take plural verbs. ("*Everybody is* invited to the meeting, but a *few are* staying at their desks to answer the phones.")

- **THE CAUSE-AND-EFFECT OUTLINE.** Use this when you want to describe how something happened. Make an outline that clearly relates the cause and the ensuing consequences.

Outlining may seem time-consuming, but it will save you much rethinking and rewriting time down the line. (Happily, word processing software is available that aids the outlining process.) An outline will also help you stay on track as you write. It's often tempting to follow an interesting tangent, to add unnecessary details, or to drop in an amusing comment or personal story. But the people who read your writing have time constraints, too. They want you to get to the point quickly and make your case clearly; every extraneous bit of writing becomes a distraction and a delay.

These days, there's a tendency to believe that organization somehow cripples creativity. But even the most brilliant artists keep their paints in tubes and their brushes clean. And even the most unconventional businesses open their doors on time, answer their telephones, and know where their employees are.

BE CONSISTENT

When Ralph Waldo Emerson wrote that "consistency is the hobgoblin of little minds," he wasn't writing a business letter. Consistency in business writing is a virtue, essential to clarity and unity in terms of point of view, tense, and mood.

- **POINT OF VIEW.** This is one of the most obvious inconsistencies in writing. When you begin to write, you adopt a point of view—first person ("I," "me," "my," "mine," "we," "us," "our," "ours"); second person ("you," "your," "yours"); or third person ("he," "she," "it," "him," "her," "his," "hers," "its," "they," "them," "their," "theirs"). Your job is to select a point of view and stick with it. Readers find it hard to follow any piece of writing that shifts from one perspective to another.
  - **FIRST PERSON.** Business writers frequently use this point of view, especially in letters, memos, and internal reports. It offers an individualized, personalized perspective. The first person can be found in formal writing but is most often used when the writer wishes to set a friendly, more casual tone.
  - **SECOND PERSON.** This is less common because it adopts the viewpoint of the reader rather than the writer. It is most appropriate in writing that instructs (this book, for example). The second person can also be used in letters. Be careful, though: Second-person writing can easily become accusatory, judgmental, and hostile: "You should know that . . . " or "Your duty is . . . "

The Good Writer

309

- **THIRD PERSON.** This is an objective viewpoint. It allows the writer to be detached—an observer of the action rather than a direct participant. The third person generally sets a more formal tone than the first person. In the language of journalism, it is the reportorial, not editorial, point of view.

- **TENSE.** Tense is the grammatical term for the time of an action or occurrence. All verbs have tense to indicate whether something is happening in the present, happened in the past, or will happen in the future: "I eat at the Greasy Spoon"; "I ate at The Greasy Spoon last Tuesday"; "I will never eat at The Greasy Spoon again."

  Changes in tense sow confusion: "Your fax machine is broken. It was repaired yesterday." Should the reader expect a broken machine or a repaired one? Unless there is a clear difference in time ("We received your broken fax machine yesterday, and we will repair it next week"), select the tense that expresses the time frame of your writing and use it consistently.

- **MOOD.** A final unifying element in writing is mood. This is the attitude of the writer, reflected in the tone of the writing. You may wish to take a serious tone to reflect your knowledge and professionalism when writing a report or proposal. Conversely, you might choose a light, joking tone when writing a memo about the annual Christmas party to members of your work team. You will probably want to adopt a conciliatory and polite tone when writing to a customer with a complaint, whereas a tougher, no-nonsense tone could be the best choice in a performance review for an employee who constantly procrastinates on assignments.

  Whatever mood you adopt, be sure that it is the most appropriate for your purpose: "Boy, did we have a wild year!" hardly sets the right tone for the annual report of a company that has suffered major financial losses. Maintain that tone throughout. Sudden changes in mood—what might be called manic-depressive writing—will disorient the reader and leave the impression that the writer is uncertain or conflicted about the subject.

WHICH WORD TO PICK?

There are words and phrases that trouble even the most conscientious writers. The difference between "affect" and "effect," for instance, or the "comprise" versus "compose" question can trip you up every time. The following list includes a number of examples, and you can doubtless add many more. The point is not to memorize every jot and tittle of correct usage, but to be alert for language problems and correct them before they sneak into your writing.

O f all the common grammar errors, dangling modifiers (also referred to as misplaced modifiers) are undoubtedly the silliest. Modifiers are adjectives, adverbs, prepositional phrases, participial phrases, infinitive phrases, and certain subordinate clauses that describe, identify, or limit the meaning of another part of speech. When modifiers are placed incorrectly in a sentence, the results can be misleading, inappropriate—and downright funny.

Consider these bloopers:

- "Meeting today after lunch, the contract negotiations kept us busy till late in the evening." (And did those negotiations enjoy a full meal?)
- "Dressed in a Givenchy gown, the bride's Rolls Royce was given a police escort." (We've heard of overdoing it, but dressing a *car*?)
- "Shot on location in Santa Monica, Antonio [the film's leading man] did all of his own stunts." (Poor guy. Is being wounded one of the prices people pay for stardom?)

Dangling or misplaced modifies are more than grammatical errors. Despite their potential to entertain, they are classic examples of poor or muddled thinking. Although we hear them all the time—television journalists are particularly culpable—danglers stand out like flashing red lights in any kind of written communication. Pity the poor job seeker who writes, "As an applicant for this position, my resume and references are enclosed."

- **ACRONYMS AND INITIALS.** Acronyms are words formed from the initial letters or syllables of words in a group: *r*adar/*r*adio *d*etection *a*nd *r*anging system; NASA/*N*ational *A*eronautics and *S*pace *A*dministration; MADD/*M*others *A*gainst *D*runk *D*riving. Initials are often used as stand-ins for longer names and phrases: IBM (*I*nternational *B*usiness *M*achines); CBS (*C*olumbia *B*roadcasting *S*ystem). Unless the word or initials have become so ingrained in common usage that no explanation is needed, write the full name in the first reference, followed by the acronym or initials in parentheses. Then use the shortcut version in all following references.
- **AFFECT/EFFECT.** The verb "affect" means to influence, alter, or produce an effect on someone or something. The verb "effect" means to cause, bring about, or accomplish. As a noun, "effect" indicates the outcome, appearance, or influence. ("The consultants were sent to *effect* changes in the way business was done. Their visions for the company *affected* senior

The Good Writer

management in a negative way. The *effects* of the experiment were unpleasant for both groups.")

- **BETWEEN/AMONG/AMID.** "Between" indicates something in the middle of two things. "Among" is used when something is in the company of three or more things. "Amid" is close in meaning to "among" but indicates that a thing is surrounded by something uncountable. ("*Amid* all the troubles with his boss, Jeffrey found himself facing a choice *between* staying and quitting. *Among* his many complaints were his late hours, long business trips, and weekends at the office.")

- **COMPRISE/COMPOSE.** The whole of a thing *comprises* its parts: "Gertrude's proposal *comprises* a description of the concept and notes on budgeting and marketing." The parts *compose* the whole: "Two pens, a holder, and an ink blotter *compose* a desk set." To say that something "is comprised of" is incorrect. Instead, use "includes," "consists of," "is composed of," "contains," or "is made of."

- **CONCERN/FIRM.** When applied to companies, "concern" connotes a business or manufacturing organization. "Firm" applies to a professional group.

- **DECIMATE/ANNIHILATE.** "Decimate" literally means to reduce by 10 percent and commonly indicates a reduction in part. "Annihilate" means to destroy totally. "Annihilate completely" is redundant.

- **FULSOME.** "Fulsome" does not just mean full, complete, or even nicely stuffed. It has more sinister connotations of overblown and excessive, insincere to the point of being offensive: "Everyone was clearly embarrassed when the account manager heaped *fulsome* praise on the client."

- **ITS/IT'S.** "Its" is the possessive form of "it." "It's" is the contraction of "it is." ("*It's* a wonder that her report found *its* way to Human Resources.")

- **LIE/LAY.** See Commonly Confused Words, page 281.

- **MARGINAL.** In financial writing, "marginal" refers to the difference between the cost to sell something and the small profit gained. In general usage, "marginal" means relegated to the edge or outside the mainstream. "Marginal" is not synonymous with minimal or minor.

- **NOISOME.** "Noisome" has nothing to do with the sounds from your cubicle neighbor's radio. It means noxious, harmful, destructive, and is especially related to odors. Do not confuse "noisome" with "noisy": "When we finally traced that *noisome* smell to some old paint supplies, we made a *noisy* protest to the building manager."

- **SCRUTINY.** "Scrutiny" is a close examination or a careful observation. The verb "scrutinize" means to look something over in minute detail. "Close scrutiny" or "scrutinizing carefully" are therefore redundant expressions.

WRETCHED EXCESSES

Words and phrases work their way into our conversation and writing for no better reason than the speaker's or writer's need to appear smarter or more sophisticated. These are the wretched excesses that crowd too much business writing. A good example is "at this point in time"—a phrase much loved by television commentators and public relations officers. "At this point in time," and its evil twin "at the present time," are the windbag's way of saying "now."

In good business writing, it is always preferable to use the simple word rather than the overblown phrase. A few examples:

WINDBAG STYLE	SIMPLE STYLE
ANY AND ALL	all
AS TO HOW	how
DUE TO THE FACT THAT	because
IN CONNECTION WITH	about
PREVIOUS TO/PRIOR TO	before
SUBSEQUENT TO	after
-WISE ATTACHED TO ANY WORD (BUSINESSWISE, EMPLOYMENTWISE, ETIQUETTEWISE, AD NAUSEAM)	about or concerning

Other wretched excess are redundancies: words that repeat themselves and can challenge common sense. Take "advance warning," for example: Since warning means to give notice beforehand, "advance warning" really means "*advance*, advance warning." Other common redundancies include "final conclusion," "mix together," "basic fundamentals" and "basic essentials," "meet together," and "consensus of opinion."

CHAPTER 25

EFFECTIVE BUSINESS LETTERS

The old-fashioned, personal business letter—written on pristine, high-quality paper, sealed in an envelope, and delivered by post or by hand—remains the single most impressive written ambassador for your company. A letter has a dignity that cannot be equaled by electronic mail or faxed correspondence. E-mail and faxes have a spontaneous, off-the-cuff quality akin to a telephone call. A letter, by contrast, says that someone has planned, written, edited and revised, typed, and perhaps retyped a message. In other words, the sender has expended that precious commodity *time* to communicate with the recipient.

Obviously, all letters are not created equal. A form letter can be helpful and informative, but it lacks the intrinsic personality of a personal letter. It's a shame, then, that so many businesspeople regard the writing of business letters as a chore. But if you keep in mind the tests of clarity, unity, and consistency and follow the basic rules of form and grammar, you can master the craft of writing business letters and even come to enjoy the process.

THE STATIONERY DRAWER

Think of business stationery as a form of public relations. Whenever a piece of paper goes out, it should look good and suit the occasion because its appearance will reflect on the image and character of the business. If you place large or frequent orders for stationary, establish a relationship with a printer and paper supplier who will watch out for your interests and see that your stationery standards are maintained. Following are the items of a stationery drawer worthy of pride.

- **CORPORATE LETTERHEAD.** This is an 8½" x 11" sheet of good-quality (high cotton-fiber) paper that is imprinted with the company name and other pertinent information, including full address and telephone number, fax number, and e-mail address. Law firms, medical partnerships, and other professional groups may include a complete list of partners on the letterhead. (Note: This can be costly, considering that the letterhead must be reprinted whenever a partner joins or leaves.)

If the name and title of a company officer or a partner are printed on the letterhead, that paper is used only by that person. Otherwise, letterhead can be used by anyone in the company for official correspondence. The name and address of the company should be printed on the face side of the matching envelope.

If a letter runs to more than a single page (generally, it should not), then second sheets are of the same paper but do not carry the letterhead. If you are responsible for ordering letterhead, remember to order matching plain sheets.

- **MONARCH SHEETS.** Also called executive sheets, these measure 7¼" x 10½" and are used by individuals for personal business letters. Monarch sheets and their matching envelopes are imprinted with the name of the individual and the address of the business, but not the business name.

  Monarch sheets are sometimes used as business letterhead by physicians, lawyers, consultants, and other professionals. In this instance, it is correct to print the name of the company or firm, address, and telephone and telecommunications numbers on the sheet. Monarch sheets used as corporate letterhead also may require second sheets in the same paper.

- **CORRESPONDENCE CARDS.** These are used for short, personal messages, including thank-you notes. The cards are printed with the individual's name only; the name and business address are printed on the matching envelope. Correspondence cards are made of a heavier weight paper and do not fold. Usually 4¼" x 6½", these cards are of heavy stock.

- **ENVELOPES.** Envelopes should match your corporate letterhead and other papers in size, quality, color, and printing style. Generally, return names and addresses are printed on the face side of envelopes to meet postal regulations. In fact, before placing any stationery orders, it's a smart idea to check with your local postal authority for the most up-to-date rules. This applies to all mailings you send out, including windowed billing envelopes and response envelopes, as well as prepaid stamped envelopes of any kind.

- **BUSINESS CARDS.** The last basic item in the stationery drawer is the business card, which is customarily presented during business occasions. Although there seems to be no end to the gimmicks offered for these small essentials, the standard is a 3½" x 2" card of heavy paper stock in white or ecru, printed in black or gray ink. The card should include only pertinent information: name and business title, business name, address, telephone and fax numbers, and e-mail address. If your name is ambiguous (Marion, for example, or Pat), include your courtesy title (Mr. Marion Brown, Ms. Pat Di Beradino); otherwise, use your full name only. (See also Your Trusty Business Card, page 226.)

*Effective
Business
Letters*

A card printed on a special form to fit roll-style address holders can be a real convenience for clients, suppliers, and others who frequently contact you by phone, fax, or e-mail. Naturally, these cards should include the same information as your business card.

Companies may also provide their employees with social business cards—printed with only the name and business telephone number of the individual—for use on strictly social occasions. Business and social business cards should always be handed out discreetly (never give out your card in the first minutes of meeting someone or during a meal) and accepted graciously. The information on your cards should also be kept up-to-date, and the cards themselves should be clean and never folded.

LOGOS AND GRAPHICS

The look of business stationery was once limited to white, ecru, or pale gray papers and black or gray ink. Today, businesses are free to be as creative as they like. Major businesses spend small fortunes on the development of complete graphics programs, and your company may have a graphics standards manual that specifies the exact look, placement, and use of everything from invoice forms to parking lot signage. Logotypes are pervasive, and their usage is protected with the same diligence as that given the crown jewels.

A word to the wise: Before spending a great deal of money on graphic design development, think carefully about your real needs. Will an expensive logo that is just another geometric shape really complement your corporate identity? Is that shocking pink letterhead going to enhance your image in business-to-business correspondence? Will that oversize or gimmicky business card attract positive attention, or will it be tossed away because it doesn't fit into a wallet or cardholder? Don't overlook the traditional forms just because they are traditional. In the long run, your smartest investment may well be the quality of the papers and the visual clarity of the design you select—not the flash and glitter.

Just as you write for the benefit of your readers, consider them when printing. If you print your letters and reports in gray ink on blue paper, your written communications can simply be too hard to read. Your word processing program offers a wealth of typefaces, but many of them—old world and script styles—are difficult to read in text and may look frivolous. For printed text, select readable typefaces—serif styles—in sizes of at least 10- or 12-point type.

WHAT'S IN A NAME?

In business correspondence, little is more important than getting a person's name and title correct. Not only do name and title identify a person, but they also signify position and rank, achievement, even self-concept. The person who receives your letter has an ego, and it may be a large one. If you have a history of correspondence, check your file letters from him or her; the courtesy and business title from their typed signature line will indicate the person's preference. This information may also be found on an executive letterhead or in a company directory or annual report. There's nothing wrong with calling your addressee's business and inquiring; asking for the right name—including spelling—and title shows concern on your part.

THE PARTS OF A BUSINESS LETTER

Business letters are set up in a standardized format, and there are excellent reasons for this conformity. No one will brew a cup of tea, curl up in a comfortable chair before a roaring fire, and settle back to savor the subtle nuances of your business correspondence. Businesspeople are busy people, and they want to get on with their work. If your writing is to succeed, it needs to be free of digressions and misdirection. Traditional business letter form—both its look and written style—eliminates clutter and visual confusion and helps the writer get down to business. By following these standards, you assist the reader not only to read your letter the first time but also to refer back to it when responding.

The format of the standard business letter includes these parts:

Dateline. The dateline comprises month, day, and year. The month should be spelled out, and the numbers written in numerals (January 1, 2005, not Jan. 1 or January 1st). The date is typed two to six lines below the letterhead, usually on the right side of the page, although flush left and centered datelines are perfectly acceptable.

Reference line. Some letters require specific reference to file, account, invoice, order, or policy numbers. These references are usually typed below the dateline, but they may also be centered on the page. When the letter runs longer than one page, the reference line should be repeated on each subsequent sheet.

Special notations. When necessary, letters may include notation of the means of delivery—certified mail or registered mail—or on-arrival instructions, such as personal (to be opened and read by the addressee only) or confidential (for the addressee or other authorized personnel). These lines are typed in all

Effective Business Letters

capital letters and placed flush left, four or five spaces below the date line and two lines above the inside address. On-arrival notations are also printed in capital letters on the face side of the envelope.

Inside address of the recipient. The inside address is usually typed from three to eight lines below the dateline. When a letter is addressed to an individual, the inside address includes:

- ADDRESSEE'S COURTESY TITLE AND FULL NAME. With the advent of political correctness, determining an individual's correct courtesy title can sometimes become a serious research project. If you are writing to a woman you don't know, do you address her as *Mrs.*, *Miss*, or *Ms.*? (*Ms.* is convenient, but not all women like it.) If your recipient holds a doctoral degree, should you use the courtesy title *Dr.*? (Some Ph.D. holders revere their hard-earned title, while others dispense with it entirely.) What about a physician—*Dr.* Smith or Jane Smith, *M.D.*? (The latter is the newer form, but some doctors prefer the traditional title.) It's important to know, because the wrong courtesy title indicates inattention on the writer's part.

    Some names just refuse to reveal the sex of an individual, causing headaches in both address and salutation. Pat, Jan, Leslie, Alex, Hillary, and Lynn, as well as surnames that are used as given names (Marshall, Tyler, Craig, etc.), are examples of these unisex names. Names from other cultures can also be problematic. If you cannot discover the sex of the person, you should drop the courtesy title in the address and the salutation (Jan White; Dear Jan White:). It's awkward but better than risking an unintended insult.

- ADDRESSEE'S BUSINESS TITLE, WHEN REQUIRED. A similar problem arises with business titles, especially when an individual holds more than one position in a company. Do you use all titles or just one? It depends on the purpose of the letter and the recipient's preference. But do not substitute a business title for a courtesy title: Address your letter to "Mr. Richard Lambert, President, Alpha Company," not "President Richard Lambert."

- NAME OF THE BUSINESS. It is equally important to write the name of the company or organization exactly. Look for details: Is *Company*, *Corporation*, or *Incorporated* spelled out or abbreviated? Does the company name include commas, hyphens, periods, or ampersands? Are words run together? Which letters are capitalized? Find out by checking letterhead, corporate publications, or the telephone book.

- FULL ADDRESS. In the address, numbers are generally written in numeral form unless they are part of the name of a building (One Town Plaza). As a rule, street numbers are written in numerals (123 East 17th Street) though First through Twelfth are often written in full, as is any number that may cause confusion (32 Fourteenth Street, not 32 14th Street). City names are written in full unless an abbreviation is the accepted spelling (St. Louis). State names can be written out, or the two-letter Postal Service abbreviation can be used—followed by the zip code. Foreign addresses should conform to the standards in the country of receipt.

For a letter to a business or organization, the address line includes:

- Full name of the company, firm, or institution
- Department name, if necessary
- Full address

If you are writing a company in general or company department, you may also want to include an attention line that directs your letter to a specific individual (Attention: Mr. Benjamin Hayes, or Attention: Director of Health Benefits). The attention line is placed two spaces below the address and two lines above the salutation, but the salutation itself is directed to the company or department.

Salutation. Your salutation is your greeting. In most cases, it is a simple "Dear Mr. _____" or "Dear Dr. _____," followed by a colon. It is a rule of thumb that you salute a person in a business letter with the same name form you use in person, so a business salutation uses a first name only when you know the addressee well or have agreed to correspond on a first-name basis. (For a complete chart showing forms of address, see page 330.)

But what should you write when you are addressing a company rather than an identifiable person? The old-fashioned "Gentlemen" is obviously unacceptable unless the organization includes no females. "Sir or Madam" and "Ladies and Gentlemen" sound stilted. "To whom it may concern" is both coldly formal and clichéd. The best solution is probably to address the company ("Dear Blue Sky Investments:") or department ("Dear Investor Relations:") or to direct your salutation to a specific position ("Dear Human Resources Director:"). A salutation such as "Dear Sales Representative" is also acceptable.

The body. You have arrived at the main course of your letter. You may write a single paragraph or several, but here is where your business will be done, or undone. The first rule is brevity—the test of your organizational skills. It isn't often that business letters require more than one page, so you need to state your message as efficiently as possible. The trick is to be concise and to the point, but never discourteous.

Your first sentence will set the mood, or tone, for the entire letter. "In regard to your request of January 9, a full response will be forwarded within two days" conveys a robotic coldness that may well be taken as rudeness. It is just as easy, and far nicer, to write "I have received your letter requesting information about the Kruppenbach Organization's public-service program. I am preparing a complete review and will be sending it to you within the next two days." The second version may be a few words longer, but it manages to acknowledge the addressee as a person, to restate the request for information (so the recipient knows that you understand what is wanted), and to indicate the writer's personal involvement in fulfilling the request within a specified time. The tone is professional but friendly and should be maintained throughout the letter. (See also Mood, page 310.)

Every good business writer is a good business thinker, and every effective business letter—from an order for spare parts to a new business solicitation—is carefully thought out. Remember that getting your letter read is only part of the job. The bulk of business letters solicit some sort of response, and experience teaches that few readers will respond to writing that bores or confuses them. For the body of your letter, here are guidelines to getting your message across. Use them as standards for all business writing:

Grammar Alert
WHO, WHICH, OR THAT?

The words "who," "whom," "whose," "that," and "which" are relative pronouns that often introduce subordinate (dependent) clauses referring or describing someone or something. But they are not exactly interchangeable.

- "Who" and "whom" refer to human beings: "Here is the job applicant *whom* you wanted to see." "Who" and "whom" can also refer to an animal with a name: "Our cat Gracie, *who* is very finicky, won't eat dry food."
- "That" refers to animals and things but can occasionally refer to people when they are collective or anonymous: "Teenagers *that* complete high school have better employment opportunities."
- "Which" never refers to people, only animals and things: "Mrs. Alvarez has a cost-cutting idea, *which* is what we need to meet our budget."
- "Whose" is the possessive form of "who," so it refers to people. Because "that" and "which" have no possessive forms, "whose" can also refer to animals and things: "Bogan & Ledwith is one of the companies *whose* earnings rose this quarter."

- **KEEP IT SIMPLE.** Some writers like to show off by using big or obscure words, but straightforward language is always preferable. Simple doesn't mean simplistic: The vocabulary of everyday speech is rich and varied. A cautionary note: Don't use a word you find in a thesaurus unless you are absolutely certain of its meaning. A thesaurus can be as dangerous as a loaded gun because it can explode in the writer's face. A thesaurus lists undefined synonyms and antonyms but does not convey the subtle and not-so-subtle differences between meanings of similar words. "Concentrated," "desperate," "exquisite," "fierce," "furious," "terrible," "vehement," "vicious," and "violent" are all listed in Webster's as synonyms for "intense," but there is a world of difference between "concentrated" and "violent."

- **BE CLEAR.** Be sure that technical and specialized terms are clearly defined. Avoid jargon unless you are writing to someone who shares your insider's vocabulary. For example, if you are instructing your reader to turn on an appliance, don't use "boot up" unless you are referring to a computer. (See also Jargon, Et Cetera, page 281.)

- **USE ACTIVE WORDS AND SENTENCE STRUCTURE.** Use verbs that express *doing* rather than standing back and watching the action. "The marketing department recommends immediate cancellation of the contract" expresses active involvement, urgency, and firm conviction. "It is the recommendation of the marketing department that the contract be terminated at the earliest possible time" backs into the proposition. Worse than being wordy, this second sentence is passive, shy, insecure—and hardly likely to bring about the desired result. (Passive voice is best employed when the recipient of the action is more important than the actor: "The files were lost in the fire.")

- **GET SPECIFIC.** Avoid abstraction by choosing language that is specific and precise. "A *Fortune* 100 company" conveys considerably more information than "a large company." If you write "In the adverse economic environment of the early 1990s," your reader may be distracted into a history question. "In the recession of 1990–1991" gets straight to the point.

- **VARY SENTENCE STRUCTURE.** When every sentence in your letter is constructed in the same style, the writing quickly becomes monotonous and dull. Compare these two examples and decide which is more likely to interest a personnel director:

  LETTER A

  I am writing in response to your ad of January 2. I am applying for the position of assistant restaurant manager. I have three years' experience in retail sales. I also worked in the food-service industry while I was in college. I received my BA degree in economics from State University in 1997.

Your January 2 advertisement for an assistant manager was just what I am looking for. After three years as an assistant buyer for a retail department store, I am well prepared for this responsible management position. I also have front-line knowledge of the food-service industry. To support myself while I earned my BA degree in economics from State University (class of 1997), I worked as a short-order cook for the University Grill in Collegetown.

Business letter writing requires frequent use of the pronoun "I," but you can take the edge off by beginning some sentences with explanatory or descriptive phrases and clauses ("After three years as an assistant, I . . . ").

• **GIVE THE READER CLEAR DIRECTIONS.**
Transitional words and phrases are verbal road signs that move your writing smoothly from one idea to the next: "Last month, Universal Manufacturing received a major new contract. *As a result*, we will be doubling our research and development staff in the next three months, and I know you can locate the right people for our needs. *Unlike past positions, however*, successful applicants must be prepared for immediate relocation."

Transitions including "also," "in addition," "likewise," "next," and "just as important" are complementary: They signal that you are adding one idea to another. ("We are looking for experienced systems-design engineers. *Just as important*, we need people who can hit the ground running.")

To show a cause-effect relationship, use terms such as "because," "consequently," "as a result," "thus," and "therefore." ("We know the situation is unusual; *therefore,* we are offering substantial employment bonuses.")

Words and phrases including "although," "in contrast," "in spite of," "nevertheless," "on the contrary," and "on the other hand" show contrast between ideas. ("*Despite* the urgency of the project, it is essential that we still interview any qualified candidates.")

Chronological transitions such as "after," "afterwards," "as soon as," "at last," "at the same time," "before," "later," "then," and "while" indicate that actions or ideas are related in time. ("I will fax you a list of job specifications as soon as they are complete; *then* we can discuss any questions you may have.")

• **USE PARAGRAPHS—AND KEEP THEM TIGHT.**
A paragraph indicates a change to a new topic. Paragraphs also give the reader a visual break. Paragraphs should not run on and on: A reasonable maximum is four or five sentences. But don't go to the opposite extreme by filling your writing with one-sentence paragraphs. Paragraphing is easier when you work from an outline: As a general rule, each of your major topics

will deserve a paragraph. The conclusion of a business letter is always written as a separate paragraph.

- **TIE IT UP.** When ending your message, stay friendly and brief. If you know the recipient, it's fine to end on a personal note: "Please give my best to your wife" or "I enjoyed seeing you at the trade show and hope your trip home was as pleasant as you expected." Even if you don't know the person, your closing can be friendly and helpful. ("I look forward to talking with you soon." Or "Please call me directly at 555–1212 if you need additional copies of the brochure.") It is always polite to say thank you for a service or attention. Do not, however, thank someone for something they have not yet done: "Thank you in advance" is presumptuous.

Complimentary close and signature. A complimentary close is used on most letters, typed two lines below the last line of your message and usually positioned flush left on the page. Some writers agonize over this little phrase: How personal should it be? Should it express formality or casualness?

In most business letters, you want to end on a friendly but not too familiar note. Use variations of "truly" (Yours truly, Yours very truly, Very truly yours) or "sincerely" (Most sincerely, Very sincerely, Sincerely yours, Sincerely). "Cordially" and its variations are proper closings for general business letters, especially when the writer and the recipient know each other. If you are on a first-name basis with your addressee, informal closings are appropriate (As ever, Best wishes, Regards, Kindest regards, Kindest personal regards). Closes such as "Respectfully" or "Respectfully yours" indicate not only respect but also subservience; although seen in diplomatic or ecclesiastical writing, they are too obsequious for most business letters.

Your handwritten signature will appear below the complimentary close, followed by the typed signature. Your business title and company name may be needed, but don't repeat information that already appears in the corporate letterhead. Your name is typed just as in the handwritten signature. The courtesy titles "Mrs.," "Miss," or "Ms." may be added to indicate the writer's preference. Academic degrees (Ph.D., LL.D) and professional ratings (CPA) may also be included in the typed signature. If more than one writer is signing a letter, the written and typed signature blocks either can be placed side-by-side or vertically.

Final notations. If your letter is typed by someone else, the typist's initials may be included two lines below the signature block. Once standard in business letters, the use of initials is now a matter of corporate style. (If you do your own

COMMA CONFUSION

Where, oh, where do the commas belong? Some writers are so intimidated by commas that they shovel these wonderful little marks onto their sentences like mulch. Think of commas as indicating the shortest of hesitations: If a period is a full stop, a comma is just the slightest pressure on the brakes. Commas are primarily used in these three cases:

- To separate three or more items in a series: "The files in the cabinet were color-coded in red, green, and yellow."
- To separate main clauses in compound sentences: "I'll research the facts, and you can write the proposal."
- To set off parenthetical or non-restrictive elements: "Chairman Rochester, alas, had already left the meeting."

Oddly, even writers with comma-itis (the compulsion to punctuate) often fail to use commas where they are always needed: to set off introductory elements. Generally, if a declarative sentence begins with any element—word, phrase, or clause—that is not part of the subject, the element is followed by a comma:

- Introductory expressions such as "yes," "no," "oh," "well," or "why": "Well, well, you certainly have impressed the boss."
- Words of direct address: "You, get off that fresh paint!" or "Mr. Harris, you are expected to attend Ms. Bernstein's meeting at two o'clock."
- Opening participles, participial phrases, and prepositional phrases: "Steaming with rage, Roger dashed off his letter of resignation."

---

typing, don't give in to the temptation to include phony initials. This little bit of self-importance can cause embarrassment and worse when it is discovered.)

When you are enclosing materials with your letter, the notation "Enclosure," "enc.," or "encl.," sometimes with an indication of the number of enclosed pieces—Enclosures (2)—is typed below the signature block. The notation "Separate mailing:" or "Under separate cover:" followed by the name of the piece or pieces (Separate mailing: 1999 Annual Report) appears when materials are being sent separately.

Courtesy copies—notated as "cc:" or "Copies to"—indicate that your letter is to be distributed to other people. The names of these recipients are listed alphabetically, and you may also include their addresses if this will be helpful to your recipient.

A postscript, or P.S., can be added below the last notation and should be initialed by the letter-writer. Postscripts are a common tactic in contemporary direct-mail advertising, as if the writer had one last brilliant reason for you to buy the product. With word processing, however, P.S.'s are rarely necessary and may signal to the reader that you did a poor job of organizing your thoughts if you left important information out of the body of your letter.

WRITING MEMORANDA

By definition, a memorandum is an informal written communication. Memoranda—memos—are usually sent within an office or company for quick and concise communication of news, requests and responses, procedures, reporting, and some employment-related information.

A memo is a For Your Information business note—but definitely not For Your Eyes Only. Memos tend to float around, sometimes for months or years. Proposal and report memos often become the basis for formal communications that are transmitted outside the office. For this reason, write letters, not memos, when your message is private. Avoid sending blind copies (copies to individuals who are not named on the memo itself), because they rarely stay blind for long.

The format for memos differs from business letters in address, salutation, content, and close. Memos can be typed on letterhead, but companies often have a standard memo form, printed or part of a word processing program. The basic address style is:

TO: Name(s) of primary recipient(s) or group
FROM: Name of sender
DATE: Day of sending
SUBJECT or RE: a brief but precise title, such as Thursday's New Business
    Presentation or Changes in Employee Health Insurance
COPIES: Name(s) of other recipient(s)

List names by order of established management hierarchy—highest to lowest position—or alphabetically. Use an alphabetized listing when the recipients are roughly on the same job level or share responsibility for a project. For memos with wide distribution, you may want to address them to a group (The Staff; Purchasing Department; Birthday Party Planners).

Don't try to make petty statements when listing memo recipients. It's true that people will often read some significance into the ranking of names on a memo list, but "demoting" coworkers or leaving them out of a list says more about the writer than the intended victim. An alphabetical listing is safer.

A memo does not have a "Dear _____" salutation; the memo writer goes to the point in a more direct manner than a typical business letter. The tone is usually casual and friendly, though the rules of good grammar and clear construction are always in effect. The informality of memos means that the writing is closer to conversational style, that jargon and even company slang are acceptable among colleagues, and that humor is permissible and often welcome. Still, a business memo is not a personal letter, and memos should never waste the reader's time by straying from the topic into marginal or unrelated issues.

THE INVERTED PYRAMID

The established organizational pattern for effective memos starts with the most important point or idea and proceeds to the least important. A well-constructed memo is like a well-written news story because it follows an "inverted pyramid" plan: It opens with the big news (the who, what, when, where, how, why) and then adds supporting information in descending order of importance. This organization has the advantage of immediately focusing the reader's attention on the heart of your message.

There is no optimal length for a memo, except that it should never be longer than necessary. Some memos may run for two or more pages (for example, a memo that details assignments and duties for a major business presentation); others may include only a paragraph or two. If the writer carefully organizes his or her thoughts before writing, the memo will be the right length for the message.

Memos do not include the complimentary closing of business letters and are not signed by the sender, although some writers initial their memos. But it never hurts to conclude with thanks or compliments or words of encouragement. ("We all know that this project is our first real shot at national recognition, and I really appreciate your willingness to burn the midnight oil.")

Here is an example of a memo that gets its point across in an easygoing yet informative fashion:

TO: The Creative and Copy Departments
FROM: Charles Fung
DATE: October 10, 1999
SUBJECT: Chewy Bread Annual Campaign

It's here again, folks. The time has come to plan the Chewy Bread ad campaign for 2002, and this year the Chewy people are making it exciting for us. They have asked for something "completely different" to sell a new line of health breads and snack foods.

Our first planning meeting will be this Thursday (October 14) at 4:30 P.M. in the Creative Conference Room. Account Service, Media, and the research team will give us the lowdown on marketing strategy, and I expect the meeting to run about two hours. (Food, cold drinks, and coffee will be plentiful.)

I hope everyone who is not otherwise profitably engaged will attend, because we are going to need all your smart ideas on this one. If you can't make it, please notify Carl Palazzolo by 2 P.M. on Thursday.

Note the conversational style: This short memo sounds as chatty as water-cooler talk. But it is also clearly organized to convey the specifics of an important meeting and encourage attendance.

WRITING REPORTS

Reports can be formal or informal and may be written as memos, in letter style, or in short or formal report format.

The format for short reports generally comprises the following:

- Title page
- Summary page
- Letter of authorization for the project
- Statement of purpose or assignment
- Findings and conclusions
- Recommendations

The summary page is a concise overview of the report and emphasizes the conclusions and recommendations. It will often be used as a quick reference or included in follow-up reports.

FORMAL REPORTS

Formal reports are longer and more sophisticated both in writing style and presentation than other reports. Printed on high-quality paper and bound under a separate cover, formal reports expand on the elements in a short report by including an acknowledgment page; foreword; table of contents; lists of tables, figures, and illustrations; footnotes or endnotes; appendix or appendices; glossary; bibliography or works cited; and index.

The formal report is frequently used for business plans and proposals, as well as research and project reports. The body of a formal report may be quite lengthy, but it must meet the tests of clarity, unity, and coherence that apply to all good business writing. Several people may contribute to a report, so it's a

MANNERLY MEMOS

Memos are so efficient for interoffice communication that there's a tendency to abuse the form. But the best memo writers always observe their memo manners, as detailed here.

- **THE FEWER THE BETTER.** Remember that your fellow employees are busy at their jobs, so send and copy memos only to the people directly concerned with your message. In the snowstorm of papers and blitz of e-mail messages that workers receive these days, an irrelevant memo is a nuisance and reflects badly on the sender.

- **ONLY WHEN NEEDED.** In addition to taking up others' time needlessly, excessive memo-writing tends to devalue the writer's messages, and even important memos are tossed into the wastebasket without being read.

- **BE POSITIVE.** Avoid negative personal comments. A critical memo can point out problems without ad hominem remarks. When you have negative criticism to deliver, don't go on the offensive. Try to open your memo with a positive statement; then, focus on the problem rather than the person: "Your plan for the restructuring of the purchasing department is very well organized, and I really like your suggestions for simplifying the ordering procedures. I'd like you to give more thought, however, to the reporting relationships you've recommended and how we can pass authority down the line." If you must deliver personal comments, a private meeting is the place to do so, possibly followed up with a formal letter. Another important reminder: Never terminate anyone's employment in a memo.

- **BE NICE.** Even the most senior executives should use a friendly tone in memos. In large companies, employees often receive memos from senior officers whom they have never even seen, and employees will form their attitudes about the company from these written communications. If the tone of the memo is brusque or condescending, the recipients will logically assume that the executive is uncaring or self-serving. Think of memos as internal public relations for the company and yourself.

- **DON'T BLINDSIDE.** Don't use memos to make end-runs around other people. If you need to go above a supervisor with a problem or complaint, for example, a face-to-face meeting with a higher-ranking manager is probably the best route. Remember that memos are rarely private and no place for confidential material.

good idea to make one person the editor. It's likely that your best writer will do the editing, but not always. Sometimes an objective outsider can spot problems and errors that those involved in the project will miss. You may want to hire a freelance writer or editor to polish your work to perfection.

Computers now make it relatively easy to incorporate charts, graphs, tables, photography, and illustration in your reports. Such graphics not only provide useful information, but they also break up the visual monotony of long pages of text and help the reader along. But don't overdo; clever visuals can't hide shallow content, weak organization, or poor writing.

For guidance in formatting the various components of a report—footnotes, bibliography, index, glossary, etc.—consult a college-level grammar and composition text or thesis-writing guide. They will help you avoid mistakes, such as confusing "i.e." (that is) and "e.g." (for example) or leaving the page citations out of footnotes.

HIGHLIGHTING

Highlighting can be an effective way to emphasize important points and give visual interest to a written page—and with a computer, it's a breeze. Your word-processing program allows you to <u>underline</u> and *italicize* and print words in **boldface.** You can make lists of items stand out with bullets:
Our graphics department includes:

- Eight innovative design specialists under the direction of *Ad Magazine's* "Art Director of the Year" for 1999
- Two award-winning copywriters
- The latest electronic design technology

But don't get carried away. Too much highlighting will result in visual clutter; don't, for example, use your computer's capabilities to print your company name in its logo form in letters and reports. (Logos in 10 or 12 point type tend to look like ink spots on the page.) Also, if you highlight everything, then nothing is important.

FORMS OF ADDRESS

	INSIDE & ENVELOPE	SALUTATION
CLERICAL AND RELIGIOUS		
POPE	His Holiness the Pope *or* His Holiness Pope Paul	*Your Holiness; Most Holy Father*
PATRIARCH	His Beatitude the Patriarch of ____	*Most Reverend Lord*
CARDINAL	His Eminence Ian Cardinal Green *or* His Eminence Cardinal Green	*Your Eminence; Dear Cardinal Green*
ARCHBISHOP	The Most Reverend Archbishop of ___ *or* The Most Reverend Ian M. Green Archbishop of _____	*Your Excellency; Dear Archbishop Green*
CATHOLIC PRIEST	The Reverend Father Green *or* The Reverend Ian M. Green	*Dear Father Green*
EPISCOPAL BISHOP	The Right Reverend Ian M. Green; Bishop of _____	*Right Reverend Sir (Madam); Dear Bishop Green*
METHODIST BISHOP	The Reverend Ian M. Green; Bishop of _____	*Dear Bishop Green*
MORMON BISHOP	Bishop Ian M. Green; Church of Jesus Christ of Latter-day Saints	*Dear Bishop Green; Sir*
PROTESTANT CLERGY	The Reverend Jane F. Jones *or* The Reverend Dr. Jane F. Jones	*Dear Ms. Jones; Dear Dr. Jones*
RABBI	Dear Rabbi David A. Schiff *or* Rabbi David A. Schiff, D.D.	*Dear Rabbi Schiff; Dear Dr. Schiff*
GOVERNMENT OFFICIALS—UNITED STATES		
PRESIDENT	The President *or* The Honorable Ian A. Green; President of the United States	*Mr. (Madam) President; Dear Mr. (Madam) President*
FIRST LADY	Mrs. Green *(no first names)*	*Dear Mrs. Green*
PRESIDENT-ELECT	The Honorable Jane F. Jones; President-elect of the United States	*Dear Madam (Sir); Dear Ms. Jones*

	INSIDE & ENVELOPE	SALUTATION
FORMER PRESIDENT	The Honorable Ian A. Green	*Sir (Madam);* *Dear Mr. Green*
VICE PRESIDENT	The Vice President *or* Vice President Jane F. Jones	*Madam (Sir);* *Dear Madam (Mr.)* *Vice President*
U.S. ATTORNEY GENERAL	The Honorable Jane F. Jones; The Attorney General	*Dear Madam (Mr.);* *Attorney General*
U.S. CABINET OFFICER	The Honorable Ian M. Green; Secretary of ____ (*or* The Secretary of ___)	*Sir (Madam);* *Dear Mr. (Madam) Secretary*
U.S. POSTMASTER	The Honorable Jane F. Jones, The Postmaster General	*Madam (Sir);* *Dear Madam (Sir)* *Postmaster General*
SUPREME COURT (CHIEF JUSTICE)	The Chief Justice of the United States; The Supreme Court of the United States *or* The Chief Justice; The Supreme Court	*Sir (Madam);* *Dear Mr. (Madam)* *Chief Justice*
SUPREME COURT (ASSOCIATE JUSTICE)	Ms. Justice Jones; The Supreme Court of the United States	*Madam (Sir);* *Madam (Mr.) Justice;* *Dear Madam Justice Jones*
FEDERAL JUDGE	The Honorable Ian M. Green; Judge of the United States (*name of*) Court	*Sir (Madam);* *Dear Judge Green*
U.S. SENATOR	The Honorable Jane F. Jones; United States Senate; (*Use same forms for state senators, with the indication* The Senate of _____.)	*Madam (Sir);* *Dear Senator Jones*
U.S. REPRESENTATIVE	The Honorable Ian M. Green; United States House of Representatives; (*Use same forms for state representatives, with indication* House of Representatives, The State Assembly, *or* The House of Delegates.)	*Sir (Madam);* *Dear Representative Green;* *Dear Mr. Green*
STATE GOVERNOR	The Honorable Ian M. Green; Governor of _____	*Sir (Madam);* *Dear Governor Green*

	INSIDE & ENVELOPE	SALUTATION

	INSIDE & ENVELOPE	SALUTATION
STATE SUPREME COURT	The Honorable Jane F. Jones; Chief Justice of the Supreme Court of ____;	*Madam (Sir); Dear Madam (Mr.) Chief Justice;*
	The Honorable Ian M. Green; Associate Justice of the Supreme Court of __	*Sir (Madam); Dear Justice Green*
MAYOR	The Honorable Jane F. Jones; Mayor of _____	*Dear Ms. Jones; Dear Mayor Jones*
ALDERMAN OR COUNCILMAN (ALDERWOMAN OR COUNCILWOMAN)	The Honorable Ian M. Green; Alderman Ian M. Green;	*Dear Mr. Green; Dear Alderman Green;*
	The Honorable Jane F. Jones; Councilwoman Jane F. Jones	*Dear Ms. Jones; Dear Councilwoman Jones*

FOREIGN AND DIPLOMATIC

	INSIDE & ENVELOPE	SALUTATION
FOREIGN HEAD OF STATE	His Excellency Ian M. Green; Premier (President) of _____	*Excellency; Dear Mr. (Madam) Premier*
PRIME MINISTER	Her Excellency Jane F. Jones	*Excellency; Dear Madam (Mr.) Prime Minister*
CANADIAN PRIME MINISTER	The Right Honorable _____, P.C., M.P.; Prime Minister of Canada	*Sir or Madam; Dear Mr. or Madam Prime Minister*
ROYALTY (CORRECT FORM IS TO ADDRESS A REPRESENTATIVE OF THE ROYAL PERSON)	The Private Secretary to Her Majesty, the Queen (His or Her Royal Highness *for members of royal families)*	*Sir (Madam)*
U.S. AMBASSADOR	The Honorable Ian M. Green; American Ambassador; *in Canada and Latin America:* The Honorable Jane F. Jones; Ambassador of the United States of America	*Sir (Madam); Dear Mr. (Madam) Ambassador*

	INSIDE & ENVELOPE	SALUTATION
FOREIGN AMBASSADOR	His Excellency Ian M. Green; Ambassador of _____	*Excellency; Dear Mr. (Madam) Ambassador*

U.S. MILITARY

Military titles are numerous. The basic address form is: Rank, Full Name, Service Initials. *In the address, rank may be written in full or abbreviated* (Major *or* MAJ). *Salutation style is* Dear Rank *or* Mr./Ms. Surname.

	INSIDE & ENVELOPE	SALUTATION
SERVICES	United States Army (USA); United States Navy (USN); United States Air Force; (USAF); United States Marine Corps (USMC); United States Coast Guard (USCG)	
EXAMPLES	General Jane F. Jones, USA (*or* GEN Jane F. Jones);	*Dear General Jones;*
	Commander (*or* CDR) Ian M. Green, USN;	*Dear Commander Green;*
	Colonel (*or* COL) Jane F. Jones, USAF;	*Dear Colonel Jones;*
	First Sergeant (*or* 1SG) Ian M. Green, USA;	*Dear Sergeant Green;*
	Lieutenant (j.g.) Jane F. Jones, USCG (*or* LTJG)	*Dear Ms. Jones; (Use Mr., Ms. or Miss for Navy and Coast Guard officers below the rank of Lieutenant Commander.)*
MILITARY ACADEMY	Private (PVT) Ian M. Green, USMC;	*Dear Private Green;*
	Cadet Jane F. Jones; United States Military Academy *or* United States Air Force Academy;	*Dear Cadet Jones;*
	Midshipman Ian M. Green; United States Naval Academy; United States Coast Guard Academy	*Dear Midshipman Green*
RETIRED OFFICERS	Major Jane F. Jones, USA, Retired	*Dear Major Jones*

	INSIDE & ENVELOPE	SALUTATION
PROFESSIONAL TITLES		
ATTORNEY	Ms. Jane F. Jones, Attorney-at-Law *or* Jane F. Jones, Esq.	*Dear Ms. Jones*
CERTIFIED PUBLIC ACCOUNTANT	Ian M. Green, C.P.A. *or* Mr. Ian M. Green *(Follow this address form for all professionals whose names may be followed by credentials, as* Ian M. Green, R.N. *or* Mr. Ian M. Green)	*Dear Mr. Green*
DENTIST	Jane F. Jones, D.D.S. *or* Dr. Jane F. Jones	*Dear Dr. Jones*
PHYSICIAN	Ian M. Green, M.D. *or* Dr. Ian M. Green	*Dear Dr. Green*
VETERINARIAN	Jane F. Jones, D.V.M. *or* Dr. Jane F. Jones	*Dear Dr. Jones*
COLLEGE/UNIVERSITY OFFICERS	Dr. Ian M. Green; President (Chancellor, Dean, etc.) *or* President Ian M. Green	*Dear Dr. Green*
PROFESSOR	Dr. Jane F. Jones or Jane F. Jones, Ph.D.; Professor of _____ *or* Professor Jane F. Jones	*Dear Dr. Jones;* *Dear Professor Jones;* *Dear Ms. Jones*
MULTIPLE NAMES		
MEN WITH DIFFERENT SURNAMES	Mr. Ian M. Green; Mr. James L. Black *or* Messrs. I. M. Green and J. L Black *or* Messrs. Green and Black	*Dear Mr. Green and* *Mr. Black;* *Dear Messrs. Green and* *Black;* *Gentlemen*
WOMEN WITH DIFFERENT SURNAMES	Mrs. Jane F. Jones;	*Dear Mrs. Jones and* *Mrs. Smith;*

	INSIDE & ENVELOPE	SALUTATION
WOMEN WITH DIFFERENT SURNAMES (CONTINUED)	Mrs. Ann B. Smith *or* Mesdames J.F. Jones and A.B. Smith *or* Mesdames Jones and Smith;	*Dear Mesdames Jones and Smith;* *Mesdames*
	Use Mrs./Mesdames *for married women;* Miss/Misses *for single women;* Ms. *for women whose status is unknown or who prefer the generic title* (Ms. J. F. Jones and Ms. Ann B. Smith/Dear Ms. Jones and Ms. Smith).	
MEN OR WOMEN WITH THE SAME SURNAME (BECAUSE THESE FORMS IMPLY FAMILIAL RELATIONSHIPS, YOU MAY WANT TO USE THEM FOR RELATED PERSONS ONLY.)	Mr. Ian M. Green; Mr. Richard Z. Green *or* Messrs. I. M. and R. Z. Green *or* The Messrs. Green;	*Dear Messrs. Green;* *Gentlemen;*
	Miss Jane F. Jones (Mrs./Ms.); Miss Betty B. Jones *or* Misses Jane and Betty Jones (Mesdames) *or* The Misses Jones (The Mesdames)	*Dear Misses Jones;* *(Mesdames Jones);* *(Ms. Jane and Betty Jones)*
PHYSICIANS IN JOINT PRACTICE	Dr. Ian M. Green, Dr. Jane F. Jones, and Dr. Ann B. Smith	*Dear Drs. Green, Jones, and Smith*
MARRIED COUPLES	Mr. and Mrs. Ian M. Green;	*Dear Mr. and Mrs. Green;*
	Mr. Ian M. Green and Ms. Jane F. Jones;	*Dear Mr. Green and Ms. Jones;*
	President and Mrs. Ian M. Green *or* The President and Mrs. Green;	*Dear President and Mrs. Green*
	Dr. Ian M. Green and Dr. Jane F. Jones;	*Dear Drs. Green and Jones;*
	Dr. Ian M. Green and Dr. Jane J. Green;	*Dear Drs. Green;*
	The Reverend Jane J. Green and Mr. Green;	*Dear Rev. and Mr. Green;*
	MAJ Jane J. Green and CPT Ian M. Green; *(address married couples in the military in order of higher rank)*	*Dear Major and Captain Green, USA*

CHAPTER 26

TYPES OF CORRESPONDENCE

Computer programs and the business section of your bookstore both offer advice on writing business letters, and they can be very helpful. But beware the book that promises form letters for you to copy; such quick fixes can result in serious problems. Most obvious is the embarrassment when your "borrowed" letter is exactly the same as a competitor's because he used the same source! More important, formulated letters are by necessity generic. Even when adapted for your purposes, they have all the heart and soul of the ingredients list on a cereal box. They leave out the first essential of effective writing—thinking. This chapter takes a different tack, offering sample letters not as models but as examples that contain the elements that should be a part of various kinds of business letters, from those that have to do with employment to the thanking of business associates. A great deal of the advice applies as much to electronic mail as to what the happily wired call "snail mail."

EMPLOYMENT LETTERS

Letters about employment—of recommendation and reference, post-interview thank-you letters, job offers, job rejections, resignations, and terminations—require serious attention because what is said will affect someone's life. Whether you are conveying good news or bad, all letters about employment issues should be personal, courteous, and crystal clear.

These types of business letters can be the most difficult to write—especially for job seekers. That's because it is so hard to "sell" ourselves without seeming self-centered or conceited. But every resume sent out must be accompanied by a cover letter, and a good cover letter is your best opportunity to introduce yourself to a prospective employer in the most positive light. (Given its importance to the job search, the cover letter—technically, a letter of application—is covered in Resumes and Application Letters, page 21. Also covered elsewhere are post-interview thank-you notes, on page 46.)

With the exception of reference and resignation letters, the employment letters on the following pages are generally written from the manager's point of view—but the principles by which they're constructed are the same no matter what job level the writer holds.

REFERENCE AND RECOMMENDATION LETTERS

When you are asked to write a recommendation or reference letter, give some thought to your own feelings. Do you know this person well or only casually? Are you enthusiastic about his or her employment capabilities or only lukewarm? Are there any negative issues that may cloud your recommendation? Your letter must be honest, so it is much kinder to politely refuse to write a recommendation than to write a letter that, despite your best efforts, will quite possibly betray your feelings.

Recommendation letters should always be addressed to an individual, never "To whom it may concern." The letter will include information about your relationship (employer, supervisor, client, teacher, etc.) to the person you are recommending and the length of your acquaintance. When possible, offer your evaluation of the person's employment qualifications. If you can cite examples of workplace experience, so much the better:

> Ms. Jones first demonstrated her organization and leadership abilities when she took on the direction of a major new client presentation during her first few months as my administrative assistant. In this and every project she has handled since, Ms. Jones has proved to be a natural self-starter, an imaginative planner, and a gifted team leader.

Limit your comments to employment-related information, and don't hesitate to be enthusiastic. Just be absolutely certain that the person can live up to your glowing comments. If you've agreed to be a reference, include a telephone number and times when you can be reached.

Negative referrals can be tricky. Think twice before saying something that calls into question a former employee's qualities or skills. Your company probably has a policy regarding what can be said and how, since negative information can have legal repercussions.

JOB-OFFER LETTERS

These are obviously easier to write than rejections. But when you are offering someone a job, be sure that you include all pertinent information. State exactly the position ("assistant manager of Happy Burger's Richmond Road store" or "pediatric nurse in the University Medical Center's Child Oncology Unit"), and be clear that the offer is formal and official. Give exact job expectations and requirements and reporting relationships ("systems designer reporting directly to the Research Director"). Confirm salary, benefits, and any performance or salary review policies. In other words, leave no stone unturned when you describe the position you are offering. Include a starting date and mention any materials (birth certificate, photo ID, immigration papers, and such) that the person needs to provide.

Job offers can be formal and legalistic, or they can be informal. It is fine to make the informal offer by telephone and follow up at once with a formal letter. Whatever approach an employer takes, it is important to remember that this is the one step in the process when the ball is in the applicant's court. If you really want the person to work for you, make him or her feel welcome.

REJECTION LETTERS

Rejection letters are rarely long, but they are often cold and sometimes cruel. It's hard to turn down an applicant, especially one who has made a good impression. But everyone who applies for a position deserves common courtesy; someone who has gone through multiple interviews and risen to the rank of final contender deserves some form of explanation.

The following example illustrates how to reject an applicant without destroying dignity:

James Wilson, Esquire
123 Common Law Street
San Francisco, CA 41072

Dear James:

I had hoped to write a different letter, but the firm has decided to offer the associate's position to another attorney. This is a real disappointment for me because I have been genuinely impressed by your qualifications, your intelligence, and your great energy. But the successful candidate has experience in the areas of intellectual copyright and East Asian law and languages that is nearly unique. Even so, the competition was close, and all the partners are truly grateful for all the time and effort you put into the process.

I feel certain that you will have a position that suits your exceptional talents very soon. In fact, I would like to recommend you to a colleague of mine if you agree. Please call me at your earliest convenience so that we can discuss his firm and the opportunities there for an attorney of your caliber.

Let me say how much I have enjoyed getting to know you. I look forward to hearing from you soon.

Yours truly,

Charles King
Senior Partner
King, Prince, Duke and Earl

Notice how the writer gives the bad news in the opening sentence and then goes on to explain the cause of the rejection. He compliments the applicant and validates his words by offering to provide a recommendation for another position. Employers don't usually follow up on an applicant, but in this case, the offer is specific and genuine.

RESIGNATION LETTERS

The first rule of resignation letters: Never write one when you are mad. No job is perfect, after all, and no one leaves a job without some degree of dissatisfaction. But it is a terrible mistake to leave behind an impression of rage and hostility. When crafting a letter of resignation, keep in mind the old saying about not burning any bridges.

A resignation can be brief and to the point: "Please accept my resignation from ABC Industries effective June 19, 1999." This type of letter is normally intended for file purposes and simply confirms a detailed, personal discussion. You may, however, want to write at length and provide an explanation for your departure: Your spouse has taken a job in another city; you've been offered an opportunity that your current employer cannot match; you have decided to change fields or start your own business—there are all kinds of good reasons for resigning, and employers usually appreciate understanding knowing the situation. Gracious resignation letters will convey your gratitude to your employer and express an honest degree of regret at leaving.

But what do you say when you have serious disagreements or dissatisfactions? The goal in the following resignation letter is to state serious conflicts calmly, rationally, and with grace.

Annabelle Kiber, MD
Director of Medical Services
Good Folks Memorial Hospital
111 Healing Way
Atlanta, GA 30305

Dear Dr. Kiber:

I am resigning my position as Chief of Orthopedic Rehabilitation Services effective immediately. While I have found virtually every day of my employment with Good Folks Hospital to be rewarding—particularly because of the quality of the staff and their dedication to our patients—the recent vote of the Board to cut funding for rehabilitation services displays a lack of insight that makes my position intolerable.

I realize that the Board's decision does not reflect your thinking, and I am sincerely grateful for your efforts to keep our capabilities up to standard. But I am convinced that the Board plans to privatize rehab services and dramatically alter its medical mission. You know my feelings about "practice for profit," and I'm confident that you will understand my choice to resign now rather than participate in the dismantling of my department.

Please know how deeply I regret this action, but it is my only option in the circumstances.

Yours sincerely,

Robert W. Thompson, MD

The writer of this letter manages to combine serious criticism with sincere regret. The letter thanks the recipient for her support, however inadequate, and directs the criticism to the responsible parties. Notice that it is a relatively short letter and does not end on a high note that would sound false. Doubtless the writer's first draft was much more heated and explicit, but the letter shows the value of judicious rewriting and editing.

TERMINATION LETTERS

Termination letters are hard to write and harder to receive. There is no euphemism—downsized, laid off, outplaced, let go—adequate to relieve the shock of being fired. Even if the termination is anticipated, when the ax finally falls, it hurts. Every employer handles the situation in his or her own way. And every *worker* knows the horror stories—the office that has been cleared out when the employee returns from vacation; the curt letter left on the employee's desk on Friday afternoon; the registered letter to the employee's home.

Companies that use these kinds of tactics are probably not good employers; they are more concerned with their own discomfort than the feelings of their employees. It is amazing that people who would never send a telegram saying "Your wife is dead Stop" will blithely deliver an impersonal letter that says "Your job is gone." For this reason, a termination letter should take a backseat to a one-on-one meeting. (*Never* fire an employee in front of their fellow workers.) Explain the reasons and, if possible, offer assistance such as job counseling and letters of reference. Don't go into a lot of details; if there is information that the fired employee will need, such as insurance papers or profit-plan data, these can be included in a short letter that formally confirms the termination. Do not indulge in spoken or written recriminations that can come back to haunt you. Be firm (a firing is not negotiable), but kind and sympathetic. (See also When You Fire, page 190.)

REQUEST AND RESPONSE LETTERS

Most of the millions of business letters mailed each day are asking for something or answering a request, and, in general, these letters will be short and sweet. Whether the writer is ordering new office furniture, booking a plane flight, confirming action on an insurance claim, or quoting sales prices, request and response letters should follow standard business-letter format, contain all necessary information, and be crafted with courtesy.

MAKING A REQUEST

If you are making the request, get to the point in the first sentence: "I am writing to request a price quotation for production of a four-color sales brochure to camera-ready stage." Then proceed to give all the information that the reader needs to fulfill your request. Include any special requirements such as a rush delivery, and note any enclosures. Request letters are rarely longer than one page and often only a couple of paragraphs.

RESPONDING TO A REQUEST

When you respond to a request, do it promptly. Response letters should follow the rule of brevity, but never write so little that your response is incomplete. It's smart to keep the request letter at your side as you compose your reply and use it as a checklist. Be sure to answer each point.

If filling a request involves further action or correspondence, be specific about how you will follow up: "Our summer price list will be available on March 1, and I will immediately forward to you the fifteen copies you request." An explanation is essential if you are unable to fulfill the request. You might even suggest an alternative source: "Last fall, we eliminated children's hosiery from our product line, so I regret that we cannot fill your order. You may wish to contact Sox Manufacturing, which offers a full catalog of specialty children's items." It never hurts to go the extra mile.

Conclude your request or response letter with an expression of appreciation and, when appropriate, a brief personal comment or compliment. People notice the small niceties: A simple "Thank you for your assistance" or "We appreciate your business" may expedite your request or keep a valued customer happy.

These following examples of request and response letters demonstrate how to write succinctly but graciously. This request for information is sufficiently specific, yet appropriately noncommittal:

Ms. Martha P. Benfield
Sales and Marketing Director
Chain Hotel East
789 Hospitality Street
Columbus, OH 43216

Dear Ms. Benfield:

Following on our telephone conversation of July 10, I am writing to request further information about accommodations and meeting spaces for the SureThing Company's regional sales conference to be held Thursday–Saturday, May 18–20, 2000. Although I cannot confirm numbers until registration for the conference, I have estimated, based on past attendance, that we will require:

- 40 single guest rooms
- 25 double guest rooms
- 2 guest suites
- 2½ days' use of the Overlook Room and breakout meeting spaces
  (Full days: 8 A.M. to 6 P.M. Half-day: 8 A.M. to 11 A.M.)
- Friday evening's use of the Presidential Ballroom, including audio-visual equipment, and adjacent foyer.

My goal is to finalize our site choice within the next six weeks. If we select Chain Hotel East (and your beautiful hotel certainly has the facilities to meet our needs), I look forward to working with you and your Meeting Planner on the specifics of food service and transportation.

Thank you very much for your interest and assistance.

Yours sincerely,

Monica R. Welles
Vice President, Sales

The response is lengthier than the request, but the writer is wisely "adding value" to her offer. She provides additional materials, points out important services, and extends a personal invitation:

Ms. Monica R. Welles
Vice President, Sales
SureThing Company
2222 Easy Street
Chicago, IL 60601

Dear Ms. Welles:

I am delighted that Chain Hotel East is under consideration for your regional sales conference on March 18–20, 2000. We are very proud of our corporate facilities and services, and I know that we can meet all your expectations.

The Overlook Room and the Presidential Ballroom are available for the dates of your conference, but because they are always in demand, I hope we can reserve them for you as soon as possible.

Chain East has 250 guest rooms and six luxury suites, and for a group your size, we offer excellent corporate rates. Corporate discounts are based on the number of rooms you reserve, and I am enclosing a sheet that fully explains our corporate pricing and cancellation policies. We are also able to book rooms in blocks, so you can have maximum control over the logistics of your conference. I have prepared two schematic drawings that show how blocks of guest rooms can be located for convenient access to our meeting rooms and ballrooms without traffic through public areas of the hotel.

I am including a customized Meeting and Events planning package, which includes information that may help with your decision. In particular, the Facilities brochure has specifics about each meeting space, including dimensions, seating capacities, and equipment (A/V, computers, teleconferencing, videoconferencing). The package includes details about our food and transportation capabilities. And please look over our Business Services brochure; we really do provide "the perfect office" for our corporate guests.

I also want to invite you and members of your staff for a Red Carpet tour of Chain East. Please call me with a time that is convenient for you and if there is any further information you need. My direct line is (614) 555–1234.

All of us at Chain East look forward to welcoming you and SureThing Company to our hotel.

Yours very truly,

Martha Benfield
Sales and Marketing Director

BUSINESS-LETTER CHECKLIST

This checklist will help you decide whether your letter meets the basic requirements of effective business writing:

- Does your letter follow the standard business format described on pages 317–325?
- Did you begin with an outline of your major points as described on page 308 and then write a rough draft?
- Is your message stated clearly and concisely?
- Did you include all necessary information, and are you sure the facts are accurate?
- Have you set a friendly, natural tone? Even when a letter conveys negative criticism or bad news, it should be courteous and considerate of the reader.
- Finally, did you check and double-check every detail—including grammar, spelling, and punctuation—before adding your signature?

LETTERS OF COMPLAINT

When a writer wants satisfaction for a complaint, the difference between success and failure often boils down to attitude. If anger and frustration erupt in a complaint letter, the chances of having the matter corrected are diminished. Also, the person who receives the letter very well may be both innocent and ignorant of the problem. So write with a positive tone (at least in your first letter) and avoid accusations, threats, and snide or derogatory comments. More than any other business letter, a complaint letter requires a cooling-off period between the draft and the final version.

- Address your complaint to the highest person up the chain of command, and use the correct name and title.
- Demonstrate professionalism by using the standard business-letter format, typed or printed.
- State your complaint clearly in the opening paragraph; then, give all the particulars necessary for the recipient to identify the source or cause of the problem. If the difficulty is with an order or invoice, for example, include the identification number. (This is a good time to use a reference number at the top of your letter.)
- Include all information that supports your complaint, but avoid negative or hurtful personal remarks. "The hotel desk clerk was unable to find any record of my reservation, credit card information, or confirmation" is clear.

"Your idiot desk clerk couldn't find snow at the North Pole, much less my room reservation" manages to insult both the clerk and the reader.

- Propose a solution and make it reasonable. For example, when an order has gone astray, it is reasonable to ask for a repeat order to be sent express, with the shipper covering the cost of the mailing. Do not expect a free order unless you want to sound both irrational and greedy.

- Close on a positive note. You don't have to say "thank you," but you might remind the reader of your past experiences: "We have been dealing with Bromide Pharmaceuticals for more than a decade, and we have always appreciated your strong customer orientation." Or end with a brief statement of your expectations: "I would appreciate a response to this matter as quickly as possible."

These days, the fear of lawsuits is pervasive in business, so if you really want to have your problem made right, don't threaten or hint at legal action. Threats will only delay resolution. You may eventually have to follow up an unanswered complaint with legal correspondence, but be certain that you really understand the law, or use a competent attorney. Before taking this route, it is essential that you have the authority to discuss any legal matters, and a wise employee will clear all complaint letters with a superior.

Sometimes a problem arises for which there is no reasonable compensation. For instance, your recent orders have consistently been delivered a day behind schedule, or you received rude treatment from a sales representative. Smart managers and executives want to know about even minor difficulties that can affect their bottom line, and they generally appreciate complaint letters that alert them to a potential problem. When you write a "red flag" letter, do it in a collegial spirit—one businessperson to another. Don't offer advice or a solution unless it pertains to your needs. And don't worry that your letter will hurt the reader's feelings; chances are, he or she will be grateful for the heads-up.

ANSWERING COMPLAINTS

It is hard to be too apologetic or too polite when answering complaints, even ones that seem trivial or unreasonable. Companies that spend millions on polishing their corporate image can lose it all if they acquire the reputation of being unresponsive. With this in mind, extend corporate courtesy not only to customers and investors, but to suppliers, employees, independent contractors, and the general public.

Types of Correspondence

It's important to acknowledge the specific problem at the start of the letter: "Thank you for your letter describing the problems you have experienced with the 555–7-A model of our recharging drill." Then state what you will do to correct the problem: "Although it is possible to repair the defect in the unit, we want you to have what you purchased. A new drill will be shipped to you today via Federal Express Overnight. Please call me directly if the shipment has not arrived by Friday." Finally, assure the person that you appreciate his or her business or patronage and want to continue the relationship: "Your satisfaction is our first concern at Dynamite Drills, and we always want to know when there is any problem with our products or service."

- Always acknowledge a complaint promptly, whether or not you have completely resolved the problem. Most people with complaints want to know that you are aware of the difficulty and are working to correct it.
- Be sensitive about offering compensatory freebies: Coupons for free meals may soothe a customer who received poor service at your restaurant, but the same coupons are likely to seem callous and thoughtless to a person who suffered food poisoning.
- Don't use your response letter to assign individual blame for a problem. Even when the complaint involves a personal failure (a rude salesperson or an incompetent technician, for example), keep your response on a professional level. It's better to describe any positive action you are taking: "The mechanic who incorrectly installed your muffler is now enrolled in a certified technical training course."

CLAIMS AND ADJUSTMENT LETTERS

When a mistake is made in a business transaction—the exchange of a product or service does not go as expected—a claim letter from the customer is called for. In turn, the company will respond with a letter of adjustment.

CLAIM LETTERS

Claim letters are similar to complaints: They deal with problems and ask for compensation. Typically, a claim letter involves a request for a refund or some form of financial entitlement, such as a product discount. Insurance claims, claims against estates, and legal actions such as bankruptcies are all too common. Although insurance companies provide claim forms, a brief cover letter may speed action on your account.

Claim letters are written in standard business-letter format. The style is professional, and the content is thorough. Be sure to explain all the details necessary for the recipient to understand your claim and make a fair and rational decision. Enclose photocopies (never originals) of all supporting materials, such as sales slips, invoices, bills of lading, shipping orders, postmarked envelopes, advertisements that make offers, warranties, guarantees, previous related correspondence, canceled checks, and credit card receipts or bills. In a claim letter, you need to prove your case, demonstrating why your claim is legitimate. As in complaint letters, avoid hostile language and threats, and maintain a courteous and businesslike attitude.

ADJUSTMENT LETTERS

Adjustment letters are the answers to claims. When the claim is allowed, the letter is relatively easy to write. You are, after all, conveying good news. But don't forget to include all relevant information. How will the claim be honored—enclosed check, check by separate post, credit to account, rebilling? When will the claim be honored? Are there any conditions? Are there forms to be completed and signed?

A polite apology is probably necessary. It's a mistake for a company to become defensive when honoring a claim, so if there was a breakdown in your billing department, for example, explain the problem briefly and express sincere (but not excessive) regret. Keep in mind that the person making the claim is a customer or client whose business you want to keep.

An adjustment letter that disallows a claim or offers only partial compensation is more difficult. It is extremely important to explain clearly the circumstances and to support your decision with evidence. Again, keep your letter businesslike and courteous. Don't dramatize the situation or assign blame.

The following example illustrates how a negative adjustment letter can be composed in the right spirit:

Mr. Daniel D. Anderson
Bill's Hardware & General Store
123 Problem Plaza
Phoenix, AZ 85007

Dear Mr. Anderson:

    We appreciate your letter regarding the billing for your recent order of 12 gross of International Items. We completely understand your surprise at the amount charged, since you anticipated receiving the 15 percent volume discount advertised in our winter catalog. Thank you for including the documentation, which has been very helpful in sorting out this problem.

In order to explain our position, I want to review the relevant details. Your order was received by International on November 20, 1999. More important, your purchase order (98766-N) was dated November 18, 1999. The discount offer made in International's winter catalog, however, was clearly limited to orders received by October 31, 1999. While we occasionally allow a few days' grace to account for mailing delays, your order was dated and received almost three weeks after the deadline for the discount offer. In keeping with long-standing corporate policy, we cannot extend the discount when so much time has passed between the cutoff date for the discount and the placement of an order.

I hope you will understand that our decision is a matter of policy and fairness to all our customers.

Yours sincerely,

Albert Hall
Vice President, Sales

The letter opens in a conciliatory tone. The writer uses the "royal we" because the rejection is based on company policy, not his individual decision. The writer also states the facts before giving the rejection. To the end, this letter is clear and courteous, but not apologetic.

SOCIAL BUSINESS LETTERS

There are endless opportunities to write social letters that are business-connected. Examples are the invitation to the new office opening, the special thank you to the planner who saved the day at your shareholders' meeting, the note of congratulations for a colleague's recent promotion, and the letter of sympathy at the death of a valued client.

- **BE TIMELY.** The key to social correspondence is timeliness. The time to write a thank-you note is immediately after the occasion. The time to send an invitation is sufficiently in advance of the event. The time to extend condolences is when the loss happens. There's really only one valid excuse for a late social note or letter: that you simply did not know about an occurrence.
- **BE CAREFUL.** A second concern is appropriateness. For years, insurance agents have dutifully mailed birthday cards to their life insurance customers. It may seem a nice gesture, but many recipients regard their annual birthday card as ghoulish, as though the insurer were thanking them for another year without a payout. Appropriateness derives from the purpose

of the message and an understanding of the recipient. For example, companies with a diverse client list have learned not to send overtly religious Christmas cards, but to wish their clients "Happy Holidays" or a "Prosperous New Year."

There are some social notes that people hate to write—thank yous and sympathy notes in particular. Perhaps the reluctance is related to the formulaic nature of these notes; they often seem inadequate to express heartfelt emotions. But remember that the mere act of writing, in an age when so many people just reach for the phone, shows genuine care and concern. What you say is important, of course—that you bothered to say it in writing is meaningful.

GOOD SOCIAL FORM

Business social letters may be typed or handwritten. If your penmanship is good, writing by hand is a gracious way to express the personal nature of your message. But typed letters and notes are just as acceptable, especially when legibility is a concern.

Notes of condolence at a death, however, should always be handwritten. Printed sympathy cards are an impersonal convenience to be avoided. (Printed responses to sympathy notes, however, are often an unavoidable necessity when the volume of replies is large.)

Business social stationery is varied. Executives often use monarch-size sheets or flat social cards for their notes. Corporate letterhead is usually fine, too, although short notes tend to look skimpy on a large sheet. The point is to use a good-quality paper and matching envelope. If you use letterhead or another piece of stationery that includes your company's name, be sure that your letter or note is business-related.

Employees should keep a stock of personal stationery for personal correspondence. Never use business paper for personal matters without permission. If you are writing a thank you for a job interview with another company or a recommendation for an old school chum, use your personal stationery. Corporate letterheads imply corporate sanction of your words, so be careful.

FORMAL INVITATIONS AND ANNOUNCEMENTS

There was a time when business invitations and announcements followed strict rules of composition. Today, they offer opportunities to be creative and fun.

Formal or informal? It depends on the occasion and the culture of your business. An old-line law firm, for example, may prefer to keep its announcements (new partners, for example, or change of address) as formal as white tie and tails, in keeping with the image of the group as serious and proper. An up-and-coming printing company might do just the opposite, using trendy design to display both their capabilities and their cutting-edge aesthetics.

But whatever style is chosen, business invitations and announcements must be complete. One advantage of the old-fashioned, formally worded, engraved announcement or invitation is that it elevates substance above style. The chance of leaving out essential information is minimal. But pity the trade association that issued the six-color, blind-embossed, die-cut, multifold invitation to its annual awards banquet and nowhere in the clever copy was the location of the event mentioned. Every invitation had to be followed by an embarrassed phone call to impart the essential details.

For all their seeming stuffiness, formal invitations and announcements have the virtues of absolute clarity and sophistication. At one time, all formal correspondence of this type was engraved, but this process is now too costly for most needs. High-quality paper and expert printing (not the cheapest printer you can find) will give the right impression. Corporate invitations and announcements often include the company name or logo printed or embossed at the center top of the page.

INVITATIONS

The company person in charge of drawing up the guest list should start by consulting every department head to make sure no key clients or customers are overlooked. Once the list is compiled, the invitation is written so that recipients are told everything they need to know before accepting and attending. For a large event, invitations should be mailed four to six weeks in advance; for cocktail parties of any sort, three weeks in advance.

Whether your invitation is formal or fanciful, the mailing envelopes can be addressed in type or printing, though handwritten addresses are preferred. Write in ink, not ballpoint pen. Don't go overboard with showy calligraphy, and never use address labels.

- **WHO IS HOSTING.** Adding a CEO's or executive's name to that of the company or organization hosting the party personalizes the invitation and makes it easier for the recipient to address a thank-you note to an individual.

- **THE PURPOSE.** The reason for the party should be made clear: to celebrate a merger or to honor or bid farewell to a certain person, for example, or to launch a product, mark a special anniversary, or welcome an important new client.

- **THE STYLE OF DRESS.** Dress should be specified as either formal, business dress, or casual. On invitations for formal affairs, the notation "Black Tie" is seen; invitations for informal affairs may use either "Informal Dress" or "Casual Dress." (See After Dark, page 179).

- **WHETHER THERE WILL BE FOOD AND/OR DANCING.** An invitation that specifies "Dinner" means the guests will dine seated at tables. "Cocktails" implies only hors d'oeuvres, while "Cocktail Buffet" means a selection of more substantial food. (See also The Ideal Mixer, page 438.) "Buffet Supper" indicates that a full meal will be served—usually at an event held in the later hours, but without the formality of a sit-down dinner. If there is to be dancing, the word "Dancing" is placed below the notation specifying dress.

- **WHETHER A REPLY IS EXPECTED.** RSVP, seen in the bottom left corner of the invitation, means the recipient is expected to tell the sender whether he is accepting or not. "Regrets Only" means that only those who are declining the invitation need respond. Most invitations for large events include a stamped return card for the purpose—an especially important enclosure for a sit-down dinner, for which a more accurate head count is necessary. If no RSVP card is enclosed, a phone number for recipients to call will appear in the bottom left corner. Only the most formal invitations neither enclose a card nor list a phone number, meaning the recipient responds in writing.

- **OTHER ENCLOSURES.** If the party site is out of the way and could be hard to find, it's considerate to enclose a map or give instructions about transportation routes and the availability of parking. Another invitation option is an admission card, which will note whether it admits one or two. A second notation on the card—"This invitation is nontransferable"—attributes a certain exclusivity to the event, and should always be heeded.

A formal invitation is engraved in black on white or ecru quality paper and is usually a double-fold card. But unless the company's image calls for such formality, lighter designs that set the mood are perfectly acceptable. Wording, too, can vary according to the event's character: "Phillip Mitchell, of Cowles & Gregory, Ltd., requests the pleasure of your company . . . " is less formal than "requests the honor of your presence . . . " Some invitations are designed for

Formal invitations are set in a traditional cursive typeface; the numerals are spelled out. For a more personal touch, the example shown here includes the recipients' names, which are handwritten.

> [corporate logo]
> *In honor of*
> **The Zerfoss Group, Limited**
> **Judith Alexander**
> *of Alexander & Anderson Industries*
> *requests the honor of*
>
> Mr. & Mrs. Richard Bailey's
>
> *presence at a cocktail buffet*
> *on Wednesday, January twelfth*
> **Two thousand** *at*
> *six o'clock*
> **The St. Regis Hotel**
> **New York City**
> **RSVP Card Enclosed • Black Tie**
> **Dancing**

An invitation for a more informal event uses numerals for the date and time as well as a less traditional typeface. Information for RSVPs—name, address, and telephone number—is also supplied.

> [corporate logo]
> Gordon & Muse Advertising
> James Evans
> President
> requests the pleasure of your company
> in honoring
> Molly Collins of Blacklock Products, Inc.
> at a cocktail buffet
> on Tuesday, September 29
> 6 to 9 P.M.
> Atlanta Botanical Gardens
> RSVP • Business Dress
> Lily Yarborough
> 71 Maddox Drive
> Atlanta, GA 30305
> (404) 555–1212

the recipient's name to be handwritten into the printed text: ". . . requests the pleasure of Mr. and Mrs. Scott Kraft's presence at . . . " or "Ashley Dixon and Gerald Burns are cordially invited to attend . . . "

FORMAL ANNOUNCEMENTS

From time to time, companies send out formal, printed announcements—notices of change of address and new office openings, additions to staff, promotions, deaths. Whether these announcements are conservative or creative depends on the company's general graphic standards, its corporate image, and the occasion. Announcements should focus on a single item, and as with all good business writing, they should get quickly to the point. Grammatically, a company or business name is always treated as a singular noun and requires a singular verb: "Smythe, Smythe, & Jones is pleased to announce . . . " but "The Directors and Officers of Jones Company are pleased to announce . . . " Announcement cards and matching envelopes are ordered when needed. A formal announcement would read:

THE BOARD OF TRUSTEES OF HIGH Q UNIVERSITY

IS HONORED TO ANNOUNCE THAT

MICHAEL KEMERLING, PH.D.

HAS BEEN ELECTED TO

THE FORTESCUE CHAIR OF MEDIEVAL LITERATURE

AND WILL ASSUME THE POST

ON THE FIRST OF FEBRUARY

TWO THOUSAND.

THANK-YOU NOTES

Aim to get all thank-you notes mailed within 24 hours of the event or action. Most thank-you notes are short—three to five sentences. It's not necessary to go into every item on the menu in order to thank a colleague for lunch. The best guide is to be gracious and stick to the point.

Dear Larry,

Thanks so much for the lunch today—and for introducing me to the Pot o' Gold. I can understand why it's your favorite restaurant. The conversation was almost as delicious as the Beef Bourguignon, and I really appreciated your wise counsel about the transfer offer.

Yours,

Sarah

A similar note to a superior or a client will strike a somewhat more formal tone:

Dear Ms. Jones,

Thank you so much for lunch today. The restaurant was lovely, and the meal was delicious. Most of all, I appreciate your ideas and guidance about my decision to transfer to the Seattle office. Your suggestions really helped me to get my priorities in order. I look forward to entertaining you on your next visit to the Northwest.

Sincerely,

Mark Dawson

Written thank-you notes are not always necessary. If Sarah, of the first note, chose to call her friend Larry and say thanks for lunch, there would be no etiquette breach. But the second note, from Mark Dawson to Ms. Jones, indicates a difference in rank and degree of acquaintance, so the written note is definitely correct. (See also Is a Thank-You Note in Order?, page 424.)

Written notes are used to express gratitude or heap praise. Write them when you receive a gift or attend a business social event, and after job interviews and sales calls.

People who overdo their thank yous may well be accused of grandstanding. It is not appropriate to write your thanks for everyday business, as when a coworker shares information or does a small favor for you. Simply saying "thank you" is enough. But when anyone goes out of his or her way to help or provide a service, put your appreciation in writing. This applies to employees and suppliers as well as paying customers. In the following example, the writer addresses the note to a department head but thanks everyone:

Dear Janis,

I want to thank you and everyone in the Shipping Department for the fantastic way you handled MegaCorp's rush deliveries on Tuesday. Those orders were crucial, and you and your staff really went above and beyond the call of duty to get them out on time. The CEO of MegaCorp, Mr. Harris, just called to tell us that the orders arrived in tip-top shape, and he is delighted with our performance. We couldn't have done it without you. Please express my deepest appreciation to everyone in your department for the hard work, long hours, and cheerful attitudes.

Yours gratefully,

Elliot Middleton

WAYS TO A SUCCESSFUL LETTER

Most of the fundamentals for creating successful business letters have to do with simplicity and directness—the hallmarks of good writing of any kind.

- **LET IT SIMMER.** Organize your thoughts before you start, and always write a rough draft of your letter. If you have the time, put your draft aside for at least a half hour. You will be amazed how you can improve your writing if you allow it to "simmer" for awhile.
- **KEEP IT SHORT.** Write only as much as you need to get your message across. But don't be so terse that you leave out important information that supports your case.
- **WRITE IN THE FIRST PERSON.** Avoid the "royal we" unless you are writing as a representative of your company as a whole.
- **BE NATURAL.** Make your writing as much like your manner of speaking as you can. But always write in complete sentences, and leave out interjections and excessive use of pronouns and contractions.
- **AVOID CLICHÉS AND BUZZWORDS.** If you use a word such as *paradigm* or *leveraged*, be sure you know what it means.
- **AVOID JARGON.** Avoid technical jargon and specialized language unless your reader is certain to be familiar with the field.
- **PROOFREAD.** Read and reread your letter for spelling, grammar, and punctuation errors. Never rely totally on your computer's spelling- and grammar-checking programs: "Pleas sea hour lay test add" will pass the spelling checker as easily as "Please see our latest ad."

CHAPTER 27

COMMUNICATING
ELECTRONICALLY

E-mail is one of the brightest manifestations of the new technology, but electronic transmission of data is hardly a new phenomenon. Samuel Morse invented his magnetic telegraph in the 1830s; ticker tape transmitted stock prices for most of the 20th century; and the telex has been in common use since World War II. But the computerization of the modern office at the end of the 20th century means that just about anybody can send and receive messages just about any time and anywhere, changing the ways people communicate—if not on paper, then certainly on the keyboard.

The business etiquette of electronic communication is still being developed, and what passes for manners in this brave new world of electronica often reflects the enthusiasms of the media's youthful masters. The coinage of the term "netiquette" for online etiquette is just one example of the playful approach to good behavior in cyberspace.

This chapter looks at a few of the problems of e-mailing (the absence of privacy included) and using the Internet and suggests ways to manage them.

THE BASICS

There are two basic modes of interoffice electronic communication, or e-mail: 1) private, internal networks that link computers within a business, sometimes including computers at distant geographic locations; and 2) public systems operated by the major long-distance telephone providers and such companies as America Online.

For businesses, e-mail can be an efficient saver of time and paper. Consider its advantages:

- E-mail eliminates the need for many types of printed memos.
- It facilitates the exchange of computer files.

- It allows off-site employees and contract workers to cooperate on projects as easily as if they were in neighboring offices.
- It enables quick transmission of data between businesses, and greatly speeds approvals and authorizations.

But because it is so easy and ubiquitous, e-mail is ripe for abuse. The Electronic Messaging Association estimated that more than 5.5 trillion e-mail messages were sent in 1999. As anyone who faces the daily deletion of a flood of pointless, useless, and irrelevant messages from the e-mail in-box can testify, quantity is no measure of quality.

E-MAIL CULTURE

The first rule of business e-mailing is to give it some thought, both for the content and the act of sending, which if done carelessly can put information into the wrong hands more easily than ever before. Also, it may be the case that "anything goes" with friends, but at the office, e-mail is designed for business messages—not office gossip, the latest jokes, rants, or anything that gets too personal. As with memos, e-mail messages should have a point.

Three etiquette precepts have emerged in e-mail culture:

- **ALWAYS RESPOND.** Junk mail and forwards are one thing, but you should always respond to a real business message, whether it's to invite you to a meeting or to provide information you requested.
- **KEEP IT SHORT.** In some places, e-mail in-box logs can be stacked high by midmorning, and having to plow through mailings more than a paragraph or two long is inconvenient for the recipient.
- **DON'T GET EMOTIONAL.** Even though e-mail messages are familiar in tone, keep your emotions in check. Save "I'm so upset I could die" for your closest friends. Also, sharing tidbits of your personal life with a business associate you know mainly through e-mail is not the best idea. (See also Watch Your Language, page 360.)

HANDLE WITH CARE

Making mistakes or misusing e-mail can have consequences a letter writer never dreamed of. Consider the following at all times:

- **PRIVACY.** E-mail privacy is an oxymoron, a contradiction in terms. Whatever e-mail you compose, send, and receive on your office PC or laptop,

Communicating Electronically

whether by interoffice network or Internet, belongs to your employer. After all, your employer owns the computer, your time, and the work you produce while in his employ. Think of your e-mail as a postcard anyone can read.

When you're connected to a common server, remember to write your messages with an eye toward the fact that your coworkers will know "where you've been," with your business followed by any prying eyes that so see fit. The same applies to surfing the Net: Your visits to compromising sites, especially pornographic ones, could come back to haunt you.

- **CONFIDENTIALITY.** Be cautious about sending confidential or sensitive information materials—contracts, business plans, salary and sales information. Again, e-mail is not private, and messages can be accidentally or intentionally intercepted or easily forwarded to unintended recipients without your knowledge or consent. There are encryption programs available which code your message so that it cannot be read until it is decoded by the recipient. But it is generally more prudent to use the Post Office or other traditional forms of transmission for private materials.

- **KNOW WHEN IT'S INAPPROPRIATE.** The more serious the message, the less appropriate e-mail becomes as the medium. E-mail has a reputation for informality, and it isn't appropriate for formal communications. Plus, it is potentially dangerous to rely on it for any kind of truly important message because it can easily be duplicated, altered, and forged. Once your e-mail is sent, it is no longer within your control.

A RIGHT TO PRIVACY? FORGET IT.

Face this fact and weigh it well: Unless laws are enacted, your employer has the right to monitor and intercept your e-mail, to access e-mail you have received, even to retrieve from your computer's hard drive e-mail that you long ago dumped or deleted—and your employer is free to act on what he or she finds.

Remember that sending racist or sexist jokes to a workmate is the same as telling them in the office corridor. Posting pornographic writing or pictures by e-mail is the same as tacking nudie pictures to your office wall. Sending proprietary company data to a friend is the same as stealing confidential documents from a file. And insulting bosses or the company in an e-mail note is the same as slapping them in the face.

More companies are setting e-mail policies and communicating them to workers, requiring new employees to sign statements that they have read and understand these policies. Some employers post warnings on their office computers. But it's a mistake to assume that in the absence of a policy statement, you are free to use office e-mail as you like.

Nor is e-mail the appropriate medium for delivering bad news of any kind. Never, for example, send an e-mail letter of resignation. Similarly, don't issue serious complaints or criticisms by e-mail; try to arrange a personal meeting to discuss problems, or write a business complaint letter or confidential memo if a one-on-one conversation isn't possible.

- **ATTENTIVENESS.** Pity the poor person who intends something for one coworker's eyes only and accidentally hits "memo all." E-mail's ability to blanket the masses has proved the undoing of more than a few hapless employees. In a word, pay attention to addresses. Once sent, e-mail can rarely be retrieved. Horror stories are legion: The intern who criticized the way the company was run in less than polite language; the woman who trashed the new boss; the man who made mincemeat of a rival coworker. Never e-mail something about someone you wouldn't say to his or her face.

  So what do you do in case of accidents? If you've accidentally sent something private to the wrong individual (not group), immediately phone him and ask him to delete before reading it—then hope to high heaven he isn't curious enough to look. If, however, your message has gone out to virtually everyone, you have no place to hide. All you can do is transmit a blanket apology and say you hope no one has been offended or angered. Getting in a dig at the technology ("If the system were better designed, mistakes like this wouldn't happen") is a futile ploy that will fool no one. You might, however, use the error as a warning to others: "I now speak from experience when I say that you should be as careful when you hit 'Send' as you are when you perform brain surgery."

- **DISCRETION.** Be careful what you forward. If a former employee sends you a brilliantly acerbic and funny rant on his former boss or department head, keep it to yourself. Broadcasting it to a few friends can backfire if it's gotten wind of by management or Human Resources—and often has.

  If the sickening realization that you made a mistake in broadcasting a message dawns five minutes afterward, you're stuck. (A second message telling everyone to delete the message before reading it will only make sure they practically break their necks getting it open.) An apology flogging yourself for having such bad judgment is the best you can do. Personally apologizing to whomever the rancor was directed may somewhat lessen the trouble you're in for, but don't count on it.

- **PERSONAL USE.** Virtually everybody uses office e-mail for communicating with their friends, and few companies make such back-and-forthing off-limits. But voluminous correspondence with friends can become an issue, especially if the company decides to do a random read and just happens to decide your "Sent" file might be interesting.

How to prevent that particular potentiality? Easy: Save your personal e-mail communications for your home computer. But what if it's too late? Your options are limited because you've left an electronic trail, incriminating evidence that makes the paper trail of old look like child's play. You could say you'd rather not have responded to all your friends' missives but didn't want to appear rude, but what if 80 percent were originated by *you*? The best course of action is to admit your abuse of privilege, promising never to do it again. Then keep your word. It may not be grounds for discipline this time, but you never know what the next violation may bring.

- **THOUGHTFULNESS.** Don't send attached files unless you know that the person receiving them has compatible software. It's more than frustrating to receive an important file that can't be opened or translates into gobbledygook. This problem most often comes about when you are sending files to people outside your office, so check beforehand with the recipient to be sure you have the same software program. If not, you can save your file in ASCII or "Text" format.

- **PATIENCE.** Be patient with the technophobes in your business. There are still plenty of people who aren't up-to-speed on the new technology, who don't trust electronic messaging, or who simply hate it. If you have a colleague who doesn't check his or her e-mail frequently (or ever), put your communications in more traditional forms: Use the telephone or send written notes. If you have the time, you might offer your assistance to the technophobe. And have some sympathy.

On the other side of the coin, the technophobe who refuses to use the new technology risks losing business or a job for being abstinent.

WATCH YOUR LANGUAGE

Tailor your style to whomever it is you're writing. In industries where e-mail is the lifeblood of communication, the use of informal, hip language is actually expected—it shows you belong to the club. Even e-mail messages between people who work in stuffier fields tend to be more informal. The occasional off-the-cuff aside and humorous turn of phrase is part of the game, and most people like to play ball. Only if your correspondent is an adamant defender of traditional business letter prose do you need to write in complete sentences.

Still, even e-mail isn't an excuse for misspellings and grammatical errors— your familiarity with such rules should shine through no matter what the

SURF WARNINGS

The Internet should be a boon to workers, allowing them to get information quickly that once took hours of digging and multiple trips to the library. But employees with PCs and Internet access quickly discover that the Net is much more than a research tool. Games, sports scores, market updates, the latest news and juiciest gossip, recipes, catalogue shopping, music, movie reviews, chat rooms, even day trading on the stock market—it's all there at a click or a keystroke. Problem is, much of what workers do on the Internet is not work, and employers, in self-defense, are increasingly monitoring workplace Internet use.

As with e-mail, there is no serious legal privacy protection for on-the-job Internet surfers. Employers can monitor and audit their employees' computers for Internet use, checking on sites visited, time spent at each site, and software downloads. Downloading software is a particular concern because of the danger of violating copyrights or a company's purchasing policies, or the possibility of importing viruses into the company's system. An employee who accesses pornographic material or engages in sexist, racist, or other prejudiced online conversation can put the company in jeopardy of sexual harassment and discrimination charges or defamation actions.

The absence of a stated company policy on Internet use does not mean employees are free to cruise the Net at will. Internet usage should be strictly confined to job-related tasks. Some companies limit Internet access to specific computers or personnel, and these restrictions should be respected. Before spending any questionable time on the Internet or downloading software, check with a supervisor or the company's Information Systems specialist.

If you're caught idly surfing, 'fess up and hope it doesn't cost you your job, your bonus, or your promotion. Avoid getting into such a bind in the first place by remembering that Internet access is there for a reason—and not the one you were using it for.

A special warning: Never do job-hunting research or apply for a job on the Internet. Having your boss or anyone else in your company come across it means the cat's out of the bag and you will have to suffer the consequences.

medium. The spell-check feature found in many modern e-mail programs will be of help, but it's anything but perfect (see Ways to a Successful Letter, page 355).

Your tone matters, too. "Flaming" is the online term for messages that are highly emotional, angry, or insulting. Although flaming is most likely to occur in

Communicating Electronically

chat rooms, when members of a group are engaged in back-and-forth conversation, it can happen in any message.

Online users have developed a vocabulary of symbols to indicate emotional state, including the following:

:-)	"happy, laugh"
:-(	"sad, unhappy"
:-O	"yelling, shocked"
{{***}}	"hugs and kisses"

These are perfectly fine so long as they are part of the electronic parlance of the people you do business with; if they're not, the use of these symbols may mean nothing to the recipient and annoy at the same time. The same goes for online abbreviations—IMHO for "in my humble opinion"; IOW for "in other words"; BTW for "by the way." If you use these as a matter of course in every e-mail you send, there's a very good chance that at times some recipients will have no idea what you mean.

Another online convention is to avoid typing in all capital letters because CAPS INDICATE THAT YOU ARE SHOUTING YOUR MESSAGE. Readability studies show that all-caps messages are also much harder to read. Use capitalized words sparingly, for emphasis: They're the e-mail equivalent of italics in regular writing, putting STRESS on words as needed. Then again, sometimes this happens because people inadvertently leave the "caps lock" key on—so make sure it's toggled off.

CUT THE SPAM

There is an online term for sending messages indiscriminately—"spamming"—and it's not a compliment. In what some see as a blessing and many more a curse, e-mail enables the writer to send copies, including blind ones, to any number of people, from a select few to everyone in the corporate database. Don't give in to the temptation to blanket the world: Be certain that your messages go only to those who need them or you'll end up as the object of everyone's ire. People who send spam are universally regarded as thoughtless (not to mention obnoxious) because they waste the time of coworkers. The danger of spamming is that the sender quickly earns a "little boy who cried wolf" reputation: By posting frequent e-mail to everyone on a list or database, the sender risks having all messages deleted before they are read.

PART VIII

—

THE
BUSINESS
MEETING

———

*I*f everybody from the CEO down really hates meetings as much as they claim, then why are there so many? The truth is that well-planned and executed meetings are extremely productive, but too many meetings are boring, pointless, and very, very long. Planning an efficient meeting is a something like planning a military campaign, requiring clear objectives, attention to logistics and supplies, and well-trained troops who won't desert under fire.

The two chapters in this section discuss meetings from the perspectives of the planners/leaders and the participants. Meetings that work—from garden variety, informal, "in my office" get-togethers to training seminars to large, multi-day international conferences—take serious forethought and ruthless dedication to details.

The section begins with an overview of meeting planning with emphasis on critical decisions, including whom to invite and what belongs in your agenda, then looks at conducting meetings and the requirements of different types of sessions. The second chapter tells participants how to get the most out of meetings and put their best foot forward making a good impression. Also here are tips for speakers, plus advice about the advantages and disadvantages of audio/visual aids.

CHAPTER 28

THE ALMOST PERFECT MEETING

If any aspect of life at the office makes workers want to cup their heads in their hands and emit a piercing collective scream, it's the meeting. It has been estimated that today's businesspeople spend at least of a quarter of their working hours in meetings, and the higher you rise in the company, the more you attend. Going hand in hand with meeting overload is the fact that too many sessions are unproductive time-wasters—a discourtesy that falls directly on the shoulders of the person who calls them. But if planning and running a perfect meeting is an almost impossible task, pulling off a near-perfect one is not.

This chapter looks at the meetings from the perspective of the person planning and running meetings—usually a middle manager or above. But much of the advice applies to group dynamics at every level. Even a junior employee who's taking her turn hosting a brainstorming session will benefit from knowing something about keeping people in a group happy and productive.

Bear in mind that managing a meeting is an art, not a science. A science is a set of rules for doing things; an art is the ability to appropriately adapt to each situation. This explains why some people put on great meetings and others masterfully botch the job. For all the suggestions made here, there are dozens of other approaches that will work. Artfully adapting requires that you be observant, be yourself, be firm in your willingness to lead and control, and be respectful of individuals and the group as a whole.

SO WHAT'S THE PROBLEM?

Despite their damaged reputation, meetings are one of the most effective tools available for getting things done. Think about it: They provide an efficient forum for the dissemination of information; they enable people to come together in a common purpose and be motivated as a team; they promote group thinking and the creative sparking of ideas that occurs when several minds are applied to a single objective. From the boardroom to the factory floor, meetings facilitate group discussion and decision-making.

All the benefits just stated presume that meetings are well planned and managed. But poorly planned and haphazardly run meetings are like pouring time down the drain. Studies indicate that more than half the time spent in meetings is wasted, and workers who are routinely subjected to inefficient meetings will tell you that the amount of wasted time is usually in direct proportion to the lack of planning and direction. Unproductive meetings are often boring, soporific experiences that work against achievement of common goals. You may actually find yourself envying the colleague who can sleep through a pointless meeting; he, at least, puts the time to good use.

True, meetings are prime opportunities for vote-taking and decision-making. But they are also excellent ways for wishy-washy bosses to delay decisions. If you've ever had an employer or supervisor who hated making decisions, then you know how meetings are used to put off commitment. Decision delayers can always find a reason to call one more meeting on the subject at hand or to appoint one more study committee that must meet and meet again before it can make its recommendations.

A QUESTION OF PURPOSE

People call meetings for lots of reasons, not all serious or businesslike. As said before, some managers hold meetings to delay decision-making. Others do it because they're sociable and like to get together with their coworkers. Some bosses use meetings as a control mechanism, to count heads and remind their employees of who's in charge. There are even a few employers around who still call weekly or biweekly meetings in order to pass out paychecks—the ultimate exercise of power. These are the kinds of ego-motivated meetings that can drive employees crazy.

A genuine business meeting, by contrast, has a genuine business purpose. Know exactly *why* you want to have a meeting and what outcome you seek at its end. Then proceed with the how, who, where, and when.

THE MANY FORMS

By understanding the basic components of a good meeting, you'll be able to see that your meetings are soundly planned and effectively implemented. It may help to begin by clarifying the terms "formal" and "informal," which apply primarily to the structure of the gathering. An informal brainstorming session, for example, will have only the barest of agendas, allow active interplay among all participants, and be flexible about time limits. A technical seminar will be more formally structured, with a carefully planned agenda or schedule and set periods for instruction or lectures followed by question-and-answer exchanges and group discussion.

While the word "meeting" means a gathering of two or more people for any reason, there are finer shades of meaning in meeting terminology.

- **THE REGULARLY SCHEDULED MEETING.** This meeting, variously called the Monday morning department meeting, the weekly job review meeting, or the work-in-progress meeting, can have a structure all its own that evolves over time, ranging from formal to informal.
- **THE SINGLE-SUBJECT MEETING.** Taking many forms, this meeting may focus on a work environment issue or a specific project with a client. It is not the time to bring up other matters, especially minor ones, such as who's leaving their dirty dishes in the kitchen sink.
- **THE CRISIS MEETING.** Usually, this is a hastily arranged meeting dealing with an immediate problem, be it internal or external. If asked to attend, understand that your attendance is mandatory.
- **THE TELECONFERENCE.** Also known as the conference call, the teleconference is conducted over speakerphones.
- **THE VIDEOCONFERENCE.** Videoconferences are teleconferences in which the participants, from different locales, are seen as well as heard. They are generally held in rooms equipped with a stationary video camera operated by a technician.
- **THE PRESENTATION.** This meeting may be informal or formal, but the format is usually highly structured so that the leader or moderator can maintain full control over the proceedings.
- **THE CONFERENCE.** This is a meeting usually focused on discussion of a single subject. Conferences can involve a few people or hundreds, but the agenda and format are formalized.
- **THE BUSINESS SEMINAR.** Usually planned as a formal event, this is a meeting with an educational twist. Seminars are generally led by instructors or experts who convey information to a group.

THINKING IT OUT

It's your meeting, and your responsibility. When it comes to holding a successful session, the devil, as the saying goes, is in the details. In addition to basic logistics (see Comfort and Care, page 378), you'll want to be certain that you've prepared for every aspect of the meeting.

An essential part of your preparation is to determine how your meeting will be organized. Do you want a loose, informal structure that promotes free-flowing give-and-take? Do you want a more tightly managed meeting with times carefully (but not inflexibly) allocated for presentations and discussion? Do you want a rigidly formal meeting that moves like clockwork from one agenda item to the next?

You don't have to know chapter and verse of *Robert's Rules of Order* to understand that productive meetings require structure. Consider your meeting subject, your participants, and your own past experiences. Try to visualize everyone together in your meeting room: How are they interacting? What is being done? Is your vision of the meeting accomplishing what you want? You might want to employ techniques you've learned elsewhere to activate your participants: A role-playing session, for example, may help salespeople identify hidden customer-service problems.

Whatever you do, never try to organize a meeting on a wing and a prayer. Anticipate problems that are likely to bog down the meeting: Is that lengthy statistical presentation really necessary or can it be handled with printed hand-outs and a short summary? Review your agenda to be sure you haven't planned too much; you can always revise the agenda before the meeting if need be.

DEFINING THE PROBLEM OR ISSUE

Ask yourself how a certain matter can best be handled. Is a large meeting appropriate (and worth calling people away from their other duties), or can the problem be assigned to one or two employees in an informal get-together? Could you accomplish your purpose in a memo or report? Never call a meeting simply because you don't know what else to do.

Now determine what you want your meeting to accomplish. Do you want to inform your participants about the issue and get their feedback? Do you want to brainstorm ideas? Do you want to assign tasks? Is there more than one issue to consider? Is decision-making involved? Although much can be done in a meeting, planners sometimes expect too much of their participants. For example, a meeting in which a wholly new problem is presented may not accomplish your goals if you also rush your attendees into making decisions at the same time. They need time to mull the issues, and meetings aren't designed for thoughtful reflection.

ELECTRONIC MEETINGS

Teleconferences and videoconferences are one of the small miracles of our age. They allow real time voice-to-voice or face-to-face communication between people in multiple locations and time zones. But to make the most of electronic conferencing requires forethought.

Timing and notification are critical. Be alert to time differences when planning the conference. Three in the afternoon may be perfect for you, but not for your colleague in London, where it is ten at night. Be sure that everybody who will participate in the call has been notified and their availability confirmed. If specific materials are needed, send them early and confirm they have been received. Check your conferencing equipment in advance; if you are uncomfortable with the technology, you may want to book an off-site location where knowledgeable folks can manage the conference for you. Also, be prepared for the worst: Have a backup plan ready when your lines go dead in the middle of the meeting or you lose one of your parties. It's a good idea to have a second phone line ready so you can fall back on old-fashioned dialing and talking.

Long-distance conferencing can be expensive, so have an agenda and stick to it. Try to focus on a single topic or issue; an electronic meeting is generally not the best venue for brainstorming or freewheeling discussion. If you are videoconferencing with large display screens, visual aids can be very effective—but don't expect your colleague with the standard computer screen to be able to decipher complex growth charts held up to the camera. Finally, end your meeting on time and avoid extended good-byes. (See also Using a Speakerphone, page 289.)

WHO TO INVITE

The right size for a meeting is a subject of constant debate, and it's wiser to consider not the quantity but the *quality* of the participants. It may, for instance, be important to include junior managers and trainees in the initial planning meetings for an upcoming business presentation; their ideas and perceptions can be valuable and, as future executives, they need to be introduced to senior management and to become acquainted with a company's meeting style. On the other hand, those same junior-level employees will be properly excluded from decision-making meetings.

When developing your list of invitees (whether all in-house, all clients or customers, or a mix of both), decide who will help accomplish your purpose. Resist the temptation to include anyone else, but consider the list carefully so that you won't inadvertently leave out a key player. It's always a mistake to manipulate meeting invitations to play office politics, either to impress a higher-up or to spite a colleague; chances are that everyone else who attends the meeting will see this kind of pettiness for what it is.

In short, the size of a meeting depends entirely on its purpose. When the meeting objective is clear, the participants almost choose themselves; you invite the people who can help achieve your goal.

PART-TIME INVITEES

You may want to plan for certain people to attend only part of the meeting. For example, an advertising executive calls a morning-long meeting to discuss creative planning for a new client; she asks representatives from the media department to attend for the first hour only and thoughtfully plans a break so that the media buyers can make a gracious getaway. Segmenting like this allows busy people to participate when they are needed, without feeling obliged to remain when their involvement is done.

GETTING ORGANIZED

Even for informal weekly staff meetings, you'll want to have some sort of agenda. Depending on the purpose of the meeting and the company culture, it can range from a list of topics the leader has jotted down on a pad to printed copies laying out the agenda piece by piece.

At more formal meetings, make the agenda more specific and detailed. You'll probably want to consult with key participants to establish topics for discussion and format. You may want guest speakers and will need to coordinate presentation topics and times with them.

Some planners recommend scheduling action items (decision-making and problem-solving) first as a way to motivate attendance. Others prefer discussion first and then proceeding to decisions. However you organize your meeting, you want to include adequate time at the end for wrapping up—summarizing discussion points, clarifying assignments, reviewing decisions, setting deadlines, and (only if necessary, remember) scheduling a subsequent meeting.

A HINT: As the meeting leader, keep a private agenda that lists the items that must absolutely be acted on. As the meeting progresses, make sure you steer the proceedings to accomplish your must-dos before a key player has to excuse herself from the meeting.

As you organize, you'll be able to estimate closely the amount of time needed for each agenda item. Plan breaks if the meeting will be lengthy; no one should be expected to sit for longer than an hour and a half.

WHEN AND WHERE?

With the agenda and the list of invitees determined, you have the tools to decide on time and location. The number of participants, format, and style of the meeting (casual or formal, in-house or with clients) will tell you what size room you need and how it should be furnished. If it's a simple announcement meeting for employees, you can jam a lot of people into a small room for five or ten minutes and ask them to stand without any discomfort. If it's an all-day seminar, you'll need a room with comfortable tables and chairs and plenty of elbow room. Be sure to book and confirm your meeting space well in advance; many a meeting has had an embarrassing start because the proposed meeting site was already in use.

LOCATION

Meetings can be held virtually anywhere, although the tone of a meeting can be affected by its location. Even small businesses may provide more than one conference room on-site—a room impressively decorated and furnished for client and board or shareholder meetings, and a room or rooms that are deliberately dressed down to encourage jackets-off, get-down-to-business meetings among employees. Many companies like to hold training seminars or brainstorming meetings away from their premises in settings that are conducive to concentrated learning or creative thinking and where phone calls and other interruptions can be controlled.

Consider carefully where to hold a meeting with a client. Convenience may dictate that it be at her office, but having her on your own turf means she won't be interrupted by the goings-on at her own. For an intense meeting, it's often best to choose a neutral site where the participants can roll up their sleeves and be free from the distractions of their respective workplaces.

TIME

Think of your invitees' schedules when you set the meeting time. Friday afternoon, for example, is usually disastrous because participants' minds have already left for the weekend, even though their bodies are in the chairs. Also be attuned to the rhythm of your workplace: Are your coworkers most harried in the morning? Then meet in the afternoon. The more people invited to your meeting, the more difficult scheduling will be, so you should at least check with key participants (including any guest speakers) before locking in an inconvenient time.

*The
Almost
Perfect
Meeting*

PRE-MEETING PREP

What materials do you need to provide? Always bring sufficient copies of the agenda to the meeting. Be sure that you have background information, reports of previous meetings, and research reports for all participants. For the participant's convenience, you can prepare labeled file folders.

Try to know something about each person you're inviting to the meeting, especially if you have included people who don't know one another or with whom you have never worked. Meetings often begin with a meet-and-greet period, and you have to be the spark plug to get things moving. Be sure that you can make friendly, courteous introductions.

ISSUING INVITATIONS

Let the nature of your meeting decide how you issue the invitations. If you're calling a small, informal meeting, a telephone invitation may be just fine, but a written notice (memo, letter, or e-mail) is even better. *Always* send written invitations for formal meetings. But only gatherings such as corporate shareholders' meetings and annual board meetings require formal, printed invitations.

Although it's not always possible, try to give your invitees as much advance notice as possible—at least a week for in-house meetings, two to four weeks for formal meetings. Remember, too, that the longer the meeting, the more schedule-shifting it will require for participants. If your invitees will be coming from distant locations, four to six weeks' notice is appropriate.

For all but the most informal meetings, you'll want to include the agenda with your invitation. You may also want to include a list of all participants. (Advance lists of attendees are normally provided for large, professional conferences and international meetings.) Be sure to provide some kind of response mechanism—your name and phone number for an informal notice, RSVP information or reply card for formal invitations. It's a good idea to ask for the response by a certain date, so that you can reschedule the meeting if too many invitees are unable to attend. To guarantee good attendance, you or your assistant should give your invitees confirmation calls on the day before the meeting and remind participants of time, location, and any materials they need to bring.

Many companies now make use of integrated calendar-scheduling software programs that simplify scheduling meetings. After you type in the participants, the time, the date, and duration, the software tells you if anyone has a scheduling conflict. Invitations and responses are also made through the software, establishing an electronic trail that makes it hard for anyone to claim that she didn't know the meeting was being held.

OFF AND RUNNING

The biggest mistake a meeting organizer can make is assuming that a well-planned meeting can run itself. That's like assuming that if you peel the vegetables and cube the beef, the stew will make itself. Managing a meeting is analogous to a chef cooking a great meal: Following a recipe, you prepare the ingredients, set the temperatures, mix and blend, juggle pots and pans, time everything to perfection, and bring the finished elements together on a plate.

The following advice is essential to all formal meetings, but many of the points will help leaders of even the most informal meetings make them productive. Manage well and you can cook up the results you want.

START ON TIME

A late meeting start sets an unfortunate tone, signaling to participants that you are not in control and that you're not altogether respectful of their schedules. In your introduction, explain the ground rules, clearly informing participants of how you expect the meeting to proceed. For example, can participants interrupt presenters with questions or should they hold all questions until the end?

Introduce speakers and special guests at the beginning of the meeting. (Participants can be intimidated by the presence of strangers or management bigwigs.) If the CFO, who is usually closeted in his office, decides to come to your departmental meeting, your attendees may be inclined to think the worst (cut-backs? layoffs?) unless you explain: "I'm so glad our CFO, Bob Moore, has joined us today. You may not know this, but Mr. Moore was the originator of the employee investment plan we're going to discuss, and he has agreed to tell us about the history of the plan."

KEEP THINGS ON TRACK

Use the agenda to keep your meeting on track. Every meeting is rife with opportunities to run away onto interesting but irrelevant tangents. Your job is to keep the proceedings headed in your direction. Be polite, but firm. "That's an interesting point, Sarah, and I'd like to discuss it with you after the meeting. But right now, I want to stay with the problem of . . . "

If the discussion strays, you will have to steer it round to the agenda. You may want to build some time into your meeting schedule for side issues, but sooner or later you must get the discussion back on target. Again, the rule is polite but firm. You can often redirect the flow by asking a pointed question: "Well, now we know how complicated the whole issue of service contracts is.

But let's get down to the problem of setting up a 24-hour help line. Do we have the personnel to operate it, or will we have to hire?"

ENCOURAGE FULL PARTICIPATION

Be alert to your group. Who is speaking, and who isn't? Why? Some people simply reserve their comments until they have a full grasp of the issues, and you don't want to pressure them. But others—especially junior-level and new employees, and attendees who are new to your group—may need active encouragement. Draw them in by directing appropriate questions their way ("Brad, you're a recent college graduate. How do you think the 18- to 24-year-olds will react to our proposal?") and listen with interest to what they say. If shy or hesitant attendees know that their ideas will be received with attention and respect, they'll feel comfortable speaking up again.

DEALING WITH PROBLEM PARTICIPANTS

Every meeting has them—the manager who is only happy when he is dominating the discussion, the department head who can't stick to the subject, the know-it-all who can't resist displays of her superior grasp of the facts, the devil's advocate who feels compelled to shoot down every new idea, the constant interrupter, the chronic latecomer. You can't change them, so you'll have to deal with them as best you can.

The Dominator, the Know-It-All, and the Devil's Advocate usually thrive in open discussions, but you can thwart them by either directing questions to others or, if necessary, politely cutting them off. You could stop the Interrupter with comments such as "Can you save that thought until the Q-and-A?" and "I think Mrs. Rodriguez was getting to that point. Let's let her finish." As for the Latecomer, she'll usually slip in and apologize later, but if she enters armed with elaborate excuses, signal her to be quiet and hope she gets your message. Some meeting leaders manage latecomers by the simple expedient of locking the door when the meeting begins.

The point is that you can't fully control everyone's bad habits. You do, however, want to make genuine efforts to deal with problem people and difficult situations. Even if you're ineffective, your other participants will see that you recognize the problem and are willing to correct it within the limits of common courtesy. (See also Problem People?, page 386).

USING AUDIOVISUALS

Computer slide shows and overhead transparencies can support your presentations, reinforce your key points, and keep you from wandering from your topic. Your audience will benefit because they'll *see* your key points as well as hear them.

There was a time a decade or so ago when audio-visuals threatened to take over most meetings. Participants in even small gatherings were subjected to multiscreened video assaults, and new product presentations seemed flat if not accompanied by laser lights, fogmachines, and mega-wattage musical scores.

THE SEMINAR

A business seminar is distinguished from other business meetings by its educational or instructional purpose and its high degree of structure. Employee training is often organized in seminars, as are motivational and continuing-education programs. In many cases, the organizer does not actually conduct the meetings; however, he or she is responsible for the near-clockwork timing required to maximize the impact of the event.

A critical planning decision is where to hold a seminar: On-site is convenient if the business has adequate facilities and the meeting space is removed from the hurly-burly of every-day business activity. But an off-site location—a hotel, inn, retreat—may be preferable because it provides psychological as well as physical distance, helping participants to focus on the content of the seminar and to bond as a group (often a primary goal in motivational training). Off-site is obviously more expensive than on-site, but cost should be weighed against anticipated outcomes.

The presenter or facilitator will determine many of the key elements of the seminar—agenda, materials, meeting style—but it is important for the organizer to work with the facilitator on the invitation list. For example, should junior and senior managers be mingled? This may be fine when the subject is purely technical, but if the topic is, for example, "Improving Corporate Management Style," the presence of senior executives will certainly intimidate or silence younger managers. It is also up to the organizer to assure attendance, including the delicate task of convincing department heads to do without their employees for a morning, a day, or longer. Employees, as well, may need encouragement to participate. (It's not unusual for the worker who most needs skills updating to balk like a mule at attending a training seminar.)

It's essential to carry out serious post-seminar evaluation. Despite the bright promises of presenters, all seminars are not effective; organizers will want to follow up by tracking not only immediate, post-seminar reactions but long-term gains. Motivational training, for instance, is notorious for producing instantaneous bursts of energy and collegiality among participants. But as with sugar candies, the long-range effects can be minimal or even counterproductive.

Fortunately, good sense has prevailed, for the most part, and the rule that "simpler is better" has been revived.

Remember that audiovisuals are aids: Do use them to support and enhance presentations; don't use them to cover weak content or inadequate information—and don't use audiovisuals simply because you think you should. Every A/V should serve a specific purpose and be seamlessly integrated with the full context of your presentation. A few more dos and don'ts:

- **DO** ask the help of a coworker whose presentations you admire if you've never created audiovisual aids before. Also ask for constructive criticism.
- **DO** make your visual aids easy to read and understand. Pie charts, for instance, are easier to grasp than columns of percentages. Keep images sharp and uncluttered. Color adds interest to many graphics, but don't overdo it. Your printer may be capable of producing transparencies in every shade of the spectrum, but the resulting graphics can be a psychedelic nightmare.
- **DO** remove visuals when you are not speaking about them. Any kind of visual—a slide, overhead page, enlarged photo, even a literal object—will continue to attract attention when you have moved on to another point. Insert black transparencies or slides where there are breaks in your visual presentation. Flip your chart or easel pad to a blank page.
- **DON'T** ever put a video on pause during a presentation; your audience will be entranced by the fractured image on the monitor and hear little of what you are saying. (Videos are really not suited for stop-and-start presentations; no matter how agile you are with the control buttons, you will find yourself doing too much fast-forwarding and rewinding if you try to interrupt a video program.)

NEEDS FOR THE DISABLED

If any of the meeting's participants are disabled, pay special attention to seating. Check beforehand to see whether any accommodations are needed, such as reserving seats next to electrical outlets for people who need to use electrical equipment. Attendees who are deaf or hard of hearing will need a good seat for viewing the speaker and an interpreter or transcriber, if there is one. If a wheelchair user will be attending, think about how the person can get around the meeting space. Remove chairs if necessary to give him or her a choice of seats and a clear path in and out of the room. Someone with low vision or blindness will face a barrier if visual aids are used; make sure the person sitting next to him knows to quietly describe visuals so that the person won't feel left out.

- **DON'T** expect your audience to be "interactive" with your meeting technology. Don't, for example, seat participants at PCs or laptop computers unless you know that everyone is familiar with the equipment and the software.
- **DON'T** pass photographs, books, or other singular items among participants.
- **DON'T** supply handouts until the end of the meeting unless your group will be working with them. Avoid anything that distracts from the business at hand. If you are delivering a report or a business proposal, *never* provide copies before your presentation is completed; participants cannot resist reading ahead and literally jumping to your conclusions. Instead, show excerpts from your report as you discuss them.

WRAPPING UP

Leave enough time near the end of the meeting for a purposeful summing up. Your wrap-up gives you the chance to delineate what has been accomplished in the meeting in an organized manner, and to clarify assignments and responsibilities. It also allows you to:

1. Present a basic action plan, including deadlines for assigned tasks and a future meeting date or dates.
2. Address any final questions (although you don't want to open up new discussion at this point).
3. Thank special guests and participants.

If the meeting has been heated or rancorous, you can also use your conclusion to smooth any ruffled feathers. Even the smallest, most casual meetings need a summing up so that the participants leave with a clear understanding of future expectations.

It is permissible to run over by five or perhaps ten minutes, but any longer amounts to rudeness. Even when a meeting is going particularly well, don't assume that you have general consent to extend it. Besides, people tend to react to scheduled ending times as psychological breaking points. When the clock ticks over the allotted time, their minds are free to wander, and they quickly lapse into inattention at best, resentment at worst. On the other hand, if it seems valuable to continue, you should ask everyone in attendance if they agree and whether they're able to stay. If they say yes and really mean it, proceed. Otherwise determine the next best time to reconvene.

The Almost Perfect Meeting

FOLLOWING UP

It is always smart to follow up your meeting within a day or two with a thorough recap memo or letter to all of the participants. Your memo will elaborate on the details of your summary assignments and schedules and will include confirmations of any formal decisions or votes. At most times, the memo is a sufficient thank you to participants, but you will want to write formal thank-you notes to speakers, special guests, and anyone else who has contributed to the success of the event.

COMFORT AND CARE

The first courtesy a meeting organizer pays to attendees is to make sure the content of the meeting is worth their time. Assuming a worthwhile agenda, the second courtesy is to assure the comfort of participants. Comfort is the product of thoughtful planning and careful attention to details. Although not every one of the following items applies to every meeting, this logistical checklist will guide you through the basics:

- THE MEETING ROOM. Is it large enough to accommodate all your participants, but not so large that your meeting will seem small and insignificant? Is it conveniently located? Are directional signs clearly posted? Is the room clean? Is it relatively quiet? Is there an adequate coatroom?

- ACOUSTICS. Can participants hear from any part of the room? Does sound echo, or is it muffled? Is an amplification system required? Do you need to provide microphones?

- SEATING. Are there adequate chairs and tables for your seating plan? Are the chairs comfortable? (Like Goldilocks, you should look for chairs that are neither too hard nor too soft, but just right.) Is the seating plan most efficient for the type of meeting? For working meetings, are the tables large enough to allow each participant to spread materials out?

- ENVIRONMENT. Is the lighting adequate? Are there dark spots or harsh glares in the room? Is sunlight a problem at any time of the day? Are windows draped, and can the room be completely darkened? Can you adjust the room temperature? It's preferable to have a room slightly cool at the start of a meeting; a too-warm room will lull participants into inattention. Adjust the temperature as the meeting proceeds. Remember, too, that a room that feels cool when you arrive will quickly warm up once it is filled with bodies.

- SUPPLIES. Do you have all the materials that participants will need? Notepads, pencils, and pens? Sufficient copies of all handouts, including the agenda? Product samples? Do you have easy access to a photocopier? If meeting participants do not know one another, do you want to provide name tags?

Take time to evaluate your meeting. Be ruthlessly honest. Did the meeting accomplish what you wanted? If not, why not? Was the agenda flawed? Did you lose control at any point? Did you invite the right people for your purpose? Was your organization too rigid or too loose? Did a problem crop up that you should have anticipated? Too many managers become wedded to a meeting format instead of learning from their mistakes. But by analyzing each meeting you hold—good, bad, or indifferent—and doing it while the particulars are fresh in your memory, you open the door to constant improvement.

- **SPECIAL CONSIDERATIONS.** Can physically handicapped attendees get to the meeting room and other locations such as reception areas? Is the room equipped for wheelchairs? Do you need to provide interpreters for the hearing-impaired or multilingual translation?
- **FOOD AND DRINK.** What and how much do you want to serve? Be sure to offer a variety of drinks (caffeine and caffeine-free) and bottled water. Finger snacks should be low on sugar and high on neatness—bagels instead of sticky buns, for example, or pretzels instead of crumbly chips. If you plan for participants to order food during a meeting, decide in advance on a source and a limited selection to avoid time-wasting debates. If the meeting includes full meals, be sure to ask invitees about special dietary needs (Kosher, heart-healthy, diabetic, and such).
- **BREAKS.** How many? How often? (Ninety minutes is considered the maximum session time between breaks.) How long? Be sure to tell participants the exact time when the meeting will resume. Don't announce a "ten-minute break"; 10 minutes inevitably means 20 to talkers and stragglers so specify a time.
- **INTERRUPTIONS.** Have you arranged for someone to take phone messages? Have you shut down phones in the meeting room? Clarify with the person managing the phone when it is acceptable to ring in or interrupt the meeting. If people tend to pop in and out of the room, put a sign on the door: "Meeting in Progress. Please Don't Disturb."
- **KEEPING A RECORD.** Be sure that the proceedings are recorded. Designate a note-taker or employ a stenographer. If you make an audiotape record, check your equipment in advance, have a supply of tapes and batteries at hand, and test the tape recorder in the meeting room so that you can be sure it picks up all conversation. Because many people are uncomfortable with taping, always tell your participants that you are using a recorder and place it in plain sight. (Unless there is a very good reason to have a visual record of the meeting, videotaping is intrusive and intimidating.)
- **SPEAKERS' NEEDS.** Do you need a podium? Microphone? A/V equipment? (Be certain the room's electrical outlets are conveniently placed for the connection.) Projection screen? Video monitors? Easels and pads? Pens, tape, thumbtacks?

CHAPTER 29

WHEN YOU ATTEND

You may love meetings, hate them for all you're worth, or fall somewhere in the middle. But take a moment to reflect: Meetings give you, the participant, the chance to display your skills and talents—to show off in a positive way—and to take the measure of your colleagues. And consider this: More than a few advancement-minded workers have undercut their own interests by failing to demonstrate the most basic meeting manners.

The advice that follows is directed to participants at business meetings of any kind, from those around the office conference table to those off-site with clients. It also spans all job levels, from junior staff to executives; when people are thrown together, the rules of behavior are much the same for everyone. Frequently, there's another participant added to the mix: the guest speaker, who has his or her own things to take into consideration (see page 385).

RESPONDING TO THE INVITATION

Your first mannerly step is to respond to all meeting invitations, whether your attendance is compulsory or not. As soon as you receive a notice, check your schedule to make sure there's no conflict and then make your reply. Even if your invitation doesn't specifically ask for a response, do it; a quick phone call will usually suffice. If you can't attend an optional meeting, it's a good idea to explain why, particularly if you have a business-related conflict. This tells the person calling the meeting that your absence is justified; it may also alert him or her to reschedule the meeting at a more convenient time.

IF YOU'RE ATTENDING

If you're able to go to the meeting, prepare in advance. Study the agenda and determine what you can do to be ready to join in discussions. If you don't receive an agenda or your invitation doesn't include particulars of the meeting, ask the meeting organizer what you should do to prepare or whether there are materials you should bring. To avoid implying the organizer has been remiss by not including an agenda, couch your questions in terms of seeking direction so that you can be up to speed for the meeting.

YOU CAN'T ATTEND?

It's an annoying fact of business life that some people can never get their organizational act together and are continually calling last-minute meetings. But remember that spur-of-the-moment doesn't necessarily mean frivolous or unimportant. If you can't attend a last-minute meeting, be sure to follow up as soon as possible by getting a report of the proceedings. You may want to send a surrogate, but always check with the meeting organizer first. Follow up on meetings you miss: Find out what happened and if you have assigned tasks.

YOU'RE NOT INVITED?

Unless you're a dyed-in-the-wool curmudgeon, there will be some meetings you're actually eager to be a part of. But what if you are excluded? First of all, realize that it happens to everyone. Being left out is sometimes a mistake on the organizer's part, but it is both impolite and impolitic to confront the meeting planner directly. The greater likelihood is that you've been left out because you are not needed, and a challenge to the planner's decision will be embarrassing to both of you.

Try not to interpret exclusion as an affront. It may happen simply because the organizer believes your time is better spent at something else, or that decisions above your level will be made. If you have a close relationship with your supervisor, you may want to ask why you were not invited; if the exclusion was a mistake, your supervisor is in the best position to correct it. But whatever the cause, take it in stride, and *never* try to force or wangle your way into a meeting. Being excluded is a temporary disappointment, but a reputation for manipulation and bad temper has longer-lasting consequences.

THE IMPORTANCE OF PUNCTUALITY

Arrive on time—not too early, and certainly not late. First, the early bird: Most meeting specialists warn strongly against arriving more than a few minutes early. The person holding the meeting may be involved in last-minute preparations or may be trying to clear away other business before the meeting's start, and he or she will feel compelled to stop and greet early arrivals.

There's really no justifiable reason to come early to an in-house meeting, since you're on the premises. But for meetings at a customer or client's office, you may find yourself there well before you're supposed to be—you made better time than you expected because the traffic was light or the bus came just as you got to the bus stop. If you arrive more than ten minutes early for a meeting being held outside your office, tell the receptionist that you prefer not to disturb your host and will wait until the scheduled meeting time.

COMING IN LATE

Arriving late is sometimes unavoidable, whether the meeting is in-house or elsewhere. If you know you'll be tardy, tell the meeting organizer as soon as you can; he or she may want to adjust the agenda if your participation is needed at a certain point. With advance notice, the organizer can also save a chair for you in a spot least likely to cause distraction. If you're delayed on the way to a meeting, try to call ahead. If you can't call, then do everything possible to get there as quickly as you can.

Entering a meeting in progress should be done as unobtrusively as possible. Walk in, apologize briefly without interrupting anyone (don't make your excuses until the meeting is ended), and take your seat. It helps to have anything you need, such as pen and pad, at hand when you enter the room. Above all, don't disturb the meeting by rattling papers, snapping a briefcase open and shut, shedding a coat or jacket, getting coffee, or whispering to your neighbors. Use your printed agenda to determine what is going on.

If a formal presentation is in progress when you arrive, you may want to delay your entrance until there is a natural break and you can slip inside the meeting room. Late arrivals are the bane of speakers because they inevitably distract the audience and break the flow of the presentation.

OTHER TIMING ISSUES

Even the best-planned meetings can run overtime, so it's wise to pad your schedule a bit to accommodate late endings. Allow an extra 20 or 30 minutes to cover most situations, and don't make appointments based on the exact end time on the agenda.

If you must leave a meeting early or right on schedule, tell the leader in advance. Seating can be arranged so that you can depart without disturbing others.

THE POLITICS OF SEATING

Where to sit at a meeting sometimes seems to be a political decision of Machiavellian proportions. Some people advise sitting opposite the most important person in the room; others counsel sitting at his or her side. Some say that sitting to the right of the meeting leader is a less powerful position than sitting to the left. Some believe that sitting at the corner of a conference table conveys an image of strength. But if everyone is jockeying for power positions at a meeting, the spectacle calls to mind a Keystone Cops routine. If people have mastered the subject, ask insightful questions, and make concise, relevant observations, they are important no matter where they sit.

If seating isn't assigned, let the key participants take their places first and then fill in around them. Don't head for the top or bottom of a conference table unless you're the leader. A good organizer will tell everyone where to sit, but if the seating order is unclear, ask the leader where he or she would like you to be. Even if you're an important guest (the client rep at a business presentation, for instance), check with the meeting leader about seating; there may be a reason, such as vision line, to seat you somewhere other than the head of the table. In a seminar or open seating arrangement, find a place where you can see and hear clearly, and leave the bad seats to the latecomers.

DO YOUR PART

Whether the organizational skills of the meeting manager are brilliant or nonexistent, you have not been invited to a meeting to sit on your hands. Your participation is needed regardless. When you've prepared well and followed the proceedings attentively, participating should be no problem. If your opinion is requested, give it. If you have an idea, state it. If you need more information or clarification, ask for it.

But contrary to the old saying, there *are* stupid questions—and they're usually asked by people who haven't done their homework. If Henry is forever asking for information that was clearly stated in meeting invitation memos or covered in previous meetings, the odds are good that Henry will sooner or later be dropped from the meetings list.

There are times, of course, to remain quiet—for example, your department is making a new business pitch to a prospective client. Although the mood of the meeting is as folksy and casual as a country hoe-down, every step has been carefully choreographed and rehearsed. You and the other members

THE BRAINSTORMING SESSION

Many companies have meetings to brainstorm ideas, and these lively sessions have an etiquette all their own. The meetings can range from four people wheeling extra chairs into someone's office to three-day off-site meetings where groups keep to a tight schedule and then either record or make presentations of their ideas.

Some things to remember:

- The idea that "nothing is off-limits" applies to ideas, not manners. Although brainstorming is blissfully free-form, talking over one another and interrupting will probably neither contribute to the freshness of the concepts nor spark any new ones. If you're bursting to get an idea out, jot it down on paper until there's an opening to speak.
- Don't shoot other people's idea down with "we've tried that before." Also, never disparage an idea, no matter how bizarre it may be. Remember that brainstorming is the forum for off-the-wall ideas that are eventually reshaped into marketable ones. If, however, someone's idea is so ill-conceived that it's ludicrous, don't say so flatly. When you point out its shortcomings, start with the positive things about it and then come up with ways it could be made stronger.
- If a group has to work individually at a communal table to get their ideas on paper or disk for a presentation, keep distractions to a minimum. Bringing in food (especially the crunchy kind) can not only affect other people's concentration but drive them up the wall.
- If your writing skills are strong and you know someone else's aren't, offer to look over their work, but only if they've made noises about how "I can't do this! I'm an engineer, not a writer!"

A NOTE TO BRAINSTORM LEADERS: If the meeting is off-site and the word processing equipment is different from that at work, arrange for tech-support people to be on the premises. The frustration of learning how to use new equipment can turn the creative thought processes that are the point of a brainstorming session into murderous thoughts.

of your team have been assigned specific roles in the presentation. This is not the occasion to speak out of turn or propose an untested idea.

Most meetings, however, get their energy from full participation; you don't want to be the only dud match in the box.

AVOID INTERRUPTIONS

Leave behind your pagers, cell phones, watches with timers, and anything else that tends to go off noisily and unexpectedly. (Another hint is to eat something before a meeting to avoid a grumbling stomach.) If you have an assistant, inform him or her (or the office receptionist, if necessary) that you will be in a meeting until such-and-such time and under what circumstances, if any, you are to be disturbed.

FOLLOW THE LEADER

It is up to the meeting's manager to set the style and tone, and up to you to follow his or her lead. If the purpose of the meeting is to convey information, for example, hold your questions until the manager asks for them; by studying the agenda, you can avoid the embarrassment of raising issues that are scheduled to be discussed later. If you're new to a group, take your cues from more experienced attendees. (Do juniors defer to senior managers, or is seniority ignored? Are off-the-cuff comments encouraged or frowned on?) By being watchful, you'll quickly catch on to both the style and the pecking order of every meeting.

CHECK YOUR GRUDGES

A meeting is not the place to even scores, display your grudges, or make known your opinion of other people's shortcomings. Check any animosities at the door. Even if you think the leader is a dunce or worse, don't challenge him too directly. Don't start a fight with another participant over something that could better be discussed one-on-one. Be careful about finger-pointing, too: If you're reviewing a joint project and don't like what the other department has done, don't couch your criticisms in an accusatory way. Instead, offer an alternative, and say why you think it's stronger.

IF YOU'RE A GUEST SPEAKER

Should you ever be called on to speak at a meeting, you won't necessarily be taking part in the meeting itself but imparting your wisdom from a podium. Unless you're an old hand at public speaking, you'll have to learn that there's more to the assignment than the content of your speech, regardless of the size of meeting you're asked to address.

First of all, you must understand the assignment thoroughly. What is the subject? Are you the only speaker or one of several? Are there particular issues you should address? Are there problems or situations you should be aware of? (Your surefire joke about the CEO on his deathbed will not go down well if your host business has just lost its beloved president.)

There's a story about a well-known chef who was invited (and handsomely paid) to address the spring luncheon of a large Jewish women's organization.

He duly spoke to the group, delivering a fulsome presentation on the planning of Easter activities and preparation of the perfect Easter ham! This is an extreme example of poor preparation, but it illustrates some of the common pitfalls of public speaking.

GETTING THINGS STRAIGHT

A speaker should always research the inviting group and the location of the event: Who will comprise the audience? How many? What are their interests? What are the unique characteristics of the business or organization and their location? An attentive speaker can win friends and influence people by customizing even a canned speech with local references.

PROBLEM PEOPLE?

Business meetings, like meeting participants, have distinct personalities. You may enjoy some meetings because they are warm and personable. You will probably hate meetings that are cold or cantankerous. Primary responsibility for setting the tone obviously falls to the organizer and leader, but meetings have inherent dynamics that can never be totally controlled. After all, business meetings are made up of people, and people have a way of marching to their own drummers.

Remember your third- or fourth-grade classroom? Most of the children were well behaved, but a few stood out: the show-off kid whose hand was forever waving for attention; the class clown who made a joke of everything; the bully whose reason for getting up in the morning was to fight you for your lunch money; the little boy who whined about every little thing; the painfully shy girl who broke out in hives whenever the teacher called on her. Well, guess what happened? They all grew up, and now they attend meetings with you.

Think about that faraway classroom again. Chances are, what made it interesting and memorable were those very kids who drove you nuts. Love 'em or hate 'em, they added spice to the stew, just as their grown-up counterparts can do today: The show-off is the Dominator who never knows when to stop interrupting. The bully is now a meeting Pit Bull, determined to have things his way and incapable of sharing credit. The whiner has become the Incessant Inquirer who asks the same questions at every meeting. The Clown is still cracking jokes. The Shy One is still hiding her light under a basket. You know the types, and there are more.

At the same time, you should provide all necessary information to the organizers. What will you need for your presentation? Equipment such as easels and projection screens? Have you any special requirements such as transportation or dietary needs? Once prepared, proceed:

- **APPRECIATE THE AGENDA.** Arrive on time, stick to the program, and don't run over your allotted time. Clarify in advance whether your presentation is to include a question-and-answer session. Be alert to time cues from the organizer.
- **MEET AND GREET.** Plan to arrive early if you can. Check out the environment. Get a sense of the audience and mingle if possible. Speakers can learn a great deal from a relatively few minutes of pre-event chitchat with some of the audience members.

As unlikely as it seems, people like these can be thought of as making a contribution of a sorts. It's not that you condone their behavior, but there's no reason to get tied up in knots over something you can't control. Try to look at things in a different light: The Dominator is someone the meeting leader can always count on to have something to say, starting the discussion ball rolling by energizing passive participants to speak up. The Incessant Questioner, at some point in his litany, will eventually ask something important and force others to come up with satisfactory replies. The Clown can cut through a tense moment with a quip. The Shy One may have little to say but be the best synthesizer in the group, zeroing in on the most salient points.

As a participant, your options are relatively few beyond tolerating foibles and not becoming intimidated by the actions or words of problem people. For instance, it simply doesn't pay to fight with the Pit Bull when he seems determined to take credit for your ideas. Make your points clearly, and then trust your colleagues and superiors to know where credit truly belongs. If you roll your eyes and snicker when the Incessant Questioner poses yet another seemingly silly question, your body language can boomerang and you may be perceived as intolerant or snobbish.

The objective of every meeting is communal, not individual, accomplishment. If you look at meetings as competitive events for you to win or lose, you have missed the point. A writer (and no shrinking violet) who has participated in hundreds of ego-laden creative sessions likes to say that after a satisfactory meeting, nobody remembers where the good ideas came from. Individual recognition comes when the ideas are implemented.

The common dynamic that drives every successful meeting is team spirit, and teams need all kinds of people. Wise men and women learn to look for the value in every meeting participant, to judge by outcomes rather than personalities, and to bask in the warmth of group achievements.

- **BE GRACIOUS.** When something goes awry—a glitch in the microphone or a last-minute change of room—don't take it as a personal insult.
- **SAY THANKS.** Highly paid speakers sometimes forget that they are not speaking from the goodness of their hearts. But all speakers should be grateful for the opportunity and the platform to express themselves. Thank-you notes to organizers are a must.

AT MEETING'S END

Wait until the meeting is over to gather your things; then leave. Naturally, you'll want to thank the leader politely, but unless a post-meeting event has been scheduled, it's best to depart promptly. You have other business to attend to, and so does everyone else. If there has been a guest speaker and you want to have a word with him or her, be extremely conscious of the person's time constraints. If you have questions that weren't answered during a presentation, it's preferable to write any speakers, telling them where and when you met and asking for a response at their convenience.

FOLLOWING UP

For participants, following up a meeting generally means doing what you were assigned to do. You may need to clarify assignments with the meeting leader, although you should receive a post-meeting confirmation or summary memo. Thank-you notes are not appropriate for the majority of meetings, although it's always nice to compliment the meeting organizer at the first opportunity. Thank-you notes or letters may be written for large conferences, seminars, and formal meetings that involve social activities, as well as for some informal meetings, such as lunch at the invitation of a client.

PART IX

BUSINESS ENTERTAIN-MENTS

G oing hand in hand with the wheelings and dealings of a business relationship are the social activities that allow people to show their more personal sides—the power lunch, the business dinner, and entertainments that range from a formal corporate event to an afternoon at the ballpark. The following four chapters venture into the business entertaining sphere, territory that many businesspeople find the most fraught with perils.

Never has it been more important to acquit yourself well when entertaining a customer or client or being entertained. How well you handle yourself at the dinner table, a party, a golf course or tennis court, a business associate's private club, or the theater says much about who you are. On these pages you will find advice on business entertainments presented from varying perspectives—the basics of appearing confident and at ease at business meals and other outings; hosting at-home parties (a chapter complete with fail-safe instructions for putting on an informal dinner or buffet); and mingling at a large-scale event of the black-tie sort, including making sense of formal place settings, glassware, and other details.

CHAPTER 30

BUSINESS MEALS

Essentially meetings, business meals come in all shapes and sizes. What all have in common is a measure of sociability over and above that of an office-bound appointment. But as important as the fellowship fostered by a business meal is your own behavior. Remember: This is the only time when your conversational abilities, your self-possession, and your table manners are all on display at once. Also bear in mind that your manners reflect on the company you represent. The desire to make a good impression hardly means rehearsing your across-the-table banter or becoming a wine connoisseur. It *does* mean knowing how to use the cutlery, eating your food with certain civilities kept in mind, and appearing at ease with those around you.

This chapter touches on business meals in their many incarnations: the relaxed one-on-one lunch that sets the stage for business to be done later; the true working lunch, held for the purpose of discussing or solving a particular problem; the posh restaurant dinner for eight that, on the surface at least, is purely social; and the business breakfast, which ranges from the "power breakfast" (an '80s-born phenomenon that conjures up top-level executives hammering out earthshaking deals) to a quick danishes-and-coffee meeting with data sheets spread over the table.

LUNCH, BREAKFAST, OR DINNER?

Whether you choose lunch, breakfast, or dinner obviously depends mainly on which one of these meals best fits the time constraints of the participants. Also take into account what you wish to accomplish. Breakfast, for example, may be the answer when the aim is a quick straight-to-the-point meeting, while evening is undoubtedly the best time for a more relaxed business meal.

THE BUSINESS LUNCH

Lunch is the traditional workhorse of the business meal. Because the participants have to return to the office, the meeting stays relatively short and focused. There are other advantages as well: Unlike a business dinner, lunch is more informal and relaxed; it doesn't cut into someone's personal time; and it doesn't require the inclusion of a spouse or partner.

Any restaurant that's reasonably quiet, conveniently located for both host and guest, and has lighting bright enough to make it easy to read any materials that are brought is an appropriate place to lunch. Places with quick turn-arounds—coffee shops and other fast-service establishments that prefer customers to eat, pay up, and be gone—can be poor choices if your meeting might take more than an hour. (On the other hand, such a choice might just suit you and your guest if you're both in the mood for a burger and fries.) Also, a familiar restaurant that has proved to have an efficient staff and dependable food is a

"HOW DO YOU LIKE YOUR TEA?"

The business tea, with its echoes of a more genteel era, has become increasingly popular in recent years. The usual venue is a fine hotel or a members-only social club that offers a quiet and unhurried atmosphere. Teas are not only calm and relaxing but also have the virtue of being brief, usually lasting only an hour or so. Better still, those held at the end of the day (the usual starting time is from 3:30 to 5:00) allow guests to go straight home instead of returning to the office. Another plus: Alcohol isn't expected at a tea, although a single glass of sherry is often part of the traditional British ritual. As with any other business meal, the host issues the invitation, chooses the place, and pays.

On a given day, an in-the-office tea may seem just the right thing for a meeting among employees, providing a needed break that also lifts the spirits. Any small conference room or an office with plenty of chairs can serve as the site. But take note: Unless you serve a proper tea, an occasion that is meant as something special will be much like any other meeting, with the usual sea of coffee mugs sporting teabags slung over their sides.

A proper tea is one that includes good china cups and saucers, cloth napkins, and a pot of freshly brewed loose tea; a second pot of hot water is used to dilute the well-steeped tea and is poured directly into the cup. Also on hand are sugar, lemon slices, and milk (milk, not cream, is the traditional addition). Crustless finger sandwiches filled with watercress, cucumber, pâté, or salmon are the standard accompaniments. Alternate food choices include slices of date-nut bread spread with cream cheese or an assortment of muffins or biscuits warmed and served with two or three jams. For originality's sake, you could offer a classic Devonshire tea—a pot of English Breakfast or Earl Grey tea served with scones, strawberry preserves, and clotted cream, a British specialty available at some gourmet markets.

better choice than one that has never been tested; botched service or a noisy crowd will end up distracting from the work at hand.

The typical business lunch lasts from just over an hour to two hours, but a participant who's on a tight schedule shouldn't take this for granted. Instead, she should announce her time constraints from the start: "Before we get busy, I should tell you that I have a meeting at the office at 1:30—bad luck, I know, but it was called at the last minute." (Note: The excuse should be real, not made up.) Stating this or something similar not only puts the person's mind at ease but avoids catching everyone by surprise when she suddenly has to leave.

THE BUSINESS BREAKFAST

Just because someone decides to do business over a morning meal doesn't mean he's jumping on the power-breakfast bandwagon. Even a garden-variety breakfast meeting has real benefits: Many people are at their sharpest early in the morning; as with lunch, a morning meeting's timing helps it stay short and focused; *unlike* lunch, it barely interrupts the workday, if at all; and breakfast is less costly than both lunch and dinner.

A business breakfast can be held at any location that is handy to both host and guest: a restaurant or coffee shop, a hotel dining room, or perhaps a private club. If it's convenient for all concerned, guests can even be invited to breakfast in the host's office. Putting out a selection of danishes or muffins and coffee or tea requires little preparation and lends the meeting the affable touch of an away-from-the-office meal.

THE BUSINESS DINNER

Whether it takes place at a table for two or involves a large group, this most special of business meals is generally oriented toward camaraderie. Because no one has to get back to work, dinner also proceeds at a more leisurely pace. At the same time, dinner's longer time span can work to its advantage when doing serious business is the goal.

Dinner is the most meaningful meal with which to mark special occasions—the retirement of a longtime employee, for instance, or to welcome a new client into the fold. It is also the more logical choice when entertaining a business associate from out of town who is traveling with his or her spouse. On occasions such as these, business will doubtless come up as a conversational topic, but the aim is usually the strengthening of relationships, with an eye on mutual rewards to be gained in the future.

Business Meals

PRE-MEAL PREP

I f you're hosting a business meal, remember that a little careful preparation will go a long way toward keeping the occasion trouble free.

- CONSIDER YOUR GUEST'S TASTE. If possible, find out if your guest(s) especially likes or dislikes certain foods or ethnic cuisines; you can simply ask when extending the invitation, or calling an assistant might give you the answer. You could also give the guest a choice of two or three restaurants. If you're hosting a group, choose a restaurant with a wide-ranging menu so that everyone present will find something to his or her taste.

- CHOOSE A RESTAURANT YOU KNOW. Even a popular new place with the hottest chef in town may have snaillike service or be so noisy or cramped that it's hard to carry on a conversation. Also keep in mind that if anyone is going to travel fairly far to reach the restaurant, it should be you, not your guest.

- INVITE WELL IN ADVANCE. You or your assistant should arrange a business lunch or breakfast at least a week in advance so that the guest can fit it into his schedule and have time to prepare for the meeting.

- MAKE IT CLEAR YOU ARE—OR AREN'T—THE HOST. So there is no question of who's footing the bill, ask "Will you be my guest for lunch?" On the other hand, if you and the other person see each other frequently and have developed a close working relationship, you might want to go Dutch. If so, a simple "Do you want to have lunch next Tuesday?" or "How about if we split lunch next week?" is a graceful way to suggest it.

- TELL YOUR GUEST WHAT TO EXPECT. So that your meal partner can prepare and bring any pertinent materials, be specific about business topics you want to discuss and how deeply you'll be delving into them.

- RESERVE A TABLE AHEAD OF TIME. Failing to reserve a table risks getting the meal off to a late start—a real problem at lunch or breakfast, where time is at a premium. If you have a preference for seating—a spot that's especially quiet, for example—let it be known when the reservation is made.

- RECONFIRM WITH YOUR GUEST. This is a must, saving real embarrassment later on. Call on the morning of a lunch or dinner; if you've scheduled breakfast, call the day before. At the same time, you might want to tell the guest to go ahead and be seated if he arrives early.

ARRIVING AND SEATING

At any business meal, it is preferable for the host to arrive a few minutes before the guests; receiving guests as they enter the restaurant relieves them of the anxiety of wondering whether they should proceed to the table. The host can either wait in the foyer or at the table; if waiting at the table, he should give the maître d' the names of the guests, asking that they be directed there on arrival. A female host should make clear to the maitre d' that the check is to be presented to her and her alone, warding off the potential embarrassment of the waiter automatically presenting it to a male.

If the host is waiting in the foyer for several guests and some are more than ten minutes late, he should go ahead and ask for the group to be seated, requesting that the maitre d' show tardy guests to the table. (Note: Tradition says that if the maitre d' leads the way to the table, the host walks behind the guests; otherwise, the host leads.) Once seated, the punctual guests needn't wait to start ordering drinks and looking at menus. When a latecomer arrives, the host stands up to welcome him or her; if the person is a woman, true gentlemen at the table will also want to stand.

Two tips for guests who arrive before the host:

1. It's fine to go ahead and take a seat at the reserved table—but don't order anything other than water and refrain from eating the bread.
2. Never criticize the choice of table to the maitre d', no matter how much you dislike its location; the host alone should request a switch. Furthermore, for all you know the table in question might have been specifically requested, especially if the host is a regular.

THE NO-SHOW

If it's 15 to 20 minutes after the appointed time and your lunch or dinner date hasn't shown up, phone his or her office. If he's not there and an assistant can't tell you his whereabouts, wait another half-hour at most. Then write a note and leave it with the maitre d': "Jim, I waited almost an hour, and hope everything's all right. Would you please give me a call at the office? Rita." Before you leave, tip the maitre d'; doing so acknowledges you've held a table that would otherwise have been occupied by paying customers. Later, when the no-show phones to explain, don't sound annoyed or out of sorts. Simply accept his apologies and reschedule the meal.

If you are a guest and running late, call the restaurant and ask that the host be told you're on your way. When you finally arrive, don't waste even more time by offering an elaborate excuse, which might add insult to injury; a quick but sincere apology will do.

SEATING

The host has probably decided beforehand which seating arrangement will be most amenable to him or her and will direct guests to chairs accordingly. Then again, he may not have, in which case a guest should ask, in some form, "Where shall I sit?" In any event, a polite host should see to it that guests take the better seats—those that look out on the restaurant or a window onto scenery, not at a wall or the kitchen door.

Also to be considered is the traditional seating at a meal. The host and hostess customarily sit opposite each other, and couples are split up so that they'll have a chance to chat with people other than their spouses. If there is a guest of honor present, he or she is seated to the host's right.

DECODING THE TABLE SETTING

Unless your business meal takes place at a diner or deli, the table will hold more than one plate and any number of utensils, glasses of different shapes, and an assortment of other items, depending on the formality of the meal. A china- and cutlery-laden table poses few worries for many people, but it may be intimidating to others. For the novice, the first step toward feeling at ease is to learn a bit about every item on the table.

PLATES

At more formal restaurants, a service plate (the large plate at the center of the place setting) and a bread plate (just above the forks and slightly to the left) will be on the table at the start. Small first-course and salad plates will be brought out by the waiter as needed and then set on the service plate. (Note: At some restaurants, the salad plate may already be on the table, in which case it is placed to the left of the napkin.) The service plate will be replaced by your plate of food when the waiter brings in the main courses.

GLASSWARE AND NAPKINS

The usual glasses are the water goblet (placed just above the knife) and two wineglasses (just above the right-hand utensils)—the larger one for red wine, the smaller for white. At restaurants with more formal table settings, there may be additional glasses: the cylindrical champagne flute, which is better at keeping the wine bubbly than the saucer-shaped champagne glass of old; and a sherry glass, also cylindrical but smaller. (See also Glassware, page 436.)

The napkin, either folded into a rectangle or rolled and inserted into a napkin ring, will be to the left of the forks or in the center of the service plate. Napkins that have been decoratively folded (usually in a fan shape) are sometimes set inside the water goblets.

FLATWARE

Today even the most formal restaurants rarely set tables with every utensil under the sun—the daunting ten-piece place settings that run the gamut from oyster fork to fruit knife. Utensils usually are kept to a minimum, with additional ones brought out whenever ordered dishes require them. However lavish or sparse the table setting, having a rudimentary knowledge of flatware placement will make any diner more comfortable.

The most traditional place setting is the "outside-in," meaning you start with the outermost utensils and work your way toward the plate. Some other setting styles are more or less free-form, or even unique to a particular restaurant. For this reason, it also helps to be able to recognize utensils by shape as well as by order of use.

The following notes on utensils describe what might typically be found at your place setting as you sit down for a business meal. Starting at the outside and working in, you would find the following:

Salad fork. If the salad is served before the entrée, this smaller fork will be to the left of the dinner fork; if served after the entrée, in the European manner and also at some formal meals, the salad fork will be placed to the right of the dinner fork.

Dinner fork. This is the largest fork and is used for eating the main course (entrée) and any accompanying dishes.

Soup spoon/fruit spoon. If soup or fruit is being served as a first course, this spoon is the outside utensil on the right side of the plate.

Dinner knife. This large knife is used for the entrée and is placed just to the right of the plate.

Butter knife. This small knife is placed across the edge of the bread plate. It is replaced there after each buttering.

Dessert fork/dessert spoon. These could be presented in one of two ways: They might be paired and placed above the dinner plate from the beginning of the meal. Or, they might be brought to you when dessert is served.

Business Meals

*An Informal
Place Setting*

If coffee is served with the meal, the cup and saucer go to the right of the setting, with the spoon on the right side of the saucer.

On the off chance you encounter a salt cellar (a small open dish) instead of a shaker, a tiny spoon might be alongside. If no spoon comes with the cellar and you are sharing the cellar with others, dip the tip of your unused knife into the salt and deposit a little mound of it on the edge of your dinner place. Traditionally, you use knife tip to obtain the salt and sprinkle it over your food as necessary; but if you have your own cellar at your place setting, taking a pinch of salt with your fingers shouldn't raise any eyebrows. Note: Do taste your food before salting it. You cannot possibly know how much salt was added during preparation until you taste the food.

ORDERING DRINKS, FOOD, AND WINE

Alongside the usual host-guest protocol observed during a business meal is the thought that goes into ordering, from choosing predinner cocktails to the various food courses to the wines served during the meal.

ORDERING DRINKS

To drink or not? The days of the three-martini lunch are a distant memory, but that doesn't mean alcohol is automatically banned at a business meal. That said, having no alcohol is the smartest choice to make. Period. Yes, ordering alcohol is a personal decision based on one's knowledge of how much he or she is affected by a glassful of wine, a beer, or a cocktail—but quaffing even one means you won't be as mentally alert as you could be, no matter how well you hold your liquor.

There is more than one school of thought about the protocol of ordering drinks. Some people regard it as standard for a host to follow the guests' lead when ordering (mainly whether to have alcohol and, if so, how many drinks to have), while others think it should be the other way around. There is also disagreement over whether a host or guest waiting alone at the table or bar should order a glass of something before the other person arrives. Other viewpoints see "rules" governing these behaviors as beside the point, and not without reason: Such differences in opinion point up just how much the precepts of good manners are relative to the situation at hand. What is appropriate depends on the circumstances, the personalities and attitudes of the people concerned, and the degree of their personal closeness.

In any event, a smart guest keeps his eye out for certain cues. An example: By not ordering alcohol herself, the host may be signaling that she wishes everyone to stay as clearheaded as possible. Guests should also take note of what their fellow diners are ordering and then stay in line. In a free-spirited group where an anything-goes philosophy prevails, tequila shots or a Singapore Sling decked out with an umbrella may not raise an eyebrow, but in the real world, such choices are a bad idea if everyone else is having iced tea or club soda.

Naturally, a host who chooses to order alcohol doesn't urge a guest to follow suit. For his part, the guest should order at least *some* kind of beverage to more or less join in. Ordering also shows that he is not concerned that drink orders might slow down the meal.

Whatever you decide, orders for beverages may be given the first time the waiter or waitress asks for them, even if every guest hasn't arrived; latecomers will usually get the chance to order when the waiter returns with the first round. If she chooses, the host can take charge and ask the guests what they want, especially if she needs to make it clear she is paying.

Business
Meals

ORDERING MEALS

The protocol of ordering meals is more straightforward, with two considerations of prime importance:

- The host makes sure her guests feel free to order anything on the menu, getting the message across by either recommending a dish at the higher end of the price scale or telling guests what she's having (again, near the high end). Pointing out that a particular appetizer "looks delicious" lets guests know that the meal will include a range of courses.
- In general, guests should try to keep their selections to the midprice range. Even when the host urges "Please don't hesitate to order anything you want," a guest should avoid the most expensive dish on the menu.

Some upscale restaurants have menus that show no prices. If the host doesn't blink when the menus are opened and points out how tempting the Roasted Pheasant with White Truffles looks, guests may presume to order freely. If doubtful, however, they should choose food that is normally lower-priced—a pork or chicken dish, perhaps, instead of an expensive game bird or a roast tenderloin.

Likewise, prices oftentimes remain a mystery when a waiter or waitress recites a list of daily specials. In deference to the host, a guest should refrain from asking the cost of each (unless, that is, everyone has agreed to go Dutch). If the host herself asks the prices, it might be taken as a hint that cost matters to some degree.

Cost isn't the only consideration. Another is ordering food that can be eaten easily while talking between bites. Some foods are messier to eat than others—among them, lobster or crab in the shell (wresting the meat out); unboned fish (removing bones from the mouth); some types of pasta (dealing with wayward strands hanging from the fork); and French onion soup (the strand of cheese that stretches unbroken from the bowl to your mouth). Diners should also remember that a business meal isn't the time to experiment with unfamiliar foods. Unless someone knows how to eat, say, an artichoke or tackle the crab claw in a bouillabaisse, sticking with a dish that poses no unexpected challenges is the best idea. (See also Problematic Foods, page 409.)

ORDERING WINE

Dinner wine is really a condiment for food; consequently, it is ordered after the menu choices have been made, with the most qualified person at the table choosing a wine that goes well with the greatest number of dishes. Alternatively, ask the advice of the waiter (or, in tonier restaurants, the sommelier, identifiable by the symbolic cellar key hanging around his neck) while offering an idea of the types of wine preferred—a light white wine for a fish course, for example, and a hearty red for steak or game. Easier still, wine can be ordered by the glass; although taking this route narrows the selection, it allows each diner to tailor the wine to his or her meal.(See also "Why Don't You Choose the Wine?", page 402.)

If you've been the one to order, the waiter will show you the unopened bottle when he brings it; assuming it's the one you chose, give confirmation with a nod. The waiter then uncorks the bottle and pours a small amount into your glass, from which you take a sip; unless its taste is "off," either nod or say, "That's fine." If the waiter hands you the cork, put it directly on the service plate; the idea that the cork should be sniffed or squeezed to test for spoilage is an archaic restaurant ritual (not to mention pretentious in the eyes of many), especially since tasting the wine is the better way to judge.

The waiter will then pour wine into the glasses, serving the host (or person ordering) last. (Those who don't care to have wine with the meal should momentarily place their fingers over their glass when it comes their turn; turning the glass upside down is a practice no longer in vogue.) After the first glass has been served, it's up to the host to refill the guests' glasses if the waiter doesn't return to pour. White wine glasses are traditionally filled three-quarters full; the larger red wine glasses are filled halfway.

TABLE TALK

It wasn't so long ago that etiquette directed diners to wait until coffee was served before bringing up business. But in today's more harried atmosphere, it's sometimes the other way around: At a working business lunch, for example, small talk is usually confined to the period before the food has been ordered. As a matter of fact, choosing the best time to discuss business has less to do with adhering to some "proper" standard than with practicality, along with your own idea of how much time you can afford to devote to casual chat. At dinner, of course, business talk usually takes a backseat to congenial conversation throughout the meal.

When not discussing business, avoid touchy subjects. While politics, religion, and many other topics that people feel passionate about are no longer considered entirely off-limits, discussing them could risk nettling a business associate and getting the meal off on the wrong foot. Also avoid talking about

"WHY DON'T YOU CHOOSE THE WINE?"

The menus have been perused, the chit-chat gathers steam, and the host abruptly thrusts a wine list the size of a small book in your direction: "Harry, why don't you choose the wine?" Bewildered, you haven't a clue where to start.

One response is to be honest: "I'd love to, but I know so little about wine I think I should leave it up to you." (Note: Never be embarrassed by your lack of wine savvy; truth be told, it is someone who sees you as somehow lacking who has the problem, and even alleged "wine experts" usually are clueless about pairing wines with food.) An alternative is to ask the other guests for suggestions as you look over the list: "Which red do you think will go best with the dishes we're having?" What you should *never* do is fake it; otherwise, you could end up with a wine that overpowers the food and pleases no one—with you as the guilty party.

With this in mind, learning a few basics will put you on relatively safe ground for the future. Boning up on wine is also easier than you might think: A number of small books on wine appreciation take the mystery out of choosing and are entertaining to boot.

Listed in this chart are wines that generally go well with certain kinds of dishes. Even though the wines are grouped as whites and reds, the recommendation of each is based less on color (the old advice being to stick with white for fish or chicken and red for meat) than on the balance of sweetness and acidity that makes for a food-friendly wine. Some wines, especially American ones, are named for the grape variety, such as Chardonnay and Pinot Noir; others, usually European, for the region where the wine originated, such as Burgundy and Bordeaux.

FISH, MILD		
	Whites	Chablis, German Riesling, Loire Sauvignon Blanc (Sancerre, Pouilly-Fumé)
	Light Reds	Dry Rosé, Beaujolais, lightest Pinot Noir
FISH, OILY		
	Whites	New Zealand or Loire Sauvignon Blanc (Sancerre, Pouilly-Fumé), Chenin Blanc, Gewürztraminer, white Burgundy
	Light Reds	Pinot Noir, Beaujolais, Barbera, Loire Cabernet Franc
SHELLFISH		
	Whites	Loire Sauvignon Blanc (Sancerre, Pouilly-Fumé), Muscadet, dry Chenin Blanc
OYSTERS		
	Whites	Chablis, Austrian Gruner Veltliner, dry sparkling wines, dry German Riesling

POULTRY
Whites   German or Alsace Riesling, Chardonnay, Pinot Blanc
Reds   Australian Shiraz, California Syrah, Zinfandel, Pinot Noir

PORK
Whites   French Chardonnay, Chenin Blanc, German or Alsace Riesling
Reds   Pinot Noir, Cabernet Franc, Chianti, Spanish reds (Rioja)

BEEF AND LAMB
Reds   Cabernet Sauvignon, Merlot, Rhone reds, Zinfandel

VEAL
Whites   German Auslese Riesling, Alsace whites, Rhone whites
Reds   Loire Cabernet Franc, Pinot Noir, Chianti, Spanish reds (Rioja)

GAME
Reds   Burgundy, Rhone reds, Australian Shiraz, Zinfandel

GAME BIRDS
Reds   Cabernet Sauvignon, Amarone, Burgundy, Rhone reds

PASTA WITH RED SAUCE
Whites   New Zealand Sauvignon Blanc
Reds   Barbera, Chianti, Zinfandel, Loire Cabernet Franc

PASTA WITH CREAM SAUCE
Whites   Soave, Pinot Grigio, Sauvignon Blanc, Champagne

SALAD AND VEGETABLES
Whites   Sauvignon Blanc, dry Chenin Blanc, dry Riesling, Gruner Veltliner

INDIAN, CAJUN, AND OTHER SPICY FOODS
Whites   German Gewürztraminer, German Riesling, Chenin Blanc, Sauvignon Blanc
Reds   Beaujolais, Barbera, Pinot Noir, Rosé

anything bleak or unappetizing, including illness or surgery—two topics that are especially off-putting when people are eating.

Traditionally, the host initiates the business discussion. However, a guest may find that he or she needs to take the initiative if the host shows signs of going on at length about sports, his rose-growing hobby, or something that happened in his college days. Just be sure his tale is complete before you change the subject. Try something such as "What a wonderful story. I *loved* the Seventies! Now, I'm eager to find out what you think about the Heifner contract." (See also Talking Business, page 284.)

While conversing, sit up straight and don't fidget. As for the elbows-on-the-table taboo, it applies only when you are actually eating; whenever your utensils aren't in hand, putting your elbows on the table is acceptable. In fact, doing so while clasping your hands together—and leaning slightly forward—shows you're listening intently to what is being said. Another major concern: Unless you deal in matters of life and death, as doctors do, turn off your cell phone ringer from the moment you walk into a restaurant to the moment you leave. The same goes for beepers that emit audible signals.

PAPERWORK

If work materials must be looked over during the meal, a booth is a better seating choice than a table; briefcases and papers can be set beside the diner instead of propped against a chair. If notes are being taken, it's a good idea to keep handy a small notebook, which can be retrieved and stashed away as

---

THE WAIT STAFF

When dining out, you needn't thank waiters and waitresses for every little task they perform, but the occasional expression of gratitude is definitely in order. A caution: No matter how absorbed you are in the details of a business deal, treating the servers as if they were part of the furniture is unforgivably rude. Worse still, an imperious or condescending manner shows you not as superior but small.

Call the waiter by catching his eye and discreetly raising your hand to face level. You can also softly call out or mouth "Waiter?" Snapping your fingers or addressing your server by anything but his or her name (which, these days, you will no doubt know), "waiter," or "waitress" (or "Miss") is less than polite. In particular, "boy" for a male and such casual terms of endearment as "honey" and "sweetie" for females are strictly off-limits.

needed. If papers are to be spread out on the table, do this after the dishes have been cleared away; it's hard to eat and read or write at the same time, and your papers won't risk being stained by food or droplets.

TABLE MANNERS, COURSE BY COURSE

Although codes of dress and some other aspects of business etiquette are less demanding today, table manners matter as much as ever—or perhaps even more, given the coming of age of a generation whose working parents rarely had the luxury of teaching many of the basics. The hard truth: Exhibiting good table manners is essential for any businessperson who wants to make a positive impression. At the same time, keep things in perspective: While eating noisily or chewing with your mouth open are clearly serious blunders, using the wrong fork hardly spells the end of the world.

Beyond the challenge presented by the table setting lie other potential problems. A few that might crop up: What to do when you're faced with an unfamiliar food; how to deal with spilled food or drink; whether something you think of as a finger food requires a fork on this occasion; and any number of civilities and procedures, right down to buttering your bread.

USING YOUR NAPKIN

Put your napkin in your lap shortly after you sit down. The rule about waiting until your host does so is less rigid today, but other mannerly habits remain unchanged. For one, your napkin should be simply unfolded rather than shaken open with a quick jerk of the wrist. For another, it is never tucked into your collar, your belt, or between the buttons of your shirt or blouse. (Some diners in Italian restaurants tuck napkins into their collars in the belief this is customary in Italy—a misconception.) Also, blotting or patting your lips with the napkin is preferable to a washcloth-style wipe.

When temporarily excusing yourself from the table, place your napkin in loose folds (soiled side down) to the left of your plate. When the meal is finished, avoid placing your napkin on the table until the host or hostess has done so, signaling the meal's end.

BREAD AND BUTTER

This is the first food put on the table by the waiter. If you want a piece of bread and the breadbasket is close to your place setting, pick up the basket and ask, "Bread, anyone?" After everyone has been served, pick out a piece and put it on your bread plate, along with two or three foil-wrapped pats of butter; if the butter comes in a dish, use your butter knife to scoop out a good-size portion and then deposit it on the edge of the bread plate. The bread plate is also the place to put portions of jam or jelly, as well as olives or any other finger foods served before the meal.

NOTE: Once you've taken a piece of bread from the basket, it's yours—don't tear off a piece and put the rest back in the basket.

Break off (don't cut) one or two bites' worth of your bread piece, butter it, and eat it, repeating the procedure each time. Never hold a drink with one hand and bread in the other—good table manners require using one hand at a time for everything except cutting food and taking a helping from a serving dish.

When the breadbasket holds an uncut loaf, the host—or whoever is closest to the basket—cuts two or three slices and then puts the loaf and slices back

---

"WHAT DO I DO WHEN . . . ?"

It's the rare restaurant meal during which at least one perplexing question doesn't arise ("Should I ask for a doggy bag?") or a glitch doesn't occur ("Is that a foreign body in my water?"). These pointers will help you cope.

- **THE FOOD ARRIVES AT DIFFERENT TIMES?** If your dining partner's food arrives before yours does, encourage her to eat before it gets cold. Likewise, if your own food has to be sent back for any reason, urge her to continue eating. If three or so people at a large table receive their food and there is a wait for the rest, they may start eating so their meals won't get cold.

- **I'VE DROPPED SOMETHING?** Don't pick up a dropped utensil and put it back on the table, helpful though that may be. It's the staff's job to retrieve it and bring you a new one; politely ask the waiter to bring you another one, pointing out the dropped one. This rule applies even more to food. If, say, a spoonful of rice pudding falls to the floor, quietly inform the waiter at the end of the meal so that it can be cleaned up before the next diners are seated.

- **MY FORK OR GLASS IS UNCLEAN?** If your yet-to-be-filled water goblet seems soiled, or any utensil shows a bit of dried crust, don't announce it to everyone at the table—especially the host. The next time a server stops by, discreetly ask for a replacement.

- **I SPOT A HAIR OR BUG?** If there is a speck floating in your water or a pest of some kind in your food (or even worse, a hair), simply refrain from drinking or put down your

into the basket. As the basket is passed around the table, diners cut slices for themselves as necessary.

Eat as much bread as you like, but remember that the custom is to leave the last piece of bread in the basket—a small nod to the golden rule of putting other people first.

FIRST COURSES AND FISH COURSES

An appetizer is generally brought out on a small plate, which is then set on the service plate. It is eaten with the small fork to the left of the dinner fork. If a platter for sharing has been ordered—say, of antipasti or stuffed mushrooms—it is passed around the table, with each diner holding it as the person next to him serves himself. As with every course that follows, wait for the host to start eating before picking up your fork. A considerate host always urges others to go ahead and start, especially if there is a lapse in the service.

---

fork until you catch the attention of the waiter. While it's probably impossible to keep the rest of the table from knowing something is amiss, try your best not to cause a fuss.

- **MY DINING PARTNER HAS FOOD ON HIS FACE?** If you notice a speck of food on someone's face (or, in the case of a man, on his beard), you're doing her or him a favor by subtly calling attention to it. Do so with a light "Oops, there's something on your cheek." You might signal silently by cocking an eyebrow while using your index finger to lightly tap your chin or whatever part of the face is affected. As prevention for yourself, the occasional dab with your napkin will help ensure no wayward bits of food stay put for long.
- **I HAVE SPINACH IN MY TEETH BUT DON'T KNOW IT?** Occasionally running your tongue over your teeth may let you know whether you have food (the usual culprit: spinach) caught between your teeth. If you can execute a quick wipe of your teeth with your napkin without attracting attention, do so. If the food stays lodged there, it may be better to excuse yourself from the table and go to the rest room to remove it rather than worrying about it for the rest of the meal.
- **I KNOCK OVER MY DRINK?** Immediately set the glass upright and apologize to all present: "Oh, I'm so sorry. Could I be any clumsier?" Don't feel as if you have to crawl under a chair; accidents happen to everyone. If it was wine that was spilled, discreetly signal the waiter or busboy, who will put a cloth over the stain.
- **I'M FINISHED, BUT MY PLATE IS STILL HALF FULL?** At a business meal, forget the doggy bag unless you're going Dutch and are with a good friend. Even then, don't load up the bag with butter, sugar packets, and any other item.

For a seafood first course, special utensils may be on the table: the fish fork and the small, swordlike fish knife. The knife is gripped as if it were a pencil, and the broad side of its blade is used to gingerly lift and separate a section of fish. (Boneless fillets make the knife unnecessary; just cut the fillet with the edge of your fish fork.) If eating Continental style (see page 411), you can use the knife, already in hand, as a pusher.

SOUP

The soup spoon, held by resting the end of the handle on your middle finger with your thumb on top, is dipped sideways into the soup at the near edge of the bowl and then skimmed toward the opposite edge; this makes it less likely you'll splash soup on your clothes. The soup is then quietly sipped—*never* slurped—from the side of the spoon. To retrieve the last spoonful of soup, slightly tip the bowl away from you and spoon in the way that works best.

If oyster crackers come with the soup, place them on the underplate (the plate the bowl sits on) and add a few at a time to your soup; using your fingers for this is fine. Larger crackers, however, should stay out of the soup; eat them with the fingers instead of crumbling them into the bowl.

Garnish the soups that come with such optional toppings as croutons, chopped onions, or chopped peppers before you begin eating. With your clean soup spoon, spoon a portion from the serving dish and sprinkle it directly into the soup; there is no need to place it on the bread plate unless you think you'll be wanting more.

If you want a bite of bread while eating your soup, don't hold the bread in one hand and your soup spoon in the other. Instead, place the spoon on the underplate and then use the same hand to take the bread to your mouth.

SALAD

When you order a salad, be aware that it won't necessarily be served first, especially in more formal restaurants. In fact, having the salad course before the main course is a relatively new idea in the United States; until the 1950s it was usually served afterwards, as in most other countries. The reason? The vinegar in the dressing affects the taste of the wine drunk during the main course.

The salad fork is smaller than the dinner fork; its placement will depend on when the salad is served—before or after the main course. Some settings also include a small salad knife. When a leaf has to be cut to bite size, use either the knife or the edge of the fork.

On the occasion that the main course and salad are served at the same time, it's fine to use the dinner fork for both.

THE MAIN COURSE

Although minding one's table manners is a meal-long concern, the lengthy period spent eating the main course is especially ripe for missteps. Following are notes on some of the concerns that might arise or situations you may face.

Sending food back. As a rule, send a dish back only if it isn't what you ordered; it isn't cooked to order (a supposedly medium-well filet arrives bleeding, for instance); it tastes spoiled; or you discover a hair or a pest. If you are a guest and the food simply isn't to your liking, keep this to yourself to avoid embarrassing the host; concentrate on the other portions of the meal and eat only as much of the undesirable food as you can tolerate.

Side dishes. When vegetables are served in individual small dishes, it's perfectly proper to eat them directly from the dish. If you choose to transfer the food to your dinner plate, either use a serving spoon (not your fork) or carefully slide them onto the plate. Ask the waiter to remove the empty dishes so that the table isn't overcrowded.

Sharing food. Accepting another person's offer to taste a morsel of his or her dish—or offering a bite of yours—is fine as long as it's handled unobtrusively. Either hand your fork to the person, who can spear a bite-size piece from his plate and hand the fork back to you, or (if the person is sitting close by) hold your plate toward him so that he can put a morsel on the edge. Don't be tempted to hold a forkful of food to somebody's mouth or reach over and spear something off another plate.

Unfamiliar foods. A business meal isn't exactly the most appropriate time to experiment with unfamiliar foods, since you may not be sure how to approach them; what's more, they might not be to your taste. You may nevertheless encounter something new if it comes on a platter of appetizers meant to be shared. In this case, either wait until someone else starts to eat and take your cues from him or her, or avoid eating the food altogether.

Problematic foods. Obviously, some foods are harder to eat than others, including the somewhat messy (spaghetti and linguine); those that leave a bit of something in the mouth (a pit or a bone); and any that require using the fingers (lobster or crab). Because dealing with a hard-to-eat dish at a business meal will give you one more thing to worry about and may embarrass you as well, think twice before ordering one. Here's a sampling:

- **FRENCH ONION SOUP.** This soup is topped with a slice of French bread (an extra-large crouton) and melted Swiss cheese, notorious for stretching from the bowl to your mouth in an unbroken strand. First, to get to the soup, take a small amount of cheese on your spoon and then twirl the spoon until the strand forms a small clump; cut it off neatly by pressing the spoon edge against the rim of the bowl. If this doesn't work, enlist the aid of a knife or fork to make the cut. (Note: Eat the portion of cheese left on the spoon with your first sip of soup.) If at any time a strand manages to reach your mouth, bite it cleanly so that it falls into the bowl of your spoon.
- **FISH, UNBONED.** If you detect a fish bone in your mouth, work it to your lips unobtrusively, raise your empty fork, and then push the bone onto the tip of it with your tongue. Deposit the bone on the side of your dinner plate—not the bread plate, where it will be more visible. If you must use your fingers, pick the bone out discreetly, with your cupped hand screening the procedure.
- **LOBSTER.** This comes with a cracking tool. Hold the lobster steady with one hand and the cracker in the other; then twist off the claws and place them on the side of your plate. Crack each claw (slowly, so the juice doesn't squirt), and then pull out the meat with a fish fork or knife. Pull the meat out of the tail in two solid pieces, one side at a time. Cut the meat into bite-size pieces, spear one with your fork, and dip it into the drawn butter or sauce before eating.
- **OLIVES.** The olives on an antipasti platter are eaten with the fingers; you can also use your fingers to remove the pit from your mouth while cupping your hand as a screen. When olives come in a salad, eat them with your fork. If they are not pitted, remove a pit from your mouth by pushing it with your tongue onto the fork tip and then deposit it on the edge of your plate.
- **SPAGHETTI, LINGUINE, FETTUCCINE.** Put the fork vertically into the pasta until the tines touch the plate and then twirl it until the strands have formed a fairly neat clump. When the fork is taken to the mouth, any dangling strands should be bitten off neatly so as to fall back onto the fork. An alternative, less used today, is to hold the fork in one hand and a large, dessert-size spoon in the other. Take a few strands of the pasta on the fork and place the tines against the bowl of the spoon, twirling the fork to neatly wrap the strands.
- **PEAS.** To capture runaway peas, use your knife as a pusher to pile them onto your fork. Alternatively, use the tines of the fork to spear a few peas at a time. Never mash peas, no matter how impatient you become.
- **SHRIMP, UNPEELED.** In some shrimp dishes, including garlic prawns, shrimp are unpeeled when served. Pick up a shrimp, insert a thumb-

HANDLING UTENSILS

There are two styles for handling the knife and fork while dining: the American style and the Continental (also called European) style, which is used not only by Europeans but by Americans who think it somehow more correct. Is one more proper than the other? Certainly not. In fact, there's no reason not to use both during a meal: You might want to cut the meat in the American way and eat the other dishes European style.

- **AMERICAN STYLE.** This entails cutting food with the fork in the left hand and the knife in the right (or reversed, if you're left-handed). Then you place (not prop) the knife on the edge of the plate and switch the fork to your right hand before raising it, tines up, to your mouth. The fork should rest on the middle finger of your hand, with your index finger and thumb gripping the handle slightly above.
- **CONTINENTAL STYLE.** In the European style, the food is cut in the same way. The knife, however, is kept in hand as the other hand lifts the fork to the mouth. The fork is held tines down with the index finger touching the neck of the handle. (Note: The tines down rule is by no means written in stone. But whichever style you choose—American, Continental, up, down—never grip the fork in your fist and use it as a spear or shovel. And do not cut food into more than two or three pieces at a time.)

The method for cutting food is the same in both styles: Hold the knife in the right hand with your index finger pressed just below where the handle meets the blade. Hold the fork, tines down, in your left hand and spear the food to steady it, pressing the base of the handle with your index finger. As you cut food, keep your elbows just slightly above table level—not raised high.

RESTING UTENSILS

Throughout the meal, never place a fork or spoon you've been using directly on the table—only on your plate, and then diagonally on the edge, not propped against the plate like an oar. Note that flatware is usually removed after you finish a course, although some restaurants expect diners to keep some utensils for the next course. Assume flatware will be removed and replaced unless the waiter tells you otherwise.

How you place your utensils on your plate is a code to the waiter, letting him know whether you have finished a course. Two positions:

- When you pause to take a sip of wine or engage someone in conversation, cross your fork (tines down) and knife on your plate, angling them so they almost touch at the plate's top-center. This tells the waiter you're not yet finished.
- To signal the waiter that your plate for any course can be removed, lay the knife and fork side by side in the center to center-right of the plate. In the American style, the tines of the fork face upward; in the Continental style, downward.

nail under the shell at the top end to loosen it, and then work the shell free. An extra plate will be provided to hold the discarded shells.

- **SUSHI.** Sushi, which is usually raw fish but includes dishes made with scrambled eggs, slightly cured seafood, and grilled fish, is eaten with chopsticks. Take a piece from the platter with the wrong end of your chopstick and then put it on your plate. Dipping a piece only lightly in your own dish of soy sauce is considered more polite than dousing your food. From a more practical standpoint, be especially cautious with the *wasabe*—a soft-green mustard that is decidedly hotter than it looks.

Fingers or fork? Certain foods are always eaten with the fingers. Others that are typically hands-on at home are eaten with a knife and fork at a restaurant. Following is a sampling of foods liable to raise the question.

- **ARTICHOKES.** Starting with the outermost leaves and working your way in, pluck off a leaf with your fingers and dip its meaty base into the melted butter or sauce provided; then place it between your front teeth and pull forward. Continue leaf by leaf (placing discarded ones on the edge of your plate) until either you've reached the artichoke's thistle-like choke or the leaves are too small and unmeaty to eat. Use your knife to slice off the remaining leaves and the choke, exposing the artichoke heart; then cut the heart into bite-size pieces and eat with a fork.
- **ASPARAGUS.** Traditionally, asparagus that is served without sauce (or is sauced only on the tips) is eaten with the fingers; when smothered in sauce, it is eaten with a knife and fork. If you find that others at the table are eating even plain asparagus with a knife and fork, you may follow their lead.
- **BACON.** Eat breakfast bacon, if it is limp, with a fork. If it is crisp and dry, it is fine to use your fingers.
- **BREAKFAST PASTRIES.** Cut danishes or sticky buns in half or in quarters and then eat with either fingers or a fork. Muffins are halved with a knife and then eaten with the fingers; it's fine to butter both halves at once, especially if the muffins are warm.
- **CHICKEN AND OTHER FOWL.** Whenever you are the only person at the table who has ordered fried chicken, stay on the safe side by eating it with a knife and fork. If other guests have ordered it, wait to see whether they use their fingers before doing so yourself. The same goes for a chicken or turkey drumstick, which at an informal meal is often eaten with the fingers after utensils have been used for the first, easily-cut-off pieces.
- **CHOPS.** Among friends or at home, the last juicy morsels of pork, lamb, and veal chops can be captured with the teeth—but at all but the most casual restaurant meals, either use a fork or go without.

- **FRENCH FRIES.** Whenever these accompany such finger foods as hamburgers or sandwiches, you may eat them with the fingers. Otherwise, cut them in bite-sized pieces and eat with a fork.
- **FRUIT.** See page 414.
- **PIZZA.** Take your pick: Fold a pizza slice vertically at the center (to keep the toppings intact) and eat it with your fingers, or leave the slice on the plate and cut bite-size pieces with a knife and fork.
- **SANDWICHES.** Sandwiches more than an inch thick should be cut into halves or quarters before being picked up and held in the fingers of both hands. Hot open-face sandwiches served with gravy are always eaten with a knife and fork.
- **SHELLFISH.** Oysters, clams, and mussels are held steady with the fingers as they are speared with a fork. Empty mussel shells may be picked up and used to scoop up a bit of broth, which is then sucked directly off the shell. Lobster and crab are picked up as the shells are being cracked and the meat is extracted, but the meat is always eaten with a fork.
- **TACOS AND TORTILLAS.** Eat tortillas and tacos (both soft and crisp) with the hands, but eat any filling that falls to the plate with a fork.

BEVERAGES

Before taking a sip of water, wine, or any other beverage, blot your lips with your napkin to keep the glass from becoming soiled. Remember that the water goblet is not a substitute for a finger bowl; if you want to clean your fingers, your napkin will have to suffice. (See also Ordering Drinks, page 399; Ordering Wine, page 400; Coffee and Tea, page 415.)

SALT AND PEPPER

Salting your food before tasting it is considered an insult to the chef. Why? Because assuming that the dish is well-seasoned to begin with is an implicit compliment to both the chef and the host. After the first taste, you may salt away.

When someone asks for salt or pepper to be passed, pass both; these items always travel together, even when a saltcellar is used.

When using a saltcellar, use the tiny spoon to place a small mound of salt at the edge of your plate and then dip each forkful of food into the salt as needed. If no spoon comes with the cellar, use the tip of a clean knife or, if the saltcellar is for your use only, take a pinch with your fingers.

Business Meals

OTHER CONDIMENTS

Pouring ketchup or steak sauce over your main course is fine if you're dining at a steakhouse or barbecue shack. In most other restaurants, it is considered gauche to even request these. An exception is made when ordering French fries, for which ketchup is the usual condiment. Just be sure not to smother your fries with ketchup; instead, pour a small pool at the edge of your plate and dip the fries in one by one.

At Indian, Chinese, and Mexican restaurants, several separate condiment dishes will probably be set in the middle of the table. Spoon a small portion of the sauce or chopped vegetable onto the edge of your plate, replenishing it as needed. Never dip your food directly into a communal condiment dish.

FINGER BOWLS

When you encounter a finger bowl, use it either after eating a hands-on meal such as lobster (often there is a lemon slice in the water) or at a more formal meal, to be used when dessert is served. Dip your fingers, one hand at a time, into the water, and then dry them on your napkin. If the finger bowl is brought out just before dessert is put on the table, it is sometimes set on the dessert plate, sitting atop a doily. If this is the case, lift the doily and bowl as a unit and set them at the upper left of your place setting.

FRUIT AND CHEESE

There is the possibility that a fruit course may be served at some point during the meal—either with the salad, following a salad served after the main course (in this case, with cheese), or as dessert. The days of peeling your own fruit are long past in most restaurants, but a whole fruit should be quartered, cut up, and eaten with a knife and fork.

Cheese, which is making a comeback as a course in some upscale restaurants, is served before the dessert course. The server (a *fromager* if male, *fromagère* if female) will either bring a tray of cheeses or wheel out a cart, suggesting which types go best with the wine you're finishing. Slices of different types are then arranged on a separate plate (often centered with a piece of fruit or a wedge of fig or plum cake) for each diner. While the cheese can be eaten with bread, the full flavor is better appreciated if you eat it singly, using a knife and fork. Start with the milder cheeses and progress to the strongest.

DESSERT

The dessert utensils—a spoon and fork—are often placed horizontally above your dinner plate. Dessert may be eaten with spoon or fork, or both. Diners who use both often use the fork for eating and the spoon as a pusher. Eating cake offers an example of how both utensils may be used. If the cake is served by itself a fork is used; if it is served à la mode, the spoon is also used.

COFFEE AND TEA

If a waiter places a pot of coffee or tea on the table but doesn't pour, the person nearest the pot should offer to do the honors, filling his or her own cup last. Three other points:

1. Any empty paper or plastic packets of sugar and cream should be crumpled and placed on the edge of the saucer or butter plate, not in an ashtray.
2. Do not take ice from your water glass to cool a hot drink.
3. Do not dunk doughnuts, biscotti, or anything else into your coffee.

HOT TOWELS

In some restaurants, moist, steamed hand towels held in tongs are brought at the end of the meal and given to diners. Use the towel to wipe your hands and, if necessary, the area around your mouth. Do not use it to wipe the back of your neck or behind your ears; you are at a restaurant table, not in a rest room or sauna.

Most waiters will take the towel away as soon as you've finished. If not, leave the towel at the left of your plate, on top of your loosely folded napkin so that the tablecloth stays dry.

THE MEAL'S END

With the meal complete, it's time to wind up the conversation, pay the check, and bid good-bye. A polite host sees his guests off until the last minute, even escorting them to the entrance, to the parking garage, or to the corner to hail a taxi, if necessary.

PAYING THE CHECK

If you are the host, it's a good idea to let the maître d' or waiter know beforehand that the check should be given to you. This is especially important for women hosts, since many waiters automatically present the check to a man. (These days, it is becoming more common for the check to be placed in the

TWELVE TABOOS

There are certain kinds of behavior that a restaurant patron should avoid at all costs—especially at a business meal, where a good impression counts all the more. Some have to do with table manners and overall finesse, others with being considerate of everyone around you.

- **BRIBING.** People who charge to the front of the line in a busy restaurant and flash a large bill at the maitre d' insult not only the restaurant management but the people they have pushed past. A tip for a maitre d' who has given you a good table and attentive service is acceptable, but trying to buy a good table is out of line.
- **COMPLAINING.** When you are the guest, never complain about the food or service. Sounding dissatisfied could make it appear that you question the judgment of the host.
- **SLOUCHING.** Your posture transmits messages, and you want it to say alertness and confidence. Never slouch in your chair, and do not stoop to eat your food. Be aware of the rest of your body language, too: Don't fidget with your tie or jewelry, drum your fingers, or jiggle your knee.
- **SMACKING AND CRUNCHING.** Good table manners require eating as quietly as possible. For many, other people's smacking noises are akin to fingernails on a blackboard. Crunching the ice from your drink is equally crude.
- **CHEWING IMPROPERLY.** Keep bites reasonably small and chew with your mouth closed. Under no circumstances should you form food into a ball in one cheek, nor should you take a sip of anything while chewing.
- **REACHING.** Do not execute the boardinghouse reach. Reach for something only if it is within the invisible boundary that separates your personal space from that of the other diners.

center of the table, an acknowledgment of changing times.) If you've been unable to clue in the maitre d' or waiter beforehand, put your credit card next to your place setting as a signal. Keep the check out of view as you look it over. Not that it's a secret document, but it's not a guest's business to know what the cost of the meal came to—nor yours to disclose it to him.

You should consider it your responsibility to pay your guest's coat-check tab, but don't argue if he insists on paying it himself. Remember that the coat-check counter is a good place for offering a guest your business card.

TIPPING

Whoever is paying should make sure a gratuity hasn't already been included in the total—something that is standard procedure at some restaurants. Other

- **SOPPING AND PLATE-PUSHING.** Occasionally dipping a piece of bread in a pool of sauce with your fork is acceptable, but don't sop the plate as if you were using a kitchen sponge. When you finish the meal, leave your plate exactly where it is: Pushing it away, even slightly, is the bumpkin cousin of the boardinghouse reach.
- **SHOWING OFF.** Money talks—and louder than ever. A noisy table of revelers flaunting the spoils of prosperity by ordering bottle after bottle of extravagantly priced wines (not to mention puffing away on cigars) not only appalls everyone around them but does no favor to the image of whatever professional field they belong to.
- **OVERINDULGING.** Drinking too much alcohol usually means a precipitous rise in voice volume and laughter—something to remember at a group dinner in particular. Few things annoy restaurant patrons more than the tipsy table that erupts periodically in sudden whoops and hollers.
- **TAKING OVER.** Groups celebrating a special occasion sometimes appear to think they have rented a private room. Balloons are tied to chairs, chairs are perched on to make speeches, and toasts inspire much shouting and clapping—to the chagrin of restaurant patrons and staff.
- **GROOMING.** Never use a comb or run your fingers through your hair while at the table. A businesswoman should also refrain from applying makeup while seated; such primping at the table may lead her dining companions to question her judgment about other things as well.
- **PICKING TEETH.** Do not, at any time, be seen using a toothpick. If you pick one out of a dispenser on your way out of the restaurant, use it only in the privacy of your car or once you are alone. Also refrain from noisily cleaning your teeth with your tongue at the meal's end, which is equally unattractive.

restaurants may include a gratuity only for large groups. On most occasions, you'll be tipping not only the waiter but other restaurant staff as well. (See also How Much to Tip?, page 254.) Tip according to these general guidelines.

- **THE WAITER OR WAITRESS.**
  15 to 20 percent of the bill total
- **THE SOMMELIER, OR WINE STEWARD.**
  Either 15 percent of the cost of the bottle or $3 to $5 per bottle
- **THE BARTENDER.**
  15 to 20 percent of the tab, with a minimum of 50 cents
- **THE COATROOM ATTENDANT.**
  $1 per coat
- **THE PARKING VALET OR GARAGE ATTENDANT.**
  $1 to $2

Business Meals

THE FOLLOW-UP

A note sent by the guest serves as a thank-you for the meal and an enjoyable time, as well as a confirmation of any decisions that were made. The host should also write, telling the guest how nice it was to dine with him or her and briefly recapping any business details. A follow-up phone call by either party could be made instead, but a note has two advantages: It doesn't interrupt the other person's day, and it comes across as warmer and more gracious.

REPAYING INVITATIONS

Does inviting someone to a business lunch, dinner, or breakfast mean it's tit for tat? Not necessarily. The rules governing the reciprocating of invitations vary from situation to situation.

- You are not expected to repay an invitation to a strictly-business meal (especially one charged to an expense account), no matter who invited you—a customer, a client, or your boss. But you may certainly do so if you have continuing business together.
- A client who is entertained by a salesperson or supplier is not expected to return the invitation, even if his spouse or family was invited.
- Do return social invitations from coworkers and other business associates, whether they've extended the hand of friendship to cement a business relationship or simply because you enjoy one another's company away from the office. You needn't reciprocate in kind. For example, you could have your associate join you for a cookout as your thank-you for a restaurant dinner.

CHAPTER 31

OTHER ENTERTAINMENTS

Inviting business associates to dine at a fabulous restaurant remains a welcome choice for a night on the town, but the possibilities for business entertaining have grown to include everything from a jazz concert or play to a party aboard a yacht. Sports activities are more varied as well, reflecting the free-and-easy spirit of the times. For every businessperson who entertains with a round of golf at a country club there is one who whoops it up with his guests at a baseball or football game. The following pages dip into the particulars of various outings, with pointers for hosts and guests alike.

AT COUNTRY CLUBS

The country club is a mainstay of business entertaining. Its golf courses, tennis courts, and swimming pools have been the scene of an infinite number of friendly competitions between business associates of one kind or another, with company executives inviting clients or customers to enjoy an afternoon in the sun and their guests returning the favor. It has long been said, only partly tongue-in-cheek, that more major business decisions are made on the green than in the executive office.

The country club is an ideal place to entertain even when no sports are involved: The setting is superb, and there is usually only one sitting at lunch and dinner, which means you can linger at your table for as long as you like. When sports are the central activity, lunch or after-game cocktails are usually on the agenda to ensure there is ample time to talk, whether of business or life in general. Lunch may be the climax of a morning spent on the golf links or tennis court or the prelude to an afternoon game, assuming that no more than a half day is to be devoted to the outing.

WHO PAYS FOR WHAT?

Many businesspeople simply take turns paying for everything at their respective clubs. At other times, certain customs are common when a match is taking place:

- A one-day golf or tennis tournament typically has an all-inclusive price that includes greens fees and a meal, and there is an understanding that the host usually takes care of the cost.
- For individual golf games, country clubs charge guests with green fees, with price varying by region and the nature of the club. The polite guest offers to pay his own green fees; if the host insists on paying, the guest should offer to pay or reimburse the host for both his own and the host's caddie fees.
- Most clubs don't allow tipping of waiters and other staff. However, tip locker-room attendants who shine shoes or bring you a drink. Parking attendants, too, deserve a dollar or two.

AT SPECTATOR SPORTS

It makes sense for a host who invites a business associate to a spectator sport of any kind—tennis or hockey, baseball or basketball—to order tickets in advance. Reserving a car for transport to the stadium or arena will prevent any parking problems. Beyond taking these steps and behaving himself, the host has little else to consider. But guests will be wise to do the following:

- Take your cues from the host. Ask him what he's wearing before you don your jeans, and then have a beer only if he does. If he's the kind who likes to concentrate on the game instead of chatting, let him initiate the small talk.
- Unless your hometown team is playing and the host would think it silly for you not to give it your unqualified support, show some enthusiasm for his team. If your team wins, offer commiseration and don't gloat.
- Volunteer to buy a snack and a drink for your host and any other guests.
- When the spectators stand as a unit, either rise with them or miss out on the action. The idea is to go with the flow: Asking people to sit down is appropriate only when they are standing alone—and ask politely. The entreaty to "Get down in front!" is better voiced as "Would you mind sitting so that we can see?"
- At tennis tournaments, where intense concentration is required by the players, try your best not to leave your seat during the game. If you must, get up and return only when there is a break in the action.

AT MEMBERS-ONLY SOCIAL CLUBS

Members-only social clubs are the descendants of the gentlemen's club, that rarefied men-only world symbolized in a thousand old movies by the monocled and mustachioed stuffed shirt who shows his displeasure at the slightest rattling

Whenever you're invited to a business associate's country club for a round of golf or a game of tennis, don't automatically accept unless you 1) know the rules of the game and 2) can play well enough not to slow others down. Don't assume that a loose acquaintance with the rules is sufficient; whether they show it or not, people who play regularly will likely resent any delays caused by your tentativeness and uncertainty. Being honest about your knowledge and abilities will allow the host to decide whether to suggest another sport or limit the occasion to lunch.

If, on the other hand, you feel perfectly secure with the sport of choice, accept with enthusiasm. On the day of the game, make a point of arriving early: Road conditions and traffic are unpredictable, and you don't want to be the person responsible for getting things off to a late start. As a token of your appreciation, you might bring a sleeve of golf balls or a can of tennis balls. You should also offer to pay your own greens and caddie fees.

During the game, if anyone takes a break to make a phone call or down some bottled water at the bar, let it be the host, not you. Rather than implying meekness, deferring to the host is simple good manners. And keep quiet, please. Loud talking or other distractions—including cell phones and beepers—are especially inappropriate as a fellow golfer sizes up his shot. Unless you're a doctor who's on call, turn the devices off.

SPORTSMANSHIP

In a time when more than a few professional athletes alternately grandstand and sulk, the word "sportsmanship" almost seems old-fashioned. Business associates who take to the course or the court can do their part for basic civility by remembering to do the following:

- If you are so proficient at the sport that you're approaching pro status, keep it to yourself; your performance on the court or links will speak for itself, and nobody likes a braggart.
- Let a bad call by your tennis opponent go unchallenged when, for instance, he insists a serve was inside the line and you know for a fact that it wasn't. Likewise, don't gripe about lapses in your own performance (and, naturally, *never* your partner's); this is a friendly entertainment, not a heated competition.
- Watch your expletives. A foul word that may not offend close friends is inappropriate when you're with a business associate, not to mention risky.
- As important as being a good loser is being a gracious winner. When you come out on top, compliment your opponent on his skill and say that luck just seemed to be on your side.
- A country club is carefully maintained, and the grounds should be treated accordingly. Stretch the tennis net tight after your game, replace a divot or fix a ball mark on the green, pick up litter, and return equipment to the locker room.

of a newspaper. Now open to women, these clubs still maintain an air of exclusivity. Another type of members-only club is the university club, with anyone who has at some point been enrolled at a given college or university eligible for membership. Both are places where tradition is important, and they share the same trappings: dining rooms with a first-class menu and expert staff, a lounge, a library, and various fitness facilities.

Unless a private room is rented for the purpose, business is not conducted in the public areas of most of these clubs. Many even have by-laws specifying that business entertainment reimbursements from a member's company are not allowed; all expenses, including dues, must be paid personally. While business may be discussed, using an item of business paraphernalia, be it a cellular phone or a notepad, is off-limits.

When a guest is invited to a members-only club, he or she should ask the host what to wear; many have strict dress codes. (A guest who's too shy to ask can simply call the club's office and find out.) For the host's part, it's never out of line for him or her to mention the type of dress expected at the club when the invitation is extended. Guests who are unaware of the club's customs will be grateful for the information; showing up completely over- or underdressed could end up embarrassing both parties.

Hints for guests:

- Don't strike out on a tour of the club. You should enter the library or lounge only if escorted by your host.
- If you have drinks at the bar before dinner, limit yourself to one. Also remember that confining your drinking to soda or spring water will be just fine—sherry is not mandatory.
- Don't be stiff, but behave impeccably. Here, your actions reflect not only on your company but on your host as well.

AT THE THEATER

For culturally minded businesspeople, an invitation to a play, a concert, the opera, or the ballet is an excellent choice, particularly when spouses are included. Beginning or topping off the evening with dinner makes for an even more memorable occasion. Unless you, as the host, are already familiar with your guests' tastes in such things, ask which kind of entertainment they favor; people who love musical comedies might find it hard to stay awake at the ballet. When you determine what best fits the bill, purchase tickets in advance and ask for the best seats possible; if you have to settle for the peanut gallery, try another show of the same type.

ARRIVING AND BEING SEATED

It is mandatory to arrive on time, even more so if you are picking up the tickets at the box office. Most theaters hold reserved tickets until 20 minutes before curtain time and then sell them first-come, first-serve. Also remember that, along with talkers, late arrivals are a source of resentment for theatergoers. While at most performances latecomers aren't allowed to be seated until a scene change, the right-minded patrons who have been punctual (and quite possibly are already absorbed in the performance) find it distracting to have to stand to let other people stumble past.

Traditionally, there is protocol for seating, starting with the host taking the aisle seat after his guests have entered the row. If there are two couples, the spouse of the guest sits next to the host, and vice versa. When there are several couples, the host's spouse leads the way into the row and the others follow, with women and men alternating. If any of the party are carrying their coats (on the assumption they face an interminable wait at the coat check), they should hold them close to their chests as they edge to their seats so that they don't brush the heads of the people in the forward row. They should also excuse themselves to every person they move past.

Other Entertainments

Any able-bodied person who is seated should let new arrivals into the row by standing up; shifting the knees to the right or left in an effort to make room makes it more difficult for the person to pass and is better left to kids.

Noise

Little is more annoying than someone who talks or even whispers during a performance, be it a symphony or a play. Nevertheless, just as many of today's theatergoers see no reason to dress for the theater, many forget there's a difference between watching a live performance in the presence of others and commenting on the action of a television situation comedy.

In terms of etiquette, what's the proper thing to do when someone nearby is talking and spoiling the performance? In the 1955 edition of *Etiquette,* Emily Post took up the question under the heading of "Theatre Pests." The intervening years have offered no better solution: "If those behind you insist on talking," she wrote, "it is always bad manners to turn around and glare. If you are young, they pay no attention, and if you are older, most young people think an angry older person the funniest sight on earth! The only thing you can do is to say amiably, 'I'm sorry, but I can't hear anything while you talk.' If they still persist, you can ask an usher to call the manager."

Coughers deserve more sympathy, but anyone who is hacking away and expects to continue to cough during a performance should consider not attending. A cough at the wrong point during a play or a concerto will earn the ire of virtually everyone in the house.

Any theatergoer carrying a portable phone or beeper should keep it turned off during the performance. Doctors and other audience members who

---

SOMETHING SPECIAL

Treat going to the theater as the special event it is. Regardless of the quality of the play or the expertness of the acting, every performance is a thing unto itself, never to be duplicated again. Despite the blue jeans, Bermuda shorts, and even jogging suits that you will doubtless see around you, wear business dress to the theater—and on the dressy side, at that. It is only respectful to the actors, who are giving their all on the stage, to show that you appreciate the difference between an afternoon at the ballpark and an evening at the theater.

must be on call are wise to bring a beeper that signals a page with a light, a low-volume tone, or a silent vibration. Cellular phones, too, come in models that vibrate rather than ring.

Another potential noisemaker is jewelry. The thoughtful woman makes sure her bracelet and earrings don't jangle. Anyone whose watch can be heard ticking should take it off and slip it into a pocket or handbag.

FOOD AND DRINK

In most theaters and concert halls, refreshments are not allowed in the auditorium. But even if they are, wait until intermission and enjoy your snacks in the lobby. Ice rattling in a cup and crinkling candy wrappers may be expected at a movie house, but particularly out of place at the theater. Chewing gum is to be avoided as well: Even if you chew so quietly that people are unaware, a working jaw will be a visible distraction to those beside or behind you.

APPLAUSE

When it comes to applauding, the risk of making a faux pas lies with too much, not too little. Few seem to remember that applause isn't a robotic response but rather a way of showing either appreciation for a job well done (at the end of solo, for instance) or respect (when the orchestra conductor walks onto the stage). An example of overkill: applauding the set when the curtain rises.

If you're not sure when to clap, wait to see what everyone else does; little is more embarrassing than breaking out in applause while the rest of the audience stays quiet. Remember, too, that a standing ovation should be reserved for performances that have approached greatness—which is rare. The more audiences rise to their feet for any performance at all, the less meaningful such an ovation becomes for performances that truly warrant it.

ON A BOAT OR SHIP

A town or city graced with a harbor, lake, or river provide the opportunity for companies to consider another party locale: a boat. A number of river towns and harborside cities have moored historic vessels at jetties and turned them into party boats outfitted with dining rooms and reception rooms. Old paddle steamers are popular in the South, with some moored at a dock and others plying the river. Despite their evocative atmosphere, moored vessels are much like any other restaurant or party facility.

IS A THANK-YOU NOTE IN ORDER?

The answer to "Should I write a note?" is usually yes, but not always. Here are some situations where the question may arise. Ideally, any notes you write should be mailed within a few days after the event. The warmth of a handwritten note is preferable to one that is typed. (If your handwriting is illegible, however, a typed note will do.)

WHEN THEY'RE NECESSARY . . .

- When a business lunch is a first meeting or an infrequent one, a short note is called for, whether typed by your secretary on business letterhead or handwritten by you.
- When you've been entertained at a business-related occasion that crosses from business to social—whether at a dinner or an evening out with your spouse, at a weekend house party at the home of an employer, or as guest of honor at an office party—a thank-you note is in order.
- When the occasion is a social one, your thank-you note should be addressed to your host (spouse or partner included) and sent to his or her home. Social thank-you notes are handwritten on informal or personal stationery.
- Business-occasion thank-you notes come in several varieties. If your company honors you with a dinner celebrating your 25 years with the firm, for example, a handwritten note on personal stationery is called for, addressed to your immediate boss. A separate note to the president of the company if he or she attended the gathering is also a good idea.
- When you thank those who have interviewed you or helped with your job search.

THOSE GRAYER AREAS . . .

- When you are one of many guests at an office party or at a restaurant where you share a meal in the ordinary course of business, a verbal thanks at the end of the occasion is sufficient. While it's never wrong to write a note, you may reiterate your thanks in your next business correspondence in place of a separate thank-you note.
- If you, as the client, have been a lunch guest, a thank-you note is in order. But if you speak to your host often, a verbal thanks is sufficient.
- If you are the lunch guest of a client you see regularly, a separate note of thanks is not necessary. You would, instead, mention your thanks for the lunch in your next letter: "Thanks again, Jim, for joining me for lunch [or "Thanks again for lunch" if your client treated]. We really accomplished a lot. I'll have that proposal to you by next week."
- If you've been entertained at a club, a verbal thank you the day after is sufficient for business associates with whom you have a close relationship. Otherwise, write a note.
- The more expensive the entertainment, the more the need for a note. A verbal thank you is appropriate for an afternoon at the ballpark with someone you know well, while dinner and the theater requires a note.

An invitation should make clear whether the party is on a moored boat or one that will cruise. Dinner cruises are popular, especially in cities where the skyline forms a glittering backdrop. But a party boat that sets sail brings a new set of concerns. Because people are unable to leave when they choose, the cruise should be kept to two hours or less; this way, they won't drink more than they normally would. In any case, it's wise to stock up on nonalcoholic drinks. The host should also make sure there is seasick medicine on board if the cruise will be in waters that could turn choppy.

AT CORPORATE EVENTS

Some business entertainments are in a class by themselves: large, formal, or semiformal events put on by the company. As often as not, these are occasions where the dress is black tie and no expense is spared. The purpose may be to launch a new product, garner publicity, or simply to create goodwill among customers and clients; large parties limited to the company's employees might be held to mark an anniversary or to toast the retirement of a prominent executive. In days past, most events of this kind were held in the ballroom of a hotel, at a full-service party facility known for its elegance and efficiency, or at a private club. Today, the sky's the limit, with a museum, park, historic house, botanical garden, or zoo as a feasible locale.

While this chapter touches lightly on the actual planning of formal and semiformal company parties, the more important topic is behavior, with the emphasis on the guests. The event used as a prototype is a formal dinner that begins with predinner drinks and hors d'oeuvres and finishes with toasts. (See also Business Meals, page 391.)

DRINKS AND HORS D'OEUVRES

At a business event with a formal dinner as its centerpiece, predinner drinks and hors d'oeuvres will more than likely be served—from a bar, buffet tables of various kinds, trays carried by waiters who circulate through the room, or any combination thereof. An etiquette précis of this phase:

- **THE BAR.** If there is no true bar on the premises, bartenders will serve from a table, mixing drinks or pouring wine or beer as requested. Before ordering, be certain it's your turn; if in doubt, ask anyone who arrived at the bar or drinks table before you did whether he or she has been served.

  Waiters, too, will probably be serving wine, passing through the room with trays. Don't make a beeline to a waiter to grab a glass; either wait patiently until the waiter comes your way or go stand in line at the drinks table or bar. Take a napkin and keep it wrapped around the base of the glass;

FROM THE COMPANY PERSPECTIVE

The first task for a company holding a large party is to consider the image it wants to project and then choose the site for the event accordingly. A conservative law firm or bank that wants to strike a conservative pose might prefer a museum or historic building; an advertising or entertainment agency may go for an avant-garde art gallery or a zoo. Other possible locales range all the way from a golf clubhouse to the reception room of an ornate old theater.

The choice also depends, of course, on 1) how well the available space accommodates the number of guests invited, and 2) whether kitchen facilities are available for an event that will be catered. If a hotel is chosen as the party site, any catering problems are probably already solved: Larger hotels have the built-in advantage of offering function rooms of varying sizes and usually have personnel who are experienced in handling parties and meals; they also offer valet parking, coat checks, and taxi ranks. On the minus side, a hotel's menu will usually be more limited than a caterer's; also, there may be a stipulation that clients are not allowed to supply their own liquor.

Caterers often furnish more imaginative menus and decor than hotels do. Some also go a step further and provide full service, which means that in addition to taking care of the food, they will contract with florists, lighting contractors, and musicians. Hiring a caterer also allows more leeway in setting the party's style, be it formal or informal, conservative or offbeat.

In any case, the innumerable details of putting on large-scale events may also be placed in the hands of a professional party planner, who will scout locations, propose theme and decor ideas, and hire the caterers, florists, decorators, and musicians who bring it all to fruition. (For notes on sending invitations, see Invitations, page 350.)

---

also remember to keep the drink in your left hand so that your right one is ready for handshakes. (A finer point of wine etiquette: To keep the wine from warming, hold a wineglass by the stem, not the bowl.) When your glass is empty, look for a sideboard or tables where used glasses and plates are deposited; if you can't find one, ask a waiter or the bartender what to do with your glass and then thank him when he more than likely takes it.

Do not tip the bartender unless there is a cash bar, in which case you will pay for your drinks—an arrangement unlikely at most formal affairs, but a possibility. Gratuities are built into the wait staff's fees, and leaving money on the table or tray puts the bartenders and waiters in an awkward position.

- **PASSED TRAY FOOD SERVICE.** This may be the only food service, or it might be combined with self-service at a buffet table. Waiters circulate with trays of hors d'oeuvres, stopping to offer them to guests. Take a napkin from the tray and leave it in your hand as long as you plan to partake, keeping it under your plate when not using it to dab your lips. Never take the food directly from the tray to your mouth; instead, put it on your plate or napkin before picking it up to eat. Also remember not to eat, talk, and drink at the same time; one activity at a time is the rule for events like these.

What to do with food skewers or toothpicks after you've eaten an hors d'oeuvre? There's usually a small receptacle (or sometimes a halved orange, which becomes a kind of pincushion) on the waiter's tray for used ones. If not, hold any items (including drink stirrers) in your napkin until you find a waste-basket. Don't place used items on the buffet table unless you see a waste receptacle there.

Another question: How on earth do you juggle your drink and your plate and shake hands at the same time? Only with great difficulty, of course, meaning that a nod and smile will often have to substitute for a handshake. Standing close to a table could solve the problem, giving you a place to put your drink. Just make sure the table isn't set or decorated in such a way that even the temporary addition of a wineglass risks spoiling the effect.

- A BUFFET TABLE. Hors d'oeuvres and canapés will be set out on a buffet table, with guests picking up plates and helping themselves to both finger foods and dishes that require a fork. Take small portions, and don't return for plateful after plateful; the food at this stage of the party takes a backseat to the people around you, not the other way around.
- FOOD STATIONS. Food stations are smaller tables set in strategic locations around the room, each holding a different kind of food—ethnic specialties, perhaps, or all vegetarian dishes. The idea is to create several shorter lines instead of one long one. Try not to frequent only one food station; many other guests may be just as fond of Mexican food as you are, and you don't want to be responsible for the sudden dearth of quesadillas.

GREETINGS AND COURTESIES

Arriving fashionably late is absolutely de rigueur for some people, but at a business function even the chicest of the chic should be reasonably punctual. It's not necessary to arrive on the dot, but being no more than 15 or 20 minutes late is clearly the considerate thing to do. As a rule, punctuality is expected more at a business affair than at a purely social one.

How guests go about meeting the host is often orchestrated beforehand and may involve the designation of greeters. These may be two or three staff members who've been asked to take on the task and then prepare themselves by carefully going over the guest list. The job consists of greeting arriving guests and escorting them to the host for an introduction or brief chat. Greeters may also introduce guests to one another during the course of the party, especially if they sense anyone is feeling left out.

During the party's early stage, the host should avoid spending too much time with one group so that he'll be able to speak briefly with everyone. Greeters help make this possible: If the host finds himself caught in a lengthy talk, the very arrival of a greeter with guests in tow will allow him to turn his attention away from his conversation partner without seeming rude.

Once a guest has been introduced to the host, the greeter directs him or her to the buffet table or bar—unless, of course, the guest and host have struck up a conversation that promises to continue for a few minutes.

Is There a Receiving Line?

Because a receiving line speeds introductions, arranging for one is a smart company choice for functions of more than 60 people. The duration obviously depends on the size of the party, but an hour and a half is the usual limit; guests who arrive to find the line disbanded must accept not only that they may not meet the host but that the host may never know they were present.

It's fine for guests to hold a drink while waiting in a receiving line, but they should finish the drink and dispose of the glass before it is their turn to go through. Once the moment arrives, a guest shakes hands and briefly exchanges a few pleasant words with each member of the line.

If the party has no receiving line, the host may appoint two or three people as introducers, who serve much the same function as greeters. Introducers make sure that every person who arrives eventually meets the host at some point during the evening. To help ensure the success of a business party, the host should avoid spending an inordinately long time with one group so that he will be able to speak, if only for a moment, with each of the guests or couples.

The Art of Mingling

Employees of the host company are expected to take part in the festivities at a corporate event. If you feel intimidated by the sheer formality of the occasion, remember that many, if not most, of your gowned and tuxedoed fellow partygoers probably feel the same. Parties of this kind also provide the opportunity to mingle with people in the higher echelons; indeed, this is part of the purpose, and shying away from taking part will be all the more noticeable. If, on the

At Corporate Events

other hand, you consider yourself anything but timid, be careful not to go over-board. Monopolizing the CEO's time just because you've finally grabbed the chance will make it hard for him to speak with others.

If as a guest you find yourself on the sidelines, don't be embarrassed to introduce yourself to someone. When the person is standing alone, the ritual poses no problems (see Introducing Yourself, page 270). Slightly more difficult is introducing yourself into a group conversation, although there are ways this can be done gracefully. (While some body language experts hold that people who form a circle are signaling exclusion, remember that this configuration is only logical at a party.)

The easiest way to join a group is to walk past and register the conversational topic. Not that you want to eavesdrop, but everybody knows this is a party, not a private meeting. If the subject is politics, sports, computers, the state of the economy, or any other subject of an impersonal nature, you've found a conversation anyone could join. Wearing a pleasant look, make eye contact with one or two people and listen to what's being said. Be patient, and eventually you'll probably be asked to join in. Look for cues: If someone looks over and smiles, stick around until you find an opening to speak.

If a private or personal topic is the subject or the discussion is about people you don't know, move on. Likewise, if people engaged in a perfectly innocuous conversation make no move to invite you in, try another group. There's no reason to take this personally: The partygoers concerned may be so caught up in their subject that they simply fail to notice you.

Whether you have to work at mingling or it comes naturally, there are some conversational topics you'll want to avoid, both with peers and higher-ups. For one, put aside any shoptalk of the critical kind; even a sip or two of wine can loosen the tongue, and you never know who might overhear you. For another, avoid any political issues you feel passionate about; save these for friends to avoid offending a stranger who may not share your views.

As important as knowing what topics to avoid is being an attentive listener. Stand up straight and show your interest by making eye contact and occasionally paraphrasing what the other person is saying to show you understand. Also make sure to keep your voice volume to a reasonable level, so as not to add to the din.

Finally, keep a close rein on drinking. Nothing has as much potential to undermine a good impression as alcohol. Even if after a few drinks you feel yourself a raconteur *par excellence,* you may be mortified to wake up the next morning and realize you were really just blabbering on. Decide before the party the limits you'll place on your drink consumption—say, one cocktail or glass of wine during the predinner gathering, one glass of white wine and one glass of red at dinner, and an after-dinner liqueur, if one is served. Then do not give in and have more, no matter how festive the occasion and how great the temptation.

THANKING THE HOSTS

You may or may not be able to spend time with the host, but at some point in the evening you must seek him out (and preferably his or her spouse) to offer thanks for a wonderful evening; not to do so is rude. If it's impossible to thank the host because at the party's end he is swamped by people trying to do the same, write a note the next day—actually, something you should be doing in any event—and express regrets that you weren't able to thank him in person.

AT THE TABLE

At a large sit-down dinner, you'll often be seated with strangers—but only momentarily, considering introductions all around are essential. People seated together at a table always introduce themselves as a sign of courtesy and respect, even when they expect to conduct separate conversations.

PLACE CARDS AND MENU CARDS

The presence of place cards on the table—or alternatively, a card given to you citing your table number—means the hosts have decided where you're to sit. Only the most boorish guests will alter the arrangement of the cards or switch them with those from another table as a means of getting closer to the head table or a better view—yet some people do, if only on the sly. An exception to the rule is when two couples have come together but are placed at separate tables. In this case, it's permissible to ask other guests whether they would mind switching, but never to insist. Request a change only while seats are being taken, not after someone has settled in and begun to chat with others.

On truly formal occasions, you'll probably find only your surname inscribed on the card, along with a courtesy title: "Mr. Lichtenstein" or "Dr. MacWilliams." At dinners where guests from the same family have been invited or a surname is shared by two or more guests, first names are added: "Mr. Michael Lichtenstein" and "Mr. Pavel Lichtenstein."

Menu cards, which list the courses of the meal as a courtesy to the diners, may also be on the table at a formal dinner, placed in a small stand. A single card may be near the center of the table, or there may be separate cards

At Corporate Events

Place cards are expected at formal affairs, and there is standard protocol regarding who sits where. As with introductions, "importance" comes into play, regardless of gender. Tradition says that a guest of honor (not necessarily someone for whom the party is given, but sometimes a person of rank instead) is always seated to the host's right, with those lower in the business hierarchy seated progressively farther down the table.

If this arrangement seems shockingly undemocratic, keep in mind that top executives and foreign visitors often adhere to protocol and expect the same of everyone else. In any event, that some seats at the table are better than others is rarely apparent to observers.

---

between every two guests. If it's obvious that the cards are meant as souvenirs, put one in your breast pocket or handbag only when leaving the table for good.

OPEN SEATING

If no place cards are on the tables, guests may sit wherever they choose. At the same time, they should never seat themselves without asking those already at the table for permission: "Do you mind if I join you?" or "Excuse me. Are these chairs taken?" (A chair tilted against the table is the traditional signal that the place is reserved, but this custom is seen less today.) If you are given the go-ahead, introduce yourself, along with your spouse or partner, as you sit down. Shaking hands with everyone at the table isn't necessary, but after the meal ends a handshake is a nice parting gesture for anyone with whom you've spoken.

FORMAL PLACE SETTING

Large, no-holds-barred business events are the most likely place to encounter formal table settings, complete with an array of drinking glasses and flatware. Predinner drinks and cocktail buffets bring still more glasses onto the scene, including those originally designed for classic cocktails and cordials.

UTENSILS

The number of courses in a formal dinner runs from four to six. In Victorian England, the determination of the newly rich to maintain class distinctions led to the design and manufacture of so many new utensils for dining—as specific as a sauce-tasting spoon (used at the table)—that even the most avid social climber was at a loss for what to do with which. Thankfully, most of these contrivances fell out of fashion, and working one's way through a formal place setting is no longer as daunting as it once was. Following are shown the utensils and table items that may be encountered at a formal dinner.

A Formal Place Setting

- **FISH FORK.** When this fork appears in a place setting, it is at the outside left since it is the first fork used.
- **DINNER FORK.** Also called the place fork, this largest of the forks is used to eat the entrée and side dishes. At times, the dinner fork (rather than a fish fork) is used to eat the fish course as well.
- **SALAD FORK.** The smaller salad fork is more likely to be to the right of the dinner fork at a formal dinner, meaning the salad will be served after the entrée in the European manner.
- **OYSTER FORK.** This small utensil is used for oysters, shrimp, clams, and similar first-course shellfish. This is the only fork placed on the right. It is found beyond the spoon, sometimes resting in the bowl of the soup spoon.
- **SOUP OR FRUIT SPOON.** If soup or fruit is being served, this spoon is placed to the right of the knives.
- **FISH KNIFE.** Positioned to the right of the dinner knife.
- **DINNER KNIFE.** This largest knife is used for the entrée and is placed to the right of the plate.

- **STEAK KNIFE.** If you have ordered beef or game, this knife might be brought out by the waiter as a replacement for the dinner knife.
- **BUTTER KNIFE.** This small knife is placed across the edge of the bread plate and is replaced there each time it is used.
- **TEA OR COFFEE SPOON.** This small spoon is presented to the diner at the end of the meal, when coffee is served.

At a formal meal, the dessert spoon and fork are brought in just before dessert is served.

GLASSWARE

Aside from the water goblets and wineglasses on the table, cocktail, liqueur, or punch glasses may be used at various times during the party, with a server bringing them out as necessary. Knowing their finer differences may be of some value on future occasions. Following is a guide.

- **WATER GOBLET.** This bowl-shaped glass with a stem is correct for both formal lunches and dinners. The usual capacity is 10 ounces or slightly more.
- **ALL-PURPOSE WINEGLASS.** A straight-sided glass with a capacity of 6 to 9 ounces may be used for both white and red wine. It is filled three-quarters or less full.
- **RED WINE.** The classic bowl has a slight tulip shape. Although the total capacity is 8 to 10 ounces, the glass should be one-half or less full.
- **WHITE WINE.** This differs from the red wine glass by having straight sides and a smaller capacity—5 to 8 ounces. It is filled three-quarters full or less.
- **SHERRY.** The traditional shape is a narrow V, and the total capacity is from 2 to 3 ounces. Fill to about half an inch from the top.
- **CHAMPAGNE.** Called a flute, this cylindrical glass has replaced the traditional saucer-shaped glass because it keeps the champagne bubblier. Its capacity is 5 to 7 ounces.
- **MARTINI GLASS.** This wide V-shaped glass holds from 4 to 6 ounces and should be filled to about ¾-inch from the top.
- **HIGHBALL GLASS.** Used for the gin-and-tonic and similar cocktails served on the rocks, this straight-sided glass holds 10 to 12 ounces.
- **OLD-FASHIONED GLASS.** This glass can be used for any drink on the rocks. The standard size has a capacity of 8 ounces, but taller versions are also seen.
- **SHOT GLASS.** This is for drinking whisky neat. The most popular size is 1½ ounces, but some shot glasses hold 3 ounces.

Red Wine Glass

White Wine Glass

Champagne Flute

- **LIQUEUR GLASS.** Also called a cordial glass (cordial being another name for liqueur), this small glass has a capacity of 1 to 2 ounces.
- **BRANDY SNIFTER.** The design of this glass—a small neck and a balloon-shaped bowl—is meant to hold in the brandy's aroma. Snifters range in capacity up to 20 ounces or so, but only about 2 ounces of liquor are poured into the snifter at one time. Brandy may also be served in a liqueur glass.
- **PUNCH CUP.** The total capacity is usually 4 to 5 ounces. Fill ⅔ full.

DINNER IS SERVED

At most formal dinners, an empty service plate—also called a place plate—will be set at each diner's place from the beginning; a folded napkin may be in the center. Alternatively, a cold first course may already be set on the serving plate when the diners are seated, with the napkin to the left of the forks. The only time a plate will not be before guests is just before dessert, when a waiter clears all the dishes from the table and crumbs the tablecloth.

Table service comes in three traditional forms:

- **PLATE SERVICE.** Waiters remove the service plates and bring guests dinner plates holding their food.
- **RUSSIAN SERVICE.** Service plates are replaced with warm dinner plates, and then courses are served from platters by the wait staff. One waiter at a time serves the vegetables, the meat, and any other courses.
- **FRENCH SERVICE.** Two waiters serve each course, with one holding the platter and the other serving guests individually.

If a first course is followed by soup, the serving plate remains until the

From the company's perspective, cocktail parties, buffets, and receptions are the consummate solution for a firm or concern that wants to entertain clients and customers without spending a fortune and being caught in a morass of details. Because mingling is the evening's central activity, these more relaxed parties are the best choice when the aim is for people to meet and become acquainted—employees and clients, for example, or staff members from a company's different branches. The style of invitations will reflect the style of the party, with printed cards following standard protocol for more formal parties, and attractive commercial fill-in cards acceptable for others. (See Invitations, pages 74 and 350.)

A function of this kind also allows more flexibility in the degree of formality. Some companies might seek to exploit the cocktail party's sophisticated image to the hilt by making it a black-tie affair. Others may specify casual dress on the invitation. Whatever dress is specified, guests should lean toward the dressier side of the category. While "Casual Dress" on the invitation lets men know that they need not wear a tie, they should be aware that proper attire is on the order of a navy blazer, gray slacks, and an unpatterned open-collared shirt or turtleneck—not the standard khaki slacks/plaid shirt look. Likewise, "Business Dress" should be on the dressier side—a black suit and silk tie rather than a brown one with knit neckwear. For women, business dress in this case means something a step above the standard two-piece suit that is worn to the office. She might wear, for example, a dressier suit, a dress, or pants suit.

As a guest, keep in mind that the tenets of etiquette take on even more meaning at a business event, where looking polished is all the more to your advantage. Remember the basics

soup course is finished; from the right, the waiter will remove the soup bowl and its underplate from the service plate and replace it with a warm dinner plate or (with plated service) a plate already holding the main course.

Possible additions to the usual china, flatware, and glassware of a formal dinner are finger bowls (see page 414) and saltcellars (pages 398 and 413). The former are used if any finger foods are part of the meal. The latter, a small bowl with a spoon, replaces a salt shaker.

However elaborate the table setting, remember that the way you treat those around you—not to mention your sparkling wit and tasteful attire—is longer remembered than your misuse of a fish fork. Table manners are a vital concern, but not to be fretted over so much that your anxiety will overshadow your comfort and ease. (See also Table Manners, Course by Course, page 405.)

for making introductions, to hold your drink in your left hand to leave your right one available for shaking, to mind your manners while eating, and to converse with charm and ease.

- **THE COCKTAIL PARTY.** The most informal, this party traditionally lasts two hours, starting and ending anytime between 5:00 and 8:30 P.M. Both hot and cold hors d'oeuvres are served, with cocktails, wine, beer, and soft drinks as the standard beverages. In addition to the fully stocked bar of liquors, there should be a choice of nonalcoholic drinks—mineral water, both sparkling and still; fruit juices; and sparkling ciders. Although a few tables and chairs should be placed around the room, people expect to stand most of the time.

- **THE COCKTAIL BUFFET.** Somewhere between 6:00 and 9:00 P.M. is the usual time for a cocktail buffet, where business dress is appropriate. Because more substantial food is served, it is necessary to provide tables and chairs for open seating, with guests alternately occupying the tables over the course of the evening. The food is generally more varied than that at a sit-down dinner, especially if food stations are placed around the room. Food stations, each offering a different kind of cuisine, also afford the chance for the food presentation to shine, albeit at a higher price. A truly memorable affair could be created by offering Provençal dishes at one table, Spanish tapas at a second, and Japanese sushi at a third, all prepared and served on the spot by chefs and staff worthy of the very finest restaurant.

- **THE COCKTAIL RECEPTION.** This most formal of cocktail parties often marks a special event or honors a prominent guest. Dressy business attire, or even black tie, is called for. If the reception is held before an evening event, it usually runs from 6:00 to 8:00 P.M., with hors d'oeuvres as the food. If it is held after an evening event, 10:30 to midnight is the usual time, and a late supper menu—egg and cheese dishes, vegetable dishes, and desserts—is served. Champagne is an essential addition to the usual range of drinks.

MAKING TOASTS

At many large parties, toasting the guest of honor or the host with wine or champagne may be expected. "Cheers" or "To your health" or variations thereof are standard, while other toasts are longer and more personal, expressing admiration for the person's good qualities.

Anyone considering making a toast should prepare beforehand, if only to rehearse mentally so as not to fumble the words. Keep whatever you say short and to the point unless your toast has been designated as the principal one of the evening. The principal toast is a small speech of sorts, and it should be composed in writing and rehearsed by the speaker in advance. A glance at your notes is acceptable, but try to speak as extemporaneously as possible. The protocol points of toasting:

- The host is the first to toast, attracting the crowd's attention by standing and raising his or her glass; banging on a glass with a knife should be considered a measure of last resort.
- At formal occasions, the toaster stands, as do the people toasting; the person being toasted remains seated.
- The guests respond by taking a sip of their drinks—but never draining the glass. A person who doesn't drink alcohol joins in as well, toasting with a soft drink or even water.

FOREIGN-LANGUAGE TOASTS

I f the person being toasted is from overseas and speaks a different language, make a point to learn his country's traditional toast, usually the equivalent of "To your health!" or "Cheers!" Following is a sampling of international toasts, with their pronunciations shown in informal phonetics; capital letters indicate the syllable(s) to stress.

LANGUAGE	TOAST	PRONUNCIATION
Cantonese	Yung sing	YOUNG-SING
Czech	Nazdravī	nahz-DRAHV-ee
Dutch	Proost	PROWST
Finnish	Kippis	KIP-pis
French	A votre santé	ah-votruh-san-TAY
German	Prosit	PROHST, with guttural R
Greek	Stin egia sas	steen-ee-YAH-sahs
Hebrew	L'Chayim	luh-CHI-um, with guttural CH
Hungarian	Egészségedre	eh-geh-sheh-GEHD-ruh
Italian	Salute	sah-LOO-tay
Japanese	Kampai	KAHM-PYE
Korean	Gan bei	kahn-BAY
Malaysian	Slimat minim	seh-lah-maht MEE-noom
Polish	Na zdrowie	nahz-DROH-vee-ah
Portuguese	Brindare	brin-DAH-ray, first R slightly trilled
Russian	Na zdorovie	nahz-doh-ROH-vee-ah
Scandinavian *	Skål	SKOAL
Spanish	Salud	sah-LOOD
Turkish	Serefe	sheh-REH-feh
Thai	Choc-tee	chock-DEE

(Danish, Swedish, Norwegian)

- The person being toasted does not drink to himself.
- After being toasted, the person rises, bows his acknowledgment, and says thank you. He may also raise his own glass to propose a toast to the host, the chef, or anyone else he sees fit to so honor.
- At private or small informal dinners, it is acceptable, of course, for everyone—toaster and toastee included—to remain seated.

CHAPTER 33

ENTERTAINING AT HOME

A more personal way to entertain is to invite people to your home. Business dinners or parties are those that center around people you either do business with or work for, while an at-home gathering consisting solely of coworkers and peers is really just another party, despite the inevitable shoptalk. Though a business party's purpose is mostly social, too, as the host you'll want to stay on your toes even more—for better or worse, your spouse, your home, and your entertaining style all reflect who you are. How well you carry off a social gathering is part of a larger picture, and your proficiency in getting the party organized, keeping it running smoothly, and staying cheerful and relaxed strikes business associates favorably and stands you in good stead.

INVITING GUESTS

If you're inviting, say, a client who's in town for a few days, a simple phone call is sufficient. The same goes for inviting local clients or customers, although in this case you should include spouses or partners. You might also want to invite a few nonbusiness friends, whose presence will lessen the likelihood of your company or professional field ending up as the evening's one and only topic.

A written invitation is more appropriate when inviting your boss or others of high rank, unless the two of you have developed such a close working relationship that it would seem artificial to stand on ceremony. Just remember to include the person's spouse or partner.

Inviting people with whom you work presents a special challenge: not offending other officemates. Either keep the invitation private or invite those who weren't on the list the last time you entertained. Some executives and managers who entertain regularly make a ritual of inviting each staff member once a year, one at a time; others choose to throw parties with small groups; still others may prefer to invite the entire staff at once.

NOTES FOR THE HOST—AND SPOUSE

It goes without saying that when businessmen or -women entertain at home, their spouses or partners do their part to get things organized and make guests feel comfortable. Since there will undoubtedly be a great deal of job-related chat among people they may or may not know, spouses should appear interested—to listen, to ask questions. At the same time, they should feel free to discuss their own professional or personal interests.

Although your spouse isn't expected to join you as you greet arriving guests at the door, introduce him or her as soon as the opportunity arises. (If you're living with someone but aren't married, it's up to you whether to inform arriving guests of the situation. All that's necessary is a standard introduction that gives your partner's full name.) If the party is small, you (or your spouse or partner) take newly arrived guests around the room, introducing them to anyone they haven't met; just wait for a break in the conversation. At a larger gathering, workmates will usually assume this responsibility themselves, introducing their spouses to colleagues.

SINGLE HOSTS AND HOSTESSES

A single man or woman might consider asking a friend to act as a co-host. It makes sense because some of the guests (the business associates) are already acquainted, whereas much of the rest of the crowd (mostly wives, husbands, or dates) are not. With two hosts sharing the duties of refilling drinks, replenishing food trays, and chatting with guests, it's less likely that spouses, dates, or the unattached will be left standing alone and feeling awkward.

HOSTING A SIT-DOWN DINNER

Dinners are less formal than they once were, and often more imaginative. Exotic dishes—perhaps a spectacular Spanish paella or a Middle Eastern menu built around chicken with feta and apricots served over saffron rice—can make a memorable meal for guests, while a traditional Southern-fried meal of braised pork chops, fresh okra, and spoon bread may be an adventure for guests visiting from the North. This doesn't mean that you should necessarily shy away from a formal dinner with a classic French menu and a 10-piece place setting: You could put one on for the sheer fun of bucking the trend toward informality—or even as an excuse to show off every last piece of your wedding china and silver. (For formal table settings, see Utensils and Glassware, page 434.)

Entertainming
at Home

443

Whatever cuisine or serving style you choose, there are things to consider beforehand, most obviously your available space and the tastes of your guests. When it comes to the latter, before planning a menu the smart host makes an effort to learn if guests dislike any foods in particular or have food allergies, whether real or only suspected. You'll also want to be able to accommodate vegetarians, some of whom forgo even dairy products and eggs. In any case, remember that the goal is to have enough variety in courses to please everyone, not to tailor the meal to one person's needs.

Planning the Menu

Unless you wish to hire a caterer, you'll probably be planning every detail of the menu yourself. But consider the limitations of your kitchen before giving your creativity free rein. If you have only one stove and plan to cook a roast, don't accompany it with baked dishes that have to share the oven—more than likely, they'll have different cooking temperatures and times. Preparing side dishes on the stove top hardly crimps your style, considering that many classic vegetable dishes (ratatouille, creamed pearl onions, and green beans amandine, for example)—not to mention comforting down-home ones (mashed potatoes, corn on the cob)—are either boiled, simmered, sautéed, steamed, or braised.

Pay attention, too, to balance. Alternate an especially rich dish with a simple one: Coquilles St. Jacques (scallops in a thick cream sauce), for example, might be followed by sauce-free grilled medallions of lamb, while the course after a creamy pasta carbonara could be a simple broiled fish with lemon. Also, balance the flavors, which means avoiding a succession of spicy or sweet foods. A meal that features duck basted with currant jelly, a fruit salad as the side dish, and a raspberry trifle as dessert piles sweet upon sweet; while each dish may be delicious in itself, it becomes monotonous when eaten with the others.

It's also a good idea to include a few dishes that can be prepared ahead of time and reheated before serving. The reason is simple: By spending less time in the kitchen, you're showing consideration to your guests. Some dishes—among them soups, stews, and curries—taste even better after being refrigerated overnight, giving the flavors time, as the French say, "to marry."

GETTING READY

Putting on even a casual business dinner entails a number of details, including deciding on how to set the table and how you want it to look. While the most important consideration is the happiness of your guests, the nuts and bolts of entertaining have to be sorted out beforehand. When will you serve the salad? Should you serve liqueurs after dinner? What do you do when you have 12 guests but only eight place settings of your good china?

TABLECLOTHS AND PLACE MATS

Although a formal dinner calls for both a tablecloth and place mats, at informal dinners a tablecloth is largely a matter of choice. A bare table with place mats is the alternative.

THE BOSS IS COMING?

Inviting the person to whom you answer at the office needn't result in the nervous hand-wringing it classically calls to mind. Today's executives and managers run the gamut, from the free spirit who arrives at work in jeans to the adamant defender of tradition. You may want to invite your boss and his or her spouse simply to introduce them to your family, or to repay an invitation extended to you before. If your boss—or any other guest of high rank from your company—is of the old school, keep the following four things in mind.

- If you and your boss don't socialize regularly at work, you'll probably feel more relaxed if you include a few other guests. Select people with interests similar to his or hers.
- Don't put on airs. Act as you normally act and entertain as you normally entertain. Don't hire special help unless you ordinarily do, and don't serve a hard-to-carve roast unless you can handle it. In other words, be yourself. Being gracious and interested will impress the boss far more than outdoing yourself in a way that he, more than anyone, knows you can't afford.
- If you have small children, by all means introduce them to your guests, who will surely be delighted to meet them. But after a few minutes have passed, retire the little ones to another room. Even though your boss may be fond of children, having them underfoot for most of the party can be wearying. If possible, hire a baby-sitter to keep them entertained in another room until they're called out to bid your guests good-bye.
- If you work in the kind of highly traditional office where workers address a person of higher rank as "Mr." or "Ms.," don't suddenly switch to "Ralph" or "Rhonda"—either in the invitation or while chatting during the evening. You and your spouse should do so only once you've been asked to.

You may think a tablecloth essential to the overall look you want to achieve, or it may serve to hide the scratches on a less-than-perfect table. On the other hand, the wood surface of a table can become a design element in itself. The gleaming mahogany of a fine dining table is nicely set off by crisp, white broadcloth place mats and napkins paired with copper or pewter serving dishes. The weathered wood of a rustic table makes a good foil for terra-cotta or hand-painted Italian serving bowls and platters, which can be combined with napkins and mats in natural earth tones.

China and Flatware

If your good china and flatware won't stretch to meet the number of guests, you have two alternatives. The first is to set a second, smaller table with your pottery or everyday dinnerware, or even with dishes and place settings borrowed from a relative or friend.

The second choice, appropriate for truly casual affairs, is to mix and match. After all, making sure that every piece of china and flatware matches is less important than the conversation and the quality and presentation of the food. Worn or chipped plates, cups, and saucers won't make the grade, but using different patterns or colors is acceptable as long as they're somewhat in keeping—no plastic wineglasses with bone china, please. The idea is to create a harmonious whole.

Centerpieces, Candles, Et Cetera

The centerpiece is just that: flowers or something else ornamental placed in the exact center of the table. Fresh flowers are the obvious choice, but an arrangement of imitation flowers crafted from silk or glass can also be used. Plastic flowers? Never, unless you're having a retro theme party complete with lava lamps and a *Partridge Family* LP. Alternatives to flowers are bowls of fruit (think of a still-life by an Old Master), ornamental vegetables, or a striking antique or contemporary glass ornament. Whatever you choose, make sure the centerpiece doesn't stand so tall your guests can't see over it.

Candles, if meant to be merely ornamental, are placed on either side of the centerpiece. If you want to create a more dramatic mood by using candles as the only source of light, you might want to place one above each place setting so that guests can clearly see their food. While white is the traditional candle color for a formal dinner, color isn't an issue at informal affairs: Simply choose whatever you think looks best with the china and linens you're using.

If your table seats eight or more, place a set of salt and pepper shakers or grinders at each end. Even at the most informal meal these two basics should be a cut above those you use every day. Wooden, pewter, and smartly designed clear glass shakers or grinders are some of the countless choices.

INFORMAL PLACE SETTING

There's no mystery to setting a proper table—especially an informal one, which calls for fewer utensils. The basic rule: Utensils are placed in the order of use, from the outside toward the plate. A second rule, although with a few exceptions: Forks go to the left of the plate, knives and spoons to the right.

The typical place setting for an informal three-course dinner includes these utensils and dishes.

- **TWO FORKS.** A large one (the dinner fork) for the main course, and a small one for a salad or appetizer. If salad is to be served as the first course, the small fork goes to the left of the dinner fork; if you're serving the salad European (or Continental style)—i.e., after the main course—it goes to the dinner fork's right.

- **DINNER PLATE.** Sometimes there are no dinner plates are on the informal table when guests sit down. The plates will be heated and brought out by the host or server just as the food is ready, making sure food stays warm while everyone at the table is being served.

- **ONE KNIFE.** The dinner knife is set immediately to the right of the plate, its cutting edge facing inward; it may be a steak knife if the main course is meat or chicken. It can also be used, if necessary, with any first course.

- **SPOONS.** Spoons go to the right of the knife, with a soup spoon (used first) farthest to the right and a dessert spoon (used last) to its left.

- **GLASSES.** A water goblet and one wineglass (or two, if two wines are being served) are placed at the top right of the dinner plate. If wine is not a part of the meal, the goblet can be used for either water or iced tea.

- **NAPKIN.** Place a folded cloth napkin in the center of the place setting or to the left of the forks.

Other dishes and utensils are optional, depending on your menu or the style of service.

- **SALAD PLATE.** This is placed to the left of the forks. If the salad is to be served with the meal rather than before or after, you may eliminate this piece of china and serve salad directly on the dinner plate—but do this only at meals where the main course won't come with a pool of sauce or gravy.

Entertainming at Home

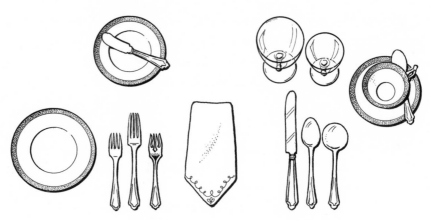

Informal Place Setting with No Dinner Plate, Napkin in Center, and Dessert Spoon and Soup Spoon to Right

- **BREAD PLATE WITH BUTTER KNIFE.** Place the bread plate above the forks, with the butter knife resting across the edge. If your china doesn't include bread plates, buy clear glass ones, which will match any color or pattern.
- **DESSERT SPOON AND FORK.** These can either be placed horizontally above the dinner plate (the spoon at the top and its handle to the right; the knife below and its handle to the left) or beside the plate. If beside the plate, the fork goes on the left-hand side, closest to the plate; the spoon goes on the right-hand side of the plate, to the left of the soup spoon.
- **COFFEE CUP AND SAUCER.** If coffee is to be drunk during the meal, the cup and saucer go just above and slightly to the right of the knife and spoons. If it is served after dinner, the cups and saucers are brought to the table.

Informal Place Setting with Dinner Plate in Center and Dessert Spoon and Fork Above

THE PARTY BEGINS

Before your guests arrive, you've made sure the house is clean, any extra furniture is set up, and the bathrooms are outfitted with hand towels, pretty bars of soap, and perhaps a candle or a small flower arrangement. The evening's star attraction—your table—is properly set, and the party begins.

BEFORE-DINNER DRINKS

If predinner drinks or cocktails are being served, plan for dinner to start about an hour later than the time specified on the invitation. If drinks are not part of the plan, you should still wait for 20 minutes to a half hour before serving the meal; this allows time for any late arrivals to say their hellos.

Don't forget to provide soda, juices, and mineral water for those who want to forgo alcohol. If you offer snacks or hors d'oeuvres, keep them fairly light so that they don't compete with the meal. Choice appetizers include pita bread points with an herbed yogurt dip or a salmon pâté with thin crackers. On the more elaborate side are such classics as baked stuffed mushrooms or a hot artichoke dip laced with mayonnaise and Parmesan cheese.

THE CALL TO DINNER

Before you call your guests to dinner, the butter and condiments should be on the table, the water glasses filled, any candles lit, the plates warming in the oven, and the wine either in a cooler beside the host or within reach on the table. A first course, if served cold or at room temperature, should also be set out when the guests are seated. (Note: Long-stemmed glass bowls holding shrimp cocktail or other seafood are set on underplates, with both dishes removed before the main course is served.)

When the time comes, simply say, "Dinner is ready. Shall we go in?" Suggest to guests who are holding drinks that they bring them to the table, and then lead the way into the dining room.

Part of making your guests feel comfortable is relieving them of the anxiety of choosing a chair at the dinner table. One might be thinking, "Would Laura rather sit next to Bruce than to me?" as another wonders, "Will the hostess think I'm pushy if I sit next to the guest of honor?"

Traditionally, the host or hostess sees to it that couples are split up at the dinner table so that each guest has a chance to visit with someone other than his or her partner. But if your intuition tells you that a couple who are considered inseparable would rather sit together, by all means encourage them to do

Entertainming at Home

so. Another tradition: If there is a guest of honor, he or she—or both, if a couple—is seated at the host or hostess's right.

As you politely motion guests to their seats, use common sense to figure out who's a good fit with whom: "Angela, why don't you sit there, across from Bryan?" If someone is hard of hearing, either seat him with his best ear toward the conversation or beside people who speak forcefully. The seat of choice for a left-hander is obviously at a corner, where he or she will be spared the embarrassment of bumping elbows with a neighbor.

When guests are seated at two tables, it's only polite that the host sit at one and the hostess at the other. If there are more than two tables, ask a good friend to act as a surrogate host, seeing that wine is served and plates are refilled.

SERVING THE FOOD

As the host, you can either dish the guests' food into the plates and pass them down or let the guests pass the serving bowls to one another. If you choose to do the former, have the warm dinner plates stacked beside your place setting, along with the food and the necessary serving implements. When guests are seated, dish food into the first plate and hand it to the guest of honor (if any), saying, "This is for you"; this lets her know not to pass it down. The second plate is passed down the right side of the table to whomever sits opposite the host; the guests to the left are then served in order, working back toward host. A more casual approach is to let guests serve themselves as they pass the side dishes around the table; tradition says to pass counterclockwise, but the point is for the food to be moving in only one direction. Serving the salad this way especially makes sense; as host, you may either dress the salad before serving or let each person add dressing to his or her taste.

TWO MORE SERVING OPTIONS: Place the dishes on a sideboard buffet-style and let guests serve themselves before being seated. Or if you don't have regular help, hire a couple of high school or college students to serve dinner and clean up; they could also pass hors d'oeuvres before the meal.

If the meal includes two or three sauces or other condiments, it's smart to serve these in a divided dish or on a small, easily managed tray; this ensures that they are passed together and the guests see all the choices.

When it comes time for dessert, either bring what you may consider your *pièce de résistance* to the table on individual dessert plates or serve it from the bowl or pan, which is set by your place at the table. The filled dishes are then passed to the guests.

LATECOMERS

The before-dinner drinks have been quaffed, the olive pits dispatched to the wastebasket, and the first course is ready and waiting. But a guest (or guests) has yet to show up. What to do? Etiquette says that the host waits for 15 minutes before serving dinner. But take note: Tacking on a grace period of even five minutes shows inconsideration to the many for the sake of the few. When the latecomer finally enters the dining room, he (or she or they) should immediately apologize to the group at large for delaying the meal. If the grace period has expired and the meal has begun, the tardy one is served whatever course is being eaten at the time. If this happens to be dessert, the host sees to it that he gets a plateful of the main course from the kitchen, though past its prime it will be.

SERVING WINE

The simplest way to offer wine at the dinner table is for you to do the pouring. Place the opened bottle on the table in front of you, preferably on a coaster or in a wine holder to prevent any drops from staining the tablecloth. Then ask guests to pass their glasses down. If several guests are present, a second bottle is placed at the other end of the table, with your spouse or a guest doing the pouring. Alternatively, walk around the table to fill the first glass for guests and then pass the bottle for refills.

SECOND HELPINGS

If you have a sideboard or serving table, using it as a halfway station between the dinner table and the kitchen makes it easy to offer second helpings to your guests. Keep the serving bowls here (preferably on a warming tray), along with extra flatware and plates. When a guest follows your suggestion that he have another serving—or remarks that a particular dish is so delicious that he thinks he'll have a little more—retrieve the serving bowl and hold it as he serves himself.

CLEARING THE TABLE

When it comes time to clear the table, never scrape or stack dishes; instead, remove them two at a time. Salt and pepper containers, salad and bread plates, condiment dishes, and unused flatware can be taken away on a serving tray. Each time something is whisked away to the kitchen, you can save time by bringing dessert plates (with or without dessert) on the return trip.

Entertainming at Home

If guests offer to help you clear, implore them to stay put: "No, thank you. Really, it is easier to do it myself." Otherwise, you may find everyone darting back and forth to the kitchen. If necessary, designate a helpmate in advance—your son or daughter, perhaps, or a close friend. Your other guests should be just that—guests—and remain at the table.

AFTER-DINNER COFFEE

Because a simple cup of coffee isn't what it used to be, it's the rare dinner party where individual guests want it the same way—or want any at all, for that matter. Unless you stock your cupboard with the works—regular coffee, decaffeinated coffee, cappuccino and espresso (both regular and decaffeinated), real tea (standard or flavored), and an assortment of herbal teas—politely ask your guests when inviting them: "Do you drink coffee or anything else after the meal?" Then ask what they prefer. Or, instead of inquiring beforehand, have ready a variety of choices—a pot of brewed coffee, a pot of decaffeinated coffee, and a pot of hot water with a choice of tea bags, both herbal and real.

AFTER-DINNER DRINKS

Offering after-dinner drinks can bring an especially cordial touch to the evening's end. If you're serving coffee at the table, a tray holding bottles of liqueurs, brandy, and cognac—along with the appropriate glasses—may be brought in at the same time. Then ask each guest which he or she would prefer. If you're having coffee in the living room, the tray is placed on the coffee table or a sideboard, with individual orders either being taken by the host or the guests helping themselves.

HOSTING A BUFFET

In addition to allowing you to serve a wider range of dishes and make sure most tastes are satisfied, a buffet—the self-service version of the dinner party—can be an easier task to undertake. When carefully chosen, prepared foods from a gourmet market will not only make a beautiful table but keep your kitchen time to a minimum. Then again, for enthusiastic cooks a buffet provides the chance to share several of their most prized recipes. The buffet has three more advantages over a sit-down dinner:

- **YOU CAN ACCOMMODATE MORE GUESTS.** An advantage, yes—but don't go overboard and invite so many people that there aren't enough places to sit. Also make sure there's enough elbow room for guests to move about with ease.

- **IT ALLOWS YOU MORE TIME FOR VISITING.** Because most of the food will have been prepared in advance and guests serve themselves, you can spend time mingling and chatting instead of dashing about in the kitchen.

- **IT'S MORE RELAXED.** A buffet gives your guests the freedom to sit in one place before dinner, go into the dining room and forage for themselves, and then either return to the same place or decide on a new one. Plus, unlike at a sit-down dinner, they are able to choose their dinner companions.

Planning a Buffet Menu

The menu for a buffet depends partly on whether your guests will be seated at tables or dining from their laps. If the latter, choose foods that are easy to manage with a fork alone; also avoid those that are soupy. Consider, too, the time of day. At a dinner buffet you'll want heavier food, and more of it; at lunch, a lighter menu is more appealing.

No matter what the seating arrangements, steer clear of dishes that have to be eaten just after being taken from the oven, such as soufflés. Beyond that, use simple common sense when planning the menu. When it comes to potatoes, for example, remember that French fries get soggy, while stuffed potatoes do fine at room temperature. Another bit of common sense: When serving cheese, meat, or anything else that needs slicing, slice it in advance so that the buffet line doesn't come to a standstill as guests take on the task themselves.

A buffet is also the ideal time to have fun with ethnic or regional cuisines. An Italian spread could include a white-bean-and-tuna salad, bruschetta (toasted bread slices topped with olive oil, garlic, and finely chopped vegetables of choice), and a platterful of alternating slices of good-quality tomatoes, smoked mozzarella, and basil leaves drizzled with olive oil. Perennial Mexican favorites are tortilla chips served with a bean dip mixed with sour cream and green chiles, hot cheese-and-salsa dips (in a chafing dish), and sugar-dusted sopapillas or buñuelos as sweets. A Southern buffet might feature baked garlic-cheese grits (as good at room temperature as straight from the oven), pickled black-eyed peas (served cold), and cheese straws with a hint of cayenne.

THE ULTIMATE COURTESY

Obvious though it may be, making sure no buffet guest gets an upset stomach—or an even worse illness—from simply partaking of the bounty should be foremost in any host's or hostess's mind. Some bacteria are partial to party-crashing, and it's your job to keep them at bay. When putting out food for a buffet, taking four simple steps will help ensure the food stays not only fresh-tasting but safe.

1. WASH YOUR HANDS. Bacteria that cause food-borne illness can't be smelled or tasted but are probably on your hands nonetheless.
2. REWASH YOUR PLATES AND KITCHEN EQUIPMENT. Pay special attention to rewashing plates, cutting boards, and knives that have come in contact with raw meat or poultry.
3. DIVIDE FOOD INTO SMALL PORTIONS. Instead of setting out all the food for a buffet at once, keep most of it in the refrigerator. Then, when replacing an empty platter, either wash it or fetch a new one before adding fresh food. Put out larger servings of foods that are going quickly and smaller ones for foods that are less in demand.
4. KEEP HOT FOOD HOT. At a buffet, serve hot food in a chafing dish or on a warming tray, keeping the food at 140°F or above.

Following are some common buffet foods, with notes on how long they can be left out after being taken from the refrigerator. If you have doubts about any food's keeping quality, you can ring the U.S. Department of Agriculture's Meat and Poultry Hotline (800–535–4555).

- CHEESE. So that its full flavor is savored, cheese is always served at room temperature, never straight from the refrigerator. But take care with soft varieties: Such favorites as goat cheese and French double or triple crèmes should be left out for no more than two hours. Firm cheeses, including gouda, cheddar, and Järlsburg, are less risky and can be left out for the length of the party in all but the hottest places.
- TUNA OR CHICKEN SALADS AND COLD CUTS. Mayonnaise-laced salads made with seafood or meat should be left out no longer than two hours at room temperature. The same goes for cold cuts. On an outdoor deck or room with an air temperature of 90°F or above, the limit is one hour. Nesting the serving bowls in larger bowls of ice will be safer still; just be sure to keep dishes cold by replenishing the ice as it melts.
- COOKED DISHES. Keep cooked foods either hot or cold, not lukewarm. Hot foods should be held at 140°F on a warming tray or in a chafing dish or Crock-Pot. Cold foods should be held at 40°F or cooler; set them out in small amounts, and replace empty platters rather than adding fresh food to half-empty ones.
- DESSERTS. Cookies and most cakes can be left out for the length of the party. But if any desserts (cakes included) have whipped cream or custard as an ingredient or topping, two hours is the on-the-table limit.

If your party is fairly large and the room is spacious enough, place the buffet table in the center of the room; this way, two lines of guests may serve themselves on both sides at once. Set plates in two stacks at one end of the table, with napkins and flatware alongside. Individual sets of utensils can be either rolled in a cloth napkin or set upright in attractive canisters—forks in one, knives in the second, spoons in the third. Choose a centerpiece that makes a colorful focal point but isn't so elaborate that it takes up space better used for the food. If you must place the table against the wall, put the plates and the main dish at the end that allows for the best flow of traffic.

When setting out the food, put twin dishes of the main dish (or dishes), vegetables, salads, bread, and sauces and condiments on both sides of the table so that guests need only pass down one side; this speeds the service and keeps bumps and tangles to a minimum.

Outfitted Buffet Table in Center of Room;
Sideboard Nearby Holding Beverages

Entertainming
at Home

SEATED OR NOT?

If the buffet is a seated one, you'll probably be using the dining table and a few folding card tables, which should be covered with tablecloths unless they have a particularly nice finish. Set the places just as you would for any seated dinner (see page 447). A major plus: Since the guests need not carry flatware, napkins, or glasses with them, considerable space is saved on the buffet table.

If you're not setting tables for your buffet, see to it that there is enough room for every guest to be able to sit down somewhere, hold a plate, and set down a glass. You can avoid accidents—and make things easier for your guests at the same time—by placing a small folding table near each chair that isn't within reach of a coffee table or side table.

THE FOOD IS SERVED

When all the guests have arrived and the allotted time for drinks is over, announce that dinnertime has arrived. Your guests, who are always served before the host and hostess, should then form a line around the table, helping themselves to your artfully arranged buffet.

After serving themselves, guests simply take their plates and sit wherever they choose, whether tables are set or not. Guests then return to the table for as many helpings as they like. When finished, they remove their empty plates to a designated table or sideboard unless there is a server to pick them up. If small side tables have been placed around the room, you or your help should remove them after the meal to provide room for conversational groups or planned activities, if any.

BUFFET BEVERAGES

If possible, place beverages and glasses on a separate sideboard or nearby table. If the buffet is a seated one, place water glasses on the tables and fill them before guests sit down. Wineglasses should also be at the places but should never be filled in advance; instead, the host (or a server) passes the wine when everyone is seated. Alternatively, one or two opened bottles of wine can be placed on each table and poured by anyone who chooses.

As host, you'll be more relaxed at a large informal buffet—and your guests more appreciative—if you suggest that all help themselves to drinks from the sideboard or fridge. When you spot someone who's engaged in a conversation and holding an empty glass, do ask if you can refill it. But try not to interrupt:

At informal dinners or buffets, there are some things a polite guest remembers to do simply as a matter of course. (For behavior at the table, see Business Meals, page 391.) He or she is likely to . . .

- BRING SOMETHING. A bottle of wine is the usual hostess gift. It is the prerogative of the host or hostess to serve the wine at the party. The guest might make it easy for them to have the wine later, saying something on the order of "You and Kathy may want to save this for your next candlelight dinner." Other choices might be a small houseplant or a top-of-the-line English marmalade or jam. Cut flowers are better sent to a hostess on the day of the party or the day after as a thank you; showing up with them unannounced gives a busy hostess one more thing to do.

- FORGO THE HOUSE TOUR. Respect your host's privacy and don't wander uninvited into other rooms. Another dictum: No matter how hard it is to resist peeking into the medicine cabinet, don't. It's the host's prerogative to decide what you will see in his home and what you won't.

- OFFER TO HELP YOUR HOSTS. It's possible that at some point you'll be standing with the host or hostess in the kitchen as they go about readying the food. Ask if there is anything you can do. You may be asked to chop the onions or wash and dry the lettuce, or you may not—but your gesture will be appreciated.

- LOOK OUT FOR OTHERS. At a buffet, it's only polite to offer to fill the plate for elderly people who may have trouble doing it for themselves, or for those who are disabled.

- BE FLEXIBLE ABOUT SEATING. If the host makes no suggestion about which chair at the table you should take, ask the group as a whole: "Well, who wants to sit next to whom? I'll be fine anywhere."

- ACT SATISFIED. Asking for steak sauce or anything else when it's not on the table may suggest you think the meal somehow insufficient. If something on your plate is not to your liking, at least take a bite or two, and refrain from announcing "I'm not really a big fan of Brussels sprouts."

- OFFER TO HELP STRAIGHTEN UP. You can volunteer to collect bottles and glasses and cart them to the kitchen, scrape plates into the garbage, or even wash and dry the dishes. Take no for an answer only if your hosts insist.

- THANK THE HOST TWICE. In some parts of the country, a second thank you by phone is customary the day after the party (the first having been delivered on leaving the party, of course)—a gesture that's equally gracious anywhere. If the business dinner or buffet was given by your boss, someone senior to you, or a client, a written thank-you note is in order. In fact, your fellow coworker would be pleased to receive your note as well.

Signaling the guest with a questioning look will probably be responded to with a smile and a glass held out in your direction.

If iced beverages are served, stacks of coasters should be set out around the room so that sweating glasses won't leave rings on tabletops. Also, it's smart to use tumblers or highball glasses, which are steadier than goblets—if a guest is sitting out of reach of a raised surface and must set her glass on the floor, her drink is less likely to spill.

If coffee has been placed on the sideboard, guests may serve themselves at any time. Otherwise, the host or hostess takes a tray set with cups, a coffeepot, cream, and sugar into the living room to serve after dinner.

PART X

DOING
BUSINESS
ABROAD

The United States may be the economic powerhouse of the world economy, but the era of the Ugly American is over. When on foreign shores or just across the border, smart business travelers understand that they must leave certain behaviors and habits behind; to do business abroad requires respect for and adherence to local cultures and customs. After all, you are a guest in someone else's home country—a guest who will be welcomed back if you show an appreciation of and a sensitivity to your hosts' ways of living and working.

Long-term international relationships can rise and fall on real or perceived slights and discourtesies, and the following chapters examine the ways you can avoid cross-cultural missteps and mistakes that can jeopardize a profitable business deal. The first shows you how to prepare for encountering a new culture and provides tips on taking care of such practical matters as passports and credit cards. The second discusses dealing with language barriers, as well as general considerations about dining, dress, and gift-giving. The final chapter gives country-by-country advice for behavior for the businessperson in more than 50 foreign countries—variations in business and social styles as well as tips on how to leave your own cultural and political baggage at home.

CHAPTER 34

BEFORE YOU GO

B e prepared" takes on new meaning whenever you travel overseas with the aim of doing business. When as an American you land on foreign soil, pass through customs, and step out into an unfamiliar world, remind yourself of this: You are representing your country as much as your company. How you behave will either reinforce or counteract your hosts' conception of Americans, which in turn will affect the outcome of your business negotiations.

A shrinking globe has made citizens of the United States more aware of the world outside their country, and few traces of the arrogant, jingoistic Ugly American of the post-World War II era remain. Ignorance, rather than arrogance, is today's businessperson's unpardonable sin. With more nations our trade partners than ever before, there are customs and courtesies to be learned—a respectful undertaking that shows your cultural sensitivity.

Naturally, one of the first steps you or your company should take is finding out whether there are any State Department warnings you ought to know about before traveling to your destination. The State Department's Web site at http://travel.state.gov/travel_warnings.html gives you not only warnings of political unrest but of currency, entry regulations, driving conditions, and more. That done, you should prepare an itinerary for your hosts, your office, and your family. (See The Thoughtful Traveler, page 244.)

CUSTOMS AND CULTURE

At minimum you should know the basic facts about the country you're visiting (see page 463). But when you exhibit more than a nodding acquaintance, you impress your hosts and all others you meet with your appreciation of the nation, the culture, and the individuals themselves.

Begin your minicourse on a country by skimming the surface and then digging deeper. If you have access to the Internet, use travel or society links to find basic facts and explore specific areas of a country's culture. An almanac and encyclopedia will do nicely. Whether your search begins electronically or between book covers, graduate to perusing a few travel guidebooks for background on history and culture. (Note that some guidebooks are better than others at probing the native culture.) You could then check your local library and bookstores for histories and other books (say, translations of classic and current literature), and choose one or two that interest you. Once you arrive, keep abreast of local events by reading regional English-language newspapers.

Be warned, however, that culture is not determined solely by national boundaries. Basque and Andalucia, regions of Spain, have distinctly different cultures, as do Sicily and Tuscany, in Italy. Not all Asian countries have the same manners and mores as Japan. Nor does language determine culture—witness the Americans and the British.

SEX, POLITICS, AND RELIGION

The saying that one should never discuss religion, politics, or sex in polite company applies twice over in foreign countries. Sex as a topic (in the sense of gender as well as in the sense of sex) is definitely off-limits, since you could end up on the wrong side of even a seemingly objective discussion of women in the workplace. As one writer on cultural diversity has put it, the greatest cultural divide is gender.

A Hot Topic

Politics is a hot topic in much of the world—usually too hot to touch. Never criticize the leaders or government of your host country, and never criticize your own. If, as is likely, you're quizzed about American politics or policy (either national or international), graciously admit that you're no expert in such matters. Explain that because your views are no more valid than those of any other American, you'd rather not say anything that might be taken as a representative national view. If you think this too circumspect, remember how quickly affairs can change at home and in the rest of the world, as hot spots erupt unexpectedly: An acceptable view you hold today may by next week become provocative to your host. Remember, too, that a businessperson is more of an ambassador for his or her country than is a garden-variety tourist.

It's hard to draw a line between discussions of world affairs and politics. Although you probably know it's rarely wise to be drawn into conversation about the Middle East, for example, talk of economics, development, and other subjects that touch on world politics are not off-limits in most other countries.

The important thing is to be well informed and open-minded—and to remember that all the world loves a good listener.

Concerning Religion

Wherever you're headed, make yourself aware of the country's dominant religion. Also take note of its religious and secular holidays. You don't want to ask for a business appointment on July 14 in France—it's Bastille Day; neither do you want to arrive for a business meeting in Jerusalem on a Friday afternoon, when everything is closed in preparation for the Jewish Sabbath.

KNOW THE BASICS

If before you travel you're unable to scratch beneath the surface of a country, at the very least acquaint yourself with the framework of its society. Reliable quick sources of basic facts are the Internet and almanacs, followed by recent editions of encyclopedias. Look up the following:

- **The correct name of the country you're visiting.** Mexico is officially the United Mexican States. Germany is the Federal Republic of Germany, even though there's no longer a German Democratic Republic (East Germany).
- **The form of government**—e.g., a parliamentary democracy, a constitutional democracy—and what that means. A country can call itself a republic and still be a dictatorship.
- **The nation's capital.**
- **Names of the ruler or top government official.** Note that in most countries, the president is not as important as the prime minister.
- **Whether there is a national religion and what it is.** Do not assume that all Arab countries are Muslim or vice versa.
- **National holidays,** including religious holidays and official days of rest.
- **What dietary laws are observed.**
- **Leading industries and agricultural products.**
- **Prominent geographical features.** If you're visiting, say, Wuerzburg in Germany, you should know its river is the Main, not the Rhine.
- **Great cultural landmarks:** museums, temples, mosques, cathedrals, seats of learning.
- **Great men and women:** Nobel Prize winners for peace and literature and in the field your host may be working in, such as chemistry or medicine; famous musicians, writers, and artists; famous athletes and other popular culture figures.
- **The country's most popular sports.**

Religious customs are a still more important concern. If you're on your way to Thailand, have you learned that it's sacrilegious to photograph any statue or other image of Buddha? Or that if you're accompanying your Muslim host in Saudi Arabia he may stop for prayer several times during the day? Such are the vagaries of religions of which you may know little, but whose orthodoxies and conventions you must nonetheless respect. This, in turn, shows respect for your host and translates into more successful business dealings.

PRACTICAL CONCERNS

What do passports, visas, credit cards, currency, and other paraphernalia of overseas travel have to do with behavior? Nothing in themselves, but your lack of attention to such items can disrupt your visit (and wreak havoc in some cases), creating embarrassment for you and inconvenience for your hosts.

PASSPORTS AND VISAS

To leave or enter the United States, you must generally have a passport. Whether needed or not, a valid passport is the best documentation of U.S. citizenship. When applying for a passport for the first time, you must appear in person at either 1) a passport agency, 2) a county, state, or federal clerk's office, or 3) a Post Office that accepts passport applications. Passport agencies are found in several major cities and tend to have the longest lines during the first six months of the year. Clerk of Courts offices (of which there are some 2,500 nationwide) and designated Post Offices (around 1,100) are less crowded at any time of the year.

As a first-time applicant, you have to present evidence of citizenship, such as a certified copy of your birth certificate or your certificate of naturalization; a driver's license or other piece of personal identification with a picture; and two passport photos, which you can have taken quickly and cheaply (usually with a Polaroid camera) at photo processing stores or other designated outlets. (Since the requirements for these photos are very specific, don't attempt to take them yourself.) You must also complete an application form and pay fees.

If you lose your passport in the United States, notify the nearest passport agency or Passport Services in Washington, D.C. If the loss occurs in a foreign country, report it to the nearest U.S. Embassy or Consulate or the local police department. It's easier to replace a lost passport if you photocopy the data page ahead of time and keep the copy in a separate place when you travel.

Certain countries will not allow you to enter without a visa. To find out whether a visa is required and how to obtain one, call the consulate or embassy of the country you plan to visit, not an agency of the United States; the responsibility to grant and issue visas is the country's alone.

MONEY AND CREDIT CARDS

In the days before you take your trip, start checking the currency conversion tables in your newspaper. Although you'll get a better rate when you exchange dollars for currency overseas, you should arrive with enough of the local currency to pay for your transportation from the airport to your hotel—even if you plan to be met by your host or a driver.

In addition to a small amount of foreign currency, you'll need to take along U.S. dollars, travelers' checks, your ATM card, and two credit cards—one or the other of which may not be accepted everywhere, especially outside large cities. Probably the easiest and least expensive way to obtain local currency while traveling is to use a local bank's ATM machine. Before you leave, find out whether you'll be able to use your regular PIN number or whether the bank must issue you a new one for your travels.

ANOTHER PRECAUTION TO TAKE BEFORE YOU LEAVE: Let your credit card companies know that you're traveling, and where. Given the eagerness of credit card companies to prevent fraud, the computer may reject your card in a new, faraway place, thinking it could have been stolen. Also, if you use a corporate credit card, make sure your company authorizes your using it abroad; otherwise, it, too, could be rejected.

It's a good idea to photocopy your credit cards before you leave; if a card is lost or stolen, you'll have the number on hand to report it. Also take with you copies of the toll-free numbers of your credit card companies; keep one copy in your suitcase, another in a briefcase or tucked in your inside jacket pocket.

The chance that credit cards may not be accepted means making sure that you have enough local currency on hand to cover all foreseen expenses as you begin the day—meals, transportation, and entertainment. Getting caught without local money—and having to put the pinch on your host—could lose you much more than "face." Learn as quickly as you can what the local currency looks like—the denominations of the bills and the coins, and the amounts signified by the various coins.

You can carry your bank checkbook with you, but don't plan on using it except in cases of extreme emergency. Checks are difficult to cash in most places abroad, and your money needs should be covered by cash, traveler's checks, your ATM card, and credit cards.

IN CASE OF EMERGENCY

The U.S. Consulate is the first place to call in emergencies, so learn of its location and telephone number in the country you're visiting. Should you need the name of an English-speaking doctor or a hospital, the Consulate can give you one. Their personnel can also help if you should get into trouble with the police or want to know whether a political crisis warrants your leaving the country. If you're going to be in the country for any length of time or are concerned about potential danger, be sure to register with the consulate once you've arrived. Registering will give them permission to give your family and friends information about your welfare.

Another resource in emergencies is the Citizens Emergency Center at 202–647–5225 or, on the Internet, the State Department's Web site at http://travel. state.gov/travel_warnings.html.

BUSINESS CARDS

One writer on international trade declares that your business card, carefully created for use in the country you visit, is the one card you should never leave home without. The expense is smaller than you might think. But what should you put on it for the convenience of your international cohorts?

- After your name, your title—as well as your function—should be shown. For example, if you function as the associate director of training for the Human Resources department, give an additional title if you have one, such as assistant vice president. In case your title or position is one that a foreigner might not understand, consider putting a "plain English" version is parentheses—for example, "Human Resources (Personnel)."
- Don't omit your title, even if it's a junior one. In many countries, particularly Latin American ones, hosts who don't know your title won't know how to treat you or whom they should designate to do business with you. But avoid any temptation to exaggerate your position—being found out could have serious consequences, even to the point of wrecking the planned negotiations.
- If English isn't commonly spoken in your destination, print one side of your card in English and the other in the native language. Even in countries where English is the second language, you'll be less likely to find English speakers in small towns than in the larger centers of trade.
- Some experts suggest that you can have your cards printed once you are overseas—but if you don't know the language yourself, be careful who you give this assignment to. Ask for a recommendation from your hosts.

EXCHANGING CARDS

In many countries, the exchange of cards follows a certain protocol. There may be a designated time for presenting cards—for example, at the beginning of a meeting or after you've been introduced. In some countries, good manners dictate that you present the card with both hands, or with the foreign-language side up. When you receive a card, don't just stick it in your pocket. Read it right away and place it in your own card case or briefcase.

You may be surprised at how many cards identify the person as "Doctor," particularly in Europe. Unlike in the United States, men and women with advanced degrees, or even university graduates, legitimately go by the title. Even if to you the title isn't meaningful, it's a faux pas not to use it.

CHAPTER 35

LANGUAGE AND OTHER MATTERS

While the United States has the world's largest economy and its business practices are for the most part respected, the way business is done in the rest of the world remains strictly local. Take this statement very seriously: Unless you accept the validity of other cultures' ways of conducting business and try to abide by them, your dealings will be less effective than they could be or, worse, fail. Major differences often have less to do with negotiating and decision-making than with how well you'll be able to communicate with your foreign counterparts, along with an understanding of the social aspects.

Social aspects? Yes. In the U.S., efficiency comes first and foremost when doing business, but the production-line mentality doesn't always carry over in other countries. Though your training and inclination may tell you to get right down to brass tacks, on other continents such haste may be considered inappropriate. In the Middle East, for example, your host may serve rounds and rounds of tea before touching on business matters.

The finer points of negotiating and decision-making depend on the specific organization with which you're dealing, and in which country and which field. For these particulars, an excellent teacher can be a fellow American who has had experience doing business at the same company and can tell you what to expect. This chapter briefly reviews the broader areas of concern for business people abroad—pointers about communication, forms of address, attitudes toward punctuality, business dress, visiting and entertaining, and gift giving. (For more specific information, see Adjusting Your Cultural Lens, page 479.)

FORGING PERSONAL RELATIONSHIPS

In many countries, forging a personal relationship is an important part of your business dealings. While socializing, your hosts get to know you. If you're patient, you'll establish trust—an important element in your foreign counterparts' decisions to do business with you. Conversely, if you appear too eager to talk business, they may think you begrudge the time you spend with them.

Learn to be the gracious guest, starting with a self-taught mini-course on the culture of the country (see Customs and Culture, page 461). Answer questions about American life in a way that can't be conceived as boasting. Don't be surprised if the conversation turns to music, gardening, good places to vacation in winter, or preferences in wine or beer. Such sociability does not, however, give you permission to ask personal questions; the American's readiness to "open up" isn't typical of the rest of the world.

THE IMPORTANCE OF NAMES AND TITLES

As for names, don't confuse developing social relationships with familiarity; remember that for an American, foreign names and forms of address are ripe with the opportunity for mistakes and embarrassment. Doing research ahead of time helps, but you still need to pay especially close attention to names during introductions—a truth well illustrated by the fact that in Spanish-speaking countries a person bears both his parents' surnames (see page 481).

Always address people by their proper titles. Señor and Madame are straightforward, but others can be confusing—for example, Herr Docktor, the German title given not only to a medical doctor but any man with an advanced degree. When in England, don't automatically call a dentist "Doctor"; surprisingly, "Mister" or "Miss" ["Ms."] is the proper title for people at dentistry's highest levels. An engineer in the United States is known simply as "Mister," but in South America, Europe, and Asia, address him as "Engineer."

About the use of first names: In most countries outside the United States, it will be a long time before you're on a first-name basis with your host and others you meet formally—perhaps never. Let your overseas business colleague suggest using first names, but do not do it yourself.

DEFERRING TO AGE

The youth culture hasn't pervaded other cultures to the degree it has in America. Even if you're in your thirties and on the fast track back home, when abroad show respect for businesspeople who are older than you are—even those in a lower position. Be deferential, holding the door for them and allowing them to be seated first. Show similar respect for anyone who has a more senior position than you do. If you happen to be younger than anyone around,

Language and Other Matters

dress and act in the most mature manner you can muster, a way of demonstrating your business experience and acumen.

RESPECTING WORK ETHICS

Don't be surprised when you don't meet a lot of workaholics abroad. In many places, family and private life, not work, is the most important part of the businessperson's world. If you feel you could close the deal or end the meeting if you and your host were to work for an extra couple of hours, resist the temptation to suggest it; it's likely that you'll be either rejected or resented. Never interpret this difference in attitude to mean that your foreign counterparts are lazy or indifferent. They may be every bit as serious and meticulous about their work but just have a different attitude toward timing than many Americans have; in general, closing shop for the day is not seen as a reason for feeling guilty.

A QUESTION OF TIMING

Business hours may vary from those in the United States, and it's easy enough to learn what they are. In former times, it was common practice in Europe and Latin America for businesses to close for two or more hours during the day, a custom that still persists in Greece, Italy, and some other southerly countries. Also know that retail stores often close for an hour or two during the lunch hour, even in countries that otherwise keep American-style hours.

Workweeks also vary. Shops as well as offices may close on Saturday afternoons. In China, the business week is Monday through Saturday, as it is in Japan and other non-Muslim countries in Asia. In Israel, the workweek is Sunday through Friday, with stores and offices closing on Friday at about noon. Muslim countries observe Friday as their Sabbath, and no business is done, with Thursdays sometimes only a half day. This doesn't necessarily mean, however, that some people don't work beyond their official business hours.

Punctuality will not be faulted in any country, but don't consider it an affront if you're kept waiting for half an hour or so, especially in Latin America. Also, don't forget that traffic jams are hardly confined to the industrialized West.

DEALING WITH LANGUAGE BARRIERS

Americans don't seem to mind being counted among the least linguistically sophisticated people in the developed world. As the globe shrinks and international trade booms, language requirements in U.S. schools and colleges remain minimal. The United States is situated directly north of Spanish-speaking Mexico and Central and South America; yet while all are major trading partners, few Americans other than those whose native language is Spanish can claim fluency in the language. What's more, a reading knowledge of French or German, the other major international languages after English, is required for many graduate studies—but not for MBAs. Too many of us think of French as unpronounceable and German as unmanageable, and let it go at that.

If you think that in most countries businesspeople speak English, you're right. One study shows that English is the native language of 12 countries and the official or second language of more than 40 others. In most of the rest of the world, English is widely studied. But don't let these facts lull you into complacency. American English is loaded with idioms and eccentric circumlocutions, and people who speak English as a second language may be familiar with all or none. While you may think they understand what you're saying, they may be hearing something else.

SPEAKING ENGLISH ABROAD

Conversational bloopers may make funny stories over the dinner table, but when you're in a business situation they can have serious consequences. Do everything you can to help other people understand you and to make your conversation in English easier for them.

- **EASY DOES IT.** Speak clearly and not too fast, enunciating carefully. If you have a regional accent, try to use standard English pronunciations. Your Southern accent may charm other Americans, but in Spain or Sweden it could make you difficult to understand.
- **KEEP VOCABULARY SIMPLE.** Don't use slang, regionalisms, colloquialisms, euphemisms, neologisms, or similes. If you ask where the bathroom or rest room is, you may never get there in time; simply ask for the toilet or lavatory. Similarly, if you say that something is "dead as a doornail" or "grows like Topsy," anticipate a puzzled look.
- **DEFINE TERMS.** Make sure that your overseas counterpart has the same understanding of business and legal terms as you. It may be that in your specialized area, such as computer technology, the same terms are used worldwide—but you shouldn't always assume so.
- **BE CAREFUL WITH NUMBERS.** When using numbers in a business discussion, it may be necessary to write them down and show them, since numbers can be expressed in different ways. To the English a billion is a million million, but to Americans, only 1,000 million. In Germany, 87 is

TRANSLATING FROM THE ENGLISH

In Britain, Australia, New Zealand, and other countries where English is the native language, you'll hear words and idioms that are likely to confound you. In most of the Commonwealth, the hood of a car is a "bonnet," and the "boot" is the trunk. The word "napkin" means "diaper," and a "serviette" is what Americans call a napkin. The toilet is often referred to as the "loo," and when someone excuses himself "to spend a penny," that's where he's going. In England, "buggered" is a rude word, but in Australia it means exhausted. In either place, if someone says he'll "knock you up," don't let your jaw drop; it means he'll stop by to pick you up for your meeting.

With its citizens' fondness for shortening words, Australia is the international capital of the diminutive. Breakfast is "brekky," a pregnant woman is said to be "preggers," a garbageman is a "garbo" (no relation to the late screen legend), a milkman, a "milko." And speaking of milk, what Americans know as a corner shop or deli the Australians often call a "milk bar."

expressed as seven and eighty, and a German quickly making the translation might think you mean 78.

- **WATCH FOR SIGNS.** Watch the faces of your listeners; you won't have a hard time noticing when they've lost the train of conversation.
- **OVER AND AGAIN.** Repeat what you are saying as often as necessary to make sure you're correctly understood.

UNDERSTANDING BODY LANGUAGE

Two words you should know about body language: Watch it. Watch it in yourself and look for it in others. Although your facial expressions, stance, and gestures are basic to communication, they are easily misunderstood. An example: In the United States, when you look directly at the speaker's face in a meeting you mean to show he or she has your full attention. But in Asian countries, making eye contact is considered impolite. Even in the United States extreme eye contact, or staring, is rude, and in some countries it could get you into trouble.

Gestures are similarly perilous. You'll be well advised never to point your finger or to snap your fingers. Beckoning with a curled index finger is widely considered offensive. Waving your hand, arm raised, in greeting or to get someone's attention may be misunderstood as a "no" signal. The following gestures should be avoided unless you're absolutely sure that they have the same meaning in your host country as in the United States:

The Etiquette Advantage in Business

472

- Thumbs up.
- The OK sign—making a circle with your thumb and forefinger (obscene in Japan and elsewhere).
- "V" for victory.

Also, when in Bulgaria, remember that shaking your head from side to side means yes, not no.

PERSONAL SPACE AND OTHER BASICS

Once you've been in a country for a while, you'll probably get the feel of the local body language. Meanwhile, here are a few guidelines:

- **SPACING YOURSELF.** "Give me space" is a byword in the United States and other parts of the world, and you should take it literally. The distance kept between yourself and others is important, and getting too close or moving too far away can be misconstrued as unwanted familiarity or standoffishness. North Americans and Europeans alike are comfortable standing some two to three feet apart. The Japanese and other Asians require more space, but the rest of the world gets closer.
- **HANDSHAKES.** In North America and Europe, a firm handshake is an appropriate form of greeting. In Asia and the Middle East, where hand-shaking is still relatively new, the grip is gentler; a too-hearty grip could be interpreted as aggressive.

  In Islamic countries, offering your hand to a woman is highly offensive. At the other extreme, it's said that you can never shake hands too much in France, where women shake hands as freely and often as men.
- **BOWING AND SIMILAR GREETINGS.** In Japan and some other Asian countries, the bow is the equivalent of the handshake. In rank-conscious Japan, the person of inferior rank bows first and lowest. The Indians and Thai may place their hands together at the chest in a prayerlike gesture as a form of greeting.
- **TOUCHING.** North Americans don't engage in casual touching, but Latin Americans and southern Europeans do. If a native jabs you with his finger to make a point or touches your arm in conversation, don't be offended. In Arab, Southeast Asian, and Pacific Island nations, a man may even find his male host taking his hand. Do not misconstrue these gestures, but don't try to copy them either.

Language and Other Matters

SPEAKING IN A FOREIGN LANGUAGE

It is a courtesy to your foreign hosts to have some small familiarity with their language—knowing the words for "please," "thank you," "good morning," "good afternoon," "good night," "hello," and "good-bye." Carry a pocket foreign-language dictionary so that you can look up words and communicate with people who may not understand English—hotel and restaurant employees, for example.

Because your hosts will usually have a better grasp of the English language than you do of theirs (even though you may have studied their language for several years in high school or college), you'd be wise not to converse with them in their language. Certainly never conduct business in a foreign language without an interpreter present, and refrain from prolonged social conversation in your host's language until you've established a good relationship with him or her; the chances of making an embarrassing error are too great. Furthermore, although many natives appreciate a stranger's attempt to speak their language, some can be intolerant of poor execution.

USING TRANSLATORS AND INTERPRETERS

The word interpreter usually brings to mind those phenomenal men and women who translate as the speaker speaks, their words following at a fast clip. Known as simultaneous translators, they are not the kind of interpreter the average businessperson uses. More widely used are consecutive interpreters, who speak after the speaker has completed a few sentences. Though you may think this is easy for anyone who is fluent in two languages—yours and the language of the person with whom you're dealing—it is not.

To make sure you get what you bargained for, use only professional translators. To avoid a conflict of interest, make sure that they are in your employ, not hired by your counterpart. Ask for recommendations from friends who have done business in your destination, or see whether your company can handle the hiring.

BEFORE THE MEETING

To let your interpreter get acquainted with your way of speaking, spend some time with him or her beforehand. This will also help you to gauge whether her English is idiomatic. Go over the agenda for the meeting, and make sure she can handle technical as well as business terms.

Prepare visual aids, if possible, to clarify and reinforce your and your translator's spoken words. Use both languages on charts and graphs, which can also serve later as confirmation of what you said. Acquaint your interpreter with the visual aids before the meeting.

Let your interpreter know the appropriate dress for the occasion. If you think she should wear business clothes, make sure she knows it. Her clothing should be subdued and unobtrusive; it is you, not she, who's the center of attention. If the occasion is formal, ask her to wear a formal dress; for a male interpreter, ask him to wear black-tie attire, or at least a dark suit.

AT THE MEETING

The translator is usually seated at the table between the two major players who need her—for example, you and your host. On more formal occasions, such as a dinner, she will sit slightly behind them. Although she does not expect to join you in eating dinner, see to it that she has a meal either before or after the occasion.

When you speak through an interpreter, many of the same rules apply as when you speak English with a non-native speaker. Speak slowly and distinctly, avoid slang and regionalisms, and watch the host for signs that he's tuning out. Always address the listener, not the interpreter.

Keep your sentences short, and speak only a few before stopping for translation. Intermittently ask your host whether he is clear about what you're saying or has any questions. Be expressive as you speak, and show concentration as you listen. Smile, but don't tell jokes; despite your interpreter's best efforts, humor rarely translates well.

Don't interrupt your interpreter, but also don't hesitate to stop the meeting to ask him about anything that isn't clear to you. When the meeting is over, have the interpreter go over what was said and her impressions of your counterpart's reactions. Also ask her about anything you did not understand. Finally, have a report drafted in English of the conclusions or agreements reached during the meeting.

TO TRANSLATE CORRESPONDENCE?

In most cases, you won't need a translation for your English-language correspondence with an overseas organization. Many businessmen who wouldn't trust themselves to negotiate with you verbally are perfectly able to read and understand your letters and to answer them in English. When you do need a

Language and Other Matters

translator for your business letters, make sure you hire a true professional—one who can convey your meaning, not one who will merely translate words literally from one language to another.

DIFFERENCES IN DRESS

Whether the adage "clothes make the man" holds true today is debatable, but clothes do *reveal* the businessman and businesswoman. Until you've visited a country a few times and know the dress code, dress conservatively. For men, a dark suit and dark tie are safe bets, and white shirts are the prevailing choice in most countries. Although the buttoned-up look may not appeal to you, you discard it at your own risk—and the risk of your business. For women, sticking to the traditional dress code is key, and on the modest side at that.

In most countries, fabrics that are obviously synthetic signify a tourist. If you are traveling for pleasure you may not care what others think, but on business trips you should either wear natural fabrics (cotton, wool, linen, silk) or rayon and other synthetics that have been retooled to lose their unattractive sheen.

MEN'S CLOTHING

In warmer climates, men can wear light-colored suits. For cool comfort, do as the natives do: In Singapore, men wear long-sleeved shirts and carry their jackets (in case of over-air-conditioned rooms). In Latin American countries, men wear loose shirts called *guayaberas,* which are not tucked in, and some Asian countries have similar comfortable regulation dress for men. First check with your host to see whether it is appropriate for you to wear the traditional garment or whether you would merely look silly. If you get the go-ahead, don't scour your hometown in search of such shirts; wear your own white shirt until you have the chance to buy some local garb.

Ties, too, can be problematic. In England, if you wear a striped tie, there's the chance you could be sporting some Englishman's "old school tie." In other countries, certain colors are inappropriate; white, for example, is a color symbolic of mourning. To be safe, stick to dark, solid colors.

WOMEN'S CLOTHING

Businesswomen should generally choose conservative suits and dresses (not slacks) and "sensible shoes" with medium height heels. Skirts and dresses should not go far above the knee in Western countries; in other countries, keep the hemline below the knee and avoid sleeveless blouses and tops, as well as scoop-neck or other low necklines. Wear only quality jewelry and not too much of it; rings on every finger, or a stud in your nose, will only cause ridicule in most places. Similarly, keep your cosmetics understated. Avoid religious jewelry, too.

DINING AND DRINKING

Whether you are the guest or the host, be prompt. As the host, make arrangements in advance. If you need help in finding a suitable restaurant, ask for the hotel concierge's help. When ordering dinner or wine, you may ask your guests if he can suggest local specialties. When invited to someone's home, send flowers or take along a box of fine chocolates.

Do as your mother told you when she said to pick up the same fork your hostess does. In other words, always watch your native host or guest and follow his example. If you're traveling to China or Japan, you should learn to handle chopsticks. In Middle Eastern countries, never eat with your left hand, which is considered unclean. If you find yourself being served a strange dish anywhere, eat it whether or not you like it—or even know what it is. One travel expert suggests that you not ask what animal the dish came from—it's easier to down a sheep's eyeball when it remains unidentified.

Toasting

Except in Muslim countries, drinking usually accompanies dining—and drinking calls for toasting. (Remember that if you're a nondrinker, this is one time that your hosts should show their understanding; it's perfectly fine to toast with a drink that is nonalcoholic.) For occasions that are somewhat formal, you should have a toast prepared in advance unless you're an accomplished extemporaneous speaker. Make it short and gracious, acknowledging the hospitality of your host. Wherever you are, etiquette calls for the host to make the first toast, so you can take your cue from him. Don't attempt a humorous toast—it could be misunderstood or considered in bad taste.

When drinking informally, you may be expected to utter a short one-word or one-phrase toast—*"a votre santé"* in France, or just *"santé"* (health); in Germany, *"prosit"* means the same. Americans unaccustomed to toasting may find themselves drinking more than they intended, so beware. (See also Foreign-Language Toasts, page 440.)

GIFT GIVING

In countries outside the United States, many rules pertain to the giving of gifts, and not following them is a serious breach of etiquette. One rule common to virtually all countries is to have the gift beautifully wrapped. (As necessary, gift-giving advice is included in Adjusting Your Cultural Lens, page 479.)

A sampling of customs: The Japanese give and expect gifts on numerous occasions, and the wrapping is perhaps as important as the present itself. In some Asian countries, clocks and handkerchiefs symbolize mourning and are not given as gifts. In other countries, bringing wine to a dinner party indicates that you think either that the host will not have enough or that it won't be of sufficient quality. The French, it is said, appreciate music or a book, and the fatter the book the better; American bestsellers are a good choice. In any country, it would be hard to go wrong giving a fine pen or pen-and-pencil set or a coffee-table picture book with an American theme.

Never give liquor to someone of the Muslim religion or nonkosher food to an Orthodox Jew in Israel (or elsewhere). Nor should you give gifts of clothing, perfume, or cosmetics, which are in poor taste almost everywhere, as are corporate gifts with a logo that is less than subtle.

MAKE IT FIT

Your gift should be tasteful but not too expensive. Moreover, it should be fitting. What you give or send to the host who has entertained you one evening in his home is not what you should give a department head who has spent one or two days attending your presentations, introducing you to his colleagues, and arranging meetings for you. To the former you might bring fresh flowers or a box of fine chocolates. To the latter you should give a more lasting present, one from the United States and better yet from your state; it is acceptable to send it after you return home. The more you research the custom of your host's country and his individual taste, the more likely your gift will successfully convey your appreciation.

CHAPTER 36

ADJUSTING YOUR CULTURAL LENS

Seasoned international business travelers who spend much of their time in Tokyo or Berlin know the score. They step off the plane equipped with the finer points of doing business the Japanese or German way as part and parcel of their baggage—the nuances of negotiating, the demands of decision-making. But not everyone is so lucky. In the beginning, businesspeople who are new to the game and take a seat at the conference table in São Paulo, Seoul, or Stockholm have little more to fall back on than acquainting themselves with the culture—culture being the larger context within which dynamics of the international business meeting are juggled.

Cultural sensitivity to local social customs is the topic of this chapter, a sensitivity that crosses over into any business dealings you undertake. Brief overviews, their lengths weighted to the country's prominence in the global business arena, acquaint you with things you should know about meeting, greeting, and—in many cases—being entertained and exchanging gifts. A sampling of social taboos warns of potentially serious faux pas.

N O T E : Books devoted entirely to the subject of doing business abroad and discussions with people who are experienced in doing business in specific countries are your best sources before you travel internationally on business. The observations that follow are intended to encapsulate the differences in attitude and customs of some 60 countries on five continents—to whet your appetite for what, with proper preparation, can become a rich meal.

CANADA

Canada is without doubt the place that presents the fewest challenges to American business people, what with the shared border and culture. But that hardly means that Americans should act as if they've simply crossed into another state. Canadians recognize their particular heritage and expect Americans to do the same. As befits the residents of a former British colony whose ties to the mother country were never broken by rebellion and war, the businesspeople of Canada are slightly more reserved than their U.S. counterparts. Realize, too, that Canadians are ethnically diverse, with large numbers of immigrants from Asia, Africa, and Europe, in addition to the indigenous Indians and Inuit.

French-speaking Quebec is a country within a country, where an independence party continues its quest for sovereignty. Although strict French-language requirements exist in Quebec, the reality is that the Quebecois do business in English, and in much the same way as their English-speaking counterparts.

Meeting and greeting. Business meetings, usually held in the morning, are generally formal and start on time. Once the subject is tackled, Canadians are less likely than their U.S. counterparts to stray from it. The American propensity for hype is quickly recognized by Canadians, who generally expect the proceedings to be stripped of all but the facts.

Behavior during introductions is virtually identical to that in the U.S., except that both English-speaking and French Canadians are less likely to use first names straight off. French Canadians tend to shake hands on leaving as well as greeting and often embrace or kiss the cheeks of close friends.

Visiting and entertaining. Canadian businesspeople normally entertain at a restaurant instead of inviting you to their homes; in the western provinces, you may be invited to an outdoor barbecue. Business dinners are considered primarily social.

Gifts. Gifts are sometimes exchanged (and unwrapped on the spot) after a business deal is closed, but they should be kept on the modest side lest 1they suggest ostentation— something the Canadians frown on.

Social taboos. Except in the North American geographical sense, don't speak of Canadians as part of "us." The V for victory sign, when flashed with the palm inward, is taken as an insult. In Quebec, it's bad manners to eat while walking down the street.

LATIN AMERICA

In Latin America, being "fashionably late" for business meetings and social functions is more than just a figure of speech—it's something of a lifestyle. While visitors are expected to show up at the appointed hour for business appointments, their Latin hosts prefer to assume a looser concept of time—a fact of Latin American life that is often frustrating for North Americans conducting business there. Don't expect those in charge to set a precedent in punctuality, either: The higher up your Latin host is on the executive ladder, the later he is likely to be.

Few succeed at wrapping up a business deal in a Latin American country in one trip. Not only are your hosts likely to arrive to a meeting late, but once they do show up it may be hours, even days, before they decide to discuss business. In general, Latins prefer to conduct business at a leisurely pace, placing great import on establishing a friendly relationship before moving on to work matters.

GREETING AND SOCIALIZING

Forging close business relationships in Latin America is usually not difficult; Latin Americans are known to be warm, effusive, and unfailingly polite. Be prepared to be greeted with a friendly handshake. Male friends embrace in what is known as an *abrazo,* or a warm hug; close women friends will lightly kiss each other on both cheeks accompanied by a light touch on the arm. When conversing, Latins like to stand close to the person to whom they are talking; backing away will only draw them closer. While you may not feel comfortable conversing in such close proximity, you should maintain solid eye contact with your Latin American associates at all times.

It's important to remember that most Latins have two surnames; the first is from their father and the second is from their mother. Use the first when addressing someone. For example, Señor Eduardo Perez Montaldo would be greeted as Señor Eduardo Perez. Titles are important to many Latins; when introducing or greeting someone, take care not to leave titles out.

You will need to have a contact or come with introductions to do serious business in Latin America. You may also need to retain an interpreter if you are not fluent in Spanish. Keep in mind that the spoken Spanish is slightly different in each country, much like dialects and accents differ from region to region in the United States. Make sure that your business cards contain information in both English and Spanish.

Establishing a friendly relationship means plenty of socializing—and Latins love to entertain. If you're an early-to-bed, early-to-rise type, be prepared to adjust your internal clock. In many Latin American countries, dining late is customary. In Argentina or Colombia, for example, a meal in a restaurant often doesn't start until after 10 P.M.

ATTITUDES IN GENERAL

Work is not something most Latins live and die for. The family is the heart and soul of the Latin American social structure. Although the culture is rapidly evolving, the Latin men's attitude toward women remains loving, respectful— and rooted in chauvinism. To most Latin men, women are subordinates; in Latin American culture, it is the woman's role to take care of the home and family and leave business matters to the men. Visiting businesswomen should not be surprised if they are treated with politeness and friendliness but less deference than that accorded their male colleagues. They should try to remain respectful of their hosts yet crisply professional at all times; an attitude that is too casual and offhand can be misconstrued as flirtation, while one that is too aggressive is seen as rude and pushy. Dress can also send the wrong message: In most of Latin America, women should opt for conservative clothing—generally dresses or suits, neither flashy nor revealing, with jewelry kept to a minimum.

You don't want to offend the traditional Latin American machismo in other ways: Never make a comment that in some way dishonors or belittles your host, even if you are only making a joke. Also, don't make the mistake of comparing the way Latins do things with the way it is done "in America." Remember: Latin Americans are Americans, too.

SENSITIVE TOPICS

Many countries in Latin America, and in particular Central America, have suffered years of volatile political circumstances. In these countries, it is best to avoid discussing politics. Latin America is also overwhelmingly Catholic; you should never treat the subject of religion lightly. The presence of severe poverty, too, can be a sensitive issue. The disparity between rich and poor is glaringly evident, particularly in countries such as Brazil, where street waifs and shanty-towns are a jarring presence amid manicured city streets and hillsides. In Latin America, entrenched class division is a fact of life. Try to avoid comparing your host country to a neighboring nation, as well—many countries, such as Bolivia and Chile, have long histories of border wars. If you're casting about for the right topic to set a congenial tone, look no further than sports. Most Latins are avid sports fans and are passionate about soccer and baseball.

ARGENTINA

With promises of great wealth, the second-largest country in Latin America lured European immigrants in great numbers in the late 1800s and early 1900s. The fact that many succeeded is underscored in the old saying "rich as an Argentine." The result was a country composed of a melting pot of cultures and a populace with both a European reserve and a Latin sensibility. Argentina's capital, Buenos Aires, a stylish and sophisticated center of high culture, is considered the most European of Latin American cities, with expansive, Parisian-style boulevards and architecture.

Meeting and greeting. Don't expect to enjoy the kind of fast-track, getting-down-to-brass-tacks business meeting you may be used to in North America. Argentines are typical Latins and place great weight on developing a friendly relationship with foreign business associates before getting down to work. Rushing through an agenda and dashing out is considered impolite. Expect to be greeted with a brief handshake, and maintain good eye contact with your hosts throughout the meeting.

Visiting and entertaining. Argentines work long hours and don't usually eat dinner until after 10 P.M. They often stop for a break between 4 P.M. and 6 P.M., when they may have a snack and coffee. Argentina's cattle industry is renowned for producing prime cuts of beef, and Argentine steakhouses are a likely choice for dinner. If you're a vegetarian, you may want to let your hosts know before you arrive.

Business attire. Argentines are more formal than citizens of other Latin American countries, and the dress by comparison is conservative—and often, quite elegant.

Social taboos. Yawning in public or eating on the street are considered rude. Placing your hands on your hips is construed as a challenge. Never put your feet up on a table.

BRAZIL

Big and brassy, Brazil is the largest country in Latin America, both in land size and population. Less formal in dress and demeanor than citizens of other Latin countries, Brazilians like to have fun, particularly during Carnivale, when the romantic city of Rio de Janeiro transforms itself into the world's biggest party. In Brazil, the family rules, and nepotism is an accepted route to employment. The official language is Portuguese, not Spanish, and most Brazilians do not consider themselves Hispanic.

Meeting and greeting. Brazilians are physically demonstrative and effusive, but when it comes to doing business, they prefer a leisurely tack. Leave the aggressive business tactics at home. When the meeting ends, say good-bye to each person, not the group. Men and women shake hands when greeting, and men may prolong the shake for an introduction.

Visiting and entertaining. Although business lunches are more common than business dinners, after-hours entertaining is often to be expected in Brazil. Dinnertime is a loose concept here; you may sit down to dine anywhere from 6 P.M. to 11 P.M. Parties in Brazilian homes can last into the wee morning hours.

Business attire. While the dress in Brazil is considerably less formal than that in other Latin American countries, businessmen and -women should dress conservatively.

Social taboos. The sign for OK in the United States (thumb and forefinger touching) is considered a vulgar gesture in Brazil.

CHILE

Geographically isolated from the rest of Latin America, this long, slender thread of land lies between the Andes mountain range and the Pacific Ocean. Isolation has resulted in a country where the population is ethnically homogenous (the majority are *mestizo*, a mix of European and Indian blood), and the Spanish spoken is comparatively pure. In demeanor, Chileans are thoughtful and kind; politically and socially, they are conservative. At the same time, Chilean men are less obviously chauvinistic toward women than their Latin American counterparts.

Adjusting Your Cultural Lens

483

Meeting and greeting. When making arrangements for business meetings, keep in mind that many Chileans take vacations in January and February. Initial meetings are usually a time to get acquainted, making further meetings necessary.

When meeting a Chilean for the first time, it is considered bad form to ask a person with whom you're not doing business what line of work he's in. Let him broach the subject first.

Visiting and entertaining. When dining, keep your hands above the table, not in your lap, and pour wine with your right hand only—or let your hosts do the pouring (Chileans have specific wine-pouring rituals). If you're invited into a Chilean home, it is customary to select a gift to present to your host. Flowers are always welcome, but avoid yellow flowers, which symbolize contempt.

Business attire. Although not as formal as the Argentines, Chileans are conservative and dress accordingly. Men are expected to adhere to the traditional business dress code. Chileans look askance at a businesswoman who wears revealing outfits or is too done up.

Social taboos. Avoid discussing religion or politics in this conservative country. Don't raise your right fist to head level, which is taken as a Communist sign.

COSTA RICA

The most politically stable and democratic of the Central American countries, Costa Rica has become a favorite travel destination for North Americans. Indeed, so many North American expatriates and retirees have made it their home that the tempo of the traditionally leisurely Latin way of doing business has accelerated—albeit ever so slightly. In this tropical paradise of white-sand beaches and lush rain forests, English is a strong second language.

The people of Costa Rica have the highest per-capita income in Central America and are among Latin America's most highly educated. One indication: The country boasts more lawyers than any other in Latin America. Although Costa Ricans are not as effusively demonstrative as their Latin neighbors, they still put a high premium on establishing a personal relationship with business associates before actually getting down to business.

MEXICO

The major barriers to free trade between Mexico and North American countries were erased in 1996 with the signing of NAFTA (North American Free Trade Agreement). Nevertheless, Mexicans still abide by the traditional Latin way of doing business: on Latin American time, which tends toward the slow and leisurely. Initially, your time will be spent developing a friendly relationship with your Mexican associates. Expect invitations to social occasions in private homes and restaurants—but don't plan on discussing business there; it's simply not done. Plus, if your Mexican friends say they will get to something mañana, that doesn't necessarily mean you'll have it in hand the next day.

Business partnerships in Mexico are unlikely to succeed if a friendship has not been established. Expect your Mexican hosts to be unfailingly polite—so polite, in fact, that they may agree to do the impossible simply to avoid letting their guests down. Although Mexican businesspeople are polite, they often appear wary in the beginning; stay the course by being courteous and diplomatic, and your friendship will develop. Also keep in mind that the family is of utmost importance to Mexicans, and nepotism is rampant.

Meeting and greeting. Meetings tend to be disorganized by American standards, with schedules and attendance lists not always strictly adhered to. Meetings also usually run longer than expected and are frequently interrupted. Whenever this happens, never betray any irritation or you will be seen as impolite.

Men shake hands with men, women with women; the exception is when a woman extends her hand to a man. When being introduced to a woman, it is polite for a man to slightly bow. Eye contact during introductions is considered especially important.

Visiting and entertaining. Mexicans love entertaining and festive occasions. Business lunches are long, drawn-out affairs, generally lasting from 2 P.M. to 4 P.M. Dinners and parties in a private home are usually for socializing, not discussing business. When you enter a party, give a slight bow to everyone in the room.

Business attire. The standard of your attire is taken as signaling your attitude toward the people with whom you're doing business. In Mexico City, men and women should dress fashionably yet conservatively, and men should refrain from taking their jackets off unless the host suggests it. In smaller towns, traditional business attire is often seen as showing off.

Social taboos. As with other Latins, Mexicans are very physical and like to get close to whomever they are talking with. Try to avoid pulling away; it is considered rude. Keep your hands out of your pockets. If you are taking your host a party gift, avoid yellow flowers, which symbolize death, and knives, which symbolize the severing of a friendship.

PANAMA

Panama is the wealthiest nation in Central America, and no wonder: The presence of the Panama Canal, the U.S.-built waterway wonder linking the Atlantic and Pacific oceans, has made it a natural center of trade and for many years the recipient of North American largesse. The United States served as caretaker of the canal and its surrounding support services for 85 years; the stroke of midnight on December 31, 1999, marks the transfer of control from the United States to Panama.

The longtime presence of U.S. citizens living and working in Panama, combined with the continued dominance in Panamanian society of *los rabiblancos,* the English-speaking class of Panamanians of European descent, has made doing business in this country relatively smooth for North Americans.

*Adjusting
Your
Cultural Lens*

Many Panamanians are passionate about sports, but in general they are easygoing. In fact, "taking it easy" is said to be a national sport in these hot, humid environs. In Panamanian society, the elderly are given preferential treatment and are usually introduced first.

PERU

Peru has one of Latin America's most highly stratified societies. Its population of Amerindians—the largest concentration of Indians in the Americas—live in deep poverty, many barely eking out a living in the country's hardscrabble high-mountain terrain. The country's high altitude can bring on altitude sickness in visitors used to living at lower sea levels. As a whole, the people of Peru are more formal than the citizens of other Latin countries. Your Peruvian counterparts will likely be dignified, diplomatic, and reserved—and they will expect the same from you. Aggressive behavior is considered disrespectful. "Doctor" is used not only as a physician's title but also as a title of respect for members of the elite or well-educated classes.

Meeting and greeting. Meetings are more structured than in many Latin American countries. At the same time, Peruvians are not particularly punctual, although they expect you to be on time. They also share the Latin propensity for establishing a personal relationship before getting down to business, meaning that a series of meetings will be held.

Men and women shake hands when greeting and saying good-bye, and friends of the same sex sometimes walk arm in arm.

Visiting and entertaining. Although business lunches are very popular, true business discussions are often unlikely during lunch and even more so at a business dinner. When dining, keep both hands on the table, not in your lap. Sending flowers to Peruvian hosts before or after a party in their home is fine; sending red roses, however, may be perceived as a romantic gesture.

Business attire. Traditional business dress is expected, with anything that appears overstated or revealing—loud colors, extravagant ties, showy jewelry, and low-cut dresses—considered inappropriate. For casual dress, shorts are frowned on for both women and men.

Social taboos. Do not wear native Indian clothing, which can cause offense. Refrain from discussing local politics.

VENEZUELA

This status-conscious country built its wealth on its tremendous natural mineral and petroleum reserves. But the oil bust in the 1980s brought with it tough times, and the country is still recovering. Venezuela has been called the most Caribbean of Latin American countries; the landscape and climate resembles that of Caribbean islands, and the mood is similarly relaxed.

Meetings and greetings. Venezuelans often like to get more or less straight to the point in meetings, a practice influenced by the large amount of international business dealings they've become accustomed to. Still, never rush or pressure a businessperson (Venezuelan businesswomen have become an increasingly larger presence in recent years) to get directly to business matters; let the Venezuelan assume control and direct the socialization period so common in Latin America. Venezuelans are a demonstrative people, always ready to hail a friend with a hearty *abrazo*. They also stand closer together when talking than other Latin Americans normally do.

Visiting and entertaining. Business lunches are generally initiated by your Venezuelan business associates, not you. Because Venezuelans rarely entertain at home, it is a high honor to be invited into one; be sure to give your hosts effusive thanks and a quality gift, such as imported liquor.

Business attire. Venezuelans tend to be more fashion-conscious than citizens in many other Latin American countries, and appreciate fine accessories; still, women should never dress in revealing clothing, no matter how fashionable a style is back home. As in Peru, shorts are not appropriate casual dress for visitors, although jeans are worn with a jacket.

Social taboos. Avoid being too attentive to a member of the opposite sex, particularly a Venezuelan business associate's spouse; your intentions might easily be misinterpreted.

WESTERN EUROPE

The group of nations that were commonly called the Common Market or the European Economic Community (EEC) are now the European Community and have begun to share a common currency. After decades of economic integration, and with the newly adopted euro replacing local currencies such as marks, francs, and lira, Western Europe now enjoys greater unity of outlook and behavior than at any time since the Middle Ages. Once again, money and goods flow freely from city to city. As business methods become standardized throughout the region, manners, too, take on an increasingly international hue.

Not all national differences have entirely vanished, to be sure, and Switzerland and Norway remain outside the European Community. More basically, a clear difference in temperament distinguishes the colder northern tier of nations from those that border the Mediterranean. The Germans, with their highly organized turn of mind, look with dismay at the flexible time schedules of the Spaniards and the Greeks. The notoriously taciturn Finns hardly know what to make of the talkative, gesticulating Italians. Yet setting aside these national traits, there are common traditions of polite behavior that hold true throughout Western Europe.

Compared with the United States, both Western European dress and behavior tend to be more formal. Whatever seems mildly sloppy to an Ameri-

Adjusting Your Cultural Lens

can—chewing gum, slouching in a chair, and putting your feet on the table—becomes a serious breach of etiquette in Europe. A Frenchman would never dream of conducting a conversation with his hands in his pockets. An Italian might grasp you gently by the arm, but unless he is your closest friend he would be appalled by a hearty slap on the back.

TIME AND SPACE

The most evident distinction in manners between northern and southern Europe regards time. Scandinavians, Germans, and other northern people plan their schedules with care and believe in sticking to them. When a Frankfort executive calls a meeting for 14:15, that is when it starts; the meeting moves along point by point, usually following a written agenda, and it ends precisely as designated—not a minute sooner nor a minute later. By contrast, in Spain or Portugal a visitor might be kept waiting as much as 30 minutes or more and then is greeted with utmost courtesy, perhaps given coffee, regaled with a discourse on soccer teams or Catalan painting, asked about his travels, interrupted by phone calls, taken to lunch, and finally sent home for a siesta. No business will have been settled—but nobody expected a quick resolution in any case.

The other great dividing line between north and south is the matter of personal space. Each culture has a physical comfort zone that marks the distance at which people like to stand while talking. For northerners, the distance is about 4 feet, and anything closer is seen as an invasion of privacy. But for southerners the distance shrinks to about 2 feet. An Italian conversing with a Swede at a cocktail party steps forward, hoping to establish a personal rapport. The Swede instinctively backs away. Neither one is being rude, just attempting to maintain what he thinks is the proper personal distance.

GREETINGS

The standard greeting throughout Europe is the handshake, for both men and women. It is usually polite for a woman to extend her hand first. Most continentals shake hands before and after every meeting, while in England a single introductory shake is considered sufficient. Fashionable women in France and Italy may greet friends of either sex with a kiss on both cheeks. Hand kissing and heel clicking, however, have long since gone the way of the silent film.

BUSINESS CARDS

In business situations, cards are normally exchanged. Because most European businesspeople speak English, an English-language business card is often acceptable, particularly in northern countries. In Mediterranean areas, a card in the language of the country is a sign of courtesy, but it is neither expected nor mandatory. Throughout the continent, people are addressed by professional title: Herr Doktor Schmitt, Signor Avvocato Manzini. No one calls another person by his or her first name until clearly invited to do so.

DRESS

Europeans are extremely style-conscious and invariably pay attention to the cut of people's clothes. But as in America, appropriate dress depends largely on one's profession. The everyday dress of a successful investment banker from London is a dark Savile Row suit, while a book editor is more likely to go about in professorial tweeds. As a general rule, suit jackets stay on in offices and restaurants, and women wear skirts, not slacks.

GIFT GIVING

The giving of expensive presents is rarely an important part of European business culture. Taking colleagues to lunch at a good restaurant is perhaps the best way for a visitor to express his generosity. Gifts bearing a company logo are generally regarded as advertising. In some instances, however, they are willingly accepted, particularly if the logo is small and tastefully displayed; in others, it is best to leave them behind.

When invited to a colleague's home for dinner—a rare privilege in most countries—a bouquet of flowers is usually appropriate. But there is a protocol for flower-giving, and it pertains to most of Europe. As in the United States, red roses are likely to signal amorous intent. Also, white lilies and chrysanthemums are to be avoided, associated as they are with cemeteries.

BELGIUM

When two peoples of different backgrounds share a single living space, questions of etiquette are bound to arise. Such is the case in Belgium, with two distinct ethnic groups. The Flemish think, speak, and behave much like the Dutch, their close cousins to the north. The Walloons are basically French in language, manner, and temperament. To complicate matters further, many Belgians are of German descent.

*Adjusting
Your
Cultural Lens*

For all the differences in language and customs, Brussels is in a way the "capital" of Europe, given that it has long been the headquarters for both the European Economic Community and NATO. With more gleaming tall buildings than are found in most European cities, some travelers see it as the European equivalent of New York.

Meeting and greeting. Business meetings tend to be formal and highly focused; punctuality is essential. Address colleagues by their surnames, prefaced by "Mr.," "Mrs.," or "Miss" in Flemish circles, and by "Monsieur" or "Madame" when dealing with French speakers. Shake hands with everyone, both on your arrival and when taking your leave. Women hold important positions in both business and government and are treated with utmost courtesy and respect.

Visiting and entertaining. Belgians justly pride themselves on their food, which features such culinary delights as mussels, waffles, chocolate, beef cooked in beer, and French fries—which the Belgians claim to have invented. When invited to dine, make sure to show your appreciation.

Business attire. A conservative approach is always best. Standard business attire leans toward dark suits, white shirts, and subdued ties. Wear lace-up shoes rather than loafers, and keep them well polished.

Social taboos. Belgians tend to be reserved and private, so avoid asking personal questions. "What do you do?" is not the way to start. Never enter a room or an office without knocking. Even when a receptionist says her boss is ready to see you, knock first (the door will be closed), and listen for a response before going in. Also, know whom you are talking with: To confuse a Flemish person with a Walloon, or vice versa, would be an unforgivable lapse.

FRANCE

It's only logical: In matters of civilized behavior, the French know best. The excellence of French civilization shows itself in the stylishness of its women, the glories of its cuisine, the beauty and precision of its language, the vision of its painters, the liveliness of its wit, the sharpness of its intellect. Paris was the cultural capital of the Western world throughout the 19th and much of the 20th centuries, and few cities are more triumphantly beautiful. No question, the French know how to live. While French women have yet to break into top positions in corporate management, their talents are highly regarded in fields such as education, fashion, and the arts.

In business, the French adhere to tradition and feel comfortable with a bit of ceremony. Business dress is conservative, manners reserved and diplomatic. People address each other by surname, prefaced when appropriate by a title such as doctor or professor. Corporate hierarchies are carefully maintained, with juniors showing courteous deference to higher-ranking colleagues.

The same formal courtesy extends to meetings. Expect each point to be presented with cogent, meticulous logic. Yet, paradoxically, a lively spontaneity usually prevails. Ideas tumble out, voices rise, the discussion veers off into unexpected avenues. No one holds back. The French prefer every opinion to be forthrightly, if briefly, expressed.

So it is in social life. The French love a good argument, whether it be about wine, books, cinema, or the state of the world. Conversation is the national amusement, an opportunity to display one's knowledge and wit. The talk is never linear, but moves rapidly from topic to topic in an impressive dance of verbal dexterity.

Needless to say, it helps to have a working command of the French language. But be warned: To a Frenchman the language is sacred, and nothing pains him more than to see it misused.

Meeting and greeting. Meetings begin punctually. There will be formal introductions and exchanges of cards. Find out in advance if French or English will be spoken, and bring a translator if needed. Presentations should be formal, logical, and complete. Avoid subjective hunches; each point should be supported by concise, carefully reasoned argument.

The French handshake, a light grasp and a single shake, is delivered on both meeting and departure. (Avoid enthusiastic arm-pumping, which is considered gauche.) Women and higher-ranking individuals are expected to offer their hands first. In social settings, women will greet friends with *les bises*—a pair of cheek-to-cheek kisses for both males and females.

Business attire. The French are famously conscious of personal style. Dark suits and subdued ties are worn year-round in Paris and other northern cities; in the south, men often substitute a blue blazer and slacks. Women should always wear suits in a business setting.

Visiting and entertaining. Dining is a serious matter in France, and while business is often conducted over lunch or dinner, the food itself deserves your enthusiastic attention. Do not dull your palate with hard liquor before a meal, and don't launch into shoptalk before expressing your admiration for the food. A dinner invitation to a French home is a rare honor. The traditional protocol is to send flowers the day before, and follow up with a handwritten thank-you note the next day.

Social taboos. Do not open a conversation with a personal question. Always knock before entering a room. Avoid backslapping, loud braying laughter, or excessive heartiness. While dining, keep your hands above the table; never put them in your lap. Do not chew gum in public.

GERMANY

Germany is the most punctiliously formal country in Europe—not surprising in a land that has a place for everything and where everything is kept in its place. Even at purely social gatherings, people are introduced to each other by professional title and university degree: Herr Direktor Doktor Braun, Frau Professor Dr. Rinehart. Men rise when a woman enters a room or gets up from a dinner table. (On the street, the man walks on the left; if there are two men, the woman walks between them. When two men walk alone, the younger man stays on the left.) Everything is planned in advance, even a trip to the grocery store. Things happen on time, whether it be the start of a meeting, the departure of a train, or the serving of dinner.

The same formality pervades German business life. Executives often keep their office doors closed, juniors defer to their seniors, instructions move down the hierarchy, and there is little frivolity around the water cooler.

Meeting and greeting. Arrive on time; a delay of even a few minutes can be taken as an insult. Most likely, you will be introduced to a senior person by a lower-ranking associate. The proper form is a brief, firm handshake all around, accompanied by a slight nod; if the group is large, a single handshake with the senior member may suffice. Be ready to offer your card, which will win points if it lists any higher university degrees and professional honors.

Meetings begin with a bare minimum of pleasantries, and the atmosphere is serious and businesslike. Inquire in advance if the meeting will be in German or English, and if necessary bring an interpreter. Avoid hype and exaggeration, which become an instant turn-off. Save jokes and humor until after business hours.

Business attire. Business dress is ultraconservative—dark suits, subdued ties, white shirts. Erect posture and a well-tailored appearance are expected of both men and women.

Visiting and entertaining. Restaurant lunches are the most common form of business entertainment, and they begin at the appointed hour. You may discuss business before and after the meal itself, but never while eating it. When finished, place your knife and fork vertically on your plate. Insist on paying the bill only when you have issued the invitation.

Social taboos. Never place a business call to a German's home telephone; family and business life are kept rigidly separate. Speak in complete sentences, and avoid letting a thought trail off unfinished. Try to restrain excessive gestures and body language. An American "okay" sign, where the thumb and index finger make a circle, is considered obscene. Keep your hands out of your pockets. Avoid waving or calling someone's name in a public place.

GREAT BRITAIN

England and America, the playwright George Bernard Shaw once famously remarked, are "two countries separated by a common language." The differences runs deeper, however, than an Englishman calling the trunk of his car a "boot" or asking for "bitter" when he wants a beer. From the viewpoint of most Americans, the British tend to be conservative, deliberate, understated, rather vague, and perhaps even a bit standoffish. They can also be immensely entertaining, full of charm, with a lively gift for humor and an enviable command of the mother tongue.

While the formal class structure that has marked British society for many centuries is beginning to loosen, it still exerts influence. One Englishman will judge another by subtle clues of accent, dress, mannerisms, and schooling. A degree from Oxford or Cambridge, for example, means more than one from a "red brick" university in an industrial city. Such distinctions carry the most weight in London and southern England. Elsewhere—in the midlands and northern England, and in Scotland and Wales—the straightforward middle-class values of honesty, hard work, native ability, and experience are more likely to prevail.

Nearly half of Britain's workforce is female, and women are moving into upper management. Women executives expect to speak with the same authority and receive the same respect as their male counterparts.

A NOTE OF CAUTION: Everyone from Great Britain is British, but only people from England proper are called English. The others are either Scots—never Scotch (something you drink)—or Welsh or Irish. And none of them, despite Britain's membership in the European Community, think of themselves as Europeans. Europe means the Continent, across the English Channel.

Meeting and greeting. The business community in London and elsewhere is often a tightly knit web of "old-boy" relationships that visitors may have difficulty penetrating. Advance appointments are essential and preferably made after an introduction by a third party. Initial meetings tend to be formal. Be prompt. You will shake hands on arriving but never on leaving. Business cards are sometimes exchanged, though not always: The continental rituals of card swapping are not taken so seriously here.

In subsequent meetings, as your relationship develops, a more casual atmosphere usually takes hold. Suit jackets come off, sleeves are rolled up, and people will start using first names. Jokes may be exchanged. The slide toward informality in style does not extend to content, however. The British want facts and figures in well-thought-out detail, backed up by written documentation. Understatement sells better than an aggressive presentation.

Visiting and entertaining. Most business entertaining takes place in pubs and restaurants. When dinner is over, the principal guest is expected to initiate the departure. Generally speaking, it is considered bad form to discuss business after office hours.

If invited to a meal in someone's house, you may arrive ten minutes late but never a minute early. No gift is expected. The British maintain the tradition of holding doors open for women and rising from their chairs when a woman enters the room. The following day, send a handwritten thank-you note.

Business attire. Dark suits with pinstripes are the classic look for the British businessman, so keep your own clothing on the conservative side. Striped ties are risky because you could unknowingly be showing the same colors as one of your business associate's regiment or club ties. Women should dress stylishly but conservatively and should save the slacks for sightseeing.

Social taboos. Never use the American conversational gambit "What do you do?" Not only is the phrase meaningless here, but inquiring about a person's livelihood is deemed rude and intrusive. Even asking what part of England someone comes from can be a bit too personal. Avoid talking shop at social events. To call someone "clever" can be taken as a veiled personal insult. When it comes to shoes, wear lace-ups rather than loafers.

GREECE

Western civilization owes its origins to the achievements of the ancient Greeks, from the wisdom of Aristotle to the ballot boxes of Periclean Athens. Yet of all Europe's nations, modern Greece remains one of the most traditional. In many ways it still exhibits a village mentality, where the values of family obligation, loyalty to friends, and respect for the elderly prevail. In business, personal relationships can be as important as strict adherence to the bottom line. Many businesses are family operations, with the lines of authority running back to a family patriarch.

Meeting and greeting. Patience and courtesy are essential tactics in developing the personal trust required for doing business. Expect long conversations over strong coffee and ouzo, the anise-flavored national drink. The Greeks are highly verbal and physically expressive; they love to haggle and expect you to haggle back. Meetings frequently start late, and they will be frequently interrupted. An attempt to hurry a decision will be taken as an insult.

Greeks shake hands when greeting each other, but they may also embrace and even kiss on both cheeks. Use last name and title when meeting someone, but expect an early invitation to address colleagues by their first name. In this cradle of democracy, avoid pretension.

Visiting and entertaining. Greek hospitality can be overwhelmingly generous, and you should accept every invitation lest you offend your hosts. When invited to a Greek home, bring flowers or small cakes, and perhaps small gifts for the children.

Business attire. Despite the conception some have of sunny Greece, conservative business attire is expected—suits and ties for men, suits or dresses for women.

Social taboos. Avoid thrusting your open palm toward someone, which can be taken as a "go to you-know-where" gesture.

ITALY

Italians tend to be outgoing, verbal, intelligent, expressive, hospitable, family-oriented, regionally proud, and genuinely interested in each person they meet. Expect to be asked what town you are from, what movies you like, how many children you have, what friends you may have in common. At the same time, deep cultural rifts mark Italian society—not surprising in a nation that achieved political unity only toward the end of the last century. Communities separated by little more than a row of hills may speak entirely different dialects. Tuscans remain proudly Tuscan and do not like to be confused with Romans, Neapolitans, or Sicilians.

The sharpest differences occur between Italy's heavily industrialized north, with its shoe factories and automobile plants, and the rural, less prosperous south. Business in the north is often conducted with a brisk efficiency that can seem almost American. Southerners tend to have a more leisurely, traditional way of doing things. Italian women, while they have long held positions in cultural areas, are only just beginning to make headway in the male-dominated world of business.

One factor that all regions have in common is the double burden of a slow-moving bureaucracy and a highly complex legal system. Some Italian laws date back 2,000 years to the Roman Empire, and more are added each year. Tax codes are similarly cumbersome and contradictory.

Meeting and greeting. Northern Italians tend to be reasonably prompt, and they expect the same from you. (In the south, 20 minutes late is still on time.) The atmosphere at business gatherings is informal. Meetings begin with an exchange of pleasantries designed to establish the close personal rapport that is essential for doing business here. Presentations should be polished and articulate, but be prepared for interruptions. As momentum gathers, you may expect everyone to start talking at once. Do not be dismayed—it is Italian to vocalize.

Italians shake hands with everyone on both meeting and leaving; good friends may embrace. Everyone with a university degree will have a title: *dottore* in liberal arts, *avvocato* in law, *ingengere* in technical fields, and *professore* in medicine and academia. Use these titles until invited to do otherwise.

Business attire. Every Italian tries to present *una bella figura*—a seamless combination of gracious manner and stylish dress. Italian designers set fashion trends around the world, and well-cut suits and expensive ties are normal attire for male executives. Women wear either slacks or dresses, fashionable and understated.

Visiting and entertaining. Restaurant dinners are an important part of business life in Italy; it is rude to refuse an invitation. Since generosity brings prestige, you may find it difficult to grab the check. Don't be surprised if your Italian counterpart has cued the waiter in advance to slip the bill to him.

Social taboos. At a social gathering, it is tactless to ask anyone about his or her profession. Do not embarrass your hosts by arriving too promptly; allow at least 15 minutes leeway, and more in the south. Avoid giving gifts that are obviously a vehicle for your company logo. Remove dark glasses when entering a building.

When stepping into a Dutch elevator you say "good day" to everyone. You do the same when entering a shop, a railroad compartment, a doctor's waiting room. It's just good manners in this extraordinarily egalitarian country to treat each individual, including service personnel, with equal courtesy. No one puts on airs. Even the late Queen Juliana would travel around town on her bicycle, exactly like one of her subjects.

The Netherlands is heir to the Calvinist ethic of modesty, frugality, honesty, and hard work. "In Rotterdam," the saying goes, "shirts are sold with the sleeves rolled up." People tend to be formal and reserved in public, avoiding undue familiarity and extravagant display. On closer acquaintance they unbend, often revealing a good-natured, sometimes earthy sense of humor. One of the more conservative aspects of Dutch society is its attitude toward women, who still tend to focus their lives on family and home.

Meeting and greeting. Business meetings begin promptly and tend to move quickly to the matter at hand. If you are late, you will be considered unreliable. Presentations should be factual, straightforward, and free of hype or hyperbole. Visuals are useful when filled with facts and figures, but be aware that the information they contain will be carefully cross-checked when you leave. High-pressure sales techniques will be seen as rude and obnoxious.

The Dutch greet everyone, including children, with a firm handshake on both meeting and departure. Direct eye contact is important. Traditionally, only close friends and family members use first names, but executives familiar with American ways may soon move to a first-name basis. (The correct form of address in all correspondence is full business title, however.)

Business attire. In banking circles the dress is formal and sedate: dark suits and white shirts for both men and women. But executives in some industries strike a more casual note, removing both ties and jackets while in the office. By an odd reversal, executives in high positions may dress more informally than their subordinates.

Visiting and entertaining. Business gatherings may continue with lunch at a restaurant; it is perfectly acceptable to continue the morning's discussion over food. You may also be invited to a colleague's home after business hours, where the entertainment may take the form of drinks, coffee, and heavy hors d'oeuvres. If invited to a sit-down dinner, take flowers (unwrapped) but not wine; a gift of even the finest vintage may be interpreted as a comment on your host's wine cellar.

Social taboos. Modesty is always the best policy in the Netherlands: Avoid ostentation, hype, and exaggeration. When encountering a friend in a public place, you may wave but never call out. When entering a room, shake hands with everyone and introduce yourself; do not appear standoffish. Remember that the Dutch sense of humor does not include verbal repartee or sarcasm.

Norway, an oil-rich country with fewer than 5 million people, awards the Nobel Prizes. Denmark, only slightly more populous, boasts one of the world's highest living standards. Sweden, whose entire population of about 9 million is roughly that of the New York City metropolitan area, ranks among the world's most advanced industrial societies. Together, these three Scandinavian nations and their neighbor Finland, whose architects' modernist styles were spread throughout the globe, amount to an economic powerhouse.

Denmark, Norway, and Sweden are constitutional monarchies with a deep commitment to social equality. Finland, a republic, is by definition a land of equals. All four demonstrate that even in the context of cradle-to-grave welfare socialism, free enterprise will grow and prosper.

Manners in Scandinavia strike a careful balance between formality and ease, reticence and relaxation. Few Europeans have a more tightly held sense of personal privacy. Scandinavians tend to be honest, reliable, self-contained, understated, suspicious of hype and verbosity, meticulously punctual, and cautious to react and decide. (The frequent silences at a meeting of Finns would drive most southern Europeans to distraction.) Yet the convivial rapport that develops at a banquet, after numerous toasts with aquavit, seems to break all social barriers.

For all their similarities, the Scandinavians and Finns are acutely aware of their national differences. Each nation is proudly independent, with diverging histories that date back to the time of their Viking ancestors; the Finns speak a Finno-Ugric language that is unrelated to the Indo-European tongues of their neighbors. A thoughtful visitor will show appreciation for the virtues that make each country unique. As a general rule, Danes and Swedes tend to be more formal than Finns and Norwegians.

Meeting and greeting. Business meetings should be scheduled at least two weeks in advance and tend to follow a planned agenda. It is essential to arrive on time. Scandinavians get down to business without delay; they will have done their homework and they expect you to have facts and figures at your fingertips. Avoid exaggeration. Speak softly and dispassionately, avoiding a hard sell. Look people directly in the eye.

Expect a firm handshake from men and women alike, given on arrival and departure. People are introduced by their family name and title—Mrs. Andersen, Dr. Thorvold—except in Finland, where the first name is often included. Do not use first names until asked to do so, however. The invitation is likely to come quickly, particularly in Norway, and sooner from younger people than from their seniors.

The standard greeting in Denmark is "Heij," much like an American's "Hi!" In Norway people say "Morn!" no matter what the hour of the day. Upper-class Swedes, in order to avoid the excessive familiarity of the pronoun "you," will ask your health in the third person: "And how is Mr. Smith today?" You should respond in kind.

Business attire. The Danes dress with a high degree of formality, often wearing double-breasted suits or suits with vests. Bow ties and flashy suspenders are considered frivolous. Dress in Sweden can be more relaxed, depending on the industry, but colors are subdued and sport jackets are accompanied by ties. In Norway and Finland, people may wear suits in winter, but in summer months they may switch to jackets with or without ties. Even when going casual, the Finns in particular have a keen eye for style. In banking circles throughout Scandinavia and Finland, the uniform is conservative: subdued clothes for both men and women.

Visiting and entertaining. Business often extends into lunch, which may range from sandwiches and coffee to a full buffet-style smorgasbord. If a woman extends the invitation, she will pick up the check. The invitation you hope for, however, is dinner at a private home.

The protocols vary only slightly from country to country. Always arrive at the appointed time; there is no such thing as being "fashionably late." A gift of flowers or chocolates will be appreciated. You may be served a drink before dinner, or you may be ushered directly into the dining room. The host or hostess will tell you where to sit; the guest of honor will usually be placed at the hostess' left. Then the toasts begin. To toast is to *skål,* and when done properly it follows a time-honored formula—particularly in Sweden and Denmark. No one touches his glass until the host proposes the first toast. Thereafter, the rule is never to toast anyone senior to you in age or rank until they have toasted you first.

Social taboos. Other than shaking hands, avoid physical contact. Scandinavians and Finns tend to stand at least four feet apart while conversing. Talking with your hands in your pockets seems overly casual, but folding your arms looks like arrogance. Refrain from asking personal questions. Keep body language subdued, and contain any urge toward exuberance.

SPAIN

At a conference room in Madrid, delegates from a large German corporation are presenting their company's product to a group of local businessmen. There are lengthy documents, all translated into Spanish, detailed wall charts, and a video. But as the German spokesman methodically lays out facts and figures, his Spanish listeners pay little attention to what he is saying. Instead, they focus on the man himself. What kind of person is he? Is he someone they want to work with?

Nothing in Spain matters more than personal relationships. These take time to develop. They begin, whenever possible, with a third-party introduction, and they build through a succession of office meetings, long lunches and dinners, the give and take of extended bargaining, until all parties reach an oral understanding based on mutual trust. Finally, a written agreement takes shape. There is no way to hurry the process.

In both business and social life, the Spanish combine a formal manner with a warm, diplomatic courtesy. Their sense of personal dignity and honor is world renowned. Invariably, a person's character is valued more highly than any amount of financial wizardry or technological know-how. Spanish women, often highly educated and career-minded, have long since begun to assume important roles in business, government, and the professions.

Meeting and greeting. During business meetings, the first half hour will be taken up by polite conversation as your colleagues try to set you at ease. Then, as negotiations proceed, expect frequent interruptions and cross conversations. For a Mediterranean people, the Spanish can be unusually direct. Respond diplomatically: The last thing you want is to offend a Spaniard's pride. When making appointments, be advised that the Spanish take a leisurely approach to time; as much as an hour may pass before your colleague is ready to see you.

Spanish friends sometimes greet each other with an *abrazo,* or hug, but business greetings are more reserved. Handshakes with everyone are normal, accompanied by an exchange of cards at the first introduction. Visitors should have cards printed in both English and Spanish and present them with the Spanish side facing the recipient.

Business attire. Men dress in muted colors and suits of conservative cut; in some professions, sport jackets or blazers may be worn. Women strive for quiet elegance.

Visiting and entertaining. The Spanish use meals to cement a business relationship. A restaurant lunch may begin at 1 P.M. and continue until 3 P.M. When office hours end, usually around 5 or 6 P.M., many business people can be seen migrating through a succession of bars and *tabernas* for a movable feast of tapas—hors d'oeuvres that range from salted nuts to saucers of squid, sausage, or potato omelet. Then at 10 or 11 P.M., people sit down to dinner. Invitations to dine at home are a rare honor. The proper etiquette is to decline at first and then accept when pressed.

Social taboos. Until invited to do so, do not address colleagues by first names or use the familiar *tu* form when speaking Spanish. Even at a business lunch, do not bring up business matters before coffee. In conversation, avoid sensitive topics such as religion, as well as separatist movements among Basques and Catalans. Say nothing derogatory about bullfighting.

SWITZERLAND

Ever since its founding in 1291, when a number of cantons from the Holy Roman Empire united to form a single federation, Switzerland has been a land of cultural diversity. It has four official languages: French, German, Italian, and a Latinate dialect called Romanish. Manners and customs vary from region to region, depending on the language spoken. Residents of Zurich behave and think like Germans, while in Geneva the cultural climate is distinctly French.

Certain character traits are common to all areas, however. The Swiss share a tradition of hard work, punctuality, formal courtesy, personal privacy, and a serious attitude toward life in general. People do not mix business with pleasure. Even in French areas, long business lunches are unusual.

When dealing with the Swiss, a conservative approach is best. Wear dark, well-tailored clothing. On public transportation, give your seat to anyone who is older. Do not slouch or gesticulate. You'll need two cards for every business appointment, one for the secretary and one for the person you are meeting. Avoid high-pressure tactics, do not ask personal questions, and be on time! (For the nuances of etiquette within each of Switzerland's main cultural groups, see the entries for France, page 490; Germany, page 491; and Italy, page 494.)

EASTERN EUROPE

The roiling inner turmoil that has defined the political and economic landscape of Eastern Europe in the 1990s has made doing business there unpredictable at best and inadvisable at worst. For most of the countries, the changing of the guard, from Communist rule to something approaching a free-market economy, has not been a smooth transition. The battle for power in Eastern Europe has ushered in unstable leadership, ethnic infighting, and unsettled economies. In some countries, such as Russia, the instability has opened the door to organized crime and corruption. In other countries, such as the Czech Republic, the break from authoritarian Communist rule has been relatively smooth and free of conflict. For others, such as Yugoslavia, the situation is much more grave: long-simmering ethnic tensions have resulted in rampant genocide, under the guise of "ethnic cleansing," and subsequent occupation by NATO.

In spite of the instability brought on by the fall of Communism, foreigners are indeed conducting business in Eastern Europe. Women will be happy to know that in most Eastern European countries (with a few notable exceptions, such as Poland) foreign businesswomen are accorded equal treatment and respect as that given to men.

Westerners are often frustrated by the slow progress of conducting business in Eastern Europe as well as the often inefficient infrastructure and unreliable equipment; these are, after all, nations in serious economic, political, and social flux. Be patient: It will likely take several trips or multiple meetings to wrap up business dealings. Be sure to set up your meetings far in advance; it may take months to acquire the proper documents and finalize arrangements.

When meeting Eastern European business associates, always call them by their titles and surnames unless asked to do otherwise; only good friends refer to each other on a first-name basis. Handshakes are the typical form of greeting in Eastern Europe. Hungarians, Poles, and Czechs are not inclined to be any more physical than that, and they typically stand a couple of feet apart when conversing. In Russia, good friends express themselves in a more physical way, greeting one another with hearty bear hugs or kisses on alternate cheeks. When in doubt, simply follow your hosts' lead.

A TASTE FOR ENTERTAINING

As a whole, Eastern Europeans love to entertain. Hungarians, for example, will fête foreigners with lavish meals that go on for hours. Poles, too, love to stay up late socializing. One of the pitfalls of being entertained Eastern European–style is the abundance of alcohol—especially vodka, the Eastern European drink of choice. Expect your Eastern European associates to entertain with copious amounts of alcohol, fueled by endless rounds of toasts. It's perfectly fine, in most countries, to simply take a sip of your drink after each toast rather than downing the entire glass.

Being invited to a social occasion in a private home is considered an honor in most Eastern European cultures. Taking a gift—flowers or chocolates, for example—is the polite thing to do. Avoid yellow flowers, which many Eastern Europeans associate with mourning. Be sure to bring along plenty of business cards as well, printed both in English and in the language of the country you're visiting. In countries with outdated phone books and electronic equipment, business cards are a major communication tool.

The three major Eastern European nations doing business with Westerners are the Czech Republic, Poland, and Russia. The breakup of the Soviet Union has splintered much of the former empire into small, independent nations, many of which have yet to develop an infrastructure for conducting business relations with foreigners. Other places, in the throes of domestic turmoil, are simply off-limits to civilians. The republics that once comprised Yugoslavia, for example, have been torn by ethnic wars and are too dangerous for foreign travel.

THE CZECH REPUBLIC

The Czech Republic has weathered the transition from Communist rule to a free-market state in a much more amicable and less tumultuous fashion than

Adjusting Your Cultural Lens

many of its Eastern European counterparts. The relative stability of the country's economy, paired with the great wealth of historic architecture and natural beauty, makes the Czech Republic a desirable place for Westerners to do business. The business of getting down to business assumes an old-world pace, however—so don't expect immediate decisions or resolutions.

When conducting business in the Czech Republic, know that the Czechs hold their elderly in great esteem and would question the validity of a company that would send a person younger than 40 to do business there.

Meeting and greeting. When making appointments in the Czech Republic, keep in mind that Czechs consider Friday afternoons the beginning of the weekend. Businesses open early every day, usually around 8 A.M., and close at 3 or 4 P.M. You're expected to be punctual for meetings. The typical Czech greeting is handshakes all around, to everyone in the room, both during arrival and departure.

Visiting and entertaining. Your Czech business associates will want to establish a personal relationship before getting down to business, and that will probably include invitations to restaurants and parties in private homes. Business, however, should not be conducted during a meal or social occasion. It will please your hosts to no end if you master a few words or phrases in Czech. A bouquet of flowers is just the right gift to take to your hosts. In some households, it is the custom to remove your shoes upon entering the home; others do not observe this old tradition. Toasting throughout the main meal is common.

Business attire. Conservative business attire is recommended.

Social taboos. When a man and woman walk down the street, the man should never take the inside position; he should always walk closest to the curb.

POLAND

Once home to one of Eastern Europe's most cultured and intellectual populations, Poland was hard hit by the suffering caused during World War II, when some 6 million Poles were killed. Democracy of sorts came to Poland in 1989 after the Solidarity union movement succeeded in pulling the country out from under Soviet Communist rule.

Poles are among the most genial and hospitable people of Eastern Europe—in spite of what might appear to be a somber demeanor. Expect to forge a personal relationship and establish a bond of trust with your Polish business associates before getting down to business. Be patient; the process will be a leisurely, unhurried one.

Meeting and greeting. In Poland, the workday begins early, around 8:00 A.M. While you should certainly try to be punctual for meetings, don't always expect the same from your Polish business associates. Be prepared to shake hands, but try not to do so over a door threshold; the Poles consider it bad luck.

Visiting and entertaining. Poles love to socialize and enjoy staying up late doing so. When being entertained in restaurants or private homes, stay the course—it is considered rude to leave your hosts early. An invitation to get together over drinks may be conveyed through body language; when a Pole wants a friend to join him for a drink, he will flick his finger against his neck.

Business attire. Conservative business attire is recommended, with suits and ties for men and dresses or business suits for women.

Social taboos. Shouting is a no-no: Poles speak softly and expect others to do the same. Don't litter or throw trash in anything but a trash receptacle. When dining, keep your hands out of your lap and above the table.

RUSSIA

The former Soviet Union has of late fallen on tough times. The breakup in 1991 of the Soviet Union resulted in the complete independence of three formerly Russian-dominated republics and the somewhat loose alliance of the remaining 12 in the Commonwealth of Independent States. Still, the breakup of the U.S.S.R. and the downfall of Communist leadership has resulted in internal havoc, with the Russian economy in disarray and the country's future uncertain. Entrenched bureaucracy, an unraveling business infrastructure, outdated equipment, and a volatile social, economic, and political landscape make doing business in Russia a challenge for foreigners.

Street crime and petty thievery are reputed problems in the Russian cities. Be sure to check with your hosts or hotelier about the safety of the areas you'll be visiting.

Meeting and greeting. You should be punctual for any meeting, even though your Russian associates may not always be on time. On first meeting, your Russian counterparts will often state their names as you shake hands. Be sure to maintain direct eye contact. Address each Russian business associate by using his title and surname, unless otherwise directed. (Remember that most Russian wives add an "a" to the end of their husband's surname.) Know that Russian business people are very cautious in making business decisions; don't get impatient if time drags on and plans have not been finalized. Don't expect your business associates to be receptive to compromise, which can be regarded as a sign of weakness; your hosts may prefer to wait out any deadlock. Also be prepared to witness some emotional "acting out" on the part of your Russian counterparts, who may walk out of a meeting in a huff more than once. Be patient: They'll be back.

When shaking hands, Russians generally say your name, and you are expected to respond in kind.

Visiting and entertaining. Russians go all out when entertaining at home. Expect lavish meals accompanied by lots of vodka and toasts. Keep in mind the Russians' love of children and respect for the elderly when considering appropriate topics of conversation.

Business attire. Very conservative is the way to go; leave the flashy jewelry and revealing clothing at home.

Social taboos. Drop off your coat in the cloakroom before entering a public building and don't loiter. Avoid shouting or laughing loudly in public. As in Poland, don't litter:

Most Russians consider doing so offensive. When dining, place wrists lightly on the table and keep your hands out of your lap.

THE MIDDLE EAST

What is a visitor to do? While negotiating a deal in a major oil-producing country, an American businessman made the mistake of openly admiring a pair of handsome gold cufflinks worn by his host. "They are yours!" the host replied—and promptly handed them over. Such are the perils of desert hospitality: If you lavish praise on any item belonging to someone else—wristwatch, book, coffee pot, Cézanne watercolor—you are all too likely to receive it as a gift. Then, at the first opportunity, you are expected to reciprocate with something of equal value.

Nothing is as important as the give and take of personal relationships. Throughout the Middle East, people will strike you as being warmly outgoing, highly vocal, generous, proud, inquisitive, impulsive, effusively polite, and given to wonderfully improbable flights of eloquence. Arab men greet each other with elaborate compliments, often embracing and exchanging cheek-to-cheek kisses. In conversation, they gesture and touch (but never point—it's impolite), their heads move closer, and personal space diminishes. No one says "no," for fear of giving offense; a fatalistic shrug, and perhaps the word "maybe," is as close as most Middle Easterners will come to a negative response.

Whenever possible, business is conducted on the basis of who you know rather than through official channels. Even in the most intense negotiations, friendship and personal respect are made to seem more important than what ends up on the bottom line.

CONCERNING RELIGION

Religion is a dominant fact of life, and in most countries the religion is Islam. Even in a secular state, such as Turkey—where people drink wine, women dress in European style, and government is nonclerical—the culture of Islam predominates. In fact, in traditional societies, such as Saudi Arabia, Islam touches every corner. Here, the workweek runs from Saturday through Thursday morning, with the Sabbath being Friday. Prayers are said five times each day: at dawn, midday, afternoon, evening, and night; business stops for prayers. Consumption of alcohol is a criminal offense; pork is forbidden; dogs are unclean; a pair of shorts is an insult to decency; and Saudi woman (who by law wear veils in public) are deemed invisible. So strict is the separation between the sexes in some Arab states, in fact, that it is a breach of manners to ask the health of your counterpart's wife or daughters. Even when invited to a private home, a visiting male might never meet a Muslim female.

In some Middle Eastern nations, the business sector has been thoroughly Westernized. While most countries follow Islam, not all are Arab. The Turks, whose ancestors arrived a millennium ago from Central Asia, speak their own non-Arabic language and take pride in their own unique heritage. So do the Farsi-speaking Iranians, heirs to the ancient Persian Empire. But religious conservatism remains strong. In Israel—the one exception to this region's Islamic umbrella—questions of religious practice and belief need to be treated with utmost sensitivity.

UNDERSTANDING NAMES

Arabic names sometimes mystify Westerners, but the formula is simple. The given name comes first and then usually the father's given name followed by the family name; in between come syllables indicating the relationship. Thus, Abdul bin Khalid al-Saud is Abdul, son of Khalid, of the Saud family. Since the

IN MUSLIM COUNTRIES

Certain customs must be observed by businesspeople who travel to countries with large Muslim populations. These taboos apply in the following countries that are treated in this chapter: All of those in the Middle East, Egypt, and large portions of the populations of Indonesia, Malaysia, and India.

- Avoid using your left hand; it is symbolically unclean. Do not offer your left hand in a handshake, do not give a gift to your host with your left hand, and do not eat with your left hand.
- When seated in a chair keep both feet on the floor, and never show the soles of your feet.
- Don't touch anyone on the head, which is considered sacred.
- Keep in mind that you will not conduct business on Fridays—it is the Muslim holy day.
- Always remove your shoes before entering a mosque.
- Remember that five times each day, business stops for prayers.
- Do not ask a Muslim male about his wife or daughters.
- Wear only long pants, not shorts.
- Refrain from kissing or holding hands in public places with a member of the opposite sex.
- When giving gifts, avoid giving pictures of animals or people, since Islam frowns on realistic images of living creatures. Also, never give alcohol or objects made of pigskin.

house of Saud is the ruling dynasty of Saudi Arabia, Abdul bin Khalid is probably of royal blood and should be addressed as Prince Abdul.

THE GULF STATES

The oil kingdoms that border the Persian Gulf—Kuwait, Qatar, Bahrain, Oman, and the United Arab Emirates—are overwhelmingly Arabic in population and culture. The workweek starts Saturday and ends Wednesday afternoon or Thursday morning. Family pride, personal honor, and one-on-one relationships always come before the hard-nosed practicalities of business. Yet in most Gulf States, the precepts of Islam are applied with a certain flexibility.

Even though Islam prohibits alcohol, many first-class hotels and restaurants serve drinks. Bahrain in particular, with its luxurious beach resorts, is noted for its Western-style entertainment. Women generally enjoy greater freedom, and many wear European dress. In Kuwait and Oman, women may hold managerial positions in business and government. As in all Arab countries, conservative attire and a demure, businesslike stance is appropriate for female visitors. (See also In Muslim Countries, page 505.)

ISRAEL

Israelis are overwhelmingly Jewish (85 percent), and most non-Jews are Arabs. Among the Arabs is a small Christian population. Yet no other country of equal size contains such a variety of people from different countries and cultural backgrounds. Some Jews are deeply Orthodox, others thoroughly secular in outlook and belief. Many are recent immigrants. Each group tends to stick together, with little social overlap. At the same time, the business atmosphere tends to be open, informal, and accommodating, with little emphasis on rank or protocol. More than any other Middle Eastern people, Israelis are likely to follow American business practices.

Meeting and greeting. Meetings should be scheduled in advance, and they usually begin on time. But because of the sometimes hectic pace of business—and the fact that Israelis love to talk and argue—you may find yourself running late. Patience is advised. Business negotiations are relatively casual and unstructured, and people tend to use first names. While decisions may move slowly, Israelis are more likely than other Middle Easterners to address issues in an open, straightforward manner.

In most cases, a warm handshake is the standard greeting. Arabs may hug or kiss. The first rule is to know whom you are dealing with—something that is true of every negotiation. Government offices and most businesses follow a Jewish week—Sunday through Thursday, with the Sabbath beginning at sunset Friday and continuing through Saturday. Arabs observe the Sabbath a day earlier, while for Christians it is Sunday.

Business attire. Informality is the byword. Many Israeli men wear slacks and open-necked shirts to work. Women favor conservative suits or dresses; if planning to visit a synagogue or mosque, make sure the dress covers your elbows and knees. Engraved business cards are preferred.

Visiting and entertaining. Bring a gift of flowers or candy when invited to a meal at an Israeli home. If your host follows dietary laws, be sure your gift is kosher.

Social taboos. Israelis with European or American backgrounds tend to be more forgiving of social lapses. Still, it's best to steer the conversation away from politics and religion. With Orthodox Jews and Arabs, avoid discussions of regional politics and religion.

SAUDI ARABIA

As the homeland of Mohammed, and guardian of Islam's holy cities (including Mecca), this desert kingdom is one of the region's most traditional states. Alcohol is banned, bathing-suit ads are pornographic, and women have few legal rights. Life centers around family, religion, and an extended network of personal friendships and obligations.

In business, honor and status are as important as technical proficiency. Meetings tend to follow an "open door" pattern that took shape in the tents of tribal leaders, where anyone could enter to ask a favor or propose a deal. Often a dozen people will be speaking at the same time, on a dozen different topics. Saudis seem to thrive in this apparent chaos and have an uncanny ability to absorb and respond intelligently to a number of conversations simultaneously.

N O T E : Saudi legal codes and religious structures make this a difficult place for foreign women to do business.

Meeting and greeting. Make appointments well in advance, and arrive on time—but don't expect your Saudi counterpart to follow exactly the same schedule you do. It is customary to make visitors wait. Dress conservatively: coat and tie for men, and for women long skirts, high necklines, and long sleeves. Greetings are warm and effusive, with the hand often grasped and held rather than shaken. Use formal titles of address: Dr. Mahmoud, Prince Abdul. Business cards will be exchanged; yours should be in English on one side, Arabic on the other. Expect lengthy conversation, multiple participants, numerous cups of coffee, and frequent interruptions. Decisions may take months—and then occur with startling, almost spontaneous rapidity.

Visiting and entertaining. Skip a meal before you go to dinner at a Saudi home. Arab hospitality is proverbially lavish. Refuse nothing, and eat with relish—but not with the left hand. In a traditional home, be prepared to remove your shoes. A small gift—flowers or candy—is appreciated but not expected.

Social taboos. The "thumbs up" gesture is considered rude. Be careful never to criticize or correct anyone, not even on obvious points of fact. Refrain from discussing religion, regional politics, or sex. Avoid telling jokes, which may be misinterpreted. If your Saudi colleague embraces you or takes your hand, don't pull away: He's only being polite. (See also In Muslim Countries, page 505.)

Adjusting Your Cultural Lens

TURKEY

The city of Istanbul straddles the Bosporus, half in Europe and the other half in Asia, and Turkey, like its ancient capital, remains a hybrid—a complex and vibrant blend of East and West. Its government is a secular democracy, its population 99 percent Muslim. Every city has its mosques and bazaars. Yet the alphabet is roman, dress and manners are largely European, and business follows a Monday-through-Friday Western schedule.

This is a land of hustle and bustle, where marketplace haggling is a way of life—both in downtown carpet stores and in corporate boardrooms. The work ethic runs strong, and everyone puts in long hours. At the same time, much of the business day is devoted to nurturing a close personal rapport with both clients and coworkers. Companies here are often family enterprises, and the business culture reflects it.

Turkish women play increasingly important roles. They are doctors, lawyers, and journalists, and they hold high posts in government. Still, Turkey has a long history of male dominance, and men often make the final decisions.

Meeting and greeting. Make appointments well in advance, preferably with a letter of introduction from a mutual friend. Be prompt; Turkish businesspeople tend to follow Western time schedules. A handshake is the accepted greeting for both men and women. Address people by their last name, preceded by a title where appropriate; formal good manners are highly prized. Meetings start with extensive small talk designed to establish friendship and trust. Then the haggling begins. Age commands respect, and so always defer to the eldest person at the table. In most negotiations, an elder will make the final decision.

Business attire. Turks often judge others by the way they dress, and it's best to go conservative. Men wear dark suits and neckties. Women should choose long sleeves, modest necklines, and hemlines that cover the knees. Bring plenty of business cards.

Visiting and entertaining. Most entertaining occurs at restaurants—and you'll find it next to impossible to pick up the check; unless you're the host, don't even try. If invited to a private home, take flowers or candy, or a bottle of wine if you know your host imbibes.

Social taboos. Unless you know someone very well, use last names only. Don't cross your legs or show the soles of your shoes. Show respect to elders: Shake hands with the oldest person first, rise when an older person enters a room, and never precede an older person through a doorway. Do not cross your arms when facing someone, and keep your hands out of your pockets. Never openly disagree with a colleague in public: You'll cause him to loose face. (See also In Muslim Countries, page 505.)

ASIA

In Japan be prepared to bow from the waist, arms straight by your sides. Hong Kong businesspeople shake hands both on meeting and leaving. The traditional greeting in Thailand is to place your palms together and incline your head. A

Filipino friend in Manila may pat you on the back. Close friends in Pakistan commonly embrace.

Each time you get off an airplane in Asia, you encounter a whole new set of social customs. No region on earth contains such diversity of language, manners, religions, social outlook, and tradition. The Indian subcontinent has been invaded and colonized by Aryans, Muslims, Portuguese, French, and English, and each group has left its cultural imprint. China's national identity reaches back without interruption for more than 5,000 years; it is one of the world's oldest civilizations. Japan closed its doors to the outside world in 1638 and in its isolation spawned a code of behavior so intricate that only native-born Japanese seem to understand it thoroughly.

For all their differences, the people of Asia hold one trait in common: a rigorous, deeply ingrained sense of courtesy. The forms of social correctness vary from place to place, yet their underlying principles seldom change: respect for the elderly, personal humility, subordination to the group, unquestioning regard for authority, and meticulous avoidance of controversy or confrontation. Never should a person be allowed to lose face. Nothing must disturb the harmonious flow of proper social intercourse.

In order to save face and maintain harmony, Asians will go to almost any extreme to avoid bringing up inconvenient facts or ideas. Whatever your question or request, it will rarely be answered with the word "no." Instead you will hear a polite evasion, such as "Perhaps, but not yet" or "Very interesting. . . . We'll certainly consider it."

For the same reason, decisions tend to be reached by consensus—with proper deference, of course, to persons of rank and seniority. The process takes time, but time in Asia has a meaning of its own. No one has a keener sense of its value than, say, the production boss of a Toyota assembly line: The pace is breathtaking. Yet negotiations with company management may take weeks or even months. Schedules are put on hold, and no agreement is final until each issue is resolved to everyone's satisfaction. Not surprisingly, one of the supreme Asiatic virtues is patience.

CHINA

As Asia's oldest and largest nation, China is the cultural fatherland of virtually every other population in East Asia. Its past emperors and sages have shaped thought and behavior from the Himalayan mountains to the islands of the Pacific. Much of China's authority comes from the system of ethics spelled out by the fifth-century Confucius, who urged respect for superiors, duty toward family, loyalty to friends, hard work, education, thrift, humility, and punctilious courtesy toward all. If everyone follows these precepts, Confucius believed, universal harmony will prevail.

Even before the advent of Communism, China was a group-oriented culture where duty to one's family and village was more important than any personal need or desire. At the same time, personal status is vitally important. An individual of superior rank should never be kept waiting, for example. At meetings, the senior executive does the talking—and woe to the junior member who is brash enough to interrupt.

A surprising number of customs originate from Chinese folklore. Certain days are deemed more propitious than others. Buildings and offices are laid out according to the precepts of *feng shui,* which warns against unlucky alignments of doors, mirrors, and other elements. Every color has a symbolic meaning. Unlucky actions, such as placing chopsticks in parallel across the top of a rice bowl, are shunned.

At the same time, the Chinese have an innately practical turn of mind that serves them well in commerce and business. They love to deal, and they hold money in high esteem.

While Chinese women enjoy many of the same legal rights as men, they are still second-class citizens in business and society. Western women should meet with no discrimination in China, however, provided they act and dress in a modest, formal manner.

Meeting and greeting. A gentle bow of the head and a handshake is appropriate, with a lowering of the eyes to signify respect. Address people by title or position followed by last name: Systems Director Chin. Your business cards—and take plenty—should be bilingual, with the Chinese characters in black or gold. Never tuck someone's card in your wallet and then put your wallet in your back pocket.

Before every meeting it is customary to send a list of your delegation in order of rank, along with a detailed paper on the items under discussion. Be punctual. Chinese visitors to your office may arrive 15 minutes early "in order to save your time." Negotiating teams usually sit on opposite sides of a conference table. The top Chinese representative will enter the room first, and he will do the talking; your side should follow suit. Speak slowly in a quiet voice, avoiding undue eloquence or emotion. Act with patience and humility; never try to hurry a meeting along—and don't be alarmed by occasional silences. There is a Chinese saying that goes "Those who know do not speak; those who speak do not know."

Business attire. The old Mao jackets are giving way to Western-style suits and ties of conservative cut. Loud colors are never appropriate for either men or women. For men, beards are a disadvantage.

Visiting and entertaining. Business entertainment usually takes the form of a restaurant banquet. These tend to be lavish affairs of two hours or more with 20 or more courses and many toasts. Arrive at the appointed hour, or even a few minutes early. The honored guest will sit facing the door. A succession of serving dishes will be placed on the table, and you should help yourself—sparingly—from each. If no serving spoon is provided, use the reverse end of your chopsticks. Never take the last morsel. Let your host make the first toast, and remember to take small sips; as soon as your glass is empty your host will insist on refilling it. Leave a bit of food on your plate at the end. The next day send a thank-you note, and before you leave China, you should reciprocate with a banquet of your own.

Gifts. The Communist law barring gifts to Chinese officials has been relaxed, and the old traditions of gift exchange are beginning to come back. As with the Japanese, these traditions follow a highly developed etiquette; in fact, most of the same rules apply (see page 515). It is good manners to refuse a gift three times and then accept it with a show of reluctance. Good gifts include scotch or cognac, food, and high-quality ballpoint pens. Avoid giving clocks, straw sandals, and handkerchiefs (which are associated with funerals), or anything sharp, such as knives or scissors (which connote the severing of a relationship). Wrap presents in bright-colored paper: red, orange, or yellow. Avoid white, the color associated with death.

Social taboos. After the initial handshake, avoid touching any but a very close friend. Avoid the colors white, black, and blue, all considered funereal. Remember that the number four is considered unlucky. Point with your whole hand, never a single finger; to beckon, hold your palm down and bring your fingers toward you in a scooping motion.

HONG KONG

Now that Hong Kong has become part of the People's Republic of China, it is entering uncharted territory. For the past hundred years, as a British Crown Colony, it was one of the world's major duty-free trading ports—a bastion of laissez faire capitalism with an English accent and a Chinese soul. Business suits in corporate boardrooms come from Savile Row or its local equivalent. Yet many Hong Kong customs, such as a strict adherence to *feng shui* (see page 510), are often more deeply traditional than in mainland China itself. Manners tend to be formal. Gifts from Asian colleagues can be so extravagant as to be embarrassing. If making a return gift of equal value is beyond your company policy, substitute a well-thought-out personal favor.

INDIA

In some respects, India is perhaps the least typical of all Asian nations. Most of the population belongs to one of Hinduism's many religious sects, with the rest being largely Muslim, plus an additional scattering of Christians, Sikhs, Buddhists, Jains, and others. But the moral ethic of Confucianism, which frames attitudes throughout the rest of Asia, is absent here. The self-effacing modesty, verbal reticence, and consensus mentality so typical of more eastern lands—none of these are Indian traits. Indians love to talk, and they do so with expansive eloquence. They make little effort to hide their opinions. Emotions—joy, grief, frustration, disappointment—are quickly vented. Decisions come unilaterally from the top down.

One characteristic the Indians share with Chinese people is a passion for bargaining. They are masters at it. There is also a strong sense of family, and many businesses have been handed down through generations from father to son. At the same time, Indians admire individual creativity and are willing to take financial risks.

Meeting and greeting. Businessmen in India shake hands on meeting, and so may Westernized Indian women. Adding a slight bow indicates respect for a person who is older or of superior rank. In more traditional areas, Indian men do not shake hands with or otherwise touch women outside their families; instead, they will place the palms of their hands together and make a bow. Indians respect punctuality but do not always observe it themselves.

Most meetings open with sweet tea and small talk, and it never pays to hurry negotiations along. When refreshments are offered, it is polite to hesitate before accepting, but don't refuse.

Business attire. Clothing tends to be casual—slacks and a short-sleeved shirt—but it should be neat. For initial meetings a jacket is advised. Women may wear slacks and a jacket or long-sleeved blouse, or a dress if it comes below the knees. From New Delhi north, the winter weather may be chilly enough to require an overcoat.

Visiting and entertaining. Most business entertaining takes the form of lunch. If invited to an Indian home for dinner, it is polite to arrive 15 to 30 minutes late. A gift of chocolates or flowers will be appreciated. In traditional Indian homes it is customary to remove your shoes. Eat and pass serving dishes with the right hand only. To thank your hosts at the end of a meal is considered insulting—far better to offer a meal in return.

Social taboos. Avoid standing with hands on hips, since the gesture will be taken as a sign of aggression. If you touch someone with your foot, or even point your foot, apologize. As in Malay cultures such as Indonesia's, a person's head is sacred and should never be touched. Wearing leather—either belt, shoes, or handbag—into a mosque or temple is an affront to religion. (See also In Muslim Countries, page 505.)

INDONESIA

With its huge population, and its 13,600 islands sprawled across more than 3,000 miles of tropical ocean, Indonesia is one of the world's most culturally diverse nations. The majority of its people, and virtually all government officials, are of Malay descent. More Muslims live in Indonesia than in any other nation. On Bali, settled in part by traders from India, strong Hindu influences remain. Local-born Chinese, whose families may have been here for centuries, dominate business and commerce; most of them are Buddhist. Some 10 percent of Indonesians are Christian. The nation has three calendars—one Western, one Islamic, and one Hindu—and a Pandora's box of languages and customs.

The traditional Pan-Asian unities apply, however. Few people are more modestly soft-spoken or more naturally polite. Family, social status, respect for elders and superiors, an instinct for consensus-building—all are important ingredients of Indonesian life. The Malay dialect of Java has 12 different ways to indicate "no" without actually saying the word. One technique is nonverbal—a quick intake of air through the teeth, implying that a proposition is full of difficulties.

The perception of time varies according to ethnic group. Malays follow a concept of "rubber time," which stretches according to the occasion. (Note, however, that a person of higher status must never be kept waiting.) One advantage is that meetings can often be scheduled on relatively short notice. The Chinese, on the other hand, tend to be punctual.

Indonesia's large Muslim population is fragmented into numerous sects, which observe Islam's taboos against pork and alcohol with varying degrees of rigor. Unlike many Islamic countries, Indonesia gives full rights to women, and women hold responsible positions in business. Almost no one wears a veil.

Meeting and greeting. On first meeting someone, Indonesians offer a gentle handshake and after that a nod or slight bow. The older the other person, the deeper the bow. Men will shake women's hands on meeting, but subsequent physical contact in public is considered unseemly. Business cards are essential, but put any given to you in your jacket pocket rather than tucking it in your wallet and then putting your wallet in a back pocket.

Business attire. Because of Indonesia's equatorial climate, people dress in lightweight cotton garments. Jackets and ties are customary for formal business meetings, but the jackets will probably be removed. Outside Jakarta, a short-sleeved shirt and tie will suffice. Women should defer to Muslim and Hindu sensibilities by wearing long sleeves and hemlines that come below the knees. Colors should be muted.

Visiting and entertaining. When invited to a social event it is customary to show up a little late. But if someone of higher rank is expected, be sure to get there first. Important people, as with royalty the world over, must be allowed to arrive after everyone else and should be the first to depart. It is polite to take flowers when invited to dinner.

Social taboos. Among both Muslims and Hindus, many of the same caveats apply (see also In Muslim Countries, page 505). Among some Indonesians it is rude to pound your fist into the palm of your hand. Don't point. Never refuse a gift, but wait until later to open it unless urged otherwise. Other than shaking hands, never touch anyone of the opposite sex in public. Don't be surprised to see men holding hands, which is customary.

JAPAN

When an American businessman meets someone, he gives his name and then the name of the organization he represents. In Japan it is the opposite. "Sony

Records Group, Regional Sales," he will say, "Associate Manager Yamadori." The priorities couldn't be more clear: For the Japanese, the organization comes first and the individual last.

No culture is more self-effacingly group conscious. The Japanese derive their sense of identity from the various groups to which they belong—family, high school, university class, age category, workplace, or corporation—and from where they rank in the hierarchy of each one. Equally important, they need to know the same particulars about you. The Japanese language is full of honorific phrases that must be adjusted to reflect the status of the person being spoken to. In theory, two Japanese cannot conduct a conversation unless each knows exactly how and where the other fits in. They often find foreigners difficult to place, and this becomes a source of social embarrassment.

Life in Japan can be seen as unfolding in a series of ceremonial events, each with its appointed forms and rituals. Most of these rituals, from how to hold a meeting to the right way to eat miso soup, take years even to comprehend, much less imitate. No one expects a visitor to get them right. Indeed, foreigners are generally put in the same category as children—innocent and charming but not yet able to behave. If you make a faux pas don't expect anyone to tell you, however, since to do so would be impolite.

Another Japanese trait that Westerners find difficult to fathom is the lack of facial expression. Joy and sorrow, anger and delight, comprehension and confusion—nothing seems to ruffle the public dignity of the Japanese. When they smile, they strike some Westerners as being insincere. Not true. Some smiles indicate pleasure and amusement, while others may hide embarrassment, confusion, anger, or disappointment.

While women find work in all spheres of business, they stand lower in the social and corporate pecking order. Foreign women, who belong to no clearly understandable hierarchy, have a distinct advantage.

Meeting and greeting. Most Japanese businessmen will shake hands with Westerners, but on meeting each other they are quite likely to bow. The more senior the other person, the deeper the bow. Cards are then exchanged; yours should be in both English and Japanese. Present it with both hands, Japanese side up and facing the recipient. When given a card, handle it with respect; never put it in your back pocket but in your jacket pocket instead. Be modest and reserved, avoiding large movements and expansive gestures. Always use last names: Dr. Saito, or Saito-san.

Business appointments should be made well in advance, and punctuality is essential. It's best to determine the agenda beforehand and stick to it, since the Japanese do not like surprises. The first 15 minutes will be devoted to social pleasantries. Early meetings are designed to get to know each other and for gathering information. Speak slowly and expect long pauses while everyone considers the issue at hand. If someone closes his eyes and appears to nod off, don't be alarmed: He's just concentrating on what you're saying. Since the Japanese prefer to move by indirection, avoid the hard sell: Hype turns them off. Don't expect any quick decisions. Never try to hurry the meeting along, and don't push too hard on schedules or deadlines or your Japanese colleagues may simply walk away from the deal. Remember, also, that the word "no" is never used.

Business attire. Wear nothing that will make you stand out. Japanese businessmen favor blue or gray suits, white shirts, and conservative ties; for women, modest sleeves and necklines, low heels, and conservative makeup. The exception is fashion and the arts, where you should take your cue from current international styles. Wearing slip-on shoes will facilitate their necessary removal in Japanese-style restaurants and homes.

Visiting and entertaining. Once office hours have ended, your real business day may just be beginning. Expect to be treated to lavish restaurant dinners and drinking parties at karaoke bars. Arrive on time. When entering a Japanese-style room with tatami floors, remove your shoes; slippers will be provided. Allow your host to do the ordering and protest that he's being too generous. Dexterity with chopsticks is advised. When you are the host, set an example by ordering from the high end of the menu; otherwise the senior Japanese person will show his modesty by opting for plain soup and salad, thereby forcing his lower-ranking colleagues to do the same. There is one situation where the rules of etiquette are placed on hold. After a festive evening, with copious libations of scotch and sake, the Japanese tend to forgive all but the most egregious lapses of decorum.

Gifts. The Japanese exchange gifts on virtually every occasion, and the ways of doing so have been refined into high art. Everything has symbolic meaning—the items given, the way they are wrapped, the methods of presentation. A few basic rules: Gifts should be wrapped in lightly tinted (never white) paper, presented and received with both hands, offered at an inconspicuous moment, and opened after the donor has departed. Prime steaks, good scotch or cognac, and luxury items from upmarket American stores all make good gifts. To avoid gift-exchange embarrassment, it's best to seek guidance from a Japanese friend or advisor.

Social taboos. After an initial handshake, avoid physical contact: Japanese people don't like to be touched. (Oddly, the noncontact rule is suspended in crowded streets and subways, which tend to resemble football scrimmages.) Avoid looking people directly in the eye lest you invade their sense of privacy. Never boast; a self-effacing manner carries you farther. Never say "no" or "I can't do it."

MALAYSIA

The same multicultural mix that distinguishes Indonesia (see page 512) will be found here. The same rules of etiquette generally apply, with native Malaysians following Muslim custom and the Chinese population doing business much like their Indonesian counterparts. Be careful not to bring up politics, a discussion of which could put Malaysians in an uncomfortable position because of the government's attitude toward dissent.

A NOTE ABOUT NAMES

In Far Eastern nations such as China and Japan the family name comes first. Li Wu Chin belongs to the Li family clan, and his given name is Wu Chin; he is properly addressed as Mr. Li. Similarly, Yamamoto Kobo is Mr. Yamamoto. But variations to this rule abound. Japanese businessmen who deal frequently with foreigners sometimes reverse the traditional order of names, putting the family name last. Similarly, overseas Chinese who have been educated in missionary schools or Western universities often add a Western first name: Mr. "Tommy" Li Wu Chin. While most Asians prefer being addressed by their family names, in Thailand it is common to use given names: Mr. Tommy. Women of Chinese descent commonly keep their maiden names.

To further complicate matters, people of Hindu or Malay origin traditionally had only one name—though often one of many syllables in length. According to custom, an initial representing the father's name would appear in front of someone's given name. Jawal's son Mehta would write his name J. Mehta. Jawal's daughter Gita would style herself J. Gita. Most educated Hindus and Malays now use Western-style family names, however. Three political leaders of modern India have carried the family name Gandhi, beginning with that nation's founding father, Mohandas Karamchand Gandhi.

Throughout Asia, it is good manners to address people by their business or professional titles: Doctor Shiga, President Chan, Chief Engineer Mehta. Because of his charismatic leadership, Gandhi earned the religious title Mahatma, meaning "great souled."

Women are perhaps less likely to shake hands with men. Because of the heat, almost no one wears a jacket. As in Singapore, be careful not to drop bits of paper or cigarette stubs in the streets of Kuala Lumpur, which has stiff penalties for littering. (See also In Muslim Countries, page 505.)

THE PHILIPPINES

It is easy for Americans to feel at home in the Philippines, with its cosmopolitan blend of Spanish, American, and native Pacific cultures. More than 80 percent of the population is Roman Catholic. English is the national language, yet Filipinos retain many of the attitudes and customs of their East Asian neighbors.

Few people have a more delicate sense of public dignity and self-esteem. The traditions of Spanish pride and Asian "face" combine to make Filipinos extremely conscious of personal status. It is vitally important to show deference toward people of high rank and advanced age, and to be polite to everyone. So careful is a Filipino not to give offense that he will apologize to a beggar for not handing him money.

The basis of Filipino life is an extended network of family connections that reaches across both society and business. It always pays to schedule meetings through a mutual friend. Meetings seldom start on time, but foreigners are expected to be reasonably prompt. (Social events—except for weddings—always begin up to half an hour late. No one will be ready if you arrive on time.) Upper-class Filipinos follow the Spanish formula of having two surnames, with the father's name coming first followed by that of the mother. Juan Antonio Rodriguez de la Rama, a scion of the Rodriguez and de la Rama families, is called Mr. Rodriguez.

More than elsewhere in Asia, Filipino women have achieved equal status with men. You will find them represented at the highest levels of government, politics, law, and business. Nonetheless, a modest, self-effacing manner on the part of women is most respected.

Meeting and greeting. Filipino businesspeople greet foreigners with a brief handshake and direct eye contact. Men do not initiate handshakes with women. Address people by title and surname until invited to do otherwise. Business cards are essential.

Business attire. Dress can be stylishly informal, but it is always neat: jacket and tie for men, matching accessories for women. Note that Filipinos are extremely fashion conscious. Do not wear shorts in the street.

Visiting and entertaining. Expect to be wined and dined by your Filipino colleagues. Most entertainment takes place in private houses, where gatherings are likely to include large numbers of relatives and guests and lavish amounts of food. Bring flowers or chocolates, and send a thank-you note the next day. At the close of a business deal, treat your Filipino partners to dinner at a restaurant. Be sure to reconfirm each invitation you give out: Filipinos expect to be asked several times.

Social taboos. Be careful to avoid any action that can be interpreted as a personal affront. If you stare at a Filipino, or point your finger, he will probably take it as an insult. Placing both hands on the hips is also an aggressive posture. Any display of anger or impatience will cause you to lose face, at the very least. In conversation, avoid anything that implies criticism or contradiction; even in bottom-line matters of business, excessive frankness or "honesty" is deemed offensive.

SINGAPORE

Like Hong Kong, Singapore is an Asian city with a British manner. Its prominence as a business center results largely from the aggressive economic policies of its first prime minister, Lee Kuan Yew, who in 1965 pulled the city out of Malaysia and declared it independent. Combining Western business efficiencies with the Confucian values of hard work and moral discipline, the Cambridge-educated Lee stamped out endemic corruption and created one of Asia's first economic miracles.

Chinese make up 75 percent of the city's population, with the rest being Malays, Indians, and Europeans. Each group tends to follow its own social customs. Business dress is neat but often informal because of the climate. Western businessmen should wear jacket and tie, but expect to remove the jacket. Women dress conservatively. Singapore authorities look severely on even minor infractions of local rules—from littering, to traffic violations, to unseemly public displays of affection or high spirits.

SOUTH KOREA

Despite its Westernized facade, Korea remains staunchly Confucian in outlook and manner. Not even the Chinese show more respect to their elders or place greater importance on the business of saving face. At the same time, Koreans are fiercely proud of their non-Chinese heritage. Their language derives from the same root as Turkish and Mongolian, and it is written in a phonetic script created centuries ago by a scholarly Korean emperor. Koreans tend to be tough-minded, physically strong, and outgoing in nature.

Despite these formalities, most Americans find Koreans easy to get along with. The secret is humor. Koreans love a good laugh, and they take keen enjoyment in life's absurdities. Remember, however, that laughter can also be a cover-up for anxiety or frustration.

Meeting and greeting. Like most East Asians, Koreans work hard and put in long hours. Business meetings follow much the same pattern as in Japan and Hong Kong. Show deference, to point of never placing anything, even important papers, on the desk of a company chairman.

Westerners are greeted with a handshake accompanied by brief eye contact, which indicates sincerity. Korean elders commonly receive a bow. Korean women do not ordinarily shake hands.

Business attire. Conservative business dress is the norm.

Visiting and entertaining. When visiting a traditional Korean house, you will be expected to remove your shoes and sit on the floor. Men sit cross-legged, women with their feet tucked under them. Never stretch your legs out straight or touch anyone with your feet. Bring a gift of fruit, flowers, liquor, or perhaps fine coffee or tea. When you receive an invitation to dinner at a restaurant, be aware that some Korean entertainments for men are lavish affairs that can run to thousands of dollars and can include entertainment by women known as *kisaeng,* the Korean equivalent of the Japanese geisha.

TAIWAN

On first impression, Taiwan seems like a place of almost raucous energy. Streets are crowded and bustling, the decibel level is high, and everyone seems to be hurrying off to some important task or rendezvous. Indeed, it is a hotbed of business activity. It is also steeped in the same Confucian sensibility as is mainland China. (Bear in mind that Taiwan's official name is the Republic of China and that the large country across the straits to the north is called mainland China.)

The Taiwanese place the same emphasis as do mainlanders on modesty, deportment, saving face, and group obligation. But while a mainlander's first loyalty is to the state, which is still the major employer, here it is to family and clan. Most businesses are family-owned and -operated. Be respectful toward elderly people; do not smoke or wear sunglasses in their presence. The protocol for business cards is the same as that of mainland China (page 510).

Styles of dress tend to be more casual than in Hong Kong or on the mainland, though a conservative choice is usually best. Women executives will find few difficulties dealing with Taiwanese businessmen, particularly in fashion-related industries; remember, however, that an assertive manner is not appreciated. As in Hong Kong, the giving and receiving of expensive gifts is a regular part of doing business.

THAILAND

Thailand bills itself as "the Land of Smiles," and few people seem to get quite so much enjoyment out of life. Laughter comes as naturally as breathing—both as an expression of happiness and also to cover any unintended lapses of manners. People are generally gentle, courteous, and friendly, and the pace of business tends to be relaxed. Decisions are arrived at slowly, with every effort to maintain harmony. As elsewhere in Asia, "yes" can mean yes, maybe, or even no, depending on the context. Gifts help make a good first impression—a bottle of scotch for an executive, perhaps, and candy or cookies for his receptionist.

Meeting and greeting. While punctuality at meetings is admired, the traffic conditions of Bangkok often make it unattainable. The traditional Thai salutation is the *wei*—palms together at chest level, accompanied by a slight bow. Foreigners, both men and women, are usually met with a handshake. Thais often address one another by first names or nicknames, usually preceded by a title. Don't be surprised when someone calls you Mr. Joe or Dr. Betty.

Visiting and entertaining. Be aware that the wives of Thai businessmen are expected to be included in business dinners.

Business attire. Great store is placed on personal neatness, with a dark jacket and tie for men and conservative dresses for women recommended for business settings.

Social taboos. Never touch anyone on the head, especially children. Don't walk in front of a person who is praying. Never touch a monk; women should avoid even handing anything to monks, who are forbidden all contact with females. It is rude to point your foot at anyone or to show the soles of your shoes. When entering a Thai home, make sure not to tread on the doorsill, since the spirit of the house is said to reside there. Outbursts of temper should be avoided, as well as public displays of affection between men and women.

AFRICA

The many faces of Africa are reflected in a wide diversity of customs that were spawned from myriad tribal traditions and the residual effects of years under foreign domination. It is a vast and complex continent, home to many distinctive and disparate cultures. Arabic and Islamic culture prevails in northern countries such as Egypt, for example, while the 250 ethnic tribes of Nigeria make this nation a rich and varied cultural stew. South Africa's customs reflect the influences of 300 years of Dutch and English settlements. The mestizo (mixed-race) population of Cape Verde have more in common with Portuguese culture (the island was uninhabited when the Portuguese settled there) than African.

In much of Africa, English is spoken, but your hosts will be most impressed if you can learn a few words of the local language. This may be more difficult than it seems; many nations in Africa are comprised of tens of indigenous tribes, each with its own language.

GREETINGS IN GENERAL

A gentle handshake is the accepted form of greeting, and you should shake the hand of everyone in the room both when you arrive and when you leave. You'll find that in most countries, however, men will not shake a woman's hand—but they will if she is from the West and if she extends her hand first. In former French colonies, the greeting will often include kisses on each cheek. Greetings are long, effusive, and endlessly upbeat—implying that everything in life is fine and going well. Prepare to do a good deal of casual chatting before getting down to business; pushy business dealings are considered rude. In South American countries, maintaining direct eye contact is important; in most African nations, the opposite applies: Prolonged eye contact should be avoided.

Africans place great import on respect for the elderly. They are also tolerant of and generous with beggars; if your host gives to a beggar, you can certainly follow suit. On the other hand, there are people who are not beggars who make their living asking for handouts from foreigners. You can tell them from real beggars by their relatively well-heeled appearance. Don't encourage these people by giving them money.

You'll find that most African people are very courteous, friendly, and giving, and they love to entertain. If you are asked to dine in a private home, however, be prepared to eat with your hands. Some traditional households, especially in more rural areas, do not use utensils. Your hosts will be happy to show you the proper way to eat by hand if that is their custom.

When visiting the countries of Africa, keep your dress conservative; it is acceptable for women to wear pants in most areas, but they should always dress modestly or risk harassment by local men. Some Africans have adopted Western dress, but many others wear traditional native garb—beautiful, elaborate, and colorfully designed *kaftans* and the embroidered robe known as the *grand boubou*.

ONGOING CHANGE

Democracy is slowly attaining a toehold in Africa's volatile political landscape. Native Africans were suppressed by foreign imperialism over the years, which left them susceptible to totalitarian rule by tyrannical rulers once their countries became independent. Real independence—and a desire by the African people to choose their own leaders and chart their own future—remains an ongoing process. Many countries—such as Rwanda, the Congo, Liberia, Somalia, and Ethiopia—are struggling with violent infighting and human-rights violations and are not recommended destinations for foreigners. Others, such as Libya, are political enemies of the United States, and passports are not valid without special validation. Therefore, the countries discussed in this section are only those African nations where travel is advised and foreign trade is encouraged as of the end of 1999.

EGYPT

This largely Islamic country was the site of one of the world's oldest and most sophisticated civilizations, whose people built fantastic monuments, tombs, and dams. Theirs is an Arabic culture—Arabic is the country's official spoken and written language. Egyptians are not uncomfortable with many Western ideas and customs. Despite the presence of extreme poverty and the resulting rise of fundamentalism and its terrorist violence toward tourists, Egyptians as a whole are friendly and respectful of outsiders. Know, however, that in Egypt, family honor and kinship mean everything, and few social ties exist outside the family environment. Don't be shocked if your business meetings are frequently interrupted by family matters and visits from friends. While family and kinship are of primary importance, that doesn't make it any easier for women in Egyptian society. A woman is simply not a man's equal here, but progress is being made, and women have more rights in Egypt than in some other Muslim countries.

Meeting and greeting. Be prompt for any meeting, but don't expect the same from your Egyptian associates. Plus, expect the business process to take much longer than in the West. You will spend much of your time in your initial meetings with Egyptian associates becoming acquainted and developing a personal relationship.

Greet your Egyptian associates with a firm handshake, but don't be put off when they maintain physical closeness. Egyptian men like to get physically close to those they are conversing with; strangers will even stand in close proximity to one another in public. Egyptians often walk hand in hand—and that includes male friends.

Visiting and entertaining. Because most Egyptians are Muslims, they are prohibited from drinking alcohol and eating pork. Private clubs and hotels often serve alcohol, though. Egyptians find great pleasure in entertaining foreigners. Dinner is often served late in the evening. It is rude to clean your plate; always leave a little something uneaten.

Business attire. Dress conservatively in Egypt, even on your days off. In Islamic culture, particularly for women, modest dress is the rule. This means wearing clothing that effectively covers arms, legs, and necklines, no matter how hot the weather.

Social taboos. Avoid crossing your legs in public or pointing at anyone. Giving someone the "thumbs-up" signal is considered rude. If you see someone tapping his forefingers together, know that it is a crude reference to sex. (See also In Muslim Countries, page 505.)

NIGERIA

The most populous nation in Africa, Nigeria is struggling at the turn of the millennium with the ramifications of a military dictatorship, a staggering growth rate, crime (Lagos, West Africa's largest city, is extremely dangerous), and chronic infighting among the country's 250 ethnic groups and tribes. Customs vary greatly among the tribes, and many different indigenous languages are spoken. For Nigerian women, however, the news is good: The business culture is one of the most open to women in Africa. Nigerian women hold prestigious positions and are not held back because of their gender.

When meeting with Nigerian business associates, be prompt and expect your hosts to be punctual as well. That doesn't mean, however, that the meeting will start at the appointed time.

The African custom of long, effusive greetings and prebusiness socializing keeps business matters at bay for some time. Business meetings thereafter are generally held during restaurant lunches or meals in private homes. Don't expect quick action, though: Business transactions often become ensnared in governmental red tape.

The potential of this dynamic, resource-rich country is unlimited, particularly if the political gains of the last five years bear fruit. The end of apartheid and white-minority rule in 1994 marked a historic milestone and a major upheaval in the political and social landscape, one in which South African citizens are still grappling with. The major groups of South Africa are the white descendants of British settlers, the white descendants of Dutch, German, or French settlers (the Afrikaners), the mixed-race group known as coloreds, and native blacks, which make up the majority population. South Africans generally speak both English and the Dutch-derivative Afrikaans.

The British and the Afrikaners are quite different temperamentally: The British are reserved and extremely polite, while the Afrikaners prefer a more brusque, "straight-shooting" style and an often closed-ranks approach to forays by foreigners into the South African business world.

South African women are not treated as equals, but Western business-women should have little trouble in their business dealings if they avoid appearing too strong or too aggressive.

Meetings and greetings. The midday heat makes the morning the best time to work; South Africans are often up and in their offices by 8 A.M., so in order to do business, you should follow suit and arrange early-morning meetings. White South Africans have a Westernized sense of punctuality and spend little time on social chatter, preferring to get right down to business. Native Africans and colored have a more flexible take on time and like to get to know their business counterparts before switching to business matters. In the native African culture, men generally precede women into and out of a room.

Visiting and entertaining. Expect to be entertained by South Africans—and expect business matters to be put aside during any social occasion. Barbecues, called *braais,* are popular forms of entertaining. Be sure to contribute to a *braai* in some way, with a bottle of wine or a dessert.

Business attire. With summer in South Africa (December through March) comes a more practical way to dress: khaki shirts and bermuda shorts help beat the heat. Otherwise, men and women should opt for typical Western business attire.

Social taboos. Handshakes differ among blacks and whites: Whites greet each other with the standard handshake only, whites and other blacks greet blacks with the standard handshake, followed by a grasping of thumbs and a return to the standard grip.

AUSTRALIA AND NEW ZEALAND

Separated by 1,100 miles of the Tasman Sea, these two countries are often thought of in the same breath—a mistake for any businessperson. Australia and New Zealand do indeed have an immigration agreement that allows them to

*Adjusting
Your
Cultural Lens*

enter and work in each other's countries. But while they both were administered as an entity by the British up to the mid 1800s, their geological and immigration histories couldn't be much farther apart, with Australia starting life as a harsh convict settlement and New Zealand as a lush green magnet for British settlers, all of whom went there of their own accord.

Still, besides remembering to take into account the friendly rivalry that exists between the two countries and behaving accordingly, American businesspeople will be more at home here than in anyplace other than Canada.

AUSTRALIA

It's said that the Aussies love the Yanks, and vice versa—and it is hard to make a faux pas here unless it's to put on airs. Moreover, the farther north you go, the more casual the atmosphere. In a parallel to the United States, the warmer the climate the more casual the people seem to be, whether in the rate of their speech or their clothing. Down Under, that means going northward, not south. The southern Australian cities of Melbourne and Adelaide are decidedly more formal than free-spirited Brisbane (capital of the northern state of Queensland) and remote Darwin (capital of the Northern Territory at the part of the continent called the Top End). The attitude in Sydney falls somewhere in between.

Egalitarianism is much in evidence in Australia, to the point that a sole taxi passenger will often sit in the front seat with the driver. This fierce sense of democracy runs parallel to what the Australians call "tall poppy syndrome," by which individuals who rise too far above their peers are cut down to size.

As in the United States and Canada, women have risen to the highest levels of business and, like their Northern Hemisphere counterparts, expect to be treated no differently than a man would under the circumstances.

Meeting and greeting. Don't be fooled into thinking that because of the easygoing nature of Australians you can be a little late to a meeting. Punctuality is important. Although Australians love humor and place special value on personal relationships, they tend to get down to business fairly quickly in an effort to make a quick decision. This doesn't mean they're not going to carefully consider all of the ramifications before closing a business deal.

Australian greeting customs are so akin to those in the United States that any missteps are unlikely. While men shake hands at the start and finish of a meeting, women rarely shake hands with one another. (The American handshake is no more forceful than the Australian and New Zealand models, but it lasts longer—so keep your handshake brisk.) Australians are informal enough to quickly move to first names.

Visiting and entertaining. An after-work visit to the pub is a long-standing Australian tradition, so don't be surprised if you're invited for a round of beers after an end-of-day meeting. Tipping customs are the same as those of New Zealand (see below). If you're invited to an Australian home, take a bottle of one of the many topnotch Australian wines.

Business attire. Some Australian men remove their jackets more readily than Americans do, especially in restaurants—but doff yours only when they do. Otherwise, standards of business dress are the same as those in America.

Social taboos. Be careful with imitating Australianisms: Saying "G'day, mate" instead of "Good morning" or "Hello" will be taken as patronizing by some businesspeople.

NEW ZEALAND

Somewhat more reserved than their Australian neighbors across the Tasman, New Zealanders nonetheless generally take to Americans just as readily. They also expect you to understand that their country is not an annex of sorts to the larger and more populous Australia. Trusting and hardworking, they are known for their socially conscious attitudes and the interest they take in national and international issues.

This doesn't portend a natural seriousness in all things, however. New Zealanders love sports and talking about the many attractions of their country, and, much like the Australians, they feel a natural affinity with Americans. At the same time, New Zealanders are somewhat less inclined to aggrandize their country than Australians are theirs.

Meeting and greeting. Meetings are often held in a hotel or restaurant, but usually after an initial meeting at the office. Arrive a little early for a meeting. Start out on the more formal side; New Zealanders will warm to you, but not as quickly as Australians. New Zealanders expect detail and completeness from people they do business with, so be especially well prepared.

Women shake hands with women, but a man should let a woman extend her hand first. (See also Meeting and Greeting, page 524.)

Visiting and entertaining. Arrive on time; the concept of fashionably late doesn't cut it here. If you are invited to dinner, it will be for social, not business, reasons. Lunch, on the other hand, is for business. Tipping isn't customary in a hotel or taxi, but is not uncommon in restaurants when it is justified. A taxi driver who goes beyond the usual run of service won't be offended by a tip.

Business attire. New Zealanders dress slightly more conservatively than Australians when doing business, but they are just as casual at other times.

Social taboos. Don't discuss race. Also, calling attention to yourself in any way, such as talking loudly or back-slapping, stands out all the more here.

PART XI

THE HOME OFFICE

I f you've ever dreamed of being your own boss, your time may have arrived. The new age of the sole proprietor working from a home office has begun, with thousands of Americans joining the ranks of the self-employed every day. But be forewarned: The facts are that small businesses fail at an alarmingly high rate, leaving disappointed customers and desperate clients in their wake. You owe these important people the courtesy of leaving no stone unturned and no detail unattended, so that your business will succeed.

The information in this section is designed to guide you through the myriad decisions and challenges of home-based work, including the essentials of setting up and getting off to a good start. The first chapter takes a hard look at the decision to become independent and the process of getting off the ground. The second turns to the many relationships you must nurture—from clients to suppliers—to keep your business purring smoothly, with advice on managing employees and farming out tasks to others. The final chapter deals with the people closest to you—family, friends, and neighbors—and how you can run your business without trampling on their needs or allowing their proximity to adversely affect your work.

CHAPTER 37

A SPECIAL OPPORTUNITY

A rhyme of sorts: "No more cubicles, no more meetings, no more bosses' daily pleadings." If you've abandoned the corporate high-rise for the adventure of going it on your own, sing it out. You're in excellent company. In the latter two decades of the 20th century, millions of Americans opted out of the traditional office environment to start their own small businesses.

The explosion in home-based work results from the move of the American worker toward independence. For the budding entrepreneur, working at home makes it possible to cut costs during the start-up of a small business; for the independent consultant, of whom today there are surely millions, it is home base for a career that may be conducted largely on the road.

No longer is home-based work limited to rugged individualists. In today's economy, home-based workers are just as likely to be the full-time employees of major businesses as the self-employed and entrepreneurial. (For home-based telecommuting, see When You Telecommute, page 114.)

PROS AND CONS

The home office is hardly new. For the greater part of human history, most work was done in and around the home. This country began as a nation of farmers and small-business owners who more than likely lived over the shop. Even with mass industrialization and corporate centralization, some workers— from Nobel laureates to the Avon lady—have always worked best from home. Its history notwithstanding, working from home presents the millions who do it with a mix of advantages and disadvantages.

ON THE BRIGHT SIDE

There are considerable advantages to home and hearth, centered around the ability to call the shots and to enjoy the fruits of self-sufficiency. Here are four:

- **FREEDOM.** Working from home gives you the freedom to move your business in your own direction. Whether your role model is Henry Thoreau or Ross Perot, entrepreneurship is the opportunity to set your own goals, operate and adapt as you see fit, and reap the rewards of your own ideas.

- **CONTROL.** You have direct control over your time and schedule. Successful self-employed workers generally find that they make far more productive use of their time when they are free from the culture of the water cooler, endless meetings, office politics, and the vagaries of the corporate power structure.
- **COMFORT.** Ah, the pleasures of informality! You can go straight to work without donning a suit or warming up the car for the 45-minute commute. You can hold client conferences (the telephone variety) in your bathrobe, eat breakfast at noon, pick up the children after school—and still get all your work done. So long as "casual" doesn't become slovenly, the lifestyle of the home worker can be a genuine pleasure.
- **SAVING.** After your initial investments, your overhead is generally lower than renting or purchasing separate office space. Despite serious inequities in federal and state tax codes, there are also tax benefits in operating a home office. Most important, you decide how your business dollars are spent, and when you get a bonus, you will know that you have earned it.

NOT SO GREAT

Despite its inherent advantages, the home office is not Nirvana. Home-based workers face a special, and often surprising, set of problems. The solution to some is often one simple word: no. "No, I won't chair the Boy Scouts fundraiser this year." "No, I can't accept that last-minute assignment." "No, I won't try to do my own income taxes." One of the first challenges facing every home-based worker is mastering the art of the gracious but firm "No."

- **FALSE PERCEPTIONS.** Many people still see working at home as less serious than office work. The image of the home-based worker as a happy-go-lucky type, doing a little work between soap operas and gossiping with the neighbors, is far from dead. Too many important people—bankers, politicians who control zoning laws, and even clients—still regard home-based work as a kind of hobby or adult toy. Women in particular must cope with the outdated but still lively stereotype of "the little homemaker who does a bit of real work on the side. How cute."
- **FALSE EXPECTATIONS.** Family and friends are inclined to take advantage of the home-based worker's time and talents. Because you are at home, you're obviously available, right? You won't mind doing a little baby-sitting or taking over that church project, right? Wrong! There's a lot of helpful advice around about dealing with children when you work at home,

but kids may get the message a good deal quicker than spouses, in-laws, and old buddies. It's tough to tell the people closest to your heart that your office hours are sacrosanct and that dropping by without an appointment is unacceptable.

- **LONELINESS.** Most self-employed workers who are entirely on their own have some degree of difficulty adjusting to the solitude. The transition from a bustling commercial site, full of interesting people and activities, to the relative quiet of a home office can be a nerve-racking experience. Even if you truly hated office work, you will likely find yourself missing the day-to-day interaction with and stimulation of colleagues and coworkers.
- **BORING DETAILS.** Being in charge of everything is not what it's cracked up to be. Anticipating freedom and independence, self-employed workers quickly find themselves immersed in arcane essentials that once were handled by someone else. Bookkeeping, taxes, business licenses and permits, insurance, marketing, business supplies, shipping and receiving, inventories, billing, collecting, payroll—on and on the responsibilities mount. It's tempting to let the boring tasks slide.
- **BEING OVEROPTIMISTIC.** Self-employed workers can be their own worst enemies. Failing to set reasonable goals and expectations, they bite off more than they can chew, taking on excessive workloads, demanding the impossible of themselves, and setting the stage for failure.

SETTING GOALS

The difficulties of setting up and operating your own business can often be prevented or ameliorated by serious goal-setting and planning. Obviously, your goal is to succeed. But succeed at what? And how? Freedom is the siren song of working from home. But the prospect of being one's own boss has lured many a would-be entrepreneur into treacherous waters.

An excellent place to start is with self-evaluation. What are your strengths and weaknesses? This is not the same as a performance review. How you perform the job you know may be less important in the long run than how well you are equipped to perform all the jobs you don't know.

Here is a checklist of critical questions to ask yourself:

- Can you afford to start your own business now? Can you afford the benefits, such as health insurance, workers' compensation, and pension plans, that an employer provides?
- Are you contemplating home-based work because you want to or because you have to? Do you see it as permanent or temporary?

A Special Opportunity

- How likely are you to adapt to an entirely new work structure? How well do you deal with unforeseen situations?
- What is your work ethic? Do you work to live, or live to work?
- Are you prepared to "sell" yourself, as well as your product or service?
- How much contact do you need with other adults in the workplace?
- Do you have the temperament to deal with frustrating customers?
- Do you enjoy your own company?

Be honest. When you understand, for example, that you are the kind of person who needs motivation or direction, you will be alert to a potential problem area when you no longer have a boss. By admitting that you rely on the security of a regular paycheck, you'll be better prepared to budget and manage your cash flow. An up-front dose of self-examination will help you refine and perhaps change your plans. If financial instability really is terrifying, for instance, you may be able to establish a telecommuting relationship with your current employer and delay full independence until you are ready. There is no way to predict everything that will happen when you work from home, but there's also no excuse for being unprepared.

HARD QUESTIONS

The self-employed home-based worker is clearly dependent on getting and keeping his or her own clients or customers. This requires marketing and promotion (not to mention an understanding that now, more than ever, mastering the fundamentals of business etiquette is not mere icing on the cake). As you plan your business, think about what you must offer potential customers beyond your unique skills. What kind of customers do you want? How well do you know the market, and what kind of research do you need to identify potential customers? Is there a niche in the market that you can fill?

Consider how you want to operate. How much service can you reasonably offer without becoming overwhelmed? What are reasonable completion and delivery deadlines? Do you need your own permanent employees? Do you have ready access to contract workers or part-timers when extra help is required? Are there reliable subcontractors available who will deliver on time (a necessity that can make or break you)? Will you be your own salesperson, or should you have an agent or representative?

Don't forget those nagging details. Will you be a sole proprietor, or should you incorporate? How will you manage your bookkeeping and billing and receivables? What professional services will you need—legal, accounting, banking, secretarial, or others?

If you're considering a franchise-type arrangement, be alert. Franchising may promise independence but impose serious restrictions and sometimes require hidden financial commitments. "There's a sucker born every minute" is a saying attributed to 19th-century showman P.T. Barnum, but it need not apply to you. Never enter into any contract without consulting a competent attorney—one experienced in contract law.

MAKING A BUSINESS PLAN

In the strictest terms, a business plan is a comprehensive proposal statement comprising business goals, purpose, and operations and including costs and earnings projections. A formal business plan is most commonly used to seek funding from banks, venture capitalists, and investors. A well-prepared, formal business plan can be compared to an architect's final blueprint and renderings; it shows precisely what is proposed, how it will be achieved, and the likely outcome.

DO YOU REALLY NEED ONE?

There is some debate about the necessity of business plans for home-based start-ups and how extensive such plans should be. If you'll be applying for business loans, including equipment leasing, you will want to make a plan. It need not be lengthy, but it should be detailed. Talk with your lender about what should be included before submitting it. There are a number of comprehensive guides to business-plan writing at your bookstore and library.

Even if a written business plan may not be required for you to do business (particularly if you are your own banker), getting your mental plan down on paper is the smart thing to do. Researching and writing your plan literally forces you to think out each step and consider every possibility. It requires you to put into black and white how you will manage the nagging essentials of running your business and managing your time. It reveals hidden strengths and weaknesses. It makes you investigate your market and how you will reach them. It demands that you translate vague ambitions into hard numbers. Most important, doing a business plan is an excellent test of the mental discipline that is the first qualification of every self-employed person. Completing your business plan also provides a surprising benefit—self-confidence. But remember that

A Special Opportunity

533

even the best business plan is not engraved in stone; like the architect's blue-print, it will change and grow along with your business.

YOUR PHYSICAL ENVIRONMENT

The decision has been made and the plans have been laid. Now it is time for you to set up shop. The first rule of having a home office: Have a home *office*. Don't work on the kitchen table or at the little desk in the corner of the family room. It is your business, after all, and it deserves at minimum a real desk and a real chair in a real room.

SPACE

Determine how much space you will need and then find it in your house. Guest room, attic, basement, the room your son left when he went off to college—don't let sentiment stand in your way. Interior decorators love to tell you how easy it is to convert a closet or alcove into a complete home office, but this is often easier said than done. The important thing is to find a space removed from the heavily used areas of your house, away from the thundering herds.

You will probably have to invest some funds in preparing your office space—telephone line or lines, computer cables, extra electrical outlets (if you plan to run a lot of equipment, have a qualified electrician check your home's

---

In Control

BE YOURSELF

For home-based self-employed workers, being yourself means never implying that your business is more than the reality. Because of still-potent negative stereotypes about the home office, it can be tempting to concoct a more grandiose business image than the little office in the basement and the part-time staff of one college intern. If you don't have a secretary, don't put phony initials on your business letters. Don't misrepresent your office as "Suite" in your business address. Don't waste your money on engraved stationery or expensive advertising just to impress clients. Be confident that societal attitudes are changing; with more and more people in every walk of life striking out on their own, prejudices against home-based work are becoming passé. In our increasingly diverse, multilayered economy, the self-employed worker is a 21st-century pioneer with every reason to be proud.

electrical capacity), and shelving. Be sure that your office has a door so that you can assure quiet and privacy, and train family and friends not to enter when the door is closed.

STORAGE

As your business prospers, you'll discover that your storage needs increase. Plan for filing cabinets and a place to store business and financial records as well as stationery and office supplies. With sufficient storage space, you can take advantage of bulk pricing on supplies. If you have inventory, be careful that your storage—your own or rental—is clean, dry, and pest-free.

DECOR

Your office decor and furnishings don't have to look corporate. In fact, home-based workers enjoy decorating their offices to reflect their own tastes and interests. But if you'll be receiving clients at home, it's wise to decorate in a style that is professional. Remember that home-based businesses are unfairly stereotyped: an office done in chintzes and frills may seem frivolous, and orange-crate seats and concrete-block bookshelves will summon up the temporary quality of a college dorm room. Above all, your furnishings should be comfortable and serviceable. Before you buy anything, try it out. Sit in those desk chairs and imagine yourself there for hours every day.

EQUIPMENT

Equipment—especially electronic items—can be costly and may become outdated or require upgrading before you have made even a few payments. You may want to lease expensive items, so talk to your banker. Take the time to research both the equipment and the provider. Look for flexibility and adaptability. Home-based workers need to be particularly concerned about servicing and repair, so look for dealers that provide in-home maintenance. (There's nothing more frustrating than being off-line for days because you've had to take your computer to the repair shop.)

YOUR IMAGE TO THE WORLD

Now, the fun part: making your decisions about the image you'll project to the world. Your business name, logo, stationery, advertising, and promotion all tell the world about you and the work you do.

What to call yourself? The choice of a name alone can have an enormous impact on your eventual success, and this decision should be made after you do some homework. Think about how your business name will be used, where it will be seen and by whom, how it will sound. Do you want to be trendy or traditional? How well will the name project the image you want? Does the name imply professionalism and stability? Or is it just too cute and faddish? Could your name be confused with another business'? Study competitors' company names; you may want to be different so that your business stands out. But do you want to be *so* different that potential customers or clients avoid you? Don't overlook your own name or variations on your name and initials.

N O T E : Give thought to your e-mail name as well—don't let the freedom to choose it tempt you to get too creative; the last thing you want is something that sounds too cutesy or unprofessional.

Put your creativity to work and make a "shopping list" of possible names. Try your favorites on friends and colleagues and gauge their reactions. Repeat the name aloud. Look at it in print. (Some names have unexpected meanings when spoken or written.) Live with it awhile and make sure it's comfortable before committing your name to stationery and ads. If you intend to register the name, consult a trademark attorney.

Business slogans. The same recommendations pertain to business slogans. Theme lines such as "Just Do It" and "Have It Your Way" work brilliantly for companies such as Nike and Burger King because these giants spend millions of advertising dollars establishing their slogans in the public consciousness. But for a home-based businessperson, a simple and straightforward statement of your activity or area of expertise is generally more serviceable. ("Bed and Country Breakfast" or "A Classic New England Inn" denotes simply and accurately what the business is; "A little bit of heaven in the hills" is unclear, imprecise, and too cute by half.)

Graphic design and logo. Once you've selected your business name, you'll doubtless want an attractive graphic design and logo. Move cautiously. Good design is costly, and bad or amateurish design is a poor reflection on your business. Unless you depend on signage or packaging to sell your products or service, a logotype may also be a wasted expenditure. Until your business is firmly established, it's advisable to settle on an attractive and legible typeface for your name. Interesting color choices in papers and inks may be just as effective as a fancy logo in your printed materials.

A HINT FOR OBTAINING A REALLY GOOD DESIGN: Make a trade. If you service business equipment, the best designer in town may

YOUR FOUR-WHEEL OFFICE

Every home office comes with a branch—your automobile. Be it a '63 Beetle or the latest luxury vehicle, your car is likely to be your most valuable piece of business equipment. Pickups and deliveries, runs to the post office and the printer, trips to clients' offices and vendors' warehouses—unless you're one of those lucky enough to have access to excellent public transportation, you're going to spend a lot of time behind the wheel. Here are a few hints for getting the most from your four-wheel office:

- **BABY YOUR CAR.** On the way to an important client meeting is no time for a break-down. Regular oil changes and tire checks are a must. Check your driver's manual for scheduled tune-ups and maintenance. Be sure that your spare tire is in good shape and that you know how to change a flat.

- **RECORD YOUR MILEAGE AND GAS PURCHASES.** Every penny of your business driving expenses is deductible. Also, check with your insurance agent about coverage of your car and contents for business use.

- **EQUIP IT WELL.** Mobile phone? A good idea if you are constantly on the go, travel long distances, or drive at night. Just remember that talking and driving have proved to be dangerous. (See In the Car, page 300.) Lay in a supply of basic office tools—stationery, notepads, pens and pencils, stamps, express mailers, paper clips, staples and stapler, tape, scissors, file folders, and anything else you may need to do business on the road. For neatness' sake, pack your supplies in a waterproof box and stow it in the trunk. Bank your nickels, dimes, and quarters for parking meters and tolls. Find a little place—an envelope or small box in the glove compartment works well—to save your business receipts.

- **THAT'S ENTERTAINMENT!** CDs or cassettes are a must, especially when you have long drives or become easily bored with standard radio fare. If you like recorded books, make the library a regular stop; the audiobooks are free.

- **REMEMBER PERSONAL ITEMS.** Some home-based workers store a complete change of clothing in the car. At minimum, keep an extra pair of shoes, socks, stockings, and a clean tie, along with basic toiletries, tissues, and hand wipes. A cloth towel, roll of paper towels, and a few plastic bags also come in handy. Never forget an umbrella and rainwear, and, for cold weather, an extra pair of warm gloves.

- **GUARD AGAINST BEING LOCKED OUT.** Keep an extra set of car keys where you can reach them. It's too easy to lock yourself out when you are dashing hither, thither, and yon.

- **CLEAN UP ON OCCASION.** Busy home-based workers tend to let their cars pile high with junk. But your rolling office should be just as clean and comfortable as your home base, especially if a client is ever a passenger.

RULES AND REGULATIONS

Your home-based business must conform to local, state, and even federal regulations, just as the largest companies do. The rapid proliferation of home-based businesses in recent years has caused chaos in local zoning ordinances and city and state health and fire codes. And when you investigate the rules governing your business and site, you may not encounter much sympathy.

Anecdotes about home businesses being closed by officious zoning authorities are legion because it is a simple fact that the home-based worker generally has little or no influence with city, county, and state bureaucrats. Sometimes permits are denied simply because a locality has no ordinances or regulations covering home offices. If you anticipate problems, the wisest course may be to contact your local councilperson and state representatives and solicit their assistance. Your Chamber of Commerce may also be of help.

It is always a mistake to try to hide your business or avoid getting the proper permits and clearances. It takes only one phone call from an irritated neighbor or jealous competitor to bring your operations to a halt. Ignorance of the law is never an acceptable excuse, because it is your responsibility to know and follow the rules. Likewise, don't let your frustration with the bureaucracy boil over; anger or sarcasm directed at low-level government workers (who doubtless have no decision-making authority) will only delay your requests, impede resolution of your issues, and complicate future dealings. Be persistent, never rude.

be happy to exchange his or her art for your repair skills. But always be clear that you are offering barter before you take up anyone's time.

Stationery. As a home-based worker, you probably need no more than letterhead, envelopes, and business cards to start. Estimate how much stationery you will require for three or four months and order that amount, even if larger orders are cheaper. This gives you the option to adjust or even change your design once you have a better sense of your needs. You'll also have to make a point of remembering to reorder *before* you run out.

Advertising and promotion. The methods for advertising and promoting home-based businesses are as varied as the types of businesses there are, and no hard and fast rules exist for selling what you do. Again, study your market and find out where your potential clients get their information. A 24-hour plumber will generate lots of calls from a small display ad in the Yellow Pages; a tax consultant may be better served by direct-mail letters to area businesses. You might want to have a brochure produced to explain your services and qualifications. Perhaps a homepage on the Internet or an ad on the local radio station or cable

TV channel will do the trick when you want to reach larger audiences. Whatever medium you choose, spend your ad budget wisely by directing your paid marketing where it can do the most for you.

Be wary of any sales representative who promises you that advertising with his station or newspaper will be all the promotion you need. If you're uncertain about what to do, get in touch with a business or marketing consultant who can help you build an integrated marketing plan that can meet your budget.

Finally, don't ignore the obvious: Word of mouth is almost always the best advertising tool, and you can start the ball rolling by telling people who you are and what you can do for them. Make appointments and see the people you want as clients. Send your business announcements to the newspapers. Join business and civic organizations that offer opportunities to mingle.

When you meet a prospective customer or referral source, follow up with a gracious, handwritten note. (It's also a good idea to send Christmas cards to clients and put a birthday tickler file in your computer for some.) You will always be your own best salesperson so long as you remember that the world will not beat a path to your door unless you tell the world (i.e., your market) why it is worth the effort.

CHAPTER 38

YOUR BUSINESS RELATIONSHIPS

When you work at home, you get to know a great many people who may never before have crossed your business radar. You are completely in charge of your operation, and that entails dealings with everyone on the business food chain—from CEOs to the delivery person. Even if you held supervisory positions in the past, you may find yourself an employer for the first time, with full- or part-time employees to direct and motivate. You may become a contractor with a far-flung network of independent suppliers. You'll also be a customer for any number of products and professional services. And you thought you were on your own!

CLIENTS AND CUSTOMERS

The people who will buy your products or services are not bosses, but they control your livelihood—and they can be bossy nonetheless. As a self-employed, home-based worker, you best be prepared to cope with the full range of human frailties and foibles. You will have to juggle patience and courtesy with firmness and self-interest. How will you handle the customer who calls six times a day to check on his order? The client who consistently delays projects but refuses to extend deadlines? The client who schedules pointless meetings with you as an excuse to get away from her office?

If you just do not have the temperament to deal with customers or if client service becomes a detriment to your overall operations—as when a client consumes so much time that your work is regularly behind schedule—then you should consider hiring a sales representative or an agent to act as your go-between. Make no mistake that the temperament question is the more serious one once you start your own business. If you really think it will be difficult for you to deal with customers, perhaps you should think twice before committing yourself to being an entrepreneur. Few people can work in a vacuum. If your work is going to involve interacting with all kinds of people all day, everyday, they will judge you even in situations that are purely social.

PHONE CONSIDERATIONS

Make it clear to the people you do business with what hours you keep—you don't want to be on call at virtually any time of day and night. By the same token, find out from individual clients what their set hours are. If they have none, ask them to give you a time frame for calling so that you don't risk waking them up or calling when they have something regularly scheduled.

When it comes to the phone, watch your p's and q's. Background noise is the most common problem for home office workers—the crying child in the next room (or on your lap), the neighbor who revs up his leaf blower at just the wrong moment. One solution is to use a cordless phone in the most soundproof room in the house, be it the bathroom or the basement. As for crying babies, you should have made clear from the beginning of your business relationship that you have a young child so that any disturbances don't come as a surprise. It goes without saying that you should time any calls you initiate during the baby's nap, if possible. But when it is you who are called in the middle of trying to calm a crying baby, you'll simply have to apologize profusely and try to schedule the call for later in the day. Most people will be understanding. (See also Telephone Tangles, page 552.)

Home office work can be lonely, and it's easy to give in to the temptation to talk longer than you actually need to, as much for the company as anything. For your sake and the other person's, don't.

COLLECTING

One of the most frustrating problems that the self-employed face involves collections. Clients who demand the nth degree of attention from you suddenly become laggards when it comes to paying their bills. They may delay by questioning every detail of your billing, or demand discounts after the work has been completed. Or their promised 30-day payment cycle drags out to 60 or even 90 days. Unless you have a Godzilla on your staff, collecting overdue payments can be a nightmare. But don't let your frustration get the best of you: By staying polite in your entreaties you have a better chance at succeeding than if you start by reading the riot act. (See also Collecting Money You're Owed, page 233.)

Once you've given all the proper notices, you may have no choice but to turn the job over to a collection agency—or even to bring a legal action—no matter who is responsible for the late payment. But even these solutions are not always productive, consuming your precious time and dollars for small returns. Written contracts may offer little security, and, sadly, it sometimes becomes necessary to take a financial loss rather than sacrifice your sanity. The point is to learn from these experiences. Be cautious when you take on new clients. Check their references; investigate their track records. Don't let yourself be swept away by glittering promises of future rewards. Generally, it's better not to discount your rates and charges just to get new business; your client will logically expect the same low rates for all your work.

Cultivate those clients who have demonstrated honorable behavior in the past, and never be tempted to give them short shrift simply because their business has become familiar. Good clients are pure gold. But a truly bad client can literally ruin your business, so be prepared to resign an account if all else fails.

TO HIRE EMPLOYEES?

Hiring employees is perhaps the most dramatic step a self-employed, home-based worker can take. As an employer, you are responsible for their livelihood, and that responsibility can weigh very heavily. Before taking on full-time employees, you will want to investigate all possibilities, including part-time workers, temporary services, interns, and even hiring family members (precarious unless they are the only hires).

Your key considerations, after deciding what you can afford to pay, involve the nature and amount of work available. Perhaps you need assistance with paperwork, filing, copying, and deliveries. Is a skilled secretary your best choice, or are the tasks substantially uncomplicated and capable of being han-

---

In Control

TIMES WILL CHANGE

Conventional wisdom holds that home-based workers have their shoulders to the wheel for 23 hours a day. True for some, but by no means all. Many home-based workers find that they are more productive within fewer hours or that work comes in intensive bursts followed by extended downtimes. Others adopt a traditional 9-to-5 schedule and rigorously observe their self-imposed office hours. The point is to use your time as *you* see fit; so long as you are meeting your goals, there's no need to feel guilty about working shorter hours or compulsive about working longer hours. Remember, however, that corporate America still tends to arrive at work at nine and leave at five. You can be as flexible as you like with your own time, but to do business with others, some degree of conformity is required.

dled by a less-qualified worker or even a college intern? Do your busiest times come sporadically or seasonally, and is there enough work to keep a full-time employee occupied during slow periods? Is the work primarily manual? Will your employee be in contact with your clients or customers? Is on-the-job transportation necessary?

Develop a detailed job description and list of requisite skills so that you, as well as your applicants, will know just what is expected. You may want to advertise the position, but responding to calls and application letters and holding interviews is a time-consuming process. Although they charge for services, reputable employment agencies can be a godsend for home employers—culling the qualified from the unqualified. If you elect to use temporary help, be sure to check out the temp service thoroughly. Talk with other small-business owners to determine whether the service will be sympathetic to your business needs.

HIRING FRIENDS AND FAMILY

There can be advantages to hiring friends or family members—you know them, trust them, enjoy their company, and so forth. But it's darned difficult to fire them. If you employ someone who is close to you personally, be very sure that person is qualified for the job. For example, if you need a good secretary, it's probably a mistake to hire your good friend who worked as a secretary two decades ago but has no computer training or bookkeeping experience. Even if a friend or family member is uniquely qualified, keep in mind that working together in an employer-employee relationship and in your home is going to be stressful even in the best of times.

HIRING SUBCONTRACTORS

A different type of employee is the subcontractor: someone who is an independent worker but contracts to work for you and under your supervision, usually for the duration of a project or for a specified time period. The subcontractor is normally proficient in a skill that you need to complete work for your clients—as when a landscaper subcontracts with a landscape architect or a book packager subcontracts with a writer and a book designer. Although under your supervision, subcontractors are not your direct employees and cannot be expected to perform tasks outside their expertise.

Relations between contractors and subcontractors are notoriously tricky, so it is generally best to assume a collegial attitude. While it's true that you are paying the subcontractor for service, it's also normally the case that your subcontractor would be difficult to replace. If you are willing to wear kid gloves when dealing with subcontractors, your reward may well be lasting and profitable relationships. An obvious benefit is that severing the relationship is much easier than firing an actual employee.

DO YOU NEED A CONSULTANT?

There are consultants for just about every phase and type of business operation, and their assistance can be invaluable. For example, when you begin to make profits, you may want to acquire a financial advisor to guide you through the arcane complexities of investment and retirement planning. Free consultant services are often provided through professional organizations and governmental agencies such as the Small Business Administration, but it is more likely that you will hire your consultants.

THE BACKGROUND CHECK

Whatever professional consultant services you need, you must be extremely careful about whom you hire. These people will often be privy to your most sensitive information and, in some cases, your money. Small businesses are attractive targets for scam artists because small employers lack the in-house expertise to track every aspect of outside contracting. You can protect yourself by requiring and *checking* references, and seeking recommendations from other people in your field.

Ask around: What is the reputation of the professional you are considering? Never hire on a hunch, but don't ignore gut feelings that something may be wrong. Also don't be intimated by fancy offices or facile sales pitches. First and foremost, you are looking for honesty, competence, and reliability. You also want someone with whom you feel comfortable sharing the intimacies of your business.

WHAT TO FARM OUT

There are some jobs that, in most cases, you as a self-employed home-based worker should not do for yourself. Here are five of them:

- **TAX PREPARATION.** Unless you're willing to spend valuable time keeping up with the latest changes in complex federal, state, and local tax codes (which means you'll have time for little else), hire an accountant.
- **PAYROLL.** This is another time-intensive area that may best be handled by an accountant or employee management service.

- **INSURANCE.** Home-based employees and the self-employed need an insurance agent with knowledge of their special needs—from liability coverage and equipment insurance to health and disability policies. (Don't make the mistake of thinking that your homeowner's insurance offers protection for your home office.)
- **LEGAL MATTERS.** Shakespeare recommended killing all the lawyers, but you will want a live one for incorporation; contracts; patents, copyrights, and trademarks; liability and compliance issues; and lawsuits. (In our litigious society, it is a dark joke among the self-employed that if you haven't been sued yet, wait a minute.) Choose your lawyer carefully: Look for a legal eagle who takes your business seriously and charges fairly.
- **MARKETING.** Promotion is vital, and at some point you will turn to experts to "sell" your business. Advertising agencies, public relations firms, graphic designers, packaging specialists, direct-mail services, broadcast producers, Internet designers—they all want your business, in large part because you offer a new creative challenge. But when you engage marketers and creative talent, there are two good rules to follow: first, be very clear about your objectives and expectations (including your budget), and second, get out of the way. You're paying these people for their creative thinking, so don't interfere with the process. Be open to new ideas.

BUSINESS SERVICES

It pays to get to know the people who can keep your business running smoothly, from office-product suppliers to delivery people and postal workers. The heads of the largest companies in the world often say that their responsibilities are to their shareholders, their customers, and their employees, yet it's rare to hear a corporate giant spare some praise for suppliers. But every self-employed worker quickly learns the value of the people who provide the products and services that keep business flowing.

NOTE: When choosing whom to do business with, it's appropriate to get several bids and in some cases to negotiate the price. Don't haggle, however, and go with your gut about who's going to give the best value.

OFFICE-PRODUCT SUPPLIERS

As you seek out office-product suppliers, you probably will consider pricing as your first criterion, and large discounters certainly offer cost savings to careful shoppers. But as a home worker, you also need to be concerned with equipment maintenance and repair. A paper clip is a paper clip, wherever you purchase it, but computers, printers, scanners, etc., cannot be tossed out when they break. Will your supplier provide service when you need it and, just as important, *where* you need it? Do they offer a reasonable service contract? Maintenance contract? If you purchase your computer and peripherals from multiple suppliers, is there a reputable and responsive maintenance and repair contractor in your local area?

SHIPPING AND MAILING

Shipping and mailing are fundamental to many home-based businesses, so you'll want to carefully research all your shipping choices. Look at where your orders are going, time between order and delivery, availability of home pickup and delivery in your area, and costs. Talk with shipping agents and ask specifically about their policies, services, and pricing for home-based businesses.

For shipments to your home, arrange with your shipper for deliveries when you are not there to sign and designate a drop-off place that is dry and out of general view. Although you will probably do most of your business with one shipper or express service, always have a backup plan; know what you will do if your shipper suddenly goes on strike. Don't forget about the U.S. Postal Service, either. Your local postmaster may be a fountain of knowledge about your best shipping options as well as postal regulations.

DELIVERY SERVICES

If you have frequent local deliveries, you will want a local delivery service—unless you really love to drive. Again, do your research and ask lots of questions. For example, does your service provide 24-hour delivery? How do they set their rates—actual mileage, zip-code areas, rush charges, and such? What is their average delivery time? Can you arrange regular pickup and delivery times if necessary? Keep the numbers of local taxi companies at hand; a cab can be a lifesaver in a pinch.

What about tipping? You needn't tip a delivery person every time he or she shows up, of course, but someone who comes regularly deserves more than a simple thank-you in the long run. A $5 or $10 tip every month or so shows that you appreciate the service. You could also give seasonal small gifts—a pot of spring bulbs, an assortment of Halloween candies, a turkey, a ham, or a Christmas cake.

Secretarial services, quick-print shops, stationery suppliers—there is a service for virtually every one of your business needs. But the key to *good* service is getting to know your suppliers. Become a valued customer. (Research suppliers and then settle on one that you want to work with rather than constantly looking for one who costs a little less.) If you can't be the biggest customer in town, be the most considerate. Don't, for example, expect your printer to routinely drop what he is doing to handle your last-minute projects. Don't berate your express shipper for failing to leave a package when you didn't provide instructions for unsigned deliveries. The relationship you establish may save you in a crunch.

THE HOME-OFFICE NETWORKER

No one can do business in a vacuum. That means you will have to get out of the house and among people who can help your business grow. Networking is the process of developing contacts within your business community and your profession. You may already have connections—PTA, Kiwanis Club, church group, for example—but when you run a home-based business, your time is at a premium. Chances are, you'll have to cut back or give up some old commitments, at least in the early stages of your business. You will probably take on some new memberships—the Chamber of Commerce, the local or state retailers' association—and you'll have to decide how much time you can give to

---

" . . . AND THIS IS ROVER "

Pets are not a social problem for the home-based worker unless you receive clients or customers in your home. Pet owners can be a myopic lot when it comes to their beloved Fluffy or Spot. But not everyone loves pets, and some of your important guests may have genuine aversions. Allergies to pets are relatively common, and your meeting will not go well if your client is sneezing and tearful. Put the family pet outside or in the garage when clients are expected. Vacuum away the pet hair. If your dog is large and likely to pounce on strangers who knock at your door, keep it leashed or penned during meetings. Also, don't "introduce" your pet to clients, expecting that they will form long-term relationships. Clients who don't enjoy being licked, pawed, or even cuddled will probably be too well-mannered to say so—and all too anxious to take their business elsewhere.

these groups. There are national trade associations and professional organizations that provide enormous assistance for their members, but again, tread carefully. Some groups with impressive names are little more than mail-order houses.

FORMER EMPLOYERS

Don't overlook your old employer or employers. Assuming that you left your old jobs in good graces, past employers can be a gold mine of information, referrals, and actual work. Many a home-based freelancer has discovered that an old boss, who already knows their skills and capabilities, makes an excellent new client. But be aware that the relationship has changed, and the person who was your boss is now a business peer. Aim for professional accommodation when you work for an old boss—not servility. Remember, the old boss may have trouble with the new relationship, so tread carefully.

FORMER COWORKERS

Keep in touch with former coworkers. In addition to the personal benefits of maintaining friendships, you will find that old colleagues usually want to see

---

In Control

FACING REALITY

Working from home is not a test of character. If your home-based employment or business doesn't work out, be prepared to move on. Keep in mind that the great majority of small businesses do fail, and there is no shame in changing direction if you are clearly headed down a blind alley. The important thing is to recognize when your plans are not succeeding and either adjust or opt out before you are financially or emotionally bankrupted.

On the other hand, your business may succeed all too well, and it is equally important to know if and when to expand. Before deciding to take on new debt, hire more workers, or relocate, you will have to ponder both your business and your personal goals. Is growth your primary objective? Are you ready to sacrifice your independence as a home-based worker? How will change affect your family? Are you overestimating your market? Is a bigger business what you really want, or are you being pushed to expand by others?

It pays to be ruthlessly honest with yourself: How much are you motivated by sound business sense and how much by ego?

your business thrive and can be valuable allies. They may be able to send opportunities your way, serve as references, and keep you informed about what's happening in the larger business community. (Be considerate, however, of their confidentiality and don't expect "insider" information that is proprietary.)

There is one serious mistake that home-based workers tend to make in the early phase of going it alone: Unused to the solitude, they may become excessively dependent on old office friends. It is fine to lunch with or call your colleagues occasionally; it's rude (and more than a bit desperate) to call or e-mail daily. You don't want to transform yourself from friend to pest.

CHAPTER 39

FAMILY AND FRIENDS

For many home-based workers, the chief advantage of the home office is achieving a more equitable balance between work and family. But one of your most difficult tasks will be to convince loved ones that *you really are working*. It has to be done. Unless you lay down specific ground rules and communicate them clearly, you will defeat the purpose of coming home to work. Then there are your friends and neighbors, for whom you have a special set of considerations. You'll want to make things run as smoothly in your relations with them as you do with your business associates.

When you explain your working rules to family and friends, be neither apologetic nor mealy-mouthed. Even the most considerate family and friends may suffer from the common misconceptions about home-based work; they must be educated. Make it clear that you are earning your livelihood, not indulging in a hobby.

OH, THOSE KIDS!

Just as children have different needs at different ages, they have different levels of understanding. Whatever their ages, they will need constant reminders of your rules. Think of home-office education like sex education—provide the information appropriate to the child's age, repeat it often, and update it when needed. A three-year-old will understand that Daddy is working; a seven-year-old may be ready for a definition of "breadwinner" and a lesson in family economics; a teenager will probably require serious discussion about the importance of advance scheduling for her school activities and trips to the mall.

Here are some tips that can help you and your children adapt to home-based work. Ask other family members to reinforce any rules you lay down. Spouses, grandparents, older siblings—many adults serve as models of behavior for children. When the other adults in the family show support for your work and respect for your rules, your kids will probably follow suit.

- **MAKE A SCHEDULE.** You are no longer on a strict 9-to–5 schedule, so you can arrange your busy times to suit your family's needs. But being flexible doesn't mean being totally freeform; you need structure in your workday. Your child-care arrangements may not be too different from the days when you left for the office, especially care for preschool children. If two parents work at home, try to schedule work hours so that family responsibilities can be alternated. Make it absolutely clear that your work hours must be honored.

- **BE HONEST.** Don't make promises to children that may not be kept. From love and guilt, all working parents are quick to promise to do things "later" or "tomorrow" in order to get through the moment. But unless you're certain you can keep your word, resist the temptation. Don't, for example, promise to attend the school play when you have an important deadline on the same day. Children will be disappointed when you must say "no." But they will be resentful when you say "yes" and then fail to meet your commitment.

- **DRESS THE PART.** Although one of the enticements of a home office is the end of everyday dressing for success, you may find that a business-like appearance helps younger children distinguish between work time and play time. If children see you in your bathrobe when they leave for school and still in your bathrobe when they return, they will logically conclude that you haven't been doing much business during the day. Without sacrificing much of your independence, you can assemble a work "uniform" as casual as jeans and jacket that nevertheless signals to children that your work has begun.

- **DEFINE "EMERGENCIES."** Of course, you want your children to interrupt your work when a real problem occurs. But don't expect children to instinctively know what constitutes an emergency. They will bother you with what seems trivial, but you can use these experiences as teaching opportunities. A fall from the swing set does require your immediate attention, but a lost Barbie head or dirty soccer uniform does not. Be patient and explain repeatedly, especially during the early stages of your business when children are making their own adjustments to your new lifestyle.

- **NO TRESPASSING.** Your office is an office and not a playroom. Until children are sufficiently responsible, they should probably not be allowed to enter your office unless you're present.

- **DO NOT TOUCH.** As a rule, do not allow children to use your business computer for homework or surfing the Internet. It's always possible they could erase an important file or put in a disk that introduces a virus with disastrous results. (Note: This is only one reason an antivirus program is essential for a home-office computer.) Also put your work supplies and materials off-limits. Just about every home-based worker with children has at least one horror story of the critical meeting notes or the client's private phone number that turned up months later glued to an art project or crumpled in a toy box.

To Take Them Along?

Include your children when appropriate. It is perfectly acceptable to take your child when you make your drop-off deliveries or do your routine errands. It is unprofessional to bring your children to meetings with your clients or employer. And never expect busy secretaries to mind your kids while you are meeting with the boss.

TELEPHONE TANGLES

Perhaps the most persistent and annoying conflicts between work-at-home parents and their children involve the telephone. Young children seem to have a special radar to detect when a parent is taking an important call; it tells them exactly when to cry or yell or bang on the floor. Older children will fight you for phone time. There's really only one solution that works—install a separate business telephone line. Take business calls in your office (and remember to shut the door to keep toddlers at bay). Be sure your business number is listed in the business section of your telephone directory and not included with your residential number. It's also advisable to invest in separate answering machines for home and home office—many an important call has been missed because

---

In Control

THE PC TRAP

The computer is a tool, not a toy, but some home-based workers find themselves falling into the PC trap. There is a strange misconception abroad that tapping into the Internet is some kind of shortcut to knowledge. With no one watching over their shoulders, home workers may be tempted to go—and stay—online in search of everything from paper clips to business ideas. The Internet can be a sound research mechanism, but it can also be a black hole that sucks you into a vast wasteland of the trite, the trivial, and the untrue. One hour at the library may well produce more usable information than eight on the Internet. Your PC and Internet connection will not make you smarter or wiser or more effective if employed indiscriminately.

someone in the family erased an important message by mistake—and record distinctly different messages for each machine.

It's also important to teach your children good telephone etiquette early. Your stodgiest client will be mightily impressed when your youngster replies with a polite "Yes, sir" and "Thank you, ma'am." Develop a simple response for your children when they answer your business phone: "Hello, this is Brown's Custom Draperies. May I help you?" or "Hello, this is Richard Mazurek's office. May I help you?" Be sure they are equally polite when answering your residential line, because you never know who's calling.

Older children can be taught to take careful message notes, and they will usually be flattered to be trusted with this important chore. You'll probably have to train children not to scream for you; kids are kids, after all, and inclined to follow the shortest route between A (the phone receiver) and B (you).

FRIENDS AND NEIGHBORS

Even the most supportive adults may find it difficult to accept the proposition that you are "at home but unavailable." People who would never call you or arrive unannounced at someone else's office will unthinkingly expect you to be ready for long chats whenever they drop by your house. You will have to be polite, but firm—very firm. Make it clear that, except for emergencies, you are not to be disturbed between such-and-such hours. Your business phone is for business calls only. Your fax machine and photocopier are not neighborhood resources. A suggestion: Don't answer the home phone while you're "at the office." Let the home answering machine be your secretary.

"WOULD YOU MIND . . . ?"

One problem common to home-based workers is coping with requests for free services. The graphic designer who sets up at home is suddenly a prime target for everyone who wants "a little help with the church newsletter" or "a nice-looking flyer for the yard sale." The accountant who works at home is deluged with friends and neighbors who want him to "look over" their 1040s at tax time. The best, and most difficult, course is to refuse everyone; a well-intended exception or two will cause resentment among the unexceptional. A strategy that may work is to meet such requests with a cost estimate. Put a dollar value on your time, and most people will get the message.

Charities and nonprofit institutions are notorious solicitors of free work, often promising (but rarely delivering) paying jobs in the future. Don't let your

KNOWING WHEN TO STOP

Long hours are not a reliable measure of productivity, so it's important to know when to stop. If you are working at home in order to see more of your family, don't stay cooped up in your home office. Even if you live alone, you still need time for yourself. Working at home doesn't require giving up your weekly golf game or lunch with friends: You need R&R if you are to be effective at your work. Don't promise yourself a future vacation while you fail to take daily breaks. Don't work when you are truly sick. Don't give up on housework. (Some home workers report that their most creative thinking comes while washing the breakfast dishes or doing a load of laundry.) The old saying that "all work and no play makes Jack a dull boy" applies to today's home-based worker. Many people enjoy a regular weekly round of golf or tennis with friends; clients will come to respect your Thursday afternoon off, knowing you'll give them more in return if you are relaxed and fresh.

sympathetic nature get the best of you. Charity clients can be the most demanding, with little sympathy for your time and professional obligations. If you take an assignment from a charity, be clear from the start that you expect payment; you may want to work for cost, but be certain the charity understands that your first priority is your paying clientele. Set reasonable goals and deadlines; if they want your work free *and* in a rush, say "no" immediately.

From humanitarian and business standpoints, charitable work is good for you and your community, so why not choose a group that you really care about and limit your "donations" to it? (You may want to select a charity that is not the traditional beneficiary of large donor funding.) The advantage of selecting only one or two charities is that you can get to know them well, become familiar with their needs and goals, and establish long-lasting relationships.

BE A GOOD NEIGHBOR

Placating the neighbors is an ongoing process. After all, your home office is probably in the midst of homes full of people who are grateful to be *away* from their offices. Your neighbors are in constant need of good public relations. They want honest assurances that your business will not disrupt their lives, endanger their safety, or damage their property values. Chances are, you won't please everyone in your neighborhood, but if you follow the Golden Rule and do for your neighbors as you'd like them to do for you, then you will avoid most hassles and unpleasant surprises. Be a good neighbor by doing the following:

- Inform close neighbors that you plan to have an office or open a business in your home and whenever you make any changes that may affect their peace and quiet. Most people are understanding when they know what's going on.
- Consider the aesthetics of the neighborhood. Even if zoning laws permit signage, exercise good taste in signs and advertising, in look, size, and placement. Think how ugly most real estate yard signs are before erecting a billboard on your front lawn.
- Control noise. Running a power saw in your workshop or cranking up the volume in your home recording studio may be acceptable at noon, but not during early morning or evening hours.
- Hold meetings or receive customers at home during standard business hours. Traffic before 9:00 A.M. and after 5:00 P.M. should be kept to a minimum.
- Do not subject your neighbors to an endless flow of cars and deliveries. Don't expect a neighbor to sign for your deliveries on a regular basis.
- Never hog the available parking. If your neighbors depend on street parking, for example, they will not appreciate walking for blocks because your customers have taken all the convenient spaces. If you share a drive with neighbors, be sure their access and egress is never blocked.

BIBLIOGRAPHY

Adams, Scott. *The Dilbert Principle*. New York: HarperBusiness, 1996.

Alessandra, Tony; Wexler, Phil; and Barrera, Rick. *Non-Manipulative Selling.*
New York: A Fireside Book, Simon & Schuster, 1992.

Axtell, Roger E. *Do's and Taboos Around the World*. New York: John Wiley & Sons,
Inc., 1993.

Axtell, Roger E. *Do's and Taboos of Using English Around the World.* New York:
John Wiley & Sons, Inc., 1995.

Baldrige, Letitia. *Letitia Baldrige's New Complete Guide to Executive Manners.*
New York: Rawson Associates, 1993.

Bell, Arthur H., and Smith, Dayle M. *Winning With Difficult People*. Second edition.
Hauppauge, New York: Barron's Educational Services, Inc., 1997.

Bernstein, Theodore M. *The Careful Writer: A Guide to Modern English Usage.*
New York: Atheneum, 1977.

Bodin, Madeline. *Using the Telephone More Effectively*. Second edition. Hauppauge,
New York: Barron's Educational Services, Inc., 1997.

Bremner, Moyra. *Modern Etiquette.* Edison, New Jersey: Chartwell Books, Inc.,
a division of Book Sales, Inc., 1994.

Brown, Steven W. *13 Fatal Errors Managers Make and How You Can Avoid Them.*
New York: Berkley Books, 1987.

Cottle, Michelle. "Working" column, *New York Times*.

Covey, Stephen R. *The Seven Habits of Highly Effective People*. New York: A Fireside
Book, Simon & Schuster, 1990.

Craig, Elizabeth. *Don't Slurp Your Soup: A Basic Guide to Business Etiquette.* St. Paul,
Minnesota: Brighton Publications, Inc., 1996.

Crystal, David. *The Cambridge Encyclopedia of the English Language.* Cambridge:
Cambridge University Press, 1995.

Dorio, Mark. *The Complete Idiot's Guide to Getting the Job You Want.* New York:
Alpha Books, a division of Macmillan General Reference, 1998.

Duncan, Melba J. *The New Executive Assistant*. New York: McGraw Hill, 1997.

Everding, Maria Perniciaro. *Panache That Pays.* St. Louis, Mo.: GME Publishing
Co., 1997.

Fisher, Anne. "Ask Annie" column, *Fortune.*

Fowler, H. Ramsey; Aaron, Jane E.; and Brittenham, Rebecca. *The Little, Brown Handbook.* Instructor's annotated edition. New York: Addison Wesley Longman, Inc., 1998.

Fowler, H.W. *A Dictionary of Modern English Usage.* Second edition, revised by Sir Ernest Gowers. New York and Oxford: Oxford University Press, 1965.

Fox, Grace. *Office Etiquette and Protocol.* New York: LearningExpress, 1998.

Garfinkel, Perry; Chichester, Brian; and Editors of Men's Health Books. *Maximum Style: Look Sharp and Feel Confident in Every Situation.* Emmaus, Pennsylvania: Rodale Press, Inc., 1997.

Geffner, Andrea B. *Business English.* New York: Barron's, 1998.

Gluckstern, Willie. *The Wine Avenger.* New York: Simon & Schuster, 1998.

Grice, George L., and Skinner, John F. *Mastering Public Speaking.* Third edition. Boston: Allyn and Bacon, 1988.

Hansen, Katharine, and Hansen, Randall S. *Dynamic Cover Letters.* Berkeley, California: Ten Speed Press, 1995.

Harvard Business Review. *Command Performance: The Art of Delivering Quality Service.* 14 articles, with a preface by John E. Martin. Boston: Harvard Business School Press, 1994.

Hesselbein, Frances, and Cohen, Paul M., editors. *Leader to Leader.* San Francisco: Drucker Foundation Leaderbooks, Jossey-Bass Publishers, 1999.

Hornstein, Harvey A., Ph.D. *Brutal Bosses and Their Prey.* New York: Riverhead Books, 1996.

Hubbartt, William S. *The New Battle Over Workplace Privacy.* New York: AMACOM/American Management Association, 1998.

Ivers, Michael. *The Random House Guide to Good Writing.* New York: Random House, 1991.

Karr, Ron, and Blohowiak, Dan. *The Complete Idiot's Guide to Great Customer Service.* New York: Alpha Books, 1997.

Klinkenberg, Hilka. *At Ease . . . Professionally.* Chicago: Bonus Books, Inc., 1992.

Lederer, Richard. *Crazy English: The Ultimate Joy Ride Through Our Language.* New York: Pocket Books, 1989.

Lewis, Richard D. *When Cultures Collide.* London: Nicholas Brealey Publishing Limited, 1996.

Lichtenberg, Ronna, with Stone, Gene. *Work Would Be Great If It Weren't for the People.* New York: Hyperion, 1998.

Lizotte, Ken, and Litwak, Barbara A. *From Secretary Track to Fast Track.* New York: AMACOM/American Management Association, 1996.

Martin, Judith. *Miss Manners' Basic Training: Communication.* New York: Crown Publishers, 1997.

Merriam-Webster's Secretarial Handbook. Third edition. Stevens, Mark A., general editor; Lindsell-Roberts, Sheryl, consulting editor. Springfield, Massachusetts: Merriam-Webster, Inc., 1993.

Miller, Llewellyn. *The Encyclopedia of Etiquette.* New York: Crown Publishers, Inc., 1967.

Morem, Susan. *How to Gain the Professional Edge: Achieve the Personal and Professional Image You Want.* Plymouth, Minn.: Better Books, 1997.

Morrison, Terri; Conaway, Wayne A.; and Douress, Joseph J. *Doing Business Around the World.* Paramus, New Jersey: Prentice-Hall, Inc., 1997.

Morrison, Terri, and Conaway, Wayne A. *The International Traveler's Guide to Doing Business in Latin America.* New York: Macmillan Spectrum, 1997.

Morrison, Terri; Conaway, Wayne A.; and Borden, George A. *Kiss, Bow, or Shake Hands.* Holbrook, Massachusetts: Adams Media Corporation, 1994.

Nelson, Robert B., and Economy, Peter. *Better Business Meetings.* Burr Ridge, Illinois: Irwin Professional Publishing, 1995.

O'Conner, Patricia T. *Woe Is I: The Grammarphobe's Guide to Better English in Plain English.* New York: G.P. Putnam's Sons, Gossett/Putnam Book, 1996.

Pachter, Barbara, and Brody, Marjorie. *Complete Business Etiquette Handbook.* Paramus, New Jersey: Prentice-Hall, 1995.

Phegan, Barry, PhD. *Developing Your Company Culture.* Berkeley, California: Context Press, 1996.

Phillips, Linda and Wayne, with Rogers, Lynne. *The Concise Guide to Executive Etiquette.* New York: Doubleday, 1990.

Pincus, Marilyn. *Everyday Business Etiquette.* New York: Barron's Educational Services, Inc., 1996.

Post, Elizabeth L. *Emily Post on Business Etiquette.* New York: HarperCollins, 1990.

Random House Webster's English Language Desk Reference. Pearsons, Enid; Baboukis, Constance A.; and Somoroff, Alice Kovac, editors. New York: Random House, 1997.

Reif, Joe, et al. *The Global Road Warrior.* San Rafael, California: World Trade Press, 1999.

Rozakis, Laurie and Bob. *The Complete Idiot's Guide to Office Politics.* New York: Macmillan General Reference, Alpha Books, 1998.

Sabath, Ann Marie. *101 Ways to Conduct Business With Charm and Savvy.* Franklin Lakes, New Jersey: Career Press, 1998.

Satterfield, Mark. *VGM's Complete Guide to Career Etiquette.* Lincolnwood, Illinois: VGM Career Horizons, NTC Publishing Group, 1996.

Shea, Virginia. *Netiquette.* San Francisco: Albion Books, 1994.

Spencer, John, and Pruss, Adrian. *The Professional Secretary's Handbook.* New York: Barron's, 1997.

Stewart, Marjabelle Young, and Faux, Marian. *Executive Etiquette in the New Workplace.* New York: St. Martin's Griffin, 1997.

Tyler, Vicki. *Scholastic's A+ Guide to Grammar.* New York: Scholastic, Inc., 1981.

Venolia, Jan. *Better Letters: A Handbook of Business and Personal Correspondence.* Second edition. Berkeley, California: Ten Speed Press, 1995.

Wall, Robert; Solum, Robert S.; and Sobol, Mark R. *The Mission-Driven Organization.* Rocklin, California: Prima Publishing, 1999.

Weinstein, Bob. *I Hate My Boss!* New York: McGraw Hill, 1998.

Zinsser, William. *On Writing Well: The Classic Guide to Writing Nonfiction.* Sixth edition, revised. New York: HarperCollins Publishers, Harper Perennial, 1998.

INDEX

Caller ID devices, 294
  on cellular phones, 298
Call to dinner
  at a buffet, 456
  at an informal dinner party, 449–50
Canada, 480–81
Candles, as centerpieces, 446
Captains, tipping, 255
Career path, and your boss, 120–21
Casual days, women's clothing for, 178
Caterers, 429
Cause-and-effect outline, 309
Cellular phones, 249, 297–300, 421, 422, 424–25. *See also* mobile phones
Centerpieces, 446
Champagne, glassware for, 396, 436–37
Charitable donations, corporate, setting policy on, 197–98
Chatting, office, 86–87
  tips for, 54–55
Cheese, 414
Chewing food, 416
Chewing gum, 67–68, 425
Chicken, how to eat, 412
Children, and the home-based business, 541, 550–52
  telephone etiquette, 553
Chile, 483–84
China (country), 470, 509–11
China (dishes)
  for a business meal, 396, 398
  for an informal dinner, 446, 447–48
Chivalry, gender-free, 134
Chops, how to eat, 412
Christmas cards, 349
  as a sales tool, 539
Chronological resumes, 22–25
Cigarette butt disposal, 146
Citizens Emergency Center, 466
Civil Rights Act of 1964, 130–31
Claim letters, 346–47
Clapping, at a performance, 425
Clearing the table, after a dinner party, 451–52
Clerical forms of address, 330

Clients, and the home-based business, 540–42
Clothing. *See* attire
Clutter, office, 91
Coat etiquette, 134
  at the theater, 423
Coatroom attendants, tipping, 417
Cocktail parties, 438–39
  informal, 80–81
Cocktails, 449
  glassware for, 436–37
Code of ethics, workplace, 185
Coffee, 415
  after-dinner, 452
  cup and saucer for, 398
  making, at the office, 218
Collection agency, 233, 541
Collections
  and the home-based business, 541–42
  of overdue payments, 233–34
Cologne, for men, 36, 164
Color, clothing
  for men's suits, 152
  seasonal, 180
  for women, 167–69
Commas, 324
Common Market, 487
Communal office equipment etiquette, 94–99
Communicating with staff, 208, 210–12
Communication skills. *See* speaking skills; writing skills
Company policy, setting
  on charitable donations, 197–98
  on dating, 193–94
  on dress code, 194
  on drinking, 198
  on drug testing, 198
  on flextime, 194–95
  on gift giving, 196–97
  policy and procedures manual, 196–97
  on privacy, 199
  on relocation costs, 195–96
  on telecommuting, 194
  on transportation costs, 195–96

Index